VICTORY AT ANY COST

The Genius of Viet Nam's Gen. Vo Nguyen Giap

CECIL B. CURREY

BRASSEY'S, INC.

Washington · London

Library of Congress Cataloging-in-Publication Data
Currey, Cecil B.
    Victory at Any Cost: the genius of Viet Nam's Gen. Vo Nguyen
Giap/Cecil B. Currey.
        p. cm.
    Includes bibliographical references and index.
    ISBN 1-57488-056-X
    1. Vo, Nguyen Giap, 1912–   2. Generals—Vietnam—Biography.
3. Vietnam. Quan doi nhan dan doi—Biography.
I. Title.
DS560.72.V6C87 1996
959.704´34´092—dc20
    [B]   96-15404

Designed by Tanya Pérez

First Edition
10   9   8   7   6   5   4   3   2   1
Printed in the United States of America

Dedicated to my grandchildren
Alessio Benjamin Barr Conte, Annalise Estelle Currey Conte, and
Mara Cheyenne Tack

and to

my adviser
Lieutenant General Vinh Loc, ARVN (Ret.)
my translator
Le Hong Lam

and

My Bright and Morning Star
They helped!

**An AUSA Book**

The Association of the United States Army, or AUSA, was founded in 1950 as a not-for-profit organization dedicated to education concerning the role of the U.S. Army, to providing material for military professional development, and to the promotion of proper recognition and appreciation of the profession of arms. Its constituencies include those who serve in the Army today, including Army National Guard, Army Reserve, and Army civilians, and the retirees and veterans who have served in the past, and all their families. A large number of public-minded citizens and business leaders are also an important constituency. The Association seeks to educate the public, elected and appointed officials, and leaders of the defense industry on crucial issues involving the adequacy of our national defense, particularly those issues affecting land warfare.

In 1988 AUSA established within its existing organization a new entity known as the Institute of Land Warfare. Its purpose is to extend the educational work of AUSA by sponsoring scholarly publications, to include books, monographs, and essays on key defense issues, as well as workshops and symposia. Among the volumes chosen for designation as "An AUSA Institute of Land Warfare Book" are both texts and reprints of titles of enduring value that are no longer in print. Topics include history, policy issues, strategy, and tactics. Publication as an AUSA book does not indicate that the Association of the United States Army and the publisher agree with everything in the book, but does suggest that the AUSA and the publisher believe this book will stimulate the thinking of AUSA members and others concerned about important issues.

CONTENTS

A single general's reputation is made out of ten thousand corpses.
—Ts'ao Sung, c. 870–920

The outcome of a battle depends . . . upon the united hearts of those who fight.
—attributed to Kusunoki Masashige, 1294–1336

A great people may be killed, but they cannot be intimidated.
—Napoleon, "Political Aphorisms," 1848

Without a people's army, the people have nothing.
—Mao Tse-tung, *On Coalition Government*, 1945

Once on the tiger's back, we cannot be sure of picking the place to dismount.
—George Ball, White House memo, October 1964

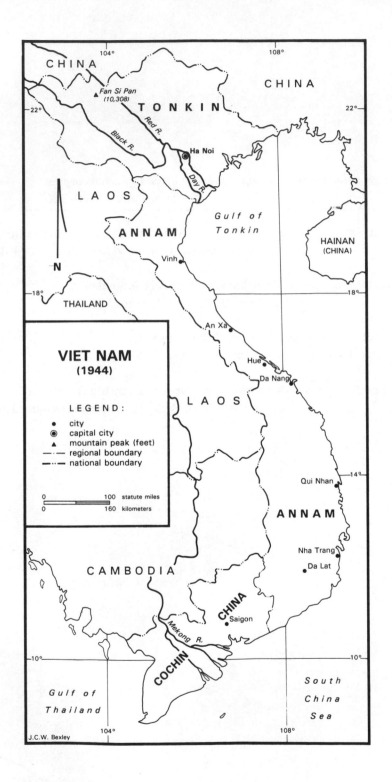

CHINA

104°

108°

CHINA

Fan Si Pan
(10,308)

22°

TONKIN

Red R.

Black R.

22°

Ha Noi

Day R.

LAOS

ANNAM

Gulf of
Tonkin

HAINAN
(CHINA)

N

Vinh

THAILAND

18°

18°

An Xa

VIET NAM

(1944)

Hue

Da Nang

LEGEND:

● city

◉ capital city

▲ mountain peak (feet)

—·— regional boundary

—··— national boundary

0   100 statute miles
0   160 kilometers

LAOS

ANNAM

Qui Nhan

14°

Nha Trang

CAMBODIA

Da Lat

CHINA

Saigon

Mekong R.

COCHIN

10°

10°

Gulf of

Thailand

South

China

Sea

104°

108°

J.C.W. Bexley

As someone who has studied and written extensively about warfare, I find *Victory at Any Cost* an impressive and important book. At last, we have a readable biography that explores and explains the military qualities of North Viet Nam's Senior General Vo Nguyen Giap. The author, Cecil B. Currey, helps us to understand why Giap may be ranked as one of the great captains of the twentieth century. *Victory at Any Cost* documents Giap's life and achievements from birth to his current tranquil retirement in Ha Noi. It also provides the most thorough and intimate look into Giap's personal life.

The author, a respected military historian, brings to this book his military experience and the knowledge gained in writing two earlier Viet Nam books: a biography of General Lansdale, the famous counter-guerrilla warrior, and a controversial description of the U.S. Army's self-destruction in Viet Nam. In this third book of his trilogy, Currey's analysis of Giap's military leadership flows out of a thorough five-year search through Giap's voluminous speeches and writings; of Vietnamese and U.S. literature and official records; and of extensive personal interviews and correspondence with General Giap, his family and colleagues, and his American military opponents. Currey paints a portrait of an extraordinary military leader whose genius lay in his organizational skills, his patience and persistence, an indomitable will, a capacity to learn, and an ability to persuade millions of his fellow Vietnamese to bear the price of victory at any cost. During three decades, Giap first helped the French drive the Japanese out of Indochina and then defeated the powerful forces fo France and, finally, of America. In the late 1970s, the army Giap had created also rejected a large Chinese force that was foolish enough to invade Vietnamese territory.

These extraordinary victories were achieved with an army Giap had created from scratch. After he and Ho Chi Minh had committed themselves to rid Viet Nam of foreign rule, Giap started his army with a few recruits and no military equipment or supplies. Giap had little military training, but studied military matters by immersing himself in the literature. He paid particular attention to Napoleon and his campaigns. These studies may have helped Giap devise his "Eastern" strategy, which used geography, time, and the avoidance of sustained engagements to defeat superior western forces that relied upon quick reaction, modern technology, and massive amounts of supplies.

In some ways Giap may be said to have adapted the Russian strategy which was so effective in defeating Napoleon. Napoleon was a military leader and military genius of enormous stature. But he eventually lost the Napoleonic Wars and left France exhausted and defeated. Cecil Currey's book is honest in pointing out the military mistakes made by Giap, sometimes through decisions taken against his advice by the North Vietnamese political leadership. The book also effectively supports Currey's evaluation that North Viet Nam's Senior General Vo Nguyen Giap is one of the great generals of history. As Currey notes succinctly, "Giap won." It is finally clear that a major reason the United States could not win its Viet Nam War was because Giap would never let that happen.

JOHN KEEGAN

Victory at Any Cost is the last of a trilogy on Viet Nam I began over fifteen years ago. The first book, *Self-Destruction* (1981), set forth the proposition that the United States lost dramatically in its efforts to maintain the southern Republic of Viet Nam as an independent, non-Communist nation. Much of the responsibility for that defeat came about because of attitudes and practices within the United States Army. It failed to know its enemy and thus could not adopt tactics specific to the particular foe it faced. Its military policies were shamefully shallow and palpably wrong. It relied too heavily on technology and the lavish use of firepower. It continued to function as if it were pursuing enemy units of the Warsaw Pact nations across the plains of central Europe. It ignored calls for change that came from within.

U.S. military leaders, then and later, refused to acknowledge mistakes they committed in Southeast Asia. An explanation often heard for the failure in Viet Nam was a renewal of the old *Dolchstosslegende* ("stab-in-the-back myth") used by the German army following its defeat in the Great War of 1914–18. The old refrain that the army failed because of political interference and social unrest at home became their theme song. The fact was simpler: military disaster in Viet Nam grew out of ineptitude at the highest ranks of the American army. It became a brittle instrument of war.

While I was writing about the United States Army's failed military intervention in Viet Nam, it became clear that more remained to be said. During my research for Self-Destruction I had repeatedly encountered traces of the activities in Southeast Asia of a shadowy, mysterious individual, Edward Geary Lansdale, whose suggestions for alternative approaches in Viet Nam carried the ring of both power and significant insight. Often he seemed only a lone witness to the possibilities for victory if the United States would follow another, more appropriate strategy in the Orient. I was fascinated and wanted to learn more. What could we have done differently in Viet Nam that might have carried America's policy there to success? Perhaps Lansdale could tell me. My efforts culminated in the publication of Edward Lansdale: The Unquiet American (1988).

Lansdale passionately advocated openness and trust in dealing with third-world peoples whose countries he helped defend against Communist insurgency. He taught that the United States' paramount object was to win over a nation's people. It was not enough for a nation threatened by revolution to rely on military operations. By themselves, they were insufficient to defeat a dedicated, internal enemy. Lansdale was one of the few Americans of his era to understand the nature of his country's foe.

The CIA sent him to Viet Nam in 1954, confident of his ability to relate to Asians. There he tried to apply his notions. He befriended and advised Ngo Dinh Diem from 1954 to 1956, guiding his faltering footsteps toward creation of a continuing, non-communist government in the South. He came within an eyelash of fashioning a stable government there. Lansdale stands as an original operational giant of modern conflict.

It was impossible to study Lansdale's career without encountering the notions of the great northern Vietnamese leader Vo Nguyen Giap, whose tactics and strategy successfully countered the best traditional military forces both France and the United States could send against his army and his nation. Thus was laid the foundation for this final work of the trilogy.

Giap was a military genius. Throughout the long decades of his career, he devised tactics and strategies that eventually brought his nation victory over powerful enemies. The circumstances of his life that helped him develop this rare talent are the subjects of this book. Readers will not find here a full-blown history of Viet Nam, or the U.S. side of the war, or any analysis of the American home front. Those who want more details about such topics may consult many available books, some of which are listed in the bibliography at the end of this book. Nothing meaningful has yet been published that does justice to Giap's extraordinary military accomplishments, and much that has been published is ridden with factual errors. The task here is to correct the record and to provide a Vietnamese perspective on the conflict in Southeast Asia and the role Giap played in defeating the French and Americans. Only with such an understanding can we ever fully understand the outcome there and the form of warfare used so effectively by Giap.

That self-taught Asian military leader learned the craft of war by fighting. In the course of a long career, Giap faced soldiers of France, Japan, the United States, the Republic of Viet Nam (his southern countrymen), Cambodia, and China. Perhaps no other general has contended with so many different enemies with such success, yet he remained relatively obscure in the West.

Anyone studying Giap quickly discovers that he has been nearly ignored in the United States despite the fact that for many years he was America's archenemy. Almost nothing has been written about the crucial twenty years of his life from 1944 to 1964 when he was creating an armed force, destabilizing French authority over Indochina, launching and winning the attack on Dien Bien Phu, utilizing guerrillas to attack the American-sponsored government south of the 17th parallel, and preparing to face the armed might of the United States. Even less has been said about his earlier life. Making matters worse, mistaken assertions have marred much of what has been written about Giap. This book is presented to provide a correct and fuller appraisal of this extraordinary man.

It was difficult to ferret out details of Giap's life; sometimes even talking to those who knew him was not fruitful. As a cultural trait, Vietnamese often have an excessive taste for secrecy. They keep details of their inner and private lives reserved and shy away from revealing information to unfamiliar and curious visitors. Perhaps they remember too well long years of Gallic domination and continuing efforts by agents of the Deuxième Bureau, French Sûreté Générale, to gather information on anyone who might prove to be a threat to their rule. Communist paranoia exacerbates that difficulty; everything in Ha Noi now is secret, and all questions are suspect.

Yet a host of information was available, ranging from Vietnamese materials translated into English, to other writings translated for me by helpful friends, to government documents, to secondary studies that either proved helpful in themselves or pointed me toward other usable sources, to Vietnamese who had known Giap and were willing to talk to me about their recollections, to Americans I interviewed who were formerly involved in U.S. intelligence or covert activities, to the government agencies where files of those earlier days have been squirreled away for half a century, to scholars in the field who kindly shared their knowledge with me.

And perhaps most helpful was that for whatever reason, Giap himself saw fit to cooperate with me in a limited way in the creation of this biography. He sat with me during December 1988 for a personal interview. After I returned home I decided to write this book. I went back to Ha Noi a year later, in December 1989, my third trip there, ready to conduct frequent and extended interviews with Giap. It was not to be. Despite my statement on my visa application that I desired to visit Ha Noi for the sole purpose of interviewing Giap, Dao Huy Ngoc, acting head of the foreign ministry's Institute for International Relations, told me upon my arrival that unnamed "senior decision-makers" believed it would be politically incorrect to allow Giap to cooperate with me. After my meeting with Ngoc, it became difficult even to meet with friends I had made on earlier visits. They were forced to slip into my hotel, creep up to my third-floor landing, and whisper to me outside my room in the protective shadows of the dark hallway. Or I hired a cyclo and rode through the streets of Ha Noi to search them out at their homes, all the while avoiding being followed by police agents. After a few frustrating weeks I returned home.

I wrote General Giap on several occasions. My letters were unanswered. I had no way of knowing whether that was because of the faulty Vietnamese postal system or because he had been given orders to ignore my correspondence. I later learned my letters had been intercepted by his government; it was keeping Giap under house watch out of fear he might lead a military coup against it. I finally got word to him of my efforts. He remembered me from our earlier meeting and expressed his pleasure, for, he said, he wanted any book written about him in the West to be done "with the honesty and the seriousness of a good historian."

He responded to written questions I submitted to him surreptitiously, and even sent photographs of himself, his wife, and his children. Page after page of the material I received from him discussed his ancestors, his parents, his home village, his school days, his early fascination with communism, his prison sentence, his work as a newspaperman, his first wife and their daughter, his teaching in a private Ha Noi lycée, his growing hatred of the French, his determination to work toward the independence of Viet Nam, his escape into China at the outbreak of World War II, his life in the northern hills during the war.

He told of the early formation of his first army, the Armed Propaganda and Liberation Brigade, of the OSS men who dropped from the sky to work in the last days of the war with Giap's Viet Minh soldiers, of his second wife and their children, her own village and parents—on and on. He responded in human terms rather than as a zealous ideological parrot. He gave a humorous response when kidded about an early nickname. He spoke of his grandchildren.

Then, despite his earlier expressed willingness to do so, Giap refused to respond to additional questions. He inevitably had an excuse to postpone action. He was "traveling," or attending "numerous ceremonies," or "celebrating historic anniversaries," or in mourning after the death of a brother. Giap finally gave only the terse explanation that he had already given me enough material and, in any case, the new questions had been "inspired by nonserious, even false and reactionary documents." He did, however, receive, date, and sign his signature to a manuscript copy of this text.

An appendix of this book, "Giap's Nation," is included as a help for those who may be unfamiliar with the history of Viet Nam. A minimal grasp of that nation's past is required in order to understand the milieu in which Giap eventually operated. Those who want to learn more about Viet Nam—its history, geography, sociology, anthropology, and culture—may wish to turn to those pages before reading the book itself. It may help them to understand better what happened in Viet Nam and in Giap's life. The appendix is there to be read or skipped. Readers may choose.

* * *

Despite his limited willingness to help, I offer my deep gratitude to Senior General Vo Nguyen Giap. He was, of course, but one among many who participated in the creation of this biography. The University of South Florida's Division of Sponsored Research and Dr. Julia Davis, former dean of the late College of Social and Behavioral Sciences, provided research assistance in 1990. The Indochina Archive, Berkeley, California, made its files on Giap available. Françoise Jean and Pascuele Lavendaire checked my translations of certain documents. Virginia Gift answered queries, investigated archives, and discovered a way for me to send questions to Giap.

Many Vietnamese, both in Viet Nam and in the United States, helped me complete this project, including Ho Thi Quang, Mme. Kim Dung Tran-Ngoc, the sisters Ha Xuyen and Ha Mai, Trinh Xuan Lang, Nguyen Dang Quang, Tran Minh Dung, Do Tin Nham, Nguyen Dang Thuyen, Pham Binh, Chau Phong, Bui Tin, General Cao Pha, General Tran Cong Man, Dinh Mien, Nguyen Thanh Long, Nguyen Quoc Hai and his wife, Ho Thi Xuan Hong, and my interpreter, traveling companion down the length of Viet Nam, friend, and "young son," Le Hong Lam, who labored mightily to make my first and second visits to his homeland so memorable. In both Thailand and Viet Nam, I received help from willing Thais: Mr. Pradorn Ucharatna, Mr. Yothin Piraphatanapong (Peter Johnson), and Vudhi Lenbury.

Helpful ideas and stimulating discussion came from T. Edward Henley, Tigard, Oregon; Mr. Will Brownell, Director, Vietnam Bibliography Project at Columbia University; and Colonel John K. Brier, USA (Ret.), Executive Director of the Tampa Bay Council for International Visitors. Colonel Brier performed yeoman service when he put me in contact with Lieutenant General Vinh Loc, ARVN (Ret.).

Working at his California home, General Vinh Loc consulted with friends and with members of the Quang Binh Association, drove significant distances to meet with acquaintances, and drew from his own vast knowledge to help me write a better book. He spent hours putting reminiscences on paper for me: life in early-twentieth-century Viet Nam, customs and traditions of the imperial court, the May Day riots of 1930, French police methods, attitudes of Vietnamese nationals toward French *colons* before World War II, primary education in Viet Nam seven decades ago, the physical plant and curriculum of the Quoc Hoc School in Hue, which Giap attended, the appearance of Giap's home village of An Xa, his own early memories of Giap, and much more. His help was far more than any author has a right to expect and I am deeply in his debt.

Sheila Simon-Derrwaldt gave cheerful, regular, and professional service as my bibliographical assistant. My cartographer, Jennifer Bexley, created maps that will more easily enable readers to understand this study of Giap's life. And there were my manuscript readers: Carl Heymann, Allison Kent Thomas, Earl

H. ("Butch") Tilford, Jr., Dr. Libby Allison-West, and Lieutenant General Phillip B. Davidson. David G. Marr also read and commented on portions of the text. They kept a restraining hand on me throughout the writing of this book. Their bold, professional challenges to my ideas often forced me to rethink many issues and some entire topics and saved me from many pitfalls. If all they desired me to say has not made its way into this text, it is not because their words were not valued or respected, but because, in the end, we found we had honest differences in some of our views.

I also thank Joshua Bilmes, JABberwocky Literary Agency, for his efforts on my behalf, and Franklin D. Margiotta, my editor and the president and publisher of Brassey's, Inc., for the time and effort he has spent on readying this book for market. After the help of all these people, any mistakes that remain in this text are most certainly my own.

Finally, I recall fondly and with appreciation the efforts of my wife, Laura Gene Currey, to provide an encouraging and loving home environment during the years of work on this biography when I was often distracted from the world around me and focused almost entirely on research, on monumental piles of notes, on the sometimes erratic behavior of my word processor, and on deadlines. She has helped me when she could, and has left me alone when she could not. I have sometimes cast many of my cares on her, for I knew she cared for me. And I her!

CECIL B. CURREY
Lutz, Florida
October 1995

PART ONE

An Xa,
1911–40

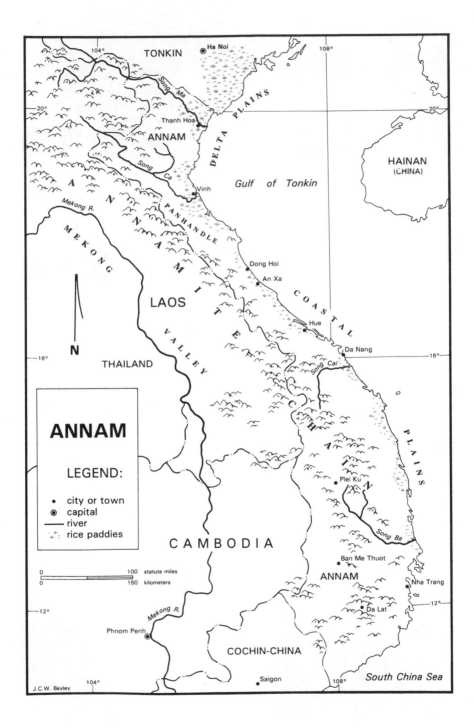

104°

TONKIN

Ha Noi

108°

Song Ma

20°

20°

Thanh Hoa

ANNAM

DELTA PLAINS

Song Ca

HAINAN
(CHINA)

Vinh

Gulf of Tonkin

Mekong R.

A

N

N

A

M

I

T

E

S

PANHANDLE

MEKONG

LAOS

Dong Hoi

An Xa

C
O
A
S
T
A
L

16°

VALLEY

N

THAILAND

Hue

Da Nang

Song Cai

16°

ANNAM

LEGEND:

• city or town
⊙ capital
— river
⋰ rice paddies

C
H
A
I
N

Plei Ku

P
L
A
I
N
S

CAMBODIA

Song Ba

0   100 statute miles
0   160 kilometers

Ban Me Thuot

ANNAM

Nha Trang

12°

Mekong R.

Da Lat

12°

Phnom Penh

COCHIN-CHINA

J.C.W. Bexley

104°

Saigon

108°

South China Sea

"The Making of a Revolutionary"

The elderly retired man sat in the rear seat of the Russian-made chauffeur-driven automobile and stared out the windows as his driver slowly steered around the worst ruts and potholes in the ruined road. As the car made its tortuous way northward, the unlined face of the old warrior gave no hint of his thoughts, but his mind was lost in memories. Senior General Vo Nguyen Giap was returning to Pac Bo in the far north of Viet Nam, just a few kilometers from its border with China, the place of his martial beginnings.[1] There he and Ho Chi Minh first worked together back when their country had yet to gain its freedom from the dominion of the French empire. "The memories," he later wrote, "have not faded."[2]

After the long trip from his spacious Ha Noi villa, Giap had rested the previous night at the tiny community of Cao Bang. "I wish the day longer and the road better," he later lamented, "so that I could revisit more easily, but that is something that I could not have." That morning, as he left to continue his journey, winter fog still covered the mountains, not lifting until they passed the hamlet of Hoa An. Seeming like pyramids, mountains around him thrust into the air above the low-hanging ground mist.

The old man's eyes lingered on scenes around him. "I know almost every mountain, stream, and town in this region," Giap wrote. "On the left side of the road is Phia But, the tallest mountain. It has a lake on one of its peaks. According to legend, many years ago a fairy came down to bathe in it. Unfortunately,

3

she was seen by people and could not return to paradise. Every year, during the rainy season, when water spills from the mountain's heights, people claim they can see her, a beautiful lady riding a horse, carrying a fan in one hand."

The automobile neared the community of Phai Khat, where Giap's soldiers once fought their first battle against the French. It had not changed much. In 1944 it boasted a dozen houses; now its size was perhaps doubled. Many people living in the area had learned that Giap would make this trip; that once again he would return to his place of beginnings. Friends from several hamlets— Nguyen Binh, Minh Tam, Hoang Hoa Tham, and Tran Hung Dai—now gathered in the community to see him once again.

"In the past, many people thought Phai Khat was just another battle of the war," the general later mused. "For me, it is much more. In 1941, the French occupied this place and turned Comrade Lac's newly built home into their headquarters." Lac's house then and now was the largest in the community. "Because of this occupation, I decided that this place would be the objective of our first battle." Someone had erected a sign in front of the house: "Phai Khat: The Start of the Revolution. 24-12-44."

Giap smiled and waved through a car window at those who had come to see him, many dressed in colorful holiday clothing. His driver steered carefully through the community, to stop finally in front of the office of the local people's committee. As Giap slowly emerged from the rear seat, two women came up to present him with flower bouquets. "It seems like a festive day," he said with a smile to those standing nearby.

Scanning the crowd, the general looked at the faces of older people, hoping to recognize some of his former comrades-in-arms. He saw Dong Phuong Quy from the Dao Truyen region, once leader of Group Three. There was Thu Son, leader of Group One, who led his forces in the battle of Phai Phat. Nearby stood Tien Luc and Le Loi, the latter a namesake of a former emperor and warrior. All were in their sixties or seventies, now retired and enjoying their final years. "When we met," Giap later remembered, "I could not restrain my emotions and cried with joy." They reminisced about the past and the heady years of revolutionary sacrifice. "Over there," the general said to them as he pointed at a buffalo pen standing adjacent to Lac's home, "this is the spot where we killed the French commander." After some time, Giap returned to his automobile and the driver resumed their journey to Pac Bo. "Without this trip," Giap reflected, "I doubt if I would ever have seen those old comrades again."

As Giap neared Pac Bo, the car in which he rode rumbled past the construction site of a national museum. Upon completion, it would become a national shrine dedicated to the memory of Ho Chi Minh. This would be the third time since the 1975 day of liberation that he had returned to Pac Bo cave. On that first trip, in April 1975, Giap had planted a tree as a memorial to the decades of national effort at independence and unification. Soon now he would plant a second, for tenderly packed away in the trunk of the car was a small tree he had taken from the garden surrounding Ho Chi Minh's carefully preserved home in Ha Noi.

The driver finally pulled to a stop. They had arrived. The old general gazed around him; the familiarity of the scene gladdened his heart. Dominating the area was the vivid green of Mac Mountain, and nearby chattered the blue water of the Lenin Stream. The golden sun seemed to occupy the whole world, and its blazing morning light shone across a waterfall, exposing the Pac Bo spring, the source of the stream. The water was so clear, the light so bright, Giap noticed, that he could see fish swimming among the rocks of its depths.

A small contingent of soldiers stationed at Pac Bo met the general's car and escorted him toward the cave that decades before had served as a headquarters and place of sanctuary for Ho, Giap, and their comrades. As always, looking at the cave entrance, Giap thought how it resembled the ear of a cat. Nearer the cave, Giap thought again of Ho and remarked later how the years of his leader's life could be configured by decades. At age twenty, using the pseudonym Nguyen Tat Thanh, Ho had left Nha Rong Port in Saigon to serve as dishwasher and cook aboard a French merchant vessel. At thirty years of age, as Nguyen Ai Quoc, he joined the French Communist Party and worked hard to promote the end of French colonial rule over Viet Nam. Aged forty, he started the Indochinese Communist Party. At fifty, he entered Viet Nam from China, where he had been living, to lead the resistance against the French. It was then that he met Giap. Now, walking in the warm sunlight, Giap was reminded of Ho wherever he looked.

The general passed the tree he had planted in 1975, now healthy and beautiful. He recalled Ho's advice: "When you plant a tree, you have to nourish it." Giap looked across the stream to a bush beside which Ho used to sit while fishing. The fish rarely bit, and when they did, Ho threw them back into the water.

Giap crossed a wooden bridge spanning the Lenin Stream and walked up to the entrance of the old cave. "We chose this cave because it was isolated and well hidden," Giap recalled. Although the opening had collapsed in 1979, Giap could still see a date—8-2-1941—scratched into the surface of a nearby rock. On that day Ho had arrived here at the end of a long, dangerous trip from China.

Giap spoke of his own impatience in those early years and how he wanted to begin immediately to carry the revolutionary struggle to the French. He thought of a cold night, of Ho sitting with him next to a campfire, and of the others present: Chi Kien, Vu Anh, and Pham Van Dong. Dressed like an old mountain man, Ho spoke to them about the future. Giap recalled his words. "In about five years," Ho said, "the revolution will be victorious and we will have a bright future. I only want to create one thing: to completely free our country and provide everyone with the necessities of life."

Speaking in simple words, Ho made the difficult and complex prospects of revolution easy to understand. One of those present that night—Giap was unsure who it had been—asked Ho, "How can we have a revolution without arms, and where are we going to find guns?"

Bac Ho replied, "We must rely on our own force with some outside help.[3] When our people absorb this beautiful idea of revolution, they will create the strongest of forces. Everything because of the people; everything for the people. People first, guns last. If we have the people on our side, then we will have guns. If we have the people, we will have everything!" It was a theme that Ho, and later Giap, would always emphasize: "If we can rely on the people, no one can defeat us." Now once again at Pac Bo, Giap still remembered Ho's words. "It's a simple idea," he commented, "but not easy to follow."

As he stood at Pac Bo for the final time, Giap luxuriated in the accomplishments of his lifetime. "Following Ho's road," he later wrote, "we have defeated all invaders and gained independence and unification. Following his road, we will have civilization, happiness, a stronger country, and the creation of a society where the development of one person's freedom is the development of everyone's freedom. The stream of Pac Bo will continue to flow."

In the Christian scriptures, the physician Luke wrote, ". . . your young men shall see visions, and your old men shall dream dreams."[4] Senior General Vo Nguyen Giap had lived long enough to do both. As a youth, glimpses of Viet Nam's potential inspired him. He had been part of that vision. At Pac Bo, as an old man, he now dreamed of the glory years long since passed away. Without his efforts, much that occurred might never have come to pass. Through long years stretching from 1944 to 1980 he fought and ordered other men into battle against the Japanese, the French, the Americans, against other Vietnamese of the southern republic, the Kampucheans, and the Chinese. He pitted his ideas about warfare and how to conduct it against two foreign powers who successively stood on Vietnamese soil, and twice he emerged unbeaten. Yet he had no prior military schooling or training to ready him for this task. Only an intense study of military history and his own experiences guided him in the part he played in the great events of recent world and Vietnamese history.

The changes that came about in Viet Nam because of Vo Nguyen Giap began quietly enough. In the twentieth century, of Tonkin, Annam, and Cochin China, Annam—nearest geographically to the remnants of the imperial court at Hue—was the most troublesome to the French, and some provinces there were more difficult than others. One of the most bothersome was Quang Binh province, with its long history of stubbornness and resistance to the French. While the colonial power believed it could remain in control of these people forever, the Viets observed the fate that had befallen them and their beloved land and waited.

In central Annam, just north of the 17th parallel, in that troublesome province of Quang Binh, canton of Dai Phong ("Great Wind" or "Tempest"), sub-district of Quang Ninh, district of Le Thuy ("Beautiful Waters"), lay the tiny village of An Xa ("Tranquil"). On 25 August 1911 a townswoman of An Xa, Nguyen Thi Kien, finished her birthing labors and presented her husband, Vo Quang Nghiem, with a lusty red-faced baby boy. They gave him the name Vo Nguyen Giap.[5] As with all Vietnamese, he would always be known by his given name.

Giap was not the first child born to Nguyen Thi Kien and Vo Quang Nghiem. He was sixth in birth order. Their first child died as a small boy. Then Kien again gave birth to a boy who also died in infancy. Kien's third child, a girl, lived for a time before dying of amebic dysentery. Nghiem and Kien must often have wondered why they were so cursed; why they seemed destined to have no children to enrich their lives and carry on their line. A family without children in Viet Nam was pitiful, pathetic, the object of both sympathy and derision to townspeople, who gathered at the marketplace to gossip endlessly.

Then Kien was again pregnant. Fear often wracked her heart as her delivery time approached. But this time Kien and Nghiem could rejoice. Their fourth child, a daughter, was a healthy baby, whom they named Vo Thi Diem. She was followed by another daughter, Vo Thi Lien. Then in 1911 Giap was born, the first male child to live, and, according to a CIA report, even he reportedly had health problems throughout his life. He was followed by Vo Thuan Nho, a brother, and another sister, Vo Thi Lai.[6]

Vo Quang Nghiem named Giap well. There are few family names in the land, perhaps fifty in all, and so many people who bear the same name may not be related. Giap's middle name, Nguyen, is one of them, but, as in his case, is not always a family name. Perhaps he bore this name to remind him of some distant lineage with the Nguyen rulers of the land. The family name, Vo, means "force"; Giap means "shield" or "armor." They were bellicose names for a tiny infant but they presaged the course of Giap's life.

Quang Binh, in which he was born, and the two provinces immediately to its north, Ha Tinh and Nghe An, formed the major portion of the thinnest part of the nation and traditionally were among the most impoverished sections of the country. Most inhabitants of the tranquil hamlet of An Xa were poor peasants. There were only three or four important landlords; others held only tiny holdings or rented their land. The hamlet was surrounded by poor, sandy soil on which grew rice and sweet potatoes. Local folk might barely eke out their living, but they were proud of Quang Binh's special landscape. There were the rivers—the Gianh, the Nhat Le, and the Kien Giang. Lake Bau Tro, two miles north of Dong Hoi, had the shape—so people said—of a Chinese ink pot. Then there was the large natural lake of Hac Hai, about one and a half miles across, with a similar shape. From these waters, rivers and lakes alike, generations of Vietnamese caught fish for their daily meals. Around the shores of Lake Hac Hai grew a variety of watermelon, so special that selected samples were offered to

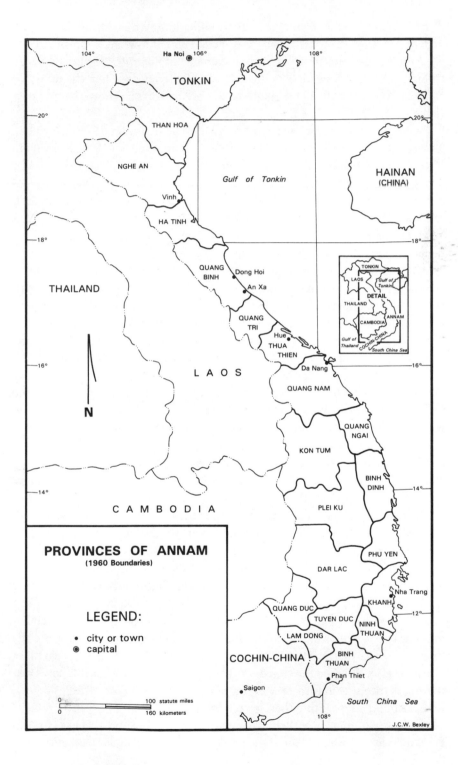

PROVINCES OF ANNAM
(1960 Boundaries)

LEGEND:
- • city or town
- ◉ capital

0 — 100 statute miles
0 — 160 kilometers

TONKIN

THAN HOA

NGHE AN

Vinh

HA TINH

Gulf of Tonkin

HAINAN
(CHINA)

QUANG BINH

Dong Hoi

An Xa

THAILAND

QUANG TRI

Hue

THUA THIEN

Da Nang

LAOS

QUANG NAM

QUANG NGAI

KON TUM

BINH DINH

CAMBODIA

PLEI KU

PHU YEN

DAR LAC

Nha Trang

KHANH

QUANG DUC

TUYEN DUC

NINH THUAN

LAM DONG

COCHIN-CHINA

BINH THUAN

Phan Thiet

Saigon

South China Sea

Ha Noi

DETAIL
TONKIN
LAOS
Gulf of Tonkin
THAILAND
ANNAM
CAMBODIA
Gulf of Thailand
COCHIN-CHINA
South China Sea

N

J.C.W. Bexley

the emperor each year in July. Nearby was the peak of Dau Mau, where children played in the caves and grottoes which dotted its slopes.

People not only were proud of their rice fields and nearby jungles and the hazy horizon of mountains but also took pleasure in knowing that from their stock were many who had risen to national prominence: esteemed scholars and writers, military advisers to emperors, poets and philosophers, tutors for royal princelings.[7] The people of An Xa and of all Quang Bing province were a rural, poor, proud, nationalistic folk, restive under French rule. They were not easy to control and had little respect for their rulers, whether Chinese, French, or Vietnamese. They rebelled against the Chinese, and against the French in the 1880s (and would do so again in 1930). They would later resist North Viet Nam's land reform program of 1956. And when Giap was a child, the adventures of local partisans were still fresh in their memories.

In An Xa, except for some few houses topped with red-tiled roofs, most family homes were of mud, straw, and bamboo. Each had a small patch of land in the rear and a tiny yard in front used for drying harvests of rice and sweet potatoes. Vo Quang Nghiem, Giap's father, was one of the fortunate few to have a tiled roof on his modest one-story home, comfortable enough by local standards. The house was easily recognizable, for in Nghiem's yard grew a large wild tea tree, which he kept pruned in topiary fashion, trimmed skillfully until it looked like a giant tiger. During the day, to passing boys and girls, it looked like a shaped tree; after dusk and at night the beast became real and alive, and children hurried their steps as they passed by or swung in wide circles to avoid it entirely.[8]

Inside the main room of the house, Vo Quang Nghiem kept his family altar, for he was a Confucian and very attached to ancestral tradition. On it stood pictures of maternal and paternal ancestors. Nearby was a large bowl on which their names were engraved in Chinese characters. Flowers decorated both sides of the altar, on which also sat a copper basin. Nghiem daily lit joss sticks, kept in a nearby ceramic bowl, and stuck them into sand in the bottom of the basin. Their perfume wafted on the currents of the thick, heavy air. The house also included a cooking area and sleeping rooms.

Vo Quang Nghiem—his given name meant "the serious one"—was a member of the tiny middle-class population of An Xa, a rice farmer who tilled his own land and rented another small parcel but for a number of years still found time to serve as a practitioner of traditional Asian medicine. After unsuccessfully treating his daughter who died of dysentery, Nghiem withdrew from the healing profession and turned to teaching local children to read. In his classes they learned to recognize both Sino-Vietnamese characters, in which much of Vietnamese literature and history was written, and the newer *quoc ngu*, or romanized alphabet, devised by Alexandre de Rhodes and favored by French rulers. By training, Nghiem was steeped in the Confucian classics.

The people of An Xa respected Nghiem and considered him to be a man of distinction, for he was a *lettré,* a scholar, and that was always a matter of importance in traditional Viet Nam.

His fellow townspeople addressed him as Ong Cuu Nghiem—Mr. Nghiem of the low mandarin rank of ninth grade, civil corps. He served as a clerk of the administrative office for the province of Quang Binh and consequently spent much time at Dong Hoi, provincial capital of Quang Binh. He served as *tong tho van,* dispatcher for all official correspondence, and this lowly post gave him much distinction within his home community.[9]

Cuu Nghiem was also a proud patriot, old enough to remember the days when northern Annam and Tonkin had been free from French control. Nghiem's father fought in the great Can Vuong uprising against the French that began in July 1885 when Emperor Ham Nghi fled their control and called for his people to save the monarchy from foreign oppression. The movement, however, lacked weapons and a coherent strategy and collapsed in 1896. Cuu Nghiem still remembered that revolt and was glad his family had been involved in the first organized resistance movement against French rule over Viet Nam.[10]

Nghiem's civil duties meant that Nguyen Thi Kien sometimes cared for the family farm in addition to her other duties as housewife. Devoted to her plants and to the land, Kien found her greatest happiness in working with her hands in the soil. A daughter of a member of the Can Vuong movement who had been a rebel commander of an entire province, she remembered that struggle against the French as well as her husband did, and delighted in telling her children, and later her grandchildren, how her father had fought against the French colonialists.

Passionately interested in Viet Nam's past, Nguyen Thi Kien had a retentive memory and, although illiterate, was able to recite by heart Vietnamese poems and sophisticated texts such as *Kim Van Kieu, Nhi Do Mai, Tong Tran, Cuc Hoa,* and others. Years later, Giap recalled: "Memories of the resistance against the occupation were still very fresh. In the evening, in the light of the oil lamp, my mother would often tell me of the grueling trials she underwent during the Can Vuong campaign, in which my grandfather had participated." Giap later told how "I can still recall my earliest childhood deeply bathed with feelings of love for our country." On some evenings, before bedtime, Giap's father also recited poems, one of which, "The Fall of Hue," told of the French sack of the imperial capital in 1833.[11] In this way his home was filled with nationalistic fervor, an emotion that would never leave him.

Cuu Nghiem taught Giap to read their language as it was written in pre-French days, when Sino-Vietnamese characters were used, during the year between his fourth and fifth birthdays. Even as a small boy, Giap liked to study, and his father encouraged him in this by keeping a glass jar near at hand, filled with the boy's favorite sweets and delicacies, to reward him for good performance. His first book in the romanized alphabet was *Au Hoc Tan Thu* ("New Manual for Small Children"), a volume filled with patriotic images of Viet Nam's past. It had only recently been published by authority of Emperor Duy Tan (1907–16), deposed by the French for efforts to incite an insurrection among Vietnamese troops used by France in the trenches of World War I. In that book, Giap later recalled, exaggerating its influence upon a small boy, "I discovered our forebears, our martyrs, our duty to expunge the disgrace of past humiliations." He learned that although his country might, as Caesar had once written, be divided into three parts, his ancestors were not "Gauls."[12]

With other village urchins, young Giap spent many hours in play. Running barefoot through the hamlet, they spun tops wound by pieces of string, shot games of marbles, fought loud battles of war, trailed after wandering ducks and geese, and threw stones. Although some older boys played soccer, the most popular game was *da kien*, which demanded both skill and patience. Many coins then had a small, square hole in their centers. Boys thrust a twist of paper or feathers or banana leaves through the hole to make a shuttlecock. The object of the game was to keep the coin spinning in the air as long as possible by kicking it with feet, knees, or ankles. When the shuttlecock fell to the ground, another player took his turn. Alternatively, two boys could play at the same time by batting a shuttlecock back and forth.

Da cau was a game similar to soccer, but the number of players was not fixed; it could be played by many or a few, depending upon how many were free from chores. Boys used a variety of makeshift balls. In season they relied on a kind of fruit that looks much like a green grapefruit but much larger. Or they could make a ball with rags or old clothes, tied tightly with thread to kick back and forth. Small boys spent endless hours and pleasant days in such fashion.[13]

As they grew older, boys of the hamlet fell heir to traditional jobs for those of their age. Dressed in short cotton jackets and pants, they took part in family chores, as Giap did. He herded ducks and watched after the family water buffalo, sitting on its rump for hours on end as it wandered grazing. He also pounded rice and, typical of the custom in Quang Binh province, sang the *ho gia gao*, rhythmic worksongs, that helped keep workers moving in harmony as they threshed rice.[14]

From the time Giap was five until he was eight, he attended school in An Xa. Even as an old man his voice softened when he recalled the first day he left home for the village's kindergarten. "My mama and I were separating for the first time," he said, "and we both wept." His school clothes consisted of a long robe that hung below his knees; in summer white, in autumn and winter black. Beneath his robe, winter and summer, he wore white trousers and black slippers, his head topped by a black turban. Morning sessions at school began at seven-thirty and ran to eleven-thirty, resumed at two-twenty and lasted until five. At noon, Giap went home, ate lunch with his parents, and, as a young boy, took a nap before returning to his classes. If he faltered in his lessons, his teachers beat him with a long, thin bamboo stick, held at the ready for use on unworthy pupils. As he grew older, he engaged more in play with friends after the schoolday ended.

His primary school, although supervised by the French, who established its curriculum, was taught by Vietnamese. A large part of his studies consisted of instruction in the Vietnamese language, and beginning in his third year, he was introduced to the French language for a few hours each week.

For centuries, Vietnamese society had been influenced by the teachings of Confucius. The basis for much of Giap's education was thus a Confucian respect for mandarins, ancestors, relatives, and parents. Many of Giap's lessons focused on how to behave in one's family and in society: younger brother to elder brother, elder son to father, family to village, village to emperor, and emperor to heaven. In the Vietnamese world, individuals and society blended into a harmonious whole. As well, he studied arithmetic, history, geography, literature, and natural science. Geography lessons initially emphasized the land of Viet Nam, but as the school years rolled by, Giap also learned of the world beyond its borders.

In history, Giap absorbed stories of past heroes: Le Loi, who wrestled independence from Chinese occupation in 1428; Tran Huong Dao, who fought the Mongols in 1283 and 1287; Phan Dinh Phung, of the Can Vuong movement; Ly Thuong Kiet, who commanded a successful invasion of Champa in 1069 and then directed a war against the Sung Dynasty of China; Nguyen Hue, who fought against a Chinese occupation of the north and then declared himself to be Emperor Quang Trung; and others. From primary school through all the remaining years of his studies, Giap gloried in committing to memory stories of the past. He learned of emperors who resorted to total war when faced with invaders. He read how they appealed to their people to rise up and smite those who desecrated the soil of Viet Nam. He learned those lessons well.

Giap's days of schooling in An Xa ended when he was eight. Nghiem enrolled him in the canton *(tong)* school at the nearby market town of Dai Phong, equivalent to the fourth- and fifth-grade classes of a modern public school. At nine, he attended district *(huyen)* school, and then at eleven he went to the province *(tinh)* school.[15]

In 1923, the twelve-year-old Giap received his official certificate for having completed his elementary studies *(diploma des études primaires complementaires)*. It was not easy for Vietnamese youth to achieve even this level of education, for French rulers limited the number of schools and encouraged illiteracy; an ignorant population was more easily controlled. The following year Giap took the entrance examination *(concours d'entrée)* to qualify for additional schooling in Hue—and failed. He spent the next months in an intensive round of study and preparation, desperately hoping to pass on his next attempt. When he took the examination again, in 1925, he finished second among all those tested that year.[16]

Cuu Nghiem enlisted the support of one of his friends, the Roman Catholic priest René Morinot, a man widely respected in the area. Father Morinot willingly recommended young Giap for further schooling in Hue. Cuu Nghiem and Kien were happy to send their eldest living son to study at the Quoc Hoc, or Lycée National, in Hue, a French-language school and a seedbed of revolution. Giap already showed signs of leadership. He would fit in well at his new school. He quickly showed his intelligence and was an excellent student, particularly in literature and history. Officials of the school posted student academic rankings at the end of each month. During his two years at the Quoc Hoc, Giap ranked first each time the grades went up except for one month when he ranked second.[17]

Annam had only three such schools: in Hue, Vinh (Nghe An), and Qui Nhon (Binh Dinh). Ngo Dinh Kha, a high court official and father of the later southern president Ngo Dinh Diem, founded the Lycée Quoc Hoc in 1909.[18] He wanted a school to provide students with an exceptional course of study in both traditional and modern education, as free from French influence as possible. It accepted students from primary schools who had received their diplomas and who were able to pass the entrance examination.

Ngo Dinh Kha put together a good faculty. Many teachers at Quoc Hoc were nationally famous. Ung Qua, professor of French literature, served as tutor to Crown Prince Bao Long. Pham Dinh Ai, who taught physics and chemistry, became ammunition technician for Giap during the years of the Viet Minh war with France, serving from 1948 to 1954. He later moved south and was elected a senator there during the second republic. Nguyen Duong Don, math and geometry teacher, became minister of national education in the government of Ngo Dinh Diem, leader of the southern half of the country from 1954 to 1963. Nguyen Huy Bao, who taught philosophy, became dean of the faculty of arts at the University of Saigon. Mai Trung Thu, teacher of drawing, was a famous artist whose paintings were exhibited many times in Paris during the 1930s. Nguyen Thieu Lau, professor of history and geography, was author of several historical research publications. Another history teacher, Nguyen Lan, edited a dictionary of Vietnamese classics.[19]

This competent faculty turned out exceptional students. Some of those who attended Lycée Quoc Hoc later became important figures in Vietnamese history, including Ho Chi Minh, Vo Nguyen Giap, Pham Van Dong (who served as prime minister of the Democratic Republic of Viet Nam from 1958 to 1988), and Ngo Dinh Diem.[20]

The curriculum at Quoc Hoc was similar to that at other French-run schools and nearly identical to what was required in France for a baccalaureate degree there. All instruction was given in French save for study of other languages. Vietnamese was a required first "foreign" language; English was the second. Pupils studied French literature from the sixteenth to the twentieth century, the history of France to the end of World War I, the geography of all departments of France and its possessions, mathematics, physics, and chemistry. It was a rigid and rugged curriculum.

After four years of study, students received the *diploma des études primaires supérieures indochinoises* (DEPSI). Those who completed seven years obtained a baccalaureate degree. Although the school was open to both boys and girls, girls were outnumbered six to one. Most girls admitted as students were graduates of the neighboring school of Dong Khanh and participated in only three of the classes offered *(classes secondaires)* at the Quoc Hoc. By the time Giap enrolled in 1925 the size of the student body was about twelve hundred.[21]

After reaching Hue, Giap rented a room in a private boardinghouse that was also home to four or five other boys enrolled at the lycée. He was eager to begin his coursework. At the lycée, he found that most of his teachers were Vietnamese, although there were a few French males assigned as instructors. One of Giap's classmates, Le Si Ngac, remembers him and the school well. "He was a nice boy, very bright, very smart, very good in school. We were in every class together. He was an excellent student. For a time we lived in the same small boardinghouse."[22]

Ngac, an aged man who now lives with his son in McLean, Virginia, recalled that "we were taught in French, except for one class. We studied French history, but very little Vietnamese history. During my time, when we graduated, we knew more about French history than our own Vietnamese past."[23]

It might not have been taught in school, but there were other ways for those boys to know the stories and legends of their country. Shortly after arriving at the Lycée Quoc Hoc, Giap came under the influence of a famous revolutionary nationalist, Phan Boi Chau, who lived under house arrest in Hue, not far from the school. Giap was not alone in this, for many of the boys looked at Chau as their hero. Giap himself recalls that "serious and hard-working, students at Quoc Hoc were very interested in politics."[24]

Le Si Ngac, Giap's roommate at the boardinghouse, was thrilled to have an opportunity to listen to such a great man. "Chau came to Quoc Hoc after his release by the French and made a speech. He attacked the French colonial system, so we were politically influenced by him. When you live under a French regime, you hate it. You hate it! Viet Nam was like a puppet, a marionette, with the French holding the strings. Everybody knew it. You resent it. Giap listened to him. . . . Giap decided to do something about it."[25]

Only recently arrived in Hue, Chau was a subject of interest wherever people stopped to talk, for he was one of the great leaders in the anticolonial movement. Seemingly destined as a youth for a bureaucratic career in one of those minor posts allowed by the French, he was led by his keen patriotism to follow a different path. He formed a nationalist group, the Restoration Society (Duy Tan

Hoi), in 1903. Two years later he fled to Japan, a popular Vietnamese refuge, where he wrote patriotic calls to anti-French feelings, asking his countrymen to join in creating a modern state in the homeland by substituting a western, scientific education for the traditional Confucianist system in place there.

Ordered to leave Japan in 1908, Chau moved to China, where, in 1912, he organized the Vietnamese Restoration Society (Viet Nam Quang Phuc Hoi), modeled after the great Sun Yat-sen's party. Imprisoned by the Chinese for a time, he was released in 1917. In Shanghai, Chau met Ho Chi Minh, then operating under the alias Ly Thuy. As heads of rival nationalist, revolutionary groups, they immediately distrusted each other, but in their quarrels Ho struck the first blow. In June 1925, for 100,000 piastres, he betrayed Chau to agents of the Deuxième Bureau, Sûreté Générale du Gouvernement Général pour l'Indochine (abbreviated as 2d Bureau)—the French police—and he was seized while passing through Shanghai's international settlement. Ly Thuy later rationalized that his was a good act. It stirred up resentment in Viet Nam against the French, which was necessary for the revolution, and the money helped Ho finance his work in Canton.[26]

Taken under guard to Ha Noi, Chau was tried by French colonial courts, convicted of treason, and sentenced to life imprisonment at hard labor. His prison term was commuted a few months later to permanent house arrest in Hue by the newly arrived French governor-general, Alexandre Varenne (1925–28). Chau lived under this arrangement for the last fourteen years of his life, dying 29 October 1940, one of the most respected Vietnamese of modern times.[27]

For whatever reason, the French allowed Chau to receive visits, and over the years many schoolboys like Giap came to his home to listen to his fiery visions. Sundays were a favorite time for Giap to visit the old revolutionary. "Often he told us about world events. On the walls of his house were portraits of Sun Yat-sen, Lenin, and Sakyamuni. We were of those youths so eagerly searching for the truth."[28]

Whether he was speaking at Lycée Quoc Hoc or to individuals and small groups at his home, Chau's message was the same: love for country, inspiration for what it could become, resolute resistance to the French, and the need for action. Time and again he spoke with Giap about democracy, the problems of Viet Nam, and abuses by the French colonial government. "The cock is crowing! Arise," he once told Giap, "arise and prepare for action!" One day Chau declaimed that "the oppressed people will rise up one day and fight for their independence. And on that day, woe to the French!"[29]

Thus from the time of his enrollment at the lycée in 1925, Giap's political awareness began to grow. Soon he invited other students to his boardinghouse room, where initially they discussed their classes at school. As their trust in one another grew, they talked, sometimes in whispers, of world problems and French colonialism in Viet Nam. Those who gathered respected Giap for his excellent

scholarship and his taste for revolution. In moments of repose, free from studies and talking politics with his friends, Giap sometimes crossed Hue's Perfume
River to the Citadel, where he stretched out on top of the bore of a French cannon standing in the shade near the gates of the old Imperial Palace. There he
continued to ponder the things he was learning and the shape his life might take
in years to come.[30] Perhaps, he thought, he might become a teacher in order "to
instill in the young feelings of patriotism and love of the freedom being trampled under foot by the foreign colonialists."[31]

"The Quoc Hoc of Hue," Giap has said, "was indeed the cradle of the student patriotic movement of Annam." His *quoc ngu* teacher, for one, emphatically
shared his own anticolonial views with students. Excited by hearing such opinions from teachers and from Chau, Giap and his friends became ever more convinced that one day France must release Viet Nam from its bondage. They passed
patriotic poems and essays around among themselves and gloried in the sentiments they read. Giap discovered nationalist newspapers such as *Le Paria* ("The
Pariah") and *Viet Nam Hon* and carefully read them.[32]

Then in 1926 during Giap's second year in school, Hai Trieu, one of his
friends, lent him a small book that would change his life. Disguised with a false
cover and title embossed in Arabic letters, the pamphlet was actually an essay
written by Ho Chi Minh, then using the pen name Nguyen Ai Quoc. Entitled *Le
procès de la colonisation française* ("Colonialism on Trial"), it inflamed Giap's
imagination. He went out into a field and climbed a tree so as to read it without
interruption. The essay, he recalled, "inspired us with so much hatred, and
thrilled us."[33] It was the first strand of the cable that would eventually bind his
fortunes with those of Ho Chi Minh and the revolutionary cause in Viet Nam.
Enraptured by the ideas of worldly revolutionaries elsewhere, Giap avidly read
French-language texts of other writings by Nguyen Ai Quoc and studied the
works of Marx and Lenin.

Feelings among Quoc Hoc boys grew ever more tense as they talked and
studied about their land's problems under the rule of France. There came a time
when talk was no longer enough. They called for actions that might demonstrate
their anti-French sentiments and patriotism. "We 'blew up' whenever chance
provided an occasion," Giap recalls, and there was an abundance of opportunity. They demonstrated when the French turned down a request from Phan
Boi Chau that he be freed from house arrest. Their ire rose again when Phan Chu
Trinh died. Trinh, an Annamite and a leading reformer, had been imprisoned
in 1908 for his part in supporting a peasant demonstration (the Revolt of the
Long Hairs) in Annam. After a time at the prison island of Poulo Condore, he
was sent into exile to France. In 1925 the French allowed him to return to Viet
Nam, where he died the following year.[34]

His funeral caused a widespread explosion of patriotic feelings. At Lycée
Quoc Hoc, in memory of Trinh, the boys dressed themselves in white mourning

clothes. According to Giap, this act enraged the French headmaster, who, with his supervisors, was in any case "hard and inquisitorial" with the students. At about that time Giap also took it upon himself to collect money to help those held in French prisons.[35]

The breaking point for Giap in his relations with the school administration came in 1927. The headmaster, whom Giap had nicknamed "the tyrant of Quoc Hoc," charged another student, Nguyen Chi Dieu, with cheating during an examination. Dieu, well known for his anticolonialist opinions, was one of Giap's close friends. Giap was certain there had been no cheating; he knew his friend too well. He believed the headmaster had made up the accusation simply as a way of ridding the school of a troublemaker. It was an injustice Giap could not overlook.

Giap and Dieu talked with their closest friends and classmates, who, in turn, talked to other students. They participated in a protest, a "quit-school movement." Both boys were surprised at the extent to which others took up this cause. It spread quickly throughout the lycée, then next door to Dong Khanh, the girls' high school, then even into area parochial secondary schools run by the Roman Catholic Church, and across the face of central Annam.[36]

Although the Quit-School Movement quickly collapsed, lycée authorities solemnly and righteously expelled Giap from the Quoc Hoc. Giap was not surprised—he had acted in full knowledge of the probable consequences—yet his expulsion still left him raging with anger. To vent his feelings, Giap wrote out an article in French—"Down with the Tyrant of Quoc Hoc"—which he submitted to Phan Van Truong, publisher of *L'Annam,* a French-language newspaper in Saigon. It was then the only newspaper openly criticizing French colonial policies and was widely read as far north as Hue. Truong published the piece. It was Giap's first venture into journalism.[37] He was sixteen years old.

Remaining in Hue after leaving the Quoc Hoc, Giap organized an underground reading library. Most of the documents he collected were supplied by French Communist organizations. For a time he and Nguyen Chi Dieu pondered the possibility of fleeing Viet Nam. Perhaps they should go abroad to join others in exile there. "Difficulties prevented us," he said later. "However, we continued to hope and wait for a favorable occasion."[38]

In those unsettled days following the end of his schooling, Giap sometimes traveled back to An Xa to see his father, Cuu Nghiem, and his mother, Kien. He was filled with turmoil, and the peace of his home village gave him an occasional sense of calm. During one of those home visits, his schoolmate Nguyen Chi Dieu visited him there and told of a newly organized group, the Tan Viet Cach Menh Dang (Revolutionary Party for a Great Viet Nam), known as Tan Viet. The secret group advocated political and social reform. Dieu was already a member. Perhaps Giap might be interested as well.[39]

"We Did Not Know How to Fight"

While an angry young Vo Nguyen Giap considered whether to join the Tan Viet, great changes were sweeping the world that would soon engulf him and mold decades of his life. The era of colonialism was coming to an end.

European nations long controlled immense expanses of Asia and Africa. Now, in the second decade of the twentieth century, that rigid structure was weakening. Millions of Japanese, intent on building a modern society, gloried in their recent defeat of Tsarist Russia at the naval battle of Tsushima Straits during the Russo-Japanese War of 1904–5, and the Russian empire shuddered and drew back. Revolution soon destroyed the tsarist regime and installed a new government under Vladimir Ulanov, known to his fellows as Nikolai Lenin. Revolution came also to China in 1911 when Sun Yat-sen brought his ideas home from his Hawaiian exile.

The Great War (1914–18) drastically weakened the countries of Europe—both financially and socially—and redrew the continent's political map. Peoples of Poland, Czechoslovakia, Yugoslavia, the Baltic states, and Finland found themselves independent, some for the first time in centuries. Many who lived under European colonial rule in Asia and Africa wondered, "Why them and not us?" Perhaps for the first time they began to realize that their masters were not wholly invincible, and they dreamed.

Threats to colonial systems became potentially graver in 1919 when Lenin ordered the creation of the Communist International (Comintern). Despite the fact that Russia was in chaos and the success of his own revolution had not yet been assured, Lenin dedicated himself to the worldwide overthrow of capitalism and its nation-state supporters. By the last years of the 1920s his Comintern agents (among whom was the young Annamite later known as Ho Chi Minh who wrote under the pen name Nguyen Ai Quoc) worked quietly and clandestinely to develop and heighten native discontent in many colonial territories around the world. When those people asked for relief and improvement in their conditions, the Dutch, English, and French reacted in shocked horror, tightening the strands by which they governed their colonists into steel bands.

In Annam, forty-three-year-old Emperor Khai Dinh met an untimely death in November 1925—the same year in which Vo Nguyen Giap entered the Lycée Quoc Hoc. Many Vietnamese raised their voices to call not for independence but for economic improvements and for a return to political conditions agreed on under the terms of the Harmand Treaty of 1883. The French seized this moment to strengthen their control. They insisted that Khai Dinh must be succeeded by the crown prince, Bao Dai, only twelve years old and a schoolboy in Paris. Until he came of age they would rule in his name. In the interim, the French *Résident Supérieur* at Hue arrogantly assumed for himself most of the last remaining remnants of imperial power, while his government arranged for Bao Dai ("Keeper of Greatness") to continue his studies in Paris for another seven years.

These actions intensified anti-French sentiments among the Vietnamese. Then came the Great Depression of 1929, which caused a disastrous plunge in the price of rice. Hardship and famine increased. Annamese nationalists and Communists, hearing of the actions of Sun Yat-sen and Mao Tse-tung in China and faced with the problems of the worldwide depression, began to organize themselves. Nationalists formed several small societies of disenchanted intellectuals who debated endlessly. Communists operated with more discipline and built upon a wider base, reaching down to include the great mass of those who labored endlessly and without surcease in rice paddies, among the trees of rubber plantations, and in the deadly mines.

Conditions on rubber plantations illustrate the neglect and savagery under which millions of Vietnamese toiled, watched by their French colonial masters. Workers labored to exhaustion from before dawn until after sunset, working in groves where the air steamed with liquid heat. Lunch consisted of a ball of sticky rice. Their drinking and cooking water came from brackish, mosquito-infested streams. At any time of the day or night they might be beaten at the whim of the *cai,* fellow Annamese overseers, many of them brutish sadists who served the French as labor foremen, police, and jailers.

One device used by *cai* consisted of beating laborers on the soles of their feet with bamboo rods and then forcing those hapless victims to run hobbling until they dropped. Replacements for workers were cheap, and so they could be beaten like animals and even killed. On every plantation was an isolation cell in which native troublemakers and the intemperate were thrown. Barracks of ragged thatch, through which water streamed from daily rains, housed laborers sometimes packed so tight many were forced to sleep seated, more than a few of them shaking with the chills of malarial fever. Wearing ragged clothes, their emaciated bodies covered with sores, these "yellows," these workers, endured agonizing days and listened receptively to whispers about a new secret organization, the Viet Nam Quoc Dan Dang, composed of nationalists and patriots working to free them from the French.

The VNQDD, or Vietnamese Nationalist Party, was founded in 1927 by Nguyen Thai Hoc, modeled after the political party of Sun Yat-sen in China. Born in the Red River Delta, Hoc was at first a moderate reformer, but became ever more inflamed when the French repeatedly ignored even mild requests for change. So Hoc's VNQDD dedicated itself to violent overthrow of the colonial regime and restoration of Viet Nam's independence. The VNQDD's lower-class origins made it, in many ways, closer to the laboring poor than were the Communists, many of whom—as Vo Nguyen Giap would be—were disenchanted and radicalized students from established middle-class families.

The VNQDD also held, rightly enough, that Communists, and Nguyen Ai Quoc in particular, were responsible for the arrest in China of Phan Boi Chau. To have treated a national hero in this way was, they said, shameful and unforgivable. In the years between 1927 and 1929, VNQDD agents organized an extensive following among radical young intellectuals, among workers, and even among soldier members of the French-run militia forces. In the summer of 1929, Hoc devised plans for an insurrection in 1930, to begin with attacks on French military posts in the Red River Delta. Lacking military experience or guidance, leaders of the insurrection made grave mistakes in coordination and control that ultimately doomed their efforts.

A competing group was composed of Indochinese Communist dissidents who worked hard to counter the appeal of the VNQDD. Lacking funds, they sometimes robbed wealthy Vietnamese, and thus many looked upon them as no more than brigands. In the political flux of those days, the Viet Nam Thanh Nien Cach Minh Dong Chi Hoi (Revolutionary Youth League), or Thanh Nien (Youth), established by Nguyen Ai Quoc in 1925, split into two factions. One formed the Duong Duong Cong San Dang (Indochina Communist Party) in 1929, and the remnant became the An Nam Cong San Dang (Annamese Communist Party). All too often these groups spent time and effort fighting each other instead of the French.

Those years between 1927 and 1929 were the same ones during which ex-schoolboy Vo Nguyen Giap joined his first secret society. Giap already knew of numerous secret societies and clandestine political parties competing with one another, all supposedly having the aim of securing Vietnamese independence.

They were also, he knew, ineffective, for they spent their time in endless discussions, in pointless meetings, in debating resolutions never carried out. Now Giap's friend Nguyen Chi Dieu offered him the opportunity to join the Tan Viet, and he did so enthusiastically in 1927.

Although the Tan Viet was a non-Communist organization, its political rhetoric sounded very Marxist. Its expressed goal was "to carry out first a national revolution and then a world revolution."[1] The party hierarchy ordered Giap to remain in Hue, working on their programs. Within a year, the Tan Viet began to split into factions, and Giap allied himself with the Communist-oriented one. Indeed, he has taken credit for organizing it, having written that "Nguyen Chi Dieu and Giap laid the foundations of the first Communist cell within the Tan Viet." Tired of debates, Giap was more and more drawn by the organization, efficiency, and discipline of the Communist Party.[2]

Enthused by his new responsibilities and as a cover for his Tan Viet activities, Giap found a job working for Huynh Thuc Khang, publisher of the *Tieng Dan* ("People's Voice") newspaper in Hue. It was the most important of the reform-minded newspapers in Annam, and although the 2d Bureau watched Khang and his employees carefully and read with care the pages he printed, for a time the police allowed it to continue in operation.

Giap threw himself into his new work and soon became familiar with every aspect of operating a newspaper and all the problems of journalism. He read everything possible, from commentaries on the world situation to social analysis. He wrote his articles with meticulous care, seeking the precise word needed to convey his exact meaning.

One story Giap wrote in which he investigated French capitalist exploitation of Viet Nam was entitled "Trading firms with capital over one million of dong." French authorities severely censured him for writing it. Authorship of the article and the subsequent censure caused Giap to adopt a tactic he followed for the rest of his life.

Giap knew he was constantly spied on by the 2d Bureau and was aware that at any moment the French could put an end both to his work at the newspaper and his duties for Tan Viet. As cover for his activities, Giap therefore began signing his articles under different aliases. He later recalled two he used while at *Tieng Dan:* Van Dinh and Hai Thanh.[3] As he sought to continue his work and avoid difficulties with the police, Giap listened to every rumor that told of the growing tension within Viet Nam between his people and the French authorities. And he held his breath, knowing that soon blood would flow.

The time for Nguyen Thai Hoc's planned VNQDD uprising in 1930 came ever closer. Although Hoc ordered attacks on major French garrisons at Hung Hoa, Lam Thao, and Ha Noi, the opening blow was to be mounted against a French hill fort, just outside the town of Yen Bay, on a curve of the Red River some sixty miles from Ha Noi. It was one of three built on jungled uplands of northern Tonkin as a first line of defense in case of a Chinese invasion.

The poorly armed VNQDD rebels hoped to persuade Vietnamese troops serving under the French to surrender their weapons or, better yet, to join the attack and turn their guns against French officers and NCOs. Disaster struck even before the attack could be mounted. When some carefully hoarded bombs accidentally exploded, French authorities realized they faced a crisis and moved swiftly to arrest VNQDD leaders. Afraid that the French would break the back of his group and all would be lost if they waited until the agreed-upon day of attack, Hoc sent word to waiting patriots for the uprising to begin on 9 February 1930. Then Hoc changed his mind and postponed the date to 15 February. VNQDD members gathering around Yen Bay did not receive these new orders. They struck out, expecting to be a part of a widespread rebellion, but they moved alone while others waited for the 15th.

VNQDD rebels gathered outside Yen Bay in the quiet hours of darkness during the night of 8/9 February 1930. Around their foreheads they wore bands of red and gold silk, red for the revolution, gold representing the people of Viet Nam. On their sleeves they wore red armbands stenciled with the words "Vietnamese Revolutionary Forces."

They attacked early on 9 February while those within the fort still slept. Lack of coordination, unwillingness on the part of many Vietnamese soldiers within the fort to join in the fray, and staunch resistance by the French all contributed to the rout of the rebels. French units came up the Red River Valley by train to cut off their retreat, although some few escaped downriver to safety among the faceless population of Ha Noi.

The raid brought terrible retribution down upon the VNQDD and anyone even suspected of sympathizing with its aims. When, a few days later, Hoc launched another raid in the lower delta against a French post there, his group became victims of the first air attack ever mounted in Indochina. The pilots were not particular who fell prey to their weapons. Flying five wood-and-fabric Potez 35 biplanes, they dropped sixty twenty-two-pound bombs and then strafed the ground with Lewis guns swivel-mounted in their cockpits. By the time they flew off, two hundred men, women, and children lay dead. Hoc himself was soon captured while trying to escape into China. Along with dozens of other members of the VNQDD, he was taken in mid-June to Yen Bay and guillotined. French reprisals decimated the party, and survivors fled into exile in southern China, where the VNQDD continued to exist as a shadow organization until an attempted return to Viet Nam during 1945–46.

Vietnamese testing of French rule did not end with the collapse of the Yen Bay risings. Communist agents, impressed by the sympathy, admiration, and increased patriotism sweeping the nation in the wake of the VNQDD attacks, decided it was time for action of their own to exploit the opportunity. The party hoped to destroy local governmental machinery and replace it with *Xo Viet* (soviet) Communist-run peasant associations. Their members spread a call for a rising, followed by factory strikes and riots on rubber plantations. A great surge of peasant support developed; to them, nothing seemingly could be worse than the famine already scourging a third of the population. On 1 May 1930—May Day—Communist-led "yellows" raised the hammer-and-sickle flag in northern Annam in the provinces of Nghe An, Ha Tinh, and Quang Ngai. These protests quickly developed into riots. The movement spread into some rich provinces of Cochin China: Ben Tre (Kien Hoa), Tra Vinh (Vinh Binh), Vinh Long, and Kien Giang.

Violence on both sides spread like a flame. The French called this period the "Red Terror," while Vietnamese nationalists and Communists knew it as the "White Terror." Peasants carrying spears and knives protested against high taxes and mandarin corruption. They burned district government offices, slew landlords and pro-French officials. Many who served the French fled for safety to Nghe An's provincial capital of Vinh.

Near-anarchy hovered over the jungles, paddies, and groves of Annam. During the summer and fall of 1930, angry Vietnamese gained control in hundreds of Annamese villages and set up a local *Xo Viet* in each that lowered taxes and rents. They seized land and redistributed it. They hunted down and punished greedy landlords who had not fled to safety. Peasants who refused to join the Communist cause were often tortured, their teeth pulled, their noses and ears cut off, and their thin beards set afire, before they were hanged or strangled or drowned.

In September, Communist leaders planned a great unarmed march of peasants into Vinh to publicize their plight and demand help from the French *résident* there. Planes from L'Armée de l'Air caught them on a long stretch of narrow road hemmed by trees and flooded paddies and bombed them, then strafed the bloodied and mutilated survivors. Over two hundred fell victim to French air power.

In a day when authorities had no fear of reporters sowing stories of repression before the court of world opinion, the French moved swiftly to destroy this threat. They systematically destroyed villages that had materially or financially supported the rebels. Troops then entered the shattered communities and systematically killed all cattle and poultry and then burned rice stocks. Bamboo hedges sheltering the villages were cut off at ground level.[4]

One man recalled those days. "As a young elementary school student in 1930, I still remember seeing many [French] posters along the streets with illustrations representing insurgents as murderers and rapists burning houses in hamlets, cutting heads off children and raping women in the middle of market places."[5]

Even distant relatives of captured rebels were condemned as criminals and refused access to jobs or prohibited from further schooling. The colonial administration imprisoned or exiled some seventy thousand nationalist and Communist Vietnamese and executed another seven hundred without even the show of a trial. This operation had not been without costs to the French. *Two* had died during that time of trouble! In a matter of months, the power and hopes of both VNQDD nationalists and the Communists had been destroyed.

The party leadership had been gutted. Many were executed, imprisoned, or exiled. Local organizations were almost totally destroyed, and those who remained alive were forced underground until the emergence of the Popular Front government in France in 1936. Yet a lesson was there for those willing to see it: the potential military and political power of rural peasants was available to those willing to cultivate their needs and interests and use them. The Communists learned and applied this knowledge during and after World War II. The nationalists did not.

Vo Nguyen Giap continued to live a double life; there was no choice for him as the White Terror of French rage coursed through the land. While openly working long hours at the *Tieng Dan* newspaper, Giap was also deeply involved in clandestine activities for the Tan Viet party. It was an arduous and dangerous life for a young man of only nineteen years. Giap needed to keep a close watch on his surroundings, aware of those in crowds around him on the street, looking to discover any who followed him. He knew he was the subject of careful investigation by agents of the 2d Bureau, who kept detailed notes of their observations and entered them into waiting files, the gist of which was regularly forwarded to Ha Noi headquarters.

It was about this time that a curious figure came like a shadow into Giap's life for a season, eventually bringing him undreamed rewards. This man was Louis Marty, Directeur des Affaires Politique des Sûreté Générale du Gouvernement Général pour l'Indochine, Viet Nam's top French cop. An old Asia hand fluent in both Chinese and Vietnamese, Marty had come to the area in the early years of the twentieth century and served successive governors-general as head of intelligence and security operations. Although ruthless enough when he felt it to be necessary, Marty hoped that the French administration in Indochina could defuse radical Vietnamese anti-Gallic attitudes by encouraging "colonization by means of books," so he encouraged publication of books and journals printed in *quoc ngu* rather than the traditional Chinese ideographs. One such publication was *Nam Phong*, edited for a time by Pham Quynh, and Marty believed all such efforts provided Vietnamese intellectuals, especially young ones, with a grand alternative to political activities that might threaten the stability of the *colons'* regime. This policy would be a *"conquête morale des habitants après la conquête matérielle du pays."*

In his Ha Noi office, located in the vicinity of the Botanical Garden near those of the governor-general of Indochina, Marty may well have kept a file on the young Giap, the material supplied to him by Martin, the police commissar at Vinh. Why not? Giap was certainly a man worth watching: he had been a student leader at Lycée Quoc Hoc; he had defied the school administration and participated in a student "quit-school movement"; he had often visited the patriot Phan Boi Chau; he had participated in the general strikes called to protest the execution of the Yen Bay insurgents; he had written articles critical of the French administration; he was certainly a militant, probably a member of the Tan Viet party, and perhaps a Communist.[6] And so Giap was watched.

By the end of 1930, in their efforts to stamp out dissidence, the French police dragnet snared a number of different suspects of all types throughout central Annam: employers, workers, peasants, intellectuals—old and young alike. Among those arrested were Giap and his brother, Vo Thuan Nho. Another man seized by the authorities was Dang Thai Mai, a professor of literature at Lycée Quoc Hoc, one of Giap's teachers, and a fellow Tan Viet member. Also arrested was Nguyen Thi Quang Thai, a fifteen-year-old schoolgirl from Lycée Dong Khanh in Hue. Giap did not know her until they became acquainted with one another during the months they spent in prison.[7]

French police arrested several other teachers from Lycée Quoc Hoc in addition to Professor Mai, and at their trials most received sentences of six to seven years, although Mai received but four. The adolescent Quang Thai faced three years. Giap initially received only a suspended two-year sentence, because he had been careful enough in his activities that little evidence existed against him. The prosecutor finally managed, however, to overturn the suspension to ensure that Giap would serve those years at hard labor.[8]

In accounts of his life, Giap has always passed over in silence the years between 1930 and 1932. He was in prison; what else was there to say? Giap, his brother Nho, Professor Dang Thai Mai, little Quang Thai, and many others learned they would serve their terms at the Lao Bao penitentiary in the mountains near the Laotian border. Yet they were the lucky ones. Many of those sent never returned. Even prisoners able to deal with the rigors of prison discipline at Lao Bao often succumbed to sickness, for the site was rife with malaria and other diseases.[9]

This imprisonment was not, however, unalloyed misery for Giap. At Lao Bao he came to know Quang Thai. Four years older than she, Giap found her to be delightful and soon realized that he was in love. Then, thirteen months after he arrived at Lao Bao to serve his sentence, Giap received word that a governmental order had been issued reducing all sentences less than four years long. Those released under its provisos, however, were not to be freed, but were to return to their home villages to serve the remainder of their time under house arrest. Giap was elated as both he and Quang Thai walked out through the gates of the prison early in 1932.[10]

Instead of obeying the official notice to return to An Xa, an undaunted and defiant Giap went instead to Hue. That was where his Tan Viet duties were, and he also had hopes of returning to work at the *Tieng Dan* newspaper. But on the second day after his arrival in Hue—in an entirely reasonable move, since Giap was violating the terms of his release—the French *résident* ordered him out of the city and back to An Xa.[11]

At home for a time, Giap decided, once again without permission, to go to Vinh, capital of Nghe An province, and promptly did so. Three reasons impelled this choice. He needed work and hoped to find a job there. Professor Dang Thai Mai, his former teacher, now also released from Lao Bao prison, lived in Vinh and might be able to help him in one way or another. More important, Vinh was the family home of Nguyen Huy Binh, father of Giap's friend from prison Nguyen Thi Quang Thai. Originally from Ha Dong, Mr. Binh worked for the railway at the Vinh train station. His two oldest children were his daughters Nguyen Thi Minh Khai, born in 1910, and Nguyen Thi Quang Thai, born in 1915.[12]

When Giap arrived in Vinh, Professor Mai opened his home to him and invited the young man to move his few belongings into his house. Now for the first time Giap met Professor Mai's family and came to know and enjoy his six children. One daughter, Dang Bich Ha, born in 1929, was eighteen years younger than Giap, and in 1932, as she toddled around the house, she thought of Giap as the young brother of her father, calling him *chu* ("uncle").[13]

Giap soon found a job, on Maréchal Foch Street, as an accountant. He also offered private tutoring in mathematics and French. It did not take Giap long to learn that Mr. Binh's family home was not far from Professor Mai's dwelling, and Quang Thai became one of his students. As he spent ever more time with her in their tutoring sessions, Giap's feelings for her deepened.[14]

Giap already knew Quang Thai's sister, Minh Khai, only a year older than he. Although both daughters of Mr. Binh were militant in their desire to see the end of French rule over Viet Nam, Minh Khai was more revolutionary. She began her anti-French activities while still a student at the College of Cao Xuan Duc in Vinh. In March 1926, when she was only sixteen, Khai joined other participants in public ceremonies mourning the death of the patriot Phan Chu Trinh, who had long called for national independence. While she demonstrated in Vinh, Giap did so also as a student at Lycée Quoc Hoc in Hue.

Both Giap and Minh Khai joined the Tan Viet in 1927, and both were drawn to its more militant wing. Recognizing her leadership abilities, fellow members elected her to the provincial committee of the party. Political activity absorbed all Minh Khai's energy. During the summer of 1930, just a few weeks before Giap's arrest and probably just in time to save herself from the French police dragnet, Minh Khai took a boat to Hong Kong, where she worked in the Asian office of the Communist International. She returned to Vinh only sporadically, and then in great secrecy. She could rarely remain at home more than a few days or a week before she had to flee again back to Hong Kong.

An extraordinarily emancipated woman for her time, Minh Khai enjoyed sports, including competition swimming, an activity unusual for Vietnamese women. British police in Hong Kong arrested her on 29 April 1931 for political activities, and she remained imprisoned until 1932. Authorities there then turned her over to Chinese authorities in Canton, who imprisoned her until 1934. Following a brief visit to Vinh, Minh Khai returned for a time to Hong Kong, where she met the man she would later marry, Le Hong Phong. Soon she was in Moscow for a course of political training at the Oriental School there.

In July 1935, Minh Khai went to Moscow as part of the Vietnamese delegation to the Seventh Congress of the Communist International. She finally returned to Viet Nam in 1937, and for a time she worked closely on party matters in Saigon with Le Hong Phong and there became his wife. Minh Khai also served as chief liaison between the Communist Party in Vinh and the central committee of the party in Ha Noi. In September 1939, with the French police closing in on her, she once again disappeared into the clandestine underground. Despite her fugitive ways, politics caused both Minh Khai and Giap to encounter one another with some frequency from 1937 until he fled into China in May 1940.[15]

Younger sister Quang Thai felt drawn toward the activism displayed by Minh Khai. She was sufficiently militant to have caused the 2d Bureau to start a dossier on her before she was fifteen. Already she boasted a prison record for patriotism. Tutored by Giap, she could only deepen her devotion to free Viet Nam from French control. And then her teacher left Vinh. When Professor Dang Thai Mai accepted a new position on the faculty of the private Lycée Thang Long in Ha Noi in 1933, Giap chose to move north with him and his family, leaving Quang Thai behind in Vinh. Before leaving he promised not to forget her. Later, in the capital city of Tonkin, Giap continued to live with Professor Mai and his family.[16]

Louis Marty, director of political affairs, whose agents had watched Giap for so long, now took a more personal interest in him, making it possible for him to complete his education. At this juncture the details may never be known. Giap himself refused to comment on Marty, asserting that all such questions were inspired by "non-serious, even false and reactionary documents."[17] It seemed to be a callous attitude toward one who provided a way for him to complete his schooling.

Whenever and however it happened, Marty came to know of the brilliant, angry young Annamese militant. Little exists to explain the reason for the humane treatment Marty was about to offer Giap. Perhaps it was enough that he believed it was easier to administer a colony inhabited by friendly junior partners than to rule over sullen foreigners. Perhaps he realized that it was better not to let such a gifted person, with the possibility of a good career, a man who might become a faithful servant of France, become lost in the seething underclass of Viet Nam. To Marty, Giap seemed to have learned his lesson, and it was time to tame and neutralize the young man. Giap may somehow have placated the terrible suspicions the French government held toward all who might threaten its hold on Indochina. He would not have been the first Annamese to be rehabilitated. But Marty committed the worst mistake of his career when he reached out to Giap, for by this act he contributed to the eventual demise of French rule in Viet Nam.[18]

Marty encouraged Giap, during meetings in 1933, to study independently and then apply to take the first part of the baccalaureat examination. That would secure for him a high school diploma, the equivalent of an American associate of arts degree. If he passed, Marty said, he would sponsor Giap's entrance to the famous Ha Noi school Lycée Albert Sarraut, named after one of Indochina's most progressive former governors (1911–14, 1917–19). "All intellectuals in Viet Nam went to Ha Noi to study. It was the center of intellectual activity. The Lycée Albert Sarraut was simply the best."[19]

What Marty proposed was to be no easy task for two reasons. Perhaps one of the gravest prohibitions imposed on the people of Viet Nam came through French regulations barring most youth from entrance to higher education and from competitive examinations for government positions. These limitations were necessary, the French claimed, to avoid overcrowding the schools and to prevent troublemakers from causing problems for the colonial administration. It was considered a very special favor when even francophile families occasionally received a special passport allowing a son to go abroad to France or elsewhere to continue his studies.

In all of Tonkin, only one center existed where students could take the final examination for their baccalaureate degree—in Ha Noi. In all of Annam, after about 1937, the same condition obtained—in Hue. And of those who took such tests, the great majority failed. In Hue in 1943, for example, three thousand students took the examination and only sixty-one received a passing grade.

The second reason posed an even graver difficulty. Under French colonial authority, young Vietnamese troublemakers never got a second chance. If they were expelled from school, their education ended. There was no recourse from this rigidity.[20] If Giap was to receive further schooling, he would need all the help he could get. Marty was ready to offer it.[21]

While he immersed himself in his books, Giap also found it necessary to obtain different small jobs to earn enough money to survive. For a time he worked as a research assistant for Pierre Gourou, the major French geographer of Indochina, author of such books as *Peasants of the Tonkin Delta* and *The Agriculture of French Indochina.*[22] When free of other duties, Giap focused on his studies, and when the next examination was held, he passed without undue difficulty. He then applied to enter Lycée Albert Sarraut in Ha Noi and, with Marty's sponsorship, was accepted.

Was there a quid pro quo for Marty? There may well have been. A curious undated (save that it was accessioned in 1972), unattributed typescript (once part of a larger whole, for its three sheets are paginated 14, 15, and 16) in the Indochina Archive lists certain salient facts about Giap's life, including the statement that from 1936 to 1939 he "acted as intermediary between the Indochinese Communist Party . . . in Hanoi when making contacts with MARTY, Director of Political Affairs of the French Security Police in Indochina." No indication is given as to what those "contacts" consisted of nor why they were necessary.[23]

What might Marty have gotten from such an arrangement? Perhaps information on plans, policies, and memberships of other political parties in competition with the Communists of Viet Nam. What might Giap have gained? Not only his education. A Vietnamese scholar suggests that Giap, "both intelligent and astute, doublecrossed the old fox Marty by applying the tactic of 'Tuong ke tuu ke,' making Marty believe he had been trapped in order better to trap, in turn, his adversary; to use his sponsor so that when the time came he would be better able to achieve his own goals."[24]

Whatever the reason, Giap seemed to lead a charmed life during the late 1930s, a time when others were in real danger. A great many things broke in his favor while all around him party members and comrades were arrested, exiled, imprisoned for lengthy terms at places like Poulo Condore, the prison island, and even guillotined. Giap emerged unscathed. His relationship with Marty seems to have ended in 1939 with the outbreak of World War II.

In September 1932, the same year in which Giap was released from prison, the French had finally allowed Crown Prince Bao Dai to return from Paris to Viet Nam, where he was crowned emperor. He was eighteen, a cosmopolitan, and out of place among his court of mandarins and the ancient etiquette that mandated all actions. Tyrannized by his mother, dubbed by French *colons* "the Tigress," he began to take long, solitary hunts in the forest and to suffer from nervous breakdowns. Yet he was determined to restore some vestige of self-government and to instigate needed internal reforms. During the time Giap was studying to pass the baccalaureate and hoping to enter Lycée Albert Sarraut, Emperor Bao Dai was taking his first steps toward reform. Powerless, lonely, and frustrated, Bao Dai revealed an independence of mind which surprised the French. They thought they had trained all such traits out of him before his return.[25]

Bao Dai certainly was no militant. He hoped to promote a loyal alliance between France and Viet Nam based upon their own treaty of 25 August 1883, but ultimately could convince neither the French nor his own people. In internal affairs at Thai Hoa palace, he halted the practice of mandarins prostrating themselves in his presence. By tradition, emperors had little direct contact with their people. Most saw him only in his pictures. Bao Dai, a shy man, wanted to simplify traditionally hallowed practices and bring himself closer to his people, so he forbade mandarins to prostrate themselves in his presence, abolished the official harem, and selected a new cabinet that included, for the first time, a man who was not a mandarin.[26]

Bao Dai was incensed at the disparity between salaries received by Vietnamese in high office and those paid to French *colons.* "A governor of a large province, like the brother of Ngo Dinh Diem, governor of Quang Nam province, earned less than a simple French policeman on duty in Hanoi," he wrote.[27] This was common practice. *Colons*—military and civilian alike—were so well treated, even coddled with excessive allowances for service in Indochina, that a saying appeared in France: *Il faudrait être fils d'Archevêque pour pouvoir être affecté en Indochine* ("It is necessary to be the son of an archbishop to get one's name on the departure list for Indochina").[28]

The case of Hoang Xuan Han serves as an example. A graduate from the Ecole Polytechnique in France and later minister of national education in Viet Nam, Han served during the 1930s as professor of sciences at Lycée Albert Sarraut in Ha Noi. Despite his education and the difficulty of the classes he taught, his salary there was but half that of the French janitor at the same school, a man who had finished only junior high school *(brevet elementaire)!*[29] It was no wonder that Bao Dai wanted such unequal treatment ended. After just eighteen months of facing French stubbornness, Bao Dai felt hopeless.

"All has been in vain," he wrote. "I now believe the nationalist insurgents were right. And I am not the only one to think so. Even in France many people share this opinion. Recently," he continued, "I read this sentence from André Malraux: 'It is hard to conceive of a courageous Vietnamese who is not a revolutionary.' " Bao Dai recalled how Pham Quynh, his minister of education, had written a decade earlier that "Vietnamese are like foreigners in their own country." That sentiment burned in his heart as well. "I also feel that way," he insisted. "During a recent trip to Tonkin I was a sovereign stranger. The French have put me in this situation. I live inside my own country as a foreign sovereign-in-exile—like my predecessors—but in exile in my own country, amidst my own people, themselves also in exile."[30]

As Emperor Bao Dai struggled to exert even some small level of influence on French colonial policy, Vo Nguyen Giap prepared himself to apply for admission to Lycée Albert Sarraut in Ha Noi, encouraged to do so by his sponsor, Marty. Giap obtained the first part of the French baccalaureate in 1933 by passing the required examination. Now it was time to enter the school itself.

Although most vacancies for the freshman class were reserved for the sons and daughters of French *colons,* Indochinese youth could qualify by passing a competitive examination, and that is what Giap did. When administrators at Albert Sarraut announced the opening of vacancies for freelance candidates, Giap applied and, on the recommendation of Marty, was accepted. He was also helped by a longtime member of the French Communist Party and professor of philosophy at the University of Ha Noi, Marcel Ner, who intervened to have admission fees dropped for Giap. Ner apologized to the authorities on behalf of Giap for his involvement in protest movements, explaining that the misguided boy had believed they were based on the ideal of the 1789 French Revolution, the study of which was a part of the instruction for all schools in Viet Nam.[31]

Giap fit well into a student body chafing under French rule. He was as determined as any of his fellows to struggle for Vietnamese freedom, but membership in the Tan Viet, his earlier problems with the 2d Bureau, and his prison term had all taught him well. He knew how to discipline himself, how to hide his emotions, and how to stay away from trouble. There is no indication during his months at Lycée Albert Sarraut that the 2d Bureau paid him any special attention. To all appearances, he had learned his lesson and would be, in the years ahead, a compliant subject of French rule in Indochina. Working with dedication and speed in regular classes, Giap soon stood ranked first in philosophy.

A former student at the school, Nguyen Dinh Tu, recalls what life there was like. Admission was the first hurdle. "We had to write an essay in French, graded both on content and spelling. Then we had to reason out the answers for mathematic problems. Lastly, we had to sing a French song. . . . I knew only one; I asked a boy who already attended the Lycée to teach it to me." Mr. Tu laughed at the memory of his simple ploy. "One day was devoted to the written examination; another for oral questions. The examination was given by the French."[32]

Mr. Tu, a man in his eighties, could remember only two Vietnamese on the faculty. There were, he recalled, about a thousand students at the school when he attended it in the early 1930s.

"From 7:30 until 11:30 A.M. and again from 2:30 to 5:30 P.M. we attended classes. Students studied very hard, but there was time to walk the streets of Ha Noi; to sit on the banks of the Hoan Kiem ["Lake of the Returned Sword"], to organize teams and play soccer against one another." There was also time to think about his country. "I was always thinking of liberating our nation from French rule. Others who shared my view, we got together, even students from other lycées, and we discussed how to fight them and to set our country free. Our own idea was how to be patriotic. We talked [most often] outside the grounds of the lycée. But we talked about that in our own way. We were not mature. Some of us were arrested because we were still very naive. We did not know how to fight."[33] Those last words formed a lament that explained the continuing plight of all militant Vietnamese. They did not yet know how to fight.

By the end of 1934, Giap had completed the second part of the baccalaureate.[34] Now that he was armed with his degree, it did not take him long to find work as a teacher at Lycée Thang Long ("Rising Dragon"), a private school in Ha Noi, where he taught history and the French language for three hours daily. Operated by Huynh Thuc Khang, Thang Long was a center of revolutionary sentiment and activity. Giap relished the atmosphere. Glad to have work and an income, Giap still wanted to continue his education. Increasingly disappointed by the lack of discipline and fervor he found within the Tan Viet party and ever more interested in a pure communism, Giap wanted to know more about political economy and so applied for and was granted admission to the School of Law (Faculté de Droit) at the University of Ha Noi.[35] As if teaching a heavy load at Thang Long while also attending graduate school at the university were not a sufficient burden, Giap soon decided also to publish his own newspaper. Before long, he was going to be busier than he had believed possible.

THREE

"They Set Their
Hopes on the Same Cause"

As a teacher at Thang Long and a graduate student at the university, Vo Nguyen Giap continued to board at Professor Mai's home. At work his students held him in high esteem, and his principal, Ton That Binh, also initially approved of him.[1] He fit right in with the mood at the school, which one man described as "seething with anticolonial feeling and Socialist debate about Viet Nam's future."[2] His students ranged in age from fourteen to eighteen, and the school itself maintained a curriculum roughly equivalent to that of a combination American senior high school and junior college. Giap used history to further his political goals. He believed that teaching it helped him "to imbue my students with patriotism."[3]

In later years, former students recalled Giap's days in the classroom. "Giap was really respected," Nguyen Dinh Tu recalled. "He was a very dedicated and strong patriot. Always he spoke of how to oust the French. Of course he did not speak of communism, only nationalism. So at the time all of us saw him as a patriot and did not think of him as a Communist." Giap, a dedicated Communist, turned many classroom lectures in history into political harangues.[4]

One student who later fled the Communist north in 1954 recalled that Giap was renowned among the student body as an excellent lecturer on historical topics, particularly military history. Many remembered him as a "fanatic fighter who never smiled and never let interlocutors convince him in anything." He remembered how Giap "could step to a blackboard and draw in the most minute detail every battle plan of Napoleon."[5] Another student was thirteen-year-old

Bui Diem, who remembered Giap as a man already "possessed by the demons of revolution and battle."

Giap's history course was to cover France from 1789 to the middle of the nineteenth century. From the very beginning, Giap made it plain that he would treat material in his own way. As he stood before his students on the term's opening day, Giap looked at them and then said, "There are a lot of books about this stuff. If you want to know about it, you can look it up. I'm only going to tell you about two things: the French Revolution and Napoleon."[6]

Half a century later, Bui Diem still clearly remembered Giap's teaching style: "his detailed descriptions of Marie Antoinette's luxury and decadence that left us with no doubts about the justice of her fate; the rousing accounts of the Committee for Public Safety, the Paris Commune, and the lives and deaths of Danton and Robespierre." Fascinated by the French Revolution and its leading figures, Giap spoke, Bui Diem recalled, "not as a mere historian but as a passionate advocate."[7]

Nervously prowling back and forth at the front of the room, Giap described "every action that demonstrated the development of Napoleon's tactics and strategy": separate battles where Napoleon flung his soldiers at the armies of Europe and even individual skirmishes between small units. All of it Giap had memorized. He wanted his students to know "why this squadron of dragoons had been positioned here or why the Imperial Guard had charged at this particular moment." His classes sat silently, infected by his contagious excitement, enthralled by his stories, as they listened to the details of Napoleon's career Giap laid before them.[8]

Despite the attention he gave to this subject, Giap later claimed that his interest in Napoleon simply grew out of his responsibility to teach his students the history of the French Revolution.[9] So Giap studied Napoleon's tactics and strategy until he knew them well.[10]

It was not long before his students gave him two nicknames: "the general" and "Napoleon." (Fifty-six years later, when asked about those nicknames, the long-retired general's only reaction was to laugh with amusement.)[11]

So rumor has it, Giap "walked and even talked in the Napoleonic manner, in short sentences, with his head hanging and his thumb stuck into his jacket." Colleagues described him as a "cold fish, with a poker face, subject to sudden anger between moments of stony silence." One day another teacher allegedly asked him, "Aren't you playing Napoleon?" to which Giap replied, "I'm going to *be* Napoleon!" He may well have thought of himself in this way, for in later days when he granted interviews, Giap regularly managed to work references to Napoleon into his monologues with reporters.[12]

Giap worked with students both in and out of class. They occasionally stopped at his home after classes to talk, and Giap regularly tried to influence their political views. Bui Diem remembers that he had a French-language copy of Karl Marx's *Das Kapital* in his bookshelf. Giap urged him to read Marx and other socialist books. "[But] the Marxist model that Giap . . . proposed," Bui Diem said, "left me cold and unconvinced."[13]

Giap expected only the best from his pupils. Just as he had worked hard at Lycée Quoc Hoc in Hue, so now he insisted upon the same devotion to study from students at Lycée Thang Long. As he demanded from them, so also did he give to his own professors at the university, and thus he made a lasting impression on them. He was pleased with what he learned in his classes in law and political economy. They were subjects that had interested him since age eighteen when he began his journalistic work at the *Tieng Dan* newspaper.[14]

In 1947, Professor Marcel Ner, Giap's Communist teacher at the University of Ha Noi, remembered him as "a sentimental and passionate man, deeply attached both to his country and to Communism."[15] Another instructor recalled that Giap was "the most brilliant student at the University at that time . . . a young man eager to learn" but "introverted."[16]

Another of Giap's instructors was also a Frenchman, Professor Gregoire Kherian, who in later years returned to Paris. In April 1945, when the Japanese took control of Ha Noi away from the French, officials of their secret police, the Kempetai, ordered faculty members to be interned. Kherian, who was then head of the political economy department at the university, received permission from one of the Japanese officers to go to his office and collect his papers. He retrieved only one pupil's dossier—that belonging to Giap, perhaps in an attempt to protect him. "He was my favorite pupil," said Kherian. "He was brilliant and very brave." When interviewed by a newsman in 1972, Kherian still had Giap's file, which included a paper he had written titled "The Balance of Payments in Indo-China." The essay, noted Kherian, was "an excellent exposé on a difficult subject." It had "clarity, method and also personality."

Kherian's most intriguing memory, however, concerned the end of Giap's university career, when he was offered the opportunity to leave Viet Nam to study in France. "Giap had passed out top [graduated] in Political Economy in 1938," Kherian noted. "Every year we had a senior economist from Paris to pass the students," he explained. "That year it was M. Gaeton Pirou. . . . He was director of the Cabinet of Paul Doumer, the Prime Minister. He told me he was very impressed by Giap's work and asked me about him. I said he had been in trouble with the authorities, that he was a hothead." Pirou then said, "We must take him out of the colonial environment. Bring him to Paris. He can study anything. We'll provide for him."

Kherian relayed the substance of his conversation with Pirou to Giap, who asked for some time to think about the offer. "The second day he came back and said he could not abandon his comrades and act like an egoist." The scholarship was given to another student, Vu Van Hien.[17] Giap thus turned down this unusual offer to accept a scholarship to France, where he might study anything he liked. His fervor made him impervious to such French efforts to co-opt bright young Vietnamese for reeducation in France where they could be influenced to follow pathways safe to the empire.

With the aid of Professor Kherian, who prepared him for his examinations, Giap received in 1937 his *licence en droit*, equivalent to a Bachelor of Law degree, with a poor grade in public law but high marks in political economy. Later asked how he felt on that occasion, he answered with a droll and simple phrase: *"Très content."* He chose not to obtain a certificate of administrative law, which would have allowed him to become an attorney. Over fifty years later, when asked why he had not become a lawyer, his answer was straightforward: "I never wished to be a lawyer."[18]

Giap continued at the University of Ha Noi during 1938, now studying at the graduate level, concentrating on his assignments in political economy, in hopes of one day receiving a doctor's degree. A voracious reader, he used the library's facilities extensively, systematically working his way through its holdings on history and communism. Other interests, however, took an increasing toll on his time, and his grades suffered accordingly. Finally, unable to keep up with his assignments and ever busier with other, more pressing interests, Giap left school forever, never receiving a doctorate in law or political science, as many western writers have claimed.[19]

The reason for the end of Giap's days as a student began two years earlier. Daily on his way to and from work at Lycée Thang Long, he walked down Trang Tien Street. It was his custom to stop at one intersection and read news accounts posted there on a bulletin board. One afternoon in May 1936, as he walked toward home, he saw on the bulletin board a notice of a momentous recent occurrence in France. The Front Populaire there, composed of several political parties, prominent among them Communists and Socialists, had won a general election. Giap was elated as he read the news. He knew the forthcoming government would change at least some of the colonial restrictions governing Viet Nam. There was no time to waste; it was a propitious moment to begin publishing a newspaper which could be filled with column after column of anti-colonial views.[20]

Giap spoke to a small group of friends, fellow teachers at Thang Long, and persuaded them to join him in his enterprise. Giap knew of an existing weekly newspaper, struggling against bankruptcy, that the owner might be willing to sell. Pooling their savings, these teachers succeeded in purchasing publishing rights to this paper, *Hon Tre* ("Soul of Youth"). Inasmuch as its owner already possessed the necessary licenses required by the colonial administration for a Vietnamese-language newspaper, Giap and his friends had no need to contend with the endless red tape required for a new application to publish.[21]

On 4 June 1936, the Socialist Léon Blum took his oath of office in Paris as France's new prime minister. Two days later, aided by a small group of friends,

Giap published the first issue of the journal *Hon Tre Tap Moi* ("Soul of Youth, New Edition"). It was the first Vietnamese-language publication to call for democracy and for amnesty for political prisoners, and to signify approval of the new French Popular Front government. It was a huge success. Giap and the others could not print sufficient copies to satisfy reader demand. After only the fifth issue, however, French authorities closed down the newspaper.[22]

Undismayed, Giap decided to circumvent the colonial demands. He had been told he could not publish a Vietnamese-language newspaper, but no one had forbidden him to print a newspaper in French. So *Hon Tre Tap Moi* shut down and on 16 September 1936 *Le Travail* ("Work") put out its first issue, with Giap serving as editor in chief. A few weeks later, one of Giap's friends came to the paper's offices. The man was Dang Xuan Khu, who, impressed with Mao's activities in China, used the alias Truong Chinh, "Long March." Just released from Son La prison, where he had been held since 1930 for anti-French activities, this man would later become one of the leading party functionaries and a Politburo member. He made his way to Ha Noi, posing as a journalist named Qua Ninh. Giap welcomed him and put him to work on the newspaper.[23]

The size of the editorial staff increased again early in 1937 when Pham Van Dong, later his country's prime minister for over thirty years, walked into the offices of *Le Travail.* Dong, like Giap, had attended Lycée Quoc Hoc in Hue. French police arrested him in 1931, and he spent the years until 1937 at Poulo Condore. Now Pham Van Dong, Truong Chinh, and Vo Nguyen Giap would work together at *Le Travail.*[24]

Giap was intrigued by stories told him by Truong Chinh and Pham Van Dong. They had been Communists for several years, and their tales of devotion and sacrifice, of discipline and order, of goals and methods, sounded ever more tempting. As he listened, Giap became ever more dissatisfied with the Tan Viet party to which he belonged. Even its Communist wing he had earlier helped organize now became simply an irrelevancy to him.

Giap wanted to work actively against the French, and now Truong Chinh and Pham Van Dong held out to him the opportunity to do so by joining the Indochinese Communist Party. Founded in February 1930 as the Vietnamese Communist Party, it had changed its name on instructions from the Comintern in Moscow because Soviet leaders believed Vietnamese revolutionaries were too weak to defeat the French colonial regime on their own. They should join with Communists in Laos and Cambodia to form a joint party representing all Indochina. Severely repressed, nearly destroyed by French authorities following the Nghe-Tinh Soviet revolt in 1930–31, survivors reestablished their organization during the Popular Front years, 1936–39, and again became the primary political organization opposed to French rule in Viet Nam. In 1937 it seemed the choice to make, and Giap gladly entered the ranks of that party.[25]

He had hopes for the future based on the past. Under Pierre Gourou he had studied the conditions and attitudes of Vietnamese peasants. First as a student and then as a teacher he had drunk deeply of the history of his own nation. Surely thoughts of the Tay Son Rebellion of 1771 and the later uprising of the VNQDD at Yen Bay went far to convince him of what could be accomplished when a mass political base was combined with the tactics of surprise, flexibility, and strategic momentum.[26]

Now with his political vision focused, Giap took his newspaper work even more seriously. On one occasion, he rode his bicycle from Ha Noi to Cam Pha, north of Haiphong, and back in order to report on a miners' strike.[27] Together with Truong Chinh (the Communist Party had sent Pham Van Dong under the alias Lam Ba Kiet on an assignment to south China), Giap organized several other newspapers that he published in French or in Vietnamese. Because of the new Popular Front government in France, which brought ripples of change even as far away as Indochina, limited political activity was permitted, including publication of nationalist newspapers.

Giap spent more and more time writing articles. Who knew how long it would be possible to publish freely? At least eleven additional weekly journals Giap and Truong Chinh initiated quickly appeared and disappeared as authorities became provoked and tracked down their locations. As well, Giap wrote articles for at least three other journals and sat on the editorial boards of still two more. In his "spare" time in 1937, Giap went as a delegate to the Congress of Newspapers of Central Viet Nam and served as chairman for the First Congress of Newspapers of Tonkin. It is little wonder that he felt overwhelmed at times.[28]

In the seven months of its existence, Giap issued thirty issues of *Le Travail*. By now he knew every facet of newspaper work: he wrote leading articles and stories of current events, composed listings for the "news in brief" comments, investigated and reported on a variety of subjects dealing with colonialism, worked with type fonts on makeup and composition, inked rollers, operated the printing press, and very often even personally delivered copies of the newspaper.

Responsibility for those duties would have been enough to wear a man down. The party demanded still more of Giap. When its leaders sent Truong Chinh and Pham Van Dong on extraordinary missions that called them away from Ha Noi, Giap remained at the newspaper offices alone. He was at his desk from six at night to six in the morning, writing and composing entire issues of the weekly newspaper, which sometimes ran to forty-eight pages. He went without sleep and had time only to swallow his breakfast before rushing headlong to his daily teaching duties at the lycée, where he continued to propagate his Marxist-Leninist ideas among his students and fellow teachers. Here was a driven man indeed. Sometimes this routine went on for days, sapping Giap of virtually all his energy.[29]

Then, on 16 April 1937, authorities closed down the newspaper. Giap might have been more resentful had he not been so tired and in need of rest and recuperation. Working at a slower pace with Truong Chinh during 1938, the pair embarked on another major venture, coauthoring a two-volume study of agrarian problems in Vietnam that they published under the title *The Peasant Problem, 1937–1938*. Both authors used pseudonyms; Giap wrote as Van Dinh and Truong Chinh used Qua Ninh, the alias he had claimed since arriving in Ha Noi. They argued that a Communist revolution could be both peasant- and proletarian-based. The author Wilfred Burchett, a later apologist for all things Communist, described the book as "a masterly analysis" and "a profound study" that ultimately formed "the basis for the Communist Party and later Vietminh policies toward the peasantry."[30]

By 1939, Giap had gone far within Viet Nam's new Communist organization. He was in a position to share with only a few others the leadership of the colony's most potent political force. Other parties were in disarray, their membership scattered, their leaders arrested and imprisoned or executed. Because of training establishments in the USSR and China, the Communists could replace their leaders more easily than other groups who did not have this outside assistance.

Apart from Ho Chi Minh, masquerading as Nguyen Ai Quoc somewhere in the Soviet Union, only two other leaders could claim high place within the party hierarchy. Pham Van Dong was one. He was immediately above Giap in party ranking and was six years older. The other was Truong Chinh, veteran of one prison sentence and destined for another close on the heels of the August 1939 Nazi-Soviet nonaggression pact and on the resultant wave of French repression in Viet Nam. Unless Giap fell prey to French authorities, he had a very bright future.

Giap's rise came about through a combination of hard work and luck. He was the right age and thus got his education through the cracks at a time when Viet Nam was beset neither by uprisings nor Japanese occupation nor French repressions. He was able both to belong to the party and to continue his schooling. He supported himself by his party writings, thus endearing himself to the hierarchy.

Other parties were not as shrewd in their analysis of Viet Nam's needs. They acted as if peasants on the land were irrelevant to any political program. Communists learned better during the Nghe-Tinh rebellions of the early 1930s. They realized they would need all the backing possible in coming days and counted on organizing the nation's masses. So while he and the party worked to prepare for the future, Giap continued to gain respect within the party.[31]

He had put aside any personal life long enough; unremitting labor had slackened and now there was time. In 1939, twenty-eight years of age, Vo

Nguyen Giap traveled to Vinh and asked Quang Thai to marry him. In many ways theirs had been more a political than a romantic courtship. Giap described it well: "Actuated by the same faith, they set their hopes on the same cause." Giap's good friend and benefactor Professor Dang Thai Mai heartily approved the union. Sometime before April 1939, Giap and Quang Thai were joined in marriage. A tiny woman, Quang Thai made a beautiful bride. She dressed for the ceremony in an embroidered Chinese red *ao dai* over white trousers, her hair worn long in traditional fashion and her head crowned by a tiara covered in rings of golden metallic thread.[32]

Giap never publicly discussed his life with Quang Thai, then or later. In this he was typical of his people, for they are often reserved about their private lives. Still, friends observed in after years that he was never happier in his life, before or after, than during the months which followed his wedding. Apart from pleasant days at Lycée Thang Long, however, he was as wedded to the party as he was to Quang Thai. Their home, located near the Lycée, became a center of party activity. Giap and Quang Thai frequently acted as hosts to many leaders of the Indochinese Communist Party.[33]

Political conditions had been changing. Since the coming of Léon Blum's Popular Front government in France in 1936, Vietnamese anticolonialists of all varieties had more opportunity to operate freely. Jules Brevié, appointed by Blum as governor-general of Indochina (1937–39), granted amnesties to political prisoners, liberalized press laws, and permitted nationalist parties to function in a legal or at least quasi-legal fashion. As 1939 opened, many who opposed French control hoped the year would bring still other opportunities to advance their cause. They were to be disappointed.

Blum's government fell in the summer of 1939, succeeded by the Daladier ministry, and Georges Catroux, a career military officer, replaced Brevié in Indochina that August. Germany invaded Poland on 1 September 1939, and the days of uneasy peace in Europe dissolved into a war that would last six years and spread around the globe. Twenty-five days later, on 26 September, French authorities banned the Communist Party both in France and in her overseas territories and issued arrest warrants for most of its top leaders. In Viet Nam, the Sûreté rounded up over a thousand party members.[34]

Giap, Quang Thai, Pham Van Dong, and all the others watched carefully and waited with apprehension, wondering if they too would be pulled in by the police dragnet. They tried to do nothing that would catch the Sûreté's attention. "[E]very movement of mine was closely watched by secret agents," Giap said, "just as they had done previously when we openly carried out journalistic activities for the Party in Ha Noi." The newlyweds may even, for a time, have left Ha Noi and returned to central Annam as a way of avoiding police.[35]

German armies rapidly changed the face of Europe. The Nazi invasion of Poland soon ended in victory. In less than three weeks the Warsaw government succumbed. Then, for some months, the *Blitzkrieg* or lightning warfare of the Germans resolved itself into a "phony war" or *Sitzkrieg* siege of the western democracies as military action was confined mainly to submarine warfare, air raids on navy bases, and occasional battles between naval ships. In the spring of 1940, Germany struck hard once again. Successive blows hammered Norway, Denmark, Belgium, the Netherlands, and France into submission. France asked for an armistice, and Germany agreed to leave a portion of that nation unoccupied. Marshal Henri-Philippe Pétain, the nation's great hero of World War I, established at Vichy a puppet government loyal to the Germans.

Nor was Germany's Pacific ally, Japan, idle during those months. By November 1939, the Meiji empire so successfully battered the reeling nation of China that Chiang Kai-shek was left with only two outlets through which he could receive vital foreign military assistance: the Burma Road and the Ha Noi–Kunming railway. After the collapse of France and the establishment of the Vichy government, its Indochinese governor-general, Georges Catroux, tried to maintain some semblance of control there.

Pressured by the Japanese to grant military privileges to their troops in Indochina, Catroux tried to interest the United States in sending an armed force to intervene. Franklin D. Roosevelt refused even to consider the notion. Again in late September the Japanese demanded the right to move their troops through Tonkin in order to launch assaults on southern China. Catroux dallied and then capitulated to Japanese demands, since by then he had little choice. For this he was somehow criticized by the new Vichy government, which had done its own share of capitulating, and recalled. He left in July 1940, replaced by Admiral Jean Decoux, commander of the French naval fleet in the Pacific, who served from 1940 to 1945.

Now the foreign ministry of the Vichy government ordered Decoux to cooperate with the Japanese. On 24 September 1940, he granted the Japanese the right to establish three air bases and garrison six thousand troops in Viet Nam. That same day, despite his signed agreement, the Japanese launched an attack on two Tonkinese cities: the French fortress of Lang Son, and Dong Dang. Lang Son surrendered two days later, and the following day all French resistance to the Japanese crumbled. The Meiji empire then moved 35,000 soldiers into Indochina. The Japanese maintained the polite fiction that they were but guests in Indochina and, despite the numbers of their soldiers located there, allowed French *colons* to continue governing under their watchful supervision. For the remaining years of the war, French authorities in Indochina collaborated with the Japanese. They supplied Japan with vast quantities of rice, coal, rubber, and other raw materials.

Decoux endeavored to maintain the illusion that France remained in control, but those over whom he ruled were quick to point out that an Asian nation had humiliated France. That fact completely destroyed the myth of white

European colonial invincibility that had endured in Viet Nam for nearly a century. A growing pro-Japanese sentiment appeared in the south of Viet Nam, while many in the north were attracted to nationalist or Communist groups. As time went on, even in the south, the bulk of the nation refused to side with the Japanese. No one wanted to become a victim of Allied air attacks, which later increased in intensity day after day.[36]

Giap and Quang Thai kept their heads down and tried to maintain a reasonably normal life. In May 1939, four months before the German war machine exploded across the fields of Poland, Giap and Quang Thai conceived a child. As her term drew closer, in the fall of 1939, they talked of the child and what its future would be. On 4 January 1940, Quang Thai gave birth to a baby girl. Giap gave his daughter the beautiful name Hong Anh, "red queen of flowers." They were happy as only new parents can be.[37]

Those quiet days lasted only a few months. In November 1939 the Indochinese Communist Party central committee decided to form a united anti-imperialist front and to make national liberation for Viet Nam its first priority. Nguyen Ai Quoc, soon to become Ho Chi Minh, now lived in southern China and was in contact with the central committee. Although under the nominal control of Chiang Kai-shek's Nationalists, south China was in a state of near anarchy, a no-man's-land that attracted revolutionaries and warlords of many kinds, and so Nguyen Ai Quoc felt reasonably safe there. On his advice, the committee decided in April 1940 to send Vo Nguyen Giap and Pham Van Dong to China. The secretary-general of the Tonkin committee, Hoang Van Thu, personally met with Giap to give him his marching orders. Among other things, they spoke about the future possibility of launching a guerrilla movement within Viet Nam.[38]

When Giap told Quang Thai of his plans, she was immediately enthusiastic and wanted to go with him. To do so would cause problems, Giap said. The trip had to be made in secret, and two could travel more safely than four, one of them a babe in arms. Hong Anh might be in danger on such a trip. What if she got sick? The party resolved matters for them. It ordered Quang Thai and her sister Minh Khai to remain in Viet Nam to act as couriers and liaison officers. Giap and Pham Van Dong would go by themselves. To complicate matters, however, Dong was ill, and Giap knew how hard it was for him to move about freely without the knowledge of the Sûreté. They prepared for their departure carefully and in complete secrecy. They hoped that before long, Quang Thai would find a safe place to leave Hong Anh and could then devote herself fully to underground activities.[39]

Giap and Quang Thai said their goodbyes on the bank of West Lake one Friday afternoon, 3 May 1940.[40] By leaving after his classes ended at Thang Long for the week, he would have all of Saturday and Sunday to work his way north. Only when he failed to show up for classes on Monday morning would anyone begin to raise questions about his absence, and even then several more hours would pass before police could be notified and an alarm raised. By that time he would be well on his way.

Giap walked away from the grounds of the Lycée "just as if going for a walk or for normal activity. Comrade Thai, with little Hong Anh in her arms, was waiting for me on the Co Ngu [now Thanh Nien] Road." With the baby in their arms, Giap and Quang Thai walked along the lake bank among others strolling nearby. Giap wore dark glasses so he would not be recognized by any of his students they might accidentally encounter. They tried to appear as just one more young, contented, loving couple among many. It was harder for Quang Thai than for Giap.

"Find someone to give the baby to so you also can go underground," Giap told his wife, stressing party needs. Quang Thai, torn by her emotions and loyalty, was crying. While she would miss her husband and wanted to go with him, she also very much wanted to work against the French. First, however, she had to find someone to care for Hong Anh. Being a mother and a revolutionary too was a very great responsibility for a young woman in love. They slowly walked back from the lake down Co Ngu Road. At last they broke apart, Giap to begin the great adventure of his life, Quang Thai to return home so she might begin looking for a safe haven for Hong Anh. They would never see each other again.[41]

Giap and Quang Thai paid in blood for their devotion to the anticolonial cause. After Giap's departure, Quang Thai and her sister Minh Khai fled Ha Noi for their home village of Vinh. Hounded by the French, Minh Khai was arrested in July 1940. Jailed and held prisoner, she was savagely tortured to force her to reveal information about the Communist Party and its activities. Despite her pain, she refused to disclose anything to her interrogators. Jailers blindfolded and shot her at Hoc Mon, near Saigon, on 25 April 1941. Her last words, screamed in hate, were "Long live the Communist Party of Indochina. Long live the victorious Vietnamese revolution."[42]

Quang Thai escaped capture until May 1941, when she also was arrested by the Sûreté in her hometown of Vinh. She had delayed placing Hong Anh in anyone else's hands. Moments before her arrest, she entrusted her year-and-a-half-old daughter to a younger sister, who managed to take Hong Anh to the home of Giap's parents in An Xa and leave the girl in their care. For the most part in the years thereafter they were her surrogate parents.[43]

The French took Quang Thai back to Ha Noi and jailed her at Hao Lo (literally, "the Oven") prison. Years later, American fliers would know it as the Hanoi Hilton. She was tried before a military court for conspiracy against the security of France and sentenced to life imprisonment at hard labor. As they had done to her sister, now also they did to this courageous young mother. Tortured to the edge of sanity and perhaps beyond, unable to endure the pain any longer, she allegedly killed herself while in her cell by swallowing her *giai rut*, a kind of soft belt material. United States intelligence reports claim she died another way:

the French hung her by the thumbs and beat her to death. Whatever the manner, Quang Thai died in 1941 within weeks of the shooting of her sister Minh Khai.[44]

For years Giap's family continued to suffer from French depredations. His daughter Hong Anh recalled the death of her grandfather Cuu Nghiem. During 1947, at a time when French troops were reoccupying her home province of Quang Binh, many within the population fled elsewhere in a torrent of refugees. "Grandfather," she wrote, "didn't want to leave . . . He said he risked nothing at all for he was an old man who had done nothing illegal or compromising. He also said he had many, many things to do." Hong Anh tells also of her own flight to safety. "We children were transported like luggage in *cai thung*"—spherical half-baskets of woven bamboo, hung at each end of a pole that rested on the shoulders of those who carried them; the age-old method used by Asians to transport burdens. She remembered how the baskets swung to the rhythm of the carrier's steps.

"I never saw my grandfather again," she recalled. Although Hong Anh did not again see him, his son Giap attempted to do so. In 1946, Giap traveled to An Xa for a reunion. A dedicated nationalist all his life, Cuu Nghiem was also a scholarly Confucian, very attached to ancestral tradition. He refused to see his son, saying that the communism Giap served was a betrayal of "the moral ideals of the nation." Even before Giap's arrival home, Nghiem had earlier scolded his son for placing himself "in the employ of a foreign ideology which had for [its] sole purpose the destruction of nationalism, the family, tradition, and the nation's religious philosophy."

Despite his repudiation of Giap's beliefs and activities, sometime after August 1947, the old man was arrested by the French during their campaign to regain control of all Annam following their capture of Hue. He was detained in the jail of Thua Thien province at Hue, located not far from Lycée Quoc Hoc. His jailers demanded that he publicly denounce his son. This Nghiem would not do, Hong Anh added. "He was tortured. One cruelty consisted of fastening Grandfather to the bumper of a car with a long rope and then dragging him." Nghiem was held in solitary confinement, and his torture continued until he agreed to broadcast appeals on the radio to his son to lay down his arms. Finally worn out by such treatment, Nghiem died in November 1947. Giap had no way to help his father, Hong Anh recollected: "My father was with the Maquis in the Viet Bac." For a time, Nghiem's body was interred in the jail's common cemetery, its location not known to his family. "Thanks to the goodwill of nice people [emissaries of Giap] we . . . were able to find his remains, a long while later. At present he reposes in the cemetery for those who died in service to our country, located at our home village."[45] If anything was still needed to cement Giap's hatred of the French, this was certainly sufficient.[46]

French treatment of Giap's family was not uncommon or unusual. Their police and Vietnamese jailers were willing to use any method to persuade prisoners to talk, including forced ingestion of water, electrical shocks, pulling fingernails, and other brutal measures. With female captives they occasionally used a variety of electric shock methods that drove many women literally mad. Jailers used eels—nasty, hard-biting creatures known for their strength and tenacity—and inserted them into the throat or vagina of women. Placed in those soft, wet areas, the eels tried to swim and bite their way to freedom. The torturers watched as their victims were bitten and electrically shocked by the sea creatures. After a time they removed the eel and continued their questioning. Resistance was sometimes magnificent. One dying woman wanted to be sure she did not speak, and allegedly bit off her tongue and spat it at her interrogator.[47]

In 1982, Will Brownell, head of the Vietnam Bibliographical Project at Columbia University, interviewed General Raoul Salan, formerly one of the commanders of the French Expeditionary Corps in Indochina. Brownell writes: "The torture of [Giap's] wife was confirmed to me in a conversation with General Raoul Salan. . . . He did not love Giap, nor did he admire him enough—but he did concede that great crimes had been done against him. The torture was conceded, tho' Salan tried to shirk it a bit by noting that it was carried out by Vietnamese auxiliaries and not done by Frenchmen. . . . General [Jacques] Massu conceded the same to me in an interview in June 1974."[48]

Giap's family suffered greatly for their aspiration that Viet Nam might be independent. In the beginning, when the French arrested his wife and sister-in-law, Giap was unaware of the dangers they faced. He was on his way to China, having just fled from his job and home in Ha Noi at the order of the Communist Party, to begin the great mission of his life. He did not know of the death of Quang Thai and Minh Khai until much later. Nor did he know of the plight of Hong Anh, his baby daughter. These sorrows were compounded by the later death of his father at the hands of the French. Those who have known him in the past believe he became the Giap of later years not just because of nationalism or his fervent belief in communism, but to avenge his family. As Hong Anh says, "He carries in his soul wounds that even time cannot heal."[49]

PART TWO

Ha Noi,
1941–46

"Neither Soft nor Warm"

When Monday morning came and students assembled for their classes at Lycée Thang Long, Giap's boys were bewildered not to find him waiting for them. In the hallways excited groups whispered rumors about his sudden disappearance. Some boys passed along the tale that he had been picked up by a Russian airplane. Others told how he was now in charge of building some new and terrible weapon. A few believed he had left to take charge of a new Chinese army on the Sino-Vietnamese frontier. One of the favorite explanations was that he had fled to the mountains along the Viet Nam–China border to avoid arrest by the 2d Bureau. Safely hidden in that vast wilderness, they said, Giap was now going to "organize guerrilla activities" against the hated French. It was a good explanation, but it was premature.[1]

After parting from Quang Thai and Hong Anh on the road to Co Ngu, Giap walked rapidly away. As he strode along, a rickshaw pulled by Minh, a trusted friend, moved alongside him. Giap slipped into the seat, and Minh pulled him by devious routes through the streets of Ha Noi to Chem in the suburbs, a safe location for the night. There Giap joined Pham Van Dong and a comrade who was making the travel arrangements for them. They were to travel separately and without luggage. On the following day, Giap and Dong went to the End-of-the-Bridge station and bought a train ticket for Lao Cai, a border town on the route leading to Kunming in China and to Nguyen Ai Quoc.[2]

The journey of the two men to China was a perilous one. There was

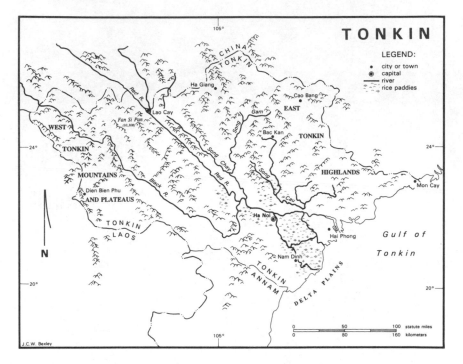

danger from possible Japanese air attacks on the narrow-gauge railway, built at the insistence of Paul Doumer, governor-general of French Indochina from 1897 to 1902. The steel rails followed the straight course of the Red River Valley as it knifed its way through the high mountains of northern Tonkin, some of which soared to ten thousand feet. It was the rainy season, and rivers were swollen. Many tributaries dumped their flooded waters into the Red River, and these swirling waters sucked at the railroad's rickety trestle bridges.

Police regularly boarded the train to search for fugitives. Consequently Pham Van Dong and Giap had to jump off the train and hide on two different occasions to avoid those who walked the aisles peering into each passenger's face, watching with suspicious eyes for traces of fear or panic. Giap and his companion left the train one station before Lao Cai and made the rest of the trip to the border on foot.

Finally reaching Lao Cai, they crossed the Nam Ti River on a bamboo raft in an isolated area. Finally they were in China, but the last part of their journey was as dangerous as the first. Rejoining the railroad, they once again took the train for Kunming. Giap remembered that each time they caught sight of railway employees and policemen boarding the train to search, they hid. At last they reached Kunming.[3]

Someone from the party met them outside the train station and drove them to the house of a Vietnamese militant living in exile there. All Giap's haste was now over. He had only to wait in Kunming for the arrival of someone identified simply as Comrade Vuong, who wished to see him. Giap was certain he knew who Vuong really was and looked forward to the meeting. Among the many Vietnamese refugees in Kunming, Giap could melt out of sight. He was but one face among many. Chiang Kai-shek's Kuomintang forces were then too busy with the Japanese invasion to concern themselves with searching for Communists hidden among the thousands of Vietnamese in the southern border area. Some of Mao's Communist soldiers were also in the area and could provide limited assistance from time to time. Nor were the Japanese particularly troublesome; their presence centered mainly on the towns and front lines, and their own rear was a chaotic area in which Chinese warlords operated with near impunity.[4]

But spring turned into summer and still Vuong did not arrive. He was busy, as he had been since the end of 1939, crisscrossing the south of China, talking with contacts and building his Communist organization, readying it for its return to Viet Nam. In the interim, Giap busied himself around his quarters; books and writing materials were at his disposal, and there were always duties of one sort or another. Life was always busy, Giap claimed. "We had to do the marketing and cooking. When my turn came, I cooked so badly that from that day on I was only entrusted with cleaning the dishes." In his spare hours, he set himself to the task of learning Chinese. He always had to act secretively when away from his housing "to avoid the watchful eyes of the Kuomintang clique lest they should assassinate us."[5]

Then one day in early June, a party apparatchik took Giap and Dong to the banks of the Tsuy-Hu River. Comrade Vuong sat in a boat drawn up on the shore, waiting for them. Giap immediately recognized him as Nguyen Ai Quoc. Vuong greeted them in a kidding manner. "Dong is not really getting old," he said with a smile. Turning to Giap, he laughed. "Giap is still beautiful like a girl," he said.[6]

In the days that followed, the three men turned to more serious matters and discussed Viet Nam's future. Vuong gave his new name to them; henceforth, he was to be known as Ho Chi Minh, "the enlightened one." Giap found in Ho a "simplicity of manner" and "lucidity of character" that was greatly appealing. "Right at that first meeting," Giap realized, "I found him very close to me as if we were old acquaintances."[7]

Ho met with Giap frequently and, as he got to know the younger man better, learned to appreciate Giap's potential. Here was a man capable of doing great things for communism and for Viet Nam. Probably no one will ever be able to determine in which order Ho put those two priorities! Before many days passed, Ho gave Giap his orders. "You will go to Yenan," he said. "There you'll enter

the Party school to study politics. Strive to study military technique as well."
Elsewhere, Giap describes this meeting as one where Ho told him to learn his
party lessons quickly so he would have time later for an internship in military
training.[8]

After that conversation, Ho left Kunming to visit the Vietnamese communities located along the railroad tracks of Yunnan. Giap packed his few belongings and in company with Pham Van Dong and another party cadreman, Cao
Hong Lanh, left Kunming for Kweiyang (in Vietnamese, Kouei Yang). The journey took three long hot days. The three men traveled aboard a Kuomintang Red
Cross truck driven by a Chinese Communist. They rode in back, jammed in
among the cargo and covered with a tarpaulin, in sweltering heat on a potholed
and rutted road. Under the tarp, they were spared the sight of the driver ca-
reening around switchbacks and hairpin curves above high sheer drop-offs on
narrow roads without guardrails. Even so, it was a ride Giap would never forget.[9]

The driver left them at the headquarters of the Eighth Route Army, a former unit of the Red Chinese army, now integrated into the Kuomintang military forces. They waited at Kweiyang for a bus to take them onward. "We had
to wait quite a long time," Giap recalled. Wait they did; weeks passed. Giap
stayed with members of the Eighth Army and was pleased that everyone, "from
the man in charge of the office to those who did the cooking, knew Ho Quang
[another pseudonym for Ho Chi Minh] very well."[10]

Since both funds and food were scarce, Giap learned gardening. "We had
to grow our own vegetables," he observed. While waiting for his bok choy and
radishes to mature, Giap spent much time in study, often using the party hall
of the local committee. It was named Viet Nam Giai Phong Dong Minh, or
League for the Liberation of Viet Nam. He pored over his books, performed propaganda work, and visited with various units of the Chinese Communist army.
The days may have been long and the food frugal, but the group were content
with the idea that soon they would return to Viet Nam to begin a revolution
against the French. Over and again they greeted one another with the phrase
Thoi co da den! ("Good prospects await us!")[11]

Giap learned as much as he could about tactics, strategy, equipment, training, and recruitment. In 1941, according to one source, he had opportunity to
visit Mao in northern China and was impressed by what he saw and heard. The
exploits of Mao and his army were on the lips of many in those days.[12] Giap was
already self-tutored in the tactics and strategies of another people's army, poorly
armed and badly equipped, officered by obscure young men and stableboys and
unknown provincial intellectuals, yet able to confront and destroy the power of
the greatest nations of its era: the units of the French sans-culottes of Napoleon's
first campaigns.

Now he drank in information about Mao and his revolutionary army. He was fascinated by an essay written by Mao in 1938, *The Strategic Problems of the Anti-Japanese War.* Giap saw that many of Mao's problems paralleled those of the Vietnamese. He also read Mao's *Struggle of the Chin-Kan-Shan Mountains,* published in 1928, which offered solutions to the problem of raising guerrilla forces. Giap digested another of Mao's books, *Guerrilla Warfare,* written in 1937. Mao's early experiences had to influence Giap. It was only common sense to build on what the Chinese Communist revolutionary had learned and to apply those lessons to Viet Nam.[13]

In this way Giap acquired two views of people's wars, to which he would add his own observations and insights. In the end he created a form of peasant guerrilla warfare that slowly but inevitably spread across the countryside of Viet Nam, instituting needed reforms without putting them off until the day of some final victory. His view was not, he said, the same as the theories of Mao, who insisted that it was impossible to start an insurrection in urban areas controlled by the enemy. "It was considered that the political struggle was predominant in the urban areas, while the armed struggle took precedence in the rural areas. . . . We combined the military, political, and diplomatic efforts in what we called 'three points of the spear.' " He incorporated the Napoleonic art of engaging an enemy on several fronts at once, keeping him divided and separately defeating scattered enemy forces with sudden lightning maneuvers. He concentrated his men and equipment on the enemy's point of gravity. And he won![14]

Growing Japanese power in Indochina made it obvious to Communists and nationalists alike that France remained in control of Viet Nam in name only. Giap believed that the main enemy was not the Japanese occupation army. He was convinced that ultimately Allied forces would crush the Axis powers. Then the French would come back after the war to reimpose their political control. "Nobody has ever seen wolves leave a fold full of sheep until they had sated their hunger or until they were driven off with gunfire" was a proverb he recalled in those dark days of exile and preparation in China.[15]

Ho Chi Minh realized that the defeat of the French army both in France and in Indochina created an opportunity for action against the *colons.* Thus in October, following the Japanese attack on Lang Son and Dong Dang in Tonkin, he sent word to Giap and Pham Van Dong that they were to meet him again, this time in the Chinese city of Kweilin, for a continuation of their earlier talks and to plan for the future. When the three gathered there to talk, they took elementary precautions against spies and assassins. Disguised as leisurely strollers, they walked through the outskirts of Kweilin or sat in some grassy spot in the shade of a tree. Giap later wrote, "Uncle [Ho] listened to our reports and gave his opinions and suggestions."

At one of those meetings Ho told the two men, "In the face of the new situation, national unity becomes all the more important. We must think of or-

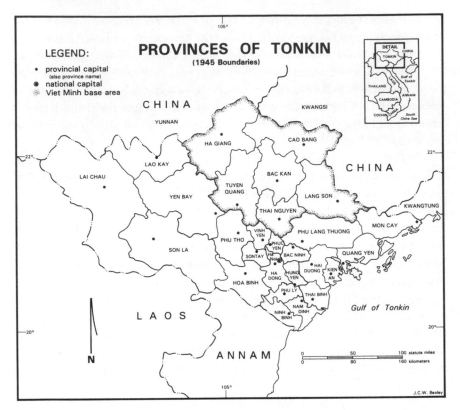

LEGEND:
- provincial capital
  (also province name)
- national capital
- Viet Minh base area

PROVINCES OF TONKIN
(1945 Boundaries)

ganizing a broad national united front, with appropriate form and name. . . . I think we had better call it Viet Nam Doc Lop Dong Minh Hoi [Viet Nam Independence League]. But that is too long for a name, so we will shorten it and call it Viet Minh. People will easily keep it in memory."[16]

Ho discussed with them other preparations they must make for the tasks that faced them. Since he had Giap in mind for military work, it was essential for the diminutive history teacher—no matter how well grounded he might believe himself to be in theoretical knowledge—to gain practical experience in the art of war. Ho assigned Giap to work with a group of young Vietnamese from Cao Bang who had recently crossed into China for safety. Currently two Vietnamese officers serving in the Kuomintang, Truong Boi Cong and Ho Ngoc Lam, were trying to organize them as a small force that could act against the Japanese. "We shall organize a training course for them," Ho ordered. "When they return to Cao Bang, they will consolidate and develop the movement further and organize communication links."[17]

In this rather casual way, Ho decided that Cao Bang would become the base for the Viet Minh revolution against the French. Or perhaps it was not so casual.

Cao Bang's revolutionary traditions went back to 1929, and it had been a strong center of resistance in the years since. Situated close to the border, it would serve both as a sanctuary and to maintain close relations with supporters in China.

Accepting his orders and traveling to Tsingsi, Giap contacted the men from Viet Nam, told them of the opportunity ahead to fight for their country, and persuaded about forty of them to join him in his first "army." As a base camp area, Giap chose the small village of Ca Ma, just inside China and a little north of the Vietnamese village of Cao Bang.

Giap seems never to have considered any other approach to his goal of weakening the French/Japanese hold on Indochina. From the beginning, he organized his training course for the refugees into a survey of minor tactics and guerrilla operations. While Giap tried to forge these men into some semblance of a military force, Ho sent another comrade, Vu Anh, south into Tonkin to locate a base camp there somewhere near Cao Bang. Anh found a suitable cave on the mountain slopes in the area of Pac Bo, twenty miles to the northeast of the provincial capital of Cao Bang and ten miles south of the Chinese village of Ca Ma.

Ho closely supervised Giap's training program. "He paid great attention to the political content as well as to the lucidity, conciseness, and intelligibility of the material," Giap realized. "Since the first time I worked with him, I was deeply impressed by his methods: concrete and cautious to the end. This style of work in that small training course had a great effect on me and guided me in my military work all through the resistance war."[18] When the course ended, Giap's refugees returned to Cao Bang to begin the great mission against the French.

Often through the remaining days of 1940, Giap made trips between China and Viet Nam in order to accomplish tasks set for him by Ho Chi Minh. Once again he adopted a pseudonym. He called himself Van and was normally addressed by his followers as Anh Van (Comrade Van). One of those duties was to determine whether or not these avid revolutionaries could count on receiving support from ethnic tribes in the northern Tonkin mountains. Perhaps as a result of his growing military knowledge, perhaps instinctively, Giap realized there was little possibility of fomenting uprisings in the lowland areas. Therefore he would establish alliances with as many highland tribes as possible: the Nung, Tho, Man, and others.[19]

These peoples lived in isolation from lowland Vietnamese and were autonomous in cultural, economic, and political life. There were nearly a million of them, and, in Giap's words, they "had never been in contact with revolutionary propaganda; they had always lived within the orbit of colonial domination." They spoke distinct languages; dialects differed from one group to another, even sometimes within the same ethnic group. Most women did not even speak Vietnamese, and Giap was obliged to learn local dialects and resort to crude drawings in order to communicate with his new allies. Eventually, Giap learned to speak a limited amount of Tai (or Tay), Dao, H'mong, Tho, Man

Trang, and Man Tien, learning from students in his self-defense training courses who were members of those tribes. Not only did such knowledge aid him in his work, his efforts allowed him to follow Ho's instructions to be in "harmony with the masses in your way of living and social contacts."[20]

One author has left a record of Giap's work in those days. "In certain remote valleys Van opened the path, operating himself according to a standard technique. He would arrive alone in a hamlet, destitute like an outlaw offering to work in the fields. In return he received his food. The days passed. First tolerated, then accepted and listened to, he assured himself of some solid support. At this moment he had won the game. The village provided intelligence and supplies for the commandos, and then furnished guerrillas. The opposition remained silent or was eliminated."[21]

Impressed with Giap's willingness to work alone and to learn tribal languages, Ho assigned him the task of translating the philosophy and ideas of the Viet Minh into French, Dao, and H'Mong languages. Carried away with his efforts, Giap even wrote a poetic saga in ethnic dialect which contained the gist of Viet Minh propaganda in easily memorized and remembered form. His work, *Viet Minh ngu tu kinh,* he writes, had a rhyming pattern that made it particularly appropriate as a teaching device for illiterate hill people. He wrote later that as he traveled across the northern country, he could sometimes hear women singing his poem, the song of the Viet Minh. It cheered Giap to enter a newly organized hamlet to hold a meeting only to find women and children reciting those Viet Minh verses by heart while they ginned cotton or pounded rice.[22]

In December 1940, Giap sought out and recruited a Nung tribesman, Chu Van Tan, to the Viet Minh cause. Born in 1909 to a large poverty-ridden peasant family in Thai Nguyen province, Tan became a youthful revolutionary. He joined the Indochinese Communist Party in 1934 after its recruiters came into his home village. Giap and Tan each judged the other to be "a man of substance," found they liked each other, and worked well together. Tan soon became a leader in the first armed resistance organization, the Army for National Salvation, which eventually merged in 1944 with Giap's new military force. Tan became a reserve three-star general in Viet Nam's People's Liberation Army and served as the first Viet Minh minister of defense after the 2 September 1945 Declaration of Independence. Giap became the strategist and Tan served as one of his best field commanders.[23]

Together this pair of thirty-year-olds worked at their cause. They taught mountain peasants to integrate both political and military action, as had been done repeatedly in the history of Viet Nam, as an essential step in the creation of armies of resistance. They chose the first group of Viet Minh cadre to be trained within Viet Nam, forty young men of the Nung tribe.

At the bottom of a quiet valley, outside a little Nung village close to the Chinese border, these young men, full of enthusiasm and courage, spent ten days in accelerated training. Their staple food was maize (corn), and they slept under the stars. They began each day by picking up firewood for nearby village people. This task of helping was a fundamental aspect of their political training and it earned them the sympathy of the local population. That was not all. In addition, Giap wrote, "we all would carry rice and maize to our quarters, husk rice, [and] grind maize. . . ."[24]

These young men learned that to survive meant total reliance on clandestine ways of living. Their activities had to be done in secretive ways. Therefore, around population centers and in certain other situations they had to observe four rules: (1) no movement during daylight; (2) no wearing of shoes, because they could leave prints in the dirt; (3) no using walking sticks or canes while climbing mountain paths, because they left marks on stones and moss; (4) no sleeping in villages, because such acts opened them to ambushes and endangered the lives of local people. The end of their training was celebrated in front of a red flag emblazoned with a five-pointed yellow star. Then graduates went back to their home villages to begin converting their families, friends, and neighbors to the new cause of revolution.[25]

Giap was pleased with the success of his group. It was not large—only ten men or so—but the members learned their lessons well and were committed. In this way Giap's recruits began to enlarge the existing clandestine area of northern Tonkin by organizing all along the frontier *hoan toan* villages, or "total villages," wholly converted to the Viet Minh cause. The Viet Minh movement grew from total villages to total cantons to total districts. A few months later, Giap could boast that out of nine districts in the Cao Bang, three were totally converted to his cause. By the end of 1941, Giap reported to Ho Chi Minh that "there were in Cao Bang province many bases for self-defense armed units."[26]

As their influence grew, so did their power. Before long, Viet Minh cadres exercised administrative power in villages, then over entire districts. The French *colons* could do nothing about their rivals. In the grip of the Japanese and caught up in other problems, the colonial administration could only fret as it saw its strength wane in the border area.

Giap believed that one important element in this growth was his use of journalism to publicize the Viet Minh cause. He pointed to the lithographed clandestine newspaper he edited, *Viet Lap*, an abbreviation for *Viet Nam Doc Lap* ("Independent Viet Nam"), which Ho ordered to be launched. Articles, he said, should run from fifty to one hundred words. "Of course it was not easy to achieve this," Giap said. "More than once I was at a loss." Although it had only a restricted circulation, it worked well, Giap believed, because "thanks to its appearance, style, and the way it was written—clear and concise—it enabled us to bring the message to all levels of the population."

The paper became quite influential and, Giap claimed, "was soon read in every village, in every salvation group." Its influence was due to the simple and short articles and "to its correct political content which suited the level of the masses . . . thereby raising their consciousness and leading them forward." While early copies of *Viet Lap* were only two pages, Giap soon expanded it to four pages and published it twice weekly. Giap's stories focused on self-defense work, on women's work, and on crimes committed against the Vietnamese by the French and Japanese.[27]

Giap's view of his journalistic abilities was not shared by Ho Chi Minh. Still in China, Ho received copies of Giap's newspaper forwarded to him and later chided Giap for his stiff prose. "We have received your articles," Ho told him with a smile, "but I didn't read them, nor did the other comrades. Usually they were long and unintelligible."[28] At another time, Pham Van Dong and Giap, who had been writing newspaper articles since 1930, showed Ho a scrapbook of their press clippings. Ho commented that what they had written could only be understood by their own party members, not by the masses. Giap tried desperately to improve his style, but even at its best—at least to western eyes and ears—his writing was not very appealing. Douglas Pike, who has probably read as many of Giap's writing as any westerner, characterizes his compositions as "the most turgid in the communist world, a distinction similar to being the tallest mountain in the Himalayas."[29]

On 8 February 1941, feeling the time was finally right, Ho Chi Minh slipped into Viet Nam and settled in at the cave of Pac Bo. The cave was well suited as a clandestine headquarters. Located in Ha Quang district of Cao Bang province, the vast and deep cavern was less than a mile from the Chinese border. It sat in a high region about three kilometers wide and six kilometers long. In front of the cave was a thick cover of reeds and rank growth, almost completely hiding the entrance, so it could not be spotted even at a short distance. At the foot of the rugged and rocky hill, honeycombed with caves, meandered a pleasant stream, swelling in places into large, near-lake-sized ponds. "Uncle called it the Lenin Stream," Giap wrote.[30]

The elevation high, the temperature cold in the thin mountain air, life at Pac Bo was hard, and Giap and his fellows had only bare necessities. Every day they rose early for physical exercises, bathed in the Lenin Stream, and then set to work. Their days were filled with meetings, with visiting nearby ethnic hill people who supported their cause, with organizing and conducting political training courses, and with teaching local children to read and write.

Giap and other cadre stopped their day's work only long enough for simple and frugal meals, often consisting of little more than rice with a slice of salted meat or fish caught in the stream. At night they slept on beds made of branches, their heads resting on wooden pillows. Those cots were, Giap recalled, "neither soft nor warm!" Nights sometimes grew so cold they could not sleep and so they rose from their beds and built fires, huddling around the flames for warmth until daybreak.[31]

The Nung ethnics who inhabited the region were, in Giap's words, "very sympathetic, good-natured people." They lived scattered along the valley and hillsides in hamlets of two or three families. The biggest hamlet comprised at most ten families. Ho knew that many who lived in Pac Bo's valley and elsewhere throughout the mountain provinces were illiterate, and so he ordered his cadre to teach them to read the Vietnamese language. In council meetings with his cadremen, Ho listened receptively to the ideas of others. Giap recalled that he never raised his voice, and he was always willing to prove himself by doing some unpleasant task first. It was his way to incorporate into his own speech the ideas, dreams, and hopes of others. For this he was appreciated, and Giap's respect for Ho constantly increased.[32]

There was also danger. Remote as the area might be, it was still visited by French patrols operating out of their posts in Soc Giang village. They arrested an occasional bootlegger and made periodic searches for revolutionaries. Despite the sense of accomplishment Giap and other cadre felt about their progress, both Japanese and French authorities regarded them as bandits and terrorists rather than as a serious and organized threat to their authority. It may have been unflattering, but had they been taken more seriously, they might well have been wiped out. At this point, Giap and the Viet Minh were hardly yet in a position to withstand an all-out pursuit should such a mission be mounted against them by either the French or the Japanese.

The revolutionaries' safety was primarily a result of this casual disregard, which allowed them the opportunity to move about more or less freely, to spread their doctrines undisturbed, and to train recruits in the doctrines of revolution. Since none of the armed might of the two occupying powers came to bear on this newly formed organization, conflicts came only suddenly, sometimes accidentally, often surprising both sides. It might happen while a French patrol searched the countryside to capture or kill bandits. Such groups arbitrarily arrested any who were believed to be Communists or sympathizers. In their rounds the French might be ambushed, one or two of their number slain. It caused them to proceed with caution and to be merciless in their reaction, and their entry upon the scene regularly forced Giap and his fellows into hiding.

"Whenever we found ourselves no longer secure," Giap recalled, "we shifted to another place, sometimes even to a place situated in the middle of a waterfall to which access was very difficult." To get there they had to ford the Lenin Stream and climb up the hill's rocky surface until they finally pulled themselves to the top of a particularly steep rock by means of a rope ladder.[33]

In rocky clefts on hillsides, deep within vast and thick forests, and in other caves, Ho, Giap, and their fellow Viet Minh cadre built hideouts for themselves, dark and humid, often hidden under canopies of broad-leaved rattan plants. Giap

described those escape holes. "Sometimes feeling that the enemy was on our trail
. . . we had to work and live separately in different caves. Once I returned there
from work in another region, and as rain had been pouring heavily, I saw snakes
and insects creeping into our cave."[34]

Life was hard under such circumstances, and in times of peril it was desperate. Giap later described how even getting enough to eat was not easy. "We
drank water from the streams. Food supply was very difficult. We ate maize or
maize gruel. . . . Sometimes maize and wild banana trunks were our only food
for a whole month."[35]

As they hid they spent long hours talking about their country's future. Giap
recalled Ho insisting, "In about five years the revolution will be victorious and
we will have a bright future. I only want to create one thing—to completely free
our country and provide everyone with the necessities of life." All of them knew
the prospects of revolution were difficult and complex, and sometimes Giap and
other cadre became confused over the problems they faced. Then Ho explained
the future in simple ways that all present could understand. One day a per-
plexed cadre asked Ho: "How can we have a revolution without arms and where
are we going to find guns?"

Bac Ho replied, "We must rely on our own force with some outside help.
When the people absorb this beautiful idea of revolution, they will create the
strongest of forces. Everything because of the people; everything for the people.
People first, guns last. If we have the people on our side, then we will have guns.
If we have the people, we will have everything." It was a lesson Giap never for-
got.[36]

In 1941, Giap was involved in more than military training measures. In
May at Pac Bo he participated in the historic meeting of the Eighth Enlarged Session of the central committee of the Indochinese Communist Party. It was at this
meeting that Ho finally gained control of the movement by convincing other delegates that the Leninist view of revolution, based on industrial workers, must
be discarded. Change in Viet Nam, Ho contended, would come using its rural
population as the base to sustain the revolution. He also gathered the support
necessary to establish national liberation for Viet Nam as the main thrust of
party policy. Under his guidance party members voted "that national liberation
was to be the central and immediate task . . . and that preparations for an armed
uprising should be made."[37]

Delegates ratified Ho's choice of name for the liberation movement—Viet
Minh Doc Lap Dong Minh Hoi—that he had earlier discussed with Giap. The Viet
Minh invited all patriots to join its movement, with no distinctions of wealth,
age, sex, religion or political outlook. In that way they could best work together
to liberate their country. For Ho, it would have the added advantage of gathering many parties under his own umbrella.

One group that answered this call was the Dang Dai Viet or simply Dai Viet, a nationalist political party formed shortly before World War II by patriotic elements among the urban middle class in Tonkin. One of its aims was to work with the Japanese occupation authorities to obtain independence from French rule. Another group that heeded Ho's summons was the remnant of the Viet Nam Quoc Dan Dang, or Vietnamese Nationalist Party, sympathetic to Chiang Kai-shek's Kuomintang in China and nearly destroyed in the aftermath of the Yen Bay uprisings in February 1930.

One organization that spurned Ho's idea of a united front was the Viet Nam Cach Menh Dong Minh Hoi, or Vietnam Revolutionary League, usually known as Dong Minh Hoi, another nationalist organization founded at Liuchow in south China in late 1942 under Chinese sponsorship to keep an eye on Japanese activities in Indochina and perhaps, after the war, to serve as the basis for a pro-Chinese government in Viet Nam. This group included the Viet Nam Phuc Quoc Dong Minh Hoi, or League for the National Restoration of Viet Nam faction, formed by Prince Cuong De at the beginning of World War II. Often simply called Phuc Quoc, this was a pro-Japanese political party composed of anti-French nationalist groups living in exile in southern China and may well have been a restoration of Phan Boi Chau's League for the Restoration of Viet Nam (Viet Nam Quang Phuc Hoi), which he had formed in 1912.

Also part of the Dong Minh Hoi were members of a previous front organization, the Viet Nam Giai Phong Dong Minh Hoi, or Vietnamese Liberation League, led by an elderly nationalist, Nguyen Hai Than, a former disciple of Phan Boi Chau. He had lived so long in China his speech had been influenced and he sounded more Chinese than Vietnamese. Yet with Kuomintang backing, for a time Than headed the Dong Minh Hoi.

The Dong Minh Hoi refused to cooperate with the Indochinese Communist Party and the Viet Minh, competing for power with them throughout the war. There were other parties and factions in wartime Viet Nam, but this suggests the complexity of the task faced by Ho and the Viet Minh in May 1941 as they sought to build a united front.[38]

Delegates to the Eighth Session meeting at Pac Bo considered further the matter of an "armed uprising" and chose Phung Chi Kien to head up a new Army for National Salvation. Trained at the Chinese Whampoa Military Academy, he later served as a unit commander in Mao's army from 1927 to 1934. To all appearances he was an appropriate man for the job. Eager to get on with his work, Kien organized his forces in the hills of northern Viet Nam and launched them against the French. He soon found half his strength destroyed and the rest of his forces slipping into hiding. His was the wrong approach.[39]

The delegates at Pac Bo also selected a new party general secretary, Truong Chinh, to replace Nguyen Van Cu, arrested by the French in June 1940 and shot in Saigon on 25 May 1941.[40]

Delegates further determined to build new guerrilla bases south of Pac Bo, for it now seemed to be an inadequate location for controlling growing Viet Minh activities, and after a few months, headquarters was relocated to Lam Son, thirty miles closer to the center of Cao Bang province. This posed security problems, however, because the French patrolled that region with great frequency.

Additional bases would speed development of revolutionary sentiment in the three crucial provinces of Cao Bang, Lang Son, and Bac Kan, which could then serve as centers for preparing the armed uprising in the Viet Bac, the term Vo Nguyen Giap and other cadre used for the provinces of Bac Thai, Cao Bang, Ha Giang, Lang Son, and Tuyen Quang.

The Pac Bo cave and Cao Bang province had been a good beginning, and now it was time to grow. In the best Leninist tradition, using their existing hub and maintaining tight liaison between centers, the Viet Minh would spread their movement southward. It was a historic moment. Nam Tien, or the March to the South, had been a part of Vietnamese culture since the restoration of their independence in the tenth century and brought on clashes with the Kingdom of Champa and with Cambodia. Once again there would be a march to the south, this time against the French.

Hardly had the Eighth Session ended when, in June 1941, Hitler shredded his two-year-old neutrality treaty with the Soviets and invaded their country in another of his *Blitzkrieg* attacks. Strangely, this proved to be a pivotal point for Viet Nam's Communists, because suddenly, along with the Russians, they became allies of the western powers in their fight against the Axis nations of Germany, Italy, and Japan. As 1941 ended, the Japanese increasingly used Indochina to prepare for their massive land and sea attacks launched in early December against Malaya and Singapore, Hong Kong, the Dutch East Indies, Guam, the Philippines, and other areas. While Japanese naval aircraft carriers steamed toward Hawaii during the night of 6 December, Japanese army units, as a precaution, closed in on all French military garrisons in Viet Nam to nip in the bud any action they might take. No French soldiers offered resistance to this gratuitous warning.

Shortly after lunch on Monday, 8 December 1941, President Franklin Delano Roosevelt addressed a joint session of Congress. The day before, he declared, had been a day of infamy: the Japanese had bombed Pearl Harbor and other American installations in the Hawaiian islands. He asked for a declaration of war. Now America too would soon become involved with Ho, Giap, and the Viet Minh.

FIVE

"Each Man Was a Soldier"

During the summer and fall of 1941, Vo Nguyen Giap continued his trips between China and northern Viet Nam at Ho's direction while still directing training courses for cadre recruits and serving as head of the March to the South. That movement would inevitably cause armed conflict with the Japanese and the French, but such potential dangers did not stop Giap's cadre. Near the end of 1941, upon a return from China, Giap found that his fellows had crisscrossed Cao Bang province, consolidating the Viet Minh hold there and establishing within its confines a number of bases for self-defense armed units. The first team established, Giap recalled proudly, was a "section," or about a squad of ten men.[1]

At the end of the year, Giap and other cadre returned to the little Nung village near the cave of Pac Bo. They spent Tet of 1942 there preparing themselves for new efforts in the coming months. Giap told how everyone paid New Year visits to families in the village. "As they already had sympathy for the Vietnamese revolution, and we correctly observed the rule governing relations with the masses, they esteemed us all the more when we lived close to them."[2]

Pleased though he might be with the results of the work thus far, Giap was not complacent. He had learned from Ho the notion "not to be complacent in periods of the high-tide of the movement and not to show pessimism when the movement receded."[3]

Giap urgently promoted establishment of a safe communication route between Cao Bang and the Red River Delta to facilitate travel both for teaching
cadre and for armed guerrillas. These intelligence/communication lines spread
out among the mountain tribal areas. In this way, Viet Minh cadre could maintain liaison during times of enemy repression and guerrilla groups could move
favorably in periods of armed activities.

Giap's agents in Cao Bang who wished to contact members of other cells
on the lowland plains and in the Red River Delta had to pass through localities
inhabited by Tho and Man Tien people, through innumerable passes, over
mountains, through fields, a march of some twenty days from beginning to
end. The Tho were already Viet Minh allies; now the Man Tien watched them
at their work. They were so taken by the dedication of these young Vietnamese
that soon Man Tien volunteers appeared, asking to join the national effort.

Man Tien probationary trainees developed their own oath to pledge prior
to admission into clandestine activities. During nighttime fire-lit ceremonies in
their hamlets, they solemnly promised to unite against the French and Japanese to save the nation and their village and to achieve the Viet Minh program,
and not to leave another in difficulty or to betray anyone. Giap was impressed
with their ritual. "The one who took the oath," he said, "would plunge the
burning incense stick he kept in hand into water to extinguish it or he would
chop off a chicken's head with one stroke."[4]

The earliest of the Man ethnic recruits was named Hoan, who became a
useful cadreman. According to Giap, Hoan worked ardently both in training and
in the field thereafter, which won him high praise among his tribe. His sacrifi-
cial work within the Communist Viet Minh promoted its growth. Then he was
captured by the French, tortured eleven separate times, and finally shot; he died
without revealing any information. Before he was shot, his jailers allowed him
a brief visit with his wife, to whom he handed a small packet of a drug concocted
from tiger bone. Keep it, Hoan told her, and pass it on to Giap. "Tell that I send
him my best wishes and want him to take this drug to preserve his health to be
able to work." She did so. Hoan's mother told Giap that although her son was
dead and despite a bad harvest, "I spare a small quantity of glutinous rice for
the guerrilla fighters. You, my sons, should kill the last French and Japanese to
enable us, the Man people, to live."[5]

As the Viet Minh movement spread to additional mountain districts, Giap
ordered the creation of "Associations for National Salvation" in every possible
village. He oversaw establishment of party cells. Before long he could boast that
there were whole villages, whole cantons, and whole districts in the mountain
region where every person belonged to a National Salvation cell.[6]

In effect, the Viet Minh now governed a growing portion of northern
Tonkin, replacing the withered colonial arm of the French and dealing with a
range of public and governmental affairs from settling land disputes to issuing

marriage licenses.[7] Converting a village to the revolutionary cause began with a visit by specially trained political commissars who explained to the inhabitants what they expected. Giap later recalled that his cadre spent little time talking about communism. "We talked about the solid organization of their strength to save the nation and the village, to implement the Viet Minh program, not to leave comrades in arms in trouble, nor yet to betray them in the face of possible enemy repression."[8]

Giap's cadre offered help in local projects. For a time they might choose to live near the village, working in it by day, sleeping elsewhere by night. Giap carefully schooled his men to be scrupulous in their behavior toward these mountain people. They must not enter a house without the owner's permission. They must sweep and clean the place where they stayed. They should not even share villagers' food if doing so would cause a shortage for a community's inhabitants.[9] Giap insisted that his men be so carefully correct around Tho women that they came to believe Viet Minh males had been "made without cocks."[10]

These visiting cadremen carefully avoided threatening anyone who opposed them because their object, after all, was not to win everyone but only to secure the allegiance of a majority. When that was accomplished, Viet Minh cadremen asked villagers to indicate who might be a traitor or French agent among them. Under the influence of their new teachers, townsfolk often pointed out village chiefs or those who collaborated with the French, rich landlords, or moneylenders. Although those charged opposed allegations made against them, often peasants supported the new way of doing things with wholehearted enthusiasm.

Locally selected village assassination committees carried out executions of those charged as antirevolutionary. After eliminating such opponents, the Viet Minh continued to cultivate its relations with the villagers and soon was able to recruit guerrillas from its population. The village now became an additional Communist base, capable of rendering effective aid on a regular basis. The cadre then moved on to convert another community.[11]

The growth of Viet Minh influence gratified Giap. "Each man was a soldier," he declaimed, "each village and hamlet a fortress and each . . . resistance committee a staff."[12] Such efforts paid handsome dividends. Recruits showed up at base camps in ever greater numbers, from mountain tribesmen to townsfolk. Hundreds of young men and women left their families and volunteered to take part in the southward march. Giap found it necessary to run his training courses once each month with about fifty students in every class. When even this proved insufficient to handle those who came, Giap launched mobile instruction teams who traveled the region, holding classes in various locations.[13]

Viet Minh expansion southward continued steadily, and Giap did not direct this movement from afar. He believed in close supervision, and he traveled regularly among villages and hamlets, visiting his cadre and urging them to greater effort. Often he had to spread palm leaves on the ground to serve as a bed for the night and he slept in the open air of the jungle.[14]

Under Giap's supervision, it was never too late for a student to confess inadequacy or too early to declare dedication. According to a perhaps apocryphal story related by Giap, during one graduation ceremony, a student who had done well in his training came to Giap and asked to be dropped from the roster of those who were about to be congratulated for completing their course. A little bewildered, Giap asked the young man, "Why do you ask to withdraw?" There is too much to remember, the student responded. He would be unable to remember it all, and this might cause him to make mistakes. "I am afraid that I am not able to fulfill my task," he ended sorrowfully. This forthrightness greatly impressed Giap, and he used this man's confession to spur other trainees into self-examination.[15]

Giap and his tribal friend Chu Van Tan simultaneously organized a clandestine network of agents throughout northern Tonkin. Giap and Tan sent intelligence collected by their people, usually about Japanese activities, to Chinese nationalists in exchange for financial and military assistance. Giap then used this aid to support his Communist organizing work in the north.[16]

Some of the funds so raised helped Giap, at Ho's orders, to establish a new location in 1942 which the Viet Minh called their party Interprovincial committee headquarters. It was located in the Lam Son region, a mountainous area where decomposing rocks formed red, porous deposits containing large amounts of aluminum and ferric hydroxides. Giap called the area their "red blockhouse region."[17] They moved into Lam Son just as their popular movement, the March to the South, was developing strongly.

The new camp was located in a dense forest on the border between Hoa An and Nguyen Binh districts. Cadre lived in a pole house erected on a mountain slope, eventually also constructing a lecture hall, dining rooms, a dormitory, and a training ground large enough to be used simultaneously by hundreds of cadre going through Giap's training course. Conditions seemed much better at the Red Blockhouse than they had been at Pac Bo.[18]

Ho Chi Minh left Tonkin early in 1942 for a trip into China because he needed to strengthen his ties with other groups that might be able to provide possible assistance. He was almost immediately arrested by the Chinese Nationalists, who were well aware of Viet Minh successes in organizing the northern portion of Tonkin. Inasmuch as the Chinese government had its own plans for that region, it knew that sidelining this revolutionary in some steaming, stinking jail would be an advantage. If nothing else, it would allow the Nationalist government to use pressure to force Ho to include politicians from other, Chinese-sponsored, nationalist groups in his upper cadre echelons.

While making his supervisory rounds of the countryside, Giap learned of the news when he received an urgent letter from Pham Van Dong asking him to return immediately to Cao Bang. Upon his arrival, Dong told him how Ho had been arrested by troops of Chiang Kai-shek. That was bad enough. Then came even worse information, based on reports Dong had heard. Ho had died in prison. It was all too much for Giap. "I fainted," he later wrote.[19]

All the Viet Minh cadre were crestfallen. Ho was their inspiration. He provided the best ideas and acted as moderator for their differences. Everyone wondered how the goals of the revolution could be achieved without him. After a few days at Cao Bang, unable to contain his sorrow and restlessness, Giap left for the Ngan Son district. To avoid French patrols and Japanese soldiers he traveled only at night, walking stealthily over desolate hills overgrown with wild reeds or struggling through deserted tiger-grass-covered mountains. The landscape seemed to mirror his own devastation. During his journey's hours, darkness lay not only upon the land but within Giap's soul. In the chilly cold, under a star-spotted sky, Giap could not contain his sadness. Through bleak eyes streaming with tears, he looked up at the stars, wallowing in his loneliness, his misery.[20]

Some days after, as he worked in Ngan Son district, a Viet Minh courier brought Giap a newspaper from China. Perusing the stories, Giap's eyes fell upon a handwritten note in the margin, unmistakably the penmanship of Ho: "I wish my brothers at home good health and good work. I am all right here," the words said. Then followed a poem. How could Ho be dead and yet these words of his appear on a recent issue of a newspaper? Giap scanned the publication date curiously. It had been printed after the supposed death of Ho. New hope crept tentatively into Giap's heart.

Back in Cao Bang, when opportunity presented itself, Giap queried the man who had first brought news of Ho's death from China. Giap recounted seeing the note and the poem. "What does all this mean? What do you think of this?" he asked. The comrade replied, "I don't know. When I was in China the Kuomintang mandarin actually told me that Uncle Ho was dead."

Giap asked the man to recall exactly what he had been told. His face narrowed in concentration, the man remembered how the mandarin had told him si-le, si-le, which meant "already dead." Giap seized on a sudden idea. Could it be, he asked, that the phrase was not si-le, si-le, but shi-le, shi-le, which meant only "yes, yes"? Yes, the other man replied shamefacedly; that was possible. "We were overjoyed," Giap cried, yet as a result of a simple misunderstanding "we had been tormented for months by pain and sorrow."[21]

Giap returned from his travels to Cao Bang on the day of the lunar New Year in 1943 to celebrate the organizational accomplishments of past months. With the close of the past year, Giap and his Viet Minh cadre had succeeded in forming many additional self-defense teams. Three northern provinces—Cao Bang, Bac Can, and Lang Son—were now so solidly controlled by the Viet Minh that Giap and his fellows simply called them Cao-Bac-Lang. Giap and others within the Viet Minh central committee, joined by workers from Cao-Bac-Lang, met with many new recruits during that Tet holiday, presenting them with flags emblazoned with the slogan "Successful Shock Work."

Giap had a right to be pleased with the success of his March to the South movement, because membership in Associations for National Salvation in 1941 had been but 1,053, and by 1943 it was 3,096. Political and military training courses increased from eleven to twenty-six, and every month another class of cadre trained in military tactics graduated from a jungle-covered school; ten schools taught literacy to area inhabitants. In some hamlets, people volunteered additional labor after their regular daily work ended. Women grew vegetables and bred silkworms; men baked charcoal to raise funds for the Viet Minh.

In turn, the party spent that windfall to support underground cadre activity. They built food reserves and dug hideouts deep in forests with baked inside walls, paved with timber and bamboo and covered over with timber and earth. These strongholds could be hidden so well that searching French patrols rarely found them. Other cadre crisscrossed from China to Viet Nam on a constant lookout for weapons to purchase.[22]

Giap even set up his own armory. He knew that daggers, spears, and antiquated flintlock rifles were not enough to displace French authority. Refusing to be daunted by overwhelming odds, he moved blacksmiths into a deep valley behind a wall of several mountains in the Red Blockhouse area so as to hide hammering noises from curious outsiders. People donated iron pots, copper trays, and brass basins. After many hard months of dangerous experimentation at the secret smithy, his men succeeded in producing their first land mine.

It was smart of those at the smithy to forge mines rather than trying to make rifles. The mine is a wonderful weapon for a disadvantaged guerrilla force. It is easy to make, simple, and cost-effective. It can be deployed by one or two people with a minimum of risk. Its potential destructiveness far outweighs the risk—a truckload of troops, a barracks, a railway line blown at precisely the right moment to derail a train. Mines strike terror into enemies, who then become afraid to move either on or off the roads. Wounds from mines far outnumber deaths, and they tend to rip off arms and legs, further preying on the mind of an enemy.

Giap and other visitors came for the field test. Spectators sat on an elevation behind huge rocks so they could watch the test without risk of being hit during the explosion by errant pig-iron shell fragments. Below them, in a rocky hole, the smiths placed their prize, attaching to it a one-hundred-meter rope. Giap waited anxiously. Comrade Cap, head of the project, shouted for one of his smiths to pull the rope. Everyone's eyes were fixed on the hole wherein the land mine lay. Nothing happened. Then Comrade Cap yanked on the rope. Smoke came boiling out, and that was all. No explosion, no hurtling fragments of metal.

"We waited for a long moment," Giap recalled. Then the silence was broken by a Tho tribal warrior who burst into hooting laughter. "It doesn't want to move," he cackled.

A little red-faced, Giap announced that the test was a failure but that efforts would continue. Comrade Cap and his smiths returned to their work, persisted in their efforts, and eventually succeeded. That workshop continued production until the August Revolution of 1945, when it was enlarged into the Lam Son arsenal. It produced a major part of the ammunition Giap's army later used. The smithy in the Red Blockhouse, Giap told others, could be considered the Viet Minh's first arsenal.[23]

There was more than a smithy hidden in the Red Blockhouse region. During 1943, under Giap's direction, coolie laborers swarmed to construct a military training camp deep within the forest. Workers built camouflaged pole houses roofed with leaves for use as barracks; buildings clung to the sides of steep slopes, the gradient requiring entries on several levels. Giap's minions quickly and quietly went on to erect a conference building, a mess hall, an armory. There was even a stadium next to the main building to be used for graduation ceremonies and training exercises.[24]

During 1943 the French at last began to realize that in the Viet Minh they had a troublesome faction that might one day become a rival for power, so patrols increased and made more intensive searches of the backcountry. At Cao Bang, as a result, Viet Minh committee headquarters came under siege. Its *Viet Lap* printing shop was shelled. Leaders of local cadre groups were ambushed and killed. French troops hung proclamations warning the populace not to help the Viet Minh or to cooperate in its activities. Families whose sons or daughters had joined the Viet Minh should contact them and order them home or face consequent action.[25]

French units unearthed and destroyed secret weapons reserves and food caches. They razed whole villages thought to be sympathetic to the revolutionary cause. They relocated remote hamlets with fewer than twenty houses into larger groupings, and countless villages throughout the Cao-Bac-Lang region sat deserted, their houses dismantled and tumbled down. Over the new settlements, the colonial administration placed curfews from 6:00 P.M. to 6:00 A.M. They held daily roll calls and tried to prevent inhabitants from taking a single grain of rice out of a village. The French knew how valuable rice was to the Viet Minh. It served as currency for the revolution. Without it the Viet Minh would be both physically and economically devastated.[26]

During searches, if French soldiers found someone in possession of Viet Minh documents he was shot on the spot. Heads and amputated arms and legs of cadre or sympathizers were prominently displayed in town markets. Devastation and desolation prowled the high mountains and sat heavily upon the aspirations of the Viet Minh. For a time Giap carried a hand grenade for "protection," or to provide for himself what the French certainly would not, a quick death. He later discovered it was a dud. "However," he said, "[I] carried [it] constantly for [its] good effect on morale."[27]

Sometimes the Viet Minh achieved small victories, and stories of these accomplishments circulated widely, told and retold, as cadre tried to salve their fears and strengthen their hopes. In one case, a French patrol probed carefully through the high jungle of what must have been a Hansel and Gretel forest looking for Viet Minh prey. Hidden all alone in nearby brush lay a young cadreman from Giap's headquarters, who, seized with sudden inspiration, leaped from the bushes and shouted, "Charge!" at the top of his lungs. The French soldiers, their nerves already frazzled from constant fear of ambush, took to their heels in a mad rush for safety.[28]

French pressure increased. Giap complained about the arrest of many families whose members had secretly joined the movement. One wonders how secret their membership was. Quite likely there were French infiltrators within the Viet Minh movement itself, providing the government with information either freely or for a price. Rewards were high. The colonial government promised thousands of piasters and generous rewards of salt—a precious commodity— to those who could bring in a revolutionary cadre's head.[29]

While this most recent "White Terror" blossomed across the land, Vo Nguyen Giap and a comrade, Thiet Hung, were conducting a training course for new recruits. French searches often required them to relocate. They marched at night to new campsites. Heavy rains poured down on them, drenching instructor and student alike. When possible they dried their clothes by the heat of a campfire and slept on piles of leaves. Rations consisted of maize or unpounded rice, mixed occasionally with bulbs of wild banana trees, boiled in salt water. Such food irritated their stomachs and weakened them at a time when strength might save their lives.[30]

Word caught up with Giap that he should return to headquarters; it was too risky to leave him at the mercy of wandering French patrols, and he was too important to the cause. Giap asked to remain where he was, fearing that if he left, local organizations would crumble and disband. That very day a French search party appeared in the area and began a careful probe. Two local volunteers tried to lead Giap and Thiet Hung out of harm's way. That entire night, in heavy showers and pitch darkness, Giap stumbled after his guides across steep slopes and through deep ravines. Even at dawn a dense mist prevented the small group from being able to see anything.

Late in the morning, as the mist cleared, Giap realized he was hiding in plain sight on a bare hill with no nearby cover. His group was not far from the village they had fled the night before, and enemy soldiers were searching at the foot of the hill on which they stood. Giap and the others quickly dropped to all fours and crawled for several kilometers until they reached the margin of a forest. They continued to walk but by noon were so exhausted they had no strength to continue. The two guides pulled Giap and Thiet Hung onward, dragging them by the arms when necessary. At about sunset they finally reached the hideout they sought.

In following days, perhaps as a result of the tribulations suffered during his narrow escape from the French, Giap fell gravely ill with malaria, and he had an almost constant fever for two and a half months. He had no quinine, and a local herbal doctor brought him decoctions of *nu ao* root, thought to be helpful under such conditions. Women comrades worried about Giap's failing health and took his tunic to a nearby soothsayer, who said prayers for his recovery. Finally, when the French withdrew from the region for a time, Giap's comrade Cap (who had been in charge at the smithy during the testing of the first land mine) came from central headquarters with a supply of quinine pills. Soon Giap was back on his feet.[31]

The French campaign against the Viet Minh continued throughout the remainder of 1943 and as late as June 1944. Yet still the Viet Minh movement grew. By the end of 1943, in some regions Giap's cadre felt bold enough to hold military reviews and to conduct sham battles involving up to fifty men in open fields during broad daylight. On some rare occasions, mock combat exercises of nearly one thousand men spread out over wide areas. Such activities could not possibly stay unnoticed indefinitely, and bloody French forays into the hills intensified right after the September rice harvest. Both sides needed the rice; mortal combat could wait until this staple vital to all was safely gathered.[32]

Giap was determined to hold on to and safeguard his carefully built-up Viet Minh infrastructure. Already enough of it was in place in the Cao-Bac-Lang region to launch an effective war and resistance zone. In the face of the French White Terror he had to maintain his organization, sustain the confidence of the local mountain people, and deepen their sympathy for and support of his cause. To accomplish these ends he applied the time-honored Communist organizational technique of the individual cell. Each cell would be small, composed of secret members who were willing to leave their families behind to live hidden in the forest. Save for its leader, members of one cell would not know those in any other cell. Neither spies nor turncoat members would be able to uncover more than one cell.

Those in each cell had to establish one contact point. It could be a cave or even a little tree-covered hut built on a mountainside or a camouflaged shanty deep within the forest. Here they would meet; messages could be left by one for another or by leader for all. They could gather for planning sessions or hide when French units came too close. Giap required them to gather enough provisions and store them at the contact point to last six months—the time necessary between rice and maize harvest. They were to live by very strict orders, adhering to a draconian schedule, dividing their activities of teaching local populations from those reserved for study, for planning, for self-criticism sessions.

According to prearranged signals, members of those secret cells left their work or homes to walk three or four kilometers across mountains and through forest, arriving at twilight at their contact point. When they gathered, they unearthed rare and hard-won weapons, opened their food caches and drew rations, talked among themselves to bolster their spirits, and set forth on missions. Supporters in local villages they passed, ignoring the menace of the French police and military, brought them provisions and supplied them with information.

The Viet Minh operated in a land where spirits, phantoms, and shadows are not only a part of lore but also a part of the way every peasant views life. They, too, were shadows, ghosts, and phantom fighters, rarely seen, but shades who inevitably left behind evidence of their passing: a dead soldier stripped of his weapons, a spy with a blackened face dangling by the neck from a braided rope, an avaricious landlord more willing to cooperate with the French than lose his land murdered in his bed. Their mission accomplished, those fighters made their way back to the contact point, sometimes sleeping alongside a river or at the edge of a rice paddy during sunlit hours. If they were lucky they could return to their hideout before the morning fog disappeared.

Because of such clandestine cells, organized by Giap and others, their popular movement was able to resist the savage persecution inflicted by the French *colons*. Yet the winter of 1943–44 was a harsh one for Giap and his men. French repression forced them to exist on strict rations, satisfied with a bag of dry cereal grain and a tube of roasted salt. On one occasion Giap and two of his men were entrapped for three days on a mountain near The Ruc. They cooked their rice in handmade bamboo tubes in water squeezed from forest vines. At other times Giap fed himself with wild tubers or roots of banana trees. And it was not only the lack of food. These ghost fighters also faced danger from exploding artillery rounds and even from forest fires lit by their enemies during the dry season to force them out of hiding.[33]

Morale might have been higher had not Ho Chi Minh still languished in prison, unable to provide needed guidance and direction to his Viet Minh followers. Then after months of stubborn resistance, at last he agreed to the proposal put to him by his Chinese jailers and promised that his Viet Minh would cooperate with Chiang Kai-shek's Nationalist Chinese Kuomintang government. With that, he was set free in Liuchow in late 1943, although the Chinese insisted he remain under parole within the city. Consequently it was not until late 1944 that he was able to return to Viet Nam.

Yet Ho still had reason to celebrate. Not only was he free from prison, but Giap managed to send him messages with the information that Viet Minh teams now controlled most of the provinces of Cao Bang, Bac Kan, and Lang Son. In late 1943 the Viet organization joined together those three provinces by converting the tiny hamlet of Nghia Ta, near Cho Don. Giap's March to the South campaign was a success. Now a cadreman could walk for nearly three weeks through mountains and forests from Cao Bang to Thai Nguyen without ever leaving Viet Minh "territory." Ever afterward the little town of Nghia Ta was known as Victory Village, and at the Tet festival celebrating the new year of 1944, the Viet Minh organized a great feast in honor of their successes.[34]

For Tet in early 1944, as the year of the goat made way for the year of the monkey, Giap returned to Cao Bang. When high-ranking members of the party gathered with him to salute the holidays, Giap ceremoniously presented a new flag representing the labor and laborers of the past. The ensign was embroidered with the slogan *Xung Phong Thang Loi*, "Victory to the Volunteers." The Viet Minh movement, Giap said, forged ahead despite French repression that had bloodied their ranks since 1941.[35]

The French antiterrorist campaign continued to rage. Giap complained that by June 1944 the "savage white repression" carried out by the French "fascists" reached unprecedented heights. They were so successful that the Viet Minh began to suffer a hemorrhage of supporters. Giap confessed that the movement "declined for some time" and that "revolutionary bases in certain regions became smaller."[36]

About the only positive item Giap now forwarded to Ho in the dispatches he regularly sent to Liuchow was the statement that "people's fighting spirit against terror ran high" and "secret groups . . . in every locality took more feverishly to training themselves militarily and to raising their political understanding." It was not quite hot air, but it was close. The Viet Minh suffered badly during those months from September 1943 to June 1944.[37]

Giap's cadre struck back as best they could. Now in addition to propaganda work, local armed platoons ambushed an occasional enemy patrol and, to use Giap's words, executed "the most reactionary elements" within the Viet Minh stronghold.[38] Non-Communist nationalists, landlords and moneylenders, members of political factions unaligned with the Viet Minh, turncoats and spies, French sympathizers, and stubborn native Roman Catholic priests and nuns who lived at the head of the Red River Delta were all fair game for Viet Minh cadre as Giap struck out in every direction to ensure the survival of his revolutionary cause. And despite the best efforts of the colonial administration, he was successful. The movement continued to grow throughout Tonkin, and Giap sent cadre as far away as the Ca Mau peninsula in the far south of the nation to create new Communist cells.

In March 1944, the Chinese Nationalist Kuomintang sponsored a conference of various Vietnamese factions and parties at Liuchow, where Ho Chi Minh still lingered under parole. For the Viet Minh it was almost a command performance; if they ever wanted to see Ho given his freedom, they must attend. The Kuomintang insisted that those present create a united front; all Vietnamese were to fight under a single banner, that of the Dong Minh Hoi. In this new organization, the Vietnamese were given only one leadership position. This could well have spelled the end for the Viet Minh except that following the close of the conference, those from other parties remained in Liuchow awaiting the coming of the Allies and the end of the war. The Viet Minh party delegation returned to the high country of Tonkin. This allowed them to claim to all patriots everywhere that the Viet Minh was nothing more than a representative of the Dong Minh Hoi and the national government-in-exile. It was a powerful recruiting pitch; in this way they gathered support from a great many non-Communist patriots who previously had shunned them.

Then world events gave the French colonial administration something other than the Viet Minh to think about. The Axis powers in Europe were suffering grievous reverses on the battlefield. Remnants of German armies retreated from Stalingrad after absorbing horrendous casualties there from the summer of 1942 to February 1943. Reinvigorated Soviet armies launched repeated offensives against their Nazi enemies. Then came the D-Day invasion of Normandy on France's northern coastline. American, Canadian, and British troops attacked Normandy and established a beachhead on the Cotentin peninsula, from which they slowly pushed inland. In July 1944, Pétain's Vichy government collapsed and all of France not then held by the Allies was occupied by the German army. The Allies liberated Paris, and de Gaulle's Free French government-in-exile declared itself the rightful authority for all France. Giap and his companions found solace in such news. They knew these changing world conditions would soon make a difference in Viet Nam.

"Boundless Was Our Joy"

Through the long months of World War II, great military leaders of many nations achieved renown and glory on sanguinary battlefields. Erwin Rommel and his Afrika Korps fought with the troops of Britain's General Bernard Law Montgomery in the arid, dusty deserts of North Africa. Germany's General Friedrich Paulus faced the stubborn Russian General Georgi Zhukov in biting winds and over snow-scarred wastelands at Stalingrad. Britain's General Orde Wingate fought the Chindit War against the Japanese in the steaming jungles of Burma along the Irrawaddy River. American General Douglas MacArthur brooded in his Australian headquarters as he planned his brilliant island-hopping attacks across the Southwest Pacific to outflank and outmaneuver Japanese forces. General Mark Clark's soldiers struggled northward along the Italian peninsula in the face of dogged German resistance from the troops of Albert Kesselring. In England, General Dwight Eisenhower planned the massive invasion of the European continent, to be carried out by dozens of subordinate generals whose names were legion: Bradley, Patton, Hodges, Collins, Patch, Gerow, Simpson, Sutherland, Cota.

These men thought in terms of tens of thousands of soldiers assigned to divisions and corps, army groups, and theater armies. They used jeeps by Willys Overland and half-tracks built by Chevrolet, tanks by Chrysler and trucks by Ford, rifles by Springfield and Singer. Industry massed behind the war effort in a way unparalleled in all history. Cargo planes, freshly christened naval vessels, great railway trains, deuce-and-a-half trucks, gliders, and parachutes carried troops into battle. The generals' planning staffs had to account for divisions capable of consuming eighty tons of ammunition a minute while in combat. Thirsty vehicles drank millions of gallons of petroleum, oil, and lubricants; without POL the entire war effort would have come literally to a grinding halt as engines turned red-hot and seized up.

Troops smoked millions of cigarettes and sent uncounted letters home to children, sweethearts, and parents by way of the Army's V-mail system. They carried chewing gum and toilet paper, K-ration chocolate bars and high-energy, high-calorie food packets. Most ate at least occasional hot meals, brought forward to them by other soldiers assigned to mobile field kitchens. Fighting men encased their feet in heavy boots and exchanged them for new ones when the old wore out. And they threw away what was not immediately essential. Battlefields and the roads leading to them were littered with the detritus of war, casually wasted by those who fought. There was always more, and still more.

Not all soldiers luxuriated in this surfeit of war-generated plenty. During those years when Giap's soon-to-be military counterparts moved vast modern armies across the plains of Europe and from island to island in the Pacific, garnering for themselves medals and glory, he scuffed along narrow paths through the jungles and mountain passes of Tonkin wearing sandals made from worn-out truck tires and sometimes dressed in the black pajamalike garb of his people. When he traveled alone, his mind buzzed with calculations as he struggled to solve the problem of logistics for his Viet Minh cadre. Everything depended upon supply and resupply. No army could fight unaided. It needed bullets and mines and rifles, machine guns and mortars and artillery; its men needed food, clothing, and shelter.

Giap's thoughts tumbled as he considered supply details: if one porter can carry fifty-four pounds of rice fifteen miles a day, or twelve miles a night, then how many porters must begin working and *when* must they begin working to sustain a four-hundred-man combat unit in a ten-day assault on a target 130 miles away? Such thoughts proved worthwhile. He came to conclusions that in the end he used to confound the best western armies in their efforts inside Viet Nam to defeat him in battle as they tried to calm the whirlwind of revolution set in motion by Ho and Giap and their fellows.[1]

The collapse of Marshal Henri-Philippe Pétain's fascist Vichy government in July 1944 and the subsequent German occupation of the rest of France not already liberated by invading Allied armies gave Giap both pause and hope. The passing of the old government in France and the emergence of a new one, he believed, might be of real help to the Viet Minh. He foresaw an inevitable coup d'état staged by the Japanese in order to destroy any remaining French power in Indochina. That would be the critical moment at which to act.[2]

At the end of July 1944, heartened by these developments during Ho's lengthy absence, Giap persuaded the Cao-Bac-Lang interprovincial committee to convene a conference to discuss whether or not the party should now launch an armed insurrection. They met at the cave of Pac Bo amid much ceremony. The meeting ground was well decorated and prepared with a triumphal arch and a display of the red banner emblazoned with the five-pointed gold star fluttering from a nearby flagpole. Inside were rows of conference tables. Dining halls and bedrooms were ready. Three successive rings of local Man warriors mounted guard. Stationed along each entry corridor through the hills and forest, they provided strict security, and these sentries were reinforced at the most sensitive locations by armed detachments of Vietnamese cadre.

"Boundless was our joy, of all of us," Giap said, "to meet together to discuss a subject which we had so much longed for, after months of arduous struggle against the terrorist campaign."[3] Giap offered the group a resolution: because of the world and domestic situation and because of the improvement thus far in Viet Minh fortunes, it was time to launch a guerrilla war.[4] He spoke for his own motion and urged his fellows to vote for an immediate uprising against the French and Japanese. His persuasiveness convinced others, and so the conferees agreed to go into action two months later, right after the September rice harvest.[5]

Giap was ecstatic and in his euphoria spoke of "People [of the land who] lived the pre-insurrection hours in hope and excitement."[6] In Giap's memory, all those who lived in Cao-Bac-Lang were enthusiastic. "People screamed with joy," he wrote, "when they heard about the . . . resolution on the launching of guerrilla warfare."[7] Preparations began in the utmost secrecy. To watching French eyes, mountain villagers seemed to continue their quiet resignation and silent suffering. Behind this facade was feverish preparation. The remainder of July and August passed as Viet Minh agents purchased and manufactured weapons. Especially sought-after were hand grenades. Giap ordered that each shotgun have 150 shells in reserve.

Food was dried to preserve it and stored in hidden caches. Giap claimed that people contributed even more grain than the quotas the Viet Minh set for them. One elderly woman, Giap recalled, sold half her belongings to buy guns for her son and daughter.[8] In September, harvest neared its completion and the still-excited Giap exulted, "The first shots of the armed action had already been fired in many localities."[9]

This was Giap's first major party decision and the strongest position he had yet taken on any issue, a fact that he quickly came to regret. For when Ho Chi Minh, who was in China, heard of Giap's decision, he sent a message to Pac Bo telling the Viet Minh to hold fast until he could return. In November he met with Giap at Pac Bo, and on the 19th, Giap reported to him. "The road to conquer the south is clear. Everybody is ready. All we need is your signal." Once again,

Ho countermanded Giap's decision and the rubber stamp given it by the conference.[10]

"Today is not the day," Ho said, shaking his head. "The masses are not fully developed. They are still divided. Premature actions will only hurt our cause."[11] Ho believed that Giap's decision was based only on the local situation in Cao-Bac-Lang and not on the entire country. Ho further explained to Giap that the younger man had "seen only part and not the whole of the problem."[12] This penchant for premature action would long remain to haunt Giap. He consistently moved too soon throughout the two later Indochina wars. Partly this was because he was a soldier and man of action who would have gladdened the heart of Napoleon. Often ignoring the cautions of Sun Tzu, he sought quick military solutions to vexing problems and in true Jominian fashion wanted to fight, to throw mass on force at the decisive point. Because of his Marxism, he also was inclined to a Clausewitzian approach, melding the political with the military. In addition, his Marxism made of him a true believer. He *believed* the people would rise to support the cause. He *believed* his enemies were often craven, lacking in courage, and morally weak. And, as time would show, he was often wrong.

There was a sufficiency of problems, Ho told Giap. There was no sure sanctuary. Any revolutionaries, Ho lectured, would be hunted down and destroyed. "How would we deal with the problem of protecting and evacuating the people when the enemy attacked every village, every mountain village, and every locality? How could we organize people's lives once we brought them into the jungle?" How could the Viet Minh continue to increase production of weapons in a time of prolonged French terrorism?[13]

As Giap looked at him with dismay, Ho continued: "At this time we need to develop new ways to cope with the new situation. The present political movement has suffered much. Our fighters are still inexperienced. We must select our best fighters and organize them into a *Doi Quan Giai Phong* [a people's revolutionary movement]." He finally convinced a crestfallen Giap that any uprising at that point would be premature and therefore extremely dangerous to the movement.[14]

That night, however, Ho threw a sop to Giap when the two men met again for an extended conversation. Giap chafed at the thought of further delay in the rising against French colonial power. Cautioning patience, Ho told his young disciple that "the period of peaceful development of the revolution is over, but that of nationwide uprising has not yet begun. . . . We must, therefore, adopt a more appropriate form in order to bring the movement forward."[15]

Ho had in mind the formation of a Viet Minh army. Giap's heart surged. This was precisely the goal he desired. A firebrand, he was ready to carry the war to his hated French enemies at the first possible moment. Then Ho passed to him the baton of leadership. "This you should carry out," Ho told him. "Can you do that? We are still weak, the enemy is strong. But we must not let them annihilate us, must we?"[16]

"Yes, I'll do it," Giap quickly responded.[17] "I was pleased with my new responsibilities," Giap recalled. "I dreamt of the day when I could put our red flag on top of Mount Phia U-oac." Knowing the difficulty of surviving a guerrilla war, Giap believed he would soon die in some battle. "I considered that my life would end in the mountains of Cao-Bac-Lang."[18]

That very night Giap lay in bed listening to Ho talk until about 3:00 A.M. Inside the chilly hut, without any light, the men leaned their heads on hard blocks of wood and planned for a guerrilla assault on French power. Ho outlined his ideas for a liberation army, its organization, its motto, its activities. He spoke of the problems of food and ammunition supply. He repeated his concern that if they relied on the people of the land the enemy would not be able to destroy them.[19]

Giap set to his task. Calling upon two trusted comrades, Vu Anh and Le Quang Ba, Giap led them to the back of the Pac Bo cave, where they discussed details of organization for the new military force and selection of its leadership. They chose Hoang Sam as military leader and Xich Thang as political commissar. The first force would consist of a platoon of three squads drawn from armed self-defense teams at Ha Quang, Hoa An, and Nguyen Binh. While they talked, Ho entered to listen, and when they turned to him, he agreed with their decisions. He reminded them always to remember that "the spirit of the people is greater than armed forces. If we can rely on the people, no one can defeat us."[20]

Late that night, Ho and Giap sat together for a long discussion. Past midnight, Ho said to Giap, "In revolution you must put the needs of the people first."[21] As they talked, Ho suggested the new military force might be named the Viet Nam Liberation Unit. The next day, however, he called Giap aside once more and ordered that the name should contain a reminder to all its members that revolutionary power grows best when the actions of soldiers are guided by political considerations. It would be called Tuyen Truyen Giai Phong Quan, or the Armed Propaganda and Liberation Unit. Its task would be to use armed struggle to mobilize and arouse the population while bowing to the notion that political activities were always more important than armed assaults; that propaganda was more vital than military attacks.[22]

In this way Giap, the former high school history teacher, now found himself at the head of a nonexistent army. Much as America's Congress in 1775 named George Washington to head a nonexistent Continental Army, so Giap found himself appointed to direct a force that was still to be raised, organized, and trained. In this way, in a dark cave lit by flaming torches, he began his long career as the primary military leader of Viet Nam. He was thirty-three years old.

While Ho Chi Minh might have left the details of raising the army to Giap, he chose not to do so. He wrote instructions providing for the formation of regular units, and in lengthy meetings with his subordinate, he and Giap reviewed French military might and their own situation. They discussed the strength of their cadres, the logistics of supplying food to troops, the regions where bases should first be established.

Over and again Ho insisted that a sudden and successful military venture must occur within a month. Winning that first battle would give the Viet Minh great help in their propaganda work. He warmed to his topic. "Be secret, rapid, active, now in the East, now in the West, arriving unexpectedly and leaving unnoticed." Ho was, of course, quoting Sun Tzu.[23]

Giap held a meeting of potential platoon leaders at Ha Quang. The sessions were enlivened by the attendance of some Vietnamese military cadets recently returned from China. They met in a dense forest around a large flat stone under an old tree. How might they best open their campaign against the French? Which target to hit? How to win without heavy losses in human life and weaponry? Should they attack a stationary target or ambush a moving column? Weapons were in short supply, but even worse was the ammunition problem; each man had only about twenty cartridges. At the end of a long day of discussion, the men shared a festive meal of monkey meat, animals shot from trees in the surrounding forest.[24]

Giap ultimately chose thirty-four men to compose the first unit of his regular army. He called them the Tran Hung Dao platoon after an early Vietnamese emperor. They were selected from among section leaders, platoon commanders, or outstanding members of local armed groups in the Dinh Ca Valley. This "army" possessed two revolvers, seventeen rifles, fourteen flintlocks, and one light machine gun! Some of those weapons had last seen service in the Russo-Japanese War of 1905.[25]

At 5:00 P.M., 22 December 1944, Giap conducted a ceremony initiating these men into his army, the forerunner of the later People's Liberation Army. It was deep winter and very cold, but the men were enthusiastic. They assembled for the first time under their gold-starred red flag. Giap made a lengthy speech emphasizing the important and heavy responsibilities they now all bore. "The political is more important than the military and propaganda is more important than fighting," he said. "Let us set high the spirit of heroic sacrifice." He called on them to pledge their blood and to adhere strictly to discipline and absolutely obey all orders of their superiors.[26]

All the men present took a ten-point oath:

1. To sacrifice everything for their fatherland so as to make Viet Nam independent.
2. To obey and to carry out orders well and without question.
3. To fight without complaint despite hardships and misery; not to lose heart even in the face of death.

4. To be alert and worthy fighters able to kill the enemy and save their country.
5. To keep absolute secrecy.
6. Never to betray their fellows even under torture.
7. To love and help their comrades-in-arms.
8. To safeguard their weapons.
9. To respect three great precepts: not to steal from, nor frighten, nor bother people; to adhere to three great principles: to respect people, to help them, and to protect them.
10. To use self-criticism for personal improvement.

Shouts of "We swear!" resounded mightily through the forest after Giap recited each point.[27]

Giap later told how those present felt lifted up by the spirit of sacrifice, and "filled with inexpressible and unforgettable sentiments."[28] To set an example of austerity, the ritual closed with a frugal meal—rice without vegetables and without salt—provided for the event by local people.[29] As darkness came on, they sat around a fire until about midnight wrapped in fog and whipped by gusts from a cold wind. "In the depths of the jungle, swept by cold winds of a chilly winter night," Giap wrote, "the army was born."[30]

Ho wanted a victory, and Giap did not plan to wait even the month Ho had allowed him before he struck at the French. Only four days after receiving his assignment from Ho, on 24 December 1944, Giap and his new army struck at French outposts at Phai Khat and Na Ngan, thirty-five kilometers from one another in the border region amid the neighboring provinces of Cao Bang, Bac Can, and Lang Son. These two outposts were ideal. French military men there occupied many homes formerly belonging to Giap's comrades. At Phai Khat, Giap sent in a twelve-year-old boy named Hoang to serve him as a spy. Each day Hoang took bread and wine to the French commander, talked to the troops, observed the food and ammunition warehouse, the mess hall, the sleeping quarters, and watch posts, and noted the schedule for meals, rest and meetings. At night he slipped out of the village through its bamboo hedge and reported what he had learned to Giap.[31]

In case he needed papers to get inside the garrisons, Giap went to the office of *Viet Nam Doc Lap* and used the typewriter there to forge patrol permits. A friend carved an official stamp from a yam tuber and used it to stamp the patrol permits with red ink next to the forged signature. "At that time," Giap wrote, "type-written letters of introduction were most valuable."[32]

These forts were garrisoned with French officers and noncommissioned officers and Vietnamese soldiers. To confuse the French, "Van" and his men dressed in clothing similar to that worn by the Mandarin militia. Van wore a conical helmet covered with indigo-dyed cloth, puttees, and a white belt. Giap's men struck first at Phai Khat and then, marching swiftly cross-country, at Na Ngan. The men of his unit, Giap reported, were all hardened and extremely devoted to the cause. Be that as it may, there seems to have been some prearrangement involved in these two battles. Giap and his men killed all the French defenders without exception and seized a large amount of ammunition, which at the time was of more value even than guns. The Vietnamese troops in service to the French surrendered with no loss of life, and there were no casualties among the attackers. Prearrangement would have brought about these results and would have been an attractive way to introduce the new army to people of the area. An initial victory makes for good feelings. A happy and feisty Giap exclaimed, "What champions we are: one meal and two battles a day!"[33]

To throw off pursuers, Giap marched his tiny force north as if to attack Dong Mu, a border community thirty miles northwest of Cao Bang. It was the first of many ruses he would use against the French. When he believed they had figured out his next objective, he halted his men and they withdrew to an already-prepared base camp at Thien Thuat, where he celebrated Tet 1945. News of his victories spread rapidly. As Giap and his men marched toward Thien Thuat, local inhabitants even in areas close to enemy posts openly carried torchlights to welcome Giap's force. Others spread festive Tet meals on tables they laid by the roadside and waited beside them for the troops to arrive so they could entertain them.[34]

At the Thien Thuat base, Giap expanded his small unit to company size by reinforcements drawn from several localities. Local people showed their support, supplying Giap's forces with buffaloes, oxen, pigs, rice, cakes, and funds for needed equipment. Now, finally, Giap could begin to train his army. The caves of Cao Bang were his initial military headquarters. Working there, Giap, some forty Viet Minh cadremen, and five hundred Montagnard guards devoted themselves to learning how to build an army. Giap wrote, thought, planned, and schemed. As resources, Giap had a few Chinese advisers, notes he had made on military matters during his two years spent in China, and knowledge derived from his historical study. With this he sought to ground himself in strategy, tactics, recruitment, training, logistics, and matériel procurement.[35]

From the beginning Giap understood that a regular army would not be sufficient by itself. Under his main armed force, he directed the creation of two subordinate groups: district armed militias and village self-defense forces. District armed militias, organized into eighty-five-man companies and three-hundred-man provincial battalions, supported the Propaganda and Liberation Army and provided Giap with local strike forces. When fully equipped, they could engage French units in sustained combat for very brief periods. They emphasized small-unit actions: ambush, sabotage, armed terrorism, and harassing fire. They served to wear down French morale, forcing the *colons* to protect isolated outposts.[36]

Village self-defense units, organized into thirty-man platoons, were the true foundations of Giap's "people's warfare." Operating at the hamlet level, these part-time militia units carried responsibility for guarding villages, harassing French military patrols, and preparing local defenses against attacks: mines, punji stakes, and booby traps. They also served as a manpower pool, offering up replacements when necessary to higher and better-armed units. Manpower losses were made up by drawing from militia units; those units drew from self-defense forces; village units conscripted from the masses of the countryside. As time progressed, the newest recruit to a local self-defense team knew that one day he might well be a member of the regular army. In this way, one writer has said, "Farming ants nourished fighting ants."[37]

Most of that nourishment—for all the levels of Giap's military organizations—came in the form of political indoctrination. From the beginning, Giap was persuaded that his soldiers needed total commitment to the revolutionary cause. Only then would they fight and die in sufficiently determined numbers. Only devotion bordering on the fanatical would drive them through the harsh days of battle yet to come with a foe that was technologically superior in every way. Such an attitude could never be cultivated solely through military training. And so Giap filled over two-thirds of the training schedule with political indoctrination classes.[38]

Giap had to bring his expectations quickly down to the level of his men's ability. When he first gave them training in close-order drill, he automatically began counting cadence in French: *un, deux, un, deux.* Many looked at him in bewilderment, so he began over, in Vietnamese: *mot, hai, mot, hai.*[39] In all their ways, Giap trained his men by the numbers until each act became part of a man's nature. When he was promoted, a man was taught a few extra movements and reactions suitable for his new responsibilities, and in these also he was drilled repeatedly until he could act upon them without hesitation, without thought.

As the years passed and Giap's men were ordered over and over again into battle with the French, there was continual promotion for those who survived combat, for casualties ran high and dead leaders needed to be replaced. After each engagement, everyone who was not killed was put through a fresh political and military conditioning course. Promising individuals were promoted to greater responsibilities and taught new motions and reflexes. In this way even the simplest man who managed to remain alive continued to improve, and some reached high positions. In later days some colonels who were barely literate but who knew their jobs by rote managed to perform on the battlefield with excellence.

Giap allowed no weakness. Everyone had to admit his faults and failings, to accuse himself of lack of dedication or skill, to repent his errors, and to promise to do better. Those who would not or could not do so were punished, sent through repeated reeducation courses, or, as a last resort, simply shot.[40]

Giap coordinated the activities of all three levels of the military and retained unified command over them all in his own hands. For a long time, Giap
was primarily concerned with teaching his men the tactics of actual battle assaults, how to move units from one point to another. Then he graduated to strategy: how did the need for a given battle harmonize with political reality? It
would still be some time before he could give serious thought to the theories to
be inferred from his work, but they would eventually come and would power-
fully affect the course of modern wars in many parts of the world.[41]

For some time the Viet Minh had been of help to the Allied war effort. Among
other things, carefully monitored by Ho, Pham Van Dong, and Giap, Viet Minh
cadre since 1942 had provided helpful information to an Allied intelligence operation, the GBT group, working within Japanese-occupied Indochina. The ini-
tials stood for Gordon-Bernard-Tan, the three members of the unit.

Laurence Gordon was a Canadian oilman with experience in Egypt, China,
and Madagascar. When war broke out in 1939, Laurie Gordon, director of operations for Cal-Texaco in Haiphong, left Indochina and returned to his California home. The English spymaster Sir William Stephenson contacted him
there and recruited him into the British Secret Service, commissioned him a captain, and helped him infiltrate back into Indochina. Acting as a freelance oil
agent, he traveled about from Ha Noi to Saigon. He was soon joined by Frank
Tan, a Chinese-American born in Massachusetts and a graduate of the Boston
Latin School, whom he had previously known, and Harry V. Bernard, who had
earlier worked for Cal-Texaco in Saigon.

GBT established an information network throughout Indochina and sent
information both to the Chinese Kuomintang government and to General Claire
Chennault's Fourteenth Air Force, based at Kunming. In 1944, GBT forwarded
a report to China that a downed American pilot, identified only as Lieutenant
Shaw, had parachuted into the Viet Minh–controlled zone. He was rescued and
kept safe from harm by one of Giap's guerrilla bands. That report stated that this
was done at the orders of an Annamite named "Hu Tze-ming [sic: Ho Chi Minh]."
Shaw was eventually brought to Pac Bo headquarters by Viet Minh cadre, and,
in one of the four trips he made into China between late 1944 and early 1945,
Ho personally accompanied Shaw to Kunming, where he was turned over to
American forces there.[42]

Those assigned to the Office of Strategic Services (OSS) in Kunming, China,
to which such reports eventually came, were interested in information about
downed American fliers and much more. In the office there was a file dating back
to 1940 detailing the activities of the Viet Minh. Included in those papers was
the first mention of Ho Chi Minh in American records. On 31 December 1942,
Clarence E. Gauss, American ambassador to China, reported that the Chinese
had, on 2 December, arrested and detained at Liuchow, Kwangsi, "an Annamite

named Ho Chih-chi(?) [sic]." OSS reports also indicated that Ho could occa-sionally be found in Kunming at the headquarters there of the Office of War In-formation.[43]

The first OSS agent in Kunming Ho contacted was Lieutenant Colonel Paul L. E. Helliwell, head of the secret intelligence branch. As an indication of interest, he gave Ho six .38 caliber revolvers and twenty thousand rounds of ammunition. Intrigued by this small, intense Asian, Helliwell reported the contact to his superiors. They authorized additional contacts and increased aid.

On one of his forays into Kunming, China, on 17 March 1945, Ho talked with Charles Fenn. In China as a war correspondent and recruited by OSS, Fenn later took marine training, was commissioned, and returned to China as a lieu-tenant assigned to OSS. His duties included acting as liaison with the GBT group in Viet Nam. In his talk with Ho, Fenn realized that here was a man who should be recruited for the war effort, and so when Ho asked if he could meet briefly with General Claire Chennault, Fenn agreed to help. For better or worse, Fenn is thus the one who "recruited" Ho's assistance for OSS efforts in Tonkin. Fenn set up the appointment but warned Ho not to ask for anything, neither supplies nor promises of support. Ho agreed. On 29 March 1945, Ho entered Chennault's of-fice and Fenn introduced the two men.

Chennault told Ho of his gratitude for Ho's helping to save the pilot Shaw. Ho replied that he was always glad to help Americans and, in particular, Chen-nault, for whom he had great admiration. For a few moments they talked about Chennault's old Flying Tiger group, a group of American volunteers he put together in the early days of the war to help Chiang Kai-shek's National-ist government combat Japanese air superiority. Chennault was pleased that the old Annamite (Ho was then only fifty-four!) knew about the famous flying group. Ho promised he would help any other downed pilots if at all possible. Neither man spoke about the French or about politics. Then Ho asked a small favor. Did the general have a picture of himself? Chennault pulled out a folder of eight-by-ten glossy pictures. Ho selected one and asked the general to au-tograph it. Chennault scrawled "Yours sincerely, Claire L. Chennault" across the bottom, and with the picture in his hand, Ho bade the general a polite farewell.[44]

Ho was elated. He held in his hand a treasure; tangible evidence he could use to demonstrate to any skeptic that he had American support behind the Viet Minh. Soon he would have more concrete help.

France's General Eugène Mordant had commanded the forces of his country in Indochina since 1940. Realigning himself with de Gaulle's Free French in 1942, he found himself under orders to head French resistance in Indochina and to prepare the way for an Allied invasion. Mordant was not a discreet man; soon even the Japanese knew of his plans. They kept a watchful eye on his activities.

Following the liberation of Paris in August 1944, de Gaulle named Mordant his delegate-general for Indochina, and Decoux, the governor-general, found himself stripped of all real authority.

The Japanese laid plans to hold on to their Indochinese bastion. They replaced garrison troops there with crack soldiers of the tactical 38th Imperial Army, commanded by Lieutenant General Yuitsu Tsuchihashi. As early as December 1944, Tsuchihashi requested permission to act against Mordant and French forces in Viet Nam. His superiors told him the time was not yet right.

In January and February 1945, Mordant sent elements of his military from their urban barracks to the northern mountains of Tonkin. He argued that in the event of a Japanese attack, his soldiers would not be trapped in the mountains and could even function as guerrillas there. Mordant further enraged the Japanese by refusing to turn over to them nine downed American pilots held by the French. Mordant also laid plans to begin an operation against the Viet Minh guerrillas to begin on 10 March.

The Japanese did not wait. On 9 March they stripped French officials of all authority and arrested and imprisoned many of them, including General Mordant. Known Gaullist sympathizers were rounded up and interned. French officers and military units were forcibly disarmed and interned. The French ironically now found themselves prisoners in their own colony. Some twelve thousand French troops located in the mountainous north tried to resist near Lang Son and Dang Dong, communities located near the Chinese border. Outnumbered and low on ammunition, several hundred finally surrendered to their Japanese attackers, who slaughtered them. Survivors began a slow fighting retreat on foot northward to China.[45] This putsch transformed the situation in Viet Nam. The eighty-year-old empire of the French colonialists collapsed in seconds and ended forever any lingering idea in the minds of the Vietnamese of French omnipotence and invulnerability.

Not one to overlook a sudden advantage, Emperor Bao Dai acted swiftly. On 11 March, only two days after the Japanese coup, he abrogated the 1884 Treaty of Protectorate and proclaimed that his Kingdom of Annam was independent. For years the Japanese had touted their Greater East Asian Co-Prosperity Sphere, with its slogan "Asia for the Asians." Now Bao Dai also joined this Japanese-sponsored and -organized group, promising to cooperate with the Japanese and trust in their goodwill toward Viet Nam. Caught by their own motto, the Japanese felt it necessary to allow some sort of Vietnamese participation in running their own country, but their adamant refusal to hand over real independence to Bao Dai or anyone else only served to strengthen the Viet Minh, who now made rapid progress following the putsch.[46] Still, Bao Dai's move came as a surprise to Ho Chi Minh and his cadre, for they wanted no other independent and patriotic rallying force in

Viet Nam save their own Viet Minh. They laid plans to deal with Bao Dai at the appropriate time.[47]

The Communist Party central committee's military commission scheduled a meeting at Bac Giang from 15 to 20 April 1945. Giap looked forward to going. It would be a chance to see comrades, to exchange news, to refine plans for military activities. Giap walked cross-country toward Bac Giang, dressed in traditional clothing: black silk shirt, white trousers, and woven bamboo conical hat. For the first time in five years he was again in the delta of the Red River.

He reveled in the sight of flooded rice paddies that increasingly appeared as he neared the delta and then spread out across the land as far as he could see. He enjoyed each hamlet he passed, his eyes taking in their impenetrable bamboo hedges. Rice fields and bamboo made his thoughts turn toward home and times of peace. He wondered about his wife, Quang Thai, and his daughter, Hong Anh. "I thought I would at last have news from my family from whom I had not heard for all these years," he said later. "I had written letters but didn't know if they ever arrived and I was thinking it would not be long until I had news."

Upon his arrival at Bac Giang, Giap found his old friend Truong Chinh already there. "When I met Truong Chinh and the other comrades . . . it was an explosion of joy," he recalled. Terrible news lay in wait for him, however. While Giap listened to others talking about how they had to move about constantly to avoid French police operations, Truong Chinh casually turned to him and, as an example of the danger in which they all lived, recalled the case of Giap's wife: "Thai was caught because she didn't have time to find someone to care for the baby. She died in prison before we could do anything."

Giap felt his blood chill and for a long moment sat still as a stunned oxen. His heart racing, he finally asked, "You say Thai is dead?"

"What?" responded Truong Chinh. "You didn't know?" He had no idea Giap had not heard from his family in all the years of hiding since they had left Ha Noi together.

Giap sat quietly, speechless, white as death for long minutes. Then he silently rose and left his fellows, desperate to find a way to accept the idea of the death of his wife. "But that was not the time for emotions," he later recalled. It was the time to plan military action; that was what had brought these men together, and when they assembled for business sessions, Giap sat stiffly among them, as his duty demanded. Ice had begun to form on the volcano.[48]

Although the Japanese now had control of the land, they had no comparable structure to replace the now-discarded French intelligence and security forces. They were unable to occupy or control more than the key towns and communication lines in Viet Nam. Rural areas fell to the Viet Minh by default. Its cadre quickly took advantage of this situation, using the opportunity for recruitment and political/military organizational work. Newly formed Viet Minh units drove south. Giap formed at least fifteen to twenty new units of his People's Liberation Army, one after the other.

At one recruiting center, three thousand young men enlisted. Patriots hoisted red flags over increasing numbers of hamlets and villages. The more daring even disarmed French troops. Everywhere it seemed that Viet Minh revolutionary committees now served as a de facto provisional government in their own areas, and the Japanese did not have the military strength to send their few troops into the high mountain areas to attack them even when Giap added Japanese targets to his guerrilla war campaign.

Truong Chinh chaired a Tonkin revolutionary military conference which met 15–20 April 1945. Attended by representatives of various armed elements from across the land, it was a party effort to create a single united front and a single command. By May 1945 a liberated zone existed, consisting of the provinces of Cao Bang, Bac Can, Lang Son, Ha Giang, Thai Nguyen, Phu Tho, Phuc Yen, Yen Bai, and Tuyen Quang, and part of Bac Giang and Vinh Yen. Then in a meeting presided over by Giap on 15 May, the People's Liberation Army was formally proclaimed in ceremonies at the Bien Thuong Buddhist temple in Cho Chu village, Thai Nguyen province. The Liberation Army spread like oil on water, and the whole northern region between Ha Noi and Cao Bang was now essentially a free area. Thus on 4 June the Viet Minh held a meeting at Kim Lung, a small village in Tuyen Quang province renamed Tan Trao by the rebels, and formally proclaimed the area a liberated zone. Tan Trao was to be its capital, and administration of this free zone was placed under the responsibility of a five-man provisional executive committee. For Giap that meeting was important for another reason: he was finally named a member of the central committee of the Indochinese Communist Party.[49]

The Viet Minh leadership anticipated that a crucial moment for their program would come with the Japanese surrender, and they wanted to be ready. To show their determination, on 4 July 1945, Giap sent his Viet Minh guerrillas against the Japanese in a major attack in the four-thousand-foot-high Tam Dao mountains in the northwest corner of the Red River Delta. A small Japanese contingent of about forty men occupied an old French outpost in the mountain resort of Tam Dao, which was used as a civilian concentration camp. Giap and his men overran the little garrison and freed the civilians from their captors.[50]

The 9 March Japanese coup against the French cut off the flow of intelligence from Viet Nam to OSS people operating out of Kunming in China. Alarmed by this loss, OSS men in Kunming contacted Ho Chi Minh to work out a new means of gathering information. Frankie Tan of the GBT group, then in Kunming, urged Ho to work with the OSS, a predisposition Ho already felt in any case. After his arrival in Kunming on 13 April 1945, Major Archimedes Patti asked Ho for permission to send an OSS team to work with his cadre and to gather intelligence on the Japanese and expand existing escape and evasion networks. On 30 June, Patti received a reply from Ho Chi Minh agreeing to receive and work with an OSS team.[51] Shortly thereafter, Charles Fenn arranged a flight for Ho and Tan from Kunming to a southern border town on China's frontier with Viet Nam. From there, Tan and Ho, with Ho's bodyguards, walked together to Pac Bo and then on to Tan Trao, the new location of Viet Minh headquarters.

Patti's OSS team was not, however, the first to reach Ho's jungle camp in northern Viet Nam. In that spring of 1945 the first American to parachute into the Viet Minh main headquarters camp was sponsored by AGAS (Air Ground Aid Section, China). He was Lieutenant Dan Phelan. Met by Frankie Tan, he was taken to the camp and introduced to Ho, Giap, and others. Phelan met with Ho on several occasions. "He kept asking me if I could remember the language of our Declaration [of Independence]. I was a normal American. I couldn't. I could have wired up to Kunming and had a copy dropped to me, of course, but all he really wanted was the flavor of the thing. The more we discussed it, the more he actually seemed to know about it than I did."[52]

It was not until 16 July that Patti's group, code-named Deer Team, parachuted into Viet Nam near the village of Kim Lung, about twenty miles east of Tuyen Quang. An advance section arrived first, headed by the team commander, Major Allison Kent Thomas. Thomas had tried since May to walk south out of China into the Viet Minh zone but had been unable to find guides. Now, leaping into the sky from the door of an old Dakota cargo plane, he and his two teammates, Private First Class Henry Prunier, his linguist, and First Sergeant William Zielski, his radio operator, plunged toward the jungled canopy below them.[53]

"Welcome to Our American Friends"

As Major Allison Kent Thomas, leader of the OSS Deer Team, swung beneath his parachute canopy he looked down at the jungle rushing up to meet him and pulled his static lines in an effort to drift toward a clear area for his landing. His struggle was unsuccessful. He crashed into a tree and came to a jarring halt thirty to forty feet above the ground without any idea what to do next. His two teammates fared better, landing without difficulty. Both PFC Prunier and 1/SGT Zielski stood on the ground below looking up at him, but Zielski, his radio operator, was the first to speak. "All you gotta do, Major, is pull your reserve chute." Thomas pulled the D-ring on his chest pack and the backup parachute slithered out of its canvas covering, its silken panels dropping to the ground. Cutting himself free from the entangled main parachute, Thomas fastened the lines of his reserve chute to a tree branch and slid to the ground. It was just after 6:00 P.M. on 16 July 1945. The American military had landed in Indochina.[1]

Quite a crowd had gathered to meet him. Thomas saw Lieutenant Dan Phelan of Air Ground Aid Station China (AGAS), who had parachuted into Viet Nam some weeks earlier, standing among what he estimated to be about two hundred guerrilla fighters. Then a man with Asian features walked up to Major Thomas and said in perfect English, "Hi, how are you? We've been expecting you." In this way he met Frankie Tan of the Gordon-Bernard-Tan (GBT) group, the covert British-American intelligence team. Tan had recently accompanied Ho on a walk into Tonkin from China.

Tan and Phelan conducted Thomas to his new home, located on the side of a forested hill, a bamboo hut with a bamboo floor raised a few feet off the ground and a roof of palm leaves. To reach it they passed under a bamboo archway on which someone had put up a sign reading "Welcome to our American Friends."[2]

Thomas, Zielski, and Prunier were introduced to "Mr. C. M. Hoo," and Ho gave them a cordial welcome. Weak from dysentery and malaria, possibly also suffering from dengue fever, Ho had just walked in from China with Frankie Tan. That first night the Deer Team members ate rice, bamboo sprouts, and barbecued steak from a freshly slaughtered cow killed in their honor, and drank Ha Noi beer captured from a Japanese convoy. As he settled down for sleep in his bamboo hut, it was all very much like a Boy Scout outing in the woods, but Thomas thought about his mission.

He was under orders to set up a guerrilla team of from fifty to one hundred men and so had brought along sufficient containers of small arms and explosives to arm such a group. They would then attack and interdict the railway as it stretched up to China from Ha Noi to Lang Son. This was to be done in support of Operation Carbonado, to hinder the movement of Japanese forces in Viet Nam, preventing them from reaching southern China in case the United States decided to land an expeditionary force there in preparation for an attack on the Japanese mainland. Thomas's second assignment was to locate Japanese military bases and depots as targets for U.S. bombing planes and to send back to Kunming OSS headquarters whatever intelligence they could gather.[3]

The next morning was the first opportunity Thomas had to examine his whereabouts. The Viet Minh camp was located on the side of a hill in a bamboo forest at the end of Kim Lung gorge, a few yards from the hut of Ho Chi Minh. Immediately to the west was the OSS drop zone, a flat valley of rice paddies surrounded by forested hills, in which sat the hamlet of Kim Lung, now called Tan Trao by the Viet Minh. Everyone with whom Thomas talked spoke with equal fervor against both the Japanese and French fascists. In further conversations with "Mr. Hoo," Ho Chi Minh told him he could receive any number of special operations teams and, with time, could infiltrate them as far south as Saigon. With Ho, Thomas spoke in English, for the Annamite did not like to use the French language; with Giap, Thomas spoke French.[4]

Ho claimed to have three thousand men under arms, operating in small bands of fifteen to twenty men each, but Thomas saw only about two hundred guerrillas in the area, armed with French rifles and a few Brens, Stens, tommies, and carbines.[5] Thomas sent off a radio request to his Kunming headquarters for requisitions ranging from toothbrushes to 60mm mortars. Air cargo transports eventually dropped more weapons: one automatic machine gun, two 60mm mortars, four bazookas, eight Bren machine guns, twenty

Thompson submachine guns, sixty M-1 carbines, four M-1 rifles, twenty Colt .45 caliber pistols, and a set of binoculars.[6]

Aided by such weapons brought in by a total of three parachute drops and by small arms crafted by the Viet Minh in their crude jungle weapons factories, Giap's army soon boasted sufficient equipment to impress people of the countryside. "To see our new company standing in neat rows and armed with new rifles and shining bayonets," Giap said, "filled us with jubilance and confidence." Giap made sure that his newly equipped units were seen by as many as possible. Wherever they went, he wrote, local people cheered and welcomed them.[7]

Unfamiliar with the language and with the nuances of Asian politics, Major Thomas also gave his headquarters in China a bit of misinformation about the Viet Minh. Perhaps in part this was because of his linguist, Henry Prunier. Prunier had some training in Vietnamese, but it was so rudimentary that it was useless. He was, according to Thomas, "a nice guy and very helpful, but not a linguist." Thomas also had little understanding of either Viet Nam or the goals of the Viet Minh movement, and he was assured by both Dan Phelan and Frankie Tan that Ho was not a Communist. In Thomas's own words: "Phelan wired back to AGAS that Ho deserved full trust and support. Likewise Tan raved over Ho, never hinting that he was a communist."[8]

Nevertheless, Thomas had seen a red flag fluttering near headquarters, and so the day after his landing he confronted Ho and asked about his political coloration. With polite indirection Ho responded that the Viet Minh was composed of many political parties.[9] In those first days in camp as Thomas tried to gain a feel for the situation, he came to know and like many of the Viet Minh cadre. For these reasons he radioed his headquarters that the group was *"not* Communist or Communist controlled or Communist led." Rather, in his opinion, they sought "freedom and reforms from French harshness."[10] That they sought independence from France is indisputable. That they chose not to emphasize their dedication to communism is an illustration of their willingness to be all things to all people in their effort to further their goals.

From 26 to 30 July, accompanied by a small group of Viet Minh, Thomas went on a reconnaisance of the area hoping to locate a usable airstrip on which Piper L-5 light planes could land and take off. He also wanted an opportunity to observe Japanese activities in the area. He was successful in both quests. He not only found his airstrip but also at one point took a leisurely swim less than a kilometer from a Japanese outpost. Wherever he traveled, people gave him a wonderful reception. He noted their kindliness in his diary. "Rum in our coffee. Honey in our tea. Bananas, eggs, pineapples, limes, chicken, duck, beef, pork, various kinds of vegetables, bamboo sprouts, greens, a sort of native potato [and] peppers." He also tasted "a special annimite [*sic*] sauce made from fish called Nuoc Mam," making him perhaps the first of uncounted thousands of American soldiers to confront this delightfully noxious concoction. He arrived back at camp so late on 30 July that he and his party lit bamboo torches in order to see the pathway.[11]

Upon his return, Thomas found the remainder of his Deer Team waiting. They had parachuted in the previous day. The assistant team leader, Second Lieutenant René Defourneaux, was now on hand. Born in France, he chose to go by the name of Douglass to avoid problems with the francophobic Viet Minh, but they still suspected him because of his accent. Present also were Staff Sergeant Lawrence Vogt, weapons instructor; Sergeant Aaron Squires, the team's photographer and handyman; and Private First Class Paul Hoagland, a medic.[12]

Thomas learned from his men that Hoagland, the medic, had found Ho sick when he arrived, visibly trembling and with a high fever. Having only recently returned to camp, Ho was suffering from general weakness, malnutrition, and malaria. Hoagland reported Ho's condition to Defourneaux, adding that the Viet Minh leader "doesn't have long for this world," and the assistant team leader told him to do what he could to help. Hoagland gave Ho quinine, sulfa drugs, and vitamin capsules.[13] Within a few days a remarkably improved Ho was up and about, well on his way back to health. The American team may well have saved his life.

The other matter which occupied Thomas upon his return was the opening of the Viet Minh communal house at Kim Lung (Tan Trao). A large crowd gathered for the festivities, and Thomas and the other Deer Team members joined them. They sang party songs and heard speeches on independence and women's suffrage. They saw simple skits on how the Japanese were wrecking the country and how to ambush their patrols. Other skits instructed the audience how to provide aid to American pilots forced to parachute onto the countryside. Thomas learned that many girls and women served in the Viet Minh. He confided to his diary how he had seen at least two of them carrying rifles. He was told that one had actually "slit the throat of a 'spy.' " He marveled at such ruthlessness, for to him many of those women looked to be about the age "of our 16 year old school girls."[14]

Working with Giap, Major Thomas began his task of training Viet Minh soldiers. In the first days of August, Giap rounded up two hundred of his men, from among whom Thomas was to pick the best half. After Deer Team ran them through their paces, the newly trained men would then be split up to share what they had learned with other of Giap's troops. On 7 August, Thomas, his men, and the newly chosen student soldiers moved about four kilometers away from the base camp to a new training area, already used as a school by the Viet Minh. The next evening, Major Thomas, Ho Chi Minh, and Giap had their evening meal at the hut of Lieutenant Dan Phelan in honor of Phelan's birthday. Thomas was fascinated by a bottle of anise which he helped dispatch; when diluted with water the liquor turned a milky white.[15]

Under Giap's watchful eye, training began the next day, 9 August, starting at 5:30 A.M. and continuing until 5:00 P.M. For the next six days, Sergeant Lawrence Vogt, the weapons instructor, and other Deer Team members taught their Viet Minh students how to fire the American M-1 rifle and M-1 carbine and how best to use light machine guns, mortars, grenades, bazookas, and Thompson submachine guns. Thomas noted that his students were very young, with little prior weapons training.[16]

Wild hilarity broke out among members of the Deer Team on 15 August when Sergeant Zielski, the radio operator, picked up a 9:00-A.M. news broadcast. The announcer declared that negotiations for the Japanese final surrender were nearly completed. Thomas issued arms to his student soldiers and told them they would all probably leave the training camp the next day. Then he started out of camp accompanied by Giap to locate Ho, but just as they set off, Ho arrived in a sedan chair, bringing the glad news that the Japanese had accepted unconditional surrender at noon.[17]

Other news followed. They learned the British would occupy the south of Viet Nam and the Chinese would move into the north for the purpose of disarming Japanese soldiers and returning them to their homeland. Thomas quickly discovered how angry that made the Viet Minh leaders he had come to know, for as they told him, the Chinese would do their best to set up their own puppet government in Viet Nam.[18]

Thomas and Giap ordered their respective troops to get ready to leave the following morning. The Americans spent the remainder of the day breaking camp and packing. That night they shot their trip flares and other pyrotechnics in celebration, and attempted to teach their Vietnamese friends to shout "Hip, Hip, Hooray." "We're a bunch of happy boys to-night," Thomas wrote in his diary while remembering the vast quantities of rice liquor they had all consumed. "Will be in pretty bad shape to leave to-morrow morning."[19]

Ready or not, Giap believed it was time to attack. The first real move to battle of his new army began on 16 August 1945. Leaving Tan Trao at about 2:30 P.M., he and his men moved on Thai Nguyen town. It was difficult going, marching over steep mountain paths, walking in streams, sometimes sloughing through mud. In the evening hours they reached the village of Dong Man and spent the night. They continued traveling on the 17th, 18th, and 19th. Major Thomas wrote that people in all the villages they came to were happy to see them, flocking out onto the paths they walked, waving Viet Minh flags.

Much of the way Thomas walked alongside Giap, who disdained the idea of looking like a soldier. Throughout 1945 and perhaps even into 1947, Giap led his soldiers while wearing a light-colored western suit, tie, and felt hat.[20] "That walk through the mountains was when I was closest to Giap," he later wrote. At one point Giap told him how both his wife and sister-in-law had died in French prisons. Thomas saw that Giap was well educated and bright, always in control of himself. "His troops looked up to him. I liked him."[21]

Giap's attack on Thai Nguyen began when Viet Minh troops moved slowly into position through the darkness between three and four o'clock in the morning on 20 August, and the attack lasted until 25 August. The first phase went smoothly, with opening shots fired about 6:00 A.M. Within half an hour the French provincial governor capitulated, and without their having fired a shot, he surrendered 160 troops of his *guard indigène*. Viet Minh soldiers quickly grabbed their rifles and ammunition.[22]

The Japanese soldiers in Thai Nguyen were a different matter. Despite the fact that their homeland had already surrendered, they refused to capitulate to the Viet Minh assault. They fired at Giap's troops whenever they saw a target, and this desultory shooting continued sporadically the remainder of the day and throughout the night. Giap housed the Deer Team members out of the way in a safe house on the outskirts of town on the opposite side from the Japanese post.[23]

At about 3:00 P.M. on 21 August, the Viet Minh mounted a concentrated assault against the Japanese defenders. For ten minutes they fired every weapon in their arsenal: captured British, French, and Japanese rifles, captured Japanese machine guns, high-explosive antitank and antipersonnel grenades, and M-1 rifles and bazookas given them by the Deer Team. Despite the volume of fire, Japanese soldiers, well installed in concrete fortifications, suffered little harm. The local townspeople, however, were duly impressed by the noise and cheered their countrymen on to victory.[24]

The battle continued until the Japanese finally decided to surrender on 26 August. Victorious Viet Minh soldiers paraded through town celebrating their feat of arms. When they tallied the war loot seized in the battle, they found they were richer by some 500 rifles, 250 pairs of shoes, seventy-two blankets, eight horses, four automobiles, over 3,000 tons of rice, large quantities of sugar, salt, and other miscellaneous items.[25]

Giap was not present at Thai Nguyen to accept congratulations for the victory because of a meeting of the Indochinese Communist Party held at Tan Trao. When Ho Chi Minh learned of the Japanese collapse he realized he needed to seize control at least of the major population centers. So he sent out a call for a party convention. Sizable numbers responded, coming from all points of the compass, some even from other countries. Delegates began to gather by 13 August, and the two-day congress opened for its initial session on 16 August. Ho cleverly showed around his autographed photo of Chennault and paraded some of Giap's soldiers, in uniform and carrying new OSS-supplied weapons.

It was a shrewd move, because not all of those who attended were sympathetic to Ho's claims of leadership. Some desired to grasp power for themselves. Others wondered whether Ho really had as much Allied support as he claimed. Both groups of contenders were impressed by Ho's display, and he managed to achieve what he wanted. Delegates at Tan Trao called for a national uprising to seize the country and welcome the arrival of the Allies. It was a critical moment, for the French were then neither equipped nor prepared to withstand a takeover of their former colony.[26]

There was no time to waste, and Ho ordered Giap to move on Ha Noi. Leaving his lieutenants to carry out the attack on Thai Nguyen, Giap gathered two sections of his troops and left for Ha Noi. He could not afford to be elsewhere. A long chapter in the history of Viet Nam was closing; a new era was opening.[27]

Many were drawn to the capital city of Tonkin in those days. One of them was Lucien Conein, an infantry officer assigned to OSS and a fluent French speaker. Some weeks earlier, following the Japanese coup against the French, OSS sent Conein into Viet Nam to contact fleeing French troops who were trying to make their way into China and help them organize for action against pursuing Japanese soldiers. Conein and a radio operator parachuted from a B-24 Liberator bomber above the jungles of northern Viet Nam. "I was a paratrooper, a *Fallschirmjäger.*"[28] "The goddam fools didn't know where to drop me," he recalled, "but tried to put me close to where they thought the French might be." He did not like the countryside where he landed. "They call the area the Hundred Thousand Peaks and it's awful! Godawful! It was harder than hell to go up and down those damn mountains."[29]

After making contact with elements of the French military, Conein worked with them. "The French had World War I equipment instead of W W slash Two, so we had to get new equipment and teach them demolitions. Some plastique. We had to completely train them. . . . Then somebody dropped the goddam bomb so the war was over. I pulled out. Left them and went into Hanoi. . . . That's where I met Giap."[30]

Conein had several opportunities during his time in Ha Noi to talk with Giap. "You didn't really *talk* to Giap. He talked to you. You'd sit down and go 'mmm, mmm.' He talked to me three or four times. He had piercing eyes and you *knew* he was sincere; he *believed* in what he was saying. Giap would give you the history about revolutionary warfare going back to the French Revolution. He was really fantastic and personable. I liked him."[31] Conein added that "Giap was a very little man. . . . He had a sort of fetish. He considered himself the Napoleon of Asia. That's what he wanted to be known as and I listened."[32]

"I was a captain in the United States Army in a place I didn't want to be," said Conein. "All I wanted to do was get the hell out of there. The war's over. I wanted to go home. Yet Ho and Giap . . . asked me to come and see them. They were *very* interested in Americans and what Americans thought and what they would do for them. How the hell did I know what they'd do for them? They wanted to hang all colonialists, that sort of thing."[33]

Conein was already in Ha Noi when, on 30 August, Major Allison Thomas learned that Patti and his team had also arrived there on 22 August. Thomas wanted to leave Thai Nguyen for the capital immediately, but Patti ordered him and his men to remain where they were until further notice.[34] Without much else to do, Thomas and his men spent their time sunning and visiting around the city. Chagrined by this enforced inaction, Thomas was not particularly mollified even when Giap sent a courier from Ha Noi to him carrying a message in French. "We have made the trip to Ha Noi. If the French come, we will fight. Ha Noi will not rest until it is the capital of a free country. . . . We have a solid heart. Viet Nam will be independent."[35] Then, on 6 September, Thomas received a gift from Giap: two bottles of champagne and a bottle of Haig & Haig scotch, sent from Ha Noi. Finally word came through: Patti had finally relented and the Deer Team members could now leave for the capital city.[36]

Impressions crowded upon Major Thomas as he and his men made their way toward Ha Noi. The countryside was beautiful, mountains crowned with forests. In each valley people worked the rice paddies, eking out their living. Along the way the group shared food with hamlet inhabitants: a diet of rice supplemented by bamboo sprouts, chickens, pigs, bananas, pineapples, grapefruit. While food was sufficient, it was also deficient in nutrients, and Thomas saw many children with distended bellies among the tribes he visited.[37]

Lou Conein met Major Al Patti and his group when they arrived in Ha Noi on 22 August. As they had done for Conein, the Viet Minh assigned Patti and his men to quarters in the city's fine old French hotel, the Metropole (now the Thang Nhat, or "Unity"). Conein was not impressed with his new superior. "I didn't like Patti. He was an arrogant Guinea. You'd never get the truth out of him."[38]

Thomas and his men finally arrived in Ha Noi at 10:00 P.M. on 9 September, completing a journey in which they had traveled by foot, sampan, rickshaw, bicycle, car, and boat. Patti's group authorized quarters for them. Thomas settled in for the night. The next day he went to the residence of the French governor, where he met with Giap and Ho. Later that day he met with Patti. Why, Thomas asked, had they been ordered to remain at Thai Nguyen? Patti wanted to maintain strict neutrality, he said, and Thomas had identified himself with the Viet Minh party. Thomas was more than irritated. "I said all we wanted to do was get home."[39]

Major Thomas spent the days from 10 to 16 September as a tourist might, wandering around the city, buying souvenirs, and saying goodbye to new friends. On 11 September he had his photograph taken with "Hoo" and "Van." He was pleased that Ho was now president of a new provisional government for the country and happy that his friend "Van" was minister of the interior. He saw Viet Minh flags flying from almost every house with their multiplicity of slogans in Vietnamese, English, Chinese, Russian, and Hindi: Welcome Allies; Welcome Peace Commission; Independence or Death; 2,000,000 People Died Under French Domination; Viet Nam for the Vietnamese. He confided to his diary, "The new government appears to be enthusiastically supported by the majority of the population in every province of Indo-China."[40]

The night before he was to leave Ha Noi for Kunming, Thomas met with Ho and Giap for a private dinner party. He was already convinced that "the ordinary uneducated peasant who was 100% Vietminh, had never heard of the word communism or knew what it meant." He had earlier reported to his OSS headquarters that Ho was not a Communist. "[I]t made no difference as HQ already knew he was, but I had not been briefed about him before the jump." Thomas wanted to clear up the matter. During the meal "I asked Ho point blank if he was a communist." In excellent English, Ho replied, "Yes, I am, but we can still be friends, can't we?" The next day Thomas flew out of Ha Noi on the beginning leg of a long trip home.[41]

Long after Thomas departed, Giap took the time to write him a friendly, gossipy letter in French, dated 20 November 1946, telling of mutual friends and recent events. He spoke of Ho's new government "in which I am actually Minister of National Defense." He closed with the words "Receive, very dear friend, the assurance of my very sincere friendship. VNG/alias Van."[42]

From the moment of the Japanese collapse and surrender, agents of Ho Chi Minh began preparing the population of Viet Nam for a Viet Minh takeover. One task was to solicit support among students in Ha Noi. It was not a difficult duty, for enthusiasm for their cause and resentment against the French ran high. "Young people tried hard every occasion possible to have new air to breathe," Vinh Loc wrote. That was enough to alarm the French.[43]

The French were eager to take up again their mantle of power in southeast Asia. As early as 24 March 1945, General Charles de Gaulle declared that following the war, France would establish an Indochinese Federation from the "countries" of Cochin China, Annam, Tonkin, Cambodia, and Laos. At the end of the war in Europe the government in Paris acted swiftly. Even before the Japanese could sign a formal capitulation aboard the battleship *Missouri*, the French mission in Calcutta dropped agents behind Japanese lines in Viet Nam as the first step in reestablishing hegemony. Military officers, colonial administrators, and intelligence agents based in China, Ceylon, and Madagascar received orders to reenter Indochina by any means possible. Some arrived by sea, while others parachuted in. Unaware of the profound changes that had taken place, they went searching for mandarins or village officials to present their papers. Most of them, including Pierre Messmer, commissioner for Tonkin, and Jean Cédile, commissioner for Cochin China, were apprehended and held, by either the Japanese or the Viet Minh.[44]

Along their route of march toward Ha Noi, Giap and his troops passed immense rice fields stretching out toward the horizon, the road down which they walked flanked and guarded by an interminable row of telegraph poles. They encountered massive demonstrations of support whipped up by agents in place. Golden-starred red flags fluttered in villages along the way. When they reached Gia Lam, a village outside the capital, Japanese outposts barred the way. After some excited wrangling, the Japanese agreed to let them go on. Finally they walked along the dikes lining the Red River and into the city, past rows of guava trees. A military band played marches as Giap's units crossed the Long Bien bridge. His fighters moved in two columns parallel with the sides of the road, carrying loaded rifles at the ready, and in this way they paraded into the capital.[45]

The rivers flooded that August and broke through long-neglected dikes. The six delta provinces, the granary of the north, were flooded, and epidemics raged. Unfortunately the flood was followed by a prolonged drought. Much of the autumn rice crop was ruined, and northern ricefields were left uncultivated. Famine had stalked the land since 1944, and about two million people died. Giap was appalled. "People lived from day to day. There were not enough garbage carts to carry the corpses of those who had died of starvation to the suburbs to dump them in mass graves. Meanwhile, starving masses of people were still pouring in through the city gates from the countryside. They staggered and wandered like dry leaves falling on a winter evening. Very frequently, just a brush of the arm from a policeman would be enough to make them collapse, never to rise again."[46]

OSS agent Lou Conein watched Giap's soldiers enter the town. He was not as impressed as they themselves were with their martial skills. "If I'd had a battalion of troops I could have knocked off the whole goddam bunch—not even a battalion, a *company* of troops. I could have knocked off the whole kit and kaboodle."[47]

Giap, on the other hand, gave almost mystical power to his soldiers. People's moods changed, he said, when they learned of the Viet Minh occupation of Ha Noi. Crime vanished. Even burglaries and theft almost stopped. Beggars vanished. Commerce gave way to revolutionary activity. All this, Giap exulted, and still people had time for songs that "resounded from morning till night. Flags with stars became . . . more numerous and . . . more beautiful."[48]

At first light on Sunday, 19 August, Giap's soldiers moved through Ha Noi and all the nearby hamlets persuading everyone to attend a Viet Minh rally in front of the opera house. Thousands obeyed and left for the meeting. Many had a festive attitude, carrying placards and flags hastily made the previous day. Cadre struggled to teach them the words and music of the anthem "Marching to the Front," and to respond at appropriate moments with cheers and slogans. As they arrived in the square they found so many others that soon the crowd backed up into nearby converging streets, singing and cheering and waving their red banners.[49]

Viet Minh soldiers marched to the palatial home of the *résident supérieur* of Tonkin until they were stopped by its high iron fence. Excited revolutionaries called on Japanese troops and Vietnamese militia to surrender, and, overwhelmed by the threatening clamor of the crowd, those frightened men did so. Like a wave cresting on a beach, the crowd flowed into the compound and captured it. Men and women of all ages marched into the barracks of the Japanese soldiers and seized their entire stock of weapons, distributing them to frantically reaching hands. Then they moved on to other public buildings, seizing them in much the same way. By early evening, the Viet Minh controlled Ha Noi.[50]

Between 19 and 30 August the Viet Minh ascended to power from the Red River to the Mekong Delta in the south. Patti, in Ha Noi, was pleased with this development. "I confirmed in my reports that French colonialism in Indochina had been one of the worst possible examples of peonage, disregard for human rights, and French cupidity, and that for more than three-quarters of a century, the Vietnamese had been cruelly exploited, brutally maltreated, and generally used as French chattel. . . . The socioeconomic conditions generated by the French colonial system fostered discontent and rebellion. . . ."[51]

The French, however, moved steadily ahead to reestablish their hold. On 16 August 1945, at a time when Vo Nguyen Giap was planning his attack on Thai Nguyen, Charles de Gaulle named General Jacques Philippe de Hautecloque, who used the name Leclerc as commander-in-chief of Far East French Forces and ordered him to deploy several infantry units to Viet Nam. Ho ordered Giap to meet Leclerc upon his arrival at the airport outside Ha Noi. Incensed at having to welcome such a man, Giap flew into a towering rage, ranting that he would never shake hands with any Frenchman. Ho Chi Minh listened patiently and then calmly laid down the law. "You have two hours before his plane arrives," he told Giap. "So why don't you go into the corner and cry your eyes out? But be at the airport!" Giap was waiting at Gia Lam airfield when LeClerc deplaned.[52]

De Gaulle also named Admiral Georges Thierry d'Argenlieu to the post of high commissioner for Indochina. Jean Sainteny, the newly appointed commissioner for Tonkin and Annam, arrived in Viet Nam by parachute on 27 August from the French mission in Kunming, China. He was immediately suspicious of the OSS working relationship with the Viet Minh. Major Patti went with Giap to meet him and presented the two men to each other. It did not help to lessen their suspicions; their differing goals made them natural antagonists.

On 28 August, Ha Noi newspapers announced the membership of the provisional government. Giap was to be minister of the interior. The standing committee also decided that the day on which they presented the new government to the people would be the day to announce officially the independence of the new nation. Before the end of the month, conferring with Truong Chinh and Giap, Ho read them a draft of his declaration of independence. Cadre worked continually to whip up the population. The streets of Ha Noi throbbed with tension and agitation. Loudspeakers broadcast news and commentaries of the provisional government. Streets were filled with placards and banners proclaiming hatred of French imperialism.[53]

Giap was formally installed in his new position as minister of the interior on 29 August, and although his old friend Chu Van Tan held the post of defense minister, Giap retained effective power as chief of the military. As head of an army he knew the dynamism of revolutionary power. As interior minister he had daily contact with westerners of all kinds—diplomats and other officials—ready to impose by force what the Vietnamese would refuse to negotiate. It was a heavy burden. He had to keep the peace and prepare for war. In those next crucial months, Giap's political understanding matured swiftly.[54]

Such a position was in line with Giap's determination never to stray too far away from politics. No matter how challenging it might be to build a revolutionary army, he was aware of the symbiotic relationship between politics and military, and Giap wanted to ensure his political position in order to guarantee that he would continue to head the military. He also knew that military solutions, in and of themselves, were ephemeral; only the solid foundation of politics could establish permanent revolutionary gain. His was an enviable position. As a member of the inner political circle, he could make certain that his military views were heard. As head of the army, he knew his fellow politicians would listen to his political ideas.

On 30 August, Emperor Bao Dai abdicated in favor of the new government being established by Ho Chi Minh and became "the humble Citizen Nguyen Vinh Thuy," "a simple citizen of a free country." He agreed to serve as a supreme counselor to the provisional government. Ho knew what he was doing, for the emperor's endorsement of any government would persuade many average people to accept and to support it.[55] He abdicated not because of his lack of interest in power and not because the Viet Minh surprised him with their organization, far stronger than his own, but because all his cabinet ministers were frightened and irresolute, refusing to resist the Communists. The Viet Minh Communists were at last in control.[56]

"We Shall Resort to Arms"

Despite the Viet Minh's best hopes, none of the wartime Allies had any intention of allowing a provisional Vietnamese government to accept the surrender of Japanese troops in Viet Nam and thus enrich itself with their weapons. Or perhaps it was more simple than that. It may well have been the case that few of the Allied powers were even aware that the Viet Minh existed, and those few who did know were opposed to native rebellions in Southeast Asia or anywhere else. At the final Allied great power meeting of World War II, held at Potsdam outside Berlin from 17 July to 2 August 1945, and attended by the heads of state for the United States, Great Britain, and the Soviet Union, Harry S Truman agreed that Chiang Kai-shek's Kuomintang soldiers would disarm the Japanese in Indochina down to the 16th parallel. British troops, crossing from Burma, would do so below that line. The first Kuomintang troops, under the command of General Lu Han, entered Ha Noi on 22 August.

Giap was not impressed with the appearance of those Kuomintang soldiers. "Their faces were puffy and jaundiced, and they looked bewildered. Their yellow uniforms, the shade of tumeric, were ragged and filthy. They lugged baskets full of junky items on poles. Some groups even brought along women and children. Many had difficulty dragging themselves along on legs swollen by beriberi. They appeared like filthy stains on the city recently washed of the stench of the colonialists."[1]

The army itself was not particularly to be feared, Giap knew, despite the

Kuomintang's paper claim to more than three hundred divisions as war came to an end. Of that number only five were estimated to be effective military units. Yet the Kuomintang, Giap worried, was "ferociously anti-Communist," wanting to destroy the Viet Minh revolution and seize his country.[2]

Ho Chi Minh tried to draw the fangs of the Kuomintang serpent. Knowing that it backed such groups as the VNQDD and Dong Minh Hoi (DMH), he gave members of those parties positions in his provisional government, in an attempt to minimize Chinese interference in his plans. Ho knew that members of the Deer Team and Al Patti generally approved of his actions. Unfortunately for the Viet Minh, another American did not. Brigadier Philip Gallagher, adviser to the Chinese general Lu Han, wired Washington on 20 September that Ho was "an old revolutionist. . . . a product of Moscow, a communist."[3]

Although nearly 200,000 Kuomintang troops eventually spread out through Tonkin, from General Lu Han down to the lowliest Chinese private they were there for gain, not to restore any French presence. Many sold their weapons to the Viet Minh, while others simply looted at will. They took everything not nailed down: plumbing fixtures, roof tiles, furniture. They piled it all on bullock carts or in trucks taken from the Japanese. If no transport was available, they carried away trophies on their backs. Captain Lucien Conein of the American OSS described those Chinese soldiers as sweeping across the land "like a band of locusts." Those few who remained under orders, however, quickly disarmed and returned Japanese troops to their island homeland.[4]

The morning of 2 September 1945 brought great excitement to people in Ha Noi. The city itself was exuberantly painted in red. Red flags fluttered from rooftops public and private, from tree branches, from poles set in the soft earth bordering the lakes. Red lamps and lanterns cast their soft glow. Red flowers decorated doorways and tables. Banners were strung across street after street proclaiming slogans in French, English, Chinese, and Russian: "Support President Ho Chi Minh," "Welcome to the Allied Delegation," "Independence or Death," "Support the Provisional Government."

Factories, shops, and marketplaces, large and small, closed down as production and commercial activities of the city came to a halt. People poured from their homes, old and young, men and women. In streams, wearing all the colors of the rainbow, they moved toward Ba Dinh Square. Members of self-defense forces came armed with spears, swords, and machetes. Some had removed scimitars from weapons racks displayed in shrines and mounted them on long poles, and now carried them proudly erect like ancient Roman legionnaires marching to battle under the eagle emblem.

Noisy and excited children darted around the legs of their elders, peasant women in yellow scarves and light green belts and workers wearing blue pants and white shirts. On cue, hastily trained Viet Minh supporters blew whistles, beat drums, stamped their feet in simple rhythms, and loudly sang revolutionary songs. Other worldly Buddhist monks and Catholic priests left their cells to stand gaping open-mouthed at the noise and confusion. A beautiful autumn sun bathed Ba Dinh Square in golden light. Honor guards solemnly surrounded a hastily constructed speakers' platform. Some have estimated that perhaps as many as a million people turned out for the special ceremony scheduled for that day.[5]

Nguyen Dinh Tu explained what happened. The chance to win the fight for freedom, he said, now fell to Ho Chi Minh. Viet Minh propaganda persuaded many who saw them struggling to create a Vietnamese government. Communist propagandists talked to ordinary people, convincing them that they were fighting for more justice. Such a "simple vision" was convincing to the majority that gave them full support. "But very, very few people was aware of what was behind, what was under the table."[6]

Lou Conein, watching the crowds on the streets from the safety of the bar at the Metropole Hotel, decided to remain indoors, later offering a cynical view of the day's proceedings: "Hell, I wasn't going to get out there and get my ass knocked off by those people. There were *thousands of people.* It was fantastic. *Everybody* was out there. They had 'orchestra' leaders, you know, leading the cheering sections. People didn't know what the hell they were doing. Something exciting was going on and everybody just came out to see what was happening. Somebody was going to make a big speech, but they didn't know who. The 'orchestra' leaders told them when to cheer."[7]

The official delegation mounted the steps of the platform accompanied by cheers from the pulsing throng. Ho had the place of honor. An emaciated man with a high forehead, bright eyes, and a sparse beard, he wore an old hat, a khaki tunic with a high collar, and white rubber sandals. A voice at the microphone introduced Ho as the liberator of the nation. While the crowd repeated the chanting of *doc lap*, "independence," he stood smiling before them. Then he raised his hands and called for silence. When he spoke his voice still bore traces of the accent of Nghe An province, his birthplace. His words were precise and clear, calm and warm as he declaimed the Declaration of Independence for Viet Nam which he had earlier written.[8]

"All men are created equal. The Creator has given us certain inviolable rights; the right to life, the right to be free, and the right to achieve happiness." Then he suddenly stopped reading and asked: "Can you hear what I'm saying?" One million voices roared back in a sound that rose and fell like thunder: YES. And so he continued. "These immortal words are taken from the Declaration of Independence of the United States of America in 1776. In a larger sense, this means that all the people on earth are born equal; all the people have the right to live, to be happy, to be free. . . . Those are undeniable truths."[9]

When Ho finished and sat down to prolonged applause, Giap spoke. Even more than had Ho, Giap traced conflicting forces at work and noted dangers still to be faced. His passionate words about independence were laced with warnings. The revolution had come quickly, and Viet Minh organizational strength was untested. Either political or social division could make the process difficult. So he repeatedly stressed unity and the need to curtail excesses. The French, he said, were already making preparations to return in force to Indochina. And, he warned, if negotiation was fruitless, "we shall resort to arms." At one point he told those listening that the United States had helped the Vietnamese cause for independence. It had fought alongside them "against fascist Japan and so the great American Republic is our good ally."[10]

The ceremony included an oath: "We, the entire Vietnamese nation, swear that with one accord, we will unfalteringly support the provisional government of the Democratic Republic of Viet Nam and President Ho Chi Minh. We swear that side by side with the government we will preserve the complete independence of our Fatherland and oppose any foreign plots of invasion even to the sacrifice of our lives." If the French invaded they swore not

—to serve in the French army,
—to collaborate with a French administration,
—to sell food supplies to the French,
—to act as guides for the French.

One million people and one million voices rose into the air as the crowd intoned, "We swear."[11]

That same day, hundreds of miles to the south, the provisional government led by Tran Van Giau organized a Saigon rally to coincide with Ho Chi Minh's announcement in Ha Noi. While people flooded the streets, French agents opened fire on them from inside the huge Gothic cathedral, Notre Dame de Saigon, in the center of the city. Forty-seven people died or were wounded. In retaliation, Viet Minh gangs attacked French *colons* in their homes, assaulting and killing several of them. The First Indochina War had not yet begun, but the killing and fighting were well under way.[12]

Members of Ho Chi Minh's provisional government held their first cabinet meeting on the morning of 3 September at the former mansion of the French *résident supérieur* in a room stripped completely bare. As Giap waited for Ho to arrive, he thought of Lenin's dictum: "It is difficult to seize power, but it is even more difficult to keep it."[13] Ho was delayed in arriving at the meeting, so Giap pondered recent events in thoughts that were, at times, almost lyrical.

The revolution, he noted, had finally come. "The newly granted rights of freedom and democracy were like showers falling on fields long parched by drought. Our people welcomed [it] like a thirsty man receiving water and a hungry man receiving food." In previous days, when France ruled, simply picking up a leaflet or shouting a slogan was enough to cause a man to be thrown into jail. Under French occupation, if a dagger was found during a house search, the entire family could be massacred. Now, Giap mused, Viet Minh flags freely hung in front of houses. People walked down streets loudly singing revolutionary songs, heads held high. Militiamen stood guard holding machetes or long spears in their hands. No one was afraid, and the land was theirs.[14]

Yet they had not won much. A few buildings, but no experienced bureaucrats. Ninety-five percent of the people were illiterate, for the French had favored prisons over schools. Unemployment accelerated. There were no rice stocks. Sometimes people had only rice gruel to eat, and many starved. A cholera epidemic broke out. There was no money. The newly formed government was bankrupt. Its treasury consisted of only 1,250,000 piastres, much of it old, disintegrating banknotes and coins.

Given a bankrupt treasury and the demands of General Lu Han, Ho had to find a way to raise money and to do so quickly. A little reluctantly, he proclaimed the week of 16–22 September to be Tuan Le Vang, "Gold Week." Pham Van Dong made a public appeal for people to offer contributions to the new government's treasury, and a pittance dribbled in. It was only when Ho himself appealed to the country that the scheme began to work. Across the northern landscape, people appeared at collecting points with offerings of gold and silver family heirlooms, wedding bands and earrings, gold pendants and chains, valuable watches and precious gems. Vo Nguyen Giap later wrote that in just a few days the Viet Minh collected some 20 million piastres and 370 kilograms of gold. People contributed even their most cherished souvenirs. One eighty-year-old woman, Giap said, contributing to the mythology of the nation, brought her life savings: a gold ingot wrapped in red silk.[15]

Nguyen Dinh Tu, a nationalist, viewed those days from a different perspective. "The Viet Minh found it very easy to make efficient propaganda. They talked only about social justice, about discrimination between yellow and white people. Many listened and believed. The peasants gave much gold because they were real patriots. Most thought that since independence had come, everybody should contribute. But long, long afterwards, they who gave realized they had been robbed and shamefully treated."[16]

Waves of foreign troops were once again entering the land, and the provisional government was powerless to prevent them from doing so. Before the Viet Minh August Revolution, Giap said, only a Japanese army of 60,000 stood on his people's soil. It did not long remain that way. In the first days of the Viet Minh government, 200,000 Chinese soldiers poured in; 5,000 British and Indian troops joined them, and tens of thousands of French expeditionary forces funneled into the land through major port cities. Other thousands of defeated colonialist soldiers in Indochina were being rearmed; those who had fled to China came back. Never before had there been so many foreign soldiers on the soil of Viet Nam, nor had the Vietnamese ever before been so willing to fight against such insuperable odds.[17]

When Ho arrived for that first cabinet meeting, he and his fellows quickly got to work. As a result of this and other meetings, the Viet Minh government moved ahead with its program of consolidation and reform. It began a campaign against illiteracy. It sought to increase agricultural production to cope with hovering famine. Everyone was asked to forgo one meal every ten days; rice thus saved was to be distributed to the hungry. It called for landlords to reduce rents by 25 percent. It abolished generational debts owed by farmers to moneylenders. It abolished head, market, and boat taxes. It forbade use of opium. It tried to teach the virtues of hard work, economy, integrity, and honesty. Disbanding the old mandarin hierarchy, it called for a general election at which a national congress would be elected by universal suffrage to be held in two months' time. Both the VNQDD and the Dong Minh Hoi (DMH) violently objected to the idea. Giap righteously insisted that on many occasions the new government told VNQDD and DMH leaders that general elections were necessary and absolutely had to be held.[18]

British troops began arriving in the south of Viet Nam on 11 September; their commander, General Douglas Gracey, flew in two days later. Although under orders from Lord Louis Mountbatten to do no more than disarm and repatriate Japanese troops, Gracey strongly supported restoration of French control and determined to impose his own version of law and order upon the troublesome Vietnamese of the south. He banned possession of weapons and announced that anyone violating this order could be shot. He not only used his own troops to enforce martial law but released and rearmed 1,400 French soldiers who had been imprisoned by the Japanese since their *coup de force* on 9 March 1945. Gracey even called on Japanese soldiers still in place to help undercut the provisional Viet Minh government in an effort to restore French rule.[19]

In his northern headquarters, Giap soon learned of these developments, but there was little he could do to help those so far away. His own plate was entirely too full with tasks in Tonkin. And so the southern Viet Minh were left to conduct a lonely struggle against the French. Leclerc boasted that it would take him no more than ten weeks to pacify the southern countryside. Still, there were some things Giap could do. He persuaded the central committee to send reinforcements. When the members agreed, Giap organized Southward March units. They arrived, Giap reported, "in the nick of time." They were assigned the task of manning frontline positions northeast of Saigon. They fought bravely, Giap recalled, and pinned down the French for an entire month, inflicting heavy casualties on them. Even when they were pushed out of south-central and southern towns and villages, Giap's warriors in the south continued to hold most of the countryside. The First Indochina War, which would last until May 1954, had begun. And from the start, American blood was shed. On 26 September 1945, A. Peter Dewey, the OSS commander in Saigon, was killed at a roadblock, apparently by soldiers of the Viet Minh forces.[20]

During the last days of September, in Ha Noi, people crowded close to public loudspeakers that blared news items from the warfront in the south. Yet they also faced their own struggle, not yet with the French, but with Chinese soldiers occupying Tonkin. Citizens faced daily harassment, if not violence.

On one occasion Giap had to go on a mission toward Ha Dong. All vehicles were required to carry permits, checked by any Chinese roving patrol or roadblock that wished to do so. Giap's automobile was stopped at the Ngo Tu So intersection despite a permit stamped with a huge red seal pasted on its window. Soldiers evicted the occupants and searched the car, turning over the seats in the process. Then they found a pistol on Giap's bodyguard. They impounded the auto and took the two hapless Vietnamese to a guard station. Asked where he worked, Giap claimed to be an employee of the China–Viet Nam Liaison Office, but even then he was detained for two hours before his release. It was not an isolated incident, Giap claimed. "Practically every night we received letters from Chiang's generals and officers . . . either making demands or threatening."[21]

The most dangerous problem faced by the northern Viet Minh during the months of Chinese occupation was the obvious favoritism those Sons of the Middle Kingdom showed to both the VNQDD and the DMH. These groups, the Chinese felt, would be more amenable to accepting an independent Viet Nam as little more than a southern satellite of its giant neighbor to the north. And many Vietnamese supported those two parties. Although the Viet Minh had collaborated with the DMH for a time, collaboration had been primarily agreed to as a way of getting Ho Chi Minh released from his Chinese prison and as a ruse to use with uncommitted people, to persuade them that the Viet Minh did indeed represent a broad-based coalition of anti-French and anti-Japanese groups, parties, and factions. There had never been any intention within the Indochinese Communist Party of sharing power with either the DMH or the long-detested VNQDD in an independent postcolonial nation. Its central committee knew that power could still slip away if these two parties gained a real foothold among the people; the Viet Minh hold on government thus far was essentially ephemeral, and political reversals might be suffered in an instant.

It struck fear in the hearts of Viet Minh leaders to see how, as the Chinese forces moved through the land, they often disarmed local Viet Minh committees and installed in their place members of the DMH and the VNQDD. Those usurpers, Giap claimed, had lived so long overseas they had lost all contact with political thought in their own country. They claimed to be Vietnamese patriots following the doctrine of nationalism, but in fact, Giap proclaimed, "they were a group of reactionaries plotting to rely on Chiang Kai-shek's Kuomintang and their rifle barrels to snatch a few crumbs." Vitriol dripped from Giap's words. "We were well aware of the savage ambition of the Chinese Kuomintang. They were the mortal enemies of the revolution. We must guard against their overthrowing us and replacing us with their lackeys."[22]

Giap's new friend Major Al Patti, the OSS man from Kunming, agreed with his view of those rival politicians. Patti talked with members of the VNQDD and DMH and found in them no sense of what must be done to meet people's needs. Although they spoke of "assuming power," none of them seemed to have any notion of what to do with it if they achieved their goal. Patti said they were "hopelessly disoriented politically," perhaps because they had lived for so long in China. He believed they were motivated primarily by "desires for personal power and economic gain."[23]

The VNQDD and DMH quickly established national headquarters in Ha Noi, where, according to Giap, they assembled local reactionaries who pestered, plundered, robbed, and killed their fellow countrymen. "Servants taking after their masters," Giap complained, "the VNQDD behaved exactly like bandits." They published newspapers with names like *Viet Nam, Coalition,* and *Realism,* which espoused their cause with "brazen and insolent arguments." Worst of all, from the Viet Minh point of view, the Chinese pressured the provisional government to include more members of the DMH and VNQDD in positions of responsibility.[24]

Nationalists, of course, had another point of view. One of them, Nguyen Duy Thanh, later wrote that in past days national leaders of many opinions rallied around Ho Chi Minh's party because "we felt that the more united we were, the stronger we would be in our fight for the common cause of the country's independence. Though we knew that Ho Chi Minh and his Party were Communists of long-standing, still, we thought that they would put first and foremost the cause of their country above all party interests. Our expectations were sadly belied. Day after day, the communists showed up their fascist tendency and adopted a hostile attitude towards the nationalists who did not brook communist ideals."[25]

Thanh spoke about Viet Minh efforts to control what people saw and heard. There was indeed freedom of the press, he said, but it was only for those papers who manufactured news favorable to communism. Only Communist books and pamphlets were put up for sale; others, even advertisements and scientific books, were subject to censorship.

Mass demonstrations favoring communism, Thanh said, were easily orchestrated. Yet, he claimed, people did not know what they were demonstrating for. He came across some women carrying slogans on cardboard signs, and he asked them what they were doing. "They frankly confessed they knew nothing about it. They were told to do so. A woman was carrying on her head a placard with the inscription: 'We Vietnamese women demand to be allowed to make our contribution to National Defence as our men do.' " A few days later, Thanh concluded sadly, the government, pressed by such "requests," allowed women to pay taxes to the national defense fund.[26]

When, on 8 September, the provisional government set the date for elections two months hence, both the VNQDD and DMH strongly opposed the idea and called for support from the Chinese. The Viet Minh, on the other hand, made the most of that reluctance to cast their rivals in a bad light. "We repeatedly told their leaders that general elections were necessary," Giap insisted, "and absolutely had to be carried out. We also expressed our desire to unite with all forces to build the country and support the southern war of resistance."[27]

Anxious to forestall additional Chinese interference, Ho bent before the wind. On 11 November 1945, he dissolved the Indochinese Communist Party, replacing it with an Indochinese Association for Marxist Studies. A few days later he organized a general conference of political parties. Representatives of both the VNQDD and DMH attended and agreed to put an end to newspaper denunciations, to unify their armies, and to form a coalition government.[28]

The coalition government was to serve only until an election could be held for a national assembly which would formally ratify a new government. Ho promised to reserve a total of seventy seats in the new assembly for the DMH and VNQDD. This would be the group that would unify the armies, organize the elections, and resign when the National Congress convened. On 19 December, the provisional government announced that general elections would be held on 6 January 1946. When, a few days later, someone complained to Ho about allowing DMH and VNQDD representatives to serve in the government, Ho responded, "Isn't manure filthy? But if it is good fertilizer for rice, won't you use it?"[29]

With differences such as these, it is little wonder that rivalry between political factions moved from public quarrels to kidnappings and assassinations. In late fall, members of the VNQDD kidnapped Giap and the propaganda minister, Tran Huy Lieu, holding them for three weeks. In negotiations for their release, Ho had to agree to drop them from their positions in his provisional government. As a result, Giap lost his ministerial rank and now became deputy defense minister to Vu Hong Khanh. In that capacity, however, he still controlled military policy through the Committee of Military Commissars.[30]

Ho's agreement was a bold move that did not ultimately help either the DMH or the VNQDD. Nationalist Nguyen Duy Thanh explained the distribution of ministerial portfolios under Ho's leadership. The ministry of defense and that of home affairs were allotted to opponents of the Viet Minh. The other eight portfolios were divided between the nationalists and Communists. "Apparently it was a fair division of power," Thanh said, "but, in reality, it was not so. For every position held by a non-communist, a communist deputy minister was attached." If a non-Communist minister refused to sign a document, his Communist deputy blithely did so.

Ministerial responsibilities were also shifted. The minister for defense, for example, became only a sort of bookkeeper. He was forbidden to examine personnel lists or to know the amounts of available arms and ammunition. Thanh himself, although named as chief of the Corps of Engineers, never learned any of the statistics dealing with his own area of responsibility. Some new nationalist ministers, having no responsibilities, never attended cabinet meetings. "The Minister for Social Works," Thanh said, "having nothing to do, applied for a job in a state-owned factory. The first and the last decree the Home Minister was ordered to sign provided that a passport was necessary for any citizen to move out from his place of residence." All this was not precisely what the VNQDD and DMH had hoped for when they agreed to participate in a coalition government.[31]

Ho assigned Giap and Tran Quoc Hoan, minister of public security, the task of counteracting DMH and VNQDD street demonstrations and halting their flow of information to the public. Honey dripped from his pen as Giap delicately described his new duties. "We had to punish the saboteurs, but . . . avoid provocations at all costs and make absolutely sure that things would not lead to a violent clash." Calling on his self-defense forces and National Salvation Association members, Giap sent them out into the streets to seek out rival political meetings and turn them into brawls. His men often invited onlookers to join in the fray. At one rally, when Viet Minh agents invaded the crowd, an exasperated nationalist fought back and shot one of Giap's men. That "crime," Giap said, provoked both indignation and anger. His men—Giap described them as the "population"—rushed the speakers. "These fellows had to hide their weapons, throw away their flags, banners and bullhorns, and flee for their lives."[32]

Members of the DMH and VNQDD were dismayed when they discovered little help to be forthcoming from the Chinese. Seeing these disturbances, Chinese soldiers sometimes fired over the heads of milling crowds, but seldom left their sandbagged bunkers to charge into such melees to disperse rioters. And so, Giap said, in such ways were agitators routed. It was effective. Even nationalists admitted their own inadequacy. Nguyen Duy Thanh remembered sadly that, deprived of Chinese support, nationalists were unable to oppose the Communists effectively.[33]

Ha Noi prepared for the first general election in its history. In preparation for that great event on 6 January 1946, workers wrote slogans on walls and hung cloth banners to wave in the breeze. Flower-bedecked cars moved through the streets. Costumed boys and girls beat drums. Government newspapers published special issues touting its program and candidates. On election day, a party atmosphere permeated towns and villages as dwellers decorated buildings with flags and flowers. Giap grumbled that "goon squads of the VNQDD tried to sabotage the voting." It gladdened his heart when he heard stories of extraordinary effort on the part of people to get to the polls, such as the one-hundred-year-old man in Phuc Yen province who asked his grandchild to lead him to the polls.[34]

People ran for offices in the new government even in French-occupied areas of the south and in parts of central Viet Nam. From north to south, people voted, Giap noted gladly, in the face of "bombs, napalm and machine guns of the enemy." When votes were tallied, Giap received the second-highest number of any candidate; in Ho's home province of Nghe An, 97 percent of those voting chose to mark their ballots with his name. Only Ho received more votes; 98.4 percent cast their ballots for him as president of the new Democratic Republic of Viet Nam. Voters chose 333 representatives to the first National Congress.[35]

While victors such as Giap extolled the virtues of the election, the VNQDD and DMH were not so certain that votes had been freely and fairly cast. Nguyen Duy Thanh lamented that 90 percent of the electorate were illiterate and were pressured to cast their votes by proxies submitted by inevitably available Communists. "In my home village," Thanh observed sorrowfully, "the polling secretary was away on some private business. The voters could not even see the voting papers. And yet fifteen candidates nominated by the Communist Party were declared duly elected by a thousand votes." Nor did he think much of the valiant efforts of those in the south to participate in the election. As it was patent that the French were in control there, "no election worth the name was held, but the Communists announced that 80 percent of the electorate had voted for ten members of the Communist party." It was, however, a done deed. An election had been held and Ho, Giap, and all their fellows now held the reins of power.[36]

Giap called upon Emperor Bao Dai, now merely First Citizen Nguyen Vinh Thuy but an "adviser" to Ho's government, to meet with recently elected members of the new cabinet. Bao Dai's support was still needed. Bao Dai later noted that membership of the cabinet generally divided into three parts. The first group consisted of "old guard" activists, chief among whom was Ho himself. Its members had spent long years in exile in Russia or China, in hiding, or in jail, and were fiercely anti-French.

The second group, Bao Dai noted, was composed of former teachers from Lycée Thang Long. Giap was representative of them all. They had been in positions of power in the Communist Party in its days of legality during Léon Blum's Popular Front government in France. Generally influenced by French culture, they had little experience of affairs outside Viet Nam and were often less fanatical than the old guard. They were intelligent, open-minded, passionately opposed to the colonial regime, and desirous of retaining the country's uneasy independence, but thought it possible to retain some sort of relationship with France.

The last group, Bao Dai wrote, numbered within it younger men, those from youth groups such as the General Association of Students or the Catholic Youth. Technicians all, they were graduates of French universities who felt betrayed because they were never able to achieve positions within the French colonial system in Viet Nam that corresponded either to their skills or their diplomas.[37]

Not long after the election, Giap decided to make an inspection visit southward to communicate to cadre there the great determination of the central committee to resist the French. He understood that no matter how serious might be the current quarrel with the Chinese, the principal enemy was France, and he wanted to focus "the flames of our struggle" directly at the colonial system. "The newly born Democratic Republic of Viet Nam, surrounded by wolves and tigers, had to summon all its strength to struggle alone . . . for survival."[38]

Bao Dai offered to accompany Giap, but his gesture was not accepted, "perhaps to prevent people from favoring me [as emperor] and cheering me." To retain the former emperor's goodwill, however, Giap went to him and made a promise: "When I return from my trip to the South I'll come and report what I saw."[39]

Giap left Ha Noi on 18 January 1946 on a warm, sunny afternoon.[40] Riding in one of the few available government cars, he headed south to determine conditions there. He was proud of those in lower Annam and Cochin China who continued to resist French efforts to reestablish their colonial authority, and Giap looked forward to talking with his brethren there. After one hundred days of fighting, those regions still stood firm. Against hopeless odds, his compatriots continued to struggle, sometimes only with "sharpened sticks" in their will to demonstrate that "resistance could not be stamped out." It persisted even in towns that the enemy believed to have been conquered.

Giap exulted, "In these moments of life and death for the Fatherland, our people quickly came up with new ways to fight the enemy, bewildering him with a new form of warfare. Towns and cities were destroyed by the same hands that had built them, people in villages absolutely refused to collaborate in any way, gardens and houses were deserted, bridges were destroyed, roads were cut to shreds."[41]

Giap knew that vast stretches of the southern countryside remained in Viet Minh hands. They had large bases in the Plain of Reeds and in the U Minh forest. He knew of others located just outside towns and cities. It was little wonder that the French urgently requested reinforcements from home.[42]

As Giap traveled southward, his spirits lifted. He no longer saw any detested soldiers of the Kuomintang, so common in Ha Noi. Even the landscape seemed to change as his car moved along Highway 1. "The smell of gasoline, the sound of the horn, brought back memories of [other] long trips," Giap commented excitedly.[43] Away from the city, his country appeared "beautiful and bright with the light of independence and freedom." He reveled in the sight of Viet Minh banners and yellow-starred red flags swinging in the wind.

He saw trains moving south on the nearby railway, their cars filled with troops going to join the fray against the French. When possible, Giap waited at crossroads stations where those trains stopped to take on water and fuel and he talked with those soldiers of the Southward March units. Most, he noted, were very young, and probably many of them were away from their home province for the first time.[44]

In Ho's home province of Nghe An, Giap watched soldiers training with wooden rifles and practicing throwing hand grenades. The next day he arrived in his own native province of Quang Binh with its long, narrow ricefields and white sand dunes. He visited with relatives in Dong Hoi and talked with them about family and country late into the night.[45]

On 20 January 1946, Giap left Quang Binh for Hue. Arriving, he relished the sight of the Perfume River, the rows of trees. He saw his own soldiers standing guard in front of the Citadel and was moved to comment that although green moss still grew on those walls, "feudal Hue was now a thing of the past."[46] Hue was the direct rear for many fronts: for battlefields in Laos and for the center and south of Viet Nam. Giap stayed at Viet Minh headquarters there two days, meeting with General Nguyen Chi Thanh to exchange ideas, to discuss their responsibilities, and to chat about changes in the country. Giap did not yet know that General Thanh would later become one of his most dangerous rivals and be responsible for efforts to destroy his career and purge him from the Politburo.[47]

Giap pushed on: to Quang Nam, to Quang Ngai, and toward Binh Dinh. Near Binh Dinh he thoughtlessly allowed his driver to pass a roadblock without permission. One guard fired at the automobile, which quickly came to a halt. Two militiamen suspiciously examined Giap's papers before allowing him to proceed.[48] On he went to Binh Dinh and then to Khanh Hoa, under attack by French airplanes when he arrived. "It was clear," Giap said, that "the enemy was trying to lift the siege of Nha Trang and to occupy a number of towns along the coast of South Central Viet Nam in order to cut the supply line from the North."[49]

Then an urgent cable from Ho summoned Giap back to Ha Noi. Although he still had not visited all the areas he hoped to see, Giap immediately ordered his driver to return to the capital. He spent the eve of Tet 1946 crossing Hai Van Pass—the Pass of Clouds—just north of Da Nang. The weather was socked in, "a vast darkness in which the sea and sky merged and became indistinguishable." As they moved higher along the road, which was bordered by a precipice on one side and rocky cliffs on the other, it began to rain. At one point they were stopped by a lonely Kuomintang soldier checking papers, and then they went on. It rained so hard the car headlights illuminated the road only five or six meters ahead. Giap thought longingly about New Year in the capital and settled down to wait out the long trip ahead of him, contemplating across the slow miles the power of the French he had seen in the south.[50]

"We Must Be Realistic"

A few days following Vo Nguyen Giap's return from his trip southward he presented himself at the villa of First Citizen and Supreme Counselor Nguyen Vinh Thuy (Emperor Bao Dai) and rang the bell at the gate. Ushered into the presence of Bao Dai, Giap said, "I am just back from my tour." He had come as he promised before leaving on his inspection trip, to brief the former emperor on what he had seen.

As it was lunchtime, Bao Dai invited him to stay and eat. He closely observed Giap as they sat at their meal. Giap seemed troubled and ate with his head down, looking toward his plate and avoiding Bao Dai's eyes. Normally, Giap was very self-contained, but on that day he had a gloomy look. Bao Dai let him finish his food without questioning him, but when Giap laid down his chopsticks, Bao Dai asked, "How is everything?"

"We must be realistic," Giap replied.

"What do you mean by that?" Bao Dai queried.

Remembering the raw military power he had seen pitted against his units in the south, Giap said sadly, "We must adapt ourselves to the return of the French."

"We have to go back to the Protectorate? Are you kidding?" Bao Dai could not believe what he was hearing.

"Yes," Giap answered. "In case of need."

Bao Dai could not contain his anger. "I no longer understand you," he shouted. "I accepted our independence from the Japanese. I abdicated to the Viet Minh. I gave you my place and now you are moving backward."

"There is no other way," responded Giap. "In the south the French have destroyed the structure we set in place with such difficulty. They have total control of everything. Soon they will land here. How can we oppose them? We have some troops but no ammunition at all." Calmer after having said this, Giap related his whole trip. One of his stories amused the emperor. He told of his stop at Vinh, his dead wife Quang Thai's home village, where he visited with members of its revolutionary committee. Giap informed them that he represented not only Ho Chi Minh, president of the Democratic Republic of Viet Nam, but also Bao Dai. They immediately asked for news of Bao Dai, and Giap told them what he knew of the former emperor's circumstances. The following day he was surprised when someone brought a large parasol and stood behind him, moving along everywhere with him. He asked Bao Dai the meaning of what had happened.

"That is not surprising," Bao Dai said. The parasol was the emblem of imperial authority. "You told them yourself that you represented me so they had to honor you with all the rites owed to the emperor himself!" It was another reminder to Giap, already fearful of French power, of how perilous and tenuous was the Viet Minh hold on government.[1]

In the weeks that followed, Giap redoubled his efforts to organize people in the north. By spring of 1946 practically every hamlet, village, street, and factory had a self-defense force that endeavored to be self-supporting and self-sufficient in weapons and supplies. Stronger units had one or two companies of men; weaker ones at least a platoon. Those in Ha Noi fared best. Members there procured knives, hunting rifles, bombs, even Japanese machine guns.[2] Assisted by the government with military training under careful party leadership, these self-defense groups even had a training school: the Ho Chi Minh Self-Defense Forces School, at which Giap regularly gave lectures.[3]

Giap had accomplished much. At the end of 1945, his military experience was only about that of a major in a western army; by 1946 he was handling responsibilities similar to those of a four-star theater commander.[4] Over a few months his army expanded tenfold in size compared to its numbers at the time the revolutionaries seized power in August 1945.[5] Nor did Giap neglect enlisting the support of those unable to serve in his military. He encouraged people everywhere to erect "fatherland altars," evoked their patriotic fervor, and impressed on them the sacred nature of their duty toward the land. His idea for these altars was borrowed from the society's traditional ancestor worship, for nearly every family had a special place in the home where they gathered to remind themselves of their obligations to ancestors and to render them honor. Family members could now pledge their loyalty to the nation before fatherland altars. Many neighborhoods in Ha Noi and elsewhere erected these memorials.[6]

Chief among Giap's many concerns was procuring more weapons. The government budgeted a large portion of its meager resources to purchase them from Japanese and Kuomintang soldiers. Despite such efforts, Giap could not meet the enormous demand for weapons and equipment for his army, which grew bigger with each passing day. Nor could he require standardized weapons as did most nations. "[A]s a result the small quantity of weapons and ammunition we had were of a wide variety [including] rifles with exceedingly long barrels produced in Tsarist times and muskets made in primitive metal workshops—over forty types of weapons firing bullets of different sizes."[7]

Giap listed some of the amazing variety used by his forces: Mousqueton rifles, Tromblon rifles with grenade launchers, 12-, 16-, and 20-gauge shotguns, Japanese short-barreled cavalry rifles, English 7.7mm rifles, American 1903 and 1917 model Remingtons, German 9mm and 7.5mm Mausers.[8] It was not what Giap wanted, but it was a start. At least his forces had *something* with which to defend themselves.

Nor was Giap reticent about calling on his army to use them. In an interview with Jean Lacouture, printed in *Paris-Saigon* on 27 February 1946, Giap ruminated on the future. "[I]f France is so shortsighted as to unleash a conflict, let it be known that we shall struggle until death, without permitting ourselves to stop for any consideration of persons or any destruction."[9]

Pressure on the Viet Minh government increased when, on 28 February 1946, diplomatic delegates signed a Sino-French accord whereby China agreed to leave Indochina between 1 and 15 March; by 31 March at the latest. France received Chinese agreement to move a limited number of troops into the north in return for France's surrendering all its claims to former concession territories in China. That would give the French a freer hand in reestablishing control over their former colonies in Indochina. Ho Chi Minh's government, barely functional since its entry into Ha Noi in August 1945, now entered upon dangerous shoals as crisis loomed for Giap and all his fellows.

Since August 1945, Ho Chi Minh had insisted on intermittent talks with the French as he sought to work out some sort of compromise to keep his government alive and in power. He insisted on two points: (1) Tonkin, Annam, and Cochin China must be considered as one political unit, and (2) Viet Nam must be independent. The French refused to consider independence, and they insisted that Cochin China, the southernmost part of Viet Nam, must have a special relationship with the mother country.

Following the Sino-French Accord, Ho realized time was running out for him. Giap was exasperated and frustrated. "Previously we had tried by every means possible to take advantage of the conflict between the French and Chiang in order to focus our strength on the French," he said. "Now our two enemies had compromised with each other. They had joined hands in a common conspiracy against us." He knew that before withdrawing their forces, the Chinese would attempt to install the VNQDD and DMH in power.

When some questioned Ho's acquiescence to the return of French troops to Tonkin, he shouted, "You fools! Don't you realize what it means if the Chinese stay? Don't you remember your history? The last time the Chinese came, they stayed one thousand years! But if the Chinese stay now, they will never leave."[10]

Both the VNQDD and DMH were increasingly restive as this new development became apparent. "They pretended to be the most zealous revolutionaries," Giap warned. "Their plot was to push us to oppose the Sino-French treaty since this would give both the French and Chiang the excuse to ally with each other to destroy the revolution." Giap explained the stance toward the French taken by the Viet Minh. "Our position . . . was to obtain *independence* at all costs and at the same time to *ally* with the French."[11]

Giap complained that those competing parties were increasing their attempts to kidnap Viet Minh leaders. They spent more time sowing discord, he said, than they did in efforts to block return of the French. When they learned Ho was in contact with the French, they accused him of betraying the nation, and they sponsored strident demonstrations in Ha Noi calling for Ho to step down in favor of a new government headed by Bao Dai.

On 16 February 1946, Ho met for diplomatic discussions with Jean Sainteny, de Gaulle's commissioner for the protectorates of Annam and Tonkin; Ho suggested the formation of an independent Viet Nam within the French Union.[12] Sainteny countered with the proposal that Tonkin and Annam might become self-governing within the Union, but that in Cochin China there would have to be a referendum to determine whether it desired linkage with the two other areas. Sainteny forwarded the substance of these conversations to Paris.

In an effort to undercut domestic criticism, Ho put together a new government on 24 February. In this rearrangement, the Viet Minh held five cabinet portfolios, the DMH and VNQDD controlled six—but Ho remained president.

The first Viet Minh National Congress convened on 2 March 1946. It met in the Ha Noi opera house, bright with flags. Giap was pleased with the turnout. "[T]here had never been such a full gathering of representatives from all over the country, including members of reactionary parties and numerous foreign guests."[13] The congress swiftly moved to ratify Ho's new cabinet. That same day, Vo Nguyen Giap was named chairman of a National Resistance Committee. "The boat of the Fatherland was hurtling toward an extremely perilous cataract," he said. Perhaps for that reason, in a cynical move, the Communist leadership persuaded the congress to adjourn that same day at 1:00 P.M., after only four hours of life![14]

Disillusioned nationalist Nguyen Duy Thanh marveled at the manipulation. "The national assembly had full legislative powers but it delegated all those powers to a committee of fifteen persons most of whom were communists. The National Assembly met only twice, once to appoint this committee."[15] Thanh sadly watched as Communists consolidated their political hold on the land in the absence of effective and organized opposition. Communists set in place machinery enabling them to watch everyone and to note any deviation from the party line. They set up secret committees to observe the actions of locally elected officials in every village, district, province, and region and to mark those who should be eliminated. Who sat on those Communist secret committees? Thanh claimed they were the country's "riff-raff." Committee officers were usually former convicts sentenced for some civil or political crime, now set free. The longer the former prison sentence, Thanh remarked, the higher the new position of those men.

Cynical to the core, Thanh recalled a time when the Viet Minh minister for external affairs paid a visit to a village near his native home. Before the Viet Minh came to power, this village was, he said, notorious for thefts and petty piracy. The visiting minister asked an old man, "How are things going on in the village now?" To which the old man replied, "It is all O.K. now, sir." The minister then asked, "What happened to the thieves and pirates?" "Sir," the fellow replied, "they are [now] all members of our executive committee."[16]

Many looked upon such officials with absolute contempt, but there was little they could do; Viet Minh secret police supervised all communal activities and maintained a nationwide network of local spies. Every official and every man of any social standing was constantly watched by a spy chosen by the police from among his friends, domestic servants, office clerks, or secretaries. Every stranger going in or out of a neighborhood was watched and reported. Some of those reports fell well within the realm of absurdity. Watchdogs noted how one woman had eighteen diapers for her child; how one official drank coffee for breakfast while his secretary had chicken for dinner. Fathers mistrusted their sons, mothers their daughters, brothers their sisters. Everyone was cautious; anyone might be a spy.[17]

The Viet Minh instituted internal passports, fearing freedom of movement, because individuals might use that opportunity to gather with others and plot against the Communists, and so one could not leave a village without permission. To cross the boundary of a military region, even if only for a few miles, one first had to walk to a passport department that might be many miles away and then, after filing an application, wait perhaps six months before receiving approval. To avoid such annoyances, people bribed officials and in that way often got their requisite permits, but at the cost of respect for those over them. Petty officials, Thanh claimed, used their power to molest women, to persecute men, and to enrich themselves with bribes. To the extent that Thanh accurately described what happened in those days, his portrayal of the Communist program was one of politics at its most base, power-seeking at its most ruthless level, but for the Viet Minh, it worked.[18]

Panic struck members of nationalist parties as Giap's reign of terror swept their ranks, dwarfing the force of previous assassination campaigns that competing political factions had launched against one another. Thousands died.[19] Those purges that began in March 1946 also sent some 25,000 nationalists to labor camps, while another 6,000, driven from their homes, managed to escape into China.[20]

By early March 1946, Viet Minh and French negotiations were still deadlocked. As a security measure, Giap ordered his armed forces to be extremely vigilant, ready to fight. All vital organs of government made careful preparations as a precaution against future trouble. A large number of old people and children evacuated the capital. City self-defense forces placed mines in the roots of trees lining boulevards. At a moment's notice those trees could be felled and their trunks used to form barricades. They were also prepared to topple electricity poles and blow tramway lines whenever Giap ordered them into action.[21]

That same month, in preparation for the coming conflict that increasing numbers of cadre believed to be inevitable, the Communist central committee named Vo Nguyen Giap as vice chairman of the Supreme Council of National Defense and promoted him to full general and commander in chief of all military forces.[22]

Ho and Sainteny continued to talk. The French reluctantly agreed to recognize Viet Nam as an autonomous state within the French Union with its own government and, its own national assembly, army, and finances. On unification of Tonkin and Annam with Cochin China, it even agreed to recognize the results of a future referendum, but the Paris government refused to concede independence. Gallic diplomats shuddered even at the use of the word.[23]

It was not enough for Ho and his followers. As Giap explained the matter, thoughts of independence and unification evoked deep emotions. "We could not," he said, "accept 'autonomy' because in doing so we would surrender in part the liberties we had won at the cost of a great deal of bloodshed, and we would agree to a certain degree to revert to a life of slavery." Warming to his subject, Giap declaimed that Cochin China "was part of Vietnamese territory—its blood was Vietnamese blood, its flesh Vietnamese flesh—and we could not allow any enemy to cut it away." Thus talks were deadlocked.[24]

To bolster their position, the French sent warships to Tonkin Gulf. Alarmed at this show of power, Ho contacted Sainteny on the morning of 6 March. Since both sides balked over the word "independence," Ho indicated he would agree to recognition of Viet Nam as a "free" state with its own government, national assembly, army, and finances and allow the issue of Cochin China to be settled later by referendum. He also insisted that no more than fifteen thousand French soldiers should return to the north to relieve the departing Chinese troops and to complete the disarming and repatriation of any remaining Japanese soldiers. Ho further wanted any French soldiers involved in that task to leave after they completed their job. Their maximum stay was to be limited to ten months. All other French forces would depart Viet Nam within five years.

Sainteny's delegation approved this approach. It was not much different from earlier proposed solutions save that "free" was substituted for "independent." Bao Dai had earlier scolded Giap for yielding to French pressure, for moving backward. Now it actually came to pass. That afternoon of 6 March 1946, at 4:00 P.M., the two sides met at 38 Ly Thai To Street to sign a Vietnamese-French Accord. Present were representatives of France, commanders of Chiang's general staff in northern Indochina, and observers from the American mission and the British consulate. Giap noted with scorn that those in attendance were "large, fat and elegant men, mostly military officers." They contrasted hugely to Ho, a frail old man who came for the signing wearing faded khaki and indigo-blue cloth shoes. "That tableau," sneered Giap, "summed up the situation: the Democratic Republic of Viet Nam surrounded by a thick circle of imperialists."[25]

Images of past humiliations flooded Giap's mind. He thought of Jules Harmand, the French *consul général* and *commissaire général* for Tonkin and Annam who, decades earlier, backed with a few cannons and a few thousand invading troops, handed the Nguyen Dynasty a draft treaty, forcing the emperor and his mandarins to bow their heads and to sign that humiliating agreement of 1883. The Patenôtre Treaty followed a year later, placing the country completely under the domination of French colonialism. From then on, Giap recalled, the nation's independence and liberties, including the right to conduct its own foreign relations, were lost.

Giap marveled at the extraordinary changes the August Revolution of 1945 had brought to the land. Shackled and miserable, Vietnamese who had lived in slavery rose up and became free people. The newly born Viet Minh government "had stood firm in the raging storm," Giap thought. "Now the enemy—supported by a large army and fully supplied with aircraft, warships and armored cars—had to negotiate with us as equals." He felt a certain triumph in that the first "to recognize a free Viet Nam were precisely the same people who sixty-three years earlier had robbed our country of all its liberties."[26]

Delegates that day initialed two agreements. The first was between Sainteny, Ho Chi Minh, and the VNQDD's Vu Hong Khanh. The second, a military annex, was signed by Sainteny, General Raoul Salan of France, and Vo Nguyen Giap. Desperate to derive some small satisfaction from the moment, Giap observed that this was "the first international treaty that the Democratic Republic of Viet Nam had signed with a foreign country."[27] The French felt a more profound pleasure in the agreement. They held on to Cochin China, the heart of their rice lands, rubber plantations, and commerce. Nor were they concerned about the outcome of any future referendum, for that promise simply gave them more time to consolidate their hold on Cochin China, and the Viet Minh had no way to hold French feet to the fire.

The French saw the same opportunities in the military annex they signed. Their promise to withdraw within five years was only as good as their *honneur*, and they believed they would have opportunity to freely introduce additional troops into the north if necessary. The Viet Minh would have to do their work for them, to maintain good order in Tonkin while ensuring that popular resentment against the *colons* did not overflow. If it did, the French could use that provocation as an excuse for military action. They were confident that their *civilisation supérieure* and their technically proficient army could crush any Viet Minh resistance without difficulty. Ultimately the Viet Minh would have to retreat into the mountains to save themselves, but on that 6 March they still had hopes that they could retain their accomplishments without war.

Embittered though he may have been by recent developments, Giap still managed to present a cordial face to his enemies. Ho sent him to Haiphong the following day, 7 March, to meet with General Leclerc. In his opening remarks, Giap referred to the Frenchman, who had fought with the underground *maquis* against the Germans during the late war, as the "first partisan of France" and described himself as the "first partisan of Viet Nam," thus equating their records and accomplishments. So far as Giap was concerned, the two were meeting as peers. He went on to speak of Paris as the capital of culture and liberty. Leclerc simply sniffed and said that while he was happy to have Vietnamese cooperation, he would do what was required with or without it. A crestfallen Giap was appalled, as he prepared to return to Ha Noi, to see in the harbor area French armored vehicles streaming down the opened ramps of beached LSTs (Landing ship, tanks). French power was growing all too rapidly.[28]

By the time Giap left the city to return to Ha Noi, armed conflict had already begun. At eight-thirty that morning, the first of those French landing vessels appeared in the mouth of Haiphong's Cua Cam River. Chinese troops stationed along the banks began firing at them. The French returned fire. Their shells resulted in blowing up a Chinese ammunition depot in the dock area, filled in part with accumulated war booty ready to be taken back to China. The firefight between the French and Chinese lasted about two hours before the Kuomintang troops backed off about 11:00 A.M. Giap observed, with some pleasure, "Many French soldiers were killed and wounded."[29]

Later that same day of 7 March, both Ho and Giap spoke in Ha Noi to some 100,000 people rounded up by the government for a mass rally. They defended the agreement they had signed the previous day with the French. This was Giap's first important public appearance since his earlier dismissal from the position of minister of the interior and was a demonstration of Ho's continued confidence in his abilities. Giap spoke first, even before Ho, at a time when "the fate of the nation was hanging by a thread."[30]

Giap made the following points. All the great powers had abandoned them; if the Democratic Republic of Viet Nam resisted French inroads, it would be forced to fight alone. Even if it resisted, revolutionary forces would be able to hang on to only a few provinces. Such resistance might be heroic, but people would suffer terribly. Desperate scorched-earth tactics necessary in such a conflict would make normal life impossible. And so it had been necessary to sign the accord.

That agreement, Giap said, was designed both to protect and reinforce the government's political, military, and economic position at a time when the young revolution was still very weak. "[T]here are terms [in the accord] which satisfy us and others which do not. Those that satisfy us, without filling us with joy, are that France recognizes the Democratic Republic of Viet Nam as a free state. Liberty is not autonomy, it is more than autonomy, but it is still not independence. Once liberty is attained, we will proceed toward . . . complete independence." Surely, he insisted, the coming referendum would bring about the reunification of Cochin China with the rest of Viet Nam, and thus it was acceptable to wait. And, Giap promised, the goal of the revolution was unchanged—complete independence for Viet Nam.[31]

As Giap spoke, the mood of the crowd changed. Hostile jeers softened into silence occasionally interrupted by a smattering of applause. The clapping became louder, the foundation for excited cheers and, finally, thunderous acclaim orchestrated by Viet Minh cadre moving within the crowd, spurring people on to respond at the proper moments. Once again the Viet Minh had achieved a respite from the terrible pressures they faced; their fingernails still maintained a tenuous, scraping hold on the heights of power.[32]

During following days, Giap did what he could to gain mileage from the 6 March accord and its military annex. To no particular avail he insisted on his right to be consulted about all French troop movements. On 22 March he joined Leclerc in a troop review and a wreath-laying ceremony at the graves of French and Vietnamese dead. On that day Giap even managed to deliver a speech in praise of the French army. It must have galled him personally, but it was still important for him and the party to reach an accommodation with France.[33]

The two sides opened an important conference at Dalat, beginning 18 April 1946. A mountain resort city located in Lam Dong province in the middle of the Central Highlands, Dalat had a relatively cool climate that made it a popular resort for sweltering Europeans. Giap attended the meeting as chief representative for his government and found opportunity there to demonstrate his political toughness. It was at Dalat that the French nicknamed him "the snow-covered volcano" (in Vietnamese, *nui lua*). Their choice was apt for it, revealed that beneath Giap's usually calm demeanor were mercurial moods and a burning hatred for the French *colons*.[34] One observer of Giap's moods in those days described him as "calm, smooth, but energetic, keeping both jaws always tightened and never smiling. His large eyes brilliant but melancholy and glum."[35]

Despite his inner feelings, Giap tried to maintain a cordial atmosphere between the opposing delegations. He was reasonably successful; at least both sides referred to one another using the French familiar pronoun *tu*. At one point, however, Giap could not control the bitterness he felt. When Giap indicated that the conference should address matters dealing with Cochin China, French delegates immediately asserted they had no authority to discuss any questions relating to the south. In any case, they said, it had already been pacified save for occasional police operations.

"To say that," Giap thundered, "is a defiance of truth. In fact, attacks continue everywhere [there]. We shall never give up our arms. . . . We want peace, yes, but peace in liberty and fairness, a peace which conforms to the spirit of the March 6 convention, and not peace in resignation, dishonor and servitude." He went on to insist that the Viet Minh position was clear. "We demand that hostilities cease against our troops" in the south, "for this tragic ignominy must cease."

Suddenly calm, Giap bent forward, with an inscrutable smile on his face, and told of his youth, how his wife had been imprisoned and killed, how his life had been destroyed. Momentarily reflecting on what he had revealed, he then said he was still able to wipe it all away, swallow his suffering, and hold out his hand in friendship. He would reserve his hatred for those responsible for such tragedies.

A French delegate, Pierre Auguste Joseph Messmer, later to become minister of the armed forces and premier, responded to Giap. He recalled an earlier forced odyssey through Tonkin, following his arrest by the Viet Minh in 1945, and his later harsh imprisonment. As he walked endless miles through the Red River Delta as a prisoner in bonds, he "was speeded on by the force of kicks in the behind." His friend, a Captain Brancourt, had been murdered by their guards, and he himself, he said, escaped that fate only through a miracle. Giap's perpetual smile slipped a little and became strained. It became even more fixed when Messmer continued his story. "If I remember well, Giap, you were then the interior minister." Giap inclined his head in agreement. Then Messmer made his point. "He too was without hate . . . he too held out his hand, and . . . all in all, they were more or less even." Messmer sat back triumphantly, enjoying his riposte.

An observer noted that as Giap listened, the glass he held in his hand trembled. He was not at all sure the two were even, and certainly that was not the case for Viet Nam and France. Redress would not come until all the hated French were long gone from Giap's country. Giap left Dalat convinced war was unavoidable. When he returned to Ha Noi, he began to prepare for it, knowing that the revolution's success would be long in coming.[36]

Shortly after the Dalat conference closed, perhaps to forestall further protests, the French announced the formation of their so-called Republic of Cochin China, with its capital in Saigon. This move was the idea of D'Argenlieu and Cédil, despite the fact that it violated the French pledge of 6 March to adhere to the results of a referendum to solve the status of the Vietnamese south.[37]

By the time this government was announced, Ho Chi Minh was no longer in Viet Nam. On 31 May 1946, Ho and a negotiating delegation led by Pham Van Dong left for Paris. They took part in what came to be known as the Fontainebleau Conference. It began on 6 July and lasted until negotiations broke down in August, at which point the other Vietnamese members of the group returned home. Ho stayed on in France, hoping to salvage at least something from his efforts on behalf of his country.

It was during Ho's four-month absence at Fontainebleau that Giap showed his mettle, while he served as acting president of the Viet Minh nation. He used the time to rid the country of rival political groups. He insisted that all parties gather themselves under the Lien Viet, or Popular National Front. Most refused, knowing that the Viet Minh held all key posts within that front organization. When they did so, however, Giap branded them as traitors and reactionaries. One way or another, in good Marxist-Leninist fashion, Giap was determined that only the Viet Minh would control power.

The presence of Chinese troops had so far guaranteed survival of the VNQDD and DMH, but they had no coherent program to offer in competition to the windy slogans of the Viet Minh, nor was their leadership of the same quality as that offered by Ho, Giap, and other top Viet Minh leaders. When the last Kuomintang soldier left on 15 June 1946, Giap acted swiftly. Targets were everywhere: the Chinese Nationalist–backed Dong Minh Hoi; the long-lived nationalist VNQDD; the Dai Viets, a pro-Japanese nationalist group; Trotskyites, of whom there were many scattered throughout Viet Nam; Francophobic nationalists; and militant Roman Catholics. He used his armed units to round up their members and to suppress their newspapers, and he ordered the deaths of literally hundreds of his political opponents.[38]

In this activity, Giap had the help not only of his regular Viet Minh cadres but of another special unit as well. In 1945, Giap had enlisted 1,500 fanatically "antiwhite" Japanese military personnel who offered their services to him following Japan's surrender to the Allies. For them it was more attractive than the idea of returning to a defeated and occupied homeland. These soldiers were led by 230 noncommissioned officers and forty-seven gendarmes of the once-dreaded Japanese Kempetai, all of whom were wanted for questioning by the Allies on charges of suspected war crimes. The entire group was commanded by Colonel Mukayama from the general staff of the 38th Imperial Army. Giap arranged for them all to receive Vietnamese citizenship and false identification papers. Mukayama became one of Giap's firm supporters and willingly served him when called upon, as he was in this instance, to attack opponents of the Viet Minh regime.[39] In these endeavors, strangely enough, Giap was supported by the French, who for whatever reason preferred to deal with the Viet Minh rather than with the multiplicity of available rivals.

So it was that on 19 June 1946, the Viet Minh newspaper in Ha Noi, *Cuu Quoc,* printed a vehement editorial attacking "reactionary saboteurs" of the 6 March Vietnamese-French Accord. Giap thus began his campaign, aided by his police and army and with the cooperation of French authorities. When the French took control of DMH territory in the Hong Ay mining district, for example, they first released Viet Minh leaders from jail and then turned administration of the area over to them as well as providing them with artillery pieces to use against a nearby position held by supporters of the Dai Viet party.

Giap ordered his agents to murder hundreds of nationalists. From 11 to 13 July, he directed a country-wide hunt for nationalist leaders, and his Viet Minh police seized the headquarters and other facilities of opposition parties. Hundreds of nationalists who might in the future provide guidance for a rival anti-French resistance movement were executed during this campaign. One method favored by Giap's hoodlums was to tie victims together in batches, like cordwood, and throw them to their deaths in the Red and other rivers. They drowned while floating out to sea—a method Giap referred to as "crab fishing."[40] The last opposition newspaper, *Viet Nam,* was shut down in early July. When it reopened a week later, on 18 July, its position had suddenly and miraculously become one of total agreement with the Communist Party line.[41]

Nor was Giap loath to blame the sudden rash of deaths around the country on his opponents. Historian Philippe Devillers, writing in 1952, claimed that in April and May 1946 the Viet Minh seized several villas used earlier by the DMH and found there "real slaughterhouses" wherein the DMH had tortured and killed a number of kidnapped French and Viet Minh prisoners. Although that party was entirely capable of having done so and in all probability actually did murder some of its opponents, such stories as were told by Devillers were later found to be fabricated by the Viet Minh.

The "affair on On Nhu Hau Street" sheds light on Giap's methods. After ordering his men to seize the main headquarters of the VNQDD on On Nhu Hau Street in Ha Noi, Giap ordered those agents to construct a chamber of horrors there. They exhumed dead bodies from graves and laid them out inside the building. Then Giap announced that they had found in the backyard a mass grave composed of corpses of their opponents killed brutally by the VNQDD. In reality many of the unidentified bodies were themselves VNQDD activists killed by Giap's security forces. Yet they told those who came to view the macabre scene that the dead had been slain by nationalists. "Look," they said, "this is the atrocious deed of the nationalists." When news of the real story began to spread,

"The On Nhu Hau Street affair opened many eyes of people who didn't then believe the red color of the Viet Minh."[42]

An era passed in French efforts to regain control of Indochina when forces commander General Leclerc was replaced on 18 July 1946 by Lieutenant General Jean Etienne Valluy. Valluy would be the first of several French generals charged specifically with the difficult task of defeating Giap and his Viet Minh troops. He was competent enough, forty-six years old and a highly decorated officer who had joined the army as a private in 1917 at the age of eighteen. A year later, following service in the trenches, he was appointed to Saint-Cyr, the nation's military academy, from which he graduated in 1918. He quickly found himself back in the frontline trenches, where he was wounded and decorated with the Croix de Guerre for valor.

Following the war, Valluy remained in the military and held several staff and command jobs, usually commanding Senegalese or Moroccan colonial auxiliary forces. A major by 1939 and the operations officer of XXI Corps, he was taken prisoner by the Germans in 1940 and released to the custody of the Vichy government in 1941. By 1944 he was a brigadier general, serving as chief of staff for General Jean de Lattre de Tassigny (who would himself later serve as commander in chief of French forces and high commissioner of Indochina from December 1950 until December 1951). In early 1946 he served as commander of French troops returning to Tonkin. On 20 February 1947 he received promotion to lieutenant general and was assigned as commander in chief of French forces in Indochina. He would be the first to fall in defeat to Giap.

Giap did not think much of Valluy. He had met him several times and worked with him during military discussions. Despite his appearance as a nice, open-minded, courteous officer, Giap suspected he was an "insidious man." On 21 June 1946, Giap's secretary interrupted him at his work to inform him that Valluy waited outside, desiring to speak with him. As Valluy entered, he offered Giap a salute and said: "I am a soldier having the task of carrying out orders from my superiors. I am here to bring a message to the Vietnamese government."

"Give me the message," Giap responded.

Valluy handed Giap a letter and stood, waiting. Giap opened the envelope and scanned the brief message addressed to him as acting president of the Democratic Republic of Viet Nam: "The French High Commissioner in Indochina, Admiral [Thierry] d'Argenlieu, has given orders to the French army to occupy the highlands of the Moi tribe as he told President Ho Chi Minh earlier in Hanoi."[43]

The Moi tribe lived in Thai Nguyen province on land considered almost sacred by the Viet Minh, for it had formerly been part of their liberated zone in northern Viet Nam during the dark days of World War II. Now d'Argenlieu intended to establish a puppet mountain republic there—a "Thai-Ky Republic"—separate from the Viet Minh regime in Ha Noi, thus further diluting their influence. This action was, Giap later remarked, "a new aggressive step taken by that malicious priest who had broken his vow." This was Giap's customary way of referring to d'Argenlieu, who in his early years had been a Carmelite monk and had risen to high position in that order. As World War II approached, d'Argenlieu left the Carmelites and resumed his naval career, joining Free French forces under de Gaulle. He was named high commissioner (the title replacing the older one of governor-general) for Indochina in August 1945.

Giap looked up at his visitor and dismissed him. "If you are here only to fulfill the task given by your superiors, then your job is done." Valluy left.[44]

Giap furiously waited for news. It was not long in coming. That evening reports filtered in to Giap's headquarters. Low-flying French aircraft had carried out bombings on Viet Minh positions; troops were sent against them. Encountering strong Viet Minh resistance, the French withdrew. The following day they attacked again and once more were forced to withdraw. On 23 June, French troops launched a surprise attack on Viet Minh soldiers on the road leading from Pleiku to Cambodia. Military activities were spreading.

Giap ordered his military units to "thwart every aggressive act [of] the French army." The French were told in unmistakable words that Ho had never agreed to any occupation of the Thai Nguyen area. Such French actions convinced Giap—if he needed any additional proof—that the only solution would be a military one. He also knew that any such conflict would be a long one; indeed, only a protracted war would provide necessary conditions for a Viet Minh victory. Neither side would be able to end a struggle with a preemptive blow. Thus he worked even harder to provide backcountry resistance centers with ammunition depots and armories capable of crafting small arms, all to be located in caves around Thai Nguyen and Hoa Binh.[45]

Provocations mounted. French soldiers repeatedly caused incidents along the Ha Noi–Lang Son road. A major incident in Bac Ninh province lasted four and one-half hours with deaths on both sides. On 25 June, French troops seized the former governor-general's mansion in Ha Noi that the Viet Minh had been using since August 1945. Giap protested this action to Valluy, who passed it off as a mistake, saying that those inside were "only a small group coming to do some maintenance work." On 27 June, in retaliation, the Viet Minh government called on people to close all markets in Ha Noi, Haiphong, and wherever there were French troops.[46]

Giap was convinced that behind these troubles lay the determination of French "reactionaries" to create incidents strong enough to undermine Ho's diplomatic negotiations at the Fontainebleau Conference. His only recourse was to hold firm in the face of French provocations.

*　　*　　*

Not all of life was dark for a harassed Giap in those weeks of late spring and summer 1946. After his return to Ha Noi in August 1945 he had gone to An Xa to visit his daughter, Hong Anh, but had decided to leave her in care of his mother until he was able to establish a home of his own. He had also been in contact with his old friend, mentor, and benefactor Professor Dang Thai Mai. The Viet Minh appointed Professor Mai as minister of national education in early 1946, and although their duties varied greatly, service in government occasionally brought both Giap and Mai together. As in older days, the professor invited Giap to his home for friendly meals when time permitted.[47]

Giap was surprised on his first visit to Professor Mai's home to see the changes wrought by the passage of years. When he lived in the professor's home in Vinh in 1932, he had enjoyed playing with one of the man's daughters, Dang Bich Ha, eighteen years younger than he, then a girl of four who enjoyed calling him *chu* ("uncle"). That small child was now seventeen, beautiful and gracious, impressed with this national hero who frequently visited her home. Giap was thirty-five, more than twice as old as she, but he was also lonely and work-brittle. And so, in 1946, he asked Professor Dang Thai Mai for permission to marry Dang Bich Ha, and her father gladly nodded his approval.[48]

After their marriage, Ha went on with her education and trained herself in the field of history, including study later in Moscow. As the years passed, Hong Anh came to live with her father and stepmother. When asked about the years of her life with Giap, Ha replied, "He has a great sense of sacrifice. It is the dominant trait of his character." And Hong Anh sounded an echo. "Father is very affectionate with us, but it is only at rare times that we have been able to profit from his presence." In 1951, Giap and Ha became the parents of a daughter, Vo Hoa Binh. The next year, Ha gave birth to a second daughter, Vo Hanh Phuc. In 1954, Giap became the father of a son, whom he named after his great victory of that year, Vo Dien Bien, and in 1956, Giap and Ha celebrated the birth of their last child, another son, Vo Hoai Nam, named after Giap's determination to create a Red South.[49] Although he loved his daughter and new wife, family would never be the center of Giap's life, and even as he began his years of marriage with Dang Bich Ha he could hear in his imagination the sound of war trumpets calling him to return to his duties and to an inevitable confrontation with the French.

"Fight to the Last Drop of Blood"

Throughout late summer of 1946 along the frontier line separating Viet Nam from China, incidents between Viet Minh and French soldiers multiplied. Men fell bloodied to the earth on both sides—on 3 August, on 10 August, on 13 August—with no end in sight. On 6 August a French envoy, Jean Albert Emile Crépin, a future *général d'armée* who had arrived in Indochina in 1945 and who later replaced Sainteny, arrived at the offices of Vo Nguyen Giap to complain about those events. "If you let such courses of action continue," Crépin said, "there certainly will be war."

Hearing that threat, Giap leaned across his desk and replied to Crépin in slow, measured tones. Recalling the shootings and aware of Admiral d'Argenlieu's recent efforts to split the land of the Viet Minh into fragments by establishing separate northern autonomous governments, the so-called Nun-Thai and Thai-Ky "republics," Giap's words were venomous: "You know very well the reason behind these shootings—those who must bear the responsibility are your troops. We have repeatedly expressed our goodwill. If you want peace, there will be peace; if you want war, there will be war!"[1]

A nervous government in Paris now ordered a new French military man, Major General Louis Constant Morlière, onto the scene in hopes that he could find a way to bring back Gallic control. Giap met Morlière at the airport and claimed that the French officer was moved by the presence of a representative of the Vietnamese government. He told Giap he "sympathized with the liberation of Viet Nam" and expressed hopes for the success of the Fontainebleau talks. Giap had to smile when Morlière introduced himself as a man with great affection for the people of Viet Nam. In one conversation with Giap, he again praised the Vietnamese. When Giap prodded him to prove his point, the hapless general could think only of one illustration. He remembered one of his servants who "had great cooking skill and honesty." Giap was unmoved by such protestations, and came to refer to Morlière as "the general of ultimatums."[2]

The Viet Minh government scheduled a show of pageantry for 2 September 1946. Its nation was exactly one year old. Everywhere people displayed flags, pictures of Ho Chi Minh, lanterns, strings of flowers, and triumphal arches. At seven o'clock on that morning sirens sounded across the city of Ha Noi and people stopped and faced south for a moment of silence to honor their compatriots fighting the French in lower Annam and in Cochin China. The military parade, with much pomp, circled Hoan Kiem Lake (the Lake of the Returned Sword). Representatives from several nations sat in the reviewing stands: Britain, the United States, China, and France. They watched as one of Giap's regiments passed in review, fully equipped, dressed in green uniforms with yellow-starred caps and leather shoes, with rifles correctly aligned on their shoulders.[3]

Then came a powerful sight: 500,000 people marched past the reviewing stands in a column over five kilometers long. Interspersed among them were floats that, while not the quality of Rose Parade standards, were nevertheless impressive. One was a giant red flag with its yellow star; another a model of the platform from which a year earlier Ho had announced the nation's Declaration of Independence; still another a yellow bird with great spread wings; and another a model of the earth symbolizing the working classes. In the evening the city was bathed in bright pink light created by tens of thousands of lanterns hung in front of people's houses. All in all, it was quite a day.[4]

Only a few days later, on 18 September, the French gunboat *Dumont d'Urville* left the port of Toulon bound for Indochina. One passenger was Ho Chi Minh. He was coming home. Giap's days as head of the Viet Minh government were nearly over. He had, however, achieved a signal success. He had shown Ho during the president's visit to France that he was utterly reliable and politically capable. As a result, Giap was firmly settled in the number-three place within the Communist Party hierarchy, immediately behind Ho and Pham Van Dong. The requirements of politics, as Giap understood them, had, however, been such that he would forever after be marked as what he actually was—an extremist. Soon he would relinquish rule to Ho. The *Dumont d'Urville* sailed through the Suez Canal into the Red Sea and, exactly a month after it set sail, entered the waters of Cam Ranh Bay. A few days later, Ho rejoined his comrades in Ha Noi.[5]

At about the time Ho returned, an October election selected members of a new national assembly. These men soon approved a new constitution, which went into effect on 8 November, establishing the Democratic Republic of Viet Nam. The assembly also elected a permanent committee to conduct affairs in its name and in its absence. The committee could vote approval of government bills, declare war, and even summon the assembly to reconvene. Having enacted these provisions, the assembly dissolved on 14 November 1946, not to be called back into session until December 1953! From now on, government would be solely within the hands of Ho Chi Minh and his inner circle.

Ho rearranged government portfolios. Now that the Dai Viet, DMH, and VNQDD had been eliminated as rivals, he felt strong enough to name more of his avowed supporters to crucial government positions. He shut out any real opponents and gave five of ten cabinet positions to fellow Communists. Remaining portfolios went to representatives of parties that were either under the control of the Viet Minh or had allied themselves with it. Giap gained the important job of minister of national defense. No thought was given to reassigning him to his former position of minister of the interior. Military planning was obviously soon going to be of more importance than internal political security. That was readily apparent throughout the fall and early winter of 1946.

The major coastal port city of Haiphong was the flashpoint that enlarged Vietnamese-French conflict into the First Indochina War. Both the Viet Minh and France used it as a port of entry for their supplies. Giap used it to bring in weapons from China; the French moored vessels at its docks while vehicles and troops from home came ashore to bolster their forces. As they enlarged their troop garrison the French began efforts to replace Viet Minh control of Haiphong's local institutions with their own. As expected, the Viet Minh resisted every step of the way, although not always successfully.

French officials, irritated that the Viet Minh controlled the collection of customs duties at the port, gave orders that this situation must end. According to Giap, on the evening of 29 August, French tanks, armored vehicles, and troops encircled the post office, the police station, and the customs office and expelled Viet Minh personnel from them. While they were seizing merchandise inbound through the port, Viet Minh troops arrived. The opposing sides exchanged gunfire, but the Viet Minh were unable to recapture the three facilities. The French did not withdraw for nearly two weeks.[6]

Only the personal intervention of General Morlière and Giap prevented an escalation of the initial gunfight into a more serious armed confrontation. French officials issued an ultimatum: the Viet Minh must turn over total control of customs activities at Haiphong by 15 October. The Viet Minh foreign minister complained to Paris, to no avail.[7]

Tension in the port city increased as the deadline passed while the Viet Minh stood firm in their refusal to comply with the French order. Then, on 20 November, French officials seized a Chinese junk they suspected of carrying arms to Giap's forces. In retaliation the Viet Minh seized three French soldiers and barricaded themselves within their enclave in Haiphong's suburbs; the city itself was by now mostly in the hands of their enemies. French troop units marched to the area and tore down the hastily erected Viet Minh abatis, and heavy fighting ensued.[8]

Giap and Morlière conferred in Ha Noi and agreed to proclaim a cease-fire to go into effect the following day at 5:00 P.M. The French high command, signaling from its headquarters in Saigon, did not want a cease-fire, and, in a move backed by both Governor-General d'Argenlieu and French prime minister Georges Bidault, ordered the Viet Minh to vacate Haiphong by 23 November—only a few hours away. When they refused, the French brought fire to bear on the city from tanks, airplanes, artillery, and naval ships in the harbor. The Viet Minh later calculated that this bit of callousness caused twenty thousand fatalities, mostly among civilian noncombatants; the French claimed that "only" six thousand died.

Then the French issued a second ultimatum. They demanded complete control over Ha Noi and the road between that city and Haiphong. Giap knew it was now time for war. At his orders, people across the land began to mobilize. Students, farmers, workers, intellectuals, old and young, male and female alike, enrolled in patriotic organizations and received assignments to attend indoctrination classes, to guard streets and bridges, to watch for French infiltrators arriving by airdrop or coastal landing parties, to serve as voluntary nurses, to collect rice for the army. Everyone had a job. Party members collected gold and jewels to be sent to the Ha Noi government to help it buy necessary weaponry.[9]

Abbott Low Moffat, chief of the Division of Southeast Asian Affairs, United States Department of State, was in Viet Nam in early December 1946. His cables home did nothing to heighten sympathy for the Viet Minh cause. For the United States, Viet Nam was an unnoticed backwater in world affairs in any case. Its attention was tightly focused on Europe, where recent Soviet intransigence caused many Americans to rethink the wartime alliance with "Uncle Joe" Stalin and to see Russian expansionism in a more realistic light. With Soviet soldiers already garrisoned across the face of central and eastern Europe, U.S. diplomats wooed France as an ally, hoping to make its soil part of the western bastion opposing communism.

President Harry S Truman's thoughts were occupied by troubles in Europe; there is little evidence that he ever saw the several letters sent to him by Ho Chi Minh, asking for support in his struggle with France. At one point, Ho even suggested his willingness to accept a relationship with the United States modeled on the one it maintained with the Philippines. His letters went unanswered. The United States had to choose between an insignificant new nation in southeast Asia and France, which was to become the cornerstone of a new defensive alliance. The choice was easily made. Support for France within America's State

Department never wavered, and postwar diplomats frowned upon the relationship with the Annamese Communists forged during the late conflict by members of the OSS. Ultimately the American government declared that it planned to respect French control of Indochina, and in October 1945 it recalled its mission from Ha Noi.

Now, a year later, Abbott Low Moffat visited the Viet Minh capital and observed the fluctuating political scene. He was so confused in his understanding of Vietnamese politics that, although he met Giap many times, at first he believed Giap was a waiter! Moffat wrote that "for ten days Morlière and Giap . . . had been calling each other names in the press." French officials described Giap to Moffat as the leader of the Vietnamese "extremists," and when Moffat met Giap informally, he remarked later, "Personally, I did not take to him, although . . . the French who know him both admire his very great intelligence and like him personally a great deal. . . . Giap had a dead-pan face which always disconcerts me. He is, of course, an avowed Communist."

Giap seemed to Moffat to be exactly "what one imagines the 'ideal' intelligent Communist party leader should be." Moffat thought the French description of Giap as "fanatical but very able" to be an accurate one. In conversation with Moffat, Giap insisted that the Viet Minh would never agree to vacate Ha Noi as the French demanded. He informed the American that "even with their tanks and planes and guns, the French could be beaten." Then, after considering his remarks, Giap modified them slightly. "[T]he Vietnamese might not win, but . . . in any event the French would not win." And then they parted.

Moffat was the last American who would see Giap for many years, the last who might have been able to sway the United States to a different course of action that might have changed the course of years, prevented the deaths of uncounted thousands, allowed immense treasure to remain unspent on war, saved the soil of Viet Nam from despoliation, and allowed the society of the United States to remain free from the ruptures of later years. Critics might well scoff at such an assertion. Moffat was not that important. He was not secretary of state; he was only a minor underling in charge of a then-unimportant division. What, they might ask, could he have accomplished even if persuaded to action? We will never know.[10]

Knowing that the French wanted to goad him into using his forces to strike at their army, Giap deliberately adopted a policy of moderation and restraint. He would not provoke the French. He sent the main part of his units out of Ha Noi and thus out of reach of the French into the northern provinces of Bac Kan, Tuyen Quang, and Thai Nguyen, the southern part of the old liberated zone where the Viet Minh had been so strong in the waning days of World War II. Giap's neighborhood self-defense forces handled local security in Ha Noi, raising barricades and preparing themselves to face the professional soldiers of France. Minor skirmishes resulted, and French units took reprisals against entire neighborhoods for instances of violence. Without result, Ho appealed to Paris.

On 19 December, the French high command called for Giap to disarm his local security forces as a sign of good intentions. His response was to order more barricades erected and to ready an operational plan for an attack on French positions. That afternoon, in a last effort, Giap talked with General Morlière, trying to find a way to reduce the growing inevitability of conflict. Morlière had no suggestions to make. It was the last time they would ever meet.[11]

Then, at 6:30 P.M., Morlière learned from intelligence sources that Giap planned an attack, and he sent out a readiness order to his troops. His garrisons were thus forewarned when, at 8:00 P.M., Giap's forces launched an attack against them. Stripped of the element of surprise, Giap's men suffered many casualties. At 9:30 P.M., 19 December 1946, Giap issued a national call to arms. The next morning, 20 December, in the name of the government and the Communist Party, Ho Chi Minh called for people everywhere to rise up, "to exterminate the enemy and save the country, to fight to the last drop of blood and, whatever the cost, to refuse re-enslavement."[12]

With the backing of the party's central committee, Giap urged the armed forces and people of Ha Noi to maintain their positions in the city for at least fifteen days to give others a chance to reach safety in the high northern mountains. They did so for two months. It was not until the night of 17 February 1947 that Giap's last soldiers crept quietly through the French tight encirclement of Ha Noi to positions of safety outside the *colons'* ring of weapons. Nor were those who fought inside the city alone in their struggle.

Across the northern countryside, local communities staged uprisings and resistance efforts as French units moved into their areas. Their fervor gladdened Giap. Villagers dug traps and tunnels, made snares and punji stakes, stalked lone French soldiers and smote them hip and thigh. As the French moved over the countryside in search-and-clear actions, some hamlets transformed themselves into fortresses of resistance. Filled with patriotism, people named their pitiful operation plan efforts after some of the great captains of their past history: Le Loi, Tran Huong Dao, Phan Dinh Phung, Ly Thuong Kiet, Quang Trung.[13]

Giap reflected that "the heroic events that occurred in the first days of the struggle . . . remain vivid." His forces, he said, "waged an extremely courageous struggle," and their toughness and stubbornness "reflected the indomitability of a small nation determined to fight a big imperialist power." All those nights of sleepless planning paid off as his units managed to pin down French forces long enough "so that our rear base could complete preparation and development of our forces."[14]

No matter their desires, no one could withstand the French juggernaut as it rolled across the landscape. By the end of March 1947, France controlled all the major coastal towns of Tonkin and northern Annam and the more urban locations of Cochin China. It occupied Ha Noi and other inland communities and controlled all the delta area of the Red River. Communication centers and the roads between them were safely in French hands, but all that did not help much as the colonial army sought to turn back the clock to the mid-1930s when only a handful of *colons* easily controlled millions of Vietnamese from the tip of the southern Ca Mau peninsula to the northern frontier with China.

Giap and the Communist Party were well prepared for their retreat to the Viet Bac. In the jungles, hills, and mountains of northern Viet Nam—the "Greenhouse," as Giap called it—they were quite safe from French depredation and attack. The country was rugged and difficult, harsh and inhospitable. Mountains rose in varying heights from two to four thousand feet above sea level and were honeycombed with caves. Eighty inches of rainfall annually blanketed the area, 75 percent of which came between May and November. The Viet Minh knew that their activities in this sanctuary would be shrouded by rain and fog. Giap took relief in his knowledge that, difficult at any time, French armored penetrations would be impossible during the rainy season. Arriving in the Viet Bac just before the rains began in 1947 gave Giap six months of total safety in which to refit, to repair, to build, and to rest.

The base area, some eighty miles north of Ha Noi, was roughly circular, with a fifty-mile radius. It was cross-compartmentalized by high ridges and steep valleys. It had few roads, and only footpaths linked tiny mountain and valley settlements. Travel by more than oxcart was simply impossible. If roads were infrequent, there were even fewer bridges to span rivers and streams that regularly intersected them. Despite all these watercourses, the only two affording travel to other than very small boats were the Clear River and its tributary the Son Gam.

The French could get close to but not into the Viet Bac. (See maps "Tonkin" and "Provinces of Tonkin.") Highway 2 went around the west side of Giap's sanctuary through Tuyen Quang to Ha Giang, close to the border with Yunnan. Highway 3 extended from Thai Nguyen through Bac Kan to Cao Bang, most of it little more than a path for oxen and their carts. Nor did its stretches look inviting to French planners, for it passed through terrain inviting ambushes from above. The last road was Highway 4, which ran along the northeastern edge of the Viet Bac enclave linking Lang Son, That Khy, Dong Khe, and Cao Bang. Giap's responsibilities were plain. Protect these roads and his base area would be safe, giving him time to form military zones and to begin fighting back.

Much had to be done before Giap could strike at the French. He watched with approval as, hidden by granite walls and shaded by bamboo and palm forests, his people poured into the safety zone. Working with unflagging energy, they erected factories and markets, military training fields and barracks, armories and smelters, scientific institutes and schools. In one school, Professor

Dang Bich Ha, the general's second wife, taught students the history of their land. Giap located his own headquarters in a straw hut.[15]

In this precarious time, Giap knew the value of good relations with local populations. Without them, he once wrote, "We shall have no information. . . . We shall be able neither to preserve secrecy, nor carry out rapid movements. The people suggest stratagems and act as guides. It finds liaison officers, hides us, protects our activities, feeds us and tends our wounded."[16]

Even more aware than Giap of the importance of civilian support, Ho strengthened the Viet Minh movement in its Viet Bac fastness by including non-Communist nationalists in his government. He could be persuasive only by acting less dogmatic. At this juncture even Bao Dai was once again sympathetic to Ho's revolutionary struggle against the French. So in July 1947, Ho formed a new cabinet which allowed nationalists more representation but no more power. Neither Giap nor Pham Van Dong held a portfolio, but Giap still remained undisputed head of the Viet Minh military effort.

Stymied by spring rains and by lack of an effective operational plan, General Valluy chose not to carry the fight to Giap immediately. Giap's forces thus had a respite until late fall to ready themselves for the inevitable French attack. Both Giap and Valluy kept one eye focused on China. The Kuomintang Nationalist government of Chiang Kai-shek was collapsing. If Mao's revolutionary Communist forces succeeded in taking over the country, both knew it would give the Viet Minh a rear-base sanctuary in which to stockpile weapons and supplies and to train Giap's fighters.

By early fall 1947, General Valluy felt it was time to move against the Viet Minh. A recent revolt on the island of Madagascar meant that fifteen thousand of his troops might be withdrawn from his command and sent there, and he could ill afford their loss. In Paris, the Chamber of Deputies was becoming increasingly querulous about voting funds necessary to fund war in Indochina. A quick victory was important for Gallic prestige, and so, in September, Valluy and his staff began to plan an assault, code-named Operation Lea.

Valluy knew that if he could kill or capture the Viet Minh leadership, rank-and-file members would no longer be much of a problem. Yet how to get into the Viet Bac to do so? There were only a few avenues of approach; Route Coloniale 2, Route Coloniale 3, Route Coloniale 4, and the Clear River–Song Gam water accessway. The Viet Minh had only to watch those few entryways in order to stymie French military excursions.

Even in the countryside held by the French they often found themselves thwarted by Viet Minh efforts. The French could successfully send out patrols; they could occupy towns and roads and bridges and railways and forts. But all the land between them belonged to the Viet Minh. They could not hold such crucial properties and simultaneously search for and destroy Giap's forces. A French military unit was safe during the day in a village; at night it might well be destroyed by a sudden mortar attack out of the darkness. The French were frustrated. If they could control less than half the country during daylight, and less than a quarter of it during the hours of darkness, how could they successfully invade the Viet Bac redoubt itself and eliminate Viet Minh leaders there?

Valluy's intelligence information provided him with the location of Viet Minh headquarters in the Viet Bac. It was sited at the wretched little village of Bac Kan astride Route Coloniale 3 north of Thai Nguyen. Valluy designed Operation Lea as a combined arms thrust, a triumphantly successful pincer movement to close on that village. One claw would move north up the Clear and Song Gam rivers while the other closed in from Route Coloniale 4, much of which was nothing more than a shallow gash cut in an enormous limestone cliff. At the moment those forces left the line of departure, an airborne force would drop on the area of the enemy headquarters. Those paratroopers would hold the Viet Minh in place until they received reinforcements from the two pincer arms as they closed, destroying the pesky Viet Minh.

The northern pincer was to have infantry, armor, and artillery elements—each with three battalions. This force was to race from Lang Son up Route 4 to Cao Bang eighty miles to the northwest, and then west to Nguyen Binh, and then south forty miles along Route 3 to Bac Kan. If Valluy recognized the difficulty of such a move he nevertheless ordered it to be done. He seemed to have forgotten that armies operate best when they follow a long-held precept, the principle of simplicity. This plan was a clear violation of that approach.

Naval landing craft would take the three infantry battalions of the southern pincer up the Clear River to the Song Gam tributary and then up the Son Gam as far as the boats could go. From that point the infantry would forge ahead along Route 3 on foot.

Valluy had only a limited number of soldiers available for Operation Lea: one engineer battalion to scout ahead, six infantry battalions, two parachute battalions, three battalions of armored vehicles, and the 4th Fighter Group of the French Air Force. Thus some fifteen thousand men were to be sent into action against sixty thousand operating in a 7,500-square-mile jungle sanctuary.[17] It appeared as if Valluy had been reading his nation's Plan XVII, designed prior to 1914 to protect France in case of German attack: "The French Army with its high morale is undefeatable in the offense."

Valluy seriously underestimated the difficulties of fighting in the jungles of Southeast Asia, and he was trapped by his earlier promise that he would eliminate all organized resistance within three months.[18] Nor did he appreciate the skill of the general facing him. Valluy's troops would have to operate on long exterior lines while cordoning off a vast area; Giap, on the other hand, could shift units from one area to another, all in close proximity to their supply bases. And how could armor and artillery and truck-transported infantry move in an area with few roads over which wheeled or tracked traffic could travel and only rickety bridges spanning some of the many small streams and rivers? It was, at best, a risky plan that could easily go wrong.

Operation Lea began 7 October 1947 when 1,137 paratroopers dropped from the skies over Bac Kan, Cho Don, and Cho Moi, an area of ten by twenty miles. Simultaneously, the northern pincer, with its elements of armor, infantry, and artillery, moved forward with appropriate speed in a desperate rush to link up with the paratroopers and augment their power. Enemy opposition soon slowed this advance, while the southern pincer did not even begin its move up the rivers for two days. The reason for its delay is uncertain.

Yet the battle went well, at first. Paratroopers closed in on Bac Kan and the Viet Minh headquarters so quickly they caught Giap and Ho flatfooted. Giap was unprepared for such an ambitious offensive aimed directly at the leadership. Both men had to flee at a moment's notice; French soldiers captured letters Ho abandoned on his desk. The enemy ring was drawn so tightly that escape was impossible; there was no way Ho and Giap could slip through the cordon. Their only chance was an extremely long one, and Giap led Ho to a hole located nearby in the jungle floor, prepared some time earlier. It was hardly big enough for both, but they covered the opening with leaves and palm fronds and sat huddled against each other.

They remained crouched there for some hours with their backs pressed together while French troops walked within yards of their hideaway, tapping the ground and searching in the jungle growth as they looked for just such hidden spider holes. Ho was the soul of the revolution, and Giap was irreplaceable by this time as military leader of the Viet Minh. How history might have changed if the French had been more persistent in their search. Eventually their footsteps faded into the distance, and finally Ho and Giap were able to slip into the cover of the jungle and make their escape.[19]

Within a day, with Giap now directing the defense, the course of battle shifted against the French as he deployed his numerically superior forces against the paratroops. As more Viet Minh units closed on them, they soon found their position desperate. Giap then ordered his men to slow down the French columns advancing from the south.

French movement on Route 4 was slow and difficult. Viet Minh sappers dropped trees across the road, destroyed bridges, and cratered the roadway itself. No broad-front movement was possible in the narrow accessway, so the French fought their way forward on a squad front. Snipers fired. The soldiers took cover. A tank edged forward to hose the surrounding area with its machine guns. Soldiers shook themselves from their cover and moved forward again, one squad behind the next, past Na Cham, through Pineapple Pass, across the Song Ky Kong River, through Loung Phai Pass to Dong Khe, on through Tunnel Pass to Cao Bang, then westward to Nguyen Binh and south toward Phu Tong Hoa, through 140 miles of Viet Minh ambushes. Giap ordered his men into an all-out effort to stop his foes at Phu Tong Hoa, ten miles north of Bac Kan. The mechanized Moroccan Colonial Infantry Regiment broke through Giap's blocking force on 16 October and finally reached Valluy's paratroopers at Bac Kan.[20]

If movement of the northern pincer was slow, that of the southern was glacial. Its men were still nowhere near their objective when on 19 October they met the paratroopers and their rescuers retreating toward them. Joining forces, the soldiers marched out of the Viet Bac. Although Valluy did not call off Operation Lea until 8 November, the entire effort failed to achieve its goals. It taught the French precious little, but Giap learned much. Never again would he leave a headquarters undefended against attack from the air. Thereafter, against the French and later the United States, he dispersed headquarters elements over a wide area, insisted that his forward operations center be highly mobile and regularly change its location, and protected key headquarters with antiaircraft fire and, later, missiles.

General Valluy began his next effort against Giap in late November, an operation he code-named Ceinture ("Belt"). The two most important towns along the southern edge of the Viet Bac—Tuyen Quang and Thai Nguyen—were under Viet Minh control, and Valluy hoped to destroy their main-force units located there. Once again he had only about the same number of soldiers as during Operation Lea, but Valluy could concentrate them more because the target area was smaller, only thirty by fifty miles. This time Giap avoided a pitched battle and recalled his regiments from the area. Although Valluy succeeded in capturing large amounts of supplies, he did no real harm to Giap's units, because they moved back into the area shortly after the French withdrew on 22 December, an auspicious date. It was the third anniversary of Giap's founding of the Armed Propaganda and Liberation Brigade.[21]

Valluy took what comfort he could from his efforts, claiming his forces had killed 9,500 Viet Minh during the actions in late 1947. The number was probably inflated, as such body counts have often been, for at the usually accepted military ratio of three wounded for every man killed, Viet Minh casualties would have numbered nearly 30,000—or half Giap's force. It is not likely that Valluy's soldiers achieved such a signal accomplishment.

Following his efforts in the Viet Bac, Valluy ordered his French forces to remain in the delta of the Red River and in the coastal plain which ran from Haiphong to the Chinese border. Others garrisoned a line of French forts along Route 4 from Lang Son to Cao Bang and clung to two outposts: one at Bac Kan until August 1948, when its main supply route became too dangerous to use any longer, and the other in the mountain town of Ha Giang, eighty miles west of Cao Bang in the Clear River Valley near the Chinese border. The French now controlled less of Viet Nam than did the Viet Minh! Unsatisfied with this state of affairs, the French military recalled Valluy and replaced him with Lieutenant General Roger C. Blaizot. He did little in the coming months. The campaign season had ended, the monsoons had come. No more extensive efforts would be possible, Blaizot believed, until the coming fall of 1948. Giap was ecstatic. His foe Valluy, trained to do battle in Europe and assigned to fight in Asia, had been unable to defeat him. Giap had shown the French that he and his forces would be no easy victory. He had demonstrated himself to be a *general!* Giap also knew the months to come would make or break the Viet Minh effort. He and his men would be busy during this interlude or dead later in battle.

PART THREE

Dien Bien Phu, 1946–54

ELEVEN

"Brandish the Banner of National Independence"

As the months of 1948 slipped away, the Viet Minh remained safe within their hundred-mile-wide strip of jungle in the far north of their country, an area of folded hills, fast-running rivers, tangled growth. Small groups armed with light weapons emerged occasionally to launch spoiling attacks on French posts in the Red River Delta, and well-trained cadre from the Viet Bac sanctuary maintained pressure on their own people who lived in French-occupied areas through the use of constant terror and unrelenting propaganda.[1]

Safe within his "Greenhouse," Vo Nguyen Giap used those weeks for reflection and planning. He had done well in his efforts to learn the craft of generalship on the battlefield, although he found it to be a most unforgiving school. Unlike many military leaders, he actually profited from his experiences, studied them, derived lessons to be learned, and applied them to new situations. As he would later say, "In war it is less profitable to win many battles and learn little than to win one battle and learn much."[2]

Giap felt he had learned a great deal, yet he did not rest content; he spent much of 1948 thinking about the coming struggle and accordingly laying plans to meet that challenge. He accepted the Maoist dictum that revolutionary war passed through three stages: strategic defense, guerrilla warfare, and the counteroffensive. Although he knew his troops could not yet win pitched battles against the French, he was also aware that the enemy no longer had the capability of ejecting him from the Viet Bac or destroying his forces within it. His fortress was, for all intents and purposes, impregnable. The initiative was his and the party's, for, with his earlier murder of so many nationalists and the consequent destruction of their infrastructure, the Viet Minh was now the only effective rallying point for his countrymen in their struggle against the French. He was ready, and his strategy and tactics confounded a succession of French and American generals and planners and finally, after 1973, the army of the southern Republic of Viet Nam. Giap's forces were often outgunned and outmanned. He lost many of his battles. He won his wars.[3]

Giap and his Viet Minh did not have to win many battles to achieve victory. They only had to make the French quit. The same could be said for the Americans at a later time. Against the French, his war aims were to gain independence from France and unite Viet Nam under a single Communist regime. In the Second Indochina War, the Politburo had three goals: (1) to disestablish the Saigon government and replace it with a Communist one, (2) to unite North and South Viet Nam under a single Communist regime, and (3) to compel the United States to withdraw, something Giap could accomplish without achieving military victory.

How is it that a man who had been only a high school history teacher and quondam journalist was able to become a successful general, capable of being ranked with some of history's best? No one in the West can be sure of the extent of Giap's military education, and he has never offered any satisfying answer when asked.[4] Some have claimed that he studied at Russian military schools or at China's Whampoa Military Academy, run by Kuomintang Nationalists. Still others have suggested he was trained by the Chinese Communists, yet there is no real evidence to support any of these views and much that disputes them. His own flip response given on several occasions was a simple one. "The only academy I ever attended was the bush."[5] That is, he learned on the job. The only problem with the bush as a military academy is that it lacks an adequate library. Clausewitz once said that there were two ways to learn about war: experience and the study of military history. Giap had a Ph.D. in experience and a more than passing knowledge of military history.

Perhaps one might as well ask where Julius Caesar received his schooling, or Timur the Lame, or Alexander. From what lofty institute did Hannibal find his way to the Alps? Which military academy did George Washington attend? Did T. E. Lawrence of Arabia receive a lieutenant's commission from Sandhurst? Like Giap, they all were self-made, self-taught, self-motivated in their study of military history, strategy, and tactics. They began with a desire to know, and they practiced their craft in settings that allowed them to learn from their mistakes. Ultimately they demonstrated their superiority over their foes just as Giap did over Leclerc, Valluy, Blaizot, Navarre, and Westmoreland.

Giap read the great masters. Driven by a sense of destiny, pressed by hatred and guided by pragmatism, he learned from his country's ancient warriors.

His classroom was indeed the bush, where learning meant living to fight again and failure was death for both Giap and the Viet Minh. Giap had to learn, to press forward, and he was not fettered by the western albatross of trying always to refight the last war. His academy was that of battle, where real leaders are always forged.[6]

We have from Giap's own pen, jotted in various places in his meandering publications, many of the sources he considered to be sufficiently important to incorporate into his own thinking and to whom he owed much in his formulation of tactics and strategy. No shrinking violet, Giap claimed that he joined the fray against the French (and later the Americans) in order to ensure Viet Nam's independence and freedom, national cultural and moral values, and a plentiful and happy life for all, and to show the revolutionary cause to other oppressed peoples throughout the world.[7]

Giap was proud of the antiquity of Viet Nam, born in ancient times out of resistance to Chinese aggression. Consequently its struggles, its uprisings, and its national wars were just ones, Giap believed, establishing in the process a glorious and proud tradition of resistance against foreign invasion.[8]

Starting with such a vantage point, he pointed with pride to past leaders of his own nation who performed heroic deeds in the long centuries of struggle against China and the Mongols. This was as it should be. One would expect a history teacher to look to annals of his own country for examples of bravery, leadership, and success. In his *Banner of People's War*, Giap wrote, "Our Party's military line has inherited, developed and improved to a new level our nation's age-old traditional strategic ability." He also acknowledged his debt to "the intelligence and strategic abilities of our ancestors."[9]

Perhaps his first debt was simply one of patriotic inspiration drawn from his own country's history. First were Trung Trac and Trung Nhi—the Trung sisters—who, in the early years of the first century of the current era, raised an army and overthrew unsuspecting garrisons of their Chinese overlords. Giap also respected Ly Bon, who led a major revolt against Chinese occupation of Viet lands in the sixth century while in simultaneous conflict with the state of Champa to the south. In 542 A.D. he overthrew the unpopular Chinese administration, and in 544 he established the independent state of Van Xuan.

Then there was Khuc Thua Du, known as Ngo Quyen, who restored Viet independence from China in 939 A.D. when, at the mouth of the Bach Dang River at the entrance to the Gulf of Tonkin, he ordered his men to sink wooden poles into the mud. When the tide fell, an invading Chinese fleet found itself impaled on those stakes and Viet warriors slaughtered their crews.

Centuries later came another of Giap's heroes, Tran Quoc Tuan, also known as Tran Hung Dao. In 1283, as commander in chief of Viet forces and faced with a Mongol invasion, Dao gave ground, inaugurated guerrilla warfare and scorched-earth tactics, and drove the invaders out. In 1287 they struck again, and for a second time Dao defeated them. For Giap, Dao was a truly great military strategist. He had used guerrilla warfare to harass a more powerful enemy. He had emphasized the importance of national unity, with the entire nation fighting as one.

Perhaps the greatest of all of Giap's national heroes was Le Loi, who in 1418 initiated a rebellion in Thanh Hoa province against Chinese overlords. Giap claims to have learned the concept of protracted war from Le Loi, writing that "our people inherently possess a tradition of persistent resistance, an art of defeating the enemy in protracted wars."[10]

Then there was Nguyen Hue, also known as Quang Trung, who, in 1771, with his two brothers, led the Tay Son rebellion. Giap considered Nguyen Hue to be a man who demonstrated the importance of the power of the masses, for he relied on the strength of peasants to topple reactionary cliques, to smash two wars of aggression by Siamese and Ching feudalists, to defend national independence, and to achieve national reunification.[11]

All those heroes and all those conflicts occurred within the framework of just wars, Giap insisted, just as his own was so. They were the triumph of a great cause over tyranny, humanitarianism over cruelty, limited resources over superior ones, small forces over larger armies, weakness triumphing over strength.[12]

Then a few capitalist countries, some with small land areas, all with small populations, but possessed of well-developed industrial bases, succeeded through cruel colonial wars, Giap believed, in conquering nearly all underdeveloped areas of the world. "The struggle of various nations," Giap wrote, "entered a dark, hopeless period." The problem for native peoples everywhere, Giap said, "appeared insoluble."[13]

Could war be used to defeat the French colonialists? "That was another new problem," Giap said, and he pondered the matter month after month, searching for solutions.[14] Giap learned from heroes of Viet Nam's past the necessity of mobilizing all people of the nation in order to win an armed struggle against invaders. This could not be accomplished if his soldiers abused or ignored civilians, and he continued to insist that they treat civilians with dignity and concern "in order to win their confidence and affection and achieve a perfect understanding between the people and the army."[15]

"Our party has always brandished the banner of national independence in order to advance the Vietnamese revolution," Giap wrote. Thus the party mobilized and inspired the entire country to arise and destroy those who would invade its soil; the struggle became a people's democratic national revolution.[16] The party—and Giap—could promise that the course of conflict with France would end foreign domination, do away with oppression and class exploitation, liberate workers and peasants, bring about social justice, and build the society mankind had always longed for—a socialist and Communist one.

Patriotism, Giap knew, served as a great spiritual force, a priceless ethical heritage, bequeathed to the living by their forefathers. The party linked patriotism with love for socialism and the new social system, showing how the path of socialism was the only road to national liberation. The more he and the party succeeded in linking their program with the cause of the people, the stronger they became. In this way the whole nation would rise to regain and protect the independence and freedom of the fatherland. "Thus," Giap said, "our political objectives have developed in terms of quality and class substance as compared with earlier uprisings and national warfare."[17]

In Giap's eyes, people were the source of the strength that generated fighting will and revolutionary heroism. One had to be aware of their needs, their desires. So within the Viet Bac and in other areas free of French control, the party gradually implemented its agrarian policy by seizing ricefields from landlords and turning them over to peasants. Their age-old dream of land to the tiller came true, Giap claimed, for the first time in his nation's history. Famine, he boasted, was eradicated. Illiteracy was wiped out among millions of people. Production accelerated, and people's living conditions improved. The armed forces developed and their combat performance became more professional. The more they fought, the more powerful they became and the greater were their victories. As a result, Giap said, "the people deeply cherished the new regime and fought courageously and sacrificed to defend it."[18]

Neither the French nor the later Americans ever mastered one basic requirement as thoroughly as did Vo Nguyen Giap: the struggle was won or lost in the allegiance of those who lived on the land. Troops from those nations came only for brief tours of duty, while Giap's soldiers were there for life. Foreigners' assignments to Viet Nam were completed before they managed to see the ultimate importance of this salient truth. Yet no matter how many arguments may have raged in American staff conferences regarding the negative impact of harassing and interdicting artillery fire and air bombardment on the lands and people of the South, little was ever done to change the situation. U.S. efforts at pacification—whether called internal defense and development or internal security or nation-building or revolutionary development or neutralization operations or rural construction or stability operations—were *always* referred to as "the other war," or some such phrase. They were secondary endeavors to be acted upon if time could be spared from the major task of finding, fixing, and finishing the enemy wherever he might be, and to do so with ever-increasing firepower. More likely those in charge simply believed that overwhelming firepower was the answer to any military problem, forgetting the biblical adage "some trust in chariots, and some in horses. . . . They are brought down and fallen."[19]

Giap taught as doctrine the need to be one with the nation's inhabitants, while foreign armies believed firepower to be sufficient to achieve their aims. Consequently they ignored or abused civilians who might well have ultimately supported them had they been treated differently. In this way France and America snubbed a host of potential Vietnamese allies, for not all of the populace favored the Communists. As a result, both nations finally bore the burden of the war all by themselves.

French and American generals believed their mission would be accomplished when they controlled the terrain. They came from nations where for generations (if not centuries) the military task was always to "control the high ground." Giap was not burdened with that tradition. He knew his primary goal was not to take and hold terrain but to gain the allegiance, or at the very least the grudging cooperation, of people of the countryside. When they were won over, along with them came the terrain, the wealth of the land, the whole existence of the nation. Giap knew that if he obtained popular loyalty and support and the French and Americans secured for themselves an overwhelming superiority in tanks, planes, artillery, and numbers of soldiers, the foreigners would still eventually fail.

French forays and American raids regularly endangered the lives of great numbers of civilians and made it impossible for them to conduct their livelihoods. As refugees, they were forced from their homes and swarmed into urban areas, a class disenchanted with the government over them, clamoring for relief and fertile ground for Communist propaganda. Trampled in combat by western conventional forces seeking to locate insurgent warriors, civilians endured plain-shirted hell as they tried to go about their daily lives—fields trampled, dikes ruined, crops wantonly poisoned or burned, harvest stores seized without compensation or replacement, homes burned, wells poisoned, animals slaughtered, wives and daughters raped, sons and husbands tortured and murdered as insurgent suspects. The unavoidable consequence of such an approach was suffering inflicted upon innocent (and sometimes not-so-innocent) bystanders and a consequent loss even of the possibility of securing their loyalty.[20]

It was easy in such circumstances for Giap, for his Viet Minh forces, and for their subsidiary organization in the south, the People's Revolutionary Party and its armed force, the National Liberation Front—usually referred to as the Viet Cong—to take the high moral ground. They proclaimed that they were saviors of the nation, protectors of human rights, and there was no rival native voice to compete effectively with them. It was easy for Giap to capitalize on resentments stirred up among countryside peasants when French troops or their African and Vietnamese auxiliaries stole someone's chickens or pigs or personal belongings, sometimes roughing up and having sport with wives or daughters in the process. It was not difficult for him to reach out to urban dwellers who were imprisoned or tortured for having the temerity to voice contrary opinions or who dared to attend clandestine political meetings. Giap believed that successful combat grew out of correct political views, that warfare without political foundations was just so much banditry, and that military leaders ignorant of political needs were only warlords.

When his soldiers were not immediately involved in battle preparations or combat, Giap used them in what that western master of insurgent doctrine Edward Lansdale later came to call "civic action." Soldiers manned shovels at rice-paddy dikes, replanted bamboo hedges which warded off the world from tiny hamlets, extended and strengthened irrigation ditches, helped to plant or fertilize or flood or harvest rice crops, and treated civilians injured in combat at military facilities. Successive foreign commanders, needing to turn the situation around quickly, found no help from local citizens. Giap's policies, including his emphasis on civic action, made that impossible. In return those civilians labored endlessly as coolies to transport for Giap the supplies his soldiers needed. They turned blank faces and mute voices toward interrogators who sought to learn Viet Minh secrets. They resisted those foreign invaders even at the cost of their lives.[21]

Giap claimed that, long ago, his nation accepted the concept of "people's wars" wherein combatants were united both militarily and politically. "The present offensive ideology of our party, armed forces, and people," he wrote, "is not disassociated from our traditional national military ideology. In our national history, generally speaking, the victorious uprisings and national liberation was led by [those] representing various processes of continuous offensive aimed at toppling the foreign feudal ruling yoke."[22]

To Madeleine Riffaud, a correspondent from L'Humanité, who interviewed him in 1968, Giap further developed his belief that the concept of people's wars was ancient. "It has existed," he said, "since mankind came into being and took shape, since they first became aware of their fundamental rights and rose up against the invader. In our most remote history, our ancestors were already saying: 'Our entire country is rising up against the invader.' " Giap used a historical example to illustrate his point. He reminded Riffaud of Nguyen Dinh Chieu, the blind poet of southern Viet Nam who wrote of "simple inhabitants of the villages who, out of love of the fatherland, have become volunteers." Everyone fought in a people's war, and Giap approvingly quoted Chieu's words about "weak and fragile women" who, because an enemy stood on the soil of their land, "rode horses, waved flags, rowed boats, loaded guns, destroyed citadels, scaled ramparts."[23]

For Giap, another man followed closely on the heels of those past national heroes—his mentor, Ho Chi Minh. "It may be rightly said that our army, which stems from the people, has been brought up according to the ideas and way of life of the Party and Uncle Ho," Giap wrote.[24] It was not military theory he learned from Ho, however, but prudence, practicality, persistence, and the need to meld political theory to military effort.[25]

Ho taught Giap that political unity was basic and must be achieved prior to beginning any military action. Ho insisted upon the necessity of safe base-area sanctuaries in case of military reverses. And he learned from Ho the need for perseverance. It was, Giap wrote, "A most valuable lesson for us before we went to the battlefront. That lesson was as [Ho] often said, 'Determination, determination, with determination one can do everything successfully.' "[26]

So also did Giap learn from Communist Party theorists, most importantly from Mao Tse-tung and Lenin. From Lenin, Giap came to understand that the goal toward which one strives is much more important than the means one uses to achieve it. Both followers and their welfare could be sacrificed without hesitation if by so doing one furthered the revolutionary struggle. So it was that Giap could willingly send thousands of his soldiers to their deaths so long as the nation moved closer to freeing itself from French and American soldiers who trampled its soil.[27]

Giap learned the value of the ideas of Karl von Clausewitz, who also insisted on the close relationship between politics and armed struggle. Giap "governed all his later campaigns by Clausewitz's basic thesis that the political object, as the original motive of war, should be the standard for determining the military objectives and the application of force to be used."[28]

Giap also studied carefully the writings of Mao Tse-tung, then the foremost philosopher of people's wars. Mao believed that all of life was governed by uniform and unchanging laws. To succeed, one had only to learn and understand those laws and to apply them. This was as true for military actions as it was for economic, political, or social endeavors. Giap could write, "Revolutionary armed struggle in any country has common fundamental laws. . . . characteristics and laws of its own."[29]

From Mao, Giap absorbed the importance of the individual in the revolutionary process. Mao wrote, "The people, and the people alone, are the motive force in the making of world history. . . . it is people, not things, that are decisive."[30] For Giap, then, constant psychological and political doctrinal reinforcement was essential if the individual parts of the "masses" were to be kept strong for the fight. "In general," says Giap, "there are two fundamental factors in war—people and weapons. Both are important, but the human factor is decisive. We had to build a new doctrine on the efficacy of few troops. We had to solve a fundamental problem of having only a few people and a small army. We were helped in this because of the basic idea that ours was a just war and had its own unique characteristics. Vietnamese military ideas are those of the people."

There were other points on which Giap agreed with Mao: the importance of establishing base and rear areas, the value of taking the initiative and the offensive, the uses of personal military experience, the necessity for concentrating a superior force on the battlefield, and the importance of the principle of economy of force.[31]

But Giap was more than a passive vessel ready to receive Mao's revolutionary waters. There were points on which he utterly disagreed with Mao, and at such times he discarded without regret what seemed to him to be arrant nonsense. Giap learned that assaults launched by moving waves of humanity—a tactic favored by Mao—were wasteful of resources, and he soon abandoned their use. Giap came to realize that the type of combat ordered needed to be based on existing field conditions rather than upon simple-minded adherence to predetermined doctrine.[32] In such ways Giap was as practical as Ho. He used what made sense and what was effective; he would not long be bound by someone else's theories when such ideas came into conflict with Giap's reality.

"How," Giap asked rhetorically, "to gain victory [over the French and later the Americans] with fewer troops? Victory goes to the most powerful. Yet our country was feudal. France, Japan, and the United States all came to Viet Nam; these three foreign nations were capitalistic with high industrial output at a time when Viet Nam was only in the handicraft stage of production. So we faced the factors of matériel, weapons, military means, and general logistics.

"We had to solve those problems. We had to learn how to use inferior means to achieve victory. We had to discover how to make poor logistics work to gain victory over our enemies. For sixty to seventy years, the Vietnamese people failed to resolve those issues. They were courageous, but that wasn't enough. Then we learned the secret method of a people's war. Thirty million people provided thirty million soldiers. Thus President Ho Chi Minh said when we began our resistance against the French, 'Who has a gun should use it; who has a knife, use it; who has not, use sticks and stones.' That is the essence of a people's war—they rose up to fight. Each had its own methods, each squad its own, each regiment had its own. But an entire nation stood up to fight for freedom and independence."[33]

Giap also had two other tutors. One was Napoleon. Although he never mentions that great French military leader in his writings, Giap did acknowledge his debt to him in a 1988 interview.[34] There was also Sun Tzu, a Chinese general and philosopher who lived from 400 to 320 B.C. A single quotation from Mao will be sufficient to show his own dependence upon Sun Tzu: "The enemy advances, we retreat; the enemy camps, we harass; the enemy tires, we attack; the enemy retreats, we pursue."[35]

To read a sampling of Sun Tzu's aphorisms immediately causes one to think of the approaches to armed conflict employed by Giap in the early years of his struggle with the French.[36] Although the similarity of Sun Tzu's doctrine to those developed by Giap is plain, when asked if he had been influenced by the aphorisms in *The Art of War*, Giap replied, "Sun Tzu has interesting ideas. I once studied him and found that he said that . . . if enemy forces are ten times larger, then we should not fight. If I had followed him we would still be in the jungle. We would never have gained victory over the French or Americans. Sun Tzu by himself would never be enough to show us how to do what we did."[37]

There was another most unlikely teacher. French officers who pitted their brains against Giap attributed his military talent not only to hard work but to constant study of geography and history. Among the works he read were the autobiographical writings of a military hero of World War I fame, T. E. Lawrence, who conducted daring exploits on behalf of Britain in Southwest Asia among the Arabs. A story circulated within the French officer corps that one day in 1946, prior to the Viet Minh expulsion from Ha Noi, Giap called on a French military officer and saw a book on the man's desk that interested him. "May I borrow the book?" the diminutive Vietnamese asked politely. "As soon as I have finished reading it myself," the Frenchman replied. The book was by T. E. Lawrence.[38]

In 1946, in a conversation with General Raoul Salan of France, Giap reportedly informed him, "My fighting gospel is T. E. Lawrence's *Seven Pillars of Wisdom.* I am never without it." And Salan himself said that Giap had been strongly influenced by Lawrence.[39]

Lawrence learned—and Giap learned from him—the importance of irregular warfare and how it can confound traditional-minded opponents. Surely such ideas were music to Giap's ears and offered his fertile mind much upon which to ponder.

In *The Evolution of a Revolt*, Lawrence stressed lessons learned from his campaigns that Giap must have appreciated.[40] "[R]ebellion must have an unassailable base," Lawrence wrote, "something guarded not merely from attack, but from the fear of it."[41] Rebellion must also, Lawrence continued, "have a sophisticated alien enemy, in the form of a disciplined army of occupation too small to fulfill the doctrine of acreage; too few to adjust number to space, in order to dominate the whole area effectively from fortified posts." No better definition could be given of the French situation in Indochina. Further, Lawrence noted, rebellion "must have a friendly population, not [necessarily] actively friendly, but sympathetic to the point of not betraying rebel movements to the enemy. Rebellions can be made by 2 per cent. active in a striking force and 98 per cent. passively sympathetic."[42] Was Lawrence writing about Arabs or Vietnamese in the midst of their efforts against the French?

Lawrence also said, "Granted mobility, security (in the form of denying targets to the enemy), time, and doctrine (the idea to convert every subject to friendliness), victory will rest with the insurgents, for the algebraical factors are in the end decisive, and against them perfections of means and spirit struggle quite in vain."[43] Given Giap's belief in the inevitability of history and in the absolute science of the military art, a passage like this would bring his immediate concurrence.[44]

Vo Nguyen Giap studied many influential men from the past and drew lessons from some. From them he learned the necessity for molding all his people into an active political base, the importance of political indoctrination of people and soldiers, and the use of protracted war to erode a stronger enemy's will.[45] He learned not only from people, but from events, from battles won or lost. And with each, his skill improved. From the August Revolution of 1945 he came to the concept "that the cities and rural areas are equally critical to the Vietnamese revolution. While rural base areas are important, cities can and must be liberated by a combination of uprising within and attack from without." His dealings with the French in 1945 and 1946 taught him that negotiations separated from military achievement seldom accomplished even minor goals. And in the use of military power he learned that the closest coordination was necessary between political and military action. Properly applied, the first became a "general uprising/insurrection," while military action became a "general offensive." A combination of the two resulted in massive upheavals capable of destroying an enemy and achieving sought-after goals.[46]

But let Giap speak for himself. In late 1988 he stated during an interview, "The origin of my military doctrine was: build on our tradition of fighting and resisting foreign invaders; heighten the power of the people to defeat new enemies through Marxist/Leninist consolidation and the establishment of the Vietnamese communist party; study and apply selected experiences of Napoleon and military men in allied countries—Russia and China—and in other countries." With a smile, he added, "I even applied some good ideas from U.S. doctrine."[47]

Giap became not only a worthy general, but an artist of war. He cleansed his brushes in the solvent of his own nation's history. He took a little paint from Le Loi, from Tran Hung Dao, from Sun Tzu, Napoleon, Lawrence, and others. He spread those colors on a canvas prepared with a background of party and people. He mixed primary colors to create brilliant secondary hues and shades of his own devising. The completed painting was entirely his own, a masterpiece of artistry.

TWELVE

"It Was
an Extremely Hard War"

During the combat lull between 1948 and 1950, Giap had opportunity to refine his own military leadership and to develop his fighting forces into something more than guerrilla bands. This timely development came about when,
in October 1949, Mao Tse-tung's Communists achieved victory in China's long
civil war, forcing Chiang Kai-shek's Nationalists to flee to the island of Formosa.
Mao immediately allowed the Viet Minh in the Viet Bac to use his southern
provinces as a sanctuary. Giap's military units could retreat there for prolonged
and advanced training in soldierly skills. In this way Giap managed to trans-
form his amateurish and adventurous troops into modern field units, armed,
through Mao's generosity, with up-to-date American weapons abandoned by
Chiang's soldiers as they fled helter-skelter toward the safety of their offshore
island.

Giap's men studied in Chinese schools learning to be effective noncommissioned and commissioned officers, memorizing skills needed to aim and fire
artillery pieces, to drive trucks and other vehicles, to link combat communication equipment. Under Chinese tutelage, Giap's soldiers discovered how to
operate as companies and battalions. Then he grouped his battalions into regiments composed of three or four battalions of six hundred men each. In late
1949 and early 1950, Giap ordered his regiments to group into fours, creating divisions of about twelve thousand men, and they practiced divisional-
sized movements. Satisfied at last with their performance, Giap established

four divisional headquarters in the Viet Bac—the 304th, 308th, 312th, and 316th Divisions—and one in northern Annam, the 320th. They would later be joined by the 351st Heavy Division, patterned after a Soviet artillery division. The 308th, known as the Iron Division, would come to rank as one of the military world's elite fighting forces. Men of those units even had uniforms, although both officers and men wore the same simple dress of thin green cotton without distinguishing badges of rank. Giap continued this practice until 1958.[1]

Giap spent much of his time planning the training of new recruits. Many, perhaps most, were illiterate peasants used to fertilizing fields and flooding rice paddies, not handling even simple weapons of war. Inasmuch as French activities in the Red River Delta in 1948 and 1949 caused Viet Minh recruiting to become ever more difficult, Giap called on the Communist Party to institute conscription. This went into effect on 4 November 1949 when both men and women aged eighteen and older became subject to the draft. For propaganda purposes, Giap knew the value of having an "all-volunteer force," so he did not often resort to conscripted levies, but it was a good club to cudgel the unwilling. In this way he was able to increase the number of his military units from thirty-two battalions in 1948 to 117 battalions in 1951.[2]

The training they achieved in southern China was important. Giap's growing army was composed of shy men, suspicious of authority, focused on the life of their own remote bamboo-hedged hamlets, unused to living or working with strangers. They were unlikely candidates for a national military force. They had grown to maturity believing in the old Vietnamese proverb "The authority of the emperor stops at the gate to the village." They had little notion of responsibility for or duty to a centralized governmental authority.

Giap knew he could not turn country bumpkins into national troops without providing them with enduring devotion and dedication to the revolution. He knew that, lacking a political education, they would melt away in the face of enemies armed with superior weapons. He had to forge their wills as well as their bodies. "Profound awareness of the aims of the Party," he wrote, "boundless loyalty to the cause of the nation and working class, and a spirit of unreserved sacrifice are fundamental questions for the army. . . . Therefore, the political work in its ranks is of first importance. *It is the soul of the army. . . .* [I]n the final analysis, victory in any war is determined by the willingness of the masses to shed blood on the battlefield."[3]

So Giap laid down orders for the political development of his troops. Well-laid plans required recruits to gather in groups and, encouraged by political officers, regale one another with tales of French persecution and the greed of absentee landlords. They recalled stories of Viet Nam's past military glories and legendary heroes. They described their own sufferings or those they had heard of from others. They extolled the virtues of being Vietnamese and denigrated outsiders. Traditional Vietnamese xenophobia made this particular task an easy one. They learned simple jokes, slogans, and songs which grew dear with repetition. Superiors promised them a responsible place in the new society to emerge following the withdrawal of a beaten French soldiery. Over and again they heard impassioned cries that victory was certain.

Familiar with the other two in these three-man groups, recruits soon transferred loyalty from family to fellows. As they came to know and sometimes to love one another, they realized how similar groups in their unit were all part of a new extended family dedicated to war, to victory, to people of the land, and to the nation. These cells met daily to discuss activities, to praise and criticize performance, to share dark secrets they harbored of ambition or vainglory or desertion or malingering—and to receive the encouragement of their brothers, or, perhaps more realistically, sometimes to be turned in to a political commissar for the sin of wrong-thinking, allowing the commissar to counsel the reluctant or recalcitrant into more perfect sacrifice and devotion. No single recruit ever knew when one of his "buddies" might turn him in for antirevolutionary thoughts or deeds.

Conversations among groups of three were regularly enhanced by larger group meetings when all men of a company attended required meetings, there to criticize their own performance and that of their fellows and officers. Perhaps the most valuable result of such sessions was that no one was spared, not even officers, and all came to believe they were valuable and worthwhile members of a unit and part of the decision-making process, from the commander to the lowliest private. Particularly for boys from remote areas, it was a heady experience and made them value their new associations and goals even more highly.

Giap's reworking of his men's psychological orientation provided him with soldiers who knew their role within the military, within society, and within the revolution. Consequently, Giap's troops—unlike the ragtag followers of warlords in south China and elsewhere in the Orient—did not treat civilian populations as sources of rapine, pillage, and plunder. The Viet Minh counted themselves as one with their civilian brothers and sisters. Each had a different role, but all were partners in the fight against the French. Giap could hardly have asked for more.[4]

During the 1948–50 hiatus with the French, in efforts to establish proper command and control procedures over ever larger units, Giap laid plans to reorganize his general staff. Previously his advisers had focused their attention and planning almost entirely on guerrilla actions. Western armies considered such planning to fall under the heading of "operations," and they were the responsibility of the G-3 of a military unit. In 1950, Giap set up his own staff on the western model: G-1 (personnel), G-2 (intelligence matters), G-3 (operations), and G-4 (logistics).[5]

Giap also established military regions—called "integrated zones" or "interzones"—covering all Viet Nam, which enabled him to retain control over his widely dispersed forces. Each interzone was directed by a combined military and political headquarters, and the interzone itself was further divided into interprovinces and intervillages, thus giving Giap vertical control over the entire revolutionary military effort. Six interzones covered Viet Nam: (1) northwest Tonkin, (2) northeast Tonkin, (3) the delta of the Red River, (4) northern Annam, (5) southern Annam, (6) Cochin China.

Giap further divided the country into free zones, occupied zones, and guerrilla zones. Free zones included (1) the Viet Bac, (2) the estuary areas of northern Annam, (3) coastal areas of Annam south of Hue, (4) the Plain of Reeds, (5) the Ca Mau peninsula of the far south. Guerrilla zones were (1) the Mekong Delta, (2) the Red River Delta, (3) central Annam's coast, (4) the central plateau of the Annamese Cordillera. Occupied areas were listed: (1) the urban areas of Saigon, Hue, Haiphong, and Ha Noi, (2) Cochin China's extensive rubber plantations, (3) certain areas of the lower Mekong River Delta. Such divisions helped Giap see more clearly the problems he faced and to plan appropriate actions suited to individual areas.[6]

Despite such chartings, it was difficult for Giap and those in his headquarters to remain in constant touch with revolutionary forces in Cochin China and other far locations. Land distances were great and travel difficult. The French carefully watched bus and train travel. Even automobile trips had their hazards. Giap often relied on radio traffic to remain in contact with far-flung subordinates, but such efforts ran the risk of triangulation by French listening posts and was unreliable even in the best of times. To these difficulties were added jealousies, petty competitions, and traditional suspicions between the north and south. Mountain boys of the north often described southerners as "fish eaters," while those from lower latitudes dismissed their Tonkinese compatriots as "northern dogs." It is little wonder that southern leaders of the revolution, supposedly under the supervision and control of Giap, began to act with a certain autonomy.[7]

Now that he had sufficient men to constitute a real army, Giap's primary worry was to discover a way to equip and supply them. Giap's manner of meeting these difficulties showed him to be one of the great logistics generals of all time. He had to build his main force units into a permanent army without losing any of their now well developed jungle-fighting skills. He was thankful that during the evacuation from Ha Noi he had ordered every movable piece of machinery capable of being used to produce weapons to be stripped from the doomed city and carried into the Viet Bac. Under the direction of an engineer, Tran Dai Nghia, who had returned from France with Ho, those machines were taken to safe hiding places deep within the "Greenhouse." There they were reassembled and put back into production, eventually producing some light- and medium-caliber weapons, including light machine guns, a few 120mm mortars, and mines, grenades, and a great deal of rifle ammunition.[8]

While such weapons might keep the French out of the Viet Bac, they were completely insufficient to force battle on the *colons* or to drive them from their own heavily fortified positions. What Giap needed was heavy weapons, and those he did not get until after Mao's victory over the Kuomintang and his subsequent willingness to help arm the Viet Minh. Even then, aid came slowly. In 1951, Giap's units received fewer than twenty tons per month from Chinese supply depots. By the next year, that pipeline brought him 250 tons per month. In 1953, he received 600 tons every thirty days, and by early 1954, 1,500 tons. By June 1954, Giap's supply lines channeled 4,000 tons per month into Viet Nam from China.[9]

Receiving supplies was one thing. Distributing them was quite another. Trucks could handily perform that task, and so, by 1954, Giap had received over one thousand Russian-built Moltova trucks from China, but they were useless in the vast wilderness of the Viet Bac, where there were no roads. Giap consequently directed the construction of new routes within his northern free zone, and he assigned vast multitudes to build them. As long as the French maintained a hold on their border outposts along the Chinese border, however, those new roads in the Viet Bac could not be linked to existing routes in south China. While trucks might one day be of great help, they were not going to solve Giap's immediate distribution problems.

He turned to a more practical solution and was grateful that he had been turning this matter over in his mind since the dark days of the early 1940s when Japanese occupation troops held sway in Viet Nam. As Giap's military forces of all types approached 300,000 in number, he determined, given the rough state of more modern transportation within the Viet Bac, that his soldiers could only be supplied through the use of porters. He calculated that he would need at least a million coolies to do the job properly, but not all of them would have to remain constantly mobilized. Most could remain in their hamlets engaged in their usual civilian activities until such times as they were needed. Only a few hundred thousand were needed as permanent laborers for his headquarters and main force units during those times when there was no active fighting going on between French and Viet Minh troops. The entire force would be required only during times of maneuver and combat with the French. On those occasions, in relays, they would pass supplies through their own area to the next, where still other coolies would carry them closer to their destination—a human labor chain, but one which Giap had available in countless numbers. As they moved repeatedly over the same routes, coolies learned the best way to transport the most supplies in the least possible time. Using them, however, had its own set of problems. They had to be recruited, organized, controlled, and fed. And they were voracious, sometimes consuming as much as 90 percent of the food they carried.[10]

Under Giap's leadership, his supply officers calculated optimal loads for coolies to carry. One man could shoulder fifty-five pounds of rice or thirty-three to forty-four pounds of arms and ammunition; he could carry the load over 15.5 miles of easy country during hours of daylight, or 12.4 miles at night. Another could bear thirty-eight pounds of rice or twenty-two to thirty-three pounds of ammunition and carry the load about 9 miles across mountainous country in one day or 7.5 miles by night. Where trails existed, a buffalo cart could be loaded with 770 pounds of material and transport them 7.5 miles each day. Horses were weaker than native water buffaloes but faster. A horse cart could carry 473 pounds up to 12.4 miles per day. In such ways, without modern means, Giap reduced everything to primitive measures, divided his needs into individual parcels moved by human and animal labor, and still supplied the ever growing appetite of his army.[11]

Giap occupied himself with thoughts of strategy and tactics, of logistics and training during 1948 and the first months of 1949. Still the French did nothing decisive to rid themselves of the Viet Minh menace to their hold on Indochina. Then in May 1949, the French government sent General Georges Revers, chief of the army general staff, on an inspection trip to assess the situation in Viet Nam and to make recommendations to end difficulties there. Many of his conclusions were obvious ones: evacuate isolated outposts strung along the Chinese border, enlarge and strengthen Vietnamese auxiliary forces, pacify the northern delta region, ask the United States for more military aid. Revers's last recommendation, however, departed from past approaches used by the French: subordinate military actions to diplomatic negotiations with the Viet Minh.[12]

Both politicians at home and French military leaders in Viet Nam gave short shrift to Revers's proposals. Those in France saw them as leading to the loss of valuable resources—rice, rubber, and tin. High military officers saw them as an admission that their own policies had not worked, and this they were unwilling to admit. As American leaders would later do also, they had been informing the home government that conditions in Viet Nam were improving. To admit now that they had underestimated Giap and his minions would be a public embarrassment, something they were unable and unwilling to accept.[13]

Military men were further convinced of their own rectitude during April, May, and June 1949 when Giap's forces launched several attacks on small French outposts along the northern border with China and failed to overrun them. They saw this as an indication of an improving situation, but in fact, Giap had not intended to take control of the area. He was simply keeping his troops in trim and the French on guard.

For years the Paris government and the French military failed to recognize that their time as overlords of Viet Nam was coming to an end. A long succession of French commanders were sent to Viet Nam to stem the revolutionary tide there. Between 1945 and 1954, eight men struggled to salvage French fortunes: General Jacques Philippe Leclerc served from 1946 to 20 February 1947, when he was replaced by Lieutenant General Jean Valluy, who was replaced in 1948 by Lieutenant General Roger Blaizot, who was replaced in September 1949 by Lieutenant General Marcel Carpentier, who abdicated his duties while there to General Marcel Alessandri. Carpentier was replaced in December 1950 by General Jean de Lattre de Tassigny, who became ill with cancer and was replaced on 20 November 1951 by General Raoul Salan, who in turn was replaced in May 1953 by General Henri-Eugène Navarre, to whom Giap gave the final *coup de grâce.*

In September 1949 the French government sent Lieutenant General Marcel Maurice Carpentier to Indochina. When promoted to captain in March 1915 during the Great War, he became the youngest man in the French army to hold that rank. Intervening years brought him constant promotions. Now the home ministry would for a time lay its hopes on him to win victory over the Viet Minh.[14]

Vastly ignorant of affairs in Indochina, Carpentier was wise enough to recognize that fact and sufficiently humble to do something about it. He turned his field command over to Major General Marcel Alessandri, an officer with years of experience in Viet Nam. He was the man who, following the 9 March 1945 Japanese coup, had marched some of his French soldiers out of Viet Nam to safety in China. Frustrated by previous commanders who had ignored his suggestions and countermanded his orders, Alessandri now found himself working for an officer willing to give him necessary backing to put into effect some of his ideas. He immediately began efforts to pacify the native population of the Tonkinese delta area.

Giap's response was quick. He kept his main force units in reserve in the Viet Bac but ordered guerrillas into action in the delta of the Red River to thwart Alessandri's work. Giap described what happened. "Our units operated in small pockets with independent companies penetrating deeply into the enemy-controlled zone to launch guerrilla warfare, establish bases, and protect local people's power. It was an extremely hard war generalized in all domains: military, economic, and political. The enemy mopped up; we fought against mopping up. They organized supplementary local Vietnamese troops and installed puppet authorities; we firmly upheld local people's power, overthrew straw men, eliminated traitors and carried out active propaganda."[15]

Alessandri's "clear and hold" tactics and his "mopping-up" operations, despite Giap's efforts, worked magnificently. The French general, for all intents and purposes, seized the whole of the delta area and did it on a shoestring. He had only twenty battalions with which to work. He began taking what was nearest—provinces, rice paddies, people. Section by section, his efforts spread outward, put into effect by from three to five French battalions at a time. These operations had names—Pomone, Diane, Ondine, and others—and in each one the French moved closer to success. Soldiers moved out, sometimes by airdrop, or marching overland, or even riding in naval LCTs (landing craft, tanks), operable on deeper rivers. With patience and tenacity, they killed guerrillas when they could find them, built forts, and recruited partisans from the Tonkinese population.

This was not as hard for Alessandri as Giap might have hoped. Giap had done his calculated best in 1945, 1946, and 1947 to wipe out all rivals who might prove dangerous to the Viet Minh cause. Those who survived the annihilation of the DMH and VNQDD maintained themselves in secret societies of the Asian kind. They did not spring from the population mass and did not love their fellow Viets as the Viet Minh professed to do, but some were still outstanding men, imbued with the Confucian moral order and mandarin traditions. Now they gladly accepted French control of the northern delta and hoped to exact revenge upon the Viet Minh, but there were only a handful of them left, not enough for Alessandri's purposes.

So the French general turned to Tonkinese Roman Catholics, more than a million of them, all fanatical in devotion to their faith. Every village had a church. The local Vietnamese curé was the manorial lord and parishioners his serfs. Peasants on the land were dominated by Asian-born priests and nuns. Within their own fiefdoms they were supreme, yet they knew the rest of the nation despised them for their western religion. They had rejected old ways and, in the nineteenth century, allowed the French to enter the land and carry out their conquest. They were chosen by God and rejected by their race. It was an uncomfortable dichotomy.

In 1945, in an attempt to heal that division, Roman Catholics eagerly embraced the new revolutionary nationalism and gladly cooperated with Ho Chi Minh and his party. But Ho wanted to establish a national church, separate from Rome, so that no one under his rule could have divided loyalties. This confronted Roman Catholics with a quandary: their faith or their nation? They chose to fix on their beliefs and to become opponents of the new Viet Minh way. Alessandri recruited them in wholesale fashion, gave them money and weapons, and allowed them to control the northern delta countryside. In this way Vietnamese Roman Catholics who in 1945 had sought to rid their country of colonial domination forever now found themselves once again the tools of French interests. Roman Catholics, nearly a fifth of the Tonkinese population, spurred on by Alessandri, came into permanent conflict with the Viet Minh. Throughout 1949 and 1950, nearly every Roman Catholic hamlet formed its own militia and turned its bamboo-hedged settlement into a fortress governed by the local curé.[16]

Alessandri also mounted a rice war against the Viet Minh. Rice was all-important in Giap's plans, for in the absence of normal economic exchange, it became the only Viet Minh currency and the basis for Ho Chi Minh's entire economic system. People paid taxes in rice, exchanged goods and services for rice, received salaries paid in rice, even offered "patriotic loans" to the Viet Minh government in rice. Government budgets were computed in kilograms of rice, soldiers and civil servants received rice as payment of their salaries. Rice harvests were sacred, for without them the whole revolutionary movement would fail. Thus at harvest time Giap allowed coolies, guerrillas, and main force unit members to go home to labor in fields and on threshing floors. Without such forbearance, famine might stalk the land again, and no revolutionary leader could allow that to happen. By 1950, because of Alessandri's successes, the Viet Minh became extremely apprehensive about its rice supplies. The French had seized vast amounts of that white treasure, mounting guards over the acres that produced it. Giap could maintain full-scale rations only for members of his army; for the rest, one bowl a day would have to suffice.[17]

Alessandri's efforts failed for three reasons. His military superiors ultimately shunted him off again to one side. Mao's willingness to aid the Viet Minh and to supply at least their minimal needs canceled out successes Alessandri achieved in the rice war. Finally, even Alessandri made little progress in persuading influential Tonkinese that he had their interests at heart. Davidson has said it best: "To the French, the native masses of the Delta were chattel pawns, inanimate objects, prizes to be fought for and used as soldiers, sources of revenue, and always, as rice producers. [But] [t]he French made no effort to spread their own values and doctrines to the people and areas they conquered, *which is understandable, since they had nothing worth propagating.*"[18]

Giap's political position within the Communist Party was not as unchallenged as his military one. During those days of contest with Alessandri, much of his attention was diverted from military planning to bolstering his place within the hierarchy. According to witnesses of that time, Giap was an able, sincere, articulate, and brilliant man with great strength of character and willpower. He possessed great charm of manner and was a quiet and gracious host, but was also a man of action with a violent temper who could be ruthless when he deemed it necessary. He needed all those attributes to deal successfully with a friend who came to mix ideology and personal rivalry into a blood feud.

Truong Chinh had been a close friend of Giap's since the early 1930s. During that decade they cooperated to produce their jointly authored book, *The Peasant Question.* Later they worked closely and harmoniously at the newspaper offices of *Le Travail* in Ha Noi prior to the outbreak of World War II. Truong Chinh frequently visited Giap's home near Lycée Thang Long.

Yet the two men were very much opposites. Although they physically resembled each other, their intellectual approach to life's problems was vastly different. Giap was a man of extensive culture, gifted with an encyclopedic intelligence, a product of the university. He was the only member of the Politburo with an advanced, essentially western intellectual background. He did not always concern himself about details. He was enthusiastic, emotional, and dramatic. He was a partisan and advocate of spectacular and imaginative actions, with little regard for resultant consequences or losses. He was usually a direct man and, when angry, prone to say whatever was on his mind. Giap was very sensitive with respect to matters affecting his own prestige, and receptive to compliments and flattery while resentful of criticism. As he gained authority within the Viet Minh movement, and particularly after he became head of the army, Giap resisted all attempts to place any controls upon his command.

Truong Chinh, on the other hand, was the son of a mandarin and a scholar of the Sino-Vietnamse school. He was devoted to the teachings of Mao Tse-tung and had a great intellectual and emotional investment in the Communist struggle for control of China. His very choice for a pseudonym—"Long March"—indicated the deep respect he held for Mao. A cold, doctrinal, deliberate, well-organized, and meticulous individual, he left nothing to chance. He countered his opponents within the party through a system of "accumulation"— carefully noting errors others committed and "holding his cards" until the most favorable moment. For him, sentiment did not exist. In one area, however, both Truong Chinh and Giap were identical. Both were "men of blood," used to liquidating their opponents. They would have numerous encounters over the years.[19]

After Giap's return to Viet Nam from China in 1940, the two men worked well together in the Viet Bac, driven by their common goal of freeing their land. In the years following the August Revolution of 1945, however, their friendship and alliance waned. While Giap focused on military matters, Truong Chinh spent his own energies on political work and built up an important following within the Communist Party he served as secretary-general.

Toward the end of March 1946, when Ho promoted Giap to the rank of general and made him commander in chief of the army, Truong Chinh sensed that Giap's power might outstrip his own. Claiming that Giap was insufficiently competent for such high posts, Truong Chinh succeeded in placing General Nguyen Son as Giap's chief of staff. Son was the only Vietnamese Communist officer with professional military training, having attended the Moscow Military Academy. He was also a dedicated Communist and, like Truong Chinh, a sinophile, having commanded a Chinese Communist regiment during Mao's Long March. Giap responded by cultivating the man and making him one of his own disciples.[20]

Giap found an opportunity to retaliate against his former friend in 1947 when Truong Chinh published a treatise on guerrilla warfare, *The Resistance Will Win.* Truong Chinh had plagiarized this writing almost directly from the works of Mao Tse-tung, and Giap publicly criticized his former friend. Perhaps as a result, Truong Chinh redoubled his own efforts to impose party control upon the army, and because of his large following, Giap was eventually obliged to make important concessions, reluctantly agreeing to allow Truong Chinh to place political commissars, under his own sole and direct control, within Giap's army. In 1949, over Giap's objections, he managed to give those military commissars even more power when he placed one of his most reliable men, General Van Tien Dung, at the head of the army's political office.[21]

Following Mao's takeover of China, it was natural for Truong Chinh to move into the leadership of the extreme pro-Chinese faction of Vietnamese Communist politics, and he urged that the Viet Minh ask for Chinese advisers and "volunteers" to help in the fighting against the French. While Giap was deeply grateful for Mao's help, he did not feel it necessary to emulate Mao's approaches in all matters and indeed was deeply suspicious of Chinese intentions. Giap declared that under no circumstances would they be allowed to fight in Viet Nam. China supplied arms, even some specialists and advisers, but its participation remained clandestine. So the two Vietnamese leaders clashed and their diverse positions pulled the party in two directions.

And Giap found those around him dying sudden deaths. Colonel Mukayama was killed in December 1947 at Cho Chu during a battle with French paratroopers. General Nguyen Son died from a bullet in the back after organizing the giant Viet Minh ambush of the Cao Bang/Lang Son garrison that ended in disaster for the French army. So Giap turned to Truong Chinh's man, General Van Tien Dung, and made of him a protégé of his own. Because of their close contact under battlefield conditions, the two men gradually became friends and close allies. This hardly pleased Truong Chinh.[22]

In the midst of this estrangement, eager to weaken Giap in any way he could, Chinh mounted a major political campaign against him in 1950. He repeatedly accused Giap of breaches of security in choosing those who worked for him, and he pilloried those unreliable subordinates. Later that year, Chinh ordered the execution of Giap's chief of logistical services, Tran Chi Chau, for alleged failings in carrying out his responsibilities. Giap was unable to stop this movement or to save his subordinate. He recognized the effort for what it was, an assault on his own power and influence. It took all of Ho Chi Minh's and Pham Van Dong's authority to avoid a major public split in the Communist leadership. Giap was able to maintain his place primarily because of Ho Chi Minh's support, despite the jealousies of Truong Chinh and his allies. Giap also pledged to himself that a time to exact retribution would one day come, and he was content to wait. Perhaps he was aware of the old Arabic proverb "Revenge is a dish that tastes best when eaten cold."[23]

In 1950, Giap finally decided to risk battle with the French. He believed his forces were ready for him to risk a change from primarily guerrilla activity to main force mobile warfare. "It is very difficult," he once said, "to say at what date we switched from guerrilla to mobile warfare since there is actually no mechanical demarcation between the two periods [but] [i]n 1950 we launched our first major campaign involving brigades. . . . The frontier liberation campaign in 1950 may be regarded as a cornerstone marking the growth of mobile warfare."[24]

As part of his preparations for this campaign, Giap renamed his old Armed Propaganda and Liberation Brigade, now calling it Brigade 209. With it and a newer Brigade (later Division) 308, he ordered operations against the French to begin. (See map "French Border Posts.") Giap's opening moves included ordering intensified military activity along Route Coloniale 4 between Cao Bang—a provincial capital near his own base in the Viet Bac—and Lang Son. French installations along Route 4—Cao Bang, Dong Khe, and That Khe, all at least three hundred miles from the French main occupation center—now came under risk, and perhaps needlessly so. For as early as May 1949, General Georges Revers, chief of the French general staff, had recommended that these isolated garrisons be evacuated. They were, Revers concluded, "a drain on French resources and could probably not withstand a serious attack."[25]

Just as he had done in April, May, and June of 1949, so now also in March and April of 1950 Giap ordered probing attacks made on isolated French garrisons. Some of them were either overrun or so threatened that the French saw fit to abandon them. "Our sections became companies, and we became strong enough to attack French garrisons," Giap said. "We gave battle only when it was profitable to us." Small units had but two rules—to give no rest to the enemy and to build up their own strength while pitting themselves against the French. Companies became battalions; battalions became regiments; regiments became divisions—and the process reversed itself when necessary. Then Giap broke off his attacks and spent the summer months planning for a fall offensive. He intended it to be a real test of strength.[26]

Dong Khe lay a little less than midway between Cao Bang and That Khe along Route Coloniale 4 in the northeast border of the Viet Bac. Giap decided to cut the road by taking and holding Dong Khe, thus severing and isolating Cao Bang from its links with That Khe. In this way, the French, distant from their own reinforcements, would discover that there were too many enemy soldiers and too few of their own to continue holding fortified military posts along Route

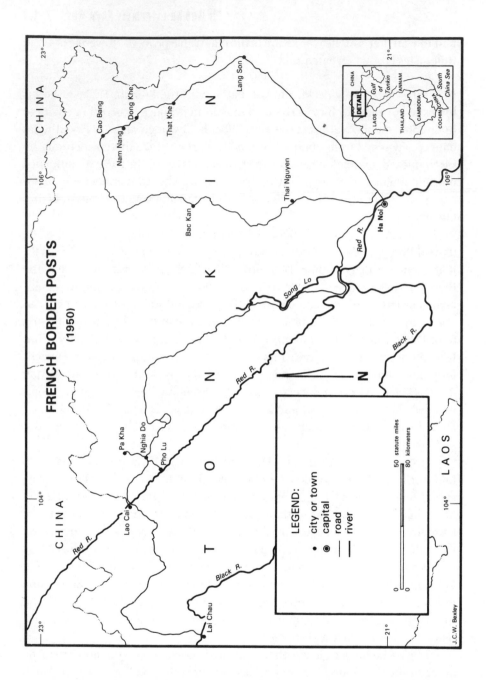

FRENCH BORDER POSTS
(1950)

LEGEND:

• city or town

◉ capital

— road

— river

50 statute miles
80 kilometers

CHINA

CHINA

LAOS

Cao Bang
Nam Nang
Dong Khe
That Khe
Lang Son
Thai Nguyen
Bac Kan
Ha Noi
Red R.
Song Lo
Black R.
Pa Kha
Nghia Do
Pho Lu
Red R.
Lao Cai
Black R.
Lai Chau

T O N K I N

DETAIL
CHINA
Gulf of Tonkin
LAOS
THAILAND
ANNAM
CAMBODIA
COCHINCHINA
South China Sea

J.C.W. Bexley

4. Giap called his plan Operation Le Hong Phong. It would be a test for his newly trained and armed divisions.

On 1 October 1950, taking advantage of prevalent ground mists in the late wet season to conceal their advance, Giap ordered his minions to move against Dong Khe. Restricted in lateral movement, unable to call on sufficient support from the south, and isolated by miles of jungle from other French positions, defenders at Dong Khe had little chance. They found themselves the target of Giap's new artillery batteries and fell prey to the first artillery duel of the Indochina War.

To the north of Dong Khe, the French commander at Cao Bang had ignored orders received earlier instructing him to destroy all his equipment and force-march his troops to Dong Khe. Meanwhile, a colonial Moroccan unit of 3,500 men was fighting its way north from That Khe to Dong Khe, intending to retake it long enough for the Cao Bang force to link up with it. It was 3 October before the garrison commander at Cao Bang decided to follow his orders, and even then he did so halfheartedly.

Told to leave his equipment and make the move on foot, the Cao Bang commander instead loaded his personnel into trucks and took with him his artillery pieces as well. In this way 2,600 soldiers and 500 civilians began their move to Dong Khe. Their route to safety stretched out over some eighty miles of mountainous terrain, ideal country for guerrilla ambushes of road-bound convoys. Giap's main force units did not disappoint the grimly determined French party.

Decimated on the way by repeated ambushes and assaults, forced to burn their trucks and supplies, finally abandoning even their artillery pieces, footweary colonial soldiers of the French empire pressed south in their effort to link up with the Moroccans at Dong Khe. Three days of savage fighting passed before they joined forces. Hot on their trail came more of Giap's Communist troops. In an effort to salvage the situation, three French paratroop battalions jumped into the fray—and disappeared as quickly as sparks drifting upward from a fire. Outnumbered three to one, finally faced with hand-to-hand fighting, all French forces were destroyed near Dong Khe on 7 October.

When the sound of the last shot faded away, the French had lost more than 6,000 soldiers, thirteen artillery pieces, 125 mortars, three platoons of tanks, 450 trucks, 940 machine guns, 1,200 submachine guns, and over 8,000 rifles—sufficient booty to equip one of Giap's newly formed divisions. The French might have held on to their key fort at Lang Son, just a little south of That Khe, but they panicked and abandoned it also. It was the greatest single defeat yet suffered by the French in the history of their colonial warfare—worse than the death of Montcalm on the Plains of Abraham during the siege of Quebec in 1759. The shock to French military officials may well have been more severe than it was four years later when their fortress at Dien Bien Phu fell to Giap's determined attacks. Things seemed so bad that Carpentier gave orders to evacuate Ha Noi, but the French government countermanded him and replaced the bewildered general.[27]

By his success, Giap now ruled the northern frontier. He had secure supply lines stretching into China. His engineers could now link roads within the Viet Bac to those in southern Chinese provinces. The war with the French would continue for three and a-half more years, but never again would they have an undoubted advantage. The Viet Minh now held the initiative.

General Jean de Lattre de Tassigny assumed command from Carpentier on 17 December 1950, charged with saving Indochina for the French empire. De Lattre believed he could do so. In an attempt to forestall Giap's forces, nibbling away at his major outposts, the new commander established his famous *ceinture* ("belt") of forts and blockhouses to defend the triangular wedge of the Ha Noi–Haiphong delta. He built no fewer than 900 forts and 2,200 pillboxes, well-fortified concrete bunkers to dominate the high places of the country and control the rebels. Laborers expended enormous effort to construct them. The project tied down 80,000 French troops and huge stockpiles of equipment. They poured 51 million cubic yards of concrete to build encapsulated bunkers normally housing nine privates and a sergeant, who spent their time peering through machine-gun slots, waiting for an attack. Viet Minh fighters maneuvered around such bunkers like water through rocks.[28] These forts still sit on the landscape, empty and pathetic, tragic reminders of false French hopes.

De Lattre also mobilized French civilians for guard duty, releasing garrison troops for combat. He refused to evacuate women and children living in Indochina, sending home empty the ship, *Le Pasteur*, that had come to carry them back to France. "As long as the women and children are here," de Lattre said, "the men won't dare let go."[29]

Pleased with his successes, itching for a fight, a cocky Giap endeavored to take immediate advantage of his victories along Route Coloniale 4. He threw himself into planning a campaign of set-piece battles that would give him control of the Red River Delta. In those campaigns he overstepped his limits and suffered successive reverses. His actions exposed one of his primary faults. He was a quick shooter, convinced that the unaided and unconquerable will of his men could overcome a superior force. Yet since mid-1950 the United States had supplied France with an abundance of high-firepower weaponry. Giap should have known better, yet he ordered his troops into the brunt of it. He would do this time and again, during both the French and American phases of the war; in 1951, 1962, 1965, 1968, and 1972. The bush still had lessons to offer this former history teacher.

THIRTEEN

"We Had to Cross Thirty Streams"

An optimistic Vo Nguyen Giap believed that now, at the start of 1951, the way to Ha Noi lay open. He was encouraged in this by his Chinese advisers, who had accompanied the aid given Giap by their government. By late 1950 these advisers, enthusiastic about the success they had achieved in Korea by human-wave attacks against their American foes, argued for similar tactics to be used against the French in Viet Nam. This strategy had worked on the northern border, where the French were dispersed and had few inner lines of communication or transport. Giap's decision to accept this viewpoint propelled him and his forces into an ill-fated campaign.

Giap listened, concurred, exaggerated the strength Chinese aid had given his army, underestimated the mobility and power of opposing French forces, and gave his orders. His soldiers then launched the first of three ill-fated campaigns against the paratroopers, Foreign Legionnaires, Moroccans, and Vietnamese auxiliary soldiers commanded by de Lattre: a strike at the town of Vinh Yen, located some thirty miles northwest of Ha Noi. It would be necessary to drive the French from their fortified positions at Vinh Yen before Giap's soldiers could push on toward the capital. Fortified by their leader's confidence, many of Giap's troops claimed they would enter Ha Noi even before the lunar New Year of Tet, just weeks away.

Preparations for the campaign gave Giap opportunity to practice his logistics skills. In earlier northern border campaigns, to support only five regiments operating in ideal terrain, he had spent at least three months mobilizing people and stockpiling resources prior to striking out against an isolated enemy. Now, preparing for a multidivisional assault on the compact and open terrain of the Red River Delta, he failed to mobilize the population into regional support forces. Such guerrilla operations might have kept the French from concentrating either their firepower or their troops.

Perhaps Giap believed his army had evolved to the point where it no longer needed support from guerrilla units. Discipline, Chinese-supplied weapons, and courage might be all that was necessary. He did, however, order stockpiles to be set up along his route of march. In an unbelievable effort, northern coolies laboriously carried into place the arms, ammunition, food, and medical supplies necessary to sustain his main force units as they struck at the French defenders of Vinh Yen. Giap insisted that his soldiers needed five thousand tons of rice, ammunition, and other supplies; moving them into position absorbed two million man-days of coolie labor. Giap then ordered his men into position. The bulk of his main-force units—sixty-one battalions of infantry, twelve heavy weapons battalions, and eight engineer battalions—were now about to face the French in combat.[1]

At 5:00 P.M. on 17 January 1951, Giap ordered his 308th and 312th Divisions into battle. Supported by heavy mortars and heavy machine guns, one division made successive ground attacks against four hills to the north and east of the town, but to no avail. Despite Chinese aid, Giap's men lacked the firepower, organization, and popular support necessary to overrun their enemies. The French reinforced the *groupement mobile* or mobile group defending Vinh Yen with two other such units. These composite units resembled U.S. Army regimental combat teams of World War II. In addition, planes dropped napalm, brought into Haiphong harbor a few days earlier by American shipping, on Giap's troops. The napalm and concentrated artillery fire caused savage casualties among Giap's soldiers. By noon on 18 January, unable to punch through French defenses, Giap ordered his troops to withdraw. Despite his best efforts, French defenders had repulsed Giap's divisions and retained control of Vinh Yen. (For the sites of this and later battles, see map "Day River and Surrounding Area.")

When the smoke cleared, Giap realized he had suffered a massive setback. Of his two divisions, six thousand were dead, five hundred were prisoners of war, and eight thousand were wounded. The majority of his casualties came from French napalm attacks. In four years of fighting, this was Giap's first—but not his last—major reversal.[2]

Somehow Giap believed it had all been a mistake. He knew that if he hit the French again he could win through to Ha Noi. Unwilling to admit defeat, Giap decided to break through French defenses around the delta of the Red River from another direction. On 23 March 1951, Giap ordered three of his infantry divisions

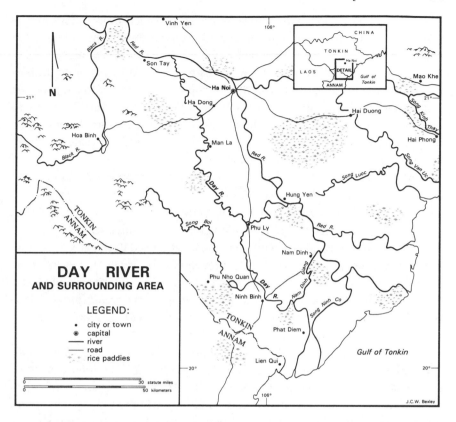

DAY RIVER
AND SURROUNDING AREA

LEGEND:
- • city or town
- ◉ capital
- —— river
- —— road
- ⸫· rice paddies

into action on the eastern edge of the French-controlled delta. They were to drive toward Haiphong and break through the *colons'* eastern defenses. They got as far as Mao Khe, fifteen miles north-northeast of Haiphong, before a series of French outposts surrounding the town brought them to a halt. After eight days of fruitless attempts, Giap called off the attack. He had lost another three thousand men, this time not to air strikes but to the French navy, whose riverine craft operating on inland waters prevented the Viet Minh from penetrating Mao Khe.[3]

A still-optimistic Giap then decided to drive along the western edge of the delta in an effort to force the French out of the Red River area along the southern flank of the delta. Giap's plan was simple. On 29 May 1951 he ordered his army across the Day River, where his 304th Division attacked Phu Ly, the 398th assaulted Ninh Binh, and the 320th struck at Phat Diem. As these three divisions hit their targets, two regiments, which had previously infiltrated the area, attacked from within.

Once again Giap demonstrated his mastery of movement and logistics. Two of those divisions traveled some 150 miles overland without being detected by the waiting French. Supporting logistics efforts required the labor of 100,000 coolies.

Giap's choice of location for the battle was, however, unfortunate, for the two armies met in an open region, which allowed the French once again to use napalm air strikes to great advantage. After some initial Viet Minh successes, the French commander swiftly threw three groupements mobiles into the battle. In addition, he assigned four artillery groups, one armored group, and the 7th Bataillon de Parachutistes Coloniaux, or Colonial Parachute Battalion, to the fray. The French also had the advantage of their Naval Infantry River Flotilla, the name recently changed to Divisions Navales d'Assaut, or Naval Assault Divisions (abbreviated in French as Dinassauts).

Although the Viet Minh gained several bridgeheads on the east bank of the Day River, the skill of the Dinassauts and the determination of the French defenders, particularly at Ninh Binh (where General de Lattre's son was killed in the fighting), prevented them from making appreciable advances.[4]

There was a second disadvantage. Those who lived in the area were neither Viet Minh nor sympathizers of the movement. They were not even ethnic minorities who had helped the Viet Minh so much in other times and places. They were hostile Roman Catholics who lustily cheered the French onward. Further disaster befell Giap's hopes when the French navy cut his supply lines. The French did not even have to commit their reserves.

The bodies of Giap's soldiers withered and crackled in napalm flames and fell on the battlefield from superior French weapons. The slaughter continued for ten days before Giap realized the immensity of the power he faced and called off the conflict.[5] Giap desperately needed to salvage what remained of his forces and regroup them. They had suffered terrible casualties in the attacks so far against the French: six thousand dead at Vinh Yen, three thousand at Mao Khe, ten thousand at the Day River. In 1952, in an attack against an isolated but powerful French base he would lose another nine thousand men.

Morale among Giap's main force units plummeted. During the summer of 1951 his soldiers deserted at an alarming rate, the highest since he had formed the army in December 1944. Never again would Giap seriously challenge the French in Viet Nam's open coastal plains. He had paid the price of well over twenty thousand killed and wounded, however, before he admitted to himself that conventional, open warfare against the French was not yet a possibility.

Truong Chinh did not delay in using these military disasters to condemn his former comrade. He accused Giap of being "responsible for useless massacres, which had no other purpose than to promote personal interests." He also denounced Giap's lack of judgment in his selection of "responsible personnel." Even Ho Chi Minh was distressed by what he had seen and by the grave battle losses. He called a meeting of the political bureau of the Communist Party to consider what course of action should be taken. During the sessions, to Truong Chinh's delight, Ho himself put on the agenda a proposal to relieve Giap of his position as commander in chief of the army. The motion was defeated, primarily because of Ho's strong opposition to his own proposal; it had been submitted to that powerful body of men in an effort to allow discussion and criticism and to clear the air of any developing movement to unseat Giap.

Giap, however, did not escape unscathed. Before the matter ended, he was forced to submit a written "auto-critique," eliminate his closest assistants, now deemed to be incompetent, give vocal agreement to the priority of political commissars over the army, and allow Chinese military advisers to be placed at all echelons. Within Vietnamese governmental circles, Truong Chinh's power now far overshadowed Giap's own.[6]

With no option available, Giap withdrew to the hills once again and fought the French only in areas which maximized his manpower and mobility while neutralizing French firepower. He had learned from his mistakes. From that time on, his strategy became one of diverting French battalions into remote areas in fruitless chases or tying them down in unproductive static positions, guarding what little still remained to them of their once and former glorious colony. Giap noted that in the future, "The countryside was to encircle the towns, the mountains were to dominate the rice lands of the plain."[7] It was a difficult time for the general, and he could find little from which to take comfort. There was only one satisfaction: those who had survived now knew their jobs and were truly an army.[8]

On such matters Giap's convictions were unshakable. His role was to defeat French forces and to send them packing from the soil of the homeland. Having admitted to the Politburo that he had been in error, Giap tried again, but this time he would not face de Lattre. Discovering he was suffering from cancer, de Lattre returned to Paris to die, and French hopes perished with him. He was posthumously named a *maréchal de France* by a grateful government.[9] *Time* magazine also honored him early in 1952 in an article about important men of 1951.

His successor, General Raoul Salan, dusted off de Lattre's plan to recapture control of Hoa Binh from Viet Minh forces. It was a key town twenty-five miles southwest of Ha Noi and controlled roads leading southward to the delta and west up the banks of key rivers. Salan launched his attack in November 1951, and French troops achieved their objective. Giap patiently resisted this French offensive as he evaluated the strength of his enemy's forces. Four weeks later, Giap ordered a counterattack, which caused heavy French losses and savaged their morale. (See map "Hoa Binh and Surrounding Area.")

By the middle of February 1952, mounting losses and increased Viet Minh activity forced the French to evacuate Hoa Binh and retreat to established defensive positions along the Red River. It took them eleven days to make their way to safety, with casualties nearly as great as they were later destined to suffer at Dien Bien Phu. They inflicted punishment of their own, however, for Giap lost another nine thousand soldiers. French military advisers were surprised at the

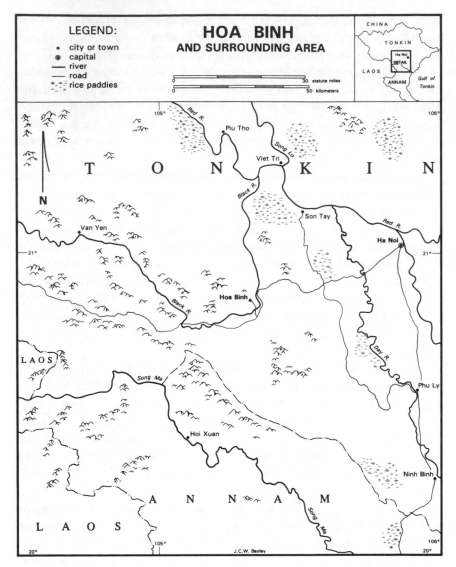

improvement in Giap's army as they watched Viet Minh main force units maneuvering in divisions, supported by both light and heavy artillery. Giap's force
was becoming an army to be reckoned with. And, finally, Giap decided not only
to act like a general but to look like one. He now adopted the practice of wearing a uniform, discarding the civilian suit, tie, and felt hat he had worn ever since
his days in the jungle during World War II.[10]

    Perhaps Giap's wastage of his troops' lives came from his having learned
the craft of war by trial and error, from the bush. Certainly he came to be philo-
sophical about casualties. He once remarked, "Every minute, hundreds of thou-

sands of people die all over the world. The life or death of a hundred, a thousand, or of tens of thousands of human beings, even if they are our own compatriots, represents really very little."[11]

Consequently, western generals and military analysts have too often dismissed Giap and refused to accord him his rightful stature, sniffing at his callous indifference to sanguinary losses. Those who sneer, however, forget that the lessons Giap learned from 1950 to 1953 paid off handsomely at Dien Bien Phu and later. He sometimes faced overwhelming odds, and while creating and directing his army he simultaneously needed to act the role of politician. Few other generals have had to face such an all-encompassing task.

His enemies had more might, more money, more machines. He fought most of the war from 1946 to 1949 without a single truck, and when he received some from China he had no roads on which to use them. He did what he could with what he had, and his casualties were high. He had to instill in his troops extraordinary morale to offset the technical superiority of his enemies. Troops with high morale sometimes take heavy casualties. These actions were necessary to let Giap exploit his strength while partially negating the power of his enemies. Yet even his sometimes staggering losses were not appalling ones in the annals of war—certainly no higher than in European conflicts, and not even by American standards.[12]

Occasionally Giap needed to play the role of a diplomat. Heartened as he was by continued Chinese aid, he traveled to Beijing in late 1951 to celebrate the seventh anniversary of the founding of the Democratic Republic of Viet Nam. Liu Shaoqi spoke there of the "unbreakable friendship" between the two nations and expressed his belief in the coming Viet Minh victory over the French. Giap declared his preference (perhaps with tongue in cheek, given his feud with Truong Chinh) for the Chinese military system over that of the Soviets. He noted that Viet Nam had learned many things from China, including both a complete system of military thought and a strategy and tactics suitable for use by a colony against a mother country. From the USSR, Giap said, he had learned only the lessons of proletarian internationalism and his tenacious and unshakable loyalty to the people's interests.[13]

At a later time he was more honest in his feelings toward China. In a blatant misstatement and dissembling greatly, Giap said in 1982, "Our military science does not owe anything to the Chinese military philosophy. We successfully carried out our revolution in the August general uprising [in Ha Noi]. Meanwhile Chinese military philosophy denies the possibility of an uprising in the cities." In Viet Nam, the revolutionary struggle grew from the power of the people, "[b]ut for them, power springs from the barrel of a gun." Or again, for decades those in the south of Viet Nam struggled and sacrificed in their military and political efforts to liberate and reunify the country, but, Giap snorted, the

Chinese "would have us keep our forces lying low for a . . . very long time. . . . They told us . . . that Viet Nam would be reunified but that it would take. . . . maybe a hundred years."[14]

Back in Viet Nam for the new year, Giap began what has come to be known as his Northwest Campaign. On 11 October 1952, Giap ordered three of his divisions into an offensive west of the Black River in the area north of the Red River Delta. His intent was to destroy remaining French outposts in the direction of Laos and to provide his units with complete freedom of movement. When possible, he threw full divisions against isolated, battalion-sized French forces. For a time during Giap's offensive, his 149th Independent Regiment occupied a small village near Laos named Dien Bien Phu. Neither side knew how important that area would be two years later.

When it appeared that Giap's efforts were grinding to a halt, General Raoul Salan launched Operation Lorraine. He sent thirty thousand French troops to penetrate Viet Minh base areas and to draw Giap back from his offensive in Laos. Lorraine terminated in November after French troops bogged down. Salan failed in his strategic aim of drawing Giap's divisions back from the country west of the Black River. Giap described Salan's frustrations: "In such a war, where is the front?" He answered himself with a quotation from Pascal: *"L'ennemi est partout et nulle part,"* the enemy is everywhere and nowhere.[15]

At about the same time, he granted Joseph R. Starobin, an American Communist, permission to visit his camp and speak with him. Starobin found Giap's headquarters a spartan one, a simple bamboo shed, open on one side with a roof of thatched leaves. Inside was a large table, covered with a green cloth on which lay the general's maps. Other maps from his 1952 campaigns were displayed on three walls, along with photos of Ho Chi Minh, Mao, and Joseph Stalin. Under the roof hung the camouflaged silk of a French parachute, a trophy from the 1952 fighting. Powered by a nearby generator, an electric lightbulb hung on a dropcord. Outside stood a single sentinel, armed with an American Thompson submachine gun. By the time of Starobin's visit, Giap had begun wearing a uniform, simple khaki without decorations. The American later published what Giap told him about logistics and other pressing matters he faced.[16]

"As a matter of fact," Giap told Starobin, "if we have to we can put all our supplies on our backs. For short distances, one peasant can carry enough provisions for one soldier." The Northwest Campaign, he said, was conducted in an area of "relatively vast distances for a country like ours. Two hundred, two hundred and fifty kilometers in width, three rivers to cross—the Clear, the Red and the Black rivers. We had to move deep into the valleys to hit the heart of the French positions. . . . We had to cross thirty streams, some of them two hundred and fifty yards wide, and make our way over very high mountains."

Giap explained, "The French officers whom we captured "told us later they did not see how we could have done it. They did not comprehend how our forces

CHINA

TONKIN

BURMA

⊙ Ha Noi

20°　　　　　　　　　　　　　　　　　　　　　　　　　20°

Luang Prabang ●

LAOS

Gulf of
Tonkin

Vientiane ⊙

● Vinh

CHINA

HAINAN
(CHINA)

THE SITUATION IN 1953
General Navarre's Map

LEGEND:

Zones entirely Viet Minh
Zones of strong Viet Minh influence

16°　　　　　　　　　　　　　　　　　　　　　　　　　16°

● Hue
● Da Nang

THAILAND

● Pak Se

ANNAM

CAMBODIA

12°　　　　　　　　　　　　　　　　　　　　　　　　　12°

● Da Lat

Gulf of Thailand

⊙ Phnom Penh

COCHIN-CHINA

● Saigon

0　　　100　statute miles
0　　　160　kilometers

South China Sea

N

104°　　　　　　　　　　　　　108°

J.C.W. Bexley

could appear . . . hundreds of kilometers from our bases. One French officer said it was a surprise to see our peasants carrying supplies for the Army, without soldiers guarding them. For the French always have to guard their porters."[17]

By the end of 1952, French control of the land was but a shadow of its former extent. Save for some coastal areas around Hue and Tourane (Da Nang), the Viet Minh held much of the country. Giap's maps showed the whole northern part of the nation shaded in red, signifying areas cleared of the French, with orange patches covering the delta of the Red River, showing guerrilla areas. Red patches dotted the Saigon delta, and the Ca Mau peninsula was solid red. Between October and December 1952, the northwest border area with Laos went red as Giap claimed control of four valleys previously controlled by 120 fortified French positions. Upper reaches of both the Red and Black rivers fell to Giap's main force units. The French retained only a small area near the Chinese border, and it had to be resupplied by air. "We just left them there," Giap commented. "Let them use up their supplies trying to hold it."[18]

Giap's guerrilla forces also continued to threaten the Hanoi–Haiphong railway and key roads in the Red River Delta necessary to French efforts. Giap was pleased at his enemy's confusion. "Either they try to extend their strong-points once again, with their depleted man-power," he said to Starobin, "in which case, they must spread themselves thin, and lay themselves open to new attacks that we can launch in regimental or divisional strength, or else they try to reduce these strong-points and consolidate them, which frees territory and population to us." Giap was satisfied with the result. "Our guerrillas and government take over within gunshot of their strong-points. In most cases, we are actually besieging them. The minute a soldier pops out of a blockhouse, he faces guerrilla fire. . . . Moreover," Giap continued, ". . . . they even destroy the dykes without which rice culture is impossible. . . . This tactic, however, rouses the people against them."[19]

In Giap's view, France faced two main problems: the difficulty of maneuvering in a land without fronts, with only a series of strongpoints amid a hostile population, and the shortage of manpower for its military. In another sense, Giap claimed, there really was no *French* army. Of the troops facing him, some 40,000 were Foreign Legionnaires. Another 50,000 consisted of soldiers from Morocco, Algeria, and Tunisia, from Senegal and French West Africa. In addition, France relied on private armies supplied by the Hoa Hao and Cao Dai religious sects. Another 50,000 were Vietnamese nationals, "puppets," the Viet Minh called them, fighting for the French. To these 140,000 troops the French added 90,000 of their own, all volunteers, 37 percent of all France's noncommissioned officers and 26 percent of her regular officers.[20]

Despite those numbers, 230,000 strong, the French had no idea how to run Giap's main force units to ground. He struck out against them all across the north, in the highlands, in the south, and even in Laos, to draw them out of their garrisons in the Red River Delta. Giap left two of his Viet Minh divisions in the northern delta region to harass, to cut communications lines, and to strike at border posts and interdict Route Coloniale 5 between Ha Noi and Haiphong. That tied down a minimum of five French battalions. In December 1953, in five days, some of Giap's units moved from Vinh, on the coast, along mountain paths into Laos, where they attacked the French at Thakhet and then turned on Seno, a French airbase, to which they laid siege for five days. The French reacted by airlifting two more battalions to Seno, one from the delta and one from Saigon, but Giap simply broke off the siege and moved onto Laos's Bolovens Plateau.

No longer was Giap's chief foe General Salan. For on 8 May 1953, General Henri-Eugène Navarre arrived and assumed command of all French forces in Indochina. His orders were to assess the military situation in Viet Nam and report what he learned to Paris so the government could negotiate an honorable peace there. The Eisenhower administration had also been criticizing the French lack of forward progress against the Viet Minh, demanding a more vigorous prosecution of the war against the Communists. Navarre had no experience in Indochina and desired none, yet he was a good officer who followed orders, and so he came to Southeast Asia. He had joined the French army during World War I and spent over two years in the trenches. By World War II he worked in French intelligence, and he fled his homeland in 1940. Joining the Resistance in 1942, he commanded an armored regiment later in the war and, much later, became chief of staff of NATO land forces.

Following an agreement signed in 1950, American aid to France had significantly increased, enabling it to continue its Indochina War. The United States supplied weapons and ammunition, aircraft and repair parts, warships, tanks, and motor vehicles, even the uniforms worn by French and auxiliary troops in Indochina. In 1951 the quantity of U.S. aid reaching Viet Nam was on average about 6,000 tons a month; by 1953 it reached a new high of over 20,000 tons. That figure was dwarfed when new French demands caused American aid in 1954 to soar to as much as 100,000 tons a month. Now the United States wanted something concrete for the millions of dollars and tons of equipment it had invested. Navarre, who would serve until July 1954, might be the one who could satisfy American demands.

Upon Navarre's arrival, however, he was dismayed to realize that over 100,000 of his troops were tied down in static defenses. Navarre further estimated that Giap had over 125,000 full-time regular soldiers disposed in six divisions, at least six independent regiments, and several independent battalions of his main force. The French had no edge in manpower. Without a change of pace or direction, France would be hard put to accomplish its *mission civilisatrice* in Indochina. And so Navarre came up with his own approach. He recognized that Indochina divided itself into two theaters of war. France would seek to avoid major confrontations with Giap during the 1953–54 campaign season in the northern theater that included northern Vietnam and northern Laos. During that time, Navarre would build up his forces there.

Navarre determined that, simultaneously, he would seek out Viet Minh forces in the southern highlands by means of a new strike, Operation Atlante. In this way he would clean out pockets of Viet Minh control in central Viet Nam and upset any plans Giap might have for a major offensive in that region. Then he would mop up in the south. Navarre also hoped to accelerate the training and growth of the Vietnamese National Army, an auxiliary force used by the French. Likewise, he intended to begin a major program of pacification in the Tonkinese Red River Delta area.

Then, during the 1954–55 campaign season, Navarre hoped to be able to seek a major set-piece battle with Giap's main battle forces in the north and destroy them. This would then provide France with an opportunity to settle the war honorably. Navarre revealed these plans to his senior commanders at a meeting in Saigon on 16 June 1953.[21]

Navarre's Operation Atlante struck at thin air. It was a landing on the southern Annam coast below Quang Tri at Tuy Hoa, along the "street without joy." French troopers found no enemy to fight, for Giap had removed his regular units and brought them north, leaving only guerrilla units to harass the French. Meanwhile he launched other heavy attacks against the French in the Central Highlands, taking Kontum and moving on Pleiku, where some of the fiercist fighting of the war occurred. Finally Giap moved his 316th Division into Laos, toward Luang Prabang. Navarre tried to corner him by sending five battalions into a blocking position, so Giap redirected his division around them and on toward the little community of Dien Bien Phu. The coming battle there would be, for Navarre, premature; he desired not to face Giap until the 1954–55 campaign season. Occurring one year too soon, it would sound the death knell for the French empire in southeast Asia and bring to Giap the lasting gratitude of his nation.

"The Sweat and
Muscle of Our Soldiers"

The time had finally come again for Giap to pit the strength of his main force units against the French. In 1951 that had meant disaster at Vinh Yen, at Mao Khe, and along the Day River. He had learned much in those intervening years and, at the demand of Truong Chinh and the Politburo, even publicly confessed his earlier lack of good judgment. As he would later write in his book *People's War, People's Army,* "All the conceptions born of impatience and aimed at obtaining speedy victory could only be gross errors. . . . It was necessary to accumulate thousands of small victories to turn them into a great success." Many small victories now lay behind him. He had built up the strength of his main force units during the actual course of the long contest with the French. Now he faced a new French general who hoped to meet him on the field of battle. Giap was ready. Successful contest with the enemy would break the back of Truong Chinh and his pro-Chinese clan and restore to Giap all his lost ground and prestige. If Navarre wanted to contest with him at Dien Bien Phu, let it be so.[1]

Yet Giap had misgivings. Speaking in April 1959 to Janos Radvanyi, a Hungarian diplomat visiting Ha Noi, Giap recalled the desperation of those days. Radvanyi summed up the general's words to him. "The battle of Dien Bien Phu . . . was the last desperate exertion of the Viet Minh army. Its forces were on the verge of complete exhaustion. The supply of rice was running out. Apathy had spread among the populace to such an extent that it was difficult to draft new fighters. Years of jungle warfare had sent morale in the fighting units to the depths."[2]

As if that were not enough, Giap also faced a new pressure, a deadline. In February 1954, in Berlin, foreign ministers of several nations met and agreed that a conference would be held at Geneva in May to settle "outstanding issues in the Far East" such as Indochina. This meant negotiation, and Ho Chi Minh was ready. "The basis for an armistice," he said to a Swedish journalist, "is that the French Government really respects Vietnam's independence."[3] If his top general was going to deliver a significant military victory—a great bargaining chip for negotiations—it would have to be soon.

Giap was proud of the caliber of his troops and believed they could stand up to pitched combat with the French. This was no longer 1946 nor 1951. His men were well prepared. They observed correct attitudes toward civilians "in order to win their confidence and affection and achieve a perfect understanding" with one another. His army, Giap claimed, had "never done injury to their property, not even a needle or a bit of thread." They were not only grounded thoroughly in doctrine, they knew how to fight, and their tactical and technical proficiency had been carefully raised through repeated training courses. So also did he feel his officers were worthy. Each one, Giap said, knew how "to show himself to be resolute, brave, to ensure discipline and internal democracy, to know how to achieve perfect unity among his men." Political work, Giap knew, was "the soul of the army."[4]

Giap knew his men were well indoctrinated with the party line. They had also done well militarily. By skillfully maneuvering his units in early 1952, Giap robbed the French of the strategic advantage they had gained by the occupation of Hoa Binh on the Black River. In late 1952, Giap launched his forces on a drive through the highlands of northwest Tonkin and on into Laos. By this strategy, he made his enemies fight on ground of his own choosing, forcing them to strengthen isolated garrisons that were much less defensible than those within the Red River Delta. Giap crowed about his achievement in transforming the French rear into his own front line. "By successively launching strong offensives on the points [the French] had left relatively unprotected, we obliged them to scatter their troops all over the place." He also gained a needed rest for his guerrillas, who had been so active within the delta region. Finally, he forced the French to choose whether to defend or abandon Laos and be content merely with coastal enclaves in Viet Nam and Cambodia.[5]

Newly arrived General Navarre, obsessed with defeating the Viet Minh in their own country and keeping them out of Laos as well, considered that he might achieve both goals by establishing a northern "mooring point," a center of operations from which French patrols could go out in search of Giap's units. Establishing such a center at Dien Bien Phu would threaten the flank of Giap's base in northwest Tonkin, force him to scatter his troops between the delta and the mountains, and provide protection for upper Laos by making it more difficult for Giap to ship supplies through that region or to maneuver his units there. This, in turn, would cut down on Viet Minh revenues from opium sales, which were financing many of Giap's weapons purchases.[6]

Indeed, Navarre thought, such an action might even end the war, perhaps within eighteen months. Navarre and his advisers estimated that the critical situation of the French Expeditionary Corps was due to its extreme dispersal in thousands of posts and garrisons scattered on all fronts to cope with Giap's guerrilla warfare; as a result, he lacked a strong mobile force to seek out Giap's main force units. To that end, Navarre ordered new units to be rushed to Indochina. By the end of 1953, Navarre commanded a total of eighty-four battalions spread over the whole of Indochina, and he concluded the time had come to launch his occupation of Dien Bien Phu, an action code-named Operation Castor, after Castor and Pollux, twin brothers in Greek mythology. It was put in motion on 20 November 1953, and seemed especially suited to the slogans that Navarre regularly relied on to inspirit his command: "Always keep the initiative" and "always on the offensive."[7]

For his plan to succeed, Navarre needed to rely heavily on two other officers, Cogny and de Castries. Navarre's subordinate commander for Tonkin was Major General René Cogny, a graduate of Saint-Cyr and a former artillery officer. He and Giap were the two most educated generals in Indochina, for Cogny had earned degrees in both political science and law. Cogny was captured twice by the Germans during World War II, in 1941, after which he escaped, and then again in 1943. Cogny made a spectacular rise through the ranks in the years after the war. Now he was commander of troops in Tonkin, and although he did not favor the Dien Bien Phu plan, neither did he plainly speak out against it.

Several days after the initial drop of the French airborne troopers into Dien Bien Phu, Navarre picked Colonel Christian Marie Ferdinand de la Croix de Castries to command the forces there. A flamboyant officer, de Castries sometimes startled guests at parties by crunching up a glass and chewing on the broken remnants. He prided himself on his athletic ability and was a daring pilot. A talented horseman, in 1933 he won the world high jump championship for horseback riding, and in competition again in 1935, won first place in the equestrian long jump. He served for a time in the French cavalry before transferring to armor. He also had been captured by the Germans in 1941, but managed to escape and join Free French forces in 1944. Always happy to live in the moment, de Castries once remarked that *la dolce vita* consisted of "a horse to ride, an enemy to kill, and a woman in bed." De Castries would have made a remarkable companion in a cavalry charge. On 8 December he took command of the forces at Dien Bien Phu.[8]

The settlement of Dien Bien Phu, a T'ai village of 112 houses, had little strategic significance, except that it was only eight miles from the Laotian border and served as a junction for three poor roads, one of which led north into China, another to the northeast, and the third south into Laos. Its name meant "the seat of the border county prefecture," perhaps better translated in English as "the location of the county government." Its main crops were rice and opium. Positioned in a flat, heart-shaped basin twelve miles long from north to south and six miles wide, the settlement was ringed with jungle and surrounded by low but steep hills. Meo tribes lived on the slopes; in the valley, T'ai tended paddy fields and lived in a few scattered tiny hamlets, the largest of which was Muong Thanh. A small river, the Nam Oum, ran through the basin from north to south. The French had earlier built two airstrips in the valley. The main one was near the village; the other, smaller one was farther to the south. They could be used to land needed personnel and equipment ferried from

Ha Noi, 170 air miles away. The area's geography made it an attractive location for Navarre, for he knew the Viet Minh would find it impossible to transport their few small artillery pieces to the site along the few narrow jungle trails through the mountains.[9]

American planes flown by French pilots carried thousands of parachute troops to the area. They included the 6th BPC, the Deuxième Bataillon, Premier Régiment de Chasseurs Parachutistes (2d Battalion, 1st Para Light Regiment), and the Premier Bataillon Etranger de Parachutistes (1st Foreign Legion Parachute Battalion, abbreviated as 1st BEP), composed, in part, of Germans of the former Nazi Schutzstaffel or SS. Thousands of soldiers and vast quantities of matériel were dropped onto the site or landed at the airstrip. The first unit in was the 17th Airborne Engineer Company; it worked on the site's defenses until 4 December 1953, when it was replaced by the 3d Company, 31st Engineer Battalion.

Giap's 148th Independent Regiment, stationed in the hills to watch the area, quietly slipped away, even as French paratroops floated downward, for the Vietnamese knew the French assault was too massive for them to stop. It was time for them to report what they had seen to their chief.[10]

Ultimately 10,814 men-at-arms of the French Expeditionary Corps waited at Dien Bien Phu for a Viet Minh attack. Of that number only about 7,000 were combat soldiers; the others were combat support. No one should be deluded that this was a purely Gallic effort. Fully one-third of the garrison was Vietnamese, members of the new National Army, established by the ever resourceful Emperor Bao Dai, now again cooperating with the French government. Other of Navarre's polyglot soldiers came from Morocco, Lebanon, Syria, Chad, Guadeloupe, and Madagascar. They dug bunkers, extended trenches, emplaced claymore mines, unrolled concertina wire. By the time they finished they had transformed the countryside into an armed camp.[11]

De Castries supervised the construction, inevitably wearing his red Spahi kepi (the headgear worn by Algerian cavalry serving with the French army) and a red scarf and carrying his riding crop. A well-known womanizer, de Castries named the artillery strongpoints constructed at outposts after three mistresses he was currently supporting, plus other earlier assignations, all of whom he wished to immortalize. He clustered his fortifications mostly near the main airstrip and the village; Huguette to the west, Claudine to the south, Eliane to the east, and Dominique to the northeast. The headquarters command bunker lay in the center. Each was located on low knolls rising up from the plain. De Castries tried to coordinate their firepower so each position could provide interlocking and mutually supporting fire to other strongpoints.

Four other independent defended areas lay slightly apart from the main fortifications. Béatrice was just a mile away on high ground to the north, blocking one of the roads. Gabrielle, two miles to the north, sat just to the east of the road to China. Anne-Marie sat perched on a rise about one and one-half miles to the northwest from the airstrip. Each of these three sites was held by one battalion of French defenders.

About four miles to the south lay Isabelle, near the small airstrip. Although it was the last position to fall to Viet Minh attack, its location was unfortunate. Positioned on that knoll were three infantry battalions (out of twelve available at Dien Bien Phu), a tank platoon, and a 105mm artillery group. One-third of all French troops defended this position, and yet its distance from other sites prevented it from playing an active role later during Viet Minh assaults elsewhere. Unbiased observers, had any been available, might have noted that the main defenses lay uncomfortably close to hills overlooking the north end of the basin.[12]

These strongpoints were poorly located. Artillery batteries at the southern strongpoint, Isabelle, were unable to support adequately other outposts of Gabrielle, Béatrice, or Anne-Marie. French fortifications also were inadequately constructed. Telephone field wire stretched along the ground when it should have been buried. Strongpoints lacked connecting trenches, a common belt of barbed wire, and even minefields. There was no overhead cover for the communications trench to the hospital, which itself was incapable of handling heavy casualties.[13]

Airborne troops, the first to arrive, were too lightly equipped to build substantial defenses, and during the early days of their occupation they did little to improve their positions. It was only about thirty days prior to the actual battle that they began serious efforts to harden their positions, and by then there was no time left to do what had to be done. Engineers calculated they were lacking at least thirty thousand tons of building material. They were able to fortify adequately only the headquarters, command post, signal center, and the X-ray room of the underground hospital.[14]

Faced with Navarre's buildup at Dien Bien Phu, Giap reacted swiftly. Within a week of the French arrival in the valley, he ordered four divisions to prepare to move to Dien Bien Phu. French air force intelligence officers estimated that Giap's forces would be about 49,000 strong, a figure which was within 10 percent of their actual size.[15] General Navarre chose to disregard this estimate. He maintained that Viet Minh troops moving toward Dien Bien Phu in late November 1953 were only elements of several divisions.[16] Even as the situation became grimmer, Navarre continued to insist that no more than one enemy division was in the region. It might be reinforced, but it would not multiply.[17]

French intelligence estimates seemed doomed to inaccuracy. They miscalculated the number of enemy soldiers ringing the site. G-2 officers projected the number of Viet Minh artillery pieces as fewer than sixty, and those only medium howitzers, capable of firing perhaps 25,000 rounds.[18] Those same men counted on their air force to interdict enemy efforts by Giap's porters to carry any sizable number of artillery rounds to battery sites.[19] Artillery and air force advisers believed they would be able to locate and knock out any strong concentration of enemy artillery before it could become more than a nuisance. Contemptuous of Giap's artillery capabilities, the French placed their own in open circular pits with no protective cover.[20]

Bernard Fall, the main chronicler of the debacle at Dien Bien Phu, believed that the greatest errors were caused by outrageous French overestimation of their own capabilities. That is, he wrote, "a national flaw of which my countrymen seem to be afflicted since before Julius Caesar's campaigns in Gaul, which, incidentally, culminated in a Gallic Dien Bien Phu at a fortress called Alesia."[21] Yet their confidence was supported and strengthened by others. High-level advisers—French and American—visited the site and pronounced themselves satisfied. Among them were General Paul Ely, chief of the French general staff, and General John "Iron Mike" O'Daniel, head of the area's U.S. Military Assistance and Advisory Group (USMAAG). Even novelist Graham Greene made an appearance. No one who came seemed to note the nearby hills or suggest that if the Viet Minh had artillery, the French would find themselves in a hopeless situation. On the contrary, like Navarre, they were elated at the prospects of victory. Their optimism was duly reported at home. *U.S. News & World Report* informed its readers that "victory in Indochina, in short, is within . . . grasp . . . in the opinion of most American experts."[22] From the beginning, an ecstatic General Navarre had been optimistic when speaking of his coming success: "A year ago none of us could see victory. There wasn't a prayer. Now we see it clearly—like light at the end of a tunnel." The analogy would be used later by others, again and again.[23]

As Navarre looked at his troops and equipment, he believed he was ready for battle. He had twelve battalions of troops, supported by two groups of 75mm and two of 105mm artillery, backed up by four 155mm howitzers and a large number of heavy mortars. A helicopter sat on the northern airstrip, waiting to serve as target spotter. Six fighter-bombers also sat on the tarmac, ready to respond to calls for close-air support. Ten light tanks, flown in disassembled, were put back together by eager crews. Men from a transport company drove their vehicles among the various positions, distributing reinforcing personnel and ammunition.

There was even a bevy of Algerian and Vietnamese whores, organized into *bordels mobiles de campagne*, "mobile field brothels," flown in to service the needs of troops. There were eleven Algerians, from the Oulad Naïl tribe, located on Dominique, and six Vietnamese (five girls and a madame) billeted on Claudine. Refusing evacuation, they lived through the fight in underground bunkers, working as auxiliary nurses in addition to performing their other duties. Four Algerian women died during the fighting. The surviving whores were among the last to surrender the following May, plying their trade until nearly the final moments. The Vietnamese were led away by their captors and never seen again. One of the Algerians, Mimi, married a fellow Algerian while in a prison hospital camp and gave birth to her first child in Communist Ha Noi.[24]

Navarre believed Giap would need to use three divisions to besiege his fortress, thus tying them up in a static role just as the French had so often suffered. It would be sweet retribution. Should they actually decide to attack across the open rice paddies, concentrated French fire would decimate them. The braver they were the more he could cripple them. He was not in the least worried about Viet Minh artillery, nor was he anxious about his own supply lines, because the airfields, surrounded by defensive positions, could not possibly be in danger.

During January 1954, while Viet Minh forces settled themselves in the area, French patrols tried to keep watch over the brooding hills. They frequently came into contact with isolated enemy positions. As the number of Giap's warriors increased, such patrols found themselves in ever increasing danger of ambush and attack and so eventually restricted themselves to close-in observation.

Those in charge seemed not to notice that they had made three grave errors in estimating the size of enemy ground forces, relative artillery strengths on both sides, and supply capabilities. Those within the fortress informed Navarre of the existence of three Viet Minh divisional command posts nearby with a fourth on the way. Nor was theirs the first voice raised in criticism. On 11 November 1953—seven days prior to Navarre's initial airborne drop of troops to the fortress—Colonel Nicot, Navarre's air transport commander, stated to him in writing that available aircraft were not capable of maintaining a heavy continuous flow of supplies to the site. As late as 25 February 1954, General Fay, chief of air staff, after an inspection trip to the site, urged Navarre to evacuate the fortress. Still Navarre maintained his mulish attitude.[25]

Giap knew that the greatest French weakness lay in the limited ability to resupply the fortress. Road-based transport was impossible for the French, leaving only the two airstrips. They would have to rely entirely on air transport. From the beginning, Giap stated, he planned "to use our artillery fire to destroy the airstrips and our antiaircraft guns to cope with the activities of enemy planes."[26]

Giap felt agonies of indecision as he considered available options while planning for the attack on Dien Bien Phu. To attack or not to attack Dien Bien Phu? If attacked, how should the assault be carried out? Two ways suggested themselves, Giap said: "Strike swiftly and win swiftly, or strike surely and advance surely."[27] He chose to strike suddenly, swiftly, without warning, "an over-all rapid attack aimed at destroying [it] within three nights and two days.

The attack was to be launched the evening of January 25th." On that very morning, however, at 10:00 A.M., Giap held a staff meeting at his forward command post near Tuan Giao.

As Giap called his group to order, he was concerned about his Chinese advisers. Mao had ordered some of his best military people to help Giap, and faced with Truong Chinh's enmity within the Politburo, Giap had no option other than to listen to them. Among those who advised him were Luo Guibo, Chu Teh, Peng Te-huai, Mei Jiashing, Wei Kuo-ch'ing, Chen Gen, and Deng Yifan. These and others worked closely with the Vietnamese high command, offering their solutions to Giap's battle plans at Cao Bang, Dong Khe, and Hoa Binh and in campaigns in northern Laos.

Ho Chi Minh wished no diminution in Mao's help. Since July 1950, with the arrival of seventy advisers known as the South China Sea Action Group, Mao had sent both experts and supplies. Because of his interest, Giap now had at Dien Bien Phu some two hundred cannon, ten thousand barrels of gasoline, three thousand rifles of all types, 2.4 million bullets, sixty thousand artillery rounds, and nearly 1.7 million tons of rice. Even a Chinese artillery division was on hand to take part in the battle. It was a bounty that could not be ignored.

In preparations for the attack on Dien Bien Phu, Giap's Chinese advisers urged him to plan a rapid attack using human-wave tactics, as they had done in Korea, in order to achieve a quick end. His staff was concerned about the level of available supplies. Giap put the question to his chief of staff and to other officers gathered around him. "Could we be certain of victory in attacking? Our decision had to depend on this consideration alone." Giap was concerned that his troops lacked experience in attacking fortified and entrenched camps.[28] "After a thorough analysis of the most recent information, I came to the conclusion that [our] quick operation *might* be crowned with success [but that] victory was not 100% certain." There was, he felt, neither certainty nor unanimity among his staff and advisers.

Giap acted without hesitation. Having spent a sleepless night considering these matters, he concluded it would be suicidal to throw his troops into battle against French artillery, tanks, and aircraft, without more preparation. "Suddenly I postponed the operation. My staff was confused, but no matter. I was in command and I demanded absolute obedience—*sans discussion, sans explication. . . .* [W]e resolutely chose . . . to strike surely and advance surely."[29]

"In taking this correct decision," Giap wrote, "we strictly followed this fundamental principle of the conduct of a revolutionary war: strike to win, strike only when success is certain; if it is not, then don't strike." Giap had certainly become more conservative than in 1951 when he attacked Vinh Yen, Mao Khe, and along the Day River without that same degree of certainty. His Chinese advisers were unhappy. Chen Gen accused Giap and other Vietnamese generals of "lacking in Bolshevik spirit" and "balking at their advisor's criticisms." He also complained that Giap "lacks honesty and frankness vis-à-vis his Chinese comrades."[30]

Nevertheless the Politburo quickly ratified Giap's decision. That afternoon, Giap recalled, after having received approval from his Pathet Lao allies in Laos, he gave the order to launch an offensive toward Luang Prabang. It was, he said, designed as a diversion to draw off the French air force while he withdrew his troops from the Dien Bien Phu area. "That decision to change our plan . . . was for me one of the most momentous decisions, one of the most difficult decisions in my life as commanding officer." That night he pulled back his infantry and artillery from their positions overlooking the French camp. "We strenuously set to work on new preparations," he said, and his forces did not reoccupy their former locations until March. Giap completely changed his plans for conducting the battle, reoriented into a protracted siege designed to ensure success. When it began, it started at 5:00 P.M. on 13 March with an attack from the east on the outer French fortress known as Béatrice.[31]

During the interim, Giap rehearsed his subordinate officers over and again, using sand-table models of the terrain and of French positions. They went through practice exercises over and again under Giap's watchful, tireless eye. If they made errors, they criticized themselves and then ran the drill once more, until they knew every nuance of their jobs and responsibilities. These officers, in turn, once they had graduated from Giap's tutelage, returned to their own men and walked them through their responsibilities in full-scale practice exercises against life-sized models of French positions. When the time to attack finally came, it would not falter because Giap's soldiers did not know their jobs.

What was needed was a transportation network, and Giap's laborers bent their backs to supply him with what he required. By 1954, the Viet Minh received a flow of goods from China and Russia amounting to more than four thousand tons a day, and even that required an incredible porter system.[32] But it was not enough. Giap gave orders for his laborers to build roads from China capable of handling trucks, to clear trails over which to haul artillery pieces, to build camouflaged firing positions around Dien Bien Phu, and to prepare a trench system around the perimeter of the French defenses.

Giap's skill at moving troops and supplies was at its best as he readied for battle. Thirty thousand of his soldiers on their way to Dien Bien Phu crossed the Black River over underwater bridges that could not be spotted from the air. One regiment pushed itself across 250 miles of mountain trails. Thousands of coolies pushed specially strengthened bicycles loaded with artillery shells along narrow paths hacked out of jungles and cliffsides.[33] Artillery pieces were dismantled, their parts slung between bicycles, and pushed into position above Dien Bien Phu. Giap later boasted that during the period of preparation, "our army men opened up the supply line from Tuan Giao [some miles north of the French fortress, where Giap located his tactical field headquarters during the course of the siege] to Dien Bien Phu; built through mountains and forests roads practicable for trucks to move artillery pieces into position; built artillery emplacements; dug trenches from the mountains to the valley . . . [and] overcame enormous obstacles."[34]

The French were about to lose a battle because of primitive coolie porters. Their analysts had calculated that Giap would not be able to emplace heavy artillery in the hills, and that his supply lines would dry up after no more than four days of combat.[35] They were twice wrong. Several of Giap's supply lines were over one hundred kilometers long with insufficient transport facing bad roads, incessantly attacked by the French air force. His men coped with those problems and with the menace of heavy rains, collapsing cliff faces, mudslides, flooding— all obstacles as big as the French bombing. Giap said, "Truck convoys valiantly crossed streams, mountains and forests; drivers [faced] sleepless nights, to bring goods and ammunition." He orchestrated thousands of loaded bicycles pushed slowly toward the front, plus hundreds of sampans and thousands of bamboo rafts plying the rivers bringing their loads to prearranged portages where they were met by hundreds of thousands of waiting coolies, who carried loads across passes and rivers. Everything, said Giap, from cooking to medical work to transport was carried on despite enemy fire from artillery and airplanes.[36]

He enlarged upon the facts when he spoke of "medical work." Bernard Fall testifies that Giap had only one full-fledged surgeon, Dr. Ton That Tung, to care for his fifty thousand soldiers at Dien Bien Phu! That lone man was supported by six assistants, but there was little they could do. With insufficient equipment and few drugs, and working in septic conditions, they must have felt particularly frustrated as they tried to cope with the savage trauma wounds that combat always produces.[37] In any case, Giap observed that never before "had so many young Vietnamese traveled so far and become acquainted with so many distant regions of their country" as did those who now continued to form around the French fortress.[38] He overspoke. His men were not on a guided tour and he was not a sightseeing director!

They were sweating, desperate men under orders to dig hundreds of kilometers of trenches; in Giap's eye they were "wonderful trenches" that enabled his forces to deploy and move in open country directly under a rain of enemy napalm and artillery shells. "Our troops," Giap wrote, "cut through mountains and hacked away jungles to build roads and haul our artillery pieces to the approaches of Dien Bien Phu. Where roads could not be built, [cannon] were moved by nothing but the sweat and muscle of our soldiers."[39]

Even as he prepared for his assault at Dien Bien Phu, Giap kept up his pressure on the French elsewhere. As early as 10 December 1953, he went on the offensive in Lai Chau province, where in ten days and nights of fighting, his troops destroyed twenty-four companies of French soldiers.[40] In partnership with Pathet Lao Communist soldiers, Giap's units continued to confront French soldiers in Laos.[41] In late January and early February, Giap's subordinates launched an offensive against Dak To in Kon Tum province; both fell to Vietnamese attacks. Giap observed that the French had to remove forces from the Red River Delta to reinforce middle Laos, then to defend in the western highlands. "Our offensive in the western highlands continued until June 1954, and scored [a] resounding victory at An Khe where we cut to pieces the mobile regiment No. 100 which had just returned from Korea, thus liberating An Khe." Besides inflicting numerous casualties, Viet Minh main forces captured numbers of badly needed vehicles and a large quantity of ammunition.[42]

Nor was that all. Giap knew he had to damage the French air resupply potential, so he sent units into the Red River Delta, where they marched into the very shadow of Ha Noi to destroy seventy-eight French planes on Cat Bi and Gia Lam airfields. They also wiped out several fortified positions and cut Route Coloniale 5, the French main supply line. Giap counted on those attacks, and they succeeded. In the south, in Cochin China, more than a thousand enemy posts were either overrun or evacuated. Giap's warriors even attacked and sank French ships in Saigon's harbor and elsewhere. Even during the battle, Giap continued to send some of his units to places two and three hundred kilometers away to launch surprise attacks on French installations; having done so, they came back to Dien Bien Phu to resume their role in the annihilation of their enemy. Everywhere he looked, Giap saw the "spirit of heroism."[43]

His enemy, Giap noted, was in difficulty on all fronts, and while French troops and commanders floundered, Giap's people's militia and guerrilla bands effectively exploited the enemy rear. This, combined with the action at Dien Bien Phu, effectively neutralized French control of the land.[44] Perhaps, thought Giap, the new slogan handed down by the party's central committee was what had infused his people with fresh enthusiasm. He approved of the motto: "dynamism, initiative, mobility, and rapidity of decision in the face of new situations."[45] Giap's troops were in place and ready. For head-down, bloody frontal assaults and trench warfare, they were superb soldiers. General Davidson has described those men well: "For what they had to do they were as good as any troops twentieth century warfare has seen."[46]

There was a marked contrast between the generals who planned and fought this great battle. Navarre wore spotless, bemedaled uniforms as he worked out of an air-conditioned office in Saigon. Cogny poured over dispatches in his suite located in an imposing French-built structure in Ha Noi. De Castries found himself in a dirty reinforced underground bunker but, true to his predilections, spruced up his surroundings as best he could, eating his meals with burnished silver utensils while seated at a table covered with a linen cloth. In contrast, Giap oversaw the operation of his army while operating from his command post located in a cave near Tuan Giao. The differences in those men, Davidson writes, represented "the amount of physical discomfort and suffering each contender was willing to suffer for victory."[47]

The initial clash of ground soldiers came early on the morning of 11 March when French troops found themselves facing two detachments of Viet Minh who had infiltrated through the concertina wire of Gabrielle under cover of darkness and dug themselves in. Fifty-eight of Giap's soldiers died before the French ejected the remainder. This small action heartened the defenders. They were confident their lines would also hold against future attacks. They did not realize what lay in store for them.

On 13 March 1954, at 5:00 P.M., Vietnamese artillery shells began crashing down on Him Lam Hill in the midst of the French fortifications at Dien Bien Phu. In the new age of atomic warfare, Giap was reviving the use of siege tactics.[48]

Giap divided his siege into three phases: (1) to destroy the airstrip in the northern subsector and capture the French strongpoints at Béatrice, Gabrielle, and Anne-Marie; (2) to tighten encirclement of the French and to destroy the central subsector crowded around the main airstrip and the village; and (3) to launch the final attack on whatever remained, including strongpoint Isabelle. Between 10–12 March (authorities differ on exactly when), Giap's guns shelled the airstrip for the first time, pockmarking it with craters and causing great dismay within the French camp as the defenders realized what was happening to their only exit. If it was destroyed, they would truly be trapped. Even the wounded could not be evacuated.[49] As Giap said, "By concentrating forces to achieve absolute superiority at [each] point, we were certain to crush the enemy."[50] When the shelling began, General René Cogny was at Dien Bien Phu on an inspection trip. He hurried to his plane and ordered the pilot to take off while there was still time![51]

The French were surprised from the start of the siege. As part of his deception plan, Giap had earlier restricted his firing batteries from using any piece larger than a 75mm howitzer. Only on 13 March did he order his larger 105mm batteries to begin firing. He had played upon the defenders' vanity and had led them to believe what they desperately hoped was true. Now they began to pay pride's price, for his capability far exceeded French intelligence estimates.

Ringing Dien Bien Phu were 144 field pieces, thirty 75mm pack howitzers, some thirty-six heavy weapons of other calibers, and, in the last few days of battle, between twelve and sixteen Soviet six-tube rocket launchers, known as Katyushas. Many of them were arduously positioned in casemates dug by tired men into hillsides facing the French, and then covered with several feet of dirt, leaving only a small hole through which the bore could fire. Special camouflaged covers hid even those openings save when the crews were working their tubes.

Giap chose wisely in the emplacement and use of his artillery weapons. His crews were not sufficiently trained nor his communication system sufficiently advanced to allow him the luxury of using forward observers who would radio or telephone target coordinates far back behind the lines to waiting "cannon cockers" as western armies did. Giap's men lacked technical proficiency for this kind of warfare. But they could, and did, learn to look down the barrel of their tubes to align them with far targets before firing. They performed with a vengeance what is technically known as "gun-target, line-of-sight fire."[52]

Far from firing only 25,000 rounds, Viet Minh battery crews loaded and launched some 103,000 shells of 75mm caliber or larger during the course of the battle.[53] Giap thus not only outwitted but outgunned the French, for their own artillery pieces larger than 57mm never exceeded sixty. Some 75 percent of French casualties came, not from infantry combat, but from artillery fire.[54]

Giap was aware of these French problems as he worked out his plan of attack. He later described his attitude at the time with words drawn both from Sun Tzu and from his own tortured reasoning. "We really knew the enemy and ourselves, mastered the laws of war and always firmly held the initiative. The French . . . lacked neither material strength and weapons, nor talented generals. But their war being unjust, they did not and could not master the laws of war."[55] Most, probably all, Great Captains have waged unjust wars. Perhaps by definition, war itself is unjust, but certainly the French (and later the Americans) had no monopoly on unjust wars, despite Giap's constant reiteration of this charge.

His men avoided artillery fire by digging trenches that steadily, inexorably moved closer to French defenders, tightening around their positions. Viet Minh soldiers even dug mine shafts under those strongpoints. In one, at the end of a forty-seven-meter shaft, coolies placed nearly three thousand pounds of TNT.[56] Many hilltops, Giap noted, were captured and recaptured over and again. Some were occupied by both sides simultaneously amid hand-to-hand fighting.[57]

Giap began the first phase of his ground attack, continued from 13 to 17 March, as soon as darkness fell on the first evening. At that point the French had about six days' supply of ammunition available; heavy fighting caused the defenders nearly to run out by the second day. Viet Minh cannoneers raked enemy positions with a savage bombardment. Advancing under cover of their own artillery fire and despite heavy enemy resistance, Viet Minh soldiers captured Béatrice by midnight. Of its defenders, not one French officer survived. In only fifteen hours, de Castries lost a good part of his artillery. Yet Giap paid a heavy price. His soldiers hung like sheaves on the wire surrounding the position. Attacks against Gabrielle and Anne-Marie were unsuccessful. During the following day, French defenders were reinforced when a paratroop battalion jumped in to bolster their ranks. The evening of 14 March, Giap asked for a four-hour impromptu truce to recover his dead. Both sides collected their casualties from the shattered wreckage of Béatrice hill.

The Viet Minh attacked again. Heavy fighting continued throughout the night on Gabrielle, and the next morning the French abandoned it. There were no hardened concrete defense positions anywhere in the French sector. Heavy shelling by Viet Minh guns made a shambles of French earthworks. Fall tells us that, as in the worst days of Verdun in World War I, enemy shells ground the whole top layer of soil into fine sand and caused trenches and bunkers to collapse.[58] Stunned survivors fell back on Dien Bien Phu. The battle was already lost. Colonel Charles Piroth, commander of artillery at the fortress, had earlier promised that he would be able to silence enemy guns quickly. That night the one-armed veteran went into his bunker, pulled the pin on a hand grenade, and committed suicide.

An auxiliary battalion defended the northern sector of Anne-Marie, the 3d Thai Battalion. For some time, Viet Minh artillery batteries had showered them with leaflet-filled shells, urging them to defect. Why, the propaganda demanded, should they sacrifice their lives for the French? These tribesmen watched as Beatrice fell, then Gabrielle. They realized they would share the same fate. Their morale plummeted and their terror increased as they became the target for intensive and murderous Viet Minh shelling. Members of the battalion began to desert as early as the night of 15 March; most of the remainder left for their homes or to defect to the Viet Minh during the night of 17 March. The French and the few Thai who stood fast then abandoned that position and retreated to Huguette. In this way phase one of the siege ended.[59]

The cost to the Viet Minh had been heavy. In that first phase, Giap used many suicidal frontal assaults and French fire decimated those who attacked. So the defenders remained sanguine, calculating they could withstand whatever Giap threw against them. Having hunted his elusive troops for so long, they found it almost a pleasure now to have them arrayed in plain sight and in full formations against their bristling guns and defenses. The main concern of the French was that the airstrip had been out of action since 15 March. Viet Minh moves against the second strip, far removed to the south, made it useless as well. From now on, supplies and reinforcements would have to come by airdrops.

Those modern-day French *poilus*, like their brethren in earlier wars, almost expected some such massive disaster. The closure of the airstrip was but the working out before their eyes of the first rule of warfare: if something can go wrong, it will. As brave soldiers do, they hunkered down behind their defenses, checked magazine clips, fingered their weapons, and peered outward, waiting for the next Viet Minh attack. They gave rueful high marks to their enemy. At least he wasn't afraid to die and had shown that willingness time and again. Nervously they waited, knowing they were more than a match for Giap's soldiers. Things might even work out.

FIFTEEN

"In the Heart
of the Battlefield"

Not everyone's morale was as high as that of the defenders at Dien Bien Phu. The French chief of staff, General Paul Ely, visited Washington and, on 26 March 1954, met with his American counterpart, the chairman of the Joint Chiefs of Staff, Admiral Arthur B. Radford. Also present was President Dwight Eisenhower and Secretary of State John Foster Dulles. Ely said that Dien Bien Phu might well fall to Giap's main force units. Although he asked for nothing save an assurance that American aid would continue, he warned that loss of the battle would have dangerous consequences for all Southeast Asia. Ely's alarum was enough to cause Eisenhower to declare gloomily on 7 April, "You have a row of dominoes set up and you knock over the first one, and what will happen to the last one is the certainty that it will go over very quickly. . . . The loss of Indochina will cause the fall of Southeast Asia like a set of dominoes."[1]

Radford proposed to Eisenhower that the United States mount a rescue action, Operation Vulture—the use of B-29s from the Philippines and aircraft from carriers to knock out Giap's artillery. If that did not work, Radford said, they should consider the use of atomic weapons. When others learned of the proposal, a scorching debate ensued. Eisenhower was of two minds. He declared that he could conceive of no greater tragedy than for his country to become involved in another land war in Asia, yet he wanted to help the French. When the French government heard of Operation Vulture, it asked Eisenhower for an immediate air strike. The president rejected the request but left open the possibility of assistance if European allies also agreed to cooperate. Dulles tried to line up support, but his efforts failed when, at a meeting of the National Security Council in late April, General Matthew Ridgway condemned the idea of nuclear weapons and said conventional air strikes could not succeed without a supporting ground base. That, inevitably, would pull the United States into an Asian land war. The next day, Dulles informed the French ambassador that there would be no American intervention.[2] Whatever was to be the solution, it would have to be found in Indochina, in northwest Tonkin, in a little basin in the hills only a few miles from Laos. Dien Bien Phu would be won or lost by the forces engaged there in a vicious and deadly battle.

While discussions swirled in Washington and Paris, Vo Nguyen Giap hunkered down in Viet Nam to ready his forces for the opening of the second phase of battle, which would last from 30 March to 30 April. He intended to ring remaining French positions with a single, huge trench and then sap inward toward his enemy's positions. Laboring mightily while working under deadly French fire, Giap's 308th Division finally established new positions within half a mile of French outposts. Other of its sister units began digging their way inward about a mile from the French outer wire. At first Giap's men dug only at night, taking cover from French air strikes during daylight hours. They expended immense efforts and created, according to Giap, "a vast network from the neighbouring hills to the plain, to encircle the central subsector and cut if off from the southern sector."[3]

The Viet Minh ring drew tighter. General Navarre decided to strengthen his force and ordered additional reinforcements. On 16 March another paratroop battalion joined units within the fortress. It did not help. On 21 March, routine French patrols between Dien Bien Phu and Isabelle to the south were driven back by Viet Minh fire. Isabelle was now isolated. Continued heavy artillery fire from the hills caused increasing numbers of French casualties. Some planes tried to land to evacuate the wounded but were driven off by heavy fire. A very few helicopters managed to ferry some injured soldiers to safety under cover of night, but their numbers could not keep up with the growing need.

Continued Viet Minh shelling, which French batteries could not silence, caused defenders to begin deepening their bunkers and burrowing underground to partial safety. French air force and navy planes scoured the skies above the valley, dropping napalm on suspected enemy positions and concentrating bombing on suspected sites of Viet Minh batteries. All this seemed to have little effect. The early arrival of monsoon rains, which transformed the French camp from a dust bowl into a swamp, caused wet foliage on the surrounding hills to be nearly immune to the ravages of napalm. The consequent dense smoke further camouflaged Viet Minh artillery pieces, which continued firing from ever-changing locations. Even worse, Giap's air defenses improved with the arrival of Chinese 37mm antiaircraft guns manned by Chinese Communist volunteers. Other Chinese joined the fray: truck drivers as well as various technicians such as radio operators and radar crews.

Despite such dangers, angry French planes floated through the skies, bombing suspected Viet Minh positions and continuing to employ napalm in hopes of consuming some of the heavy vegetation that hid enemy fire batteries within it. They dropped ordnance on Viet Minh supply routes and showered roads with delayed-action bomblets. Despite their best efforts, Giap chortled, "They could not check the flow of hundreds of thousands of voluntary workers, pack-horses and transport cars carrying food and ammunition."[4]

Just as the French air force had little success in silencing Viet Minh guns, so also did it fail to succor its own ground forces. Supply drops became increasingly hazardous, loads often drifting away from the grasping hands of defenders into and behind Viet Minh lines. Vietnamese artillery crews ran to strip the packing from those bundles and retrieve 105mm rounds intended for those within the fortress. Carrying them back to their own positions, they fired them at targets within the imperiled and entrenched camp. Yet as the perimeter shrank, French military men still volunteered to jump into the imperiled fortress to add their weight to the defense. In the course of the fighting, five battalions came to Dien Bien Phu. One was Vietnamese. One was composed of Legionnaires, mostly Germans. Three came from the French army. In addition to those armed units, 1,530 other volunteers parachuted into Dien Bien Phu as replacements for gunners, radio operators, and other specialists who had fallen casualty. Of that number, 680 had never before jumped from an airplane![5]

On 23 March, General Navarre spoke with Giap over an open radio and, for the first time, addressed his enemy using the title "general." He asked the Viet Minh not to fire on medical aircraft attempting to evacuate the wounded. His request, Fall writes, was met with "stony silence."[6]

On the afternoon of 30 March, Giap ordered his divisions to attack from trenches they had pushed close to French lines, territory that now was little more than a two-kilometer square. They assaulted Dominique in the northeast, where both sides hotly disputed every inch of ground, the intensity sometimes reaching Verdun levels. The desperate scenes and martial sounds gave Bernard Fall the title for a book: *Hell in a Very Small Place*. Defenders ran out of hand grenades and 81mm mortar shells, and still they held their ground. Fighting continued for over four days and nights at Dominique, at Eliane, at Huguette. At some points, lines were only ten to fifteen meters apart. By mid-April, Giap's forces reached the airfield and cut it from west to east.[7] His troops exhausted, casualties heavy, Giap relaxed his pressure on the French in order to bring forward reinforcements and to replenish ammunition and other supplies. Navarre had hoped the monsoons would make it impossible for Giap's logistics forces to operate. This did not happen, and supplies came steadily into the Viet Minh camp.

Navarre finally came to realize the mistakes and miscalculations he had imposed upon the Dien Bien Phu defenders.

Giap had not organized his style of warfare to accommodate prisoners of war, and the Viet Minh were unable to care properly even for their own injured, much less for captured French soldiers who suffered from wounds. On Giap's orders they returned injured men whom they had captured (and refused to accept their own back), knowing the agonies of battlefield injuries and the cries of wounded men would resound within the French positions, adding still another pressure to the many faced by their beleaguered enemies. Those fit enough to march were taken away to isolated camps selected by Giap's staff officers.

These prisoner-of-war camps were often not even enclosed; perimeters were simply arbitrarily announced. Without housing, captured soldiers often slept in the open until they could erect their own rude shelters. Their rice-based diet caused many prisoners to suffer from rampant vitamin deficiency diseases. They spoke later of enduring humiliation, arbitrary restrictions, and torture—all considered by the Viet Minh to be part of their "reeducation" and foreshadowing later treatment given to American prisoners. After the fall of Dien Bien Phu, their Viet Minh guards forced prisoners, including the injured and the ill, to march six hundred kilometers in forty days under conditions which cost many lives.[8]

For a time, French defenders at Isabelle considered fighting their way out of the trap into upper Laos. They even had a code name for any such attempt—Operation Albatross. The number of Viet Minh units in the area made such a plan no more than another form of suicide, so they abandoned the idea and continued to defend their positions, although some seventy men did finally succeed in fighting their way out of the Viet Minh trap.[9]

A possibly apocryphal story Giap later related about himself was printed in the *Armee Rundschau* ("Army Review") of the former Deutsche Demokratische Republic (DDR). He recalled a lull in the fighting that came one day, perhaps between the first two phases, perhaps between the last two. He did not specify the time. For years, Giap revealed, he was so busy with leadership of the army, surely an all-consuming lust, that he barely had time to devote himself to his second love of music. His favorite composers were Beethoven and Liszt. During that pause in the attack, singers, dancers, and musicians came to the forest, where Giap rested on a bed of leaves, nearby tables spread with war maps, and presented there a program of music for the general, his staff, and some men from adjacent units.[10]

Whether Giap listened to Beethoven—either then or at any other time—is of little consequence; the notion that entertainers came to the Viet Minh camp is, however, worth considering, for such evidence makes those soldiers more human, less a faceless, unfeeling, undifferentiated horde, as they so often seem to have been portrayed then and later. In his writings Giap indicates the concern he and the party felt for the morale of each one of his troops. "Each day," he claimed, "thousands of letters and telegrams from all over the country came to the Dien Bien Phu front. Never had Viet Nam been so anxious about her fighting sons, never had the relations between the rear and the front been so intimate."[11]

It was fortunate for his cause that Giap was concerned about his men and the sacrifices they were making. Casualties on both sides had been heavy in every engagement, but the Viet Minh took the brunt of every clash, and their losses far exceeded those of the French. By the end of the second phase of the siege, Viet Minh losses probably reached twenty thousand killed, wounded, or captured. That gruesome total was the approximate size of two of Giap's light infantry divisions. Giap recognized the awful state in which his men lived. As the French suffered, so did they: from fatigue, filth, and vermin, living like animals as they forced their trenches toward the enemy, endless labor without proper rest, inadequate diet, constant fear. Inevitably they were drenched from monsoon rains with no shelter or dry clothes, adrenaline coursing through their bodies as they rushed forward to pit their lives against the French in hand-to-hand combat, bereaved survivors mourning the loss of comrades. Week after week of such horrors sapped the bravery from the very marrow of their bones.

Within the French perimeter, defenders listened to Viet Minh radio broadcasts from lower-unit commanders informing their superiors that certain units refused any longer to obey orders. Prisoners captured by the French told how they had been made to advance by threats of being shot from behind by their own noncommissioned and commissioned officers if they lagged or faltered.[12]

Giap's dry, turgid writing describes how serious the problem of morale became: ". . . the battle having lasted a very long time, more troops . . . become fatigued and are worn and are faced with great nervous tension. . . . not able to avoid decimation. . . . there appear negative *rightist tendencies*, whose manifestations are the fear of having many killed, the fear of suffering casualties, of facing up to fatigue, difficulties, privations." Such an admission is surprising and is an indication of just how serious the morale problem had become.[13] "We found in our ranks," Giap wrote, "signs of under-estimation of the enemy . . . particularly after the second phase of the campaign." It was then, he added, "when attack and defence were equally fierce," that "negative rightist thoughts cropped up" to the detriment of the cause. When Giap learned the extent of his army's morale problem, he reported the situation to the Communist Party's political bureau. Members of the Politburo considered the matter and quickly advised Giap to rectify the problem.

Giap related that "in the heart of the battlefield" he called for "an intensive and extensive struggle" against "rightist passivity." Political cadres and commissars within all his units called meetings of their men. As the battle raged on, these political officers led discussions about courage, bravery, right thinking, devotion to the cause, dedication. Men stood and offered self-criticism. They pointed at others as examples, both good and bad. All this, Giap admitted, was necessary "for the heightening of revolutionary enthusiasm and the spirit of strict discipline." It began to work. Only through his men's rededication could Giap be sure of "ensuring the total victory of the campaign." Fired by the oratory of their commissars and the bravery of their fellows, even the recalcitrant and reluctant began to feel new zeal. "This ideological struggle was very successful," Giap sighed with relief. "This was one of the greatest achievements in political work in our army's history" and was the single factor which "led the Dien Bien Phu campaign to complete victory."[14]

One is almost driven to admire Giap's honesty and his willingness to admit the existence of such problems and to write of them in publications that eventually made their way to the West. What might have happened at Dien Bien Phu if Giap had been more of a soldier and less a politician? Reinforced by their political lessons and by other, fresh units ordered into line by Giap, the men of the Viet Minh army now stood paused, ready to resume the struggle.

Giap's third phase of the siege ran from 1 to 7 May. By this time the French held no more than one square kilometer of ground plus Isabelle to the south, and they were entirely exposed to Viet Minh firepower. Still they fought on, bolstered at 5:20 A.M. on 6 May by ninety-four paratroopers who volunteered to jump into their midst, only hours before the end. In these final days, Giap ordered no preliminary or covering barrages, perhaps because his troops were often less than one hundred yards from the French. Viet Minh soldiers simply rushed toward their enemy. They demolished bunkers, blew gaps in the wire, and fought hand-to-hand with grenades and bayonets. Fighting continued on 2 May, and that night the last French reinforcements, part of still another paratroop battalion, dropped onto the fortress. Each day the Viet Minh infantry pressed the attack while mortar rounds fell on French positions. One by one the French lost their positions and outposts, sometimes by being overrun, increasingly by abandonment as they ran out of ammunition.

On 7 May about noon the 308th Division launched a massive attack and broke through the last French defenses into the center of the last pockets of resistance. The last hour had come. In his bunker, de Castries shouted into a radio microphone, "Our resistance is going to be overwhelmed. The Viets are within a few meters of the radio transmitter where I am speaking. I have given orders to carry out maximum destruction. We will not surrender. We will fight to the end. . . . *Vive la France!*" Moments later he was seized by Viet Minh soldiers who burst into the bunker.[15] At 5:30 P.M., the French hoisted the white flag of surrender. Isabelle held out until the early-morning hours of 8 May, but then it too surrendered. The battle had lasted for fifty-five days and fifty-five nights.[16] A subdued de Castries and his staff were paraded before Giap.

Giap enjoyed statistics, and so he tolled the results of his efforts in typical exaggerated fashion, given the fact that the French garrison at Dien Bien Phu never numbered much over ten thousand troops. "On all fronts, we put out of action 112,000 enemy troops and brought down or destroyed on the ground 177 planes. At Dien Bien Phu, we put out of action 16,200 enemy troops, including . . . one general, 16 colonels, 1,749 officers and warrant-officers . . . 62 planes [and] seized armaments, ammunition and equipment." He had at last defeated the "organized gangs of myrmidons" who opposed him. For the remainder of his life, Giap would laugh at a small joke Ho Chi Minh made about the outcome of the battle. "At Dien Bien Phu," Ho chuckled, "Giap lost not a single tank or airplane."[17]

The Chinese Communist government in Peking quickly claimed that it was responsible for the Vietnamese victory. Its senior military advisers to Giap, including General Lo Kwei-Po and others, were the ones, Peking proudly announced, who had guided him to victory. Those advisers had done all the planning. Giap simply took their ideas and put them into action. Giap and the Viet Minh government laughed off this claim.[18] Giap himself announced that "the most important and most decisive factor" in the victory "was the adamant determination and very high spirit of struggle of our people and people's army."[19]

The conflict at Dien Bien Phu exhausted both armies and sucked nearly dry Giap's supply resources. Victory went, not to the strongest side, but to the combatant with the most equanimity, the one whose internal difficulties were more successfully hidden from the other camp. In his public pronouncements, Giap proclaimed what he had achieved as inevitable; the French shouted their dismay to the whole world. Only 4 percent of the French force was destroyed in the siege of Dien Bien Phu, but psychologically it was the end. The eight-year war had cost them billions and, according to Bernard Fall, 172,000 dead, wounded, or missing. Viet Nam was no longer worth the cost.[20]

On the morning of 8 May, just as the French at home were preparing to celebrate the ninth anniversary of the victorious end of World War II, news of the disaster in Indochina blazoned across the front pages of their newspapers. Reaction of the citizenry to this news was nearly unanimous. In Paris a crowd attacked a motorcade of cabinet ministers on their way to the solemn anniversary celebrations and stoned the automobiles. All over the land, thousands of spontaneous meetings came together to shout demands for peace. The Laniel-Bidault cabinet had earlier called for fighting to continue against the Viet Minh to the bitter end and had talked of "internationalizing the Indochina war." It now found itself without support. Shouting deputies in the *parlement* gave a vote of no confidence, and the Laniel cabinet resigned a few days later. A new government would now represent France at the meetings in Geneva.[21]

The victory at Dien Bien Phu was precisely what Ho Chi Minh needed for use at Geneva. Now he had total control of the north of Viet Nam and effective occupation of much of the remainder. Surely this would be recognized by the great powers, already assembled in Switzerland. With their concurrence, Ho would have the time necessary to help the north recuperate from its years of conflict. Giap would have opportunity to rebuild his army if a renewed effort became necessary to unify all Viet Nam.[22]

The new French prime minister was Pierre Mendès-France, a radical socialist. For some time he had been convinced that the Laniel government had dragged its feet in Indochina and stalled at the Geneva meetings in hopes of persuading the United States to take a more active role in the war with the Viet Minh. Mendès-France believed continuing the conflict would only further humiliate his country, and so he pledged an astonishing commitment. If he was not able to bring about peace with the Viet Minh government within thirty days, he would hand in his resignation. He kept his word, although it took him a few days longer than he had promised. Mendès-France found negotiations with the other great powers at Geneva more difficult than he had envisioned.

Present were Georges Bidault, a holdover from the Laniel cabinet, as the spokesman for the new Mendès-France government; Chou En-lai for the People's Republic of China; Vyacheslav Molotov, representative for the Union of Soviet Socialist Republics; Anthony Eden, for Great Britain; and Walter Bedell Smith, standing in for Secretary of State John Foster Dulles of the United States. Pham Van Dong, Hoang Minh Giam, and Colonel Ta Quong Buu came on behalf of the Democratic Republic of Viet Nam. Nguyen Quoc Dinh and Dr. Tran Van Do represented Bao Dai's State of Viet Nam, comprising the land from southern Annam to the Ca Mau peninsula. Laos and Cambodia also attended, the latter represented by its foreign minister, Tep Phon, and defense minister, General Nhick Tianlong.

From the beginning, Dulles looked upon the conference at Geneva with grave suspicion. He knew that some sort of settlement was inevitable, and he shuddered at the thought of the military void in Southeast Asia that would be left when the French departed. He saw there a highly complicated and dangerous international situation, and wanted the United States to gain a firm foothold in the region and use Indochina as a main link in a *cordon sanitaire* he hoped eventually to stretch around the treacherous Chinese Communists who now controlled their own vast land. In each silence around the table, U.S. representatives could hear the sounds of toppling dominoes. The American secretary of state, on 24 June, had already informed congressional leaders that the United States must assume more responsibility in that part of Asia. To ensure that freedom was kept alive there, he wanted to create a regional alliance, patterned on NATO in Europe. Yet the cards seemed stacked against the U.S. position in Geneva when Mendès-France assumed control of the French government and Dulles began to look beyond the immediate situation to the years after the conferees departed for the airport and home.

Dulles was not the only one with suspicions. Laos and Cambodia feared Vietnamese aggression and wanted assurance that they would not become targets of their neighbor's expansionist policies. Pham Van Dong argued on behalf of President Ho that, inasmuch as the Viet Minh effectively held most of their national territory, north and south, they should now fall heir to the whole of the country. Bao Dai's negotiator insisted that the State of Viet Nam must remain inviolate, out of reach of the grasping hands of northern Communists. With American encouragement, Bao Dai's government ultimately refused to be bound by the final agreement and so announced that position at the conference.

Great Britain, then involved in a guerrilla conflict of its own with Chinese insurgents operating among the rural population of the Malay Peninsula, at first supported the American position, agreeing that it was in the best interests of the West to "bar the road to Asian communism with a stout wall." Then Anthony Eden changed his mind; Viet Nam was not Malaya and French colonies were not British ones. If Mendès-France wanted a settlement, Eden was happy to accommodate him.

Then the Soviets dropped a bombshell that immediately became suspect by all freedom-loving peoples. As the diplomats sat around the conference table, Molotov announced that his government believed the answer lay simply in granting independence to all the states of Indochina and pledging them to a position of neutrality between the cold war competitions of East and West. Eden believed that to be a reasonable proposal and threw the weight of his country behind the Soviet initiative. China also accepted the suggestion.

There was, however, a hitch that caused Pham Van Dong's pulse to race and his obstinacy to surface. Viet Nam would be divided temporarily between Ho's government in the north and Bao Dai's State of Viet Nam in the south. Nationwide elections would later be scheduled to end the division and determine whether Ho's or Bao Dai's government would rule over the whole of the land. Unable to persuade the only two countries—the USSR and China—who recognized his government to abandon this position, Pham Van Dong was at the point of stalking from the conference. It took the combined efforts of Molotov, Chou En-lai, and Eden to convince him to accept the provision.

Now came hard bargaining. Where should the line be drawn? Dong wanted it placed as far south as possible, while Bidault, who still dreamed of a continuing French influence and presence in Viet Nam, insisted that it be drawn as far north as he could manage. It might be possible to retain French control in Cochin China. Under the right circumstances, even Tonkin might someday return to membership in the French Union. Consequently, Bidault hoped to push the date for elections as far into the future as he could so as to give his countrymen the chance to realize those possibilities, while Pham Van Dong wanted elections scheduled and held quickly. The Viet Minh delegation in Switzerland was not as successful as Giap had been at Dien Bien Phu.

Even while the meetings in Geneva continued, Dulles began to carry out his plans to insert the United States into the midst of the problems of Indochina. He and his brother, Allen, who was head of the Central Intelligence Agency, met in Washington with Colonel Edward G. Lansdale, an air force officer on loan to the agency. Lansdale was only recently returned from a spectacular success in the Philippines, where he had stage-managed Ramón Magsaysay into the presidency of that country and successfully introduced counterinsurgency measures that neutralized the Hukbalahap Communist-inspired rebellion there. Impressed with his exploits, the two brothers Dulles assigned Lansdale to duty in Viet Nam. His orders called for him to do everything possible to strengthen the non-Communist southern government and to weaken Ho's northern regime, including the use of covert paramilitary operations to sabotage physical installations and political/psychological black propaganda to disrupt northern support for Ho. Lansdale arrived in Saigon on 1 June 1954 and immediately began to assemble a team to work with him, which he named the Saigon Military Mission.[23]

A few days later, at his chateau in Cannes, France, Bao Dai selected Ngo Dinh Diem as his new premier for the State of Viet Nam. Diem arrived in Saigon on 26 June. Upon his arrival at Norodom Palace there, he found no supporters, no functioning bureaucracy, no government in place. On the next day he had a surprise visit from Lansdale, who encouraged him to begin his duties and to expect great help from the United States. On 7 July, Diem formally assumed the duties of his office.

The accords, or the Final Declaration of the Geneva Conference, as they were officially known, were signed a few days later on 21 July 1954. They were, of course, a compromise that pleased no one. In Viet Nam a cease-fire was to go into effect immediately; that codicil was signed by General Ta Quang Buu for the Viet Minh and General Henri Delteil for France. Laos and Cambodia were to become two independent but neutral kingdoms. Both France and Ho's government must pull their troops out of both countries.

With a stroke of the pen, Viet Nam was artificially divided in half along the 17th parallel, although the conferees were careful to stipulate that this "should not in any way be interpreted as constituting a political or territorial boundary." That division was to be only temporary. The zones would be unified before July 1956 by "free and democratic" elections. France must withdraw its forces from the north, and the Viet Minh must leave the south within three hundred days. During that time, civil populations also had the right to choose whether they wished to live in the north or south and had the right to free movement in either direction. New foreign troops were prohibited from entering upon Vietnamese soil. An International Control Commission composed of personnel from Poland, India, and Canada would monitor compliance with the accords.

The United States refused to sign the agreement and urged the southern Vietnamese to withhold their signatures. Bao Dai consequently denounced the agreements. Walter Bedell Smith, on behalf of the United States, issued a unilateral declaration that his country would refrain from the threat or use of force to disturb the agreement, would view with grave concern any renewal of aggression as a violation of the accords and a serious threat to international peace and security, and would support the coming free elections to be supervised by the United Nations.[24]

The victory at Dien Bien Phu brought Giap an international reputation. Bernard Fall wrote, "In . . . grand strategy, the little Vietnamese history professor with his largely self-taught military science had totally outguessed the French generals and colonels with their general-staff school diplomas."[25] Davidson writes that criticisms of General Giap are "superficial" and describes him as one with a "sure grasp of the fundamentals of strategy," an officer who "showed imagination," a man who "merits praise" and who "deserves great credit." An amateur turned professional, Giap earned even "higher marks" as a logistician, Davidson says, because of his ability to keep his troops at Dien Bien Phu supplied under the worst possible conditions. That was an "achievement of first rank." Yet, Davidson says, Giap accomplished an even greater one. "It was in the field of organization, administration, and motivation that he excelled. In this area he was a genius."[26]

Others have agreed. O'Neill writes, "Not only was Giap's strategy in accepting battle at Dien Bien Phu soundly based, but also his tactical control of the battle was of a high order. Particularly outstanding were his use of artillery to cut off French supplies from the air and his series of overlapping wave attacks that struck the French defences first on one side and then the other." O'Neill gives the Vietnamese leader great credit for his use of the principles of flexibility and surprise. He was, O'Neill sums up, a skillful practitioner of strategy and tactics.[27]

It is clear why Giap chose not to take his army on a victory parade into Ha Noi immediately following his victory at Dien Bien Phu. It was not the time to let up on the French army lest its leaders perceive that the Viet Minh was nearly done in. Giap's divisions had suffered savage losses. Morale had fallen and near mutiny had set in during the clash at Dien Bien Phu. Giap needed time to instill his troops with even more political indoctrination, and this could best be done with them living under wartime discipline. So he did not order his men to stand down until the date of the actual cease-fire specified by the Geneva Accords— 1 August 1954. During that summer, Giap continued his relentless pressure against the French. In the Central Highlands, in a series of ambushes, Giap's army inflicted severe casualties on the three thousand men of Group Mobile 100.

This enabled the Viet Minh to occupy several towns and plant cadres there before they withdrew north of the Ben Hai River in August.

It was 10 October 1954 before Giap, with his 308th Division, spearhead of the People's Liberation Army, marched proudly into Ha Noi. The first groups of Viet Minh cadre had not arrived until 3 October, delaying their entry for weeks out of fear of French reprisals. When the last French troops departed on 9 October, it did not take long before the highest of the Viet Minh leaders came into the city, although Ho Chi Minh did not appear until 17 October. Most of the 308th Division's soldiers had not seen or heard from their families for eight years—not since the night of 19 December 1946 when they whispered quick goodbyes and disappeared into the darkness, fleeing from the French. Now they exulted in their reunions with loved ones. Two days after his return, Giap walked into the Ha Noi power station to discuss technical problems of its operation with French engineers who still manned the installation. There was much to learn in the days of transition from French to Vietnamese rule.[28]

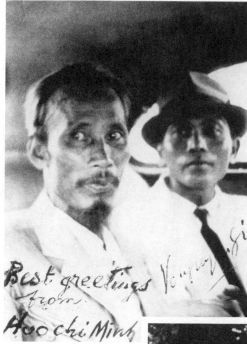

Autographed photo of Ho Chi Minh (left) and Vo Nguyen Giap (right) seated in automobile in Ha Noi in 1945. *Courtesy of Allison Kent Thomas*

Giap and Ho Chi Minh in Ha Noi, 1946. After first meeting Ho in China in 1940, Giap became his trusted lieutenant and was chosen in 1944 to form his army. *Courtesy of Vo Nguyen Giap*

Ho Chi Minh and Giap pose with members of the U.S. Deer Team, who parachuted into their camp in 1945 to assist their tiny military force with training in small arms and small-unit tactics. Standing (left to right): unidentified, René Defourneaux, Ho Chi Minh, Allison Kent Thomas, Giap, Henry Prunier, Dam Quang Trung (now a general), unidentified, Paul Hoaglund. Seated: Lawrence Vogt, Aaron Squires, unidentified.
Courtesy of Allison Kent Thomas

Ho Chi Minh reading from his recently declared declaration of independence above the crowds in Ba Dinh Square in Ha Noi on September 2, 1945. It was based in part on America's.
Courtesy of Allison Kent Thomas

Giap and second wife, Dang Bich Ha, 1956. Although Giap loved his first and second wives, his children, and his grandchildren, they always knew they were secondary to his devotion to freeing his country and ridding it of foreign control. *Courtesy of Vo Nguyen Giap*

Giap's daughter Vo Hong Anh by his first wife, with children from his second marriage: (left to right) daughter Vo Hoa Binh, son Vo Dien Bien, son Vo Hong Nam, and daughter Vo Hanh Phuc. Photo taken in 1960. *Courtesy of Vo Nguyen Giap*

Giap's primary weapon against the South and its allies: the elusive Viet Cong guerrilla.
National Archives

(Left)
In this North Vietnamese photo captured by an American soldier in 1969, the specter of Ho Chi Minh hovers over South Vietnamese soldiers as they head toward the war front during the height of U.S. involvement.
Courtesy of Dennis W. Currey

(Below)
North Vietnamese Army regulars on parade in Ha Noi during the 1960s.
National Archives

(Above)
Giap (right) chats with members of the People's Liberation Army in December 1965. Lt. Gen. Tien Dung (center, rear), chief of the general staff, trails behind.
National Archives

(Left)
Giap in full dress uniform in 1968.
Courtesy of Vo Nguyen Giap

In 1990, the Vietnamese celebrated the forty-fifth anniversary of the August Revolution in the northern Vietnamese town Kim Lung (now Tan Trao). The banyan tree shown is the one in which Maj. Allison Kent Thomas became entangled in 1945 when he and the other members of the Deer Team parachuted in to aid Giap's forces. *Courtesy of Allison Kent Thomas*

Giap and Dang Bich Ha in 1991 in front of their home in Ha Noi. *Courtesy of Vo Nguyen Giap*

The author with Giap in Ha Noi.

PART FOUR

Saigon,
1955–91

SIXTEEN

"The Party
Committed Serious Errors"

Following recognition of North Viet Nam as an independent state, Giap became vice prime minister, while simultaneously filling the post of minister of national defense and commander in chief of the army, as well as serving as a member of the Politburo. Until 1963, he was also president of the National Commission for Research. He had reached new heights of power and prestige. He was in command of an army of 350,000 men reinforced by a people's militia of 200,000. All Chinese Communist advisers had gone home. In many ways his warrant was the equivalent of the American secretary of defense combined with that of the chairman of the Joint Chiefs of Staff, with the added powers and authority held by a general in command of a field army. He had immense prestige and authority. But despite his years as a military man, he was still first a politician dedicated to Communist doctrine. His life would be shaped as much by what happened in the halls of the Politburo as by victories on the field of battle.

The central committee was important, but it met on average only twice a year. It set policy, but day-by-day implementation remained the responsibility of the Politburo, and it was Giap's membership and ranking there that gave him his real power. Those decision-makers joined in an interactive process, considering various demands and weighing limited resources and poor communications against existing priorities. Giap was in the midst of this byzantine system. He was now the headquarters man, the home office head, and those who would follow his career would have to be aware of what occurred there.[1]

After Giap's victory at Dien Bien Phu, an immediate respect grew for the North Vietnamese within the underdeveloped world. Asians and Africans, long the subject of western colonial domination, cheered the French defeat, for it confirmed what they had long hoped—that western powers could be overcome, that peoples awash in poverty and lacking modern technology could throw off the bonds that had so long chained them. Few in Asia or Africa felt much affinity for what Mao had achieved. He had, after all, only fought against other Chinese, and his country was so vast that not many could identify with it. North Viet Nam was another matter. Giap had defeated a traditionally powerful, recognized western nation, and he had accomplished this feat through fidelity to his cause, by outthinking his opponents, and by relying on the bravery of his soldiers.[2] It had been a physical battle, to be sure. Yet it had been more. The Vietnamese had drawn on the wellsprings of their spiritual and moral essence, and other peoples knew they also possessed those qualities in abundant measure. And so they honored Giap and Ho and Viet Nam and drew strength from their example.

For Giap the end of the First Indochina War was a welcome sight. His hopes were high, and he had achieved great deeds. Among the population he was now regarded as a folk hero. His party had not gained all it hoped to receive at Geneva, but it had garnered much, and that was worth celebrating. He had also grown tired of the privations of life in the bush. Now he could return to a more settled and comfortable life with his wife, Dang Bich Ha. Perhaps the two of them could make a normal home for his teenage daughter, Hong Anh. He had served his country as a soldier; now duty called out to the politician in him, for there was much to be done to establish the Communist Party solidly in the North and to carry its programs into action. He was only forty-three, a young man to have accomplished so much, yet still at an age where he could plan on many more years of service.

He may have contemplated that cheerful future on 1 January 1955 when he stood with Ho, Pham Van Dong (who would serve as foreign minister of the new government), and other luminaries on a reviewing stand over sixty feet tall. It was the day of the official victory celebration, and before them stretched out a crowd of 200,000 people, many waving flags, flowers, and pictures of Ho, Lenin, Marx, and other Communists. Both Ho and Giap spoke to the assembled throng. They knew by this time that outside forces were again poised to strike at their fledgling state; that there were those who were dedicated to making them fail.

Ho, Giap, and other leaders of the new northern government faced a set of unexpected problems caused by the implacable enmity of the American government and by the activities of a freewheeling American intelligence agent. Colonel Edward G. Lansdale had been in Saigon since the previous summer, sent by Allen and John Foster Dulles with the approval of Eisenhower, to do what he could to strengthen Bao Dai's southern government and to weaken Ho Chi Minh's hold on the reins of power in the North. On 27 June 1954, the day after the new premier, Ngo Dinh Diem, arrived at Saigon's Tan Son Nhut airport, Lansdale, with incredible chutzpah, walked into Norodom Palace (which Diem quickly renamed Doc Lap, or Independence Palace), introduced himself to Diem, and offered to help him run the country. Diem accepted.[3]

Lansdale thus found his opening to fulfill one of the two responsibilities assigned him by his superiors, and in coming months he spent a great deal of time counseling Diem. Having begun a course of action to strengthen Diem's government, Lansdale now gathered a team of young men to help him destabilize Communist rule in the North. In a disingenuous remark, Lansdale wrote, "I . . . split my small team in two. One half . . . engaged in refugee work in the North. The other half stayed with me [in Saigon] to help with other endeavors."[4] Lansdale selected Lucien Conein, one of the first Americans to parachute into Indochina in 1944 and now firmly fixed on a CIA career, to head that part of the Saigon Military Mission (SMM) team which would operate against Ho's regime in the North. Conein's task was to develop a paramilitary organization to be in position and ready for action when the French finally left the North and the Viet Minh took over in early October 1954. He was also to carry out systematic sabotage of North Viet Nam's utility, transportation, and port facilities. Conein established a headquarters in Ha Noi with a branch in Haiphong and set to work.[5]

Conein's team, among other activities, scattered carefully crafted leaflets informing Tonkinese how to behave when the Viet Minh takeover of Ha Noi occurred in early October. The finished product included items on property and money reform and called for a three-day holiday for all workers to celebrate the event. Shopkeepers were instructed to take an inventory of their goods so that the new government would know what to confiscate. The leaflet was so well prepared that when local party officials saw copies, they assumed the broadside was authentic and insisted that shopkeepers obey its demands. Viet Minh currency fell to about half its previous value. Authorities saw through the trick, however, and denounced the leaflets in radio broadcasts. Some local officials were so suspicious that they were certain the radio denunciations were no more than a French propaganda trick.[6]

The team also hired noted northern astrologers to predict imminent disasters certain to befall Viet Minh leaders and to forecast a long period of prosperous unity for those in the South. These predictions, set forth in a spurious almanac produced at SMM headquarters in Saigon, were smuggled deep into Viet Minh territory and sold there.[7]

Conein then turned his attention to organizing a Vietnamese paramilitary group to use against the Viet Minh. Most of its members were drawn from the small number of remaining northern Dai Viets still alive after repeated earlier purges of their ranks by Giap and his police.[8] This group was armed with paramilitary matériel introduced by SMM into the north by clandestine air, sea, and land shipments.[9] When Viet Minh security forces tightened control over goods coming into Haiphong's airport, SMM simply chose an alternate sea route to transport its contraband. All told, about eight and a half tons of supplies were shipped for later use by Conein's Dai Viet paramilitary units, including fourteen radios, three hundred carbines, ninety thousand rounds of rifle ammunition, fifty pistols, ten thousand rounds of handgun ammunition, and three hundred pounds of explosives. SMM delivered two and a half tons to agents already in place and, with the help of the U.S. Navy, cached the remainder at operational sites along the Red River. The operational teams infiltrated into the North around mid-April 1955.[10]

Conein and his sabotage team struck many targets and noted others for future assaults: power plants, coal mines, water systems, bridges, the telephone systems of Ha Noi and Haiphong, and oil depots and harbor facilities at Haiphong. They had to be careful, however, because the United States maintained a very small consulate and a Military Assistance and Advisory Group (MAAG) detachment in the North, and, as Conein said, "We couldn't do anything that would jeopardize them. We could have done a lot more if they hadn't been there." Time ran out before Conein and his team completed their work; they evacuated Ha Noi on 9 October 1955 along with the last French troops.[11]

Brigadier General Cao Pha, now vice director of the Institute for Military History in Ha Noi, remembers those days and the efforts of the Saigon Military Mission. "Its goals were ambitious," he said, "but preparation and organization were not sound and the project was done in haste." Wagging his finger, he added, "We were, of course, prepared for just such attempts." The Americans, he said, "had to use as agents people willing to betray the interests of their own Fatherland who were recruited from anti-Communist parties and from former secret agents of the Deuxième Bureau. . . . They were betrayers and mercenaries with no ideals. They worked for money so we had an easy job to capture them. These people quickly gave themselves up to us or . . . we found them out because our common people turned them in."

Warming to his subject, Cao Pha recalled how quickly "we discovered Conein's hidden weapons. A hasty job of hiding them had been done. The ones hidden around Haiphong and along the Red River were uncovered. Burying them was not very helpful for the South, but we were glad to add them to our arsenal."

Then Cao Pha summed up. "In brief, SMM acted in too great of haste. It relied incorrectly on betrayers to serve as agents, and its assessment of our people was incorrect. Lansdale and Conein wanted to sabotage things such as electric plants, but under communism our workers were masters of those factories so were themselves concerned about the facilities' safety. It was a constant in U.S. policy to destroy the Geneva agreements from the first days and to replace France in Viet Nam with U.S. power. There were wicked schemes we had to face. The U.S. tried to empty the sea to catch fish."[12]

As his team members worked in the North, Lansdale continued to meet with Ngo Dinh Diem and, with low-keyed, patient fervor, to offer suggestions. The South, he believed, must be made as strong as possible, and that would require, among other things, a larger population base. Lansdale wanted to encourage vast numbers of northerners to move below the 17th parallel during the three hundred days in which such relocation was allowed by the Geneva Accords. Diem had not much thought about the matter, was not interested in it, and expected no more than ten thousand refugees. Personnel at the American Agency for International Development calculated they might need tenting capable of housing about the same number. Red Cross people were laying in a supply of bandages to help a few thousand. French authorities, who had agreed to help transport those who wished to move, planned to provide for no more than thirty thousand, mostly landlords and businessmen.

Lansdale found a persuasive argument to use with Diem. "When the plebiscite comes between North and South, we have to have more people to vote on our side. . . . It would give us a chance for the future." That was a speech Diem could understand, and he authorized an effort to persuade northerners to abandon their homes for new lives in the South.[13]

Viet Minh officials reacted angrily to Lansdale's scheme. An official history complained that "under U.S. patronage, a plot was evolved for the amputation of one half of Vietnam. . . . [Using] all kinds of deceitful manoeuvres and means of corruption, the United States set up a puppet government comprising reactionary elements most hated by the Vietnamese people. . . . [T]he U.S. 'advisers' were the real masters of the country [including] Lansdale, for the secret police."[14]

Lansdale's Saigon Military Mission went into overtime in its efforts to excite northerners to relocate. Two hundred thousand needed little convincing; they were dependents of members of French military auxiliary units who had to cast their lot with Diem. Others were convinced by black propaganda rumors of Chinese army units moving into Tonkin, while merchants and landlords decided to leave because Ho's government would confiscate all their belongings and property. A number came south because of the predictions of astrologers. And hundreds of thousands came, nearly seven hundred thousand of them, because of Saigon Military Mission propaganda about the dire consequences that would befall Roman Catholics under Ho's new regime. Sixty percent of the more than one million northern Catholics made the journey. Throughout Catholic hamlets and villages of the Red River basin, fervent believers listened when their priests thundered, "The Virgin Mary is moving south and we must go with her," or heard marketplace rumors that "God is deserting the North." Fearing reprisals from Ho's government if they remained and unwilling to chance the loss of their faith if the Spirit of God was truly departing from their land, these people solemnly set their faces toward the South.[15]

Refugee registration increased dramatically in the late summer of 1954 and continued on into the spring of 1955. As registrants flooded the port of Haiphong, the city became swamped with people unable to find shelter, food, or medicine. Several nations volunteered to help out in this Great Migration of 1954. The Kuomintang government on Formosa, Great Britain, the French, and private relief agencies all provided support for this dramatic version of an oriental Dunkirk, as did the ships and men of the U.S. Seventh Fleet.[16]

Angered though he was by these departures, Vo Nguyen Giap ordered that men of his main force units should help those refugees whenever possible. Bui Tin, until recently the editor of *Nhan Dan,* was then a major commanding the 14th Battalion of Giap's 304th Division and had fought at Dien Bien Phu. His unit was stationed in Nghe An province during the Great Migration, and Major Tin saw the plight of many of his countrymen as they entered upon the life of a refugee. "They went by foot on the roads or by sea on small bamboo boats," Tin remembered. He tried to persuade some to stay, but they insisted on leaving, following the advice of their priests. On Highway 1 were thousands of people. "Many cried," he said, "for they were leaving their native soil. They said goodbye to us. Many felt contradictions between their religious and family feelings. Many were poor peasants with only a few clothes, a little rice, a sleeping mat. The countryside was poor. They had to leave quickly and were not prepared materially or spiritually. There were no cars, no trains. It was terrible."

Tin related, "The most important thing for many was to keep their crosses. Many knelt by the pillars of their houses and prayed. Some—after walking south perhaps two hundred meters—returned to their homes to hug the trees and weep. Women carried babies on their backs. It was painful for us to see ill eighty-year-old people trying to go. Most Christian people in Nghe An lived near the seacoast. In parts of the province, villages sat totally deserted. Slogans convinced them to go: 'God is leaving for the South.' "

Tin and his fellows tried to help. "At first they were afraid even to let us in their houses, for they believed the issue was one of communism versus Christianity. Our policy was not to disturb them, to look after their children, to wrap up their beds as luggage for their journey. We didn't carry guns, but were just there to help. Our soldiers were in tears to see their sorrow." Tin's soldiers gave away their food, carried luggage, held children. "Our soldiers carried some old people on their backs, ten or more kilometers to the boats, before returning to their units. More than a million went south."[17]

As refugees headed south, Giap was aware of the necessity of removing his forces from south of the 17th parallel, a provision of the Geneva Accords. What was he to do with those units? Giap had no intention of losing hard-won gains there. Although he ordered his main force units north, he sent instructions to southerners who had fought with the Viet Minh to go underground, to cache their weapons, and to disguise their tunnel openings. They had operated in War Zones C and D, north and northeast of Saigon, in the Phuoc Tuy area to the southeast of Saigon, and the Trans-Bassac region of the Ca Mau peninsula. Those base areas should be preserved, Giap ordered, and so they stored weapons, ammunition, radio sets, and explosives in well-camouflaged tunnels. (For a diagrammatic look at life in those tunnels, see illustration "Typical V.C. Underground Group Shelter.") Giap knew the struggle in the South in the two years immediately ahead would be political rather than military. Then elections would reunite the country.

Viet Minh contingents traveled north from ports at Cap St. Jacques and Qui Nhon on Polish vessels. They used American Liberty ships given to the Soviets during World War II. Their rusty, trampish appearance suggested they had not been repainted since the day they left American shipyards. Bui Tin recalled that the name of one ship was the *Belinski.* Ultimately, only about seventy thousand came north. The remainder—the most valuable parts of Giap's guerrilla infrastructure—waited, in obedience to the orders of Vo Nguyen Giap. When he needed them again, they would respond.[18]

Ho Chi Minh knew his government faced enormous challenges, not only from U.S. covert action teams such as Lansdale's Saigon Military Mission, but also because of conditions in the North caused by long years of conflict. It was also time to put into practice the Communist theories that guided the party, and so Ho immediately began to consider his priorities. In the misguided political changes which Ho implemented, Giap continued to figure prominently, and to maintain his unquestioning support of his leader. Because of his acquiescence he therefore was responsible for many of the agonies suffered by his countrymen during these years.

Since 1946, Ho, Giap, and the Communist leadership of the Viet Minh had sought to eliminate notions they believed to be dangerous or offensive. Giap himself had led the way in eliminating rivals. Now the Politburo turned its attention to the eradication of ideas. Many had already been condemned as insidious and cancerous: individualism, liberalism, romanticism, the notion of natural rights, the tolerance of differences, any influence of French thought and culture. Now, with the French gone, Ho's government moved to eradicate other evils still pervasive in his society: private property, Confucianism, feudalism, absentee landlords.[19]

All of them could be attacked through a single program that would at the same time put in place one of Ho's long-held dreams: land to the tillers. Ho chose Truong Chinh, Giap's archrival, to head up this land reform program. He adopted Ho's slogan, "land to the tillers," and promptly constituted agricultural reform "tribunals" in each community to identify those who were evil landlords so they could be stripped of their ill-gotten wealth. The result was widespread

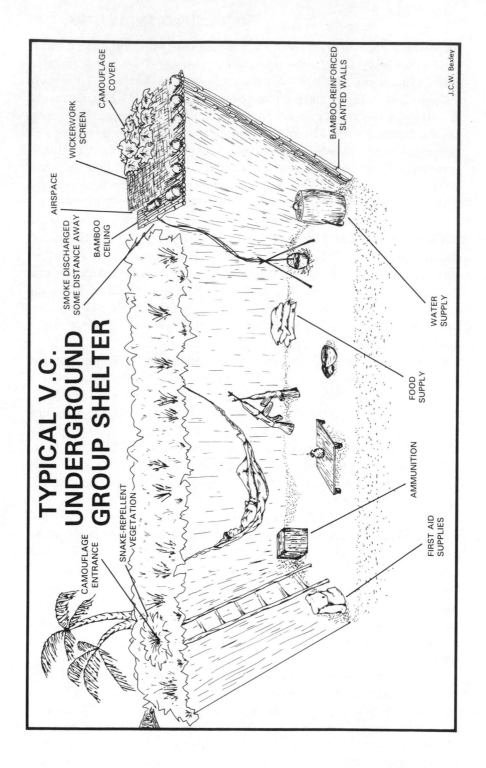

TYPICAL V.C.
UNDERGROUND
GROUP SHELTER

CAMOUFLAGE COVER

WICKERWORK SCREEN

AIRSPACE

SMOKE DISCHARGED SOME DISTANCE AWAY

BAMBOO CEILING

BAMBOO-REINFORCED SLANTED WALLS

WATER SUPPLY

FOOD SUPPLY

AMMUNITION

FIRST AID SUPPLIES

CAMOUFLAGE ENTRANCE

SNAKE-REPELLENT VEGETATION

J.C.W. Bexley

chaos throughout the north. Village harmony disappeared. Trust of others became dangerous. The situation became similar to that of medieval European manors visited by black- and brown-robed Franciscan and Dominican monks of the Holy Inquisition, when to avoid punishment themselves, fathers denounced sons and daughters their mothers, where every hand was raised against all others.[20]

Everywhere, lies and accusations poisoned community life. Those who tried to defend themselves from baseless accusations were singled out for harsh punishment, the least of which might be a sentence to a reeducation camp. Truong Chinh's minions sought to eliminate every vestige of the landowning class. He allowed landless peasants at the lowest levels of the social structure to exercise, for the first and last time in their miserable lives, great political power. Most of them were deeply in hock, owing generational debts, sometimes possessing nothing except the rags they wore. Those a little better off might possess as little as one-ninth of an acre and perhaps a few ducks. Such people were not a threat to the government; both Ho and Truong Chinh knew they could totally rely on such *misérables* to do what was necessary.

It is quite possible that Ho delayed the start of his "land to the tillers" program until after the end of the Great Migration, so as not to startle additional thousands into moving south. When the time for moving allotted by the Geneva Accords expired, Truong Chinh vigorously applied himself to agricultural reform. Peasants were informed that they were to uncover those within their midst who profited from the labor of others, who rented land or tools or sold seed, or even those who were sympathetic to such practices. Dissatisfied with results in the first months, Truong Chinh intensified his efforts in 1956. Viet Minh cadres, who lived in every village and community, began the process. They singled out those to be condemned as landlords, persuading townsmen to be the actual accusers.

O'Neill gives us a picture of community life in rural Viet Nam during that time of terror. "If a man had enjoyed a high moral reputation, then his daughter might have to denounce him for incest. A man who had been a patriotic supporter of the Viet Minh, whose sons had fought in the army, might be denounced by his wife for having signalled to a French aircraft." Those accused were assigned debts to be paid within days—virtual confiscation. Those hesitant to join in such kangaroo-court proceedings were themselves denounced and condemned at trials with punishments ranging from imprisonment to death. O'Neill suggests that as many as 100,000 were executed during the rampant idiocy of the land reform campaign.[21]

Fearful of being branded a reactionary landlord or, having fallen under the jealous eye of a neighbor, charged with having too many possessions, peasants produced only enough for their families to subsist, and agricultural production declined dramatically. Truong Chinh's program destroyed morale throughout the North, damaging both the prestige of the Communist Party and agricultural production. It was nearly September 1956 before Ho considered the harm he had caused and decided to end it. On 17 August, he wrote a public letter apologizing for errors and shortcomings in the program and promised that the wrongs would be set right. Now that Ho had spoken, his theme could be picked up by others. On 24 August, *Nhan Dan* noted that many former patriots had been dishonored, humiliated, imprisoned, and even executed. Still the nation trembled, wondering what would happen next to complicate their lives further.

In October, Ho suspended immediately the reform program and proclaimed a new Rectification of Errors campaign. He fired the minister of agriculture, Ho Viet Thang, dismissed Truong Chinh from his job as head of the land reform program, and forced him to resign from his position as secretary of the Communist Party. In a move that might well have made Giap tremble with joy as he remembered his own earlier and humiliating self-denunciation, Chinh also was made to confess publicly the mistakes he had made. Ho then assigned Giap to denounce Truong Chinh and to bring order out of the chaos. This was justice indeed. Giap began his chore with a speech to the Tenth Congress of the party's central committee, and—in what must have been a glad moment, given his feud with Truong Chinh—gave a blistering denunciation of the program.[22]

He accused those responsible of having allowed "too many deviations and executed too many honest people." They had "acted indiscriminately" and resorted to widespread terror. Unfortunately, they had treated rich peasants and landlords in the same manner, attacked tribal chieftains too strongly, and failed to respect freedom of faith and worship. Torture, Giap thundered, perhaps with tongue firmly placed in his cheek given his own past use of that technique, "came to be regarded as a normal practice."[23]

Articles in party newspapers and Giap's speech to the congress were not enough for some. They were shaken by what had occurred, and their disaffection with the party grew too strong to restrain. Disorder broke out in several locations but was the worst in Nghe An province, the birthplace both of Ho and of Vietnamese communism. In Quynh Luu district, during early November, farmers openly rioted. Giap sent his closest unit, the 325th Division, to suppress the revolt. Peasants resisted their own "people's" army, and fierce, bloody fighting continued from 2 to 20 November 1956.

This occurred about the time of the Hungarian Uprising and the Suez Canal intervention. Both of those events received great play in America's news media, yet little, if anything, was reported in the United States about this sad resistance in Viet Nam to government policies. Giap's ruthless units killed or wounded more than a thousand peasants and deported over six thousand more to work and reeducation camps before he was able to reestablish party authority. To ensure passivity, Giap left the division in place until February 1957. He may have disapproved of Truong Chinh's leadership of the land reform program, but he was not about to allow peasants to assert themselves against his beloved party and government.

There remained sufficient resentment throughout the North over the criminal land reform purges that as late as 4 March 1957 Giap still felt constrained to continue his condemnations of it. On that date, on the anniversary of the founding of the Communist Lao Dong party, he once again called it to mind. "Our movement had its ups and downs," he said, and progress had "not always gone from one victory to another." Particularly in the "Land to the Tiller" activities, "the Party committed serious errors," which caused even greater difficulties. In good Marxist fashion, however, he declared that the party had correctly applied self-criticism and adopted measures to correct those mistakes. Now, he continued, "The revolutionary leadership is an overwhelming success," and "the errors and shortcomings" were "only temporary."[24]

Some would not agree that party leadership was so successful, even after the terrors of land reform. Vu Hac Bong, until recently director of the Foreign Affairs Bureau in Saigon, told an interviewer, "Frankly speaking, we are not very good at economic management. We made mistakes from the beginning. That is why the country still suffers from problems caused by our management. Having suffered greatly from war, we wanted to build our economy rapidly. Our thinking caused mistakes. For example, we collectivized *everything!* It was a mistake."[25]

Despite Truong Chinh's condemnation by Giap and the Politburo for his failures at land reform, he was still a powerful foe. Giap kept a weather eye on him at all times. Truong Chinh still headed the pro-Chinese leadership faction, and he had scores to settle. Calling on all his "accumulations," Truong Chinh was able to weaken Giap's authority by reorganizing the ministry of defense into three separate branches: the general staff, the political department, and the logistical department. Giap remained the nominal head, but his authority was in fact limited to the general staff. Truong Chinh placed one of his own men in charge of the political department, and the logistical department became autonomous.[26]

While Giap's political infighting with Truong Chinh kept him busy, he was also involved in reorganizing what was left to him of his military command structure as he attempted to turn the Viet Nam People's Army (VPA) into a modern fighting force. He ordered "all officers and combatants" in the name of the "high command" of the army to "develop the heroic traditions of the army," to "actively carry out the . . . plans for building our army and strengthening our national defense." Giap reminded his soldiers "to maintain . . . their spirit of enduring hardship and to strengthen their solidarity with the people." While he might give public lip service to the notion of using his soldiers in civic action projects, Giap must have fumed inwardly. He saw his units assigned to tasks ranging from rebuilding irrigation systems to operating factories. While military discipline ensured that they did their work efficiently, he continued to argue against this policy, for Giap was convinced that the best use of troops in peacetime was to improve their military skills. That could only come from drilling, from practice field exercises, and from study.[27]

He did what he could. Giap's soldiers—even the best of his officers—had all begun their careers at the bottom ranks; each was promoted for conscientious performance of duty or for valor in the face of the enemy. Unlike officers in western armies, his officers had not moved from command to staff positions and back again, giving them broad-ranging knowledge and experience. They were technicians who knew only their own jobs. Now Giap established officer training schools near Ha Noi at which Chinese advisers trained his men in staff functions and in infantry and artillery combat arts, including some use of combined arms tactics.

For the first time, Giap's artillerymen received instruction in indirect, rather than direct, fire methods, and they practiced endlessly on ranges Giap ordered set up. He also established rifle ranges, insisting that his infantrymen improve their marksman skills, and he began efforts to standardize weapons and ammunition used by his infantry. Giap additionally worked to establish a small air force, sending prospective pilot candidates into China for their training and begging planes from Mao's inventory. Giap ordered the creation of a naval force, with a major headquarters at Vinh where its members trained in methods of coastal defense and learned how to operate small patrol boats.[28]

Before long a time would come when he would need all these military structures if the South was ever to be overcome, for intelligence reports filtering in from below the 17th parallel brought unwelcome news. Instead of disintegrating from its internal fragmentation and lack of a central focus of power, the southern republic seemed to be gaining a measure of strength. The more secure it became, the less chance the North would have to draw it within its own orbit.

With the help of Lansdale and other Americans, Diem slowly increased his control of the southern government. During September and October 1954, Diem's army chief of staff, General Nguyen Van Hinh, seemed to be planning a coup. Lansdale forestalled that possibility by shipping Hinh off for a vacation to the fleshpots of Manila. Through bribes, Lansdale persuaded one of Diem's rivals, Trinh Minh The, a sect leader of the Cao Dai religion, to merge his army into Diem's national Army of the Republic of Vietnam (ARVN). Similar tactics worked with warlords of the Hoa Hao cult. Upwards of ten million dollars in CIA money made its way to such men to persuade them to follow their new national leader.

Trinh Minh The received between one and two million dollars; Nguyen

Thanh Phuong, another Cao Dai general, demanded and received nearly four million plus additional monthly payments for his troops; a Hoa Hao warlord, General Tran Van Soai, cost three million dollars. It was an expensive process, but in this way Lansdale neutralized Diem's potential rivals. Invigorated, Diem launched an attack against his strongest opponent, Le Van "Bay" Vien, of the Binh Xuyen, the Vietnamese mafia. Bay had once been a river pirate who came to control vice in Saigon: gambling, prostitution, smuggling, and opium, all of which he controlled from the Grand Monde, a huge complex in Cholon. He even bought the job of police chief for Saigon and the rank of general in the Vietnamese National Army from Bao Dai at a time when the emperor was strapped for funds. Diem decided to destroy this powerful rival and his 25,000 soldiers. A sudden attack by his troops, the Army of the Republic of Viet Nam (ARVN), threw Bay Vien's troops out of Saigon and into the swamps outside the city, where for some time they continued to oppose Diem's government and, in later years, merged themselves with the Viet Cong movement.[29]

Now Diem began to ponder how best to rid himself of Bao Dai, who, from his French base, still occasionally endeavored to influence events in the South. Lansdale counseled Diem to hold a referendum to determine by popular vote who should be chief of state—Bao Dai or Diem. The premier liked the idea, and on 23 October 1955 the citizenry turned out to vote. Diem received 98 percent of the overall vote—5.7 million total as opposed to 63,000 votes cast for Bao Dai. In Saigon, Diem received 605,025 votes, one-third more than the total number of 450,000 registered voters. Before nightfall that day, Diem proclaimed himself president of the nation.[30]

Bao Dai was no longer a threat. Bay Vien's Binh Xuyen had been expelled from Saigon. The Cao Dai and Hoa Hao sects no longer mattered, their generals bribed to become part of ARVN or their armies smashed. Ngo Dinh Diem now felt sufficiently secure to reach for another goal. On 19 January 1956, he gave a speech that expressed his natural xenophobia: "The presence of foreign troops, no matter how friendly . . . [is] incompatible with Vietnam's concept of full independence." He did not have Lansdale or the small American MAAG detachment in mind. His words were directed at the French. It was time for their troops to leave the South. They protested, but the United States supported Diem in this, as in all things, and so the last vestiges of the French colonial empire in Viet Nam finally ended on 10 April 1956 when the last ten thousand French troops boarded transports in Saigon's harbor for the long journey home.[31]

The new president of the Republic of South Vietnam now turned his attention to the national elections scheduled for 1956 by the Geneva Accords. Some who knew the situation already believed that Diem could never win such an election. Allen Dulles, head of the CIA, was one who realized that unification was inevitable if the vote was held without United Nations supervision. Ho, with his extensive political apparatus in place, would win. In 1956, Dulles sent

Eisenhower a report predicting that Ho would win a landslide victory. Eisenhower knew something about such wins, and he certainly did not want one to take place in Viet Nam. There was a way out. Diem's government had not signed the Geneva Accords, and thus Diem could proclaim, as his government had done at the close of the conference in 1954, that he was not bound by them.[32]

As mid-1956 and election time approached, Giap publicly became ever more enraged over Ngo Dinh Diem's refusal to allow elections to be held. Giap, and all other Viet Minh leaders, parroted the same line. They had assumed, they said, that France would stay in the South long enough to oversee those mandatory elections. But they were gone. Now the South was an independent nation backed by inexhaustible American treasure. The United States was the new western power in Viet Nam, and its entire foreign policy revolved around opposition to communism. It wanted an anti-Communist government in Saigon—democratic or not—and it made its wants and demands plain to see. Thus encouraged, Diem staunchly refused to participate in elections scheduled by a conference whose accords he had never recognized.

Bui Tin, journalist and longtime party functionary, recalled, "Diem sabotaged the election of 1956. Many Viet Minh remained in the South, convinced that the 1956 election would reunify the country. When it was canceled, there was much sorrow. In Tri Thien province, very many local people finally decided to move north. There was no longer any reason to remain."[33] Ho denounced Diem, but there was little he could do about it. It was a *fait accompli*. Ho had no power to enforce the referendum and none of the Geneva great powers seemed willing or able to do so. "The struggle in the South," Giap proclaimed, "will be long, arduous, but certainly victorious."[34]

Giap's attitude toward America, once so favorable in the days when he walked and talked with Allison Kent Thomas and others in the service of OSS during World War II, now became ever more venomous. In late 1957, he lamented that it was unfortunate that the Vietnamese should still have to struggle for unification. He spoke of the "American interventionists and their lackeys, the Ngo Dinh Diem clique." Then suddenly, for reasons unknown, Giap disappeared from public view for several months. Rumors gained credence among his friends outside Viet Nam that the Politburo had removed him from office, but no one knew for what reason. Then, in 1958, he reappeared without explanation, and resumed his duties. Perhaps he had been ill. He had suffered great privations during the war years, and consequently for years Giap was plagued with ill health. Whatever the reason for his absence, his return was timely, for the northern Communist leaders were beginning to develop their strategy toward the "occupied" South.[35]

It was clear to all observers that the North Vietnamese regarded the 17th parallel as only a temporary demarcation, not a permanent boundary separating two independent, sovereign states. By itself, the North was an incomplete nation. Giap described it as "the liberated half of our country," and the area below the parallel was always the occupied South. Giap also referred to the North as "the vast rear of our army" and "the revolutionary base for the whole country."[36]

Communist leaders minced no words; plainly, they desired to see the "puppet" government in the South eliminated and the two halves of the nation unified under Ho's leadership. What was not then clear, perhaps even to the Politburo members themselves, was the extent to which they should involve themselves in southern affairs. Preferably, southerners would topple Diem's regime from within, through sabotage or subversion or, better yet, through a great patriotic uprising. People of the South, with appropriate encouragement and assistance, would throw off the bonds of the rotten, corrupt, and illegitimate regime that ruled over them. They would sweep away, in Giap's words, all the "spies, bandits and hirelings of the U.S. imperialists" into the dustbin of history. In the eyes of the hero of Dien Bien Phu, Ngo Dinh Diem and his supporters operated a "fascist dictatorial political regime, ferociously oppressing and exploiting the people, using every barbarous means to suppress the patriotic movement."[37]

At the same time, Giap recognized the immense amount of equipment the United States had already supplied the Republic of South Vietnam, and, if possible, he wanted to avoid a clash with America. He believed that ultimate victory would not come quickly, that it would be achieved only by once again proceeding carefully through each of the three phases of revolutionary war: guerrilla conflict, mobile warfare, and the final full offensive.

Yet all around him heated discussions swirled. How long could the North allow such a government to stand? What, if anything, should actively be done about it? Answers to these questions became the imperative that drove the policies of the Democratic Republic of Viet Nam for the next fifteen years, from 1960 to 1975.

SEVENTEEN

"Absolute Secrecy and Security Were Our Watchwords"

Leading members of North Viet Nam's Politburo argued often and sometimes bitterly in 1959 over the course of action they should follow. Should they draw closer to China or to the Soviet Union? It would be wrong to suggest that northern leaders divided solely over the question of pro-Soviet or pro-Chinese orientations; disputes in Ha Noi were probably more often based on the relative priorities of many things: production, morale, industrial development, consolidation of the North, and, always, the circumstances of the national democratic revolution in the South.

Yet members did have personal views about their two major allies, and this also was a factor in their decision-making. The USSR counseled its client states to follow a course of peaceful coexistence in their foreign policy, and that was appealing to those in Ho's government who believed their first duty was to consolidate their hold on the North and rebuild the land so wasted by years of war. The Chinese, more militant, pressed for stronger action against the new southern republic, but some Vietnamese looked with grave suspicion upon that ancient enemy. The perils of close association, politically and geographically, with China needed to be offset by strengthening ties with the Soviets. As a Ha Noi official would later say, "China used Viet Nam like a chess pawn," and many believed that China's primary interest sprang from its desire to use the north of Laos and the Democratic Republic of Viet Nam as security buffers against the growing American influence south of the 17th parallel.[1]

What about the South? What should be done there? Was active interference appropriate? Should Giap's armies mass and march across the 17th parallel? Or should the North wait for those under Diem's rule to launch a general uprising? The order of the day was the notion "Good policy is based on good information," but which of the many who argued for their own position was sharing good information?[2] Ho Chi Minh did not always see fit to impose his own views. Often it seemed better to him to allow his underlings to fight among themselves while he used his deciding influence only after long debates and arguments had drawn the battle lines. He could count on his lieutenants to speak out—all of them.

They were a mixed group. Number two man on the Politburo, just behind Ho, was Party Secretary Le Duan, who, with all his fellows, was utterly dedicated to the overthrow of the southern government. Born in Annam in 1908, son of a railway clerk, he joined Ho's Revolutionary Youth League in 1928 and was a founding member of the Indochinese Communist Party in 1930. Arrested by the French in 1931 for seditious activities, he was sentenced to five years' imprisonment.

Rearrested in 1940, Le Duan spent the war years on Poulo Condore. Following World War II, Le Duan served for a time in Ha Noi with Ho's government. Sent south, he became party secretary for the southern branch of the Viet Minh, the Central Office for South Viet Nam (COSVN). Opposed to the Geneva Accords because of his dedication to Vietnamese unification, he went along with them only on Ho's urging, but his fervor earned him the nickname "Flame of the South." During 1954–56 he consistently advocated use of armed force against the regime of Ngo Dinh Diem. Recalled to Ha Noi in 1957, he became a member of the Politburo and de facto general secretary of the Communist Party following the demotion of Truong Chinh, a position which was formalized in 1960. As Ho was in poor health, Le Duan then became the most powerful member of the Politburo.

Statements of Ha Noi leaders during periods of crisis in 1955, 1963, 1965, 1968, and 1972 point to the fact that Le Duan was more militant and more willing to take risks in the South than was Giap. The Politburo tended to favor Le Duan's proposals over those of Giap.[3]

Truong Chinh, despite his failure with the land reform program, his subsequent public apologies, the loss of his job as party secretary, and his public condemnation by Vo Nguyen Giap, remained the third-ranking member of the Politburo. An avowed Maoist, he had received much of his early training in China and was avid to maintain and strengthen Viet Nam's ties with that massive power. He gloried in the military equipment and advisory personnel China had supplied the Viet Minh during the First Indochina War. Although he kept a low profile for some time following his demotion, he once again came to prominence in late 1957 at the very time that Giap disappeared from the public eye.

Directly behind Truong Chinh in Politburo rankings was Vo Nguyen Giap, who held the number four position (until the Third Party Congress of 1960 demoted him to sixth place). Minister of defense and commander in chief of the military, Giap was a man to be reckoned with. Even when his colleagues disagreed with him, they listened carefully to his views.

Other important leaders included Le Duc Tho, whose real name was Phan Dinh Khai. Born in Nam Ha province in 1910, as a youth he attended Thang Long school in Ha Noi. Tho joined the Indochinese Communist Party soon after its founding in 1930. Later arrested by the French, he served time at Poulo Condore and other prisons. During World War II, Tho served in the Viet Bac, and later he served as deputy to Le Duan in the South. Called back to Ha Noi in 1954, he was elevated to the Politburo and served for twenty years as head of the organization department.

General Nguyen Chi Thanh, born in Annam between 1913 and 1915 to poor peasants, became active in revolutionary activities in the mid-1930s and joined the Indochinese Communist Party in 1937. He served as head of the Communist Party in Thua Thien province until 1938, when he was arrested. The French imprisoned him during most of World War II. He was released in time to attend the Tan Trao conference in 1945 and the same year was named to the central committee of the party. For a time he led party operations in Annam and then joined the People's Liberation Army. Promotions came rapidly to Thanh, and by 1950 he was in charge of the army's General Political Directorate, which supervised ideological aspects of military training. He became a general of the army in 1959, two years after being named to the Politburo. Thanh's promotion came, in large part, because he had the vocal support of Truong Chinh, who consistently maintained that Thanh was a more competent general than Giap. Whispers to that effect spread throughout the North. Never for a moment did Thanh lose sight of his belief that the fight against the French (and the Americans) must continue in full force not only in the North but in the South as well.

The General Political Directorate was not subordinate to Giap but rather to the party's central committee, so Thanh was able to advance his notion that Communist theory should have primacy over military professional training. He was a difficult opponent, for he held four-star rank, the same as did Giap, and thus could not simply be silenced by an order from his commander. This dispute between Thanh and Giap was not resolved until 15 March 1961, when Thanh was relieved of his GPD duties and transferred to the Directorate of Agricultural Collectivization. There he remained until 1964, when he was named head of COSVN and given charge of military operations in the South, where he followed a policy of big-unit warfare against U.S. forces. His high casualties stirred Giap's wrath, and finally the Politburo agreed to use a less volatile strategy. He died, depending on the source, in July 1967 during a U.S. bombing raid, from a heart attack, or of pneumonia, while formulating initial plans for the Tet offensive.

General Van Tien Dung, another of the players, was born in 1917 in the northern village of Co Nhu, Tu Liem district, Ha Dong province, to a peasant family. Dung was one of seven children. At age sixteen, having completed six years of schooling, he went to work, and in 1938 he held a job in the French-owned Cu Chung textile mill. Dung joined the Indochinese Communist Party in 1937 and became active in the Workers' League, a Communist-front organization that linked twenty-six trade unions. Twice arrested, he both times escaped. He became an apparatchik within the Communist bureaucracy as secretary of the regional committee for northern Viet Nam in 1944. Joining Giap's forces, he rose rapidly through the ranks, for Giap recognized his ability and promoted him often. In 1946 he became deputy secretary of the party's military committee, and in 1947 Giap promoted Dung to brigadier general. More stars came quickly: major general in 1954, colonel general in 1959, and senior general in 1974. For a year (1950–51) he commanded the 320th Division, but by 1953 he was Giap's chief of staff and the army's chief political commissar. For much of his career he served as Giap's deputy. He deferred often and easily to Giap and embraced his mentor's military doctrines and principles. A man of easy temperament with a modest self-image, Dung wrote much but offered little that was original, preferring instead to restate Giap's views or discuss narrow technical problems.

Like Giap, Van Tien Dung favored relations with the USSR over China. He became an alternate member of the party's central committee in 1951. In the years following Dien Bien Phu, Dung continued to serve Giap as his chief of staff. In 1960 he became a full member of the central committee. That same year he was tapped as an alternative member of the Politburo. During the first years of the Second Indochina War (1963–73), Dung and Giap divided military responsibilities. Giap focused on the war below the 17th parallel and Dung supervised northern air defenses, logistic operations on the Ho Chi Minh Trail and elsewhere, and the war in Laos. Given field responsibility in 1971, Dung carried out the 1972 Easter campaign that seized Quang Tri province in northern South Vietnam. In 1972 he also finally attained full Politburo rank. In 1974 Dung went south to command the army during the "Ho Chi Minh Campaign" which led to the fall of Saigon in April 1975, and gradually, as Giap's activities became limited by age and illness, Dung assumed full responsibility for the day-to-day command of the army. He directed the Vietnamese invasion of Cambodia in 1978 and defended Viet Nam against China in the short war which began the following February. In 1980, Dung served for a time as minister of defense.[4]

Between 1965 and 1968, therefore, Dung supervised elements of the war that were genuine successes for the Communists. Giap, on the other hand, was in charge of a southern stalemate and a tactically unsuccessful, or only marginally successful, military enterprise. As luck would have it, Dung's career was unmarked by failure while his mentor faced problem after problem. Consequently his star rose in the estimation of the Politburo at the same time that Giap's image waned.

Pham Van Dong, Giap's longtime coworker, was born in 1906 in Annam's Quang Ngai province to a mandarin and his wife. Like Giap, he was educated at the Quoc Hoc in Hue. In 1926 he traveled to Canton, there joining the Revolutionary Youth League and attending the Chinese Whampoa Military Academy. He returned to Viet Nam to work for the league's southern regional committee. Arrested in 1931, he was sent to Poulo Condore, where he remained until granted an amnesty in 1937. For a time he worked on party matters and with Giap at the newspaper in Ha Noi, until he and Giap fled to China in 1940. Involved in Communist activities in southern China, he went by the name Lin Pai-chieh. In Viet Nam he sometimes used the alias Lam Ba Kiet. In 1946, Ho named him minister of finance. Elected to the Politburo in 1951, Dong became minister of foreign affairs in 1954 and prime minister in 1955, a position he maintained for the next thirty years. He was reputed to be an effective administrator and a conciliator who could bring men with wide differences to a common meeting ground.[5]

Both these and other leaders agreed on two points: the political dimensions of people's wars were particularly important, and no matter what temporary divisions might be imposed on the land by others, Viet Nam was one and indivisible. Truong Chinh spoke for them all when he insisted that "military action can only succeed when politics are correct," and added that "politics cannot be fulfilled without the success of military action."[6]

The action necessary was the reunification of the land. Culture, language, tradition, politics, and driving ambition all spurred northerners to pursue reunification. While Vietnamese did not traditionally hold to any sense of nationalism, they certainly had a sense of themselves as a culture, with a language and values all their own that were not to be impinged upon by foreigners. The people were one even when dominated by foreign powers or separated into competing political entities. This was not only the view of Ho and Giap and other leaders in the North, but was held by politically aware southerners as well. Those from *both* halves of the nation looked toward reunification, with, of course, their own party in control of the whole. No matter what temporary divisions might be imposed on their land, Viet Nam was one and indivisible. While the seat of the Communist government might be in Ha Noi, the old warriors of the North believed they were not foreign conquerors but Vietnamese, seeking a unified country.[7]

Those who sat on Ho's Politburo never regarded the Democratic Republic of Viet Nam (DRV) as a complete political entity. To Giap, for example, the North was only "the liberated half of our country" and the DRV was no more than "a firm base of action for the reunification of the country."[8] For him, the North was "the vast rear of our army" which served as "the revolutionary base for the *whole* country." For Giap and his fellows, a divided Viet Nam was a country in crisis, suffering unnatural agonies.[9] Neither in the North nor in the South did Vietnamese leaders look upon the 17th parallel as anything more than the status granted to it in the 1954 Geneva Accords: a "military demarcation line" that was "provisional and should not in any way be interpreted as constituting a political or territorial boundary."[10]

Although Giap and Truong Chinh were increasingly rivals over position and place, they agreed that, despite the division of their nation, it was first necessary to solidify the North as the bastion of communism and to build the infrastructure of its own economy. In time, their unanimity on this subject and their resistance to the policies of Le Duan caused them to become again, if not friends, at least allies, a relationship that would endure until Truong Chinh's death.

What other choice was there? China was in no position to back up northern posturing or military adventures into the South. It was still recovering from its 1949 revolution and from the effects of its conflict in Korea with the United States, when it suffered about a million casualties, killed, wounded, or missing. Nor was the USSR about to offer unqualified backing to Ho's government, wanting no part of a conflict that might escalate into World War III. Although it would provide some level of aid, the USSR made it plain, in 1957, that it sought regional stability in Indochina when it proposed admitting both Viet Nams into the United Nations as separate entities. Perhaps reluctantly, the Politburo determined that the South would have to strive on its own for the foreseeable future. While compatriots there could defend themselves when necessary, they would have to rely on their own political action and on guerrilla war to destabilize the rule of Ngo Dinh Diem, followed, at some point, by an uprising to unseat him and unite the country. This Giap/Chinh strategy held sway from 1954 to 1959.[11]

On the orders of Ho and Giap, the southern Viet Minh during those first years following the Geneva Accords maintained a minimal level of activity. Their foremost duty was to establish proper political attitudes and behavior among the rural population of the South. They worked in hamlets and villages planting and harvesting crops, delivering rice to markets, improving community buildings and homes, providing drugs and basic medical care. In this way they built solid support for their cause among peasants working the land.[12]

Ho gave his southern comrades very specific instructions. In political discussions with villagers, they were to emphasize nationalism, not communism. Under no circumstances were they to take land from peasants. If at all possible, they must avoid antagonizing local community leaders and instead work with

and through them. Violence was to be used only selectively. If it became necessary to assassinate a village elder or some other Saigon-appointed official, they
were to use a knife, not a rifle or grenade. Such weapons too often killed innocent bystanders and raised resentment among the population, alienating peasants from the revolution. On those occasions, cadre were to make certain that
peasants were told why those killings had been necessary. They were never to
engage in military operations, for that would lead to their defeat. They simply
were not yet strong enough to face the soldiers of Ngo Dinh Diem.[13]

Diem instinctively realized that the Viet Minh within his borders were
much more a threat to his regime than any of his other rivals were. At Lansdale's suggestion, he refused to call them Viet Minh, preferring instead to de-
scribe them with the derogatory term of "Viet Cong," or Vietnamese
Communists. In late 1955, Diem launched a campaign to expunge the Viet
Cong from his land and proclaimed that those enemies were no longer even to
be considered human beings. He sent his army out on sweeps to capture or kill
them in their base areas. He ordered Viet Minh war memorials and cemeteries
to be desecrated, a heathenish act given the intensity of respect accorded ancestors in Viet Nam. During this campaign, ARVN or Ngo Dinh Nhu's secret police killed a vast number of alleged Viet Minh/Cong; estimates have ranged from
20,000 to 75,000. They captured another 100,000 who were sent to reeducation camps. By the time the campaign ended in 1958, only about 3,000 Viet
Minh still survived in the South.[14]

As a matter of safety during that dangerous time, Giap told the southern
Viet Minh to retreat to the Central Highlands. Puppet forces and their U.S. advisers, he was certain, would stay in the coastal areas and the cities. The Viet
Minh must establish safe areas and only then extend their influence into lowland jungles and the villages of the Mekong Delta. Any assault on the cities
would have to wait for a later, more propitious time.

In the midst of Diem's campaign against them, the Viet Cong, in mid-1957,
launched their own program of retribution. Their assassins targeted Saigon-
appointed rural officials. During 1958, as their own numbers increasingly fell
prey to government action, Viet Cong cadre slaughtered well over one thousand
low-level appointees of the Republic of South Viet Nam, and they increased
their assassinations to four thousand in 1959 and the years thereafter. Diem's
methods of quieting opposition to his rule had already alienated many in the
rural areas of South Viet Nam, and for the most part, peasants across the countryside—Communist and non-Communist alike—were either unmoved by the
deaths of Saigon's officials or glad to see them slain.[15]

Diem reacted as the Viet Cong hoped. He believed the crisis was caused
by a lack of security in the villages and appointed army officers to serve as government bureaucrats. By 1962, thirty-six of forty-one province chiefs were military officers, while others held positions within the rural bureaucracy down

to district levels. They were usually Roman Catholics, so Diem believed he could trust them, but they did not understand or sympathize with their largely Buddhist charges. They regularly neglected economic and social needs out of fear of alienating Diem. Worse, they lived as if in the midst of enemy territory, inside blockhouses surrounded by concertina wire and armed troop contingents.[16]

During those bitter years when the Giap/Truong Chinh policy held sway, although the North focused on its own problems, Ho's Politburo did not refuse all help to those in the South. During early 1959, Giap began thinking of a way to move men and supplies from the North into the South. On 19 May he ordered General Vo Bam to begin work on the project: "Absolute secrecy, absolute security were our watchwords." Bam did well and soon opened a "modest track" to the South. It was begun in May—the fifth month of 1959—and those who labored on the route were known as Group 559. Group 759, organized in July, studied ways to infiltrate the South by sea. In September, Giap ordered Group 959 to develop ways to provide supplies to Pathet Lao forces. He also sent military units to fight alongside Laotian rebels to secure the area, under construction by Group 559, for an infiltration route to the South.[17] (See map, "NVA Supply Routes.")

It was not enough for some. The chorus of southern voices in the northern government grew louder, and the mood of the Politburo began to shift from the Giap/Truong Chinh view to that espoused by Le Duan and his supporters. They had argued for years that the North needed to be involved actively in the effort within the South, and finally Le Duan's arguments received official Politburo support.

Dong Nghiem Bai, who later rose to prominence within the government of a united Viet Nam, remembered those days. "In November and December 1959, the Politburo made a resolution. Having assessed trends in the South, the party concluded it was now the right time to call on people there to rise up and overthrow Ngo Dinh Diem, who was isolated, repressive, a dictator who operated a barbarous repression of executions and tiger cages."[18]

Giap, despite his own misgivings, was forced into a position where he had to provide more active help to those in the South. He ordered a number of his soldiers, southern Viet Minh who had come north in 1954, to return to their home provinces, a few at a time. They brought weapons supplied by Giap or dug up those they had buried in 1954. By late 1960, the number of armed opponents to the Diem regime numbered at least ten thousand. Slowly they came to control mountainous areas of Quang Ngai province, the U Minh Forest in Kien Giang and An Xuyen provinces, the Plain of Reeds along the Cambodian border, and large portions of the swamps of the southeast. Peasants south of the 17th parallel vacillated at first but were eventually persuaded—by promises and good works, by threats and intimidation—to side with those in power at the local

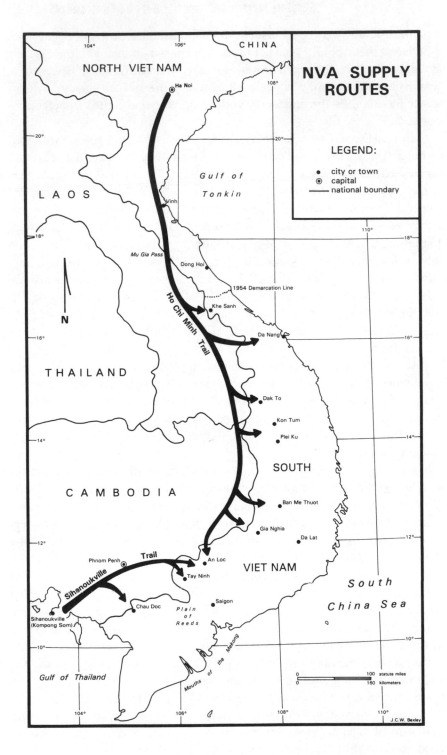

level, and gradually the Viet Cong controlled an ever-growing part of the rural southern terrain.[19]

Furious at his inability to destroy the Viet Cong, Diem ruled what was left of his nation with an increasingly rigid hand, backed by $300 million annually in U.S. economic and military aid. With good reason, Diem's suspicious mind was never far from worries about rivals, conspiracy, revolution, and assassination. His decisions of state constantly narrowed his base of support. He excluded many professionals, skilled technicians, and Buddhist religious leaders from participation in government. He allowed his brother Ngo Dinh Nhu to create an official Can Lao political party, and Diem regarded those who could or would not join it to be in the same category as the Viet Cong—enemies of the nation.

He might have ensured renewal and preservation of his people's ancient tradition of village democracy and introduced a real and vital program of land reform in the South. Had he done so, peasants might well have proclaimed undying loyalty to his government. As in older days, they might have seen their ruler cloaked with the Mandate of Heaven and given him their support. But he turned his back on those possibilities and prohibited local elections, sending his own appointees to serve as village chiefs. He supported absentee landlords and seized other land from its owners and parceled it out to his supporters, who were often Tonkinese Roman Catholics and thus, themselves, unsympathetic to southern Buddhists. Diem wrenched people from lands farmed by their families for a thousand years and thrust them into new settlements elsewhere, many of which were little more than concentration camps in which confused peasants huddled miserably and wondered whether the Viet Cong might not have a better idea. It is no wonder that the great majority of the rural peasantry was either openly hostile or silently indifferent to the Saigon government.[20]

Few advisers remained to suggest alternative courses to him. The only foreigner he had ever trusted was Edward Lansdale, and he had returned to the United States in early 1957. Even before his departure, Lansdale's moderating influence had lessened. Tran Van Don, who served Diem for a time as foreign minister, had frequent occasion to observe Lansdale's last days with Diem, and he once asked Diem to explain the estrangement. Diem answered, "Lansdale is too CIA and is an encumbrance. In politics there is no room for sentiment." Don believed that one reason for Lansdale's downfall was that he pressed too hard "to have Diem copy [the ways of Ramon] Magsaysay [of the Philippines]. . . . [T]his really hurt Diem's feelings," he said.[21]

Diem felt little respect and less liking for other Americans, believing them (correctly enough) to be monumentally ignorant about Vietnamese problems and egotistically certain that their naive and uninformed suggestions should be followed without question. As this attitude strengthened, Diem came to rely more and more only on members of his own family. His older brother Ngo Dinh Thuc served as archbishop of Hue, the Roman Catholic prelate for all Viet Nam.

In a state where Catholics were prized above all other citizens, Thuc's position greatly enhanced Diem's following among coreligionists.[22]

Diem appointed a younger brother, Ngo Dinh Luyen, to serve as international spokesman for the Ngo family, as ambassador to Great Britain and as a roving ambassador to the rest of the world. Luyen preached to everyone who would listen of the necessity for the survival of the Republic of South Viet Nam. He became extremely rich speculating in piastres, using information provided by his brothers in Viet Nam.[23]

The next brother was Ngo Dinh Can, a poorly educated man who lived reclusively with his mother in Hue. The warlord of central Viet Nam from the 17th parallel to Phan Thiet province because of the positions and trust Diem gave him, Can became a very rich man with both his own army and secret police. Diem deferred to him in all matters relating to Can's area.[24]

Ngo Dinh Nhu, another younger brother, an opium-smoking megalomaniac, was Diem's closest associate and confidant. The longer Diem was in office, the more inseparable the two became. Nhu served as political boss from Phan Thiet province south to the Ca Mau peninsula. His wife, Tran Le Xuan, known as Madame Nhu, served as Diem's hostess and had a high opinion of herself, sometimes acting as if she were a latter-day reincarnation of the Trung sisters. A self-appointed guardian of women's morals and morality, she used her own personal female army in attempts to outlaw dancing, brassieres, lipstick, and beehive hairdos. Diem positioned himself within this strange family cocoon, presenting an increasingly hostile face to outsiders. It was not a helpful situation if the southern republic was to long endure.[25]

The political situation in Diem's republic continued to deteriorate. In January 1959 the central committee of the northern party decided to begin armed insurrection in the South and gravely enacted this conclusion into policy at its Fifteenth Plenum in May of that year. In July, Giap sent about four thousand southern members of his military force to infiltrate into the Republic of Viet Nam, many to serve in their own home provinces. Now the southern Viet Minh/Cong felt sufficiently empowered to begin strikes against ARVN military bases and government facilities. On 8 July 1959, for the first time, they struck against Americans. Guerrillas infiltrated the U.S. Military Assistance and Advisory Group (USMAAG) compound at Bien Hoa air base, a little north of Saigon, and killed two U.S. Air Force men: Major Dale Buis, an officer assigned to the Army Security Agency, and Master Sergeant Chester Ovnand.[26]

The tempo increased. On 5 September 1960, at the Third Party Congress—the very same meeting at which Giap and Truong Chinh were demoted in rank—Ho's government gave public notice of its support for the southern insurgency. All hope had ended, the congress announced, of achieving its objectives through nationwide elections; now armed conflict would decide the issue.

In December 1960, Ha Noi announced that a congress held "somewhere in the South" near the Cambodian border had formed a new organization, the Mat Tran Dan Toc Giai Phong Mien Nam, or National Front for the Liberation of South Viet Nam (NFLSV; more commonly, the National Liberation Front or NLF). This "front" group, like many of two and three decades earlier, was a Communist ploy to disguise its leadership by hiding within more than a dozen other groups, non-Communist and nationalist organizations that opposed Diem. All of them defied Diem's vision of his state, and all wanted to rid their land of his government: peasant, youth, woman, writer and artist, educational, religious, cultural, and political movements. The NLF also reached out to disaffected remnants of the sects and their armies, the Cao Dai, Hoa Hao, and Binh Xuyen, hiding in their southern delta sanctuaries, and gave them new hope and purpose.

From the first, northern Communists controlled the NLF lock, stock, and barrel. All its guidance and direction came from the People's Revolutionary Party (PRP). Like the NLF, the PRP was but a mouthpiece for the northern Politburo. Organized in this way, however, the NLF and PRP could trumpet their "independence" to the world. They were homegrown southern movements and served notice on the world that North Viet Nam was not violating the agreements of Geneva by sending its military forces south of the 17th parallel. To emphasize that fictitious point, Ho relieved Vo Nguyen Giap of his total control over military operations in the South and assigned them to Giap's rival, Senior General Nguyen Chi Thanh. This was followed by Giap's demotion from fourth to sixth rank in the Politburo hierarchy.[27]

A bruised and battered Giap, long plagued by ill health, now had little option other than to follow orders and to keep a low profile, best accomplished by seeking medical treatment for his ailments, and by rest and seclusion. His opponents for a time would clearly have the upper hand in deciding how the war in the South should be fought. And they did well. Armed southern units, reinforced by northern aid and personnel, caused Diem to lose control over ever-increasing portions of his emerging state. He could not count even on his own army. In November 1960, unfriendly military units surrounded Diem's presidential palace and demanded reforms. He was saved from this sudden coup only by the timely arrival of loyal troops.

Fearful that increasing Viet Cong activity and widespread southern dissidence were but a prelude to an attack by the North, General Samuel "Hanging Sam" Williams, commander of USMAAG, stepped up his efforts to retrain ARVN soldiers. He wanted a streamlined army of 150,000 carbon copies of U.S. soldiers, as ready to resist a conventional northern invasion force as Americans were elsewhere against the USSR on the plains of Europe. Over the course of his tenure in Viet Nam, Williams was very successful, and as a consequence ARVN lost what little guerrilla-fighting technique it had formerly possessed.[28]

Even some of Diem's longtime friends despaired over the worsening situation in Viet Nam. Edward Lansdale, now working on Cuban affairs for the Of-

fice of the Secretary of Defense, returned to Viet Nam on a hastily arranged inspection trip, 2–14 January 1961. He always claimed he wanted to be out of
Washington when the CIA-sponsored invasion of Fidel's island kingdom began
at Playa Girón—the Bay of Pigs; he didn't want to be blamed for its failure![29] The
report he submitted upon his return was a gloomy one, although he believed
there might still be hope for Diem and his regime.

Ignoring Lansdale's specific recommendations, newly elected President
John F. Kennedy decided instead to increase the number of American advisers
assigned to Diem's government. As of 30 December 1960, 900 Americans
served there. A year later, 3,200 were in place; by 31 December 1962, Kennedy
authorized 11,300 military assignments to Viet Nam. At the time he was mar-
tyred in Dallas, 16,300 American soldiers served in Diem's southern republic.
Thirty-two died from enemy action in 1961 and 1962. The Pentagon decided
that USMAAG was insufficient for the task and created the Military Assistance
Command, Vietnam (USMACV). The United States was being drawn into a military La Brea tar pit.[30]

Despite his demotion, Giap continued to push for his own vision of what
was needed in the South. In 1961, he (or staff assistants) gathered a collection
of his speeches and essays and published his book *People's War, People's Army*,
called by the *Herald Tribune* "a handbook on guerrilla war, which is designed to
become the blueprint for Communist terrorist leaders in South Viet Nam."[31] In
the pages of that work, Giap told of his struggles against the French, how he won
at Dien Bien Phu, of the importance of political action over military operations,
and how people's wars require long, protracted conflicts if they are to be successful. Although the book may have raised the ire of Senior General Nguyen
Chi Thanh, now in charge of fighting below the 17th parallel, it did not succeed
in changing Ho's support for overt northern help to comrades in the South.

That same year, Giap began to improve the supply line to the South. A bigger trail was needed, west of the original route, cutting through Laos and Cambodia with dozens of spurs running off the main route. Its southern terminal was
at An Loc, seventy-five miles north of Saigon, with secret connections to the
main Viet Cong base at Cu Chi, a little northwest of the capital city.

Thirty thousand coolies labored on the project. When they finished, it contained several thousand kilometers of hard-surfaced camouflaged roads able to
bear the pounding of weighty trucks, tanks, and artillery pieces moving south.
Air raid shelters lined the route, each spaced about one hundred yards from its
nearest neighbor. Underwater bridges spanned hundreds of watercourses along
the way. Even rest and recreation facilities were built. As laborers completed new
sections, travel time greatly decreased.[32]

During late 1962, the Democratic Republic of Viet Nam intensified its opposition to U.S. activities within the Republic of Viet Nam. In September, Giap
sent an "emergency message" to Indian ambassador R. Goburdhun, chairman

of the International Supervisory and Control Commission (ISCC), which supposedly monitored violations of the Geneva Accords. Giap's message to Goburdhun is an indication of the quality of intelligence that filtered north to him in his command headquarters from the southern republic. Giap's complaint was threefold. A U.S. Navy ship had arrived in Saigon's harbor on 17 September carrying thirty-three combat helicopters and five hundred officers and men. He observed that the number of U.S. troops in the south now totaled more than ten thousand, up from eight thousand in July.

Giap also decried the August orders of USMAAG commander General Paul Harkins, who dispatched some of his units "to take a direct part in the fighting." He noticed that General Maxwell Taylor had visited Saigon only a week earlier. These matters, Giap reflected, demonstrated that the United States was "bent on expanding its armed intervention in South Viet Nam, thus creating the danger of an extension of the smoldering hotbed of war." These actions, he charged, violated Articles 17, 18, and 19 of the Geneva Accords.[33]

On 22 December, the anniversary of Giap's founding of the People's Army, in his order of the day, the general spoke of the North's active struggle for "peaceful national reunification." In the South, unfortunately, the United States was "resorting to every brutal and mischievous maneuver" to repress all hopes of ending the division between the two Viet Nams. He charged patriotic citizens with the need to "support the movement for national independence and democracy, heighten our vigilance, be ready to stay the imperialists' war-like hands, and smash all their dark designs." Much progress could be made, he urged, if every citizen actively studied politics, stepped up production, and practiced economy.[34]

The next day, at an army reception for visiting General Pavel Ivanovich Batov, deputy chief of staff of the USSR armed forces, Giap told how his own army was improving its professionalism and combat skills. He congratulated Tonkinese vigilance that had foiled schemes of the United States and the Diemists— that "rotten regime"—to "send spies and commandos to the North." Then, in an anomalous moment, the atheist Giap quoted from the Jewish Scriptures: "Those who sow the wind will reap the whirlwind."[35]

On 26 December, Giap sent another message to Goburdhun, drawing the attention of the ISCC once again to the "dark designs" of the United States and its "Diemist lackeys." He summarized American activities during the year just ending. Financial aid amounted to $510 million. Arms and war matériel arrived at an accelerated tempo—tons of ammunition for ground forces, hundreds of jet fighter planes, helicopters, toxic chemicals, napalm. Electronic telecommunication systems linked air bases at Tan Son Nhut, Bien Hoa, and Da Nang. Americans and their puppet ARVN troops, Giap said, had launched eleven thousand raiding operations of battalion size or larger. Strategic hamlets were, in effect, concentration camps. This "aggressive war" was launched and directed by the Kennedy administration, it constituted a "grave threat" to peace and violated Article 12 of the Geneva Accords.[36]

Giap celebrated Tet 1963 by writing an article, "New Year, New Successes," that appeared in *Quan Doi Nhan Dan* ("People's Army") newspaper. He spoke of past accomplishments and how the North was carefully building its technical base. "Each spring our Party . . . brings us new strength. Communism is Mankind's spring." All this showed that northerners were "firmly advancing toward a comfortable and happy life." Unfortunately, in the South, the United States was engaged in an "undeclared aggressive war," spending one and a half million dollars a day to support its puppet government while still "sinking deeper and deeper into the swamp where the French colonialists sank." The North, Giap said, would never forget the South, for it was the "brass fortress" of the nation. Final victory, he assured his readers, was certain.[37]

More and more it came to seem to those on the Politburo that Le Duan and his supporters had been correct all along. Political conditions in the South worsened daily. Diem lived with paranoia, increasing his jailing and exiling of those who offered even a whiff of opposition. His generals grumbled about politics, but their leadership of ARVN was a sham and its soldiers were ineffective. This was clearly demonstrated on 2 January 1963 at the battle of Ap Bac near the Plain of Reeds in Dinh Tuong province when two thousand troops of ARVN's 7th Division, despite a well-conceived operations plan, refused to attack the Viet Cong 514th Battalion, dug in near tiny Ap Bac village along a mile-long canal. Viet Cong soldiers held their positions and brought down five helicopters and damaged nine others. They raked the hulls of accompanying M-113 armored personnel carriers (APCs), killing their machine gunners and terrifying the drivers, who refused to continue into the face of that deadly fire. They killed or wounded two hundred confused and frightened ARVN troops and killed three USMACV advisers. ARVN seemed to those in the North to be on the point of collapse.[38]

They noted also how restive Diem's people were and took heart from the summer 1963 Buddhist crisis. In that year, the 2,587th birthday of Siddartha Sakyamuni, the Gautama Buddha, Diem decided to forbid the Buddhists' religious celebrations of parades, flags, and firecrackers. On 8 May a thousand protesters gathered at the building housing the government radio station in Hue and refused to disperse. ARVN troops fired into the crowd, killing eight. By the next day, crowds of over ten thousand angry Buddhists shouted the need for an official apology and for reparations to be paid to families of the dead and wounded. Hunger strikes spread across the land, answered by ARVN patrols manning armored APCs, by attack dogs, by tear gas.

On 11 June, Thich Quang Duc, a seventy-three-year-old Buddhist monk, brought his disciples to Saigon's Pham Dinh Phung Street. With journalists watching, a monk poured gasoline over Duc, who then lit a match and set himself on fire, his death a protest to the harsh Diem measures. Other Buddhist self-immolations followed as a horrified world watched during evening news telecasts. An intransigent Diem increased his vigilance. In mid-August he imposed martial law, suspended all civil liberties, and prohibited public gatherings. Madame Nhu, on a goodwill tour of the United States, made callous jokes about the deaths. Nhu enforced his brother's repressions of the South's Buddhists. The army had had enough. With quiet assurances from America's new ambassador, Henry Cabot Lodge, carried to them by that omnipresent CIA agent Lucien Conein, a cabal of generals led by Tran Van Don and Duong Van Minh launched a coup and, on 1 November 1963, murdered Diem and his brother Nhu.[39]

Excitement filled the minds of Ho and the members of his Politburo. Le Duan and Nguyen Chi Thanh were particularly ecstatic; events in the South seemed to prove the correctness of their political view. The South was going to self-destruct before the United States could intervene in sufficient strength to postpone its end. Chaos in the South could only work to the advantage of the North. Le Duan and his supporters whispered that they might try to purge anyone who did not wholeheartedly support their efforts in the South. By the end of 1963 there were no vocal opponents to the Le Duan strategy.

Giap certainly was in no position to object. Even though he still had doubts remaining, he admitted the possibility of a quick conclusion to the fight as Diem first floundered and then died. He probably would not have spoken out against Le Duan at that time in any case. As defenders of a discarded strategy, both he and Truong Chinh were suspected by those in ascendance, and Giap had recently been under heavy attack. Giap had made no secret of his pro-USSR/anti-Chinese attitudes, but of late the premier of the USSR, Nikita Khrushchev, had increasingly advocated peaceful coexistence. The USSR and China had forsaken their former solidarity and now followed separate and often hostile policies. Giap's Russophile past clearly put him out of harmony with his more powerful colleagues.

Not only did Nguyen Chi Thanh denigrate Giap with impunity, charging that Giap and Khrushchev corresponded on a friendly basis; he also slandered Dang Bich Ha, Giap's wife, who had studied history in the Soviet Union in the early 1960s. Thanh speculated that during her time there she had been too greatly influenced by Khrushchev. Thanh gained new ammunition during the summer of 1963 when Giap and Ha thoughtlessly used a government helicopter to fly to a resort area at beautiful Ha Long Bay just north of Haiphong. Security guards ordered other bathers from the beach so Giap and Ha could relax and swim privately. News of this incident traveled quickly to Ha Noi and aroused great resentment among those who were hardly able to afford a bicycle and would never travel anywhere.

At one point that summer, General Thanh even went to Giap's villa to lecture him on his failings. Thanh intoned to Ha that "Giap still has the attitudes of a bourgeois because of you. He does not have the virtues of a revolutionary cadre." These were serious charges for Thanh to levy, particularly because he felt free to make them against the hero of Dien Bien Phu.[40]

Thanh should have taken comfort from his power while he could. Diem was dead. The southern government lay in chaos as its generals jockeyed for position and attempted to govern its dispirited masses. The Viet Cong ruled over much of the countryside, and soldiers of the Republic of Viet Nam could control even some crucial areas only during daylight hours, for the night belonged to "Charley"—the Viet Cong.

Substantial numbers of northern folk had gone south to aid their compatriots in their struggle. Thanh and Le Duan had predicted that people there would rise in a great tide to throw off their government. But where were those masses? Why did they not act? Instead of rising, they went about their daily lives, passive, solemnly acquiescent to whatever government ruled in Saigon. Some in the North began to wonder and to reexamine the arguments that had raged for years. Perhaps Giap had been right. Maybe there was a need for a longer, more protracted struggle before the South could be won. Giap's star was about to rise again, and it would be Thanh, not Giap, who would lose his favored place in Politburo politics.

EIGHTEEN

"Only Philosophers Talk of Laws"

By 1964 the scale of warfare within the Republic of Viet Nam had grown until Viet Cong units were able to mount full regimental attacks. Equipment and supplies necessary to sustain this level of combat could not be had merely by using matériel captured from ARVN, and so General Giap ordered the flow of aid from the North to be increased. "The stubborn U.S. imperialist warmongers do not [yet] accept the need to forsake their armed plot of intervention," he noted. It had been his hope that with the death of John F. Kennedy in Dallas, the new president would have the wisdom to end American aid to the South. This had not happened. Giap observed that Johnson was just as bad as Kennedy had been. The war would continue.[1]

Giap contemplated plans for an assault on Saigon. By 1964 he had three Viet Cong divisions, all within fifty miles of the South Vietnamese capital. In time, these units might isolate Saigon, allowing his units to mount an assault against it. That, at least, was Giap's hope when in mid-April he granted an interview to Wilfred S. Burchett, a leftist journalist from Australia. Burchett had recently visited "liberated areas" in the South and then gone on to Ha Noi. The balance of forces, Giap informed Burchett, had shifted in favor of the North despite the "brutal and cynical" aggression of the United States. He chuckled that most Viet Cong supplies were marked "made in the U.S.A."; even the machines liberation forces used to make weapons were manufactured in America. The United States and its southern puppets, Giap said, were "no longer discussing . . . whether they will lose or win, but when their defeat will come."[2]

Giap's optimism and his analysis were premature. Serious debate in America over the conflict in Viet Nam had not yet torn ragged holes in the fabric of its society. A little later in the year, in a more realistic appraisal, Giap lamented that Americans "will never retreat of their own accord unless the [Vietnamese] people use all forms of revolutionary struggle to combat them."[3] Still smarting from charges made by Le Duan and Nguyen Chi Thanh that he favored a pro-USSR policy of peaceful coexistence, Giap wrote an article accusing the USSR of not knowing how to assure victory in underdeveloped countries. He claimed to regard the USSR as a partisan of capitulation; it was a nation endlessly credulous toward imperialists.[4]

In another long article written on the occasion of the tenth anniversary of the Geneva Accords, published in *Nhan Dan* on 19 July, Giap accused the United States of having violated those agreements "before the ink had dried" with "dark and perfidious" actions designed to give it control of Laos and Cambodia as well as of southern Viet Nam. Perhaps, in his rhetoric, he had forgotten that neither the South nor the United States had been a signatory to those accords and thus there was no ink to dry. Turning his attention to the Republic of Viet Nam, Giap noted scornfully that the "unlamented collapse of the Diem-Nhu brothers has turned topsy-turvy the ranks of the puppet administration and its army, sowing bewilderment and confusion among them." Giap accused the southern government of being unable to stand "on its own feet unless it clings fast to its master as a meek servant."

Giap further condemned President Lyndon Johnson's appointment of General Maxwell Taylor as the new ambassador to the Republic of Viet Nam. Arrival of this man demonstrated that the United States followed a policy of "war and terror." He ridiculed Taylor's hope that the South would be pacified within eighteen months and said that Taylor's plans would no more work than did those of successive French generals who came to Viet Nam with bright hopes of reestablishing colonial domination. Giap gave a prideful recitation of recent achievements. In the first half of the year, the Viet Cong had fought nearly 14,000 battles, razed over 400 enemy posts and forced the withdrawal from 550 others, killed or captured 42,000 ARVN soldiers and put 30,000 others out of action. One hundred and seventy planes had been shot down and 500 U.S. troops had been killed, captured, or wounded. While one wants to fault his statistics, a quick check of American sources reveals that he was correct at least in his reference to U.S. casualties. In 1963, a total of 489 Americans were killed or wounded, up four times over the previous year. About 16,500 U.S. troops served there, and U.S. aid to the southern republic amounted to about $500 million.[5]

The war was about to heat up because of unexpected results from covert intelligence missions conducted by the U.S. Navy and Marines. Known as DeSoto missions, these operations searched for northern ships bringing in supplies to southern Viet Cong units, surveyed coastal radar and other electronic installations, and recorded navigational information for use by commando teams landing along the long coastline of North Viet Nam. Three days before the assassination of President Kennedy, he gave his approval for an additional program, known as Operation Plan 34-A, or OPLAN 34-A.

Operations conducted under this new program included minor commando raids at various locations along the northern coastline. Mercenaries and South Vietnamese commando forces penetrated enemy territory, blew up defense positions and supply dumps, and endeavored to damage other targets. In support of DeSoto, Admiral Ulysses S. Grant Sharp, Jr., American commander in the Pacific (CINOPAC), ordered the aircraft carrier USS *Ticonderoga* into the entrance of the Tonkin Gulf. Meanwhile, the USS *Maddox*, a destroyer crammed with electronic interception (ELINT) gear, conducted electronic snooping along the northern coast. During the hours of darkness, 30–31 July 1964, an OPLAN 34-A group conducted raids against two small islands—Hon Me and Hon Ngu—offshore from Vinh. Using six special patrol torpedo (PT) boats, called Swifts, the strike force was unable to land any commandos but did fire on island installations before returning to base. The *Maddox*, 120 miles away, monitored resulting radar and radio transmissions.

Perhaps understandably, northern defense forces may not have been able to discriminate between DeSoto and OPLAN 34-A activities. Following the attack by the PT Swifts, electronic intercepts made by the *Maddox* indicated that the North Vietnamese were preparing military operations. By that time the *Maddox* was within three miles of Hon Me island—one of the targets of the recent OPLAN 34-A raid—which lay about fourteen miles off the coast. Captain John Herrick, commander of the *Maddox*, assumed this might mean a retaliatory attack against his ship, but his superiors told him to remain on patrol.

Then, in midafternoon on 2 August, three northern PT boats made a run at the *Maddox*. Herrick radioed the *Ticonderoga* for air support, and when the enemy boats came within ten thousand yards of his ship, he ordered his five-inch batteries to open fire. In official jargonese, Herrick "initiated a positive reply." The PT boats responded with 12.7mm machine-gun fire and launched three torpedoes. Two missed, and the third failed to explode. Fire from the *Maddox* hit and sunk one enemy PT boat. Three F-8E jets from the carrier arrived and strafed the other two PT boats, which turned and fled toward their home port. Damage to the *Maddox* consisted of one "ding" or "dent" in its superstructure from enemy machine gun fire.

When President Lyndon Johnson heard of the incident shortly thereafter (because of time differences, it was the morning of 2 August in Washington), he rejected the idea of reprisals, but ordered the *Maddox* to continue its DeSoto mission, reinforced by another destroyer, the USS *C. Turner Joy*. Admiral Sharp ordered both ships to make daylight approaches to within eight miles of the northern coast and four miles of its islands to "assert the right of freedom of the seas." Meanwhile OPLAN 34-A raids continued; two more were carried out as PT boats manned by South Vietnamese commandos attacked radar installations at Cape Vinh Son and an installation at the Cua Ron estuary.[6]

On 4 August at about 7:00 P.M., Herrick received a message from the National Security Agency (NSA). It had intercepted a North Vietnamese transmission warning of a possible attack. General Quarters bells rang throughout both ships as crews assumed their battle stations. About 8:00 P.M., Captain Herrick again called for support from the *Ticonderoga*. Aircrews were unable to identify any enemy craft in the area. A few minutes later, radar scanners on the ships plotted the course of three PT boats closing with the American vessels. Darkness closed on the area, which was overcast with heavy clouds. About 10:00 P.M., sonarmen reported the tracks of at least twenty torpedoes fired at the two ships. The vessels swung in wild, evasive maneuvers and their guns blazed as they attempted to hit unseen targets. The captain of the *C. Turner Joy* reported seeing a column of thick, black smoke, but it vanished as he tried to get a closer look. When the action ended after about two hours, ships' officers reported they had sunk two, possibly three, enemy PT boats.

In fact, later investigation showed that no one involved could positively state he had ever seen any enemy ships or heard any enemy gunfire; the "torpedo wakes" claimed by overeager and inexperienced sonarmen may have been generated by the ships' evasive maneuvers or even by a playful school of dolphins! An attack *may* have been initiated; there is little evidence that it was ever *conducted*. There is, however, one curious fact. During an award ceremony on 8 August, following the first American air strikes conducted three days earlier, Vo Nguyen Giap complimented personnel of his navy for chasing U.S. warships from northern territorial waters. He could only have referred to either the 2 August attack against the *Maddox* or the second incident on 4 August.[7]

In Washington, President Johnson learned of the incident at 9:20 A.M., 4 August, and decided a reprisal, code-named Pierce Arrow, was necessary. He met with key congressional leaders and informed them that he had scheduled imminent American air strikes against the North and of his intention to ask for a resolution of support from the Congress. As the president spoke on television that evening, telling the public, "We seek no wider war," F-8 Crusaders, A-1 Skyraiders, and A-4 Skyhawks from the carriers *Ticonderoga* and *Constellation* flew sixty-four sorties along a one-hundred-mile stretch of the Tonkin Gulf coastline. They attacked and either destroyed or damaged about half of Giap's PT boats, destroyed an oil storage depot at Phuc Loi that held about 10 percent of the North's supply, and wiped out seven antiaircraft installations at Vinh.

American officials admitted that in these raids two U.S. planes were damaged and two others shot down. The pilot of one was Lieutenant (Junior Grade) Everett Alvarez, Jr., who parachuted to safety but fractured his back, probably while ejecting from his A-4 aircraft. Such injuries were not uncommon. He landed in the water and was taken prisoner, gaining the dubious distinction of becoming the first in a long line of pilots who would be held under extremely harsh conditions by the North. He was not released until 1973, nearly nine years later. Vo Nguyen Giap, proclaiming that U.S. actions were like those of a thief crying "Stop thief," told how his forces inflicted heavier casualties than those admitted by the Pentagon. He spoke of eight planes shot down and three damaged.[8]

On 10 August 1964, the Congress quickly gave President Johnson his Tonkin Bay Resolution authorizing him to "take all necessary measures to repel any armed attack against the forces of the United States and to prevent further aggression . . . including the use of armed force." Senator Wayne Morse called the resolution the functional equivalent of a declaration of war. The president agreed, for he observed that it "was like Grandma's nightshirt. It covers everything." In the Senate, only two men opposed the move: Wayne Morse of Oregon and Ernest Gruening of Alaska.

At the end of the year, during a reception given him on the occasion of the twentieth anniversary of the founding of the Armed Propaganda and Liberation Brigade, Vo Nguyen Giap warned the United States of the dangers of continued intervention such as had been seen in the last months. He congratulated the People's Liberation Party and the National Liberation Front for their valiant efforts in the South. Still mindful of the power of Le Duan, he was careful to thank both China and the USSR for their "fraternal help" to his nation.[9]

In late 1964, following the incident in the Tonkin Gulf, Giap accelerated his timetable for action in the South. He still hoped to avoid facing off against superior American strength if it could at all be avoided. In the Central Highlands, Viet Cong units thrust from the mountains of the Annamite Cordillera near Pleiku and An Khe toward the coastal beaches in an effort to cut the South in half. It is unimportant whether Giap or General Thanh gave the orders, for although Giap still believed in protracted war he certainly was willing to exploit available opportunities. Giap reasoned that if America sent military divisions to Viet Nam, the North would still be able to stay in the fight. At the most, he might face 600,000 U.S. soldiers, reinforcing 500,000 ARVN troops. Against such an array, Giap could muster 100,000 people to help 200,000 Viet Cong, although they would have widely varying capabilities—main force units, VC regional forces, guerrillas, and self-defense forces. With sanctuaries in Laos and Cambodia, Giap was willing to face odds of three to one if necessary. In preparation, Giap moved his 325th Division from its home base near Vinh into the Central Highlands of the South.[10]

* * *

In the spring of 1965, Ha Noi made two fateful decisions. The first was to pass up an opportunity for direct negotiations with the United States, provided by a private Soviet proposal to reconvene the Geneva conference. The second was to reinforce the southern strategy of Le Duan and Nguyen Chi Thanh—to meet the prospective American buildup of ground forces by continuing to send northern regular units south of the 17th parallel and by trying to maintain offensive operations there. General Giap entered his protest to using Phase III, or large-scale, operations in the southern republic.[11]

In late February 1965, General William C. Westmoreland (who had arrived in June 1964 as deputy commander, USMACV, and had since taken over its command) requested two battalions of U.S. Marines to protect the American base at Da Nang. On 8 March, a little after 9:00 A.M., the 9th Marine Expeditionary Brigade landed on the beach at Da Nang in full battle regalia, to be met by sightseers, ARVN officers, and Vietnamese girls wearing ao dais and carrying leis. Four U.S. soldiers held a large sign which read "Welcome Gallant Marines." The Marines, however, were not "first in and last out." USAF air commandos and U.S. Army Special Forces had been swimming off that beach for nearly four years. They had also been fighting and dying. The Americans had come for the long haul; they would not leave until March 1973. Six days earlier, on Lyndon Johnson's authorization, the air force began Operation Rolling Thunder, bombing selected targets within the Democratic Republic of Viet Nam. The president was pleased over the newly initiated air war and the landing of the marines, remarking to one of his aides, "Now I have Ho Chi Minh's pecker in my pocket."[12]

Giap condemned the landings and the "bloody war of aggression in the South." Why, he asked, should America send more troops? "Who has the right to retaliate? The US imperialists, whose country is on the other side of the Pacific . . . or the South Vietnamese patriotic people exercising their sacred right to self-defense . . . under the leadership of the NFLSV [National Front for the Liberation of South Viet Nam]?" The United States, Giap continued, had miscalculated if it believed it could salvage the war in the South.[13]

For a time in 1965 the war reached a stage of equilibrium as Giap's forces and the Viet Cong faced the combined power of ARVN and the newly introduced American troops. The introduction of large U.S. ground units deprived him of a victory that was already within his grasp. The disruptive effect of American firepower and mobility became ever more evident. In a summer 1965 article published in *Hoc Tap* ("Study"), the theoretical journal of the Communist Party, Giap outlined the successive strategies of the United States in its policies toward Viet Nam. He divided them into phases; the first from 1954 to 1959, when the United States supported creation of the anticommunist Republic of Viet Nam; the second from 1960 to the coup against Diem, as the United States tried to bolster that drunkenly staggering republic; the final phase from 1963 to the present, as the United States looked for an alternative to the late Diem and finally decided itself to take a direct role in the struggle against the Viet Cong and the North.

Even American leaders, Giap claimed, bitterly admitted that they faced a very tough enemy who showed no sign of weakness. Air force generals could not forsee, he continued, that their supersonic jets, "the most up-to-date aircraft on any battlefield, could be downed by North Vietnamese militiamen with rifles and machine guns and Air-Defense units and our young Air Force." If, in Algeria, French troops could not win victory over a population of twelve million, "how can some tens of thousands of US aggressive troops defeat the 14 million South Vietnamese people?"[14] Only a few days later, Giap again wrote for *Hop Tac*, warning northern citizens, "We need to make every preparation to defeat the United States aggressors in case they expand the war to the whole of our country."[15]

It was a very real fear. Giap had no way of knowing that the United States would refrain from crossing the 17th parallel. The air war and the troop buildup in the South seemed to presage an attack upon the Democratic Republic of Viet Nam, and any commanding general who did not take steps to counter such a threat would have been derelict in his duties. Throughout every northern province, Giap organized hamlet and village self-defense forces and armed them with weapons supplied by China and the Soviet Union. In case of attack, everyone, old and young alike, was to fight until the last defender fell before the guns of the enemy. One western analyst wrote of the dangers of such a defense. "There is only one means of defeating an insurgent people who will not surrender, and that is extermination. There is only one way to control a territory that harbours resistance, and that is to turn it into a desert. Where these means cannot, for whatever reason, be used, the war is lost." Despite the desires of Curtis LeMay, head of America's Strategic Air Command, and the bulk of the air force and half the senior army, no one in a responsible position in the American government was willing to "create a desert and call it peace," and so Giap's self-defense measures were never put to the test.[16]

Besides concern over a possible invasion of the North by U.S. forces, Giap faced two other difficulties, for both of which it was imperative that he discover solutions: how to combat American ground troops within the southern republic, and how to defend against Rolling Thunder bombings of the North. When America's air war began, Giap's Democratic Republic of Viet Nam lay nearly prostrate before the sophisticated enemy war planes that soared safely through its skies. What could be done? "We had," Giap said, "to solve those problems. We had to learn how to use inferior weapons to gain victory over superior modern ones. We had to learn how to use inferior means to achieve victory."[17]

Giap fell back on a basic premise of peoples' warfare: *everyone* in the North was part of its basic air defense. "In war," he has said, "victory goes to the most powerful. That was the secret method of the peoples' war. Thirty million people provided thirty million soldiers to destroy the Americans."[18] Thus defense against Rolling Thunder was not the duty of air-defense gun crews alone, but a job for peasants in the fields and workers in factories. "I will tell an anecdote," he told a visitor many years later. "I had the idea that even a rifle could be used to shoot down a plane. I gave the order for this to be done. For some months no one could figure out how to do so, but then we learned." The breakthrough was a simple one. Heretofore those on the ground had tried to aim directly at and fire upon speeding aircraft. Inevitably they failed to hit their targets as their bullets fell hopelessly behind the swift-moving airplanes.

Then someone—even Giap does not know who—conceived the idea of using small groups firing automatic and semiautomatic rifles, emptying their weapons into a zone well ahead of an oncoming airplane. They created cones of fire in the sky into which, occasionally, low-flying planes flew and sometimes suffered fatal damage. "Afterwards," Giap recalled, "I met with both men and women of those groups who had shot down a plane with rifles. I praised them and gave them decorations. 'Why were you successful?' I asked."

One woman gave General Giap a proud reply. She was not an educated person, the general said, having completed only the equivalent of an eighth-grade education, but she was a fighter. "I kept close watch and followed the flight route of the enemy; I understand the enemy and his regulations and rules." Her answer mightily pleased Giap. "I told her she was a great philosopher, for only philosophers talk of laws."[19] For such patriots, whether individually or by units, the northern military department created a new heroism award, the "Determined to Win" award.[20] Yet Giap knew that such methods were but a stopgap. Something more had to be done.

More effective help came in the form of MiG fighter jets, antiaircraft artillery (AAA), and surface-to-air missile (SAM) batteries supplied by the Soviet Union. Along with the equipment came trainers to teach Giap's soldiers and airmen and technicians to keep the machinery in operation. The result was a great improvement in the North's air defenses. Gradually Giap's air defense teams turned northern skies into a hell of fire and flak that forced the United States to pay a heavy price in downed fliers and lost or damaged aircraft as it continued its Rolling Thunder flights. Ultimately the North became the most heavily defended piece of real estate in the history of air warfare. It emplaced some eight thousand AAA guns, over two hundred SAM launchers, a highly complex radar-detection system, and central control launchers. By November 1967, the U.S. Air Force had lost over 730 planes on missions to the North. That year, testimony before the United States Congress indicated that it had successfully destroyed some $320 million worth of North Vietnamese facilities at a cost *three times as great as that of the targets destroyed.* USAF aircraft losses alone totaled more than $911 million.[21]

But only half the job was done. It was not enough to make bombing raids over the North increasingly dangerous, for the flights continued despite Giap's best efforts. He had also to solve the problem of repairing the damage they did. It was necessary to repair railroad lines, rebuild bridges, fill in cratered roads, restore interrupted communications lines. Only if these things were accomplished could Giap continue to order men and materials to move to the southern front. In order to accomplish such tasks in the minimum time, Giap called upon the full-time labor of legions of coolies and the part-time work of additional multitudes. Decentralized, they worked in sectors, using prelocated repair materials. "Each had its own methods," Giap once said, "but an entire nation stood up to fight for freedom and independence."[22]

A long-secret CIA document reveals how little effect air force bombings had on the North. "[T]he flow of men and material from NVN into Laos and SVN continues, perhaps at an increased rate. . . . [A]t least 200,000 workers have been allocated to repair and to maintain essential lines of communications (LOCs). Pham Van Dong boasted that as a result of this effort, the average daily tonnage of goods transported south has, for many months now, exceeded the average volume reached by the end of 1964." As air force efforts increased, the northern capacity to move men and goods became more efficient![23]

There was but one way for Giap to learn how to combat American ground forces, and that was by facing them on bloody fields of battle. That time was not long in coming. On 26 June 1965, General William C. Westmoreland received Pentagon authority to assign his U.S. troops to field actions. Two days later, three thousand soldiers of his 173d Airborne Brigade, accompanied by an Australian battalion and an ARVN airborne infantry unit, moved into War Zone D, twenty miles northwest of Saigon, in search of Viet Cong units. Thus occurred the first American "search and destroy" mission of the war, called off after three days when it failed to make any major contact with the enemy; one American died and nine others, along with four Australians, were wounded. (For American corps sectors and war zones, see map, "U.S. Military Operations in South Viet Nam.")

The first significant test of the wills and tactics of Giap and Westmoreland came at the battle of Plei Me (19–27 October). For some time, Giap's northern units had been assaulting Special Forces camps in the Central Highlands. He intended to attack across the Central Highlands and drive on to the sea, splitting the Republic of Viet Nam in half preparatory to seizing the entire South.

Giap ordered a heavy attack on a U.S. Special Forces camp at Plei Me, 215 miles north of Saigon, held by four hundred Montagnards and twelve Americans. When ARVN soldiers set forth to relieve the siege at Plei Me, they did so under an umbrella of howitzers lifted into position by U.S. helicopters. Defend-

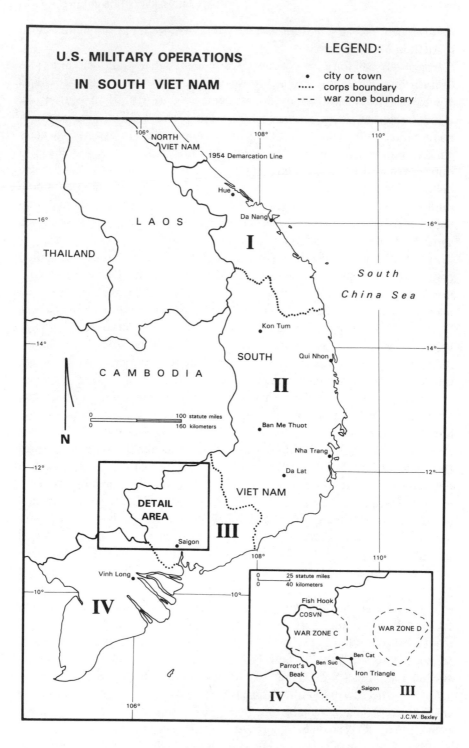

ers at the camp repelled repeated attacks by Giap's 33rd Regiment with the aid of ARVN reinforcements and numerous American air strikes. These enemy soldiers were not black-pajama-clad Viet Cong but northern regulars in khaki battle dress with pith helmets camouflaged by clumps of elephant grass. Armed with Soviet-made AK-47 automatic rifles, they carried canvas bags filled with wooden-handled potato-masher grenades. Some squads were equipped with heavy machine guns and RPG-2 shoulder-fired rockets. The siege continued for almost a week, before General Westmoreland ordered his 1st Air Cavalry Division, newly arrived from the United States, to relieve the camp at Plei Me. Its 435 helicopters enabled soldiers of the division to fly over roadblocks. Its firepower rained destruction on the enemy. On 26 October, ARVN forces broke through to the camp to end the siege. In the face of this torrent of enemy strength, Giap's general, Chu Huy Man, decided to withdraw toward the sanctuary of the Ia Drang Valley to the southwest, a part of Pleiku province near the Cambodian border, an area so remote no enemy had ever dared to penetrate it. Two regiments of Giap's foot soldiers, many of them veterans of Dien Bien Phu and part of his 325th Division, took refuge there and began to regroup.

Then came a more significant battle, a continuation of the clash at Plei Me. Westmoreland ordered the 1st Cavalry to follow Giap's fleeing soldiers into the remote, inaccessible, and unpopulated Ia Drang. He planned to break up the sanctuary and destroy enemy operational forces in the Ia Drang and the nearby mountains. The week of bitter fighting that followed became a contest known as the battle of the Ia Drang Valley (14–20 November 1965). The bloodiest contact to that point, some of it occurred in desperate hand-to-hand fighting as Giap's troops fought to protect an important supply and staging base. At times Giap's veterans faced young troopers of the 1st CAV at distances of only yards.

On 14 November, the 430 soldiers of the U.S. 1st Battalion, 7th Cavalry made a helicopter assault into a small, apparently unoccupied clearing dotted with six-foot-high termite hills. Unwittingly they had landed in the midst of a large number of Giap's forces.

North Vietnamese soldiers watched from the ridgeline on the Chu Pong massif above them. The ensuing action was so fierce that relief forces had to land a considerable distance away and attempt overland marches to aid their comrades. Even B-52s were called in from Guam to aid in the battle. On 17 November, the 2d Battalion, 7th Cavalry walked into an ambush while moving toward the scene of the original fighting. They were hit by Giap's soldiers—the NVA 8th Battalion, 66th Regiment and the 1st Battalion, 33d Regiment. They destroyed almost an entire company of Westmoreland's men in the most savage one-day battle of the war; 155 American soldiers died and another 124 were wounded. Other U.S. troops managed to hang on to their positions with the aid of heavy artillery protection and more air strikes.

There was no way Giap could finally avoid ordering his men to retreat into the safety of their Cambodian sanctuary. Westmoreland's use of U.S. helicopters meant that no place was safe for Giap's soldiers. He had no experience with the new tactic of using helicopters to move men and matériel rapidly from point to point, and he was overwhelmed by what he saw. Tactics he had successfully used against the French were not going to work against the Americans.

Giap read with growing amazement the reports from his battlefield commander, General Chu Huy Man, who told him of the combat miracles performed by the 1st Cavalry as it airlifted its 105mm howitzers over the jungle and supplied those guns with shells. Division artillery fired 33,000 shells—6,500 during one twenty-four-hour engagement. The division moved its guns overland only once during the battle; sixty-six other times it did so by air! Whole battalions were shifted forty times by helicopter, and rotary wing aircraft brought in 13,257 tons of supplies during the course of battle. Soldiers of 1st Cavalry moved seemingly at will, ferreting out food caches, underground hospitals, and headquarters. Having no answer to this awesome feat, Giap finally ordered a withdrawal only after his troops had suffered horrendous casualties, estimates ranging from 634 to 2,262 killed in action. Units of 1st Cavalry lost some 300 killed and many more wounded in an engagement which a Central Intelligence Agency analyst described as an "inconclusive battle." It was a turning point in the war. The conflict had now, irreversibly, become America's war.[24]

Both opposing generals learned from the battle for the Ia Drang. Westmoreland was encouraged, convinced now more than ever that fighting a big-unit war of attrition was absolutely the way to win. Take the war to the enemy! When Westmoreland received his assignment as commander, United States Army, Vietnam (COMUSARV), he had about 23,000 military advisers who answered to him. Soon he commanded 8,600 Marines, 20,000 logistics and engineering soldiers, and 40,000 combat troops. By the end of 1965 he was in charge of about 181,000; by the last day of 1966, Westmoreland had 385,000 servicemen under his control. Even so, he might well need need additional soldiers. It would, he believed, take massive infusions of troops to counter the depredations of the Viet Cong and Giap's People's Liberation Army, but in the Ia Drang, he had shown it could be done. The answers to the problems he faced were mobility, troop strength, and firepower.[25]

Giap reacted differently. Among other things, his observations about the actions of American soldiers convinced him that U.S. soldiers were afraid of many things: the sun, the dense forest, malaria, even ordinary Vietnamese, including old women and children, and he would have to exploit all those fears in one way or another.[26] Despite those perceived weaknesses, however, there were more important lessons to be learned. Hoang Anh Tuan, later vice minister for foreign affairs and for many years a Viet Cong general, spoke for the controversy that raged through inner councils of Giap's advisers. He recalled, "When the Americans entered the war, we spent all our time trying to figure out how to fight you. . . . [We] talked about it constantly. It was a matter of life and death. The incredible density of your shelling and your mobility were our biggest concerns. . . . Our losses were huge. We had to admit you had a terrible strength. So how could we preserve our forces, but still engage you?"[27]

Another enemy general agreed that entry of American big-unit forces had changed the face of the war. Nguyen Xuan Hoang told an interviewer, "We could not indulge in wishful thinking. . . . When you sent the 1st Cavalry to attack us . . . it gave us headaches trying to figure out what to do. General [Chu Huy] Man and I were very close to the [Ia Drang] front and several times the American troops came very near us."[28]

The analyses began. General Hoang recognized the amazing mobility of U.S. units. "With the helicopters, you could strike deep into our rear without warning. It was very effective." Then came his realization. "But your troops were never really prepared. The 1st Cavalry came out to fight us with one day's food, a week's ammunition. They sent their clothes back to Saigon to be washed. They depended on water in cans, brought in by helicopters." He compared that situation with his own. "Our only mobility was our feet, so we had to . . . . make you so dependent on [helicopters] that you would never develop the ability to meet us on our terms—on foot, lightly armed, in the jungle."[29]

Hoang Anh Tuan continued the story. "[W]e had to force you to fight our way—with chopsticks, piece by piece. And then it came to us that the way to fight the American was to 'grab him by his belt' . . . to get so close that your artillery and air power were useless. The result was interesting—our logistic forces, who were farther from the Americans, took greater losses than the combat units who engaged you."[30]

As a result of discussions like these, Giap finally reached the conclusion that "we could fight and win against the [air] cavalry troops . . . . You planned to use [air mobile helicopter] tactics as your strategy to win the war. If we could defeat your tactics—your helicopters—then we could defeat your strategy." In the Ia Drang campaign, Giap said, "We had trouble with supplies of water and food. We had no helicopters. Our people had to forage in the jungle for food and drink water from the streams. But our foot soldiers had to be very intelligent, very creative, and make their own way." He explained what he had learned. The Americans had fearsome strength: a highly mobile division with much flexibility, capable of launching sudden attacks supported by heavy firepower. "But the Americans didn't understand that we had soldiers almost everywhere; that it was very hard to surprise us."[31]

With soldiers located "almost everywhere," Giap had his own form of mobility that helped to counter the advantage helicopters gave to U.S. troops.[32] General Hoang explained how this system was made to work. "[T]he people, the Viet Cong, and our regular forces were inseparable. If you had a temporary success against one, the other would take up the battle."[33] Giap agreed with that claim.

"You Americans were very strong in modern weapons, but we were strong in something else. Our war was people's war, waged by the entire people. Our battlefield was everywhere, or nowhere, and the choice was ours." He summed up his belief: "Being on the spot, everywhere, was the best mobility of all."[34]

General Tran Cong Man agreed with his superior. "Our regular forces, compared with yours, were small, but everyone could fight—with whatever he had." In the Da Nang area, for example, "we seldom had more than one regiment in regular forces. Why couldn't you defeat us? Because we had tens of thousands of others—scouts, minelayers, spies, political cadres. . . . Without the self-defense forces, we would never have gotten you out. If you were our commander and were told to attack the Da Nang air base and destroy the planes there, how many troops would you need? Several divisions, right? Well, we did precisely that with thirty men—thirty! It was a new kind of war, and it was impossible without the self-defense forces."[35]

Giap thought about American mobility and concluded, "Even advanced weapons [such as helicopters] have weaknesses." American reliance on aerial bombings proved to be an Achilles' heel. "You staged bombing raids in advance of your [helicopter] landings." Then, when Giap's forces heard incoming helicopters, "we went on alert and prepared for battle wherever you landed." During preparatory bombings "our soldiers were in their tunnels and bunkers and took very few casualties. When your armed helicopters came we were still in our shelters. Only when the helicopters brought your troops did we emerge, and only then did we start shooting." Almost as an aside, he added, "In Viet Nam, your commanders never realized that there are limitations on power, limitations on strength. . . . [T]he most intelligent of men can do the stupidest things."[36]

Although the words belonged to General Nguyen Xuan Hoang, the notion he expressed clearly stated Giap's views. Speaking to an American interviewer, Hoang described the predicament faced by U.S. troops. "Because you depended on artillery, you built fire bases and seldom went beyond their range." Once built, such bases became semipermanent. "So we knew how to stay away from your artillery, or how to get so close you couldn't use it. Also you seldom knew where we were, and you seldom had a clear goal. So your great advantages ended up being wasted, and you spent so much of your firepower against empty jungle." As a result, said Hoang, "You fell into our trap. Our guerrillas served to keep you divided. You could not concentrate your forces on our regular troops, so your advantages were dissipated."

Hoang told how, despite many defeats and sometimes extraordinary losses, "we never stopped winning the war. Time was on our side. We did not have to defeat you militarily; we had only to avoid losing. A victory by your brave soldiers meant nothing, did nothing to change the balance of forces or to bring you any closer to victory."[37]

Giap had the last word. In mid-December 1966 he commented that American strategists had discussed at length the ratio to be maintained between their own forces and those of the people, "as if troops and weapons were enough to win a war." He appreciated the fact that the United States did not understand the characteristics of people's wars where "every man or woman can at any moment become a resolute fighter, with a perfect knowledge of the terrain, resourceful and heroic." Those who fight for the freedom of their country, Giap said, "are capable of legendary prowess." No doubt, he continued, GIs would be able to perform wonders if they had to defend their own country, but in his land they were stymied, for every hand was against them. Nor, he declaimed, did the American government know what to do next.

Should it send troops into the Mekong River Delta? Strengthen American forces along the 17th parallel? Intensify its bombing raids over the North? Reinforce the defense of Saigon? Withdraw from the Central Highlands or settle there in force? These, he said, were only some of the questions that bedeviled his enemies, who still nurtured the vain hope that "a few more divisions, a few more shiploads of bombs, napalm, poison gas, and intensified bombings may bring the Vietnamese people to their knees." He called on Americans to open their eyes. "We shall win!" he cried.[38]

Rationalize as he might, still Giap realized two fundamental facts from his experience with the 1st Cavalry in the Ia Drang. The Americans had inflicted savage losses on his units, and it was time to draw back from the Le Duan/Nguyen Chi Thanh strategy of pitting northern main force regulars face-to-face against the Americans. It was not yet time to conduct Phase III of a people's war. Protracted war, to grind down the enemy, was needed. He had long insisted on this view; now it was proved to him. It was difficult for him to understand how Le Duan and General Nguyen Chi Thanh could be so blind to reality. Although the United States would suffer "inevitable failure" regardless of the size of its troop commitment, it would not come about from battlefield victories, Giap said in January 1966. It would come because American superiority was "limited" while its weaknesses were "basic."[39]

He may have allowed his irritation toward his rivals to show too plainly. On 27 or 28 April 1966 he spoke at a meeting of the national assembly, commenting on the course of the war and arguing that conventional warfare against the United States was futile. The North, he insisted, should revert to Phase I, a temporary reemphasis on guerrilla war methods. That his remarks did not please his more powerful rivals is evident; his speech was omitted entirely by Ha Noi newspapers that ran lengthy accounts of other speeches. Thereafter, save for a single public appearance on 10 May when Giap attended a state dinner for a visiting Romanian delegation, he disappeared from view. He was not seen again by a westerner until late that year. On 22 December, he appeared, along with his rival Le Duan, at a ceremony marking the twenty-second anniversary of the founding of the army, and that same month he gave a long interview to Jacques Decornoy, a reporter for Paris's *Le Monde* newspaper.[40]

By the time Giap met with Decornoy, he was in better spirits. Decornoy wrote how for more than two hours, Giap developed his themes without "stopping even to catch his breath." Nor was this a somber talk. Although Giap insisted that the Democratic Republic of Viet Nam would win "militarily and politically" against the "special war" of the United States, he did so as a "smiling man, who sometimes bursts into laughter, literally sparkles, speaks exquisitely refined French and develops his thought with impeccable logic and skill."[41] As the internal debate over strategy continued in the halls of the northern politburo, however, the months to come would test Giap's good humor.

NINETEEN

"Washington Cannot See the End of the Tunnel"

Giap may have drawn lessons from the Ia Drang engagement, but it took time to implement them. In the interim, he wanted to see for himself how people in the war zone were coping. In another interview with Wilfred Burchett, on 20 February 1967, Giap told how, on a recent trip, he had been deeply impressed by people and scenes he had observed: unpaid laborers carrying supplies, troops on maneuvers, antiaircraft units drilling and ready to fire at attacking aircraft, engineers supervising young laborers as they repaired quays and roads, old people planting trees beside pockmarked roads, peasants growing rice in the fields, children in conical straw hats on their way to school. The vitality of his fellows, he told Burchett, gave him new strength. "How brave, active, heroic, creative, optimistic, and confident is our people's life during the sacred anti-U.S. national salvation struggle."

Becoming over-eloquent in his talk with the leftist Burchett, Giap told how this internal vitality had welded his countrymen into a force "hard as steel, as stable as brass." Then, his tongue tripping over itself, Giap described those he had seen as if they had four hands: "Hammer in one hand and rifle in the other, plow in one hand and rifle in the other." It is no wonder they were difficult to defeat! In summation, Giap told Burchett, "We are living the greatest moments in our people's history."[1] The Polish press revealed additional comments Giap had made to Burchett. The general predicted that American bombings, "cruelties," and "war crimes" would double in 1967, and would make the eventual

U.S. defeat all the more devastating. Giap made no secret of the fact that his northern government was helping the NFLSV in its struggles in the South.[2]

For months after the Ia Drang battle, Giap's regular regiments won no major battles. In June 1966, Giap launched his 324B Division south across the demilitarized zone (DMZ) in an effort to capture the northernmost provincial capital, Quang Tri city. Another division, the 341st, came from Laos into the next province to the south, Thua Thien. A difficult region, it was isolated from the rest of the country by mountains ranging from Laos to the South China Sea a little north of Da Nang. The major line of communication in the region was Highway 1, a steep, winding, two-lane road across Hai Van Pass, the Pass of Clouds, that lent itself to sudden ambush. Only a small American force of marines was diverted from another area to spoil this attack, no important ground was gained, and no little Dien Bien Phus were fought, which might have stirred American public opinion in the congressional off-year elections. It was apparent that northern plans for a quick military victory were not going to succeed.

Westmoreland ordered Operation Irving in Binh Dinh province, mauling many of Giap's soldiers, followed by the equally costly Operation Attleboro in Tay Ninh province in October 1966 that took a heavy toll of men and matériel in the long-held base area of War Zone C, the site of COSVN. Giap found it increasingly difficult to prepare for or to mount major operations without inviting highly damaging U.S. spoiling attacks. Yet Giap had lost battles, not a war. Even if he could not grasp victory, his military defeat by the United States was improbable. His main force units began 1967 larger than they were in early 1966, and the flow of men and supplies southward was adequate to maintain this new level.[3]

Giap had never agreed with the Le Duan/Nguyen Chi Thanh strategy, and as time passed he became ever more skeptical. In early 1965 his two opponents argued that the complete collapse of the southern government was imminent, yet the regime of ARVN air force general Nguyen Cao Ky showed surprising durability despite repeated crises, confounding their predictions. They had believed that a groundswell of international opinion would eventually overwhelm the conscience of America, forcing it to relinquish its operations in Viet Nam, and were disappointed when that did not occur. Growing internal problems and increasing foreign policy tensions between China and the Soviet Union exposed China as an uncertain and unstable ally.

To no avail did Giap argue against this position. Thanh countered that those who held Giap's views were "old fashioned" with "a method of viewing things that is detached from reality." Thanh insisted that to repeat "what belongs to history in the face of a new reality is adventurism." Such people looked for answers "in books, and [by] mechanically copying one's past experiences or the experiences of foreign countries . . . in accordance with a dogmatic tendency."[4] By late October 1966, it was apparent that Thanh had once again prevailed. Silenced by his rival's charges, Giap continued to seethe while his opponents argued that American opinion and politics—as had been the case with the French—would prove decisive in the long run. They had a strong incentive to hang on until the presidential campaign within the United States, and the Politburo majority agreed. Perhaps they could galvanize resentment against U.S. administration politics at that time.

In early 1967, despite Westmoreland's 389,000 troops, the Viet Cong still controlled much, but by no means all, of the Central Highlands (especially at night), and their southern base areas and supply links between their forces and the North remained in working condition. Northern forces feared a continuation of the American buildup, but the U.S. administration limited Westmoreland to a maximum of a little over 500,000 troops in-country rather than the one million that would have been necessary to give him a fighting chance to defeat the enemy.[5]

On 8 January 1967, General Westmoreland ordered elements of more than three divisions into the Iron Triangle, a heavily fortified enemy base area. This was Operation Cedar Falls, named after the hometown of a Medal of Honor recipient. Some thirty thousand soldiers had as their objective the destruction of all villages in an area forty miles square, including one named Ben Suc. The troops moved in, evacuated all inhabitants, and then burned houses and crops. All males were treated as if they were Viet Cong (perhaps because they probably were), and even women and children were regarded as hostile civilians and were relocated elsewhere to new settlements. Heavy equipment, including huge Rome plows, leveled Ben Suc and the other villages. Engineers destroyed every shack and even killed the vegetation. At Ben Suc they left behind twenty acres of wasteland.[6]

Westmoreland followed this action on 22 February with Operation Junction City, another divisional-level search-and-destroy mission penetrating War Zone C near the Cambodian border north of Tay Ninh City. More than 45,000 U.S. and ARVN soldiers jointly conducted the nearly-three-month-long Operation Junction City. These vast enterprises were remarkably unsuccessful. Not only did American forces find few enemy soldiers but they could not even locate supply dumps in any number. As the last Americans withdrew from the two areas, Viet Cong units resolutely reoccupied them.[7]

Many in the North shuddered at the thought of America's vast power and technology arrayed against them. "If we keep fighting five more years," one Ha Noi official predicted, "all that will be left of Viet Nam will be a desert." A military delegation from North Korea, Cuba, and China secretly visited the war theater, and in their exit briefing they warned of the dangers inherent in allowing the war to go on indefinitely. None of this was good news to Giap.[8] Despite such warnings, on 29 March 1967, General Giap struck in the South. His main force units attacked the villages of Cam Lo, Gio Linh, and Con Thien on the southern side of the DMZ, blanketing them with heavy artillery fire.

In April 1967, Ho Chi Minh convened the Thirteenth Plenum of the Communist Party's central committee. If Giap hoped the delegates would support his position about the proper approach to take toward the South, he was to be sorely disappointed. Led by Truong Chinh, the committee passed Resolution 13, calling for a "spontaneous uprising [in the South] in order to win a decisive victory in the shortest possible time." There would be no protracted war. The call was for an immediate and total drive for victory. Giap was not happy about the new plan, for he remained a cautious exponent of protracted warfare. Nevertheless, as a good soldier, he swallowed his objections and ordered his staff to begin planning. The first step toward the Tet offensive of 1968 had been taken.[9]

Giap's fortunes rose in July 1967. On the 4th of that month, his deadly rival Senior General Nguyen Chi Thanh either fell desperately ill from pneumonia, was wounded by bomb fragments, or suffered a heart attack while on duty in his COSVN tactical operations center. Flown to Ha Noi for treatment, he died there two days later. Now no one remained who held equal military rank with Giap. Once again his voice would be supreme—at least within military councils.[10]

In October 1967, Giap released a detailed explanation of his own victory strategy which appeared both in *Nhan Dan* ("People's Daily") and *Quan Doi Nhan Dan* ("People's Army Daily"), so lengthy it ran to fifty-four pages in its English translation. Wordy and bombastic, Giap claimed the North would fight on to complete victory. "The turning point toward defeat of the United States," he wrote, "is drawing increasingly nearer." He called U.S. tactics over the past two years a "complete failure." As was his wont, Giap called for a strategy of protracted warfare, an approach for which Americans would have no stomach. Unlike other of his writings, this piece was very stern in its call for northerners to accept additional hardship and sacrifice. Giap threatened "disciplinary measures" against individuals, military units, and even hamlets and villages "for their negligence of air defense tasks." This laxness, he said, was causing weaknesses in air defense against American bombings, in communications, and in moving supplies to the war front, and therefore would not be tolerated.[11]

Giap stubbornly continued his pro-Soviet stance. Although he was prudent enough to thank China for its aid, in an article he wrote for the Soviet *Red Star*, published 21 October, he extolled the Russian October Revolution as marking "the beginning of a new era in mankind's history." Thanks to both the USSR and China, Giap wrote, "[t]he Vietnamese People are successfully advancing on the glorious path of the October Revolution."[12]

Disagree as he might with the Politburo's decision, Giap carefully planned his new offensive against the South. He code-named his master plan TCK-TKN—

the abbreviation for Tong Cong Kich–Tong Khoi Ngia ("General Offensive–General Uprising"). His strategy envisioned an operation beginning in the fall of 1967 with attacks along the borders of the Republic of Viet Nam to tie down large numbers of U.S. troops.[13] Then would follow a coordinated general offensive against the South in all its major cities. Southern cadres were to launch a general uprising of the population which would culminate in a complete overthrow of the southern government, or at the very least installation of a Communist-dominated coalition. And Giap planned to launch another attack at the U.S. Marine outpost at Khe Sanh.

In the midst of these plans, in October, Giap accompanied Party Secretary Le Duan and Foreign Minister Nguyen Duy Trinh to Moscow to participate in celebrating the fiftieth anniversary of the Russian Revolution. During a Beijing stopover, Giap told Chinese leaders of his TCK-TKN campaign plans. Pleased that the North was abandoning all vestiges of allegiance to the Soviet call for peaceful coexistence, the Chinese gave Giap an immediate offer of help. To free up Vietnamese combat troops, they offered to send 100,000 logistics troops and truck drivers and 200,000 rail and road maintenance workers. They also promised 107mm and 240mm artillery pieces, the latter having a range of eighteen miles. Ho accepted at least part of this Chinese offer, although public acknowledgment of it did not come until 1977, when General Giap visited China and awarded the Order of Friendship to a number of military units for their contributions to the war effort. Some 120,000 men ultimately saw duty in Viet Nam, mostly along the rail line leading from Ha Noi to the border. Later, not to be outdone, the Soviets pledged to speed up shipments of armor and other weapons.[14]

As Christmas drew nearer and northern plans began to fall into place, Giap's chief of staff, General Van Tien Dung, sent new instructions for the coming "winter-spring campaign" to his field commanders. During the first days of 1968, Foreign Minister Trinh blandly announced that peace talks with the United States could begin as soon as it stopped bombing the North. His news was probably no more than a ploy to persuade the White House to declare a bombing halt, allowing Giap and COSVN to ready their attack without constantly having to watch for air raids.

Khe Sanh sat in western Quang Tri province, fourteen miles south of the DMZ and six miles from the Laotian border. Westmoreland believed it to be a position of great tactical importance. U.S. and ARVN forces could use it to mount operations into Laos. It was well located to interdict infiltration of northern soldiers and supplies moving south of the 17th parallel. American engineers built an airstrip there in 1966 to further enhance its worth. Now it could accept C-123s and C-130s— aerial logistics workhorses. A battalion of U.S. Marines defended it from attack and on 24 April 1967 fought off an assault by two northern regiments in a battle that lasted twelve days. The marines gave a good account of themselves, killing nearly nine hundred of Giap's soldiers. Despite his losses,

Giap succeeded in his intent. Westmoreland was forced to transfer additional troops to more northerly provinces instead of mounting additional southern divisional-level forays on the order of Cedar Falls and Junction City.

In late 1967, as Giap positioned his forces for the upcoming Tet offensive, American military intelligence officers partially misread his intentions. They reported that the marked increase in enemy movements signaled a forthcoming attack on Khe Sanh; some even voiced concern about the safety of the cities. General Westmoreland ordered another four thousand marines to the base as reinforcements and launched Operation Niagara against Giap's 325C Division, northwest of Khe Sanh, and the 304th Division to the southwest. The air force struck at North Vietnamese positions more than 5,000 times, dropping over 100,000 tons of explosives within an area of less than five square miles.

Westerners have sometimes criticized Giap for trying to repeat his success at Dien Bien Phu at Khe Sanh. If this was in fact the case, who could blame him for wanting to reprise such a stunning victory? On 20 January 1968, the 3d Battalion, 26th Marines forged into battle against a battalion of North Vietnamese soldiers entrenched between two hills northwest of Khe Sanh. The next day, NVA soldiers overran the village and their long-range artillery began to pound marine positions. The eyes of the world focused on Khe Sanh as Giap's soldiers and the Viet Cong positioned themselves to launch the Tet offensive. Giap's target was larger than just Khe Sanh; it was all of the Republic of Viet Nam. Westmoreland, however, believed that Giap was focused solely on Khe Sanh—that it would be another set-piece battle on the order of Dien Bien Phu. The siege of the marines there did not end until mid-April, when other American troops finally linked up with the defenders and Giap's divisions withdrew. U.S. troops eventually left Khe Sanh on 13 June.[15]

By mid-January 1968, Giap set the final date for his southern offensive, and in order to be as close to the fighting as possible, he established a tactical operations center headquarters in the southern panhandle of the Democratic Republic, not far from Khe Sanh. He faced a great task that might well produce a big victory.[16]

The coming Tet offensive would later be viewed by many as the decisive campaign of the war. American military intelligence analysts at the time were surprised by the attack. It was not that they had no information about a planned offensive; it is rather that they misread its form and shape. Giap's diversionary plans required drawing the attention of the U.S. forces away from his objective—the coastal regions of the South—by engaging them in activities around the perimeter. U.S. intelligence officers viewed such attacks as a sign of MACV's successes in 1967 in making the interior of the South safer from large-scale depredations by northern main force units. MACV further believed the Communists would focus any offensive on U.S. combat forces rather than on populated areas. So, in late 1967, General William Westmoreland ordered U.S. units away from population centers to counter any sudden enemy attack on the borders of the Republic of Viet Nam. MACV also knew that previous Tet truces had been used by the North to lay in additional logistic material rather than to launch attacks. There was no indication that the Tet holidays in 1968 would be different from earlier ones.[17]

Giap obliged the Americans. Operations along the borders served him well as training exercises for his troops. Both VC and NVA units needed more experience in fighting coordinated operations in urban areas so they would be better prepared when they attacked larger population centers and military installations. Border battles also helped Giap to continue inflicting casualties on U.S. forces; he well knew their psychological impact on American society.[18]

The offensive was originally scheduled to begin during the night of 29–30 January, but Giap ordered a twenty-four-hour delay at the last moment. Some VC units did not receive notice of the delay and so prematurely began their attacks during the first three hours of 30 January 1968 with an exchange of gunfire in Nha Trang. A few other cities in northern and central South Viet Nam also suffered from enemy artillery and ground attacks. By daylight, however, all enemy forces had been driven from their objectives. It was not until just after midnight in the early-morning hours of 31 January 1968 that Ho Chi Minh himself gave the official attack order, a poem which he read over Radio Ha Noi. "This spring shines far brighter than any before. Happy news of victories bloom across the land. South and North challenge each other to fight the U.S. aggressors. Forward! Total victory will be ours."[19]

Viet Cong and North Vietnamese units suddenly shattered the Tet holiday spirit of southern revelers as they attacked in forty-one of forty-four provincial capitals and five of the six largest cities. Giap's men held on to their advantage almost everywhere from periods of a few hours to, in Hue, twenty-seven days, where they entrenched themselves and raised their flag over the easily defended redoubt of the Citadel. In Saigon they attacked the American embassy, Tan Son Nhut air base, and ARVN's general staff headquarters. In I ("Eye") Corps, in addition to Hue, they attacked Quang Tri City and Tam Ky and attacked marines at Chu Lai and Phu Bai. In II Corps they assaulted Tuy Hoa and Phan Thiet and bases at An Khe and Bong Son. In III Corps, Viet Cong troops attacked ARVN installations at Bien Hoa and invaded the American base at Long Binh, the huge logistical home of the U.S. Field Forces in Viet Nam. They also struck at targets in IV Corps throughout the Mekong Delta area.

Giap's plans called for a lightning-swift blow after which southern organs of state power would quickly fall. For this task, Giap's commanders cautiously fragmented their units into small, platoon-sized groups and often held back other troops as supporting reserves. They thus failed to take full advantage of the principles of mass and surprise, but that would only become apparent later. Initially they made great strides against American commanders and units. From its location along the Cambodian border, COSVN constantly kept Giap informed of events as they unfolded in the South. For a time, senior American commanders insisted that Giap's raids on the cities were a strategy to divert resources away from his primary objective at Khe Sanh.

Giap made another costly mistake. He sent units into pro-government villages believing that ARVN generals would not call artillery and air strikes against them in the midst of friendly populations. That conclusion, of course, proved to be fatally wrong, as the tragedy of Ben Tre demonstrated. In that city, capital of Kien Hoa province, Viet Cong troops overran government defenses and occupied it. Following extensive American air strikes and naval bombardments, U.S. and ARVN soldiers recaptured the town. Four thousand civilians were homeless, 1,500 were wounded, 600 were dead. An unnamed major informed journalist Peter Arnett, "We had to destroy Ben Tre in order to save it."

Despite the callous sound of that quotation it is not a violation of the laws of war to strike at an enemy that has purposefully placed itself among a civilian population, as Viet Cong troops did at Ben Tre, even if that means killing innocent civilians. Giap bears the responsibility for the destruction of Ben Tre as much as or more than the American units who leveled it, if he ordered units into the town thinking that the presence of civilians would offer his forces protection.

Giap faced another problem. Since early in his career he had used sand-table models of his objectives on which to rehearse his commanders and full-scale mockups to familiarize his soldiers with their objectives. This had not been done prior to the Tet offensive, and consequently many of his troops did not perform to his expectations. Many were not even notified that they were going into combat until a few hours before the attack. Despite these weaknesses, Giap achieved great surprise and mocked charges that his soldiers and those of COSVN were too weak to stand and fight. In this offensive, Giap for a time seized the initiative from Westmoreland, forcing him to defend southern cities and, consequently, to strip the countryside of its American protection.[20]

Giap's Tet offensive also demonstrated to the South Vietnamese that their own government was unable to guarantee their security. Southerners were appalled to hear of the arrest, summary trial, and execution of civilians by northern units and Viet Cong in Hue and elsewhere. In Hue, northern soldiers with prepared lists of names seized people from their homes and either executed them on the spot or consigned them to a mass grave, later found to contain nearly five thousand corpses.

The biggest failure of the Tet offensive was not Giap's, but rather belonged to the late Senior General Nguyen Chi Thanh. Giap had opposed the project from the start, but the arguments of Thanh and Le Duan had convinced Ho Chi Minh that the attack should be carried out. Communist troops, they said, had suffered massive casualties. Northerners were weary of the continuing American bombings. The United States might decide to invade the North. A dramatic attack in the South would reveal the weakness of the government there and force the United States to withdraw. Giap reluctantly followed orders. The result was not surprising to him when American military might proved far more adaptable and responsive than Thanh and Le Duan had predicted.

Tet was a tactical disaster. Despite Giap's brilliant logistics movement of men and supplies into the South and his best-laid plans for the assault itself, none of the objectives Thanh and Le Duan had hoped for were achieved, and thus, in its very execution, the offensive demonstrated that Giap had been correct in his opposition all the time.[21] Southern front advocates in the Politburo had wanted to take pressure off the Viet Cong, yet the rapid response and overwhelming fire-power of American and ARVN soldiers to the Tet offensive destroyed the Viet Cong infrastructure, carefully built up and preserved over fourteen long years. Forty thousand Viet Cong lay dead or wounded, compared to 1,100 U.S. soldiers and 2,300 ARVN who were killed in action. Over a million people throughout the South lost their homes.

Never again was the Viet Cong able to fight in even battalion-sized units. From now on the brunt of combat would be borne by northerners, not by the Viet Cong. ARVN soldiers had not deserted their posts or surrendered their weapons to join in the fray against the southern government. Restless refugee throngs in the cities had not risen against their rulers.

Still there were, from Giap's perspective, positive results. At the very least, from the time of the first introduction of American troops into Viet Nam in 1965 to the end of the Tet offensive in 1968, Vo Nguyen Giap accomplished a military stalemate in the face of overwhelming American military technology. Given the strength of the United States and his own limited resources, that was quite a feat! One analyst rated Giap's skills highly, writing that "Giap deserves respect as one of the most skilled practitioners of his profession" since Napoleon's defeat at the hands of Wellington at Waterloo in 1815.[22]

To replace his losses, between 1 January and 5 May 1968, Giap ordered nearly ninety thousand replacements to make the long trip into the South. He and his staff worked feverishly on plans for a new offensive. His army now used the latest and best military equipment the Communist world could provide: B-40 barrage rockets, automatic rifles, 155mm artillery pieces, flamethrowers, even tanks. He had also become comfortable with the use of combined-arms— or at least coordinated—tactics. Although infantry remained the main element of his forces, it now coordinated its efforts with artillery, engineers, and crack special units. On 7 May 1968, Giap's soldiers launched Tet II—119 attacks on southern provincial and district targets. Once again, Saigon, Tan Son Nhut, and the Chinese Cholon section came under fire. Viet Cong and northern soldiers fared no better during Tet II than they had in January. They were slaughtered by the thousands in fierce combat with resolute ARVN and American units.

When it was over, nearly 200,000 more civilians were refugees. It was not much of a welcome for the new American commander in Viet Nam, General Creighton Abrams, who replaced Westmoreland in June. Still, the war, from the U.S. point of view, was "winnable." Abrams inherited an excellent tactical and operational situation because of the recent wholesale destruction of Viet Cong forces.

Americans had long hunted VC/NVA main force units, usually without success. Now those forces had come into the open where U.S. firepower could destroy them almost at will. Whatever surprise Giap achieved by his offensive, the first two weeks of this campaign gave the U.S. military its greatest killing period of the long conflict. Giap's greatest success came, not on the battlefield against the forces of MACV, but in the American homeland.

In the aftermath of Tet, *Time* magazine spoke of Giap as "a dangerous and wily foe who has become something of a legend in both Viet Nams for his stunning defeat of the French at Dien Bien Phu. . . . one of the principal developers . . . of the art of guerrilla warfare, a tactician of such talents that US military experts have compared him with German Field Marshal Erwin Rommel."[23] The tone of that reporting was quite a turnaround for *Time* from its 1954 story on Dien Bien Phu, fourteen years earlier, when its columns derided Giap as able only to pour "screaming flesh and blood against the French concrete, wire and land mines. . . . [Giap was] squandering life at Dien Bien Phu to win points at the conference table in Geneva."[24] *Newsweek* was as impressed as its rival, solemnly declaiming that Giap's "audacious Lunar New Year offensive" had, "in a single stroke, dramatically altered the complexion of the war."[25]

It had indeed. Although he had suffered a grave tactical defeat at the hands of U.S. and ARVN firepower, Giap's Tet offensive gave him, for the second time in his life, a great victory. The loss of Dien Bien Phu in 1954 forced the French government to abandon its efforts to remain in Viet Nam. Now the Tet offensive persuaded a massively growing number of Americans to look for a way out as well. Robert O'Neill put the matter succinctly: "If he planned this offensive to achieve the particular results which it did, his insight into the psychological and political problems of his enemies is brilliant."[26]

Giap felt euphoric when he met in late May or early June with Madeleine Riffaud, a correspondent for *L'Humanité*. Once again he was an undisputed member of Ha Noi's ruling clique—member of the Politburo, secretary of the military affairs committee of the party's central committee, deputy premier, and minister of national defense. Giap delighted in belittling U.S. efforts. "Westmoreland has found the way to bring the strength of the U.S. expeditionary force from some 20,000 men to more than 500,000," Giap told Riffaud, "yet Washington still cannot see any light at the end of the tunnel." He listed five objectives the Pentagon had set: to eliminate the Viet Cong threat, to pacify the countryside, to blockade the south from land and sea infiltration, to destroy the

North by bombing, and to strengthen the southern government. None, he said, had been met. Instead, "the battlefield of the South is for America a bottomless pit."[27]

It was a busy time for interviews. A week later, Giap spoke with the director of the Algerian daily newspaper *El Moudjahid*. Giap proclaimed that "current skirmishes of the People's Army in South Viet Nam constitute . . . one long battle of Dien Bien Phu, and the victory is certainly ours." The Algerian recalled that Giap's victory over the French in 1954 had led to the Geneva Accords. Might not a similar negotiation occur because of Tet? Giap dismissed the possibility. "Naturally there are analogies in history, but they are never complete." He certainly had no faith, he said, in the negotiations now in progress in Paris, and he did not believe in "the good intentions of the American imperialists." He proffered his gratefulness to the Algerians for their moral support.[28]

In America, Senator Eugene McCarthy (Democrat, Minnesota), a former schoolteacher and an antiwar activist, took 42 percent of the vote in a contest with President Johnson in the New Hampshire primary. Four days later, Robert Kennedy joined the race for president as an antiwar Democratic candidate. Senator George Aiken (Republican, Vermont) grumbled, "If [Tet] was a failure, I hope the Viet Cong never have a major success." Walter Cronkite, the country's favorite television anchorman and a longtime supporter of the war, editorialized that the war had resulted only in a bloody stalemate. One hundred and thirty-nine members of the House of Representatives called upon President Johnson to review his Viet Nam policy. Clark Clifford, the new secretary of defense, urged the president to get out of Viet Nam. It was all too much. On the evening of 31 March 1968, Johnson told a television audience, "I will not seek, and I will not accept, the nomination of my party for . . . president."

The United States began peace negotiations with the North in Paris on 13 May 1968. Ho Chi Minh's representative was Xuan Thuy. The NFLSV sent Nguyen Thi Binh to speak on its behalf. Nguyen Cao Ky, flamboyant former ARVN air force general and, from 1967 to 1971, vice president of his nation, represented the Republic of Viet Nam. W. Averell Harriman came to the conference as America's man in Paris. The talks dragged on intermittently while, in the United States, Richard Nixon defeated Vice President Hubert Humphrey for the presidency of the nation. Nixon claimed to have a secret plan to end the war. Harriman came home from Paris in January 1969, a disgusted man no closer to an agreement than when he arrived the preceding May.

In Viet Nam, General Abrams, under orders from the president, adopted a former French approach to the conflict. The United States could not continue fighting indefinitely; combat would have to be borne by the southern army. The French had called it *jaunissement*, "yellowing"; America referred to it as "Vietnamization of the war." Turning the war over to the southern army might not be an effective way to ensure the continued independence of an anti-Communist

South, but it provided the United States with a way out: it could declare the program a success and begin withdrawing its units from Viet Nam. Slowly the drawdown began and troop ceilings fell ever lower. Giap scorned the idea, saying it "will be a tragedy not [only] for the puppet army but also for the American troops." He was right.[29]

Even as the battles of Tet II raged, Truong Chinh was busy mounting his own attack on Le Duan and his clique of supporters who had for several years controlled Ha Noi's military policies. On 5 May he reported to the Politburo that a new approach was essential. The Tet offensive, he claimed, had been a blunder. Consequently, military power in the South now favored the United States and ARVN, requiring a reversion from Phase III main force offensive warfare to Phase II guerrilla tactics. Giap rejoiced and after May scheduled no additional large-scale assaults. Le Duan's desperate hope that victory could be achieved by one major offensive was doomed. Even COSVN welcomed the respite. In April 1969, COSVN issued a directive: "Never again, and under no circumstances are we going to risk our entire military force for just an offensive."[30] At long last, the Giap/Truong Chinh policies completely dominated the military policy of the North and the Le Duan faction could only grimace and hope for better opportunities in the future.

Peace negotiations in Paris opened anew on 25 January 1969. This time Henry Cabot Lodge acted the role formerly occupied by W. Averell Harriman. He found Xuan Thuy as stubborn as Harriman had. Lodge tried to discuss the neutrality of the DMZ; Thuy demanded a halt in the war. Although other meetings were held, there was no real progress in negotiations for the rest of that year. Only a month after that meeting in Paris, on 22 February, Giap launched another Tet offensive. Not nearly as successful in achieving surprise as he had been the year before, Giap called off this new campaign after three weeks. Over eleven hundred Americans died in that fighting.

Furious with the lack of progress in negotiations and angered by the 1969 Tet offensive, on 18 March 1969 Richard Nixon ordered the U.S. Air Force to begin secretly bombing Viet Cong and People's Liberation Army sanctuaries in Cambodia. Called Operation Menu, this became Nixon and Henry Kissinger's secret war, the covert phase of which lasted until March 1970 and which continued until 1973. On the president's authorization, the air force flew hundreds of B-52 raids and dropped about 550,000 tons of explosives on the soil of Cambodia. The government of Prince Norodom Sihanouk had tried for years to remain neutral in the troubles besetting Indochina, but under such pressures it became so destabilized that, during a visit to Paris, one of his generals, Lon Nol, replaced him as head of state on 18 March 1970. Five years later, on 17 April 1975, the government of Lon Nol was itself overthrown by Pol Pot, head of the Communist Khmer Rouge guerrillas, when Pot's forces entered Phnom Penh, capital of Cambodia. They launched a holocaust that eventually massacred over two million of Cambodia's estimated population of eight million people.

At a summit meeting with President Nguyen Van Thieu held at Midway Island on 8 June 1969, Richard Nixon announced that Vietnamization was working. It was now possible for him to withdraw the equivalent of a heavy combat division from Viet Nam—25,000 men. In late August the fortunate soldiers of the 9th Infantry Division began the long trip back to the United States.

In June and July, Giap delivered two speeches. The first was to a congress of antiaircraft and air force cadre; the second to the cadre of the Third Military Sector. Freed from the shackles of Nguyen Chi Thanh's insistence on Phase III actions in the South, Giap praised the power of people's wars and protracted conflicts. Of course, he said, it was the "sacred duty" of the North to liberate "the southern part of the beloved country," but it would be done slowly, using the methods of people's wars: "minimal force to oppose an overpowerful enemy and using ordinary weapons against his much better modern weapons." The North was the "great rear," the South was the "great frontline." Success was inevitable if "crack forces" applied "clever tactics." Most of all, he wanted cadre to have "revolutionary ethics, high tactical and technical standards and, as leaders, to be able to command skillfully."[31]

Ho Chi Minh's health, weakened by decades of deprivation, vitamin deficiencies, intestinal parasites, and recurrent bouts of malaria, now began to fail. Throughout 1969 he was increasingly troubled by congestive heart failure, although until the very end he kept a keen interest in the progress of the struggle against the American "imperialists" and their southern "puppet" government. He died on 2 September 1969. His funeral service a week later, held in Ba Dinh Square in Ha Noi, was accompanied by the weeping of tens of thousands of grief-stricken mourners. Sitting on a raised platform, Ho's old comrades Vo Nguyen Giap, Le Duan, and Pham Van Dong shed unabashed tears.

Following the funeral those three formed a triumvirate of collective leadership. Le Duan controlled domestic affairs, Pham Van Dong presided over foreign policy, and Vo Nguyen Giap provided leadership on all military and defense matters. Although they had clearly delineated areas of authority, as a practical matter, most issues of state demanded approval by all three. None of Ho's three heirs had his charisma. They knew that they lacked his authority and could not match his ability to extract extra sacrifices and effort from the cadre and people of the North. It would have been surprising if Ho's death had not given them a sense of uncertainty. They had their own personal ambitions and had often quarreled savagely with one another. Ho had not stifled their debates, but he was a kind of umpire whose eventual rulings they accepted, and his authority served to maintain a basic unity within top circles of the Politburo. Now he was gone, and they knew their regime would lose some of its appeal to average citizens. The triumvirate knew they would have to walk carefully.[32]

More independent and powerful as a result of Ho's death, Giap continued his policy of battlefield disengagement throughout the rest of 1969, preferring to mount only sapper and small-unit attacks and random shelling of U.S. and ARVN installations and positions. His goals were to pursue a prolonged war, to inflict setbacks to Vietnamization and pacification, to impose casualties on U.S. troops, and to keep pressure on the South Vietnamese armed forces. All of that could be achieved without mounting major meeting engagements with U.S. units. Indeed, in December 1969, Giap pointed out that the North had ignored many of the cardinal precepts of fighting a people's war and declared it imperative to repair these faults even if that meant going on the defensive temporarily.[33]

Giap was certain it was the correct approach. Interviewed by the Hungarian Ferenc Hegedus, Giap told him, "[O]ur party has endeavoured to inculcate in the people [of the South] the consciousness that they must count mainly on their own forces in the struggle for liberation." He added that if people resolutely stood up to fight and were properly motivated politically, they could defend their "freedom, independence and sacred rights." They were "completely capable of defeating any aggressor be it [even] U.S. imperialism." The late General Nguyen Chi Thanh would have blanched at such heresy, but yesterday's revisionism had now become Politburo policy.

Giap would concentrate on "high quality" war efforts and use mobile strike units rather than relying on massed forces as he had in the past when Le Duan and Nguyen Chi Thanh were ascendant. This was the most rational course of action, Giap believed, given manpower shortages in the North and a "balance of force" in the South numerically favorable to the United States. For a time the southern front, COSVN, and NFLSV would be on their own.[34]

"Rivers May Dry Up and Mountains May Erode"

Earlier in the war, Giap's troops below the 17th parallel and NFLSV Viet Cong units operated from safe base areas inside the Republic of Viet Nam: War Zone D, War Zone C, and the Iron Triangle, the last only twenty-five miles from Saigon. These three sites totaled more than two thousand square miles of sanctuary that, for all practical purposes, were immune to attack until, in 1967, General Westmoreland ordered his divisional-sized search-and-destroy missions to penetrate those vastnesses and clear them of enemy troops and storage depots. Although enemy soldiers and headquarters units filtered back after Westmoreland withdrew his units, they never again felt as safe there as they once had. As a result, Giap was forced to locate and build new sanctuaries across the border in the jungles of Cambodia. His engineers laid out huge sheltered preserves in the Parrot's Beak and Fishhook areas of Cambodia and stockpiled them with supplies brought overland on the Sihanouk trail through the jungles from the southern port of Sihanoukville, facing on the Gulf of Siam.

With those new areas completed, Giap took the time to write an important article marking the twenty-fifth anniversary of his founding of the army. Serialized for several days in December in the army newspaper, *Quan Doi Nhan Dan*, and in *Nhan Dan*, the party newspaper, it reemphasized the importance of protracted warfare. Although Giap promised a military victory "within a relatively short time" and called for intensified preparations for an uprising in the South, he stressed the need for gradualism. An all-out assault would be very danger-

, he said, because of a "great imbalance of technical equipment." Now was the time to "spur and stimulate" thought and action toward that coming day of southern liberation from the "imperialist aggressor" and its "puppet government." He was not about to order any large-scale attacks on U.S. forces.[1]

The year 1969 was a period of transition for both Communists and Americans. While the United States moved toward withdrawal under its evolving Vietnamization program, General Giap used that year to regroup and rest his forces from their efforts at Khe Sanh and during Tet in 1968 and to refit and relocate them for new operations in 1970. Tactically he was in better position than either ARVN or U.S. forces. They had no stable, definitive defense lines save for the demilitarized zone (DMZ) along the 17th parallel, which was observed most often in the breach and suffered hemorrhages of northern troops and supplies on a regular basis. U.S. and ARVN units had to keep watch everywhere. Although great in number, they were spread over a large geographical area that constantly had to be patrolled and guarded. Giap's forces, safe in their sanctuaries, had great freedom of action. They could concentrate their efforts where and when they wanted throughout the length and breadth of the Republic of Viet Nam. Giap's ability to wage war from a flanking position was extremely favorable.

Previously focused on the war in the South, Giap now turned his attention to Laos and Cambodia. Earlier actions in Laos by his units and their allies, the Pathet Lao, were chiefly undertaken to protect the Ho Chi Minh Trail and in Cambodia to preserve sanctuaries. Now, in 1970, Giap ordered new military offensives, concentrating on the conquest of southern Laos. This would allow the opening of a river route from North Viet Nam into Cambodia over the Se Kong and Mekong waterways. Success would consolidate control over Cambodia's northeastern provinces. Additional attacks in the area of Cambodia's Angkor Wat would put Giap in a position to protect portions of the vital Sihanouk Trail.[2]

Officials of the Cambodian Khmer Rouge guerrilla movement visited Ha Noi at about this time. While talking among themselves in their lodgings one evening, they recalled the centuries-long enmity between the peoples of Cambodia and Viet Nam, spoke of Vietnamese "hypocrisy," and stressed the need "to beware of North Viet Nam's desire for hegemony after [the] foreseeable joint victory over the Yankee aggressors and the [Cambodian] traitor Lon Nol." Some of the insects in their room were "bugs," and their words were duly reported to General Giap. Visibly shaking with anger, Giap complained the next day about the front leaders' remarks. Their words, he said, "hurt us deeply, since every day our soldiers, far from their dear homeland and beloved families, fight and die on the sacred soil of our Khmer brothers and sisters, side by side with them against our common enemies, to save and liberate your country, Cambodia."[3]

Curious about his American enemies, Giap made arrangements to visit a Ha Noi hospital in which lay an injured pilot, shot down over the North on a bombing mission. The man didn't recognize Giap, who stood by the bed wearing civilian clothing (and probably would not have recognized the general if he had been in full dress uniform). Giap sneered at him, "You were supposed to return to your base; instead I see you've returned safely to the Ha Noi Hilton!" Many years later, recalling the incident for an interviewer, Giap said with typical exaggeration and an air of unreality, "We learned to shoot down American aircraft with ordinary weapons! How? We had determination and creativity, which stemmed from our revolutionary heroism."

Americans, Giap said, suffered many losses of aircrews on those missions. Giap and the defense ministry, examining captured air force maps and plotting charts, were able to learn what U.S. intelligence had discovered about "the locations of our rockets and dispositions of our forces." In later years, Giap reflected about the value of those documents. "I reviewed them and found that some locations were accurately plotted and others were not because some of our sites were fake ones with mock-up guns and we protected our real ones with camouflage. We *pretended* to have more than we did." He magnified one incident in the recounting. "My youngest son, who came to one such crash, found secret documents and brought them to me. When I saw the security classifications stamped on them, I said to him, 'Maybe the Pentagon [in Vietnamese, the "five-cornered house"] intended for my defense ministry to be an exception.' "[4]

Heartened by his recent successes, Giap was glad to entertain a visiting delegation of the Palestine Liberation Organization, recently arrived in Ha Noi, the second Arab group in recent weeks.[5] Chief among those new arrivals was "Abu Ammar," a pseudonym of Yassir Arafat. Giap met with Arafat at the defense ministry and, after an exchange of pleasantries, began a lengthy monologue. It must have been sheer torture for the long-winded Arafat to be forced to listen to someone else pontificate! Giap told the Arab that there were only two essentials in people's wars: organize and organize. "Fight by any method which can achieve victory," Giap declaimed. "If regular war can do it, use it. If you cannot win by classical methods, don't use them. Any method which achieves victory is a good one. We fight with military and political means and with international support and backing."[6]

Unwilling to tolerate Giap's offensives in Laos and Cambodia any longer, President Nixon gave his approval to a new military offensive. Using American air support, ARVN would assault across the border into Cambodia's Parrot's Beak area while General Creighton Abrams's U.S. ground units would attack the nearby Fish Hook, where COSVN was supposedly currently located. ARVN forces made their move on 29 April; U.S. soldiers started on 1 May.[7] It might have become a set-piece battle had Giap been willing to risk his troops, but after two days of desperate fighting, he ordered them to abandon their laboriously constructed barracks, hospitals, supply depots, recreational fields, and headquarters buildings and flee west, farther into the Cambodian interior. Many did not make it to safety. General Abrams claimed 11,000 enemy soldiers killed and 2,500 captured, but his figures were immediately disputed by CIA analysts, who insisted that civilian noncombatant deaths were figured into Abrams's total. By 3 May, at the conclusion of the campaign, these joint ARVN/U.S. assaults resulted in the seizure of vast stores of small-arms ammunition, shoulder arms and crew-served weapons, sidearms, rice, and thousands of rounds of mortar and rocket ammunition. Buildings in the base areas were razed and burned. U.S./ARVN forces finally left Cambodia in late June. The Cambodian incursion helped achieve America's strategic goal of continued withdrawal. Had the Viet Cong or northern main force units launched another Tet-style offensive, Vietnamization would have been discredited both politically within the United States and militarily in Viet Nam.

Not everyone was impressed with this military venture. Jean Lacouture, writing in *Foreign Affairs*, claimed that Nixon's act had changed the nature of the conflict from a war in Viet Nam to the Second Indochina War. President Nixon's action, Lacouture said, was politically suicidal and militarily foolish. He quoted a statement of Vo Nguyen Giap: every extension of battle served the revolutionary cause; it was to the advantage of the side with greater firepower to concentrate rather than diffuse the field of battle, yet that was precisely what America had done.[8]

While this action badly hurt the enemy, postponing any plans Giap may have had for offensive operations in Viet Nam, it did not entirely achieve U.S. goals. Nixon hoped success would frighten the Communists into real peace negotiations in Paris. At those meetings, Henry Cabot Lodge had given way to Henry Kissinger. On 21 February 1970 he began a series of secret sessions with Le Duc Tho, successor to Xuan Thuy, who continued to serve as Tho's deputy. Tho continued to insist week upon dreary week that the United States must stop its air war over the North and agree to unilateral withdrawal from Viet Nam before real progress could be made. The Cambodian excursion did not soften his stance.

That invasion of Cambodia brought unexpected results within the United States as well, breathing new vigor into the antiwar movement. Campuses across the country erupted in protest. Ohio National Guardsmen at Kent State needlessly fired upon a crowd of shouting, angry students who were throwing objects toward them. Four students died. Further deaths resulted from a similar incident at Jackson State in Mississippi. Mammoth demonstrations filled the streets and public places in Washington, D.C. Senators talked about repealing the Tonkin Bay Resolution or requiring complete U.S. withdrawal from the Republic of Viet Nam by the close of 1971.

Giap also took umbrage from his losses. In June, in the first remarks of any high-level northerner dealing with the Cambodian excursion, Giap pledged that the arena of the war was not just the two Viet Nams, but all Indochina. His forces, he said, would "fight shoulder to shoulder with the fraternal peoples of

Laos and Cambodia for genuine independence and freedom and to lead the national liberation undertaking of the Indochinese peoples to complete victory" over the "U.S. imperialists and their lackeys."

Then in a moment of unbelievable sentiment, Giap made mention of the embalmed body of Ho Chi Minh. The countenance of the late president of the Democratic Republic of Viet Nam had, Giap asserted, "become more shiny before the revolutionary tide which is mounting everywhere on the Indochinese Peninsula, from the Plaines des Jarres to the ancient Angkor ruins."[9]

In September, Giap spoke at a military conference called to study the last four years of anti-U.S. resistance and to derive lessons learned from those experiences. The general used this opportunity to praise the toughness of those who lived in Quang Binh, his home province, in a speech peppered with unrestrained exaggeration. They had, he said, a "full grasp" of the correct party military line. This had enabled them to shoot down 572 enemy aircraft (none of which, presumably, were B-52s), to set ablaze or sink forty-five small naval surface vessels, and withstand bombings by the aggressors and their hirelings. In an incredible moment, Giap claimed that, using rifles alone, self-defense militia in Quang Binh downed fifty-three aircraft and captured a number of "air pirates." At the same time, hardworking peasants in Quang Binh increased food production and established new enterprises. They were worthy of emulation, Giap said, and he held them up as examples to his audience.[10]

Giap seemed never to tire of the sound of his own voice. It is a malady that often afflicts the great and near-great. In October 1970 he addressed an All-Army Conference on Military Science. As minister of defense, secretary of the central military committee, and senior general of his nation, he was the featured speaker, and he took advantage of that fact. He addressed those present by reading from a paper with a title so awesome it could have been drafted only by a Communist or a college professor at a major history conference: "Let Us Step Up the Task of Reviewing, Studying, and Developing Vietnamese Military Science as a Positive Contribution to Defeating the U.S. Aggressors." His presentation had an introduction and five lengthy parts, and he went through each with meticulous care so those in the audience would not miss any of his thoughts on the subject. His long-drawn text was punctuated with tired clichés, hackneyed phrases, and dogmatic jargon.

He insisted that Vietnamese military science was materially different, wholly new, for it "scientifically reflects the law of . . . proletarian revolution." It was progressive and served the just objectives of the working class. It had developed the people's offensive spirit and initiative to an ever higher degree. Giap called for more study to solve specific problems such as logistics, staffing, tasks involving medical problems, management, training, and other military tasks. Finally (his listeners must have wrinkled their brows in anticipation), everyone must thoroughly understand the scientific character of those military tasks, coordinate the comprehension of the masses, study both immediate and long-term problems, and assimilate military achievements from fraternal countries. "Vietnamese military science," Giap said in conclusion, "is an invincible one."[11]

The celebration in Ha Noi that December 1970 in honor of the twenty-sixth anniversary of Giap's founding of the People's Liberation Army also commemorated the twenty-fourth anniversary of national resistance. The party made certain that it was a festive occasion. The show it put on was typical of methods used to keep up the country's spirits and to ensure people's continued willingness to make unending sacrifices in the revolutionary struggle.

The meeting hall in Ba Dinh Square was brilliantly lit. Colorful banners with flamboyant slogans bedecked the room. "Great and Beloved President Ho Will Live Forever in Our Work." "Fulfill All Tasks, Overcome All Difficulties, Defeat All Our Enemies." "Let Us Resolutely Implement the Sacred Testament of President Ho." "Everything for the Kith-and-Kin South." "Be Ready to Fight and Sacrifice Our Lives for the Sake of Socialism." "Let Us Fight Resolutely and Strengthen Our Combat Readiness in Order to Annihilate the Enemy and Crush All His Aggressive Plots Against North Viet Nam."

Guests that night represented a broad cross section of the population. Antiaircraft artillery people gathered under their banner with its slogan: "Aim and Accurately Fire at the Enemy." Peasants came from Ha Noi's suburban collective farms. Working people stared at uniformed representatives of the air force, the radar force, engineers, military transport, artillery, infantry, and navy. Mixed with the throng were delegates from various front political parties, nationalities, religions, liaison committees of southerners visiting Ha Noi, and artists and writers. Many third-world diplomats and military attachés from fraternal countries attended as guests and spoke with foreign and domestic television and radio newsmen covering the event.

At precisely 9:30 P.M., Le Duan, Pham Van Dong, Truong Chinh, Vo Nguyen Giap, and his protégé, Colonel General Van Tien Dung, army chief of staff, and other dignitaries walked onto the platform and took seats there. Prominent behind them was a huge portrait of Ho Chi Minh and the yellow-starred red flag of the Democratic Republic of Viet Nam. On cue, children and teenagers—described as "Uncle Ho's grandchildren"—wearing red neckerchiefs signifying membership in the Communist Party's Youth Pioneers, elatedly jumped onto the platform to present bright bouquets of flowers to the dignitaries, who, with practiced smiles, accepted the offerings.

Premier Pham Van Dong gave a lengthy opening speech. Then Giap strode to the microphones. "Our people," he thundered, "are determined to drive U.S. imperialism, the common enemy, out of the Indochinese peninsula." It had become a war to free not just the South, but the whole of Indochina from an American presence. He summarized the growth of the army over the past twenty-six years, pointing out, "Our barefooted troops defeated the aggressive French colonialists' professional army. . . . because of their absolute spiritual strength and great combat ability." He condemned Nixon's Cambodian venture, Vietnamization, and the U.S. insistence on continuing the war. Such actions were, he said, nothing more than the "frenzied acts and shouts" of a nation on its way to defeat. He promised that the South would be freed. "The Vietnamese people are one—rivers may dry up and mountains may erode—but this truth will never change!"[12]

The next month, Giap celebrated the Tet New Year quietly, conveying greetings to members of his air force and planting trees at a Confucian temple in the Dong Da ward of Ha Noi.[13] That January he also spoke with Masana Wada, correspondent for Tokyo's *Akahata* newspaper. Vietnamization remained on his mind, and, fearing it might succeed, he harshly condemned it. It was, Giap said, an American policy to save its own soldiers and substitute "corpses of a different complexion" on the battlefield; the United States was openly using the southern Vietnamese "in exchange for weapons and dollars." He told Wada that the most important developments of the past year were the joint American/ARVN expedition into Cambodia that had violated his sanctuaries and the increasing emphasis on Vietnamization. No matter, he concluded. Despite the United States' posturing "like a blood-thirsty wild animal," it would not succeed in its evil quest to salvage the puppet regime. "We Vietnamese will win the final victory."[14]

Even as Giap spoke, General Abrams and his staff laid plans to test Vietnamization once again. Abrams had been so impressed with ARVN's performance in the raid on Cambodia, in fact, that he had pulled American advisers from some ARVN units, feeling they were no longer needed. Now it was time for a second test. Abrams's troop strength was now down to 335,000 men, of whom perhaps as few as 40,000 were combat soldiers. That number would continue to decrease as Nixon fulfilled his promise to bring "the boys" home. There was one looming problem that needed to be solved if the Republic of Viet Nam was ever to have any real hope of remaining separate from the North. That was the vaunted Ho Chi Minh Trail. It was not some preexisting and established transportation system which Ha Noi merely exploited. The Communists had taken a network of footpaths used by peasants and travelers for centuries to move along the Annamite chain and installed a major military logistical system. Furthermore, they did much of it on the neutral soil of Laos, and it provided the way for Ha Noi to filter men and supplies into the South. It had to be severed.

Maintained by perhaps 100,000 Vietnamese coolies and Laotian laborers, it was no longer a simple jungle footpath. It had about 12,000 miles of camouflaged roadways; there were paved two-lane stretches in some sectors. The trail reached southward to Tchepone in Laos near the border of the Republic of Viet Nam, punctuated by rest stops and bomb shelters. Beside it ran a four-inch fuel pipeline. CIA analysts concluded that from 1966 to 1971, 630,000 soldiers,

100,000 tons of food, 400,000 weapons, and 50,000 tons of ammunition came down the trail into the South.[15]

Abrams wanted to use American fighting men to sever the trail, but the Cooper-Church Amendment, passed as a result of his Cambodian excursion the previous year, forbade him to use U.S. troops outside the confines of the South. He turned to ARVN, and President Nguyen Van Thieu approved the operation, committing the use of 21,000 of his soldiers. It would be called Lam Son 719, named after the birthplace of Le Loi. American bombers and army helicopters would provide support. The attack began 8 February 1971, when ARVN moved west along Route 9, a potholed, decrepit track that paralleled the Xe Pon River, from Khe Sanh toward Tchepone, some twenty-five miles distant. To ARVN's left, south of the Xe Pon, lay a sheer escarpment rising up to mountains. The ground was sheltered by dense undergrowth and, in places, double-canopy jungle.

At first ARVN soldiers encountered only light opposition as they moved through the rugged landscape. Then the weather turned sour and rains blanketed the area. Weary foot soldiers slogged slowly ahead through clinging mud in the face of sudden and savage enemy resistance. On 11 February, ARVN simply stopped its forward movement and hunkered down in place, hiding from increasing enemy fire. Weeks passed and ARVN sat in place while its commanders wondered what to do next. Finally, on 6 March, South Vietnamese troops managed to occupy Tchepone, by now deserted and of no military value. Vigorously choosing to defend his lifeline to the South, for it was at the heart of his strategy, Giap then threw nearly 40,000 of his main force units into the battle against ARVN: elements of his 2d, 204th, 308th, 320th, and 324th Divisions, including nineteen antiaircraft battalions, one artillery regiment, and one tank regiment. Giap's defending forces exacted staggering losses on ARVN, and neither American bombing nor helicopter gunships were able to relieve ARVN's bloodied ranks. Only three days after his men forced their way into Tchepone, President Thieu ordered ARVN to fight its way back out of Laos. Even with the help of American air support, southern soldiers suffered nearly 10,000 casualties, and it still took them two weeks to retreat to their starting point at Khe Sanh. Americans watching the evening television news saw pictures of panic-stricken Vietnamese soldiers clinging to the skids of American helicopters in their efforts to escape. Neither the attack nor Vietnamization had succeeded.[16]

On 20 March, Giap spoke at a reception in Ha Noi given by the Mongolian ambassador. Lam Son 719 was fresh in his mind, and he condemned the Nixon administration for having massed the "U.S.-puppet military force" that tried to "brazenly carry out a large-scale military adventure against southern Laos." It had been a combined force—NFLSV, northern units, and Pathet Lao soldiers— "fighting side by side on the Route 9 front from Khe Sanh to southern Laos" who ignored American air power to deal ARVN those "fatal blows."[17]

Frank Margiotta, then a pilot in the air force with the rank of major, worked in the U.S. headquarters in Saigon at the time of the disastrous Lam Son 719 campaign. He reports, "So many U.S. Army helicopters were shot down that Army members at the headquarters would not discuss this issue with Air Force people. It was rumored that they were afraid of the implications for roles and mission assignments that might be drawn from chopper vulnerability."[18]

Despite Giap's victory over ARVN at Lam Son 719, he faced an array of problems that were now at least a year old. The overthrow of Cambodia's Prince Sihanouk in March 1970 cost Giap the use of Sihanoukville as a supply port for the Sihanouk Trail. General Lon Nol, the new head of government, ordered his army into action against Giap's forces and the Vietnamese-sponsored Khmer Rouge guerrillas. U.S./ARVN incursions into Cambodia in May and June 1970 not only deprived Giap of sanctuaries but expanded his area of operations by thousands of square miles, as much of Cambodia became for him hostile territory.

Lam Son 719 was another blow to Giap. For the first time in the war he was forced to fight on terrain that was vital to him—four hundred miles closer to Ha Noi than earlier battles on southern soil. In order to meet the challenge of Lam Son 719 he had to divert units earmarked to replace losses in Cambodia and the Republic of Viet Nam. This left his northern strategic reserves thinner and weaker than he liked, for even as late as 1971, despite evidence to the contrary, Giap retained his concern that the United States might actually invade northern soil. Now, as the combat sounds of Lam Son 719 faded, he was faced with writing new battle plans, recruiting and training new troops that were increasingly more difficult to find, and gathering new supplies. It would all take time, a difficult, costly, and drawn-out process.

Despite such problems, the Politburo was heartened by ARVN's debacle at Lam Son 719. In early summer, not long after Giap's victory in Laos, ranking members of the northern government authorized him to launch a major assault against the South sometime the following year, while the United States was still drawing down its forces, rather than waiting until after the departure of American units. ARVN would be no threat, and an attack would humble not only the South but the United States as well. They could smell victory, and in any case, war should end with a bang, not a whimper.[19]

Giap listened to all this with mounting dismay. He had believed that such desires were a thing of the past, dead and buried. Hoping to find a way to short-circuit such plans, he enlisted the aid of Truong Chinh, and both men vigorously opposed mounting a southern campaign. As at Tet in 1968, Giap believed it was the wrong time to undertake such a major offensive against the South. It was still too strong. ARVN had improved too much as a result of Vietnamization. American field forces might be fewer in number, but U.S. air power could still mount savage strikes against ground forces. An offensive would drain the North of too many of its units and its meager supplies. Once again, Giap's position did not convince others in the Politburo, and he was ordered to prepare a strike against the South and to achieve a battlefield victory that would enable Ha Noi to dictate the terms ending the war. Despite his misgivings, good soldier Giap took this broad directive and began to turn it into an operational plan. He called it the "Nguyen Hue offensive," after an eighteenth-century emperor who defeated invading Chinese troops in 1789.[20]

In Paris, Le Duc Tho had nearly driven American negotiators into a frenzy. By early 1972, so little had been accomplished that the most substantial achievement had been to agree upon the sizes and shapes of the negotiating tables! One central table would have a diameter of twenty-six feet. It would be flanked by two smaller rectangular tables, each three by four feet, positioned eighteen inches away and on opposite sides of the main table. With progress like that, negotiations would last into the next millennium.

Giap submitted his completed concept to the Politburo. It involved a three-pronged attack on the South. The northern thrust by North Vietnamese main force divisions would cross the DMZ with infantry, armor, and artillery in a drive on Quang Tri province with a separate and simultaneous drive toward Hue. If the attack was successful, Giap would occupy the two northern provinces of the Republic of Viet Nam and be positioned to threaten Da Nang, a little to the south, the country's second-largest city.

The second attack point would come on the central front with other northern divisions, again supported by armor and artillery, driving against Kontum and Pleiku in the Central Highlands. This would be linked to a simultaneous drive on the coastal province of Binh Dinh. Capture of these objectives would cut the South in half along Route 19, an important road leading west from the coast into the Central Highlands.

On the southern front, Giap planned to use three Viet Cong divisions to aim at Loc Ninh and the capital of Binh Long province, An Loc. Despite their name, these divisions had long since become manned by northern troops; the Viet Cong had never sufficiently recovered from their 1968 mauling to be able to man units of this size. The capture of An Loc would seriously threaten Saigon's continued safety and further weaken the stability of the southern government. Meanwhile another division would roll into the Mekong Delta to seize rice, occupy additional territory, and serve as a blocking force to prevent ARVN troops there from reinforcing actions elsewhere.[21]

Le Duan and the late Senior General Nguyen Chi Thanh had long called for this kind of action. Now Giap was ready to provide it with a vengeance; his approach to Phase III of people's wars was nearly ready. Disagree with the concept as he might, he believed it was still his duty to prepare for battle with all his skill. He would rely on the coordinated power of fully equipped and modern infantry, armor, and artillery. Their only weakness would be lack of close air support for these ground units. If all attacks on the three fronts succeeded, the Republic of Viet Nam would collapse. If even only one prevailed, the setback to the southern government would be so severe that its people and administration would be unnerved and in jeopardy. Giap set the date for the attack at noon, 30 March 1972. On the Christian calendar that was Good Friday.

Prior to the offensive, the Ha Noi government launched an unprecedented recruiting campaign to flesh out the ranks of the army. For the first time, sons of party members, university students—even those already selected for advanced studies in eastern Europe—teachers, skilled workers, and sons whose fathers and brothers had already died or been wounded now found themselves dressed in military clothing and destined to serve their fatherland on distant war fronts.[22]

On D-Day, heavy guns of the northern artillery laid down a massive barrage on ARVN units along the DMZ. As the sound of explosions lifted from the battlefield, Giap's infantry divisions moved forward, thirty thousand men and two hundred Soviet tanks. By 1 April, southern soldiers began to retreat in orderly fashion, but the next day, infected by panicked refugees moving south through their lines, their uncertain morale vanished and they abandoned their positions. As they fled their enemies, retreat turned into a rout. Northern artillery fired into those refugees crowding the roads. An estimated twenty thousand civilians died. On 1 May, Giap's troops occupied Quang Tri City and the province. It was not until 16 September that reinforced and reinvigorated ARVN units were able to retake the city under the watchful umbrella of American air support.[23]

On 27 April, while the campaign in the south raged on, Kamil Tangri, a correspondent for Bonn's *Vorwaerts* weekly newspaper, met in Ha Noi with General Giap. Tangri, half Vietnamese and the son of a northern staff officer, came from his residence in Singapore for the interview. A persistent man, Tangri asked hard questions and continually reminded Giap that he was digressing. Tangri asked Giap if the southern offensive would decide the future of Viet Nam. "That battle," Giap declaimed, "began more than twenty-five years ago. A battle, no matter how important it may be—whether Issos or Hastings, whether Philippi or Belle-Alliance—can always represent only one point of a developing situation. But the destinies of entire peoples are made according to other laws which produce currents and countercurrents until the two clash with such force that they bring about belligerent conflicts." Tangri indicated that he had wondered only about the southern offensive, not the military history of civilization itself. He tried again.

"You say that communism brings freedom to people," Tangri said to the general. "How then do you explain such obvious lack of freedom, for example, when Nobel Prize winner Solzhenitsyn finds it impossible to accept his award?

When Jews are refused permission to leave the Soviet Union? When Germans are not allowed to visit their fellow countrymen on the other side of an unnatural wall?"

Giap quickly begged the question. "I do not feel competent to make any exhaustive judgment on the internal problems of the Soviet Union, the GDR, or any other country. . . . There are many shades of socialism, such as Leninism, Maoism, Titoism, Fidelism, the experiments of Prague and Chile and we, again, go our own way. Marxism is relatively young and . . . it will take generations to perfect it."

Giap became more intense. "The freedoms you mention, after all, are insignificant for the overwhelming majority of mankind. People place more value on their own unrestrained luxury than on the freedom of their fellow men to eat three meals a day and to live without epidemics. What good does it do the masses of India vegetating in misery, that there is freedom to travel everywhere? What good does it do illiterate native Indians in Latin America that they have the freedom to buy fascist publications?"

If that was what Giap wanted to talk about, Tangri was happy to accommodate him. "Do you believe Saigonese are or feel less free," he asked, "than their fellows in Ha Noi?"

Giap's response was a snippy one. "The inhabitants of Saigon, as President Thieu put it, have the freedom to ride motorized instead of plain bicycles."

"You digressed," Tangri charged. "What goal do you pursue with your present offensive?"

With a smile, Giap replied. "To bring our people a step closer to real freedom."

Tangri tried again. "Is your offensive designed to cut South Viet Nam into two parts? Is Hue to be captured or Saigon to be threatened?"

Giap's straight-faced response was less than believable. "You would have to ask the liberation front," he said. "We are merely supporting it with troops and weapons."

Tangri could not believe what he had heard. "In fact," he said, "you are supporting it so massively that it looks to all the world like your war. After a victory over the Saigon regime will you also overrun Laos and Cambodia?"

Primly, Giap replied, "There we likewise support only the liberation struggle of the people."

Tangri fired another question. "How long will the war last?"

And just as quickly, General Giap gave a soft, hopeful response. "I would think that the war will not last as long as it has already lasted."[24]

The campaign on the central front began in early April. Here another 35,000 of Giap's soldiers gathered in Laos and moved across the border, probing toward Kontum. *Time* magazine reported, "As usual, they are fighting meticulously prepared, preset battles. Only when everything is in place—from tanks to troops to missiles and ammunition supplies—do the North Vietnamese even begin to move. Most often things have gone well."[25] Along the coast, in Binh Dinh province, northern soldiers and local Viet Cong forces cut Highway 1. From the end of April through the middle of May, the People's Liberation Army moved closer to Kontum against halfhearted ARVN defenses. On 14 May, they attacked Kontum, but were forced back by ARVN artillery fire and U.S. helicopter gunships and tactical bombing.

From 15 to 25 May, northern units probed Kontum, trying to locate weak points in its defenses. They broke through finally around midnight on 25 May and entered the outskirts of the city. By the evening of 28 May the People's Liberation Army could no longer sustain its momentum. Its troops had suffered grievously from U.S. air attacks, and neither reinforcements nor resupply was available. On 30 May they began to withdraw. In Binh Dinh province, with American air support, ARVN recaptured the area it had lost in April and May and reopened Highway 1. As in the North, now on the central front, Giap's carefully laid plans had not carried the day. This second of his thrusts had failed to achieve its objectives.[26]

The offensive along the southern front began early on 2 April when three reinforced divisions drove against Loc Ninh and An Loc in Binh Long province. Loc Ninh was overrun on 6 April, and enemy divisions moved on to threaten An Loc. A worried President Nguyen Van Thieu sent reserve units to reinforce his positions there. Giap's soldiers hit An Loc on 13 April with a massive barrage of artillery, followed by tanks and infantry. Aided again by U.S. air power, ARVN beat off the attack. The People's Liberation Army and its Viet Cong divisions tried again on 14 and 15 April and were once more repulsed. *Time* magazine noted Giap's problem with momentum. "Neither Giap nor his troops have had experience in large-scale conventional warfare, and they are not fighting a true war of maneuver. . . . Locked into preset plans and dependent upon prepositioned supplies, the communists are tied to a stop-start pattern."[27]

A new assault moved forward 19–23 April, and still ARVN managed to hold in place. The pace slackened for some days as Giap's units tried to regroup and resupply, but his primitive logistics system simply had nothing more to give. They would win or lose with what they had. They renewed their attack on 11 May, moving forward behind an artillery barrage. U.S. fighter-bombers, B-52s, and helicopter gunships stopped them in place. They tried again on 12 May and for the last time on 14 May. Stymied, morale broken, with no chance of reinforcement, Giap's forces finally melted back into the jungles to the west from which they had originally come.[28]

While the Easter campaign raged, an angry Richard Nixon unleashed his air power on the North. U.S. bombers hit targets never before designated, razing storage depots and electrical and industrial plants, dropping bridges into gorges and waterways, destroying rail lines and roads. Nixon ordered the port of Haiphong mined, completely stopping traffic in and out, on 8 May, and revealed what he had done shortly thereafter to the American public by telecast. Without shipments of war goods from his major allies, Giap could not go on. In an assault he had not wanted to mount, 100,000 of his soldiers lay dead on three battlefields.[29]

There was some small comfort for the North. Giap's divisions now occupied territory never before controlled. Unprecedented numbers of northern soldiers stood on southern soil, and the terms of the 1973 peace agreement would not require their removal. Morale in the South had been badly shaken. Vietnamization seemed as if it would not work unless backed by American air support. That was little enough reward in the face of such a serious reversal. Combat deaths were so high and expenditures of matériel so great that even the most avid Politburo supporters of southern incursions were now forced to face facts. No new offensive could be undertaken within the foreseeable future. They had lost their chance to shake the foundations of the weak Republic of Viet Nam. They had not humiliated the United States. Instead, U.S. air forces had shattered their best-laid plans and prevented the defeat of southern armies.

Prior to the campaign, Ha Noi believed it could continue the southern war and at the same time build socialism in the North. The failed offensive changed that. Additional economic development would have to await victory. The party, the press, and the radio began telling factory managers to worry less about production and more about the army's need for men. Their only option now lay in Paris; Le Duan had to order Le Duc Tho finally to negotiate seriously with Henry Kissinger.

There was, finally, another step the disappointed members of the Politburo could take. Giap had warned against the Nguyen Hue campaign. He had cautioned that it might not succeed. He had been right. That was enough to condemn him. In the ancient western world, rulers killed messengers who came bearing bad news. Although he retained his position as minister of defense, the Politburo stripped Giap of his command of the People's Liberation Army and gave it to his longtime disciple General Van Tien Dung. Three years later it would be Dung, not Giap, who would be renowned as the "conqueror of the South." In August, Dung also received full membership on the Politburo, a sure sign of his ascendancy. These actions had to strike Giap to the core. He was the founder of that army. He had taken thirty-four inexperienced men armed with primitive weapons and made them into a modern army. For twenty-eight years he had held full field command over that force. Now it was gone, given to another, and Giap's mouth must have filled with the bitter taste of gall.

Surely thoughts of what-might-have-been plagued Senior General Vo Nguyen Giap in his offices within the defense ministry. Perhaps he should have resisted more strenuously when others suggested the campaign, but that would also have cost him his job. Perhaps he should not have spread his forces over three fronts but concentrated on only one. Ignoring that military Principle of Mass may well have caused his defeat. He knew his logistics system had failed him, yet he could conceive of no other way to organize it, given his lack of heavy transport. It had been logistics which, on all three fronts, forced his troops to halt repeatedly in their attacks, waiting for resupply. Giap could *stockpile,* but he could not *transport,* and there lay the rub.

Highly mobile, conventional warfare consumed supplies with a voracious, inexhaustible hunger. Combat divisions of his American foes used tons of supplies for every minute of battle. There was no way he could satisfy even the lesser demands of his own units. Yet he had been ordered to fight conventionally, and he had overestimated his ability to do so. Nor had he known what to do with the hundreds of T-34 and T-54 tanks provided him by the Soviet Union. He was no Heinz Guderian or George Patton. Armored warfare was beyond his ken. He had used his tanks as moving gun platforms, ineffectively coordinated with infantry units, when they should have slashed through ARVN lines in armored *Blitzkrieg* penetrations, cutting off and bypassing enemy defenses, leaving them to rot. Yet no amount of recrimination would restore Giap to his position. His days of field command had ended.

By summer 1972, Giap dropped out of sight. Rumors suggested he was ill and had gone to Moscow for treatment. That is possible. Although never confirmed in the West, stories had long circulated that by 1972 Giap's health—never strong since childhood—had broken, that he suffered from Hodgkin's disease, a cancer of the lymphatic system, making it impossible for him to be as active in government as had formerly been the case. In this scenario, Le Duan's promotion of General Van Tien Dung to field command of the army had been done as a kindness to Giap—the "national treasure" of the North—in recognition of his failing health and to relieve him of some of his burdens. More likely he was only despondent over his relief and decided to keep a low profile. His health problems, which would become real enough in 1974, were now only a cover story for his absence from the limelight. There was little sign of any activity by Giap until 23 December, when, on the anniversary of his founding of the army, he paid a visit to the 77th Missile Unit detachment.[30]

That same day, officials at the Communist peace negotiating mission in Paris officially denied a report of Giap's death that had recently surfaced among southern intelligence circles in Saigon. Rumor had it that Giap had died in an explosion of a delayed-action mine while inspecting damage at the Tran Hung Dao armament depot in Haiphong. In its precipitate and premature obituary, Agence France Presse claimed that Giap had been criticized in the past "for having allowed politics to intrude on an otherwise brilliant military career." It was a ridiculous observation. It would have been more correct for AFP to assert that he was a complete politician who also knew how to organize and operate an army. This "news" surfaced even as Ha Noi radio broadcast a message from Giap calling for bravery in the face of the American Linebacker II bombing offensive that raged from 18 to 29 December 1972 as the U.S. Air Force mounted 739 sorties, 729 of which struck north of 20 degrees latitude, dropping over fifteen thousand tons of bombs until, literally, no military targets in the North remained untouched. "Ha Noi and Haiphong and other cities may be destroyed," Giap said in this broadcast, "but the Vietnamese people will not be intimidated."

Giap had been reported dead on other occasions. He was falsely reported to have been killed in an air raid in the middle 1960s, and in the months just past there had been unconfirmed reports that he had died from the effects of malaria. The December radio broadcast demonstrated that Giap was alive, still motivated by his desire for ultimate victory over his foes. That time was drawing nearer. On 23 August 1972, the U.S. Army's 3d Battalion, 21st Infantry redeployed back home—the last American combat unit to leave Viet Nam.[31]

"They've Had Me in My Grave a Dozen Times"

The long months of negotiation in Paris finally ended in early 1973. On 15 January, President Richard Nixon ordered a halt to all American military operations aimed at North Viet Nam. On 27 January, representatives of all four parties—the United States, the Republic of Viet Nam, the Democratic Republic of Viet Nam, and the Provisional Revolutionary Government of South Viet Nam (the old NFLSV)—signed their names to the peace treaty. A ccase-fire was declared in place. Prisoners of war would be exchanged. The United States would withdraw all remaining military personnel from the South within sixty days. A Council of National Reconciliation and Concord would resolve difficulties and organize new elections in the South. No further foreign military activity was to take place in Laos and Cambodia. An International Commission of Control and Supervision, composed of Canada, Hungary, Poland, and Indonesia, would monitor compliance with these provisions.

Ha Noi's government announced that same day that the national flag would fly throughout the North for eight days, from 7:00 A.M. on 28 January through the beginning of the Tet New Year on 4 February, in celebration of the successful end of the Paris peace talks.[1] Only a few days before, Giap was still trying to contend with rumors about his health.[2] Now, on 27 January, in a radio address to the nation, he turned to more important matters. "This agreement is a great victory for our Vietnamese nation. . . . [and] for the heroic Vietnamese people. . . . We are very proud and enthusiastic."[3]

On New Year's Day, Giap spoke again on radio and commented on the meaning of the new peace terms. "For the first time in one hundred years," he said, "all foreign aggressor troops will have left Viet Nam." In the South, he continued, "Our people and compatriots . . . have large liberated areas and have . . . the NFLSV, which has scored countless feats of arms, which has brought together people of all strata and all patriots. They also have the PRGSV [Provisional Revolutionary Government of South Viet Nam], the only genuine representative of our people in the south. Peace has been restored, [but] it has not yet been consolidated."[4]

Peace had not, of course, been restored. Only an agreement had been signed. Fighting inside South Viet Nam never stopped. Ha Noi increased its movement of men and supplies along the Ho Chi Minh Trail. Northerners built a MiG base at Khe Sanh and trucked SA-2 surface-to-air missiles south across the 17th parallel. Furthermore, ARVN never stopped fighting these northern moves. Southern soldiers continued sweeps against the Viet Cong and Giap's main force units inside South Viet Nam and, in 1974, nearly exhausted themselves on a major offensive.

By May 1973, Giap expressed alarm and dissatisfaction with U.S. "violations" of the peace treaty. It had, he said to correspondents from three Czech newspapers—*Obrana Lidu, Pravda,* and *Cteka*—in violation of the agreements, discontinued removing its mines from northern ports and resumed espionage flights north of the 17th parallel. Despite such intransigence, Giap promised that the North would continue to work for the "peaceful reunification of the country" and to strengthen its alliances with "fraternal parties" in Laos and Cambodia—the Pathet Lao and the Khmer Rouge.[5]

On 9 July 1973, Giap appeared at a ceremony in Ha Noi to greet Beqir Balluku, vice chairman of Albania's council of ministers and minister of national defense, who had made a state visit to the Democratic Republic of Viet Nam. Giap was not seen again until September, when he warmly greeted a visiting Fidel Castro. Then he dropped completely from sight for nearly eight months, until 1 May 1974, when he appeared at a May Day celebration and presided over a meeting of the Politburo at Ba Dinh Hall in central Ha Noi. At his appearance, he was heartily applauded by his governmental colleagues.

According to available sources, Giap had been in the Soviet Union, returning from Moscow on an Aeroflot flight under an assumed name only a day or two earlier and slipping back into Ha Noi without fanfare. Every indication suggests that he had suffered serious health problems and even upon his return had not fully recovered. Those who saw him said he looked to be at least fifteen pounds lighter, measurably thinner, with haggard, drawn features. In past years he had suffered from a variety of diseases brought on by his years in the bush and by general neglect of his own health, including chronic malaria, diabetes, and hepatitis. In late 1972 he was reputed to be suffering from Hodgkin's disease. During his long absence in 1974, rumor-mongers suggested other possible illnesses that were supposedly ravaging his system: cancer of the liver or some other abdominal cancer, perhaps even neurological cancer.[6]

In December 1973 or April 1974, depending on who told the story, unnamed western diplomats who had known Giap in Ha Noi and who "just happened" to be there saw him in a Moscow hospital's cancer ward, looking worn out. They spoke with him, but he disclosed nothing of the nature of his illness.[7]

An absence, enforced or voluntary, is always a sure way for the indispensable to learn how easily they can be replaced and forgotten. During his time in the Soviet Union, Giap missed some very important activities. Both Van Tien Dung and Song Hao, recently promoted from lieutenant general to colonel general, were introduced in their new rank to those present at the 26–27 April 1974 army conference. Giap was not there to welcome them.

When he resurfaced, Giap tried for a time to be as visible as possible.[8] It was not until 31 May that Ha Noi diplomatic sources finally admitted officially that Giap had received medical treatment in the USSR.[9] In July, the *Frankfurter Allgemeine,* a German newspaper in Frankfurt am Main, carried a story datelined Ha Noi, informing its readers that Giap was now back in Hanoi after a trip to Moscow "and Eastern Europe." The tone of the article made it seem as if he had been out of the country for diplomatic rather than for health reasons.[10] That same month, Ha Noi watchers picked up on a whispering campaign against Giap for "his complete failure in the 1972 summer offensive," while Le Duan, who had actually advocated that offensive, remained immune to criticism. As late as September, observers described Giap as "frail and emaciated, although he apparently still functions."[11]

That he had been seriously ill is undisputable, but, characteristically, neither Giap nor his government has ever precisely indicated the nature of his problem. His last word on the subject came in October 1977, during an interview with French journalist Berengère d'Aragon of *Paris Match.* Giap learned that previously she had been seriously ill and he cordially inquired about her current health. "Never listen to the doctors," he told her laughingly. "They are birds of ill-omen. Now, I have had a cancer of the pancreas, or something of the sort, according to the newspapers and the doctors, for about thirty years, I think. They've had me in my grave at least a dozen times."[12]

In the fall of 1973 the Twenty-first Plenum of the Politburo convened to reappraise its war policy in the South. For a time its members had hoped to end the long conflict through political action. There had been some expectation of success from that approach. Following the Easter offensive of 1972, the military capabilities of ARVN steadily diminished and civilian morale in the South continued to worsen, both in the face of continuing heavy cuts in U.S. aid packages. These distressing developments were heightened when North Vietnamese forces seized isolated ARVN outposts and fire support bases in the western high-lands of the South. The approach of the Politburo made sense in late 1972 and throughout 1973. They could hardly mount a major military action in the South, since neither Giap's army nor COSVN was capable of a major attack at that point. Consequently, the Republic of Viet Nam seemed able to withstand such minor setbacks and northerners fumed at their lack of progress in the po-litical war. In October 1973 at the meeting of the plenum, Politburo members argued for a different approach and so adopted a resolution calling for a new mil-itary offensive against the southern government of Nguyen Van Thieu, to cul-minate in a final push in 1976.[13]

The Politburo named Giap's successor, Senior General Van Tien Dung, as head of this military venture. If he was to succeed, he had to remedy many de-ficiencies in a short time. It was no simple task. His northern military forces had suffered grievous casualties in the 1972 Easter offensive, and his logistical sup-port had been severely curtailed by U.S. mining operations in the North and by American air strikes. Nor were COSVN's southern forces in better shape. Colonel General Tran Van Tra, commander of the southern B-2 Front, wrote that "in 1973 our cadres and men were fatigued, we had not had time to make up our losses, all units were in disarray, there was a lack of manpower, and there were shortages of food and ammunition." Both Tra and Dung did what they could.[14]

Dung called his divisions back across the DMZ to be reinforced and outfit-ted with new equipment. In early 1974, Dung restructured his divisions under four new corps headquarters and the units themselves were brought up to strength and reequipped where necessary. He supervised construction of new roads and pipelines in support of southward logistics resupply efforts. He de-manded and got improvements in the Ho Chi Minh Trail. He expanded training centers, established equipment repair shops, filled supply depots, and organized additional hospital units. By the end of 1974, his army now not only could fight again, but for the first time ever, it could be resupplied fully and in time without depending on prepositioned stockpiles and coolie-borne matériel. It had finally become a modern army.[15]

Le Duan, Le Duc Tho, and others continued to bring pressure on General Dung to begin a final offensive against the South. In meetings with the military committee, still chaired by Giap, Dung proceeded cautiously. Although he was willing to work on a southern assault, he predicted at a conference with the Politburo in late 1974 that complete victory over the Republic of Viet Nam might take several more years. Giap was more sanguine. He reminded Dung, "Our planning must provide for the contingency that it [the war] could end in 1975."[16] Dung also fretted that the United States might again intervene on be-half of the South if he launched a major invasion. The United States had, after all, promised to use its airpower, if necessary, to protect the southern republic. Dung decided to test that proposition by concentrating on a single province.

Dung selected Phuoc Long province, only forty miles from Saigon at its closest point. On 26 December 1974, Dung ordered artillery to fire on the target, and on 5 January 1975, he sent two divisions with accompanying armor and artillery toward the provincial capital. No B-52s appeared in the skies, and ARVN air support for its ground forces was negligible. Light ARVN resistance failed almost immediately, and by 6 January the province fell captive. America had *not* intervened, and, encouraged, Le Duc Tho, now number two in Politburo ranking, ordered Dung to launch a new strike at Ban Me Thuot. Dung's planned operation was a model of simplicity. He would divert ARVN's attention by attacking elsewhere and then move on Ban Me Thuot with overwhelming force.[17]

Three northern divisions attacked Ban Me Thuot on 1 March. Another force attacked west of Pleiku as a diversion. Dung's men finally fought their way into the town on 10 March. After two days of heavy fighting, the town fell. ARVN tried to mount a counterattack on 15 March, but the effort quickly collapsed. Once again there had been no last-minute intervention by the United States on behalf of its late friends in the South. Many of President Thieu's southern politicians and generals began making plans to escape the country before the end of this final confrontation. Troop commanders fled their units, leaving their men to fight on and die. Sadly enough, the higher a man's rank, the more likely it was that he would seek to save his own skin. Those weeks and the ones to follow were not the proudest ones in the history of the Republic of Viet Nam.

On 12 March, Senior General Vo Nguyen Giap, chairman of the military committee, transmitted to Dung's general headquarters the latest directives of the Politburo. Invest Pleiku. Close all roads and airports. Go forward without talking about the progress realized. Black out all news from the war front.[18]

So General Dung sent his forces south out of Quang Tri province down Highway 1 toward Hue. President Thieu abandoned the city and called for a new defense line north of Da Nang. It was no use. Da Nang fell on 29 March, and Dung's armies now held all of the South's Military Region 1. There had been no savage fighting and but few bloody casualties. ARVN had simply collapsed in panic and disappeared as a combat-ready force. Dung's units now moved to liquidate Military Region II, completing their seizure by mid-April as ARVN continued to melt away before them.

On 25 March, the Politburo ordered General Dung to seize Saigon before the arrival of monsoon rains in mid-May. After some thought, Dung asked permission to call this last effort the Ho Chi Minh Campaign, and those in Ha Noi quickly ratified his suggestion.[19] Dung now sent his superior forces toward the southern capital: over fifteen infantry divisions and hundreds of tanks and artillery; he even had limited use of the small northern air force. Antiaircraft artillery batteries proceeded with the rest in case Saigon's aircraft tried to interfere with the advance.

Many American military men, observing the order of battle of Dung's units, claimed that the North had abandoned the tactics of a people's war in favor of a highly conventional attack. One author even described Dung's assault as a carbon copy of "an American one."[20] But, as John Gates has written, no American army has ever relied upon aid from guerrilla forces, popular militia, and political cadres to facilitate and sustain offensives by U.S. regular forces.[21] Writing later, Generals Giap and Dung claimed that *"everywhere regional forces, militia, guerrillas and self-defense units* seized the opportunity to hit the enemy" during the Ho Chi Minh Campaign.[22] These forces, they wrote, "seized control in many places, wiped out or forced the withdrawal or surrender of thousands of garrisons, shattered the coercive machine of the enemy at the grassroots level, and smashed their 'popular defense' organizations." Those same fighters, by their efforts, provided "better conditions for our regular units to concentrate their attacks on the main targets of the general offensive."[23] Giap and Dung described how other sympathizers "carried out a campaign of agitation among enemy ranks to bring about their disintegration."[24] The attack was fully consonant with the principles of the third phase of a people's war of national liberation.

For the South the last grains of sand were about to fall to the bottom of the glass. As March turned to April, Dung moved eighteen divisions to within forty miles of Saigon and readied them for a five-pronged attack on the city. Each of five corps had a principal axis of advance to follow that, Dung hoped, would prevent last-ditch house-to-house defensive fighting in the city. Poised on the abyss, President Thieu fled to Taiwan on 21 April, and Vice President Ky also soon slipped away. A few days later, on 28 April, a coalition of generals and politicians named General Duong Van Minh as acting president because, he confessed, he had "connections" within the Communist camp and someone would have to negotiate with them.

Operation Frequent Wind, the American effort to extract its nationals and a few favored Vietnamese, staggered along as overloaded helicopters struggled into the sky from the roof of the U.S. embassy, assailed by the wails of those left behind. On the afternoon of 30 April, a column of North Vietnamese tanks rolled up to the presidential palace and the lead machine crashed through the heavy metal gates. Colonel Bui Tin was the first northern officer into the building. The South had at last fallen. The two entities—the Democratic Republic of Viet Nam and the Republic of Viet Nam—would henceforth be known as the Socialist Republic of Viet Nam.[25]

Giap later told an interviewer that after the liberation of Saigon "I was delirious with joy." He flew there and inspected the combat headquarters of the joint general staff there. "Everything was intact," he said, "for they fled too quickly to destroy their papers. I remember there was a map which had a computer system to locate Viet Cong areas. Next to it was a display of weapons and means of war operated by computers. I had [obviously] followed the war closely," Giap continued, "but on that day I had the profound impression that our united forces had defeated not only the soldiers but the gigantic potential of the American army and its puppet government." He drew another conclusion. All that modern equipment had been useless. "The human factor had been decisive."[26]

Of the three American generals he had faced, someone once asked him, which was the best? "I don't want to criticize them behind their backs because I do not see them in this room," he responded coyly. "The French have also asked me the same question and *they* changed generals *nine* times!" Then he became more direct and offered an actual response of sorts. "I think General Westmoreland was experienced and well trained. He came, saw the problems, and requested two hundred thousand more troops. I won't say whether I feel he was good or not, but if he thought two hundred thousand would be enough, he was wrong."

Then Giap turned to General Creighton Abrams, Westmoreland's successor, and, like him, destined later to become army chief of staff. "Abrams was different and had different fighting tactics," Giap observed. "He based his leadership on research. He studied his own and other's experiences to see what he could apply to the real situation here, but he believed he would win and was defeated." General Fred Weyand followed Abrams both to Viet Nam and to the office of the chief of staff. "For Weyand," said Giap, "it was not possible to attain victory. The situation was too different given the legacy he inherited from the two previous generals. Their mistake was that of invading us, but that was the responsibility of the U.S. government. That is all I will say."[27]

On another occasion, Giap had an opportunity to express his feelings about the abilities of U.S. soldiers. On a plane trip to Ha Noi, he recalled, he had been wearing civilian clothing but some American veterans seated nearby, on the way to revisit war scenes in Viet Nam, recognized him from the name tag on his luggage. One of them asked, "General, what did you think of U.S. soldiers?" Giap replied that "American soldiers were just like any others, when led well, they fought well." They were defeated, he added, but that was not their fault but that of their leadership. Then he said, "U.S. soldiers should never take part in a war of invasion of another country. If they love their own honor and freedom, then they should love the honor and liberty of others."[28]

Many Americans were disappointed at the outcome of the Viet Nam conflict. Charges and countercharges were hurled in attempts to resolve where the fault should be placed. One man who should have been listened to in an earlier year finally spoke to an interviewer, explaining that much of the fault lay in pride and ignorance. In his own pithy way, Lucien Conein, who spent about as many years in Southeast Asia as any American, summed up his view of U.S. experiences there. "In 1956, I was brought back [to the U.S.] after my experiences in the North and Center [of Viet Nam] and our establishing a 'democratic' regime in

Saigon. Before I went on to [assignment with] Special Forces at Ft. Bragg, I was debriefed at the Pentagon. They asked me how the French army could be whipped when they controlled the air. I said the French made mistakes. They were (1) roadbound. Highway 5 to the North. The Street of Joy. They'd get ambushed. (2) They *did* control the air, but (3) they also built these little Beau Geste outposts all over the place. And at night the Viets'd come in and ttcchhh [sic], cut the balls off the French sleeping in those little goddam outposts. I said we should not make those mistakes. So they said, we're going to do better.

"So . . . we sent ten times the amount of air force. The B-52s. Rolling Thunder. And we had our own little Beau Geste outposts which we called fire support bases. We were . . . roadbound. The same thing that happened to the French happened to us. We didn't learn one goddam thing.

"Everytime somebody new came out there, he thought he could win the war. Tell you the truth. The first week I was in Viet Nam in 1945, I knew *everything*. When I left—after sixteen years out there—I admit I knew absolutely *nothing!*"[29]

China had once served Giap as a personal haven when, in 1940, he found it necessary to flee from the clutching hand of the French 2d Bureau. Later he used its southern provinces as infantry training grounds and artillery ranges. Its Communist government provided supplies for him to use against first the French and later the Americans. Chinese "volunteers" helped the North maintain, repair, and defend its railroad lines during American bombing campaigns, and they manned some of the Ha Noi government's antiaircraft batteries. No one, least of all Giap, would have denied the valuable services China gave over twenty-five years to the Democratic Republic of Viet Nam. Yet his attitude toward its government continued to sour.

Giap was well known among northern leaders as one who favored close ties with the Soviet Union and who resisted the influence of China. Seven years after reunification, in 1982, Giap let slip to an interviewer part of the reason for his fierce antagonism toward this neighboring Communist government. It wanted, he suggested, to keep Viet Nam divided, to postpone the day of unification. The Chinese, Giap said, "would have us keep our forces lying low for a . . . very long time. . . . They told us . . . that Viet Nam would be reunified but [claimed] that it would take . . . maybe a hundred years."

Giap was unwilling to allow another Viet Nam in the South to remain separated for such a long time. Although he long advocated protracted warfare to Nguyen Chi Thanh and Le Duan, even he did not foresee allowing the situation to continue for more than a few additional years. In what may have been an unguarded moment, Giap recalled for his interviewer, "In the spring of 1975, we launched the general offensive which ended in final victory." Then he dropped his bomb. "But Peking was opposed to it."[30] That is all he said.

He did not elaborate. If true, however, it would overturn all conventional western intelligence wisdom of the time, for assessments and estimates then inevitably included the notion that China supported Ha Noi's final drive on the
South.

Perhaps the Chinese were afraid of losing too much influence in a Viet
Nam at last reunited, concerned that their neighbors to the South would revert
to their two-thousand-year-long hostility. Tonkin by itself was an acceptable
client state, too weak to oppose other Chinese efforts to extend their influence
into Laos and Cambodia. A continuation of the status quo, under those circumstances, might well have been part of Beijing's planning and thus reason
enough to oppose a final northern drive upon the South.

The silence from the battlefields was deafening to Giap. He had heard the
"mournful mutter of musketry" ringing in his ears almost without cessation for
thirty years. Although he had been a part of the Ho Chi Minh Campaign, he had
not led it as he might have wished. It had been his fate to lead two unsuccessful campaigns against U.S. forces—Tet 1968 and the Easter offensive of 1972.
Both times he had warned against those attacks, and twice he had been over-
ridden only to suffer consequent failure, condemnation from his superiors, and
demotion. He had not been allowed to cap his career with the 1975 final on-
slaught on the South. The laurels for that victory went instead to Van Tien
Dung. Giap may well have fallen into the throes of a martial postpartum depression. His whole life had been geared to war, to resistance, to national salvation campaigns, to reunification, to independence. Now all that was
accomplished—but not by him—and life no longer seemed to hold much challenge.

His doldrums remained for several months with endless boring days in his
office and quiet brooding at night in his villa until Le Duan offered a change of
scenery. How would Giap like to travel overseas on a fraternal visit to Cuba and
Algeria? Save for his time in the border regions of China during World War II,
a visit to the USSR in 1967 when he attended the fiftieth-anniversary celebrations of the October Revolution, and his more recent trip there for medical treatment, Giap was a little-traveled man. He had thought much about the history
and culture of other lands but had long since given up hope of any extended
travel. He rapidly assented to Le Duan's request to head a Vietnamese delegation. At least for the duration of the trip, diplomatic protocol would necessitate
foreign heads of state treating him as he believed he deserved.

And so as head of a diplomatic delegation, Giap and his fellows arrived in
Havana, Cuba, on Monday, 15 December 1975, for the First Congress of the
Communist Party of Cuba. Before leaving Cuba, Giap visited schools, museums,
a fertilizer plant (such visits are *de rigueur* in Communist lands!), Isla de los Piños
(Island of Pines) off the southern coast, and several cities. He paid a floral trib-

ute to the memory of José Martí, met twice for lengthy chats with Raúl Castro, and addressed meetings of army officers and politicians, offering speeches with impossible titles: "Cuba Has Been and Will Always Be an Inviolable Fortress of Independence, Freedom and Socialism, the Lighthouse of the Revolution in Latin America and the Western Hemisphere."[31]

Giap and his delegation then flew to Algiers, guests of Houari Boumediène, who held the modest title of president of the Revolutionary Council and the Algerian Democratic and Popular Republic. In his days there Giap followed the same sort of dreary tour he had endured in Cuba, observing an endless procession of revolutionary sites and socialist accomplishments.

Giap tells a possibly apocryphal event that occurred at one point, during a celebration of Algeria's Independence Day. He suddenly encountered Zbigniew Brzezinski, later national security adviser to President Jimmy Carter. "Although we did not have enough time to talk, we saluted and welcomed each other." Brzezinski indicated his appreciation of the bravery of the Vietnamese people and asked Giap about his military strategy. "Tell Americans that the strategy of Giap is one of peace, independence, freedom," he told the American. "The Vietnamese know war; war was forced on us and we had to wage it in defense of ourselves. It was an obligated war, but we are the most peace-loving people in the world. The Vietnamese people love and cherish peace." It may not have been the answer Brezhinski wanted, but he had at least given Giap the opportunity to deliver himself of a happy little speech.[32] On 21 January, the weary members of Giap's delegation returned to Ha Noi.[33]

For the remainder of 1976, Giap busied himself with a round of ceremonial appearances. It was a punishing regimen for a sixty-five-year-old man who was no longer in robust health. To all those groups, Giap gave essentially the same message, as he recalled "the day when our country was free from the shadow of any enemy, when the north and the south were united into one family . . . and when a new era opened in our country."

In those appearances, Giap also delivered a sterner message. The work of the military had not ended. Soldiers had won the war, now they had to win the peace. With no martial enemies to face, soldiers, sailors, and airmen now must carry out their task of "building the economy and, together with all the people, implement the party's policy of economic construction and development." There could be no slackening of effort. It was essential to build "the material and technical base of socialism, thus contributing to the achievement of big strides in economy, stepping up socialist industrialization and building a prosperous and strong country."[34]

There may well have been a false note in those addresses, undetectable to the ears of his audiences. For once again, General Giap steadfastly supported in public a program with which he privately disagreed and which he had excoriated in the halls of the Politburo. Public leadership for policies he opposed almost seemed to have become his lot in life. It was well and good for Vietnamese young people, during their statutory tours of required national military service, to clear jungle for new farms, to build railroads and repair roadways, to erect new buildings and restore old ones in efforts to overcome the bomb damage wrought by American air power during the long years of conflict, to plant and tend tens of thousands of hectares of rice, to create new fisheries, and to perform a multitude of other tasks. All those things, Giap agreed, desperately needed to be done for the good of the country. He was even willing to compliment those groups before whom he appeared for their hard work and faithful service.

But he did not believe that civic action projects were the responsibility of the military. In time of war the function of soldiers was to fight, to the death if necessary. In peacetime, their *only* duty was to upgrade their martial skills, to become more professional, to prepare for war. In this as in so much else during recent years, Giap was overruled. If the army was reduced in size, the staggering economy of the country would be saturated with people for whom there were no jobs. Keep them in the armed forces in case they were needed again in their primary role. Until that time, make the best use of them possible. Work bands under military discipline assigned to reconstruction projects could accomplish much at minimal cost. It was appropriate, Giap was told, for him, no longer faced with other time-consuming duties, to act as standard-bearer for these programs. He was, after all, a hero to the entire nation. His words of encouragement would mean much. And so, once again, Giap strode forth in support of a policy the wisdom of which he personally doubted and which he privately despised.

Such cabinet/Politburo solidarity was a major reason why the Vietnamese Communist Party managed to avoid major conflicts between its civilian and military members during its first three decades in power. Giap and other leaders of the army were not solely professional military men. First and always they were ranking party leaders. Giap, for example, had been active in both urban and rural political issues long before he came to head the armed anti-French resistance movement. That training and those years of discipline still remained with him always.[35] By December 1976, at the Fourth Communist Party Congress, it seemed as if Giap was being groomed for lesser things. In the past he had always given the report on military affairs; this year that task was performed by General Van Tien Dung. Giap was relegated to a smaller role. He delivered the report on science and technology.[36]

As 1977 opened, however, Giap could take pleasure in one recent accomplishment. He had long called for creation of an advanced military school. It was time for his country to modernize its officer corps and give its officers the same advantages held by their counterparts in other lands. General Giap finally got what he wanted. The Military Institute of the People's Liberation Army in Ha Noi instituted its first course on 3 January 1977. Appropriately enough, Giap gave the address at the opening ceremony. "We must try our best," he stated to that first class and to other assembled dignitaries, "to build a contingent of high-ranking military cadres absolutely loyal to the party's revolutionary cause, who have high revolutionary qualities, a high political training, a fundamental and systematic knowledge of military science, a comprehensive economic, scientific and technological standard and a high capacity for leadership and command. They must also know how to use the dialectical method in examining, analyzing and solving the strategic and tactical problems . . . confronting our army in all circumstances."[37]

Then it was time for another trip. This time Giap led a delegation on an extended visit to the Communist countries of the Soviet Union, East Germany, Hungary, and Poland to consolidate Viet Nam's relations with those nations. Giap arrived in Moscow on 10 March and was immediately caught up in a round of official ceremonies and sight-seeing tours, including the obligatory visit to the tomb of Lenin. Across the face of Russia, Giap laid wreaths at war monuments and visited hydroelectric power plants, tractor plants, and (naturally enough) a fertilizer plant.[38]

Giap then enplaned for East Germany, where he was received by Erich Honecker, general secretary of the central committee of East Germany's Socialist Unity Party. Giap spoke at a meeting of senior officers, intellectuals, workers, and collective farmers in Dresden. Filled with a broad-minded attitude of live-and-let-live he had never been able to adopt during the years he struggled for unification in his own country, Giap not surprisingly declaimed, "The Vietnamese people fully support . . . the reality that there are two coexisting independent and sovereign German states [which must] observe the principle of strict respect for each other's sovereignty and noninterference in each other's internal affairs."[39]

Next came travel to Hungary. Giap visited there at the invitation of Lieutenant General Lajos Czinege, minister of defense. Eleven days of sight-seeing and meetings took place in an "atmosphere full of militant solidarity."[40] Then it was on to Warsaw, at the invitation of Wojciech Jaruzelski, minister of national defense. Giap remained there until the end of the month, returning at last to Ha Noi on 7 May.[41] The time had been gratifyingly spent. In each country Giap's delegation had been hosted by the defense minister, in each they had been received by the Communist Party chief and treated to a standard round of talks, rallies, and banquets. Giap thoroughly enjoyed the VIP treatment and the honors accorded him because of his former military achievements.[42]

Giap was home less than a month when once again he was asked to make a diplomatic trip, this time to China, for a friendly official visit and to secure promises of continued military aid. Once again there was a round of official visits to various locations.[43] At a banquet on the evening of 6 June, General Giap awarded Viet Nam's Order of Friendship to a number of Chinese People's Liberation Army units that had made outstanding contributions to the war effort in Viet Nam during its conflict with the United States.

During the height of that war and the American bombing of the North, the People's Republic of China (PRC) sent about 120,000 men into Viet Nam, all of whom were stationed along the rail line leading from the PRC border to Ha Noi. Some were members of antiaircraft artillery units, others were railway construction engineers, and many were laborers—in the United States they would be known as gandy dancers—who repaired rail lines as rapidly as American bombs tore them apart. They left Viet Nam immediately following the cessation of the bombing at Christmastime 1972 and were not publicly acknowledged as being there at all.

Professor Harvey Nelsen, expert on the Chinese army and a former analyst for the Defense Intelligence Agency, has stated, "We knew of them at the time through communications intelligence. . . . The PRC itself provided the 120,000 figure some years after the fact. We [then] thought there were no more than 80,000" in Viet Nam.[44] Giap's award ceremony in Beijing that night was the first public indication of the extent to which China had helped Viet Nam during the late war.[45]

While in China, Giap discussed the Khmer Rouge with his hosts. In earlier years Viet Nam had sponsored and aided those Cambodian guerrillas when they fought Prince Norodom Sihancuk's government. That changed later, as the Khmer Rouge leadership overthrew the military government of Lon Nol in April 1975. The Khmer Rouge rulers slid effortlessly into primal savagery.

For the Khmer, 1975 became "Year Zero," an opportunity to start fresh. They rejected their own heritage and slaughtered fellow countrymen by the hundreds of thousands in an effort to create a new, perfect Communist utopia. Pol Pot emptied the cities and worked most of those on rural lands to death. His "Kampuchea" became, in the words of Sydney Schanberg, a correspondent for the *New York Times,* "a killing field" for a third of the nation's people. Some who were lucky fled the country, and hundreds of thousands ended across the frontier in Viet Nam. Observers there watched in horror as Pol Pot's excesses grew even more depraved.

The army of Kampuchea, not content with trampling its own people underfoot, also mounted cross-border raids on Vietnamese hamlets and villages in a constant violation of the frontier line. The Khmer explained they were only searching to bring back those who had run away. There had been a series of such brutal assaults only about a month before Giap reached China. China still supported the Khmer Rouge and provided most of its weapons and ammunition. PRC advisers served with the Khmer army. Now Giap admitted that in those recent border disputes, his army had taken Chinese advisers prisoner. It was not news the PRC wanted to hear, but Giap wanted to make plain that Ha Noi was determined to maintain its own leadership throughout the whole of Indochina. Giap basically told the Chinese to go suck a hundred-year-old egg! With that he returned home.[46]

* * *

Freed for a time from diplomatic travel, Giap returned to his ceremonial role within his homeland, addressing crowds at localities throughout the country.[47] In October Giap met with French journalist Berengère d'Aragon and spoke with her about massive problems in the South—unemployment, and the overpopulation in Saigon caused by refugees in the late war. It was necessary to return them to rural living, "but how can you make them go back to the country now that they have had a taste of city life?" He spoke of the difficulty and dangers of deactivating both friendly and enemy minefields—ugly reminders of past conflict. "And then there are all the junkies. A nice present left us by the Americans."

D'Aragon asked Giap what had been done with ARVN officers. Giap replied that they "have been accepted into our society . . . as citizens without restriction. Of course, there are exceptions; there are centers for reeducation."[48]

That same month, after lengthy study including Giap's personal assessment, the Vietnamese army initiated action against the ever more troublesome Khmer Rouge. General Van Tien Dung ordered an armored column to penetrate up to fifteen miles into Svay Rieng, a Cambodian province on the border with Viet Nam. As soon as the unit made contact with Khmer infantry, it was to falter and rapidly fall back toward its starting point. The trap worked. A battalion of Khmer followed hard on the heels of the retreating armored column, right across the border and into the jungles of western Viet Nam. Thereupon another waiting Vietnamese unit punched in from the side, cutting off the Khmer from retreat and inflicting casualties. Dung and Giap hoped this would be message enough for Pol Pot.[49]

TWENTY-TWO

"The Memories Have Not Faded"

The 1975 Communist victory in Viet Nam was accompanied by similar Communist takeovers in Laos and Cambodia. The western world, accepting the domino theory, believed that now the three Communist parties of Indochina, having seized rule in their respective countries, would work together harmoniously, bound by a fraternal ideology, to reach common goals. Even Viet Nam probably held such notions for a time, hoping to recreate the relationship of the nineteenth century when weak monarchs in Laos and Cambodia paid tribute to the Vietnamese court in a system modeled on Viet Nam's own arrangement with the Chinese court at Peking. It did not work that way. The Pathet Lao Communists, long nurtured by the Vietnamese, continued a docile relationship with their neighbor to the east. The Khmer Rouge of Cambodia, however, resisted Vietnamese domination. Pol Pot's memory was a long one, and he still blamed Viet Nam for failing to uphold Cambodian interests at the Geneva conference of 1954.

Under Pol Pot, the Khmer Rouge pursued a bitterly anti-Vietnamese policy. Almost immediately after the Communist victories in Saigon and Phnom Penh in 1975, the two nations began skirmishing along their common frontier, with most of the actions launched by Cambodia, which now, under its new dictator, had been renamed Kampuchea. Pol Pot was determined to retrieve border areas seized centuries earlier by Viet Nam in its historic drive to dominate all Indochina. His forces landed on and occupied the Vietnamese islands of Phu Quoc and Cu Xu in the Gulf of Siam. He even turned a deaf ear to suggestions from Ha Noi that such issues could be negotiated. Heavy fighting broke out along the border in May 1977, forcing Vietnamese to flee from two southern towns situated on land claimed by Kampuchea. Ha Noi propaganda spoke of the miseries inflicted by Khmer troops on hapless Vietnamese civilians: raping and disemboweling pregnant women, beheading men and disemboweling others to eat their livers, tearing apart the bodies of living children. Hundreds of thousands of hectares of land and ricefields lay fallow as peasants fled to safer locations.

In December 1977, Viet Nam struck back. In retaliation for a Khmer raid into Tay Ninh province that killed or injured some two thousand people, Viet Nam army units occupied the Parrot's Beak area of Kampuchea. This gave Pol Pot still another excuse, and fierce border fighting occurred. On 31 December that year, Pol Pot broke diplomatic relations with Viet Nam, citing "ferocious and barbarous aggression" as his reason. By January 1978, Vietnamese troops occupied four hundred square miles of Kampuchea along the frontier area between the two countries. China announced its support for Pol Pot and his program and sent advisers to work with his army. It also poured massive aid into Kampuchea, including hundreds of long-range artillery pieces, tanks, and several modern jet aircraft and combat helicopters.

Late in January 1978, Senior General Vo Nguyen Giap, minister of defense, flew to Vieng Say in northern Laos to meet with General Grigoriyevich Pavlovskiy, commander in chief of USSR ground forces. The Soviet military man had flown from his homeland for a "fraternal" visit with Laotian Communists. Pavlovskiy and Giap met quietly to discuss the increasing turmoil in Kampuchea and to consider possible solutions.

The Khmer Rouge had become a Frankenstein monster. Insatiable for blood, their malevolence increasing almost daily, the Khmer Rouge became a byword among the nations for unrestrained terror and vicious governance. While Viet Nam might tolerate Khmer activities within Kampuchea, it could not overlook increasing cross-border violations during which Khmer soldiers moved frontier markings eastward as much as twenty miles. Nor could it sit silently while Kampuchean forces terrorized frontier Vietnamese hamlets. Something had to be done. Pavlovskiy offered Giap a pragmatic solution to the Kampuchean problem. Remember the Prague Spring of 1968, he said, when the Soviets felt threatened by recent changes in Czechoslovakia made by Alexander Dubcek. Send in your armies; drive on Phnom Penh and settle the matter with armed force. Giap had much to think about on his return to Ha Noi.[1]

In the weeks thereafter, Giap's mind was occupied by thoughts of war. This showed in his addresses to various military units in which he warned his men to increase their preparedness, step up training, fully master and apply the art of military command and control, and uphold the spirit of the revolutionary offensive. There is little doubt that Giap believed his nation's armed forces would soon be once more sent off to war.[2]

While the ministry of defense gave increasing attention to actions against Kampuchea, Giap also continued to manifest some level of interest in the other area of concern toward which the Politburo had lately urged him. He visited a conference on science and technology in Ho Chi Minh City in late January, where he met "brother and sister intellectuals." This is the first indication in the records that this journalist *cum* historian *cum* military leader now regarded himself as part of his nation's intelligentsia. He urged those present "to develop their patriotism and live for socialism." Before watchful eyes, he made a great show as he "examined various types of farm machines, hand tools, new products, and technical innovations of scientific research projects which have been applied to production on an experimental basis." He called on those around him to build the former southern capital "into a modern, prosperous and beautiful socialist city."[3]

Giap penned several books that appeared in December 1979 in time for celebrations of the thirty-fifth anniversary of his founding of the army in 1944. *War for National Liberation and National Defence* included some of Giap's writings since 1970 on fundamental aspects of the party's military line. *The Whole People Determined to Defend Socialist Viet Nam* dealt with recent antagonisms between Viet Nam and China.[4]

Tensions grew, not only between Viet Nam and Kampuchea, but with China as well. On 3 July 1978, Beijing abruptly terminated its economic assistance, and on 16 July it recalled its ambassador from Ha Noi. In August both China and Viet Nam accused the other of initiating a border clash during which Vietnamese troops occupied a small portion of Chinese territory. The Politburo's interest in settling its foreign policy differences peacefully finally vanished. It would first have to deal with Pol Pot, whose seven divisions of 1975 had increased to twenty-three, with nineteen massed along the common border. With the concurrence of Giap, as minister of defense, and of the Politburo, General Van Tien Dung sent his troops into Kampuchea. As early as 14 December they had been reported as far as 112 kilometers into southern Kampuchea. On 23 December, Pol Pot ordered a major assault against Tay Ninh province. Giap and Dung reacted swiftly with a strong counterattack.

This time Dung's soldiers moved without a stop order. Quickly overrunning Khmer resistance, Vietnamese units occupied Phnom Penh on 7 January 1979. Pol Pot and the remnant of his Khmer forces fled back into the jungle whence they had come four years earlier. Ha Noi founded a new government for Kampuchea, using as its leaders former Khmers who had renounced their allegiance to Pol Pot: the Kampuchean People's Revolutionary Council, headed by Heng Samrin. Three days later, Samrin declared the establishment of the new People's Republic of Kampuchea.[5]

It was all too much for Deng Xiao-peng of the People's Republic of China. On the morning of 17 February 1979, his army launched ground attacks, supported by artillery bombardments and air strikes, along the whole of China's 480-mile-long southern border with Viet Nam, largely in retaliation over the recent invasion of Kampuchea, although there was the usual rhetoric about cross-border incursions by Vietnamese soldiers and disputes over ownership of the Spratley Islands. From 200,000 to 300,000 Chinese soldiers moved south, and were quickly confronted by an ever-stiffening Vietnamese military resistance.

Senior General Van Tien Dung was now in charge of the Vietnamese military, and Vo Nguyen Giap continued to serve as minister of defense. He refused to sit back and watch events unfold without him. He had nurtured the army from infancy to maturity. It was his creation that now faced Viet Nam's centuries-long foe to the north. And so he frequently consulted with his successor, and Dung listened. The aging Giap relished the opportunity to be of service once again with his beloved army. It is to Giap's great credit that he had so successfully trained his army that it could function without him at the helm. It could fight well, as it had in the past under Giap's single leadership, even though Dung was now officially its head. The plans of Giap and Dung and the stubborn bravery of Vietnamese soldiers at first blunted the point of the Chinese thrust and then turned it aside entirely. They gave the Chinese a good whipping.

Giap stirred the fears of his people by announcing the horrors wrought by the Chinese troops. "They used machetes and axes to behead and disembowel innocent people and hoes, shovels and clubs to smash the skulls of wounded people and chop up the bodies of the dead. They tore up infants and threw them into fires and slaughtered men and cast them into water wells. They used explosives and flamethrowers to massacre our compatriots hiding in caves and underground shelters." It was, Giap, announced, "more horrible than the [American] Son My massacre," better known in the United States as the My Lai massacre.

Fortunately, said Giap, he had anticipated just such an attack and had made necessary preparations against the dark schemes of the Chinese. "We succeeded in turning the whole northern border, which had been one of friendship for many years, into a strong defense line." He extolled brave combatants who singlehandedly "killed from one hundred to one hundred and fifty enemy troops." Many of his military units achieved a kill ratio, he said, of thirty, fifty, even one hundred or more to one. In some localities, Giap noted, entire families united to fight the enemy. "Fathers were in command, the sons fired machine guns, the daughters-in-law used submachine guns and grandchildren threw grenades to eliminate tens of enemy troops." Despite Vietnamese defenses, Chinese soldiers penetrated up to forty miles, took the provincial capital of Lang Son, and destroyed the Pac Bo historic museum complex dedicated to the memory of Ho Chi Minh and his years in the wilderness during World War II.

China claimed the assault had been necessary to punish Viet Nam for an alleged seven hundred armed "provocations" along the border in the previous six months. The war did not go well for them, however, and after a few months and the loss of some thirty thousand soldiers, on 5 March 1979, the Chinese government announced it would withdraw its troops. Having intended to teach Viet Nam a lesson, that giant northern neighbor got an unexpected one of its own. Unprepared for the extent of Viet Nam's military resistance and unwilling to expend the necessary human and matériel resources necessary for victory, the Chinese government tucked its collective tail between its legs and quickly agreed to peace talks.

Giap, never particularly fond of the Chinese, excoriated both their motives and tactics. Recalling some of his old rhetoric against France and the United States, he now recycled it: the attack by China, Giap said, was "one of the most brutal and unjust wars in history."[6] Even after the Chinese withdrawal, Giap insisted that they had not given up their "insidious designs" and continued to concentrate their troops along the border, stage provocations, and threaten new aggression.

In an interview with Daniela Kuneva, a correspondent for Bulgarian television reporting on southeast Asia, Giap warned the Chinese not to renew the conflict. Viet Nam, he said, would win "irrespective of the scale" of another attack. Once again he pulled old phrases from his memory to condemn the late invasion as "the most unjust, the most barbarous, and the dirtiest of all aggressive wars."[7]

For eight years the two sides exchanged occasional and desultory artillery fire in a war of communiqués as "peace" talks continued. China insisted that Viet Nam withdraw all forces from Kampuchea and Laos. In mid-1980, Viet Nam accused China of shelling its territory and received countercharges that it sponsored "incessant armed provocation" along the border. In February 1984, China complained of artillery shellings that killed one of its farm workers during the lunar New Year while the Socialist Republic of Viet Nam spoke of thousands of enemy artillery rounds fired into its northern provinces and penetrations by Chinese army reconnaissance squads of up to one and a half miles south of the border.

Despite this continuing problem, possibly an effort by Beijing to distract the Ha Noi government from mounting a full-scale offensive against Chinese-backed guerrillas in Kampuchea, Viet Nam continued its military actions there. On 22 July 1979, Giap claimed total victory over Pol Pot's forces in Kampuchea, but despite this announcement, Khmer guerrillas continued to attack Vietnamese forces as they tried to mop up. Viet troop strength was about 180,000 against an estimated 40,000 Khmer. Operations continued in efforts to wipe out pockets of guerrillas. That effort, never completed, would last nine years.

With foreign threats at least temporarily resolved, Giap returned to banal ceremonial duties, writing and delivering dreadfully turgid and boring lectures on education and technology, presenting awards, courteously drinking cups of offered tea while listening to bureaucratic drivel, turning symbolic spadefuls of dirt at commemorative tree plantings, speaking at dedications, and presenting flowers to little girls. At Yen So agricultural cooperative in the suburbs of Ha Noi, Giap spoke in June praising the labors of its farmers. He called upon them to achieve the objective of "one hectare per laborer, three hogs per hectare." One wonders how Giap's martial mind escaped total paralysis as he busied himself with such utterly mundane matters.[8]

October and November provided Giap with more varied vistas. Once again he was on the move, out of the country again for much of that time, heading an official government delegation on a tour of East Germany, Czechoslovakia, Algeria, Libya, and the USSR.[9] Cooperative farm visits seemed to have become a standard feature of Giap's routine. Back home, he visited still another agricultural commune, Duong Lam cooperative, in suburban Ha Noi's Ba Vi district, and listened to still another set of statistics. He urged the manager not to rest on his laurels.[10]

Tet of 1980 brought Giap bitter disappointment. At a meeting of the standing committee of the national assembly on 7 February 1980, Premier Pham Van Dong, for reasons still not clear save perhaps for Giap's long record of obstinacy on some policy matters, proposed personnel changes to the president of the Socialist Republic of Viet Nam, Ton Duc Thang. In his turn, Thang signed orders appointing new members to the council of ministers and relieving others.

Vo Nguyen Giap, that wary and controversial old warrior, had remained at the center of power and events for thirty-five years. Now, although he remained a member of the Politburo and retained his post as vice premier, he was dismissed as minister of national defense, replaced by his former protégé General Van Tien Dung. Earlier relieved of field command of the army, now Giap was removed from all military responsibilities. It hardly seemed like an appropriate way to treat a man who had given so much service to his country, but politicians in Ha Noi, like their counterparts around the world, had no permanent friends, only permanent interests. They then threw Giap a bone. He would head the ministry for science and technology. Perhaps he was prepared; he had been receiving additional assignments in this area for some time. Now it was officially his.[11]

Giap was a stubborn man, not about to let his enemies see any despondency he may have felt. Giap showed his toughness when the Politburo decided for the first time to issue party membership cards to those who were eligible. Upon receiving his in a public ceremony, Giap pledged "to struggle and forge myself all my life to remain worthy of being a Vietnamese communist party member and of great President Ho Chi Minh." He would not take the easy way and retire to private life.[12]

Now began a dreary round of visits to agricultural cooperatives where he extolled the virtues of animal husbandry, of talks before the science and technology commission, of trips to Ho Chi Minh City to speak with scientists and technicians there. He offered wise words to geological conferences, met with visiting delegations from Bulgaria's academy of science, and hosted economic and trade delegates from Czechoslovakia and East Germany.[13]

Only once did he publicly hark back to his military days that year of 1980, when he visited a historical site in Hai Hung province to celebrate the six hundredth birthday of Nguyen Trai, one of Le Loi's comrades. During his lengthy talk he reminisced about his days as a warrior and told how he had drawn inspiration from the example of Nguyen Trai by "using weakness to fight strength, taking the enemy by surprise, using few troops to fight many and making frequent use of ambushes." The ancient hero, Giap said, taught that "by avoiding an enemy's strength and attacking their weakness, we can use half the strength needed and achieve a victory twice as large."

Nguyen Trai was "very proud of his beautiful country with its imposing mountains and rivers, its abundance of produce, proud of its old civilization and unique lifestyle, proud of its brilliant and heroic history of resisting foreign aggression." Following that example, Giap could do no less. For Nguyen Trai, as for Giap, "Love of one's country had to be closely linked to love of the people because the country and people are one."

Then, perhaps for the only time in his life, Giap spoke with beauty and grace, his words suddenly devoid of the usual Communist cant and jargon. He told how, in his days in the Bac Viet, "the mountains and rivers appeared fresh and new." He elaborated, in a lyric manner unlike his normal turgid usage. "The chirp of a bird, the petal of a flower, a gentle breeze, a few drops of rain, a gust of wind in the spring, all of these could stir the soul of a poet." Then, in haiku-like lines, he said:

> "Talents were like leaves in the autumn,
> And heroes appeared like the dawn."

or again:

> "When a herdsman played his flute,
> The moon rose higher in the sky."

"Literature," Giap said in closing his tribute, "can and must elevate a man's soul."[14]

Giap made three other trips out of Viet Nam in 1980. In February he visited the Soviet Union.[15] It was not long before he was off again. With Premier Pham Van Dong, he left for a second trip to the USSR on 14 June, returning about the end of July.[16] The third trip was more extensive. Leaving in the first few days of November, he did not return until the middle of January 1981. Giap's delegation visited Yemen, Madagascar, Mozambique, Ethiopia, Guinea, Benin, Congo, Angola, and Algeria. "The Africa of 1981," he said, "is no longer the mosaic of colonies, of countries under foreign and feudal domination that they used to be. A new Africa, in full rise, displays powerful vitality and . . . nothing will be able to check its march forward."[17]

Between trips, Giap met again with the leftist reporter Wilfred Burchett, who published his interview in the London *Guardian* on 7 July 1980. Giap allowed some of his aplomb to slip during that meeting, to which he wore his general's uniform. "I still keep an eye on defence," he said. "I'm still a military man. Yesterday I was at the front of national liberation and reunification. Now, *by a party decision,* I am at the front for building socialism." He told Burchett, "Our [major] difficulty is to defend the country and build socialism at the same time."[18]

In April 1981, Giap led a high-level party delegation to Vientiane, Laos.[19] Much of the rest of his energy that year and in 1982 was expended on his continuing round of speeches to various scientific and technical groups.[20] His life was now largely given over to ceremonial functions. He greeted foreign visitors, made the occasional obligatory speech, and appeared at funerals of departed comrades who had passed on to whatever reward awaits those who deny the existence of an afterlife. He was bored, tired, and seventy-one years old, but he was still a fighter and he had recently engaged in still another battle.

From October 1980 through at least February 1981, a policy debate raged within the ranks of the party on the nature of Soviet influence within the Socialist Republic of Viet Nam and the extent to which it should reach. In a turnabout from earlier years when he prized the aid and influence of China, Party Secretary Le Duan, joined by Le Duc Tho, Do Muoi, and even General Van Tien Dung, argued that the government should be restructured along Soviet lines and they should be allowed to extend their economic and military influence down to district level.

After all those years and with China's recent 1979 invasion still fresh in his mind, old Politburo member Truong Chinh (he of the "Long March" name) violently disagreed. At the meeting in Ha Noi of the national assembly in December 1980, Truong Chinh openly criticized Le Duan's pro-Soviet position. He did not, surprisingly, call for restoration of relations with China, but called for Viet Nam to be more independent of *all* foreign powers, including the USSR, and to follow a course of neutrality between China and the Soviets. Only in this way, he said, could they truly and closely observe Ho Chi Minh's last will and testament. General Vo Nguyen Giap, who then ranked sixth within the Politburo, saw fit to endorse Truong Chinh's stand and joined in support of him. There was personal danger in his doing so. For years now he had been undergoing a gradual eclipse. In April 1973, following the Easter offensive, he was relieved of his field command of the army. In December 1976 the Fourth Party

Congress dropped him from fourth to sixth rank. He lost his position as minister of defense in February 1980 and was relegated to oversight of science and technology. In 1981 he was further demoted from first deputy premier to third deputy premier. Much was already gone, yet he still had much to lose by this public support for Truong Chinh.

The Fifth Party Plenum, originally scheduled for December 1980, was postponed until August 1981 to allow time for Politburo members to resolve this fiery debate. Yet it continued to rage that August and so was again rescheduled for 1982. During those months, rumors circulated that Giap's endorsement might put him in line to succeed Pham Van Dong as premier, for it was believed that Dong might resign in 1981 because of advanced age (he was seventy-five) and ill health, but Dong retained his position until the Sixth Party Congress in December 1986, at which time he finally resigned.

The long-awaited plenum finally convened in late March 1982. Le Duan, who had gained sufficient backing for his pro-Soviet position during the time since October 1980, took his revenge. Six recalcitrant members were dropped from the Politburo, including sixth-ranking Vo Nguyen Giap, although he retained his position on the party's central committee. *Nhan Dan* informed its readers that "along with others," Giap had decided "not to be a candidate." It had been his choice, the newspaper insisted. The maneuvering left Giap's mouth with the taste of bitter almonds, for replacing him as the number six man was General Van Tien Dung. Despite his former glory and substantial contributions, Giap was tossed away like an old shoe.[21]

It must have occurred to Giap to retire completely, from both politics and the army, in which he still held the rank of senior general. Common sense ruled. He thus kept his magnificent villa, which was a perquisite for his contributions to the state and on which he paid no rent, and he remained in public life as third deputy premier and head of science and technology. It was occasionally humiliating, as when at affairs of state, protocol demanded that he had to stand behind even the editor of *Nhan Dan* rather than near the front as had once been the case. It was better than nothing. He had been neither poor nor ignored for forty-two years, and he was unwilling to consign himself to poverty or obscurity.[22]

He continued to putter with his duties for the next several years. They were not onerous and gave him an opportunity to keep in touch with old confederates and colleagues. He might be seen at many events. He handed out prizes at an awards ceremony for students who had won mathematics and physics competitions. He gave a banner of excellence to a Ha Noi kindergarten and its teacher. He told members of the municipal chapter of the Communist Youth Union that it would be up to them to resolve the issues of producing food and consumer goods. He attended the eightieth birthday celebration of the Ha Noi Medical College, founded with six students in 1902 and grown to over three

thousand students working in forty different specialties. He complimented ge-
ographers for having completed a 1/200,000 map of Tonkin and a 1/1,500,000
map of the entire country.

Some years were a mixture of sadness and opportunity. In April 1984 he
was named president of the commission on demography and family planning.
Although he wrote an article that year on Dien Bien Phu that was published in
the monthly pictorial *Vietnam,* he was conspicuously absent from events celebrating the thirtieth anniversary of that victory, and he did not even appear at
the fortieth anniversary of the army—which he had founded. He visited a
forestry conference and brought Tet greetings in 1985 to the people of Thanh
Hoa province. In January of that year he traveled again to the Soviet Union and
met with its state committee for science and technology. Then he pressed on to
Africa for a short round of visits.

The years rolled by without much change. He reviewed programs on nutrition and listened to briefings on meterology and hydrology. In 1986 he spoke
at an international conference held in Ha Noi on applied nutrition and thanked
attending members of foreign nongovernmental organizations for their efforts
to relieve many of the besetting ills of his society. He attended a gathering of textile experts and marked 5 June 1987 as the fifteenth World Environment Day.
He encouraged construction workers in 1988 to do what they could to improve
Ha Noi's deteriorating appearance. Despite his lessened political role, his fellow
citizens still held him in awe. Dr. Do Trong Hieu, a physician at the Institute for
Women and the Newborn in Ha Noi, emphasized his appreciation of the legendary Giap. Three years earlier, Dr. Hieu had been at a performance "and this
man came past me trying to get to his seat. He said, 'I'm sorry,' as he slipped by
me. I looked up and saw Giap. How straight he was. How imposing. It is my only
contact with him but I will always remember it."[23]

On 22 June 1988 at a meeting of the national assembly, the members
elected Do Muoi premier. Do Muoi decided to reduce the number of vice premiers
from six to four, and Giap braced himself for another fall, but the new premier
announced that Giap would be one of those retained. Do Muoi gave Giap a new
responsibility. He would be in charge of education. In 1989, with relationships
easing between Viet Nam and China, Zhang Dewei, the Chinese ambassador,
briefed the old general on his government's "swift crackdown" at Tiananmen
Square "on the counterrevolutionary rebellion." Giap responded that he "ardently hoped the situation in China will surely restore social stability and normal life under the leadership of the Chinese communist party." The following
year Giap led a high-level delegation to Beijing to attend the 11th Asian Games,
the most senior Vietnamese official to visit there since the 1979 border war. He
thanked his hosts for their "great and effective support and assistance" from
1949 to 1975, adding that he was "confident that Sino-Vietnamese relations
will soon be normalized."[24]

Giap spent increasing amounts of his time at home in his villa on Hoang Dieu Street near Ba Dinh Square. Entirely surrounded by trees, the two-storied building sits about thirty meters back from the road. Just inside the entry hangs a huge photo of Giap and Ho Chi Minh, taken in 1945 just after the August Revolution. There is no air conditioning; ceiling fans stir the air. The floors are wooden, beautifully done, dating from the colonial period. The furniture is modest: in the main sitting room is a couch with pillows, footstools, and a low coffee table. Giap, who has recently suffered from a serious eye infection, spends time on the couch that faces the garden, visiting with his wife, talking with his children when they drop by, and cuddling his grandchildren. His wife, Dang Bich Ha, a pleasant woman, performs the necessary courtesies when guests arrive.[25]

Ha's hair is now streaked with gray, short, with a little permanent. She exhibits much patience and solicitude toward others. The general speaks little when guests drop by. Over eighty years old, he remains strong and active. His eyes are still bright and quick with intelligence. Sometimes, even at home, he wears a tieless uniform, and on his feet are sandals with rope ties. When she is there, Hong Anh, Giap's daughter, offers guests aromatic green tea, longans (an Asian fruit), and seeds of fresh lotus flowers. The general no longer drinks tea, remarking jokingly that at his age he takes only "white" tea, that is to say, water.[26]

Even though ostensibly retired, he continues to make news. In a September 1991 interview with Reuters, speaking for his government, he urged the United States to lift its economic embargo. In a wry moment, he expressed his willingness to meet with his old archenemy General William Childs Westmoreland, so long as Westmoreland was willing to travel to Ha Noi. In line with his government, he endorsed Viet Nam's recent move toward a market economy while explaining that what was being done did not mean any acceptance of a capitalist economy. On 20 August 1991, his government presented him with the nation's highest medal, the Ho Chi Minh Gold Star, but did so in a manner so quiet that Giap's followers were insulted. It should have been given, they claimed, in a major ceremony studded with a great number of speakers giving encomiums to Giap. Their irritation had begun a year earlier when this national treasure's eightieth birthday passed unnoticed, rather than being made a special, country-wide event by the government.

As early as 1991, the U.S.–Vietnamese emigré press began claiming that leaders of the Socialist Republic of Viet Nam feared Giap. The government suspected Giap, the press stated, of being the major spiritual force behind a planned coup d'état by army generals against the civilian administration. For this reason, the press said, Giap had been placed under close house surveillance. His movements curtailed, his contacts suspected, the gallant old general continued his occasional ceremonial functions.[27]

It was for such a reason that he returned to commemorate the newly rebuilt Ho Chi Minh Museum at Pac Bo in the far north of Viet Nam, just a few kilometers from the Chinese border, the place of his martial beginnings, the location where he and Ho Chi Minh had first worked together at a time when their country could only dream of its liberation from the dominion of the French empire. He sat in the rear of his Russian-made, chauffeur-driven automobile and stared out the windows as his driver slowly steered around the worst of the ruts and potholes in the ruined road. His mind was lost in thought. "The memories have not faded. . . . I wish the day longer and the road better," he lamented, "so that I could revisit more easily, but that is something that I could not have. . . . I know almost every mountain and stream and town in this region. . . ."[28]

An Assessment

Senior General Vo Nguyen Giap is not a nice person. Neither were more ancient warriors from Attila the Hun and Timur the Lame to Napoleon, Zhukov, Patton, and MacArthur. Nice men do not become legendary generals; they teach Sunday school classes or become professors of history or military chaplains. They do not fill the pages of books with stories of their martial prowess or battlefields with bodies of the dead. Nor can Giap recount tales of his mercy or his love, save perhaps for his relations with family and grandchildren, and even they always occupied a tertiary or quaternary role in his life.

Giap reserved his primary affection for his country and his dedication to the Communist Party. He was self-pledged to the liberation of Viet Nam from foreign domination and to its unification into one nation. These two goals commanded his attention throughout the decades of his life, and to them he committed his unbridled ambition and hubris. Though he was sufficiently detached emotionally to view lives of subordinates and troops as no more than pawns to be expended without a qualm, his icy exterior overlay a temper so fiery the French described him as a snow-covered volcano.

This book has not been written because of Giap's humanity or personality, although his lack of humanity and the tone of his personality helped to make him what he is: one of the most talented generals of the twentieth century and the greatest living expert on people's warfare. His active career as a military commander spanned the years from December 1944 to April 1973, when his protégé, Senior General Van Tien Dung, replaced him as commander of the army. Even then, Giap remained as minister of defense until February 1980, at which time he was dropped from that office in favor of Dung. Thirty-six years of power ended. Even thereafter, until July 1991, a month before his eightieth birthday, when he was dropped from membership in the Vietnamese Politburo, he was inevitably a force to be reckoned with in matters military.

During that time he became not only a legend, but perhaps the single greatest military genius of the twentieth century and one of the greatest of all time. Not because of his elegance or the brilliance of his strategies. Not because he led and inspired his legions from the front to heights of courage in a few famous battles. Not because of his charismatic persona, nor his undeniable ego. Because of his results. Giap is the only general in modern history to launch battle against his foes from a position of grave weakness, lacking equipment and financial resources, beginning with no troops, yet still able to defeat in succession the remnants of the Japanese empire; the armies of France, the second-ranking colonial empire; and the United States, one of the world's two superpowers, despite the lengthy and enormous U.S. commitment of energy, resources, manpower, and technology. He went on to oversee battle against the southern Vietnamese, Cambodia, and China. Over more than thirty years he built a victorious peasant war machine from nothing, and he did so in a poor country, all the while restricted and sometimes wrongly directed by the politics of the Communist Party. He was the driving force behind victory after victory. His record is unparalleled and his results extraordinary. That is military genius.

He was not always victorious, as witness his campaigns in 1951 against the French in the Red River Delta area or his effort against the U.S. Air Cavalry in the Ia Drang Valley in 1965. Yet he was *mostly* correct in his military insights and judgments, and for a former history teacher without formal military training, that is extraordinary. Like America's George Washington and Nathanael Greene, he learned war through war. His training, as such, came from whatever he could glean from his reading and what he learned on the job. Books were not that much help in his early efforts. Before fleeing to China at the start of World War II, he went to the main library in Ha Noi to see what he could learn. In an encyclopedia he found a section describing grenades and their detonators. "It was very difficult to understand," he later commented. He had in the past fired a shotgun, the single firearm French *colons* allowed a few influential Vietnamese to possess. The article on grenades and his experience with a shotgun, he said, were his "sole knowledge in the matter of armaments."

Giap was bright and imaginative, and he learned on the job rather than at a service academy or in ROTC classes. For him there were no basic or advanced officer schools, no war colleges, and thus no "school solutions" so eagerly sought after by military students so they can get an assignment "correct." Giap approached problems without the impediments formally trained officers often carry with them. In the early years he had a very flexible approach. Each problem called for fresh answers, which, for a time, he provided. Later, during the years he fought the Americans, his nondogmatic approach hardened into an official and approved doctrine all its own. In a sense, what at first was highly original later became doctrine. As the war and his forces expanded, Giap had to teach larger numbers at an ever greater distance.

Giap's strategy in later years was no longer original except to professionally trained, Eurocentric U.S. officers. For the most part, they looked at his tactics and strategy as cheating, much as their British forebears of two centuries earlier had frowned upon the rebelling colonists of North America. Additionally, like any great commander, Giap was only as good as his subordinates, for they were the ones who carried out his orders and fought his battles. It is little wonder that Giap believed in rote training. His army and the Viet Cong operated far from Ha Noi, at the end of a long line of command and control, communicating with Giap only by primitive means. He had to trust in their training and believe in their autonomy, for his signals communication was probably closer to that used by eighteenth-century warriors than to those of the twentieth. More often than not, it worked.

Giap's challenges made him a master of tactics, logistics, and strategy. He invented a tactical style of warfare that neither France nor the United States was able to overcome. Even Giap learned how effective it was in the decade after the 7 January 1979 occupation of Phnom Penh by Vietnamese forces when Pol Pot and his minions faded back into the jungles of Kampuchea and for the next ten years successfully used Giap's own tactics against the now more conventionally trained and organized army of Viet Nam.

In strategy he demonstrated the essential requirement to coordinate political purpose with military action. During the Tet offensive, for example, television and newspapers brought the war home to Americans always in dramatic and sometimes in misleading ways. In the middle of a tactical defeat, Giap breached a gap in the American will to continue through broadcast pictures of a burning C-130 at Khe Sanh, of sappers in the very compound grounds of the U.S. embassy in Saigon, and of the fighting for the Citadel at Hue. That gap found, Giap pushed through it, crying that he had destroyed "the outmoded belief that modern equipment and a strong force could achieve victory." He put to rest, he said, the myth about the "unsurpassable strength of U.S. troops."

In logistics, in the early years, he managed time after time to field divisions of fighting men against the French using a system more primitive than that of Caesar in Gaul! His supply lines resembled those of Hannibal as he and his elephants made their way over the Alps.

Marchers wound their way south over mountains and through jungles, across northern Viet Nam, into and through Laos, and down the long miles of Cambodia. Coolie porters carried seventy-pound packs up forty-degree slopes, while enduring insects, snakes, hunger, occasional attacks from wild animals, fatigue, and tropical diseases. Every step of the eight-hundred-mile route they were under threat from American air strikes. Yet, despite these fearsome difficulties, they delivered hillocks (if not mountains) of supplies. In the earlier years of this effort, every pair of 81mm mortar rounds fired by Giap's men in the South, for example, represented a three-month march by one man down the Ho Chi Minh Trail. It was a feat nearly beyond belief. No one was happier than he when, by the mid-1960s, the Ho Chi Minh Trail had been improved to the point that most supplies funneled south along its course were carried by trucks.

For this logistics skill, Giap has received some recognition, but few in the West have been willing to accord him greatness in tactics or strategy. As late as 7 February 1991, he was described at a scholarly meeting in Atlanta as a logistics genius but only a mediocre tactician and strategist. That is ridiculous.

A master tactician would be one who demonstrated an ability to fight and defeat a variety of superior enemies. Giap did so. From the 1940s through the 1980s, Giap's armies fought soldiers of Japan, France, the United States, South Viet Nam, Kampuchea, and China. He prepared for a long struggle, fought defensively until equilibrium of sorts was reached, and, adapting his approach to his needs, then met his enemies with massive armies capable of defeating them.

A master strategist would overcome potential disasters and learn from defeats. Giap did so. His unfortunate early campaigns against the French taught him how to command and operate an army. His initial contacts with American units gave him the idea for his "grab them by the belt" tactics; a way to maximize his own strengths and minimize those of America. Giap had his setbacks, as at Dien Bien Phu when his units, savagely attrited, nearly mutinied, and during the dark days when American high-tech weaponry seemed overwhelming.

A master strategist would understand his enemies, make use of their weaknesses, and possess a grasp of conflict in its entirety. Giap did. He understood how important to the final outcome was his primarily social and political hold on the people of the land. They became his unsung warriors. They wore down his enemies, kept them off balance, and supported his main force units in decisive battles. They protracted the French war beyond what Paris could accept and the American war longer than Washington could afford. He manipulated the collective minds of his enemies by the effects of Dien Bien Phu and Tet 1968. While neither battle was militarily decisive, both were psychologically and critically important *on his enemy's home front.* Such achievements are the hallmark of a master strategist. Giap also avoided an essentially military emphasis toward battle adhered to by his two major enemies. Clausewitz would have saluted him.

"We hold that our war strategy does not embrace purely military affairs," Giap wrote. "War must be a comprehensive and combined strategy. The political goals are basic. The army must then not only fight but educate the masses."

Thus all "citizens are soldiers; all villages and wards are fortresses and our entire country is a vast battlefield on which the enemy is besieged, attacked and defeated." He also said, "We focus on one area or another depending on the specific conditions prevailing in each period or stage. This is a very important strategic principle in conducting people's war." Important to the outcome was his belief in his own role. He once drew from his memory a sentence made famous by Napoleon, one of his military heroes, to explain why the Corsican came to head the military efforts of France. Giap first encountered this quotation when he was still young, still a student, and he was convinced that everything that followed in later years in his own life derived from this one basic premise. "We are here by the will of the people and we shall never give way!"

He fought for independence from France and then against the United States and the Republic of Viet Nam in a struggle to unify the Viet people under one government. "I belong," Giap says, "to the generation that grew up during the years following World War I. At that time my country, very much part of French Indochina . . . was subject to the infamous policy of the 'Great Exploitation.' These were dark years in the history of my people." By the will of the people, by order of his superior, and by his own determination, he dedicated himself to his goals.

As the years went by and his victories multiplied, Giap showed his sure grasp of strategy. Because of his keen imagination and his solid knowledge of the principles of war and the fundamentals of strategy, he regularly outthought his more traditionally trained opponents, even if he did not always outfight them. He was flexible, dogged, and patient. Able to suffer defeats, he tried to learn from them and return to the fray better prepared. As teacher and trainer, he inspired in his peasant troops great trust in his leadership, the courage to resist despite sometimes overpowering odds, and a willingness to sacrifice themselves in their country's cause. In many ways, he was the prime organizer of an entire nation.

Giap mastered the Asian use of evasion and understood how to use the dimensions of time and space in order to counter Western dynamic reaction and advanced technologies. He won. His military accomplishments are matched by few in history.

Giap's Nation: A Brief History of Viet Nam

The land of Viet Nam, shaped like a giant stretched-out letter S, forms the eastern portion of a long peninsula at the southeastern tip of Asia, jutting from the belly of China into the South China Sea. The northern part contains the heavily populated, highly cultivated, and very productive delta of the Red River. Moving south, those northern flatlands give way to a long, undulating coast pocketed by small, fertile plains, occasionally challenged by rocky promontories reaching out into the sea. This thin coastal strip widens farther south, eventually falling toward the rich alluvial loam of the Mekong River Delta. The inland mountains of the north slope into the Annamite chain, which merges with a group of western plateaus. From north to south, the high country follows a line parallel with that of the coast.

Millennia ago, from the Paleolithic to the Bronze Age, a river of people flooded out of China, and in the ebb and flow of their movements across trackless ocean waters, some settled the myriad islands of the western and southwestern Pacific. Others within that current moved overland, south, out of the vastness of China at a time when ruling dynasties were weak and unable to enforce their rule everywhere. Far from the imperial court, these newcomers made homes for themselves on the eastern coastal strip of the Indochina peninsula. They ignored or overpowered those already there, some of whom had resided in that region for ten thousand years. Led by one Trieu Da, the newcomers named the area they inhabited Nam Viet—Land of the Viet People of the South. Although they looked upon the city of Canton (Guangzhou) as their capital and despite the fact that they occasionally bowed to imperial decrees issued from Beijing, these peoples thought of themselves as having a separate identity and developed new ways of speaking, of living, of ruling themselves.

Then, in 111 B.C., armies of the Han Dynasty conquered the land and people of Nam Viet. The Chinese established a suzerainty that, with some exceptions and with increasing difficulty, would maintain itself for over one thousand years.

During those long centuries of Chinese overlordship, the Vietnamese drank deeply from the wisdom of Confucius. They based much of their society upon his doctrines and from them developed well-ordered patterns of living, largely unchanged for dozens of generations. Custom and law molded everyone into a rightful and proper place in life. One's primary and basic loyalty was not only to the living family, but to the dead as well. Ancestors were not to be forgotten. They played an important role in family affairs. Fathers, as heads of households, periodically consulted with them for advice and for protection. Successive generations passed away, each one spiritually linked in a continuity yoking the present and the past.

All family obligations were respected, extending even to remote cousins. Respect and obligation prevailed at all levels from brother to elder brother, wife to husband, son to father, all to ancestors. Loyalty, obedience, and status were bywords for Vietnamese families.

While Confucian doctrine undergirded Vietnamese society, faith in the teachings of Lord Buddha dominated religious thought. Brought by missionaries from India in the first century, Buddhism became the primary religion. In the tenth century, Vietnamese emperors used Buddhist monks as advisers and declared Buddhism to be the official state religion. Its influence waned among the ruling scholar class in the early fifteenth century, but it remained popular among common people.

In 939 A.D., the Viets were, for a time, able to free themselves from the rule of their giant neighbor to the north when Ngo Quyen (whom all later generations would revere as a national hero) fought the Chinese along the Bach Dang River, at the entrance to the Gulf of Tonkin. He achieved a mighty victory there by sinking wooden poles into the mud at the mouth of the river. Impaled upon those stakes, the Chinese navy was helpless to prevent Quyen's soldiers from slaughtering its infantry. That same year, following his great victory, Ngo Quyen established the first Viet ruling house, the Ngo Dynasty.

During those years of Chinese rule, the Viet portion of the Indochina peninsula was known as An Nam—the Pacified South—and the people were called Annamese. As the centuries of occupation slowly passed, the Annamese absorbed much from Chinese society: tones for their language, the Confucian philosophy, ways of governing themselves. Now, for a time, they flourished as an independent people. Sometimes calling themselves Dai Nam—the Great South—and Dai Viet—Land of the Great Viet People—they fiercely defended themselves against all attackers. In 1257 and 1287, they repulsed invasions by the Mongols.

Then in 1407 they fell once again under Chinese rule, reduced to a province under the Ming Dynasty, a shame they endured until 1418, when Le Loi, another national hero, pushed the Chinese back north across the mountains of the frontier.

In the years that followed they resisted efforts by the Sung, Ming, and Manchu dynasties of China to reconquer them. And in turn, the Viets pushed southward along the coast until they came in contact with a people who had long ago come from India to establish on the shores of the South China Sea the Kingdom of Champa. The Viets destroyed and absorbed the Chams in 1692 and continued to expand, now against the Khmer peoples of Cambodia, who recoiled in fear and crept deeper into their jungle fastnesses. Still, by 1807 the Viets were able to establish a protectorate over the Khmers, strengthened in 1846 by a joint Viet-Thai protectorate.

Almost everywhere throughout the land, people labored as rice farmers on land sacred to them because it cradled the graves of their ancestors. The family home, the hamlet of nearby huts, and the village, which was made up of two or more hamlets, formed a bucolic world where past, present, and future became one. Life was very rural, and Vietnamese drew their strength from the soil. This emphasis on the land, the village, and the extended family meant that Vietnamese lived without any real sense of nationhood and had little idea of national patriotism. This presented real problems in the twentieth century for men like Ho Chi Minh and Ngo Dinh Diem who labored to build nations out of the loyalties of such people.

Social classes and status grew out of broad-based support from these rice farmers. Above them were landowners, merchants and artisans, priests, mandarin scholars, and nobles. At the apex was the emperor as head of state. Separate from the rest were those who had failed at all other livelihoods and were thus forced to become soldiers. Such men were the least regarded class in society. They might, from time to time, have power, but never respect. Military heroes of their past were not professional soldiers but civilians— usually scholars—who, in time of need, came to the defense of their country. Vo Nguyen Giap fit well into this pattern, for he was educated and worked as a teacher of history.

The basic governmental organization was the village, consisting of a cluster of neighboring hamlets. A village population might range from a few hundred to several thousand people who shared a common leadership, a community-center house, and a market. These folk looked to one another and within themselves for guidance and direction rather than upward toward some higher government. So tied were they to their native villages they seldom traveled more than a short walk from their homes. And those villages survived the vagaries of invasion and civil war, the idiosyncrasies of successive emperors, and the French destruction of their freedom.

Heads of households, locally elected village elders, and teachers, who were given great respect because of their learning, exercised government within such villages. They inevitably offered fierce resistance over the years when rulers tried to tamper with this autonomy, for to do so ran counter to the force behind an old saying: "The law of the sovereign gives way before the custom of the village." This system embraced nearly 95 percent of the Vietnamese population, and except at tax time people had little contact with any higher echelon of government. As they said, "The authority of the emperor stops at the village gate."

Immediately above the village was the district, roughly equivalent to an American county. Here again villages played a role, for district leaders were elected by village elders. Above the district was the province, its overseers appointed by the emperor or his representatives. These state bureaucrats were mandarins, who for at least a thousand years played a fixed and important role in society. They were steeped in the lore of Confucius, and their authority grew out of their knowledge of the wisdom of the past. Their primary task was to ensure that there was little change, that society looked to old answers rather than to new ideas. In this way they guided Vietnamese conventional behavior.

Mandarins perpetuated a static worldview, providing an internal order based on obedience, loyalty, hierarchy, and respect. Social change was to be avoided; one's duty was to follow the way of the past. They thus maintained a collective society in which individual interest was always voluntarily subordinated to that of the group: the land, the family, the hamlet, the village, teachers, elders, mandarins, nobles, emperor.

At the apex of society was the emperor, a father figure and chief religious leader, who communicated directly with heavenly powers as he fulfilled his role as intermediary between the gods and his people. He lived removed, isolated, elevated from lesser folk, hidden away behind walls from the sight of the unworthy. Even courtiers could not approach him except on their knees. He held all rice lands in trust for his people and occupied his time with diplomacy and other worthy matters. His was not necessarily a hereditary throne, for his subjects believed that national misfortune such as war, drought, flood, famine, or plague was an indication that he had lost heaven's mandate and therefore ought to be replaced.

Such changes sometimes came with regularity. In 1527, Mac Dang Dung usurped the throne, proclaiming himself emperor of a new Mac Dynasty. Although he was recognized as such by the Ming court in Beijing, his own countrymen were hardly persuaded, and as early as 1533, rivals put forward their own claims. Stung and weakened by civil wars and competitions for power, the Mac Dynasty fell to the jealousies of other great families: the Le, the Trinh, and the Nguyen. Intent upon battling one another for the right to rule the land, members of those families barely noticed the arrival of Alexandre de Rhodes (1591–1660), who came to Ha Noi in 1627.

It was Rhodes who opened the door between East and West. A French Jesuit missionary, he was dedicated to spreading the Roman Catholic faith among benighted Asian heathens. To enable Viets to read the Gospel, he devised a Roman-alphabet rendering of the Viets' spoken language that came to be called *quoc ngu.* The Vietnamese still write in the fashion taught them by Rhodes.

Others from France followed in Rhodes's train. In 1787 the pretender to the Viet throne, Nguyen Anh, signed the Treaty of Versailles with Louis XVI of France. In return for financial support and the use of French naval craft and troops to defeat his rivals, Nguyen Anh granted France commercial and missionary rights, the city of Da Nang (which the French renamed Tourane), and the island of Poulo Condore, about fifty miles from the coast, essentially uninhabited, which the French soon turned into a prison colony for recalcitrant Vietnamese.

Nguyen Anh now launched a campaign against those who resisted his rule. By 1802 they were dead or in exile. Taking the dynastic name Gia Long, he declared himself emperor, placed his capital at Hue in the center of the land, and changed the name of his kingdom from Dai Viet to Viet Nam.

While Viets fought with one another, French traders, missionaries, and military men looked with ever more favor upon the exotic land. In 1858 the French fleet attacked Vietnamese naval ships in Da Nang harbor; the following year French troops conquered some land in the Mekong Delta. In 1862 came the battle of Ky Hoa, near the town later known as Saigon. In June 1862 the French wrested the Treaty of Saigon from Emperor Tu Duc, who, sickly and by nature pessimistic, was unequal to the tasks that faced him. He confirmed French ownership of Poulo Condore and ceded to the French the southern provinces of Bien Hoa, Dinh Tuong, and Gia Dinh.

Fed by a growing hunger for empire, France declared a protectorate over Cambodia in 1863 and then turned back to claim more Viet land. The Philastre Treaty, signed by Tu Duc in March 1874, ceded all remaining southern Viet provinces to the French, who now renamed the area Cochin China.

That treaty also opened the Red River (Hong Ha) Delta area of the far north to international commerce and allowed the French to open consulates in Ha Noi, Hai Phong, and Qui Nhon. Viet Nam promised to conform its foreign policy to that of France. Tu Duc thus slowly accommodated himself to increasing French domination of his country.

In 1883 the Harmand Treaty established French authority over all of north and central Viet Nam—the areas of Tonkin and Annam, reconfirmed by the Patenôtre Treaty of

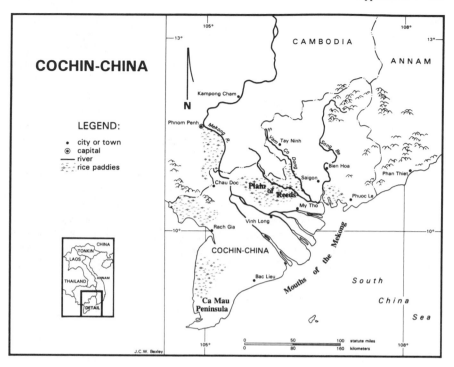

1884. After two hundred years of effort, France now controlled the ancient Annamese lands, now called Tonkin, Annam, and Cochin China, and the kingdoms of Cambodia and Laos. In 1887, the government in Paris organized them into the French Indochinese Union.

By force of arms and by threat, the French government sent sixteen thousand of its subjects to rule over fifteen million Viets. Paris called this effort its *mission civilisatrice*, its "civilizing mission" to help modernize this ancient backward land. The actions of those *colons* gave the lie to their slogan. They knew in their hearts that the brown-skinned Viets with their epicanthic eye folds were their inferiors, and in sexual, social, political, and economic matters they were quick to demonstrate the extent to which they believed in their own superiority.

French administrators occupied all governmental positions down to the lowest level. Merchants, traders, and plantation owners wrested treasures from the soil—rubber, coal, rice, hardwoods—and shipped them to Europe. French shareholders grew rich while Annamese coolies, sometimes tied like animals to their plows, or driven by whips in mines and rubber plantations, starved, grew sick, and often died in their traces. Peasants were tricked or cheated out of their tiny landholdings so that French *colons* could establish larger plantations. Merciless moneylenders provided peasants with seed and money which grew into generational debts. Grandchildren continued to pay on the usurious interests of debts that could never be repaid.

Some Annamese saw this "wave of the future" and cooperated. Often they converted to Roman Catholicism. They were repaid with minor jobs in the bureaucracy, with having their children sent to France to be educated, with colonial French passports, and with opportunities to grow wealthy under the watchful eye of the Deuxième Bureau of the Sûreté Générale du Gouvernement Général pour l'Indochine, the French police.

Others resisted. As early as July 1885, Emperor Ham Nghi, who had come to the throne at the age of twelve, fled his capital in Hue with regent Ton That Thuyet, to launch the Can Vuong (Save the King) resistance movement against French occupation. Captured in 1888, he was exiled to Algeria, where he died in 1947. Save the King rebels, however, continued widespread guerrilla activities for some years in the central provinces under the leadership of Phan Dinh Phung. When Phung died in 1896 from dysentery, this first organized resistance movement against the French collapsed.

The nationalist patriot Phan Boi Chau began an anticolonial organization in 1903, the Modernization Society (Duy Tan Hoi), to promote an insurrection that would evict the French and establish a constitutional monarchy. In 1912, he changed the name to the Vietnamese Restoration Society (Viet Nam Quang Phuc Hoi). Chau himself wandered in exile from Japan to China to Hong Kong while several attempted uprisings failed. In Japan he organized the Study in the East (Dong Du) movement to encourage Vietnamese youth to come to Japan to study while preparing for a national insurrection. The effort dissolved when Chau was evicted from Japan in 1908. Seized in China in 1925 by French agents, he was taken under guard to Ha Noi, where he was tried and convicted of treason. He spent the rest of his life under house arrest in Hue, where he died in 1940.

French police were wary even of conservative efforts to bring about change within Vietnamese society. They closed down the Tonkin Free School (Dong Kinh Nghia Thuc), founded in 1906, after only a few months of operation. Privately financed, it sought to introduce Western ideas into Vietnamese society, promote the use of *quoc ngu* as the national language, and emphasize teaching of geography, mathematics, and science. Yet the French became suspicious and swiftly closed the school.

Perhaps they were correct. Luong Ngoc Quyen, son of the founder of the school, launched a rebellion against French rule which broke out in Tonkin during August 1917. Vietnamese rebels made a disorganized attack on a colonial military garrison in Thai Nguyen province, but a counterattack quickly scattered them, and those who managed to retreat into nearby mountains were captured the following month.

Emperors had long used civil service examinations to evaluate potential candidates for the mandarinate, the imperial bureaucracy of the nation. Patterned after those given in China, these tests were first used by the Ly Dynasty in the eleventh century. At first they were open only to members of the hereditary nobility, but eventually nearly all males could qualify unless they worked in proscribed occupations or had been convicted of a crime. The baccalaureate examination was given in local centers, the master's in regional towns, and every three years, candidates for the doctorate gathered at the Imperial Palace in the capital at Hue for their test. While not all who passed became mandarins, these examinations were the best way for young men to move upward in society. As part of the plan to weaken the values of traditional Vietnamese society, the French colonial government abolished civil service examinations in Tonkin in 1915 and in Annam in 1918. In ways such as this the French increasingly came to control the destinies of those over whom they ruled. Neither benevolent nor progressive, they built more prisons than schools, and often-used guillotines, set up in public places, served as grisly reminders of their authority.

Slaves within their own country, powerless to direct their destinies, increasingly separated from their traditions and lands, the people of Viet Nam waited and watched for an opportunity to regain their freedom. They looked at their achingly beautiful land: mountains and streams and forests, rice paddies and rivers and coastal beaches, decaying temples and quiet hamlets and the tombs of long-dead emperors. Over all the land lay the mantle of French imperial control.

Now, in this richest of France's territories in Southeast Asia, even emperors bowed to the will of foreign *colons*. In the late nineteenth century, the home government of France stripped Viet Nam's rulers of their traditional powers, decreeing that a French résident supérieur, rather than the emperor, would henceforth preside over the supreme council (Co Mat), composed of the six chief ministers of the court. Two emperors, father and son, Thanh Thai (1889–1907) and Duy Tan (1907–16), who entertained hopes of throwing off the rule of France were later exiled to Réunion Island in the western Indian Ocean. In this way emperors became figureheads, shadows of their former grandeur, a symbol of the court, restricted to such inconsequential duties as an occasional award of honorary diplomas, the recognition of good and loyal service by their people, and the routine of court and family life.

The French believed their power to be too great to be challenged. The Vietnamese observed the fate that had befallen them and their beloved land, and waited. None could foresee the changes to be wrought by a man, born in the province of Quang Binh on 25 August 1911, whose parents named him Vo Nguyen Giap.

Battle Casualties Compared

The willingness of General Vo Nguyen Giap to engage foes with superior technology and firepower and to order his soldiers into bloody combat might, for some, qualify him simply as a "butcher" rather than a shrewd, careful tactician. Of course he was a butcher. All combat generals work in human abbatoirs. But was he better or worse than others of his kind? To help resolve this matter a comparison of his losses with those of other military leaders may prove helpful.

Any text on military history routinely includes battle statistics for various wars. Such books also tell a sorry tale of combat losses endured by western soldiers in battles ordered by their leaders, many of whom have been praised as skillful commanders.

At Shiloh, on a Sunday and Monday in early April 1862, came the first great bloodbath of the American Civil War. General Ulysses S. Grant ordered his men into the battle of Pittsburg Landing, where they suffered over 13,000 casualties while the Confederates lost 10,694. Both North and South were shocked at this "butcher's bill."

On 1 July 1862, General Robert E. Lee foolishly launched his men against superior Union defenses at Malvern Hill and his waves of charging Confederate infantrymen were blown to bloody bits time after time by murderous enemy artillery. After the battle, one Confederate general commented, "It was not war—it was murder." In that finale to the Seven Days Campaign, Lee lost 5,355 men in only a few hours, and in that one week alone, 20,000 of his men fell casualty while inflicting 16,000 on the Union.

On the last day of the Second Battle of Manassas (Bull Run), 29–30 August 1862, Union Brigadier General John Pope made the mistake of committing his troops to battle in piecemeal fashion. They suffered 16,000 casualties out of 60,000 committed. The Confederates absorbed 9,000 losses out of a 50,000-man force.

At Antietam on 16 September 1862, the bloodiest day of the Civil War—indeed, in all of American military history—75,000 Federals faced 40,000 Confederate defenders along an insignificant creek. Before the sun set, 4,700 men were dead, 18,440 wounded, and 3,000 missing. This butchery achieved little. The battle was at best a tactical draw and a strategic failure for both sides. Fighting renewed the next day with additional heavy casualties.

On 13 December 1862, at Fredericksburg, Union Brigadier General Ambrose E. Burnside ordered his men to attack the soldiers of Lieutenant General James Longstreet, entrenched behind and to the north of the town at Marye's Heights, as well as Thomas J. "Stonewall" Jackson's troops, crouched behind a railroad embankment on Prospect Hill. The result was a slaughter of Union men by southern shoulder-arms fire and artillery. The Federals took 12,563 casualties, inflicting 5,309 on the South.

On 31 December 1862 and 2 January 1863, General Braxton Bragg's soldiers attacked Major General William S. Rosecrans's troops and were badly defeated at Stone's River southeast of Nashville, taking over 10,000 casualties to massed northern artillery. Rosecrans's casualties were also high. Then, at the Chancellorsville campaign in May 1863, Union losses came to above 17,000; those of the Confederates tallied 12,700.

In 1863 during the three days of Gettysburg, the South inflicted 23,000 casualties while suffering 28,000 of their own—one-third of Lee's entire combat strength. The battle toll rolled on like an incoming tide. At Chickamauga Creek, 18–20 September 1863, southern losses were over 18,000, Union casualties more than 16,000. In the Battle of the Wilderness, 5–7 May 1864, the two armies slugged one another to a tactical draw at a cost of 17,500 Union losses and 7,500 for the Confederates. Grant faced Lee at Cold Harbor, 3 June 1864. When they ordered their men into battle, 7,000 Union soldiers died in less than half an hour. One Southern observer called it "inexplicable and incredible butchery." Grant's men had suffered 55,000 casualties in the single month since he launched his 1864 campaign in the Wilderness.

That was a long time ago. Was the Civil War only a bloody aberration, never again to be repeated? No. Just as Americans had learned to slaughter one another in wholesale fashion, so would European generals refine those techniques and apply them in even more deadly fashion.

During the first month of the Great War (1914–18), 200,000 Frenchmen fell casualty. At the First Battle of Ypres, 20 October–22 November 1914, total casualties on all sides reached 250,000. During the Dardanelles Campaign from February 1915 to January 1916, at Gallipoli, the Allies lost 500,000 casualties and the Turks an equal number. In April and May 1915 at the Second Battle of Ypres, the British lost 59,000 men. From 21 February to 18 December 1916, during the Battle of Verdun, German losses stood at 300,000; the French lost 460,000 killed, wounded, missing, or taken prisoner. In those ten months, 420,000 French and German soldiers died.

In the Battle of the Somme, 1 July to 19 November 1916, some 1,250,000 German, French, and English soldiers fell casualty. The British suffered 60,000 killed or wounded on the first day. The gain in that four-month battle was an Allied advance of only eight miles.

The Third Battle of Ypres, or Passchendaele, fought between 31 July and 20 November 1917, saw British commander Field Marshal Sir Douglas Haig lose 31,850 men in Flanders Fields on the first day alone. When the battle ended, the British had lost 300,000 killed or wounded and the Germans 260,000—all for an Allied advance of only nine thousand yards, a little over five miles. In that same year, following the Battle of Caporetto, the Italians listed losses of 305,000 men.

Now Americans were in France, ready to fight in the trenches. On the orders of their commander, General John J. "Blackjack" Pershing, they were soon committed to battle. In September 1918 they found themselves flung into the Meuse-Argonne Campaign, the heaviest and longest-sustained period of combat in American military history. These "doughboys" fought for forty-seven days, penetrating four successive German defensive trench lines. When the campaign ended, some 1,200,000 U.S. soldiers had participated, suffering 120,000 casualties including 26,667 dead.

All those sanguinary losses were not to be, after all, sacrificed in a successful effort to fight the "war to end all wars." Instead the hatreds engendered by the Great War and the Versailles Treaty that followed it planted the seeds of World War II. Although it started far from our shores, in China in 1937 and in Poland on 1 September 1939, it came home to America on 7 December 1941. By 1942 we were fighting Germans once again, this time in North Africa.

Americans still labor under the illusion that their ground forces during that conflict were always led by incisive and competent battlefield leaders. Glowing wartime propaganda then portrayed those generals as capable of doing no wrong. Fawning authors later nearly canonized some of those men.

They were not all giants. Sometimes they were unimaginative, plodding, inferior officers who knew only—like their predecessors in the Civil War and the Great War—how to throw masses of cannon fodder against the enemy. They depended more upon massive columns of men and inexhaustible piles of supplies than upon thoroughgoing knowledge of tactics and strategy. They lacked training, talent, and insight.

Obviously there were exceptions. Yet consider the casualties suffered in Italy in early 1944 when Major General John P. Lucas, with 40,000 U.S. and British troops, began Operation Shingle on 22 January with an over-the-beach assault at Anzio. It was to be an end run around the Germans' Gustav Line, which had stopped the Allied advance up the peninsula well south of Rome.

Landing without opposition, Lucas dallied while Luftwaffe General Albert Kesselring built up his forces, sealing off the beachhead and nearly driving the Allies into the sea. For a time the Germans referred to the Allied toehold at Anzio as the largest self-sustaining prisoner-of-war camp in the world. Only on 23 May, following Lucas's replacement by General Lucian Truscott, did the Allies fight their way out of Kesselring's encirclement, at a cost of 72,306 GI casualties.

Later that same year, just inside Germany, V Corps commander Lieutenant General Leonard T. Gerow foolishly ordered his 28th Infantry Division, commanded by Major General Norman "Dutch" Cota, to make a diversionary attack into the Huertgen Forest. The 28th was to draw German troops onto itself so that VII Corps commander General J. Lawton "Lightning Joe" Collins could attack toward the Rhine River in an attempt to seize bridges there.

From 2 to 16 November, the 28th was the only active division on the western front, allowing German units to focus on it with a vengeance and slaughter its men. Company, battalion, and regimental commanders appealed to higher headquarters to let them withdraw from that killing ground. Divisional commander Cota, corps commander Gerow, First Army commander General Courtney Hodges, and even 12th Army Group commander General Omar Bradley all refused to allow the division's men to pull back to a position of safety—even after Collins canceled his attack toward the Rhine on 5 November because of inclement weather. As a result some 23,000 American soldiers died to gain about fifteen hundred yards of useless open high meadow pastures and dark pine forest.

And then there was Vo Nguyen Giap. At Vinh Yen in January 1951 his forces suffered 14,500 casualties. At Mao Khe in March, Giap's soldiers absorbed another 3,000 losses. In May, at the Day River, Giap watched as an additional 10,000 men fell on the field of battle. In the first six months of 1951, his ranks were reduced by 27,500 men as compared, for example, to British losses of 31,850 on 31 July 1917, the first day of Passchendaele.

Though a comparison of Giap's losses with those of other wars and other military leaders may not excuse his expressed indifference to the lives of his soldiers, it does set his actions into a broader context. At least he was wise enough to admit that he had been mistaken and to withdraw from further contact with the French until his forces were strong enough and sufficiently armed to pit themselves once again in battle. And he was always willing to attempt tactics capable of confounding his enemies. This was not a passive attitude. He actively strove to do the unexpected. That has not necessarily been true of other wartime leaders.

In the United States alone, statues have been erected and counties, towns, forts, libraries, schools, and public parks have been named after past generals, many of them no more than butchers in a bloody abbatoir. An arrogant Napoleon boasted that he could spend the lives of 25,000 soldiers each month, but, devotees have always obsequiously truckled to him and other such men, writing glowing biographies and teaching their exploits in reverent tones. At the same time, because Giap lost 27,500 men in his three 1951 attacks on the French, he has been dismissed as "only a logistician."

Perhaps it is impossible for an Asian to attain in the West the status of a successful and competent general. Certainly to attribute Giap's victories to anything other than mastery of supply lines and luck would require a consequent diminution of the reputations of those stolid generals who opposed him—French and American—and that has been difficult for either French or American analysts, writers, and historians to concede.

Those wishing more information may consult any standard work on military history, including James M. Morris, *America's Armed Forces: A History* (Englewood Cliffs, N.J.: Prentice-Hall, 1991). Other information is drawn from Cecil B. Currey, *Follow Me and Die* (Briarcliff Manor, N.Y.: Stein & Day, 1984).

CHAPTER ONE
"The Making of a Revolutionary"

1. Giap's name is regularly mispronounced in the West. In the dialect of northern Viet Nam, his name is pronounced "Voh Nwin Zahp."
2. The material that follows is drawn from an article by Vo Nguyen Giap, "Pac Bo Spring," in *Nhan Dan* ("People's Daily"), 24 December 1989, pp. 5–6.
3. "Bac Ho" is a customary way Vietnamese refer to Ho Chi Minh. While "Bac" can mean "uncle" and is usually translated in the West in this way, it also means an older adult whom one admires for such traits as wisdom and concern.
4. The Acts of the Apostles 2:17b.
5. Letter, Dr. Thai Van Kiem, Archivist, University of Arts Library, Paris, to Cecil B. Currey, 28 May 1994. Early in my research I made the acquaintance of Lieutenant General Vinh Loc, formerly an officer in the Army of the Republic of Viet Nam (ARVN) and now a resident of Texas. He spent countless hours providing me with instruction in the customs and traditions of imperial Viet Nam and in sorting out information about Giap. His carefully written responses came to me in letters dated 12 February 1991, 3 March 1991, 14 April 1991, 17 April 1991, 2 May 1991, 18 June 1991, 21 August 1991, 15 September 1991, and 1 November 1991. They are here collectively cited as Vinh Loc Manuscripts.

    It is surprising that a man so important to the history of the United States since 1950 has received so little attention here. If one consults the *Reader's Guide to Periodical Literature* for the years 1945–65, for example, one finds a massive omission of studies about him. Major U.S. press articles total only a paltry three or four entries, each of but two or three pages. Consulting *Dissertations in Progress* and other such works is no more rewarding. A computer search of the archives at University Microfilms International revealed 520 dissertations written on Vietnamese topics from 1940 to the present but, interestingly, only one focused to any extent on Giap: Thomas Latimer, "Hanoi's Leaders and Their South Vietnamese Policies,

1954–1968" (Ph.D. dissertation, Georgetown University, Washington, D.C., 1972).

If budding scholars have all but ignored the man, so also have the military services. Student papers at the U.S. Army Command and General Staff College, the Army War College, and the Air War College include fewer than half a dozen studies of this signal individual. The most error-ridden biographical accounts of General Giap were those prepared by the Central Intelligence Agency! Only a very few older biographical studies, containing a number of errors, are available, and they are cited in the notes for this book and in the bibliography.

Much confusion was clarified when Senior General Vo Nguyen Giap saw fit to reply to a questionnaire I submitted to him following a long conversation we had in December 1988. His responses, dictated to his daughter Hong Anh, filled twenty-six typed, single-spaced, legal-size sheets of paper and are a treasure of information, enhanced by a letter from Dang Bich Ha, his wife. Those materials are here cited as Giap Questionnaire.

What I received in this way was not, of course, all I wanted. Submitting questions and later receiving written answers is assuredly not the best possible inter view method. Certain problems inevitably arise when we read what someone else has written about himself. Did he write what happened? Or what he thought had happened? Or what he wanted others to think had happened? Or what he wanted others to think he thought had happened? It is difficult to resolve such questions.

Follow-up questions are a critical element in all interviews. Without them, one tends to get set-piece replies, often better than no answers at all, but still far from optimum. Opportunity to ask additional questions allows an interviewer to delve deeply into contradictions or to extract more detail about particular events—to follow trails to their conclusion, often a destination an interviewee might not wish to reach.

6. Giap Questionnaire. Of the children of Kien and Nghiem who grew to maturity, only three are still living. Diem and Lien are now dead. Diem married a Vietnamese soldier with the rank of master sergeant serving in the French colonial army. Giap's younger brother, Nho, also received his baccalaureate degree, married, had children of his own, and served under the Viet Minh government following World War II as political commissar for justice for the administrative committee of Quang Binh province. Reputedly he gave orders to behead many anti–Viet Minh revolutionaries at Dong Hoi. For a time he later acted as vice minister of national education. He now resides in Paris. Giap's little sister, Lai, married and became a mother. She worked within the bureaucracy of the northern government and is now retired. See Giap Questionnaire and Vinh Loc Manuscripts. For Giap's health as a child, see Phillip B. Davidson, *Vietnam at War: The History, 1946–1975* (Novato, Calif.: Presidio Press, 1988), p. 13; and CIA Documents.

7. Vinh Loc Manuscripts. See also Georges Boudarel, *Giap!* (Paris: Editions Atlas, 1977), p. 15.

8. Vinh Loc Manuscripts.

9. By tradition, the corps of mandarins was divided into two different elements, civilian and military, each with nine different ranks. Each step consisted of a probationary and a permanent grade. Within the civil corps, the lowest or ninth grade was given to clerks, public servants, and elected village chiefs, and was used as an honorary title for notable tradesmen. Vo Quang Nghiem, a member of that rank, thus held the title Cuu. Vinh Loc Manuscripts.

10. Giap Questionnaire; letter, 28 May 1994, Dr. Thai Van Kiem, Archivist, University of Arts Library, Paris, to Cecil B. Currey; Charles Gosselin, *L'empire d'Annam* (Paris: Perrin, 1904), pp. 265ff; Dom Moraes, "The Frozen Volcano," *Asia Magazine,* 17 September 1972, p. 3.

11. Giap Questionnaire; Vinh Loc Manuscripts; Neil and Susan Sheehan, "A Reporter at Large in Vietnam," *New Yorker,* 18 November 1991, pp. 54–119. In the Giap Questionnaire, Giap recalled his mother's reciting verses from *Tong Tran.* He may have meant *Phan Tran,* a story about a man named Phan Sinh and his beloved wife, Tran Kieu Lien. *Pham Cong Cuc Hoa* is the title of a long poem about the tribulations of a husband, Pham Cong, his wife, Cuc Hoa, and their two children, whose plight is heard by the Lord Buddha.

    Occasionally Vo Quang Nghiem took his wife, Nguyen Thi Kien, with him when he traveled to the provincial capital at Dong Hoi. On those occasions, their eldest daughter, Vo Thi Diem, took over operation of the family home and land. Married to her army man, she eventually came to be called Mu Quan, or "Mrs. Master Sergeant," by local people. See Vinh Loc Manuscripts and Giap Questionnaire. See also the transcript of a 1982 filmed interview with Giap, outtakes from which formed part of the Public Broadcasting System's *Vietnam: A Television History,* part of the holdings of the William Joiner Center for the Arts, University of Massachusetts, Amherst, Mass. In that transcript Can Vuong is mistakenly spelled Con Phuong—a nonsense rendition. See also *Point de Vue et Images du Monde,* April 1991; Vinh Loc Manuscripts.

12. Sheehan, "Reporter at Large." The manuals were composed of *Nhat Thien Tu* (poems of one thousand words), *Tam Thien Tu* (poems of three thousand words), and *Ngu Thien Tu* (poems of five thousand words). They included aphorisms such as "To give a trunk full of gold to your children is not as worthy as giving them a good book that surely will make them a laureate with a purple dress in the royal court." Another advised, "In raising a child, teach him to read books; help him to find dimonds and gold in them." Giap Questionnaire; Vinh Loc Manuscripts. See also Stanley Karnow, "Giap Remembers," *New York Times Magazine,* 24 June 1990, p. 36.

13. Giap Questionnaire; Vinh Loc Manuscripts; interview, Cecil B. Currey with Nguyen Dinh Tu, Vienna, Va., 26 April 1990.

14. Giap Questionnaire.

15. Ibid.; Karnow, "Giap Remembers," pp. 36, 39.

16. Giap Questionnaire.

17. DIA Document (unnumbered); Giap Questionnaire; Vinh Loc Manuscripts.

18. Vinh Loc Manuscripts.

19. Ibid.

20. Ibid.

21. Ibid.

22. Interview, Cecil B. Currey with Le Si Ngac, McLean, Va., 16 March 1991.

23. Ibid.

24. Giap Questionnaire; Vo Nguyen Giap, *Unforgettable Months and Years,* trans. and introduction by Mai Van Elliott, foreword by George McT. Kahin (Ithaca, NY: Cornell University Southeast Asia Program Data Paper #99, May 1975), p. v; Neil L. Jamieson, *Understanding Vietnam* (Berkeley: University of California Press, 1993), pp. 57–63.

25. Currey interview with Le Si Ngac.

26. Davidson, *Vietnam at War*, p. 4.

27. Introduction by Georges Boudarel to Vo Nguyen Giap, *Banner of People's War: The Party's Military Line* (New York: Praeger, 1970), pp. xiii–xiv.

28. Vo Nguyen Giap, *The Military Art of People's War: Selected Writings of Vo Nguyen Giap*, ed. and introduction by Russell Stetler (New York: Monthly Review Press, 1970), p. 43. See also DIA Document.

29. Giap Questionnaire. See also Karnow, "Giap Remembers," p. 39; Joseph Buttinger, *Vietnam: A Dragon Embattled*, 2 vols. (New York: Praeger, 1967), vol. 1, p. 227.

30. DIA Document; Giap Questionnaire. See also Victoria Brittain, "General Vo Nguyen Giap—Communist Napoleon Who Conquered South Vietnam," *Times* (London), 2 June 1975, p. 10.

31. See English-language typescript of Mario Dolci, "The Rise of General Vo Nguyen Giap, 'Red Napoleon' of Asia," *Milan Giorni*, 18 May 1972, pp. 18–20, in Giap File, Indochina Archive, Indochina Studies Project, Institute of East Asian Studies, University of California, Berkeley, hereafter cited as Giap File.

32. Giap Questionnaire; cf. Vinh Loc Manuscripts.

33. Giap, *Military Art of People's War*, p. 42.

34. Giap Questionnaire.

35. Ibid.; and see Boudarel, *Giap!*, p. 17.

36. Giap Questionnaire.

37. Ibid.

38. Giap Questionnaire. See also Giap, *Military Art of People's War*, p. 42.

39. Giap Questionnaire.

CHAPTER TWO
"We Did Not Know How to Fight"

1. Giap, *Military Art of People's War*, p. 42; see also William J. Duiker, *Historical Dictionary of Vietnam* (Metuchen, N.J.: Scarecrow Press, 1989), p. 163.

2. Giap Questionnaire; Vinh Loc Manuscripts. See also Max Clos, "The Strategist Behind the Vietcong," *New York Times Magazine*, 16 April 1964, p. 8.

3. Giap Questionnaire. Fascinated by aliases, Giap has used many of them. At around the time of the founding of the Indochinese Communist Party in 1930, he called himself Buong Hoai Nam. (See Do Quang Tien, *Vom Troi Bien Gioi* [Ha Noi: Nha Xuat Ban Viet Bac, 1972], p. 291n.) In the early 1940s he used the names Tram Van Lam and Bay. (See Nong Van Lac, "Diary," *Tac Pham Moi* 34 [February 1974], p. 4.) During his work with the Viet Minh during World War II, Giap operated under the code name Van. (See Ban Tai Doan, *Tac Pham Moi* 35 [March 1974], pp. 66–67.) As late as February 1975, in communications with General Van Tien Dung, he signed his name as Chien and Dung was Tuan. (See Boudarel, *Giap!*, p. 120). He used the pen name Hong Nam for an article he published in the October 1978 issue of *Tap Chi Cong San*, reprinted in a collection of his speeches in a work entitled *Ca Nuoc Mot Long Bao Ve Vung Chac To Quoc Viet Nam Xa Hoi Chu Nghia* ["United as One Man, All Our People Will Firmly Defend the Socialist Vietnamese Fatherland"] (Ha Noi, Su That, 1979), pp. 9–46. Such use of aliases has been commonplace among prominent Vietnamese.

4. Vinh Loc Manuscripts.
5. Ibid. For more on the riots and French reaction, see Ellen J. Hammer, *The Struggle for Indochina, 1940–1955* (Palo Alto, Calif.: Stanford University Press, 1955), pp. 81–85.
6. See, for example, "The Red Napoleon," *Time*, 17 June 1966, p. 30.
7. Giap Questionnaire; interview, Cecil B. Currey with Christine Pelzer White, Honolulu, 10 May 1991.
8. Ibid.
9. Giap Questionnaire.
10. Ibid.
11. Ibid.
12. Ibid.; Vinh Loc Manuscripts.
13. Giap Questionnaire. Many years later, Dang Bich Ha became Giap's second wife.
14. Ibid.
15. Boudarel, *Giap!*, pp. 171–72; Huynh Kim Khanh, "A Legend Demoted," *Far Eastern Economic Review*, 116, 15 (9 April 1982), pp. 32–33; Christine Pelzer White interview; Giap Questionnaire.
16. Ibid.
17. Giap's reaction to my question about Marty was related in a letter fax from Kim Dung Tran Ngoc, Paris, 7 June 1995.
18. Ibid.; Boudarel, *Giap!*, pp. 18–19; David G. Marr, *Vietnamese Tradition on Trial, 1920–1945* (Berkeley: University of California Press, 1981), pp. 45, 68, 138, 152–53; Vinh Loc Manuscripts; "Red Napoleon," p. 30.
19. Interview, Virginia Gift with Kim Dung Tran Ngoc, Rueil-Malmaison, Paris, February/March 1991.
20. Two knowledgeable Vietnamese émigrés, Lieutenant General Vinh Loc and Dr. Phan Quang Dan, M.D., concur with this conclusion based upon their own recollections of youthful days in French-occupied Viet Nam.
21. Vinh Loc Manuscripts.
22. Currey interview with Christine Pelzer White.
23. See Giap File.
24. Letter, Dr. Thai Van Kiem, Archivist, University of Arts Library, Paris, to Cecil B. Currey, 22 April 1994.
25. Lucien Bodard, *The Quicksand War: Prelude to Vietnam*, trans. Patrick O'Brian (Boston: Little, Brown, 1967), p. 69n. Published in France by Editions Gallimard in two volumes, *L'Enlisement* (1963) and *L'Humiliation* (1965).
26. Vinh Loc Manuscripts. See also Bao Dai, *Le Dragon d'Annam: Memoirs de S.[erene] M.[ajesty] Bao Dai* (Paris: Editions Plon, 1979), p. 58. Hereafter cited as Bao Dai, *Memoirs*.
27. Ibid., p. 59; Vinh Loc Manuscripts.
28. Vinh Loc Manuscripts.
29. Ibid.
30. Bao Dai, *Memoirs*, pp. 69, 71.
31. Letter, Vinh Loc to Cecil B. Currey, 17 March 1994.
32. Currey interview with Nguyen Dinh Tu.
33. Ibid.
34. Giap Questionnaire.
35. Ibid.

CHAPTER THREE
"They Set Their Hopes on the Same Cause"

1. See Bernard Fall, "Vo Nguyen Giap—Man and Myth," in Vo Nguyen Giap, *People's War, People's Army* (New York: Praeger, 1962), p. xxxii; Vinh Loc Manuscripts.
2. Bui Diem, *In the Jaws of History* (Boston: Houghton Mifflin, 1987), p. 12.
3. Karnow, "Giap Remembers," p. 57.
4. Currey interview with Nguyen Dinh Tu. Le Duc Tho, later adversary of Henry Kissinger at the Paris peace talks, was one of Giap's students. So were Nguyen Lam, for a time northern planning minister, and General Le Quang Dao, who served under Giap in the People's Liberation Army.
5. Vinh Loc Manuscripts.
6. Bui Diem, *Jaws of History*, p. 13.
7. Ibid.
8. Ibid.
9. Giap Questionnaire.
10. Ibid.
11. "Red Napoleon," p. 30; Davidson, *Vietnam at War*, p. 6; Vinh Loc Manuscripts; Giap Questionnaire.
12. Interview, Oriana Fallaci with Vo Nguyen Giap, published as "Americans Will Lose, Says General Giap," *Washington Post*, 6 April 1969, p. B-1.
13. Bui Diem, *Jaws of History*, pp. 13–14.
14. Giap Questionnaire.
15. Fall, "Vo Nguyen Giap—Man and Myth," in *Giap, People's War, People's Army*, p. xxxvii.
16. Davidson, *Vietnam at War*, p. 6.
17. Giap Questionnaire; James Fox, "Giap—the Victor at Dien Bien Phu," *Sunday Times Magazine* (London), November 1972, p. 56.
18. Giap Questionnaire.
19. Hoang Van Chi, *From Colonialism to Communism: A Case History of North Vietnam* (New York: Praeger, 1963), p. 69.
20. Giap Questionnaire.
21. Ibid.
22. Ibid.
23. Ibid.
24. Ibid.
25. Davidson, *Vietnam at War*, p. 6; Robert J. O'Neill, *General Giap: Politician and Strategist* (New York: Praeger, 1969), p. 11.
26. Marr, *Vietnamese Tradition on Trial, 1920–1945*, p. 272.
27. Giap Questionnaire. As Giap told the story to me in 1991, his round-trip bicycle ride from Ha Noi to Cam Pha was three hundred kilometers. Told to Miguel Rivero in 1980, the trip was two hundred kilometers. Its purpose was to cover a port strike and grievances by coal miners. Cam Pha is a town on Ha Long Bay, and served as Tonkin's principal coal export harbor. See interview by Miguel Rivero with Vo Nguyen Giap published in *Verde Olivo* (Havana), 10 February 1980, pp. 4–7, English-language transcript in FBIS, Giap File.

Much of the information on Giap in this text has been derived from material compiled by the National Technical Information Service (NTIS) of the U.S. Department of Commerce. NTIS monitors foreign broadcasts, news agency transmissions, newspapers, and periodicals, and regularly reproduces translations in full or in extract of those deemed to be of importance to subscribers to its publication under the title *Foreign Broadcast Information Service, Daily Report Supplement*. These documents in the Giap file at the Indochina Archive, University of California, Berkeley, are cited herein as FBIS, Giap File.

28. In addition to *Le Travail*, weekly newspapers begun by Giap and Truong Chinh included *Notre Voix* ("Our Voice"), which served as the Communist Party's official French-language newspaper; *Rassemblement* ("Assembly Call"); *En Avant!* ("Forward!"); *Thoi The* ("The Times"); *Ha Thanh Thoi Bao* ("Ha Noi City Chronicles"); *The Gioi* ("The World"); *Doi Nay* ("Contemporary Life"); *Tin Tuc* ("The News"); *Ngay Moi* ("New Day"); *Ban Dan* ("Friend of the People"); and *Giai Phong* ("Liberation").

   Giai Phong published only three issues before authorites seized its press machinery. Other papers for which Giap wrote articles included *Nhan Dan* ("The People"), still the party's official newspaper; *Lao Dong* ("Labor"); *Rally;* and *Times*. He served on the editorial board of *La Voix du Peuple* ("Voice of the People") and *Notre Victoire* ("Our Victory"). Giap Questionnaire; Vinh Loc Manuscripts.

29. Ibid. In some ways, Giap still thinks of himself as a journalist. When, in 1991, the Vietnamese journalists' association awarded Giap the medal given only to those who have spent more than twenty-five years in the profession, he was inordinately pleased with the recognition. He wrote to me that journalism was a first love; he had never truly gotten away from it.

30. Van Dinh [Vo Nguyen Giap] and Qua Ninh [Truong Chinh], *The Peasant Problem, 1937–1938*, trans. Christine Pelzer White (Ithaca, N.Y.: Cornell University Southeast Asia Program, Data Paper #94, 1974). Also see Davidson, *Vietnam at War*, p. 6.

31. O'Neill, *General Giap*, pp. 12–15.

32. Giap Questionnaire.

33. Fall, "Vo Nguyen Giap—Man and Myth," in Giap, *People's War, People's Army*, p. xxxii.

34. Ibid.; Davidson, *Vietnam at War*, p. 7; Vinh Loc Manuscripts.

35. Giap, *Military Art of People's War*, pp. 39–40. It was Bernard Fall who suggested that Giap and Quang Thai (whom he names as Minh Thai) returned to central Annam. See Fall, "Vo Nguyen Giap—Man and Myth," in Giap, *People's War, People's Army*, p. xxxii.

36. Vinh Loc Manuscripts.

37. Giap Questionnaire.

38. Ibid.

39. Ibid.

40. Ibid.; Giap, *Military Art of People's War*, p. 40; also Fall, "Vo Nguyen Giap—Man and Myth," in Giap, *People's War, People's Army*, pp. xxxii–xxxiii. It is uncertain when Giap left Ha Noi. In his answers to me in the Giap Questionnaire, he states that "in mid-June, Giap had to be separated from his wife, his baby and go to China with Pham Van Dong." Elsewhere, however, he wrote that he left on Friday, 3 May 1940. That is the date used in this text.

41. Giap Questionnaire; Giap, *Military Art of People's War*, p. 40; Boudarel, *Giap!*, p. 21.

42. Giap Questionnaire; Boudarel, *Giap!*, pp. 171–72; Fall, "Vo Nguyen Giap—Man and Myth," in Giap, *People's War, People's Army*, pp. xxxii–xxxiii. Following the fall of Saigon in 1975, the government changed the names of many of its streets, and Rue Pasteur became Nguyen Thi Minh Khai Street.

43. Other authors who have mentioned the arrest of Giap's wife have implied that she kept Hong Anh with her and that the baby died of neglect in prison. Hong Anh—a nuclear physicist—lives today in Ha Noi. Giap Questionnaire.

44. Giap Questionnaire; Vinh Loc Manuscripts; Davidson, *Vietnam at War*, p. 7; Fall, "Vo Nguyen Giap—Man and Myth," in Giap, *People's War, People's Army*, pp. xxxii–xxxiii.

45. Hong Anh responses in Giap Questionnaire.

46. Vinh Loc Manuscripts.

47. Letter, Will Brownell to Cecil B. Currey, 13 February 1991.

48. Brownell's interview with Salan was held on 13 July 1982. Letter, Will Brownell to Cecil B. Currey, 1 July 1991.

49. Hong Anh responses in Giap Questionnaire.

CHAPTER FOUR
"Neither Soft nor Warm"

1. Bui Diem, *Jaws of History*, p. 17; Marr, *Vietnamese Tradition on Trial*, p. 327.

2. Giap Questionnaire; Giap, *Military Art of People's War*, p. 40.

3. Giap Questionnaire; Giap, *Military Art of People's War*, pp. 40–41.

4. Giap Questionnaire.

5. Giap, *Military Art of People's War*, p. 41; Giap Questionnaire.

6. Vu Anh, "From Kunming to Pac Bo," in *Days with Ho Chi Minh* (Ha Noi: Foreign Languages Publishing House, 1962), p. 167.

7. Giap, *Military Art of People's War*, p. 46.

8. Ibid., p. 48; Giap Questionnaire.

9. Ibid.

10. Giap, *Military Art of People's War*, p. 47.

11. Giap Questionnaire.

12. Edgar O'Ballance, *The Indochina War, 1945–1954: A Study in Guerrilla Warfare* (London: Faber & Faber, 1964), p. 40.

13. See Mao Tse-tung, *The Strategic Problems of the Anti-Japanese War*, 2d ed. (Beijing: Foreign Languages Press, 1960); *Struggle of the Chin-Kan-Shan Mountains* (Beijing: Foreign Languages Press, 1954); *Guerrilla Warfare* (New York: Praeger, 1961). See O'Ballance, *Indochina War*, p. 41; John C. Levanger, "General Vo Nguyen Giap: The Vietnamese Napoleon?" Student Thesis #AD-761-581, U.S. Army War College, Carlisle Barracks, Pa., 1973, pp. 14–16.

14. See Mario Dolci, "The Rise of General Vo Nguyen Giap, 'Red Napoleon' of Asia" *Milan Giorni*, 18 May 1972, pp. 18–20. See also Rivero interview with Giap, pp. 4–7.

15. Dolci, "The Rise of General Giap."

16. Giap, *Military Art of People's War*, p. 50.

17. Stetler, "Introduction," in Giap, *Military Art of People's War*, pp. 16–17, 51.

18. Giap, *Military Art of People's War*, p. 53.

19. Ibid., p. 61.

20. Giap Questionnaire; Vinh Loc Manuscripts.

21. Greg Lockhart, *Nation in Arms: The Origins of the People's Army of Vietnam* (Wellington, Australia: Allen & Unwin, 1989), p. 94.
22. Ibid.; Giap, *Military Art of People's War*, pp. 55–56; Giap, "Stemming from the People," in *A Heroic People: Memoirs from the Revolution* (Ha Noi: Foreign Languages Publishing House, 1965), p. 116.
23. Giap Questionnaire; Vinh Loc Manuscripts; Giap, *Military Art of People's War*, p. 52; Philippe Devillers, *L'histoire du Viet Nam de 1940 à 1952* (Paris: Editions du Seuil, 1952), pp. 102, 105.
24. Giap Questionnaire.
25. Giap, *Military Art of People's War*, p. 58.
26. Giap Questionnaire; Giap, *Military Art of People's War*, p. 57; Vo Nguyen Giap, "Stemming from the People," pp. 100–1.
27. Giap, *Military Art of People's War*, p. 57.
28. Giap, *Military Art of People's War*, p. 55.
29. Douglas Pike, "General Vo Nguyen Giap—Man on the Spot," typescript, May 1968, Giap File. p. 14.
30. Giap, *Military Art of People's War*, pp. 55–56.
31. Ibid.
32. Giap, "Stemming from the People," pp. 94–95; Giap, *Military Art of People's War*, pp. 55–56.
33. Giap, *Military Art of People's War*, p. 56.
34. Ibid., p. 59; Giap, "Stemming from the People," p. 94; Vo Nguyen Giap, *Ten Years of Fighting and Building of the Vietnamese People's Army* (Ha Noi: Foreign Languages Publishing House, 1955), pp. 5–15.
35. Giap, *Military Art of People's War*, pp. 55–56; Giap, "Pac Bo Spring."
36. Levanger, student thesis, p. 16.
37. Jean Lacouture, *Ho Chi Minh* (New York: Random House, 1968), p. 55 and *passim;* Giap, *Military Art of People's War*, p. 57.
38. Giap Questionnaire; Georges Boudarel, "Essai sur la pensée militaire vietnamienne," *L'Homme et la Société* 7 (January/February/March 1968), p. 188.
39. Giap Questionnaire.
40. Ibid.

CHAPTER FIVE
"Each Man Was a Soldier"

1. Giap Questionnaire; Giap, *Military Art of People's War*, p. 58.
2. Giap, *Military Art of People's War*, p. 53.
3. Giap, *Stemming from the People*, pp. 99–100.
4. Ibid., p. 112; Giap Questionnaire.
5. Giap, "Stemming from the People," p. 113.
6. Giap, *Military Art of People's War*, pp. 57–58.
7. Ibid., p. 58; Giap Questionnaire; Giap, "Stemming from the People," pp. 108–9.
8. Dolci, "Rise of Giap," pp. 18–20.
9. Clos, "Strategist Behind Vietcong," p. 9.
10. Robert Pisor, *The End of the Line: The Siege of Khe Sanh* (New York: Norton, 1982), p. 150.

11. Clos, "Strategist Behind Vietcong," p. 10.
12. Minh Tranh, review of Vo Nguyen Giap, *The Party's Great Experiences in Leadership over Armed Struggle and the Building of Revolutionary Armed Forces* (Ha Noi: Su That Publishing House, 1961), in *Nhan Dan* (Ha Noi), 21 September 1961, English typescript translation in Giap File.
13. Giap Questionnaire; Giap, *Military Art of People's War*, p. 63.
14. Giap, "Stemming from the People," p. 121.
15. Ibid., pp. 107–8.
16. Dolci, "Rise of Giap," pp. 18–20.
17. Giap, *Military Art of People's War*, p. 58.
18. Ibid., pp. 60–61.
19. Giap, *Military Art of People's War*, p. 62; Giap, "Stemming from the People," pp. 117–18.
20. Giap, *Military Art of People's War*, p. 62; Giap, "Stemming from the People," pp. 117–18.
21. In many Chinese dialects the pronunciation of the character for "death" *(si)* and the word for "yes" *(shi)* are confused in everyday conversation to the point where speakers have to draw the character in the air or on their palms in order to clarify to a listener which word is being used. In answer to the question "Is Ho Chi Minh all right?" the answer "yes" *(shi-le, she-le, "le"* merely being the final particle) could easily have been heard as "dead" *(si-le, si-le)*. This would have been especially likely for a Vietnamese foreigner speaking Chinese. For the story of this episode, see Giap, *Military Art of People's War*, pp. 62–63; Giap, "Stemming from the People," pp. 118–19.
22. Giap Questionnaire; Giap, "Stemming from the People," pp. 123–24.
23. Giap, "Stemming from the People," pp. 110–11.
24. Giap Questionnaire.
25. Giap, *Military Art of People's War*, p. 64.
26. Giap, "Stemming from the People," pp. 126–27.
27. Ibid., p. 116.
28. Ibid., p. 125.
29. Giap, *Military Art of People's War*, p. 64.
30. Giap, "Stemming from the People," pp. 131–32.
31. Ibid., pp. 114–15.
32. Ibid., p. 110; Giap Questionnaire.
33. Giap Questionnaire.
34. Ibid.
35. Ibid.
36. Giap, "Stemming from the People," pp. 115, 135.
37. Ibid., p. 115; Giap, *Military Art of People's War*, pp. 64–65.
38. Giap, *Military Art of People's War*, p. 65.

CHAPTER SIX
"Boundless Was Our Joy"

1. See Pisor, *End of the Line*, p. 148.
2. Giap, *Military Art of People's War*, p. 65.
3. Ibid., p. 66; Giap Questionnaire.

4. Interview, Huu Mai with Vo Nguyen Giap, in *Nhan Dan* (Ha Noi), 14 December 1964, pp. 2–3. English-language transcript in Giap File.
5. Giap, *Military Art of People's War*, p. 65.
6. Giap, "Stemming from the People," p. 140; Giap Questionnaire.
7. Huu Mai interview with Giap.
8. Ibid.
9. Giap Questionnaire.
10. Giap, "Pac Bo Spring." It has been impossible to work out the chronology of the events leading up to the birth of the Viet Minh Armed Propaganda and Liberation Brigade in late 1944. Archimedes L. A. Patti, *Why Vietnam? Prelude to America's Albatross* (Berkeley: University of California Press, 1980), p. 56, has Ho returning to Viet Nam in November for his criticisms of Giap's plans for an uprising. David Halberstam in *Ho* (New York: Random House, 1971), pp. 61–68, gives little indication of when he returned to Viet Nam. Nguyen Khac Huyen, *Vision Accomplished: The Enigma of Ho Chi Minh* (New York: Macmillan, 1971), p. 68, has Ho returning to Vietnam in October. Neither in the Giap Questionnaire nor in his other writings does Giap give a clear indication of the date Ho returned, although from reading Giap's writings, one could get the impression that it was only a few days after Ho's return that the brigade was formed.
11. Giap, "Pac Bo Spring." The quote from Ho Chi Minh is as given by Giap.
12. Huu Mai interview with Giap.
13. Ibid.
14. Giap, "Pac Bo Spring"; Giap, *Military Art of People's War*, p. 67. The quote from Ho Chi Minh is as given by Giap.
15. Giap, *Military Art of People's War*, p. 67. The quote from Ho Chi Minh is as given by Giap.
16. Ibid.
17. Ibid.
18. Giap, "Pac Bo Spring."
19. Ibid.
20. Ibid.; Huu Mai interview with Giap. The quote from Ho Chi Minh is as given by Giap.
21. Giap, *Military Art of People's War*, p. 67; Giap Questionnaire.
22. Giap, *Military Art of People's War*, p. 68; Huu Mai interview with Giap.
23. Giap Questionnaire; Boudarel, *Giap!*, pp. 7, 11.
24. Huu Mai interview with Giap.
25. Ibid.
26. Ibid.
27. Ibid.
28. Giap Questionnaire.
29. Huu Mai interview with Giap.
30. Ibid.
31. Ibid.
32. Ibid.
33. Giap, "Stemming from the People," p. 146.
34. Marr, *Vietnamese Tradition*, pp. 246–47, testifies that Giap included three women among the members of his first armed body. "[T]he ability of these women to both handle firearms and explain current political developments made a deep impression

on villagers." By the end of 1944, Vo Nguyen Giap had some 10,000 at his command; by June 1946, 31,000; by November 1946, 60,000. When the Viet Minh
war with the French began in 1947, Giap's army totaled 100,000. By 1952 it contained 300,000 men and by 1968 consisted of 440,000 regulars backed by
175,000 militia, and these figures do not include village self-defense forces. See
Pike, "Man on the Spot," p. 6.

35. Douglas Pike, *PAVN: People's Army of Vietnam* (Norato, Calif.: Presidio Press 1986),
p. 27.

36. Lucien Bodard, *Quicksand War*, pp. 244–47 *passim*.

37. Ibid. The role of the self-defense forces is still in question. What I have said here de-
picts their role in the early days of Viet Minh organizational activity and is not ap-
plicable to their situation during the Second Indochina War of 1965–73. By that time,
self-defense forces were generally made up of women, cripples, and old men whose
age, gender, and condition made them unsuited for combat. Did they lay mines?
Doubtful, for that is a job requiring military know-how. Did they furnish recruits to
"higher" military organizations? Again, doubtful. They were, however, a valuable
source of intelligence information, and interrogation of high-ranking POWs revealed
that by the American phase of the conflict, becoming a member of the self-defense
forces was more a political than a military statement. Membership was a political commitment. See Davidson, *Secrets of the Vietnam War* (Novato, Calif.: Presidio Press,
1990), p. 33.

38. Davidson, *Vietnam at War*, pp. 54–58.

39. Karnow, "Giap Remembers," p. 57.

40. Bodard, *Quicksand War*, pp. 244–47.

41. Boudarel, *Giap!*, p. 28.

42. Patti, *Why Vietnam?*, pp. 56–57; Boudarel, *Giap!*, p. 41; Buttinger, *Dragon Embattled*, vol. 1, p. 594; letter, Allison Kent Thomas to Cecil B. Currey, 27 November
1993.

43. Patti, *Why Vietnam?*, p. 57. Those wartime files also contained a request from Ho
asking for a visa in the name of an "Indochina-born Chinese Ho Ting-ching [Ho Chi
Minh]" to come to the United States to work for the Office of War Information. OWI
people in New York were considering using him in their radio services as they
beamed war news in the Vietnamese language to Asia.

44. Charles Fenn, *Ho Chi Minh: A Biographical Introduction* (New York: Scribner's, 1973),
pp. 76–79. See also letter, Allison Kent Thomas to Cecil B. Currey, 2 November
1991.

45. Patti, *Why Vietnam?*, pp. 36–42, 56–57, 74–75; Jean Julien Fonde, "Giap et la
maquis de Cho Ra (Mars 1945–Mars 1946)," *Revue Histoire des Armées* 30, 2 (1976),
pp. 112–27.

46. Stetler, "Introduction," in Giap, *Military Art of People's War*, pp. 21–22.

47. Patti, *Why Vietnam?*, p. 73.

48. Giap Questionnaire; Boudarel, *Giap!*, p. 40. "It is rare a man from that team
ever talked about his own past. I never heard Vo Nguyen Giap mention the killing of his wife. . . . I knew this [only] through my old acquaintance, Ta Quang
Buu [Giap's deputy and signatory for the Viet Minh at the Geneva conference
in 1954]. He told me Giap was hard stricken by the news and it dictated the
attitude he later adopted vis-à-vis the French [although he] tried to keep

his attitude toward them hidden to prove his magnanimity." Vinh Loc Manuscripts.

49. Giap Questionnaire; Giap, "Stemming from the People," pp. 145–48; Pike, *PAVN*, p. 32.
50. Patti, *Why Vietnam?*, p. 128.
51. Ibid., pp. 126, 128.
52. Letter, Allison Kent Thomas to Cecil B. Currey, 2 April 1991; "The United States and Vietnam: 1944–1947," staff study based on the Pentagon Papers, prepared for the use of the Committee on Foreign Relations, United States Senate, Study #2, 3 April 1972 (Washington, D.C.: Government Printing Office, 1972), p. 2.
53. Letters and telephone conversations between Allison Kent Thomas and Cecil B. Currey during 1991.

CHAPTER SEVEN
"Welcome to Our American Friends"

1. Allison Kent Thomas Diary, 16 July 1945 entry, Allison Kent Thomas Collection. Hereafter cited as Thomas Diary.
2. Ibid.
3. Ibid.
4. "The OSS in Indochina, 1945–1946," typescript, p. 257–58, in Giap File; also letter, Allison Kent Thomas to Cecil B. Currey, 2 November 1991.
5. "The OSS in Indochina," pp. 244–45, 266, 270–71.
6. Ibid., p. 246; Ngoc An, "Bo Doi Viet-My" (Vietnamese-American Armed Unit), in *Tap Chi Lich Su Quan Su* ("Magazine of Military History"), November 1986, p. 4, trans. Dr. Van T. Gwyn. Copy supplied the author by Allison Kent Thomas. Also see letter, Allison Kent Thomas to Cecil B. Currey, 27 February 1995.
7. Giap, *Military Art of People's War*, p. 69.
8. Letter, Allison Kent Thomas to Cecil B. Currey, 27 November 1993.
9. Ibid.
10. "The OSS in Indochina," pp. 249, 246; also letter, Allison Kent Thomas to Cecil B. Currey, 2 November 1991.
11. Thomas Diary, 26–30 July 1945 entries.
12. "The OSS in Indochina," pp. 251, 258; "Yank Helped Train Gen. Giap," *Pacific Stars and Stripes*, Saturday, 1 May 1971, p. 5; letter, Allison Kent Thomas to Cecil B. Currey, 2 April 1991.
13. Letter, Allison Kent Thomas to Cecil B. Currey, 2 April 1991.
14. Thomas Diary, 1 August 1945.
15. Ibid., 8 August 1945.
16. "The OSS in Indochina," p. 259.
17. Thomas Diary, 15 August 1945.
18. Ibid.; "The OSS in Indochina," p. 261.
19. Thomas Diary, 15 August 1945.
20. Pike, *PAVN*, p. 32; Khanh, "Legend Demoted," pp. 32–33. "He didn't wear a uniform. He wore civilian clothes." Interview, Cecil B. Currey with Lucien Conein, McLean, Va., 26 April 1990.
21. Allison Kent Thomas, "Welcome to Our American Friends," in Harry Maurer,

Strange Ground: Americans in Vietnam, 1945–1975 (New York: Henry Holt, 1989), pp. 28–37.

22. Pike, *PAVN*, p. 32.
23. "The OSS in Indochina," p. 261.
24. Ibid.
25. Ibid., pp. 263, 271.
26. Giap Questionnaire; Patti, *Why Vietnam?*, pp. 134–35, 143.
27. Giap Questionnaire.
28. Interview, Lydia Fish with Lucien Conein, McLean, Va., 30 July 1989.
29. Currey interview with Conein, 26 April 1990.
30. Ibid.
31. Ibid.
32. Fish interview with Conein.
33. Ibid.
34. "The OSS in Indochina," p. 263.
35. Photostat, letter, Van [Vo Nguyen Giap] to Allison Kent Thomas, undated [August 1945], Allison Kent Thomas Collection.
36. Thomas Diary, 30 August and 6 September 1945.
37. "The OSS in Indochina," p. 263.
38. Currey interview with Conein, 26 April, 1990.
39. Thomas Diary, 9 and 10 September 1945.
40. Ibid., 10–16 September 1945.
41. Letter, Allison Kent Thomas to Cecil B. Currey, 2 April 1991; "The OSS in Indochina," pp. 263–64.
42. Photostat, letter, Van [Vo Nguyen Giap] to Allison Kent Thomas, 20 November 1946, Allison Kent Thomas Collection; Giap Questionnaire.
43. Vinh Loc Manuscripts; Nguyen Dinh Tu interview.
44. Giap, *Unforgettable Months and Years*, p. 20.
45. Giap, *Military Art of People's War*, p. 75; Giap, *Unforgettable Months and Years*, p. 24.
46. Giap, *Unforgettable Months and Years*, p. 18.
47. Currey interview with Conein.
48. Giap, *Unforgettable Months and Years*, p. 19.
49. Pike, *PAVN*, p. 166.
50. Ibid., pp. 165, 167; Giap, *Unforgettable Months and Years*, p. 16.
51. Patti, *Why Vietnam?*, p. 132.
52. "Red Napoleon," p. 30.
53. Giap, *Unforgettable Months and Years*, pp. 24–25; report by Arthur Hale, USIA, in "The United States and Vietnam: 1944–1947," Staff Study #2, prepared for the Committee on Foreign Relations, United States Senate, 3 April 1972 (Washington, D.C.: Government Printing Office, 1972), p. 24.
54. Truong Chinh, *The August Revolution* (Ha Noi: Foreign Language Publishing House, 1947); Boudarel, "Essai sur la pensée militaire vietnamienne," pp. 188–89; Devillers, *L'histoire du Vietnam*, p. 151; Hammer, *Struggle for Indochina*, pp. 102–5.
55. Giap, *Unforgettable Months and Years*, p. 22; Patti, *Why Vietnam?*, pp. 220–21.
56. Vinh Loc Manuscripts.

CHAPTER EIGHT
"We Shall Resort to Arms"

1. Giap, *Unforgettable Months and Years*, p. 23.
2. Ibid., p. 58; Stetler, "Introduction," in Giap, *Military Art of People's War*, p. 24.
3. Gabriel Kolko, *The Politics of War: The World and United States Foreign Policy, 1943–1945* (New York: Random House, 1968), p. 610.
4. Fish interview with Conein; Giap, *Unforgettable Months and Years*, p. 30.
5. Giap, *Unforgettable Months and Years*, p. 26.
6. Currey interview with Nguyen Dinh Tu.
7. Ibid.
8. Giap, *Unforgettable Months and Years*, p. 24; Patti, *Why Vietnam?*, p. 250.
9. Patti's version of the Vietnamese Declaration of Independence differs from those usually printed, but inasmuch as he was present on that day, I have relied on his transcript. Patti, *Why Vietnam?*, p. 250.
10. Ibid., p. 251.
11. Giap, *Unforgettable Months and Years*, p. 27.
12. Peter M. Dunn, *The First Vietnam War* (New York: St. Martin's, 1985), *passim*.
13. Ibid., p. 32.
14. Ibid., pp. 53–54.
15. Ibid., p. 51; Patti, *Why Vietnam?*, pp. 337–38; Vo Nguyen Giap, *Unforgettable Days*, (Ha Noi: Foreign Languages Publishing House, 1975), p. 76. Readers of Vietnamese might also want to consult Tran Huy Lieu, *Cach Mang Thang Tam* ["The August Revolution"] (Ha Noi: Su Hoc Publishers, 1960), *passim*; and Nguyen Kien Giang, *Viet Nam Nam Dau Tien Sau Cach Mang Thang Tam* ["Viet Nam: The First Year Following the August Revolution"] (Ha Noi: Su That Publishers, 1961), *passim*.
16. Currey interview with Nguyen Dinh Tu.
17. Giap, *Unforgettable Months and Years*, pp. 32, 47, 50.
18. Ibid., p. 62.
19. George Rosie, *The British in Vietnam: How the Twenty-five-Year War Began* (London: Panther, 1970), p. 51 and *passim*.
20. Giap, *Unforgettable Months and Years*, pp. 39–40; Giap, *Military Art of People's War*, pp. 82–84; Hammer, *Struggle for Indochina*, chap. 5 and *passim*. Also see Mike Gravel, ed., The Pentagon Papers: The Defense Department History of United States Decisionmaking on Vietnam, 5 vols. (Boston: Beacon Press, 1971), vol. 1, p. 45.
21. Giap, *Unforgettable Months and Years*, p. 43.
22. Ibid., p. 29.
23. Patti, *Why Vietnam?*, p. 333.
24. Giap, *Unforgettable Months and Years*, pp. 30, 42.
25. Nguyen Duy Thanh, *My Four Years with the Viet Minh* (n.p., Democratic Research Service, n.d.), p. 1.
26. Ibid., pp. 11–12.
27. Giap, *Unforgettable Months and Years*, p. 62.
28. Ibid., pp. 62–63.
29. Ibid., p. 66.
30. O'Neill, *General Giap*, p. 39; Dcvillers, *L'histoire du Vietnam*, p. 197; Giap, *Unforgettable Months and Years*, p. 64; Pike, "Man on the Spot," p. 8.

31. Nguyen Duy Thanh, *Four Years*, pp. 2–3.
32. Giap, *Unforgettable Months and Years*, p. 64.
33. Ibid., pp. 63–64; Thanh, *Four Years*, p. 4.
34. Giap, *Unforgettable Months and Years*, p. 68.
35. Ibid., pp. 68–69.
36. Nguyen Duy Thanh, *Four Years*, p. 7.
37. Bao Dai, *Memoirs*, vol. 3, p. 130.
38. Giap, *Unforgettable Months and Years*, pp. 70, 40–49.
39. Bao Dai, *Memoirs*, vol. 3, p. 148.
40. Giap, *Unforgettable Months and Years*, p. 47.
41. Ibid., p. 70.
42. Ibid., pp. 70–71.
43. Ibid., p. 71.
44. Ibid.
45. Ibid., p. 72.
46. Ibid.
47. Ibid. Thanh became a Politburo member in 1957 and was promoted to general of the army in 1959. He advocated big-unit warfare against U.S. military units in the south, and was roundly criticized by Giap for the casualties incurred thereby. General Thanh was also a member of the National Defense Council until his death in 1967.
48. Giap, *Unforgettable Months and Years*, p. 74.
49. Ibid., p. 75.
50. Ibid., pp. 76–77.

CHAPTER NINE
"We Must Be Realistic"

1. Bao Dai, *Memoirs*, p. 148.
2. Giap, *Unforgettable Months and Years*, p. 54.
3. Ibid., p. 55.
4. Davidson, *Vietnam at War*, p. 31.
5. Giap, *Unforgettable Months and Years*, p. 55.
6. Ibid., p. 55n.
7. Ibid., pp. 55–56.
8. Ibid., p. 56.
9. As quoted in Devillers, *L'histoire du Vietnam*, p. 221.
10. Giap, *Unforgettable Months and Years*, p. 90; *Pentagon Papers*, vol. 1, p. 49.
11. Giap, *Unforgettable Months and Years*, pp. 90–91.
12. Devillers, *L'histoire du Vietnam*, p. 214.
13. Giap, *Unforgettable Months and Years*, p. 95.
14. Ibid., pp. 93, 96; Hammer, *Struggle for Indochina*, p. 144; Devillers, *L'histoire du Vietnam*, p. 220.
15. Nguyen Duy Thanh, *Four Years*, p. 7.
16. Ibid., p. 8.
17. Ibid., p. 9.
18. Ibid., pp. 9–10.

19. Bui Diem, *In the Jaws of History*, pp. 40, 46.

20. Tran Van Don, *Our Endless War: Inside Vietnam* (San Rafael, Calif.: Presidio Press, 1978), p. 27.

21. Giap, *Unforgettable Months and Years*, p. 98.

22. Some sources say he was not given this position or rank until 1947.

23. Giap, *Unforgettable Months and Years*, p. 100.

24. Ibid., p. 99.

25. Ibid., p. 101.

26. Ibid., p. 102.

27. Ibid., p. 101.

28. Devillers, *L'histoire du Vietnam*, pp. 234–35.

29. Giap, *Unforgettable Months and Years*, p. 101.

30. Translator's remark in "Introduction," Ibid., p. 12.

31. The author quoted this speech from the 8 March 1946 issue of the newspaper *Quyet Chien;* see Devillers, *L'histoire du Vietnam*, pp. 230–31.

32. Ibid.

33. Ibid., pp. 236–37; Hammer, *Struggle for Indochina*, p. 159.

34. Moraes, "Frozen Volcano," p. 6.

35. Vinh Loc Manuscripts.

36. Devillers, *L'histoire du Vietnam*, pp. 256–57, 263–64; Hammer, *Struggle for Indochina*, pp. 165–74.

37. Giap, *Unforgettable Months and Years*, pp. 56–57; Giap, *Military Art of People's War*, p. 85.

38. Vinh Loc Manuscripts; Joseph Buttinger, *Vietnam: A Political History* (New York: Praeger, 1968), p. 256.

39. DIA Document.

40. Ibid.

41. Fall, "Introduction," in Giap, *People's War, People's Army*, p. xxxvi.

42. Vinh Loc Manuscripts; Devillers, *L'histoire du Vietnam*, p. 197; Nguyen Duy Thanh, *Four Years*, p. 4; Robert F. Turner, *Vietnamese Communism: Its Origins and Development* (Stanford, Calif.: Hoover Institution Press, 1975), pp. 58–59.

43. Vo Nguyen Giap, *Those Unforgettable Months and Years*, ed. Huu Mai (Ha Noi: Van Nghe Quan Doi, December 1974), p. 57. This writing by Giap has been translated by Mai Van Elliott and excerpted by Huu Mai. Van Nghe Quan Doi had earlier published part 1 of Huu Mai's excerpts, and in 1974 published part 2, consisting of chapters 14–25. An English translation of Huu Mai's excerpts was produced by FBIS and may be consulted in Giap Files.

44. Giap, *Those Unforgettable Months and Years*, p. 58.

45. Fall, "Introduction," in Giap, *People's War, People's Army*, pp. xxxvi–xxxvii.

46. Giap, *Those Unforgettable Months and Years*, p. 58.

47. Giap Questionnaire.

48. Ibid.

49. Ibid. Giap is now grandfather to six children. At this writing in 1995, Hong Anh's son is twenty-five years old. Hoa Binh has a sixteen-year-old daughter. Hanh Phuc's daughter is fourteen, while Dien Bien has a twelve-year-old boy and Hoai Nan has two children, an eleven-year-old boy and another child of five.
    Of Dang Bich Ha's family, only two sisters survive, both of whom are

professors of literature at teacher training colleges: Dang Thanh Le (American Literature and Image of Women in Vietnamese Literature) and Dang Anh Dao. Madame Ha works as a researcher at the Southeast Asia Studies Institute, Social Science Committee, at 27 Tran Soan Xuan, Ha Noi. Her concentration is on Laos. Her father, Professor Mai, died about 1982–83. Christine Pelzer White interview.

CHAPTER TEN
"Fight to the Last Drop of Blood"

1. Giap, *Those Unforgettable Months and Years*, p. 60.
2. Ibid., p. 61.
3. Ibid., pp. 63–64.
4. Ibid., p. 66. For a list of first-year achievements as seen through Viet Minh eyes, consult Vo Nguyen Giap, *One Year of Revolutionary Achievement: Report to the Viet Nam People at Ha Noi* (Ha Noi: Vietnam News Agency, 1946), 23 pp., *passim.*
5. Giap, *Those Unforgettable Months and Years*, pp. 71–73.
6. Ibid., p. 62.
7. O'Neill, *General Giap*, p. 46.
8. Ibid.; Giap, *Military Art of People's War*, p. 86.
9. Vinh Loc Manuscripts.
10. "The United States and Viet Nam, 1944–1947," Senate Staff Study, pp. 40–43; also letter, Allison Kent Thomas to Cecil B. Currey, 2 November 1991.
11. Jean Julien Fonde, "Il y a 24 ans à Hanoi," *Revue Militaire Générale* 6 (June 1972), pp. 753–58.
12. Giap, *Military Art of People's War*, p. 86; O'Neill, *General Giap*, p. 48.
13. Vo Nguyen Giap, "A Letter to the Commemorative Congress," 13 January 1972, released by Ha Noi Domestic News Service, in Vietnamese, translated by FBIS, Giap File.
14. Ibid.
15. Interview, unnamed correspondent for the Deutsche Demokratische Republik's *Armee Rundschau* ("Army Review") with Vo Nguyen Giap, Ha Noi, November 1970, pp. 24–29, 64, English typescript translation in Giap File.
16. *New York Times* news service press release, 18 March 1968, copy in Giap File.
17. O'Neill, *General Giap*, p. 53; Davidson, *Vietnam at War*, pp. 48–49.
18. Joseph Buttinger, *Dragon Embattled*, vol. 2, p. 1023.
19. J. R. Tournoux, *Secrets d'état: Dien Bien Phu les Paras Lalger* (Paris: Editions Plon, 1960), p. 11; Bernard Fall, *Street Without Joy* (Harrisburg, Pa.: Stackpole, 1967), p. 28.
20. O'Neill, *General Giap*, p. 56–57; Davidson, *Vietnam at War*, pp. 49–50.
21. Ibid.

CHAPTER ELEVEN
"Brandish the Banner of National Independence"

1. Davidson, *Vietnam at War*, pp. 14–31 *passim.*
2. Pike, "Man on the Spot," p. 11.
3. O'Neill, *General Giap*, pp. 59–62 *passim.*

4. Vo Nguyen Giap ignored a question on this subject in responding to the Giap Questionnaire.

5. Giap said, "I have been to a military academy—that of the bush and the guerrilla war against the Japanese," quoted in Jules Roy, *The Battle of Dien Bien Phu,* trans. Robert Baldick (New York: Harper & Row, 1965), p. 315. To Victoria Brittain, he said, "The only military academy I have been to is that of the bush." See her "General Vo Nguyen Giap—Communist Napoleon," p. 10.

6. Allen T. Padgett, "The Strategy of Vo Nguyen Giap," history seminar paper, University of South Florida, Tampa, November 1989.

7. Vo Nguyen Giap, "The Invincible Strength of the Vietnamese People's War in the New Era," in *Hoc Tap* 12 (December 1974), pp. 11–43. Translated typescript in Giap File.

8. Ibid., p. 14.

9. Giap, Banner of People's War, p. 3. See also Davidson, *Vietnam at War,* pp. 15–16.

10. Giap, *Banner of People's War,* p. 68.

11. Giap, "Invincible Strength," p. 16.

12. Ibid., p. 11.

13. Ibid., p. 15.

14. Ibid., p. 18.

15. Ibid., p. 13.

16. Davidson, *Vietnam at War,* p. 17; Vo Nguyen Giap, *People's War, People's Army,* p. 56.

17. Giap, "Invincible Strength," p. 19.

18. Ibid., pp. 22, 23.

19. Psalms 20:7–8.

20. I have elsewhere written extensively on this subject. Readers interested in the topic may wish to consult *Edward Lansdale: The Unquiet American* (Boston: Houghton Mifflin, 1989); "Vietnam: Lessons Learned," in Phil Melling and John Roper, eds., *America, France and Vietnam: Cultural History and Ideas of Conflict* (London: Academic Publishing Group, 1991); "Teaching People's Wars of National Liberation," in Marc Jason Gilbert, *The Vietnam War: Teaching Approaches and Resources* (Westport, Conn.: Greenwood Press, 1991); "Introduction" to Edward G. Lansdale, *In the Midst of Wars,* 2d ed. (Bronx, N.Y.: Fordham University Press, 1991); "Preparing for the Past," *Military Review,* 69, 1 (January 1989), pp. 2–13; and "Edward G. Lansdale: LIC [Low Intensity Conflict] and the 'Ugly American,' " *Military Review* 68, 5 (May 1988), pp. 44–56.

21. Giap, *Banner of People's War,* p. 66.

22. Davidson, *Vietnam at War,* p. 17.

23. Interview, Madeleine Riffaud with Vo Nguyen Giap, Ha Noi, no date given, published in French in *Voix Ouvrière* (Geneva), 8 June 1968 and *L'Humanité* (Paris), 4 June 1968. Translation by FBIS, Giap File.

24. Giap, *Military Art of People's War,* p. 77.

25. Davidson, *Vietnam at War,* pp. 17–18, makes this point.

26. Giap, *Military Art of People's War,* p. 78; and see Davidson, *Vietnam at War,* p. 18.

27. Davidson, *Vietnam at War,* p. 18.

28. Ibid., pp. 18–19.

29. Giap, *People's War, People's Army,* p. 68; and see Davidson, *Vietnam at War,* p. 19.

30. Mao Tse-tung, *On People's War* (Peking: Foreign Languages Press, 1967), pp. 11–12.

31. Davidson, *Vietnam at War*, p. 20.
32. Ibid.
33. Interview, Cecil B. Currey with Vo Nguyen Giap, Ha Noi, 12 December 1988.
34. Ibid.
35. Mao, *On People's War*, p. 32.
36. Sun Tzu, *The Art of War*, trans. and introduction by Samuel B. Griffith (London: Oxford University Press, 1977), pp. 66–100; Giap, *People's War, People's Army*, p. 46; Rivero interview with Giap, pp. 4–7.
37. Currey interview with Giap.
38. *Time*, 17 November 1952, p. 31.
39. Ibid., p. 33; C. L. Sulzberger, "Did Giap Take the Cue from Lawrence of Arabia?" *New York Times*, Op-Ed page, 22 March 1968; and Davidson, *Vietnam at War*, p. 15. See also T. E. Lawrence, *Seven Pillars of Wisdom: A Triumph* (Garden City, N.Y.: Doubleday, Doran, 1927), *passim*.
40. T. E. Lawrence, *The Evolution of a Revolt*, ed. and introduction by Stanley and Redelle Weintraub (University Park: Pennsylvania State University Press, 1968), pp. 108–10, 113.
41. Ibid., p. 119.
42. Ibid.
43. Ibid.
44. Ibid., *passim*; Sulzberger, "Did Giap Take the Cue."
45. Giap, *Banner of People's War*, p. 47; Davidson, *Vietnam at War*, p. 23.
46. Davidson, *Vietnam at War*, pp. 24–25.
47. Currey interview with Giap.

CHAPTER TWELVE
"It Was an Extremely Hard War"

1. Javier M. Arroyo, "Vo Nguyen Giap: Military Operations: 1946–1954," history seminar paper, University of South Florida, Tampa, November 1989.
2. O'Neill, *General Giap*, pp. 66, 69; Davidson, *Vietnam at War*, pp. 57–60.
3. Giap, *Banner of People's War*, p. 97; Davidson, *Vietnam at War*, pp. 60–64, *passim*.
4. Davidson, *Vietnam at War*, pp. 62–64, *passim*.
5. Ibid., p. 58.
6. O'Neill, *General Giap*, p. 67.
7. Ibid., pp. 67–68.
8. Ibid., p. 70.
9. George K. Tanham, *Communist Revolutionary Warfare: The Vietminh in Indochina* (New York: Praeger, 1961), p. 69.
10. Davidson, *Vietnam at War*, pp. 59–60.
11. Tanham, *Communist Revolutionary Warfare*, p. 70.
12. Patti, *Why Vietnam?*, pp. 408–9; Davidson, *Vietnam at War*, p. 65.
13. Patti, *Why Vietnam?*, pp. 408–9; Davidson, *Vietnam at War*, pp. 66–67.
14. Davidson, *Vietnam at War*, pp. 67–68.
15. Giap, *Military Art of People's War*, pp. 87–88.
16. Bodard, *Quicksand War*, pp. 205–15, *passim*.
17. Ibid., pp. 215–20, *passim*.

18. Davidson, *Vietnam at War*, p. 70. Emphasis added.

19. James Fox, "The War Against America," *Sunday Times Magazine* (London), 12 November 1972, pp. 77–78; P. J. Honey, *Communism in North Vietnam: Its Role in the Sino-Soviet Dispute* (Cambridge, Mass.: MIT Press, 1963), pp. 30–31.

20. Interview, unnamed correspondent for *Verde Olivo* (Havana) with Vo Nguyen Giap, Ha Noi, 15 May 1964, released the same day in English by Viet Nam News Agency, Ha Noi, transcript by FBIS, Giap File.

21. Buttinger, *Dragon Embattled*, vol. 2, pp. 748–49.

22. Joseph R. Starobin, *Eyewitness in Indo-China* (New York: Cameron & Kahn, 1954), p. 67.

23. Ibid.; Bernard Fall, *The Two Vietnams: A Political and Military Analysis* (New York: Praeger, 1963), pp. 109–12, *passim*.

24. Pisor, *End of the Line*, p. 156; Pike, "Man on the Spot," p. 12.

25. Thomas D. Boettcher, *Vietnam: The Valor and the Sorrow* (Boston: Little, Brown, 1985), pp. 86–87; Starobin, *Eyewitness in Indo-China*, pp. 67–68.

26. Fall, *Street Without Joy*, p. 33.

27. Davidson, *Vietnam at War*, pp. 90–1. See also Fall, *Street Without Joy*, p. 30.

28. Davidson, *Vietnam at War*, p. 113. See also Thomas D. Boettcher, *Vietnam: The Valor and the Sorrow* (Boston: Little, Brown, 1985), p. 87.

29. Fall, *Street Without Joy*, p. 33 and Davidson, *Vietnam at War*, p. 102.

CHAPTER THIRTEEN
"We Had to Cross Thirty Streams"

1. Pike, "Man on the Spot," p. 15.

2. Douglas M. Eye, "The Generalship of Giap—the Myths and the Realities," student thesis, Army War College, Carlisle Barracks, Pa., 1973, pp. 8–12, *passim*; O'Neill, *General Giap*, pp. 87–88; Lockhart, *Nation in Arms*, pp. 238–41.

3. Fall, *Street Without Joy*, p. 41; Patti, *Why Vietnam?*, p. 410.

4. Arroyo, "Giap: Military Operations."

5. Pike, "Man on the Spot," p. 12.

6. Ibid.; Fall, "Vo Nguyen Giap—Man and Myth," in Giap, *People's War, People's Army*, pp. xxxvii–xxxviii.

7. Starobin, *Eyewitness in Indo-China*, p. 68; *Time*, 7 January 1952.

8. Vinh Loc Manuscripts.

9. Fall, "Vo Nguyen Giap—Man and Myth," in Giap, *People's War, People's Army*, p. xxxvii.

10. Michael W. Keaveney, "Unravelling the Giap Myth," student essay, Army War College, Carlisle Barracks, Pa., 1984, p. 23.

11. Bernard B. Fall, "Vo Nguyen Giap—Man and Myth," in Giap, *People's War, People's Army*, p. xxxvii.

12. See Appendix B, "Battle Casualties Compared."

13. DA Gongbao (Chinese News Agency), 24 December 1951, translation by FBIS, Giap File.

14. Interview, unnamed interviewer, with Vo Nguyen Giap, 1982, transcript of outtakes used for PBS series *Vietnam: A Television History*.

15. Starobin, *Eyewitness in Indo-China*, pp. 65–66.

16. Ibid., p. 73.
17. Ibid., pp. 69–70.
18. Ibid., p. 67. See also Giap, *People's War, People's Army*, pp. 20–21.
19. Starobin, *Eyewitness in Indo-China*, p. 69.
20. Ibid., p. 70.
21. O'Neill, *General Giap*, p. 124; Arroyo, "Giap: Military Operations."

CHAPTER FOURTEEN
"The Sweat and Muscle of Our Soldiers"

1. Giap, *People's War, People's Army*, pp. 28–29. No thoroughgoing self-criticism by an American general comes readily to mind. Even those who criticize general officer performance are themselves too often attacked. The American system tends to mold career officers who, as they advance in rank, are reinforced in the belief that they never make mistakes worth mentioning or worth regrets. For confirmation, consult any archival set of officer evaluation reports.
2. Janos Radvanyi, *Delusion and Reality* (South Bend, Ind.: Gateway Editions, 1978), p. 6. See also Carlyle A. Thayer, *War by Other Means: National Liberation and Revolution in Viet-Nam, 1954–1960* (Sydney, Australia: Allen & Unwin, 1989), p. 3.
3. Jean Lacouture and Philippe Devillers, *End of a War: Geneva, 1954* (New York: Praeger, 1969), p. 45.
4. Giap, *People's War, People's Army*, pp. 55, 57–58, 197.
5. Robert J. O'Neill, *The Strategy of General Giap Since 1964* (Canberra: Australian National University Press, 1969), p. 2.
6. Giap, *People's War, People's Army*, p. 197; Olson and Roberts, *Where the Domino Fell*, pp. 34–35; Bernard Fall, *Hell in a Very Small Place* (New York: Lippincott, 1967), p. 31.
7. Giap, *People's War, People's Army*, pp. 155, 193–96; Fall, *Hell in a Very Small Place*, p. 467. See also Howard R. Simpson, *Dien Bien Phu: The Epic Battle America Forgot* (Washington: Brassey's, 1994).
8. Olson and Roberts, *Where the Domino Fell*, pp. 36–37; Davidson, *Vietnam at War*, pp. 199–202; Fall, *Hell in a Very Small Place*, pp. 54–55.
9. Cincinnatus [Currey], *Self-Destruction: The Disintegration and Decay of the United States Army During the Vietnam Era* (New York: Norton, 1981), pp. 9–10; O'Ballance, *Indo-China War*, p. 213; Giap, *People's War, People's Army*, p. 208; Fall, *Hell in a Very Small Place*, p. 22.
10. Arroyo, "Giap: Military Operations"; Fall, *Hell in a Very Small Place*, p. 87.
11. Cincinnatus, *Self-Destruction*, p. 10.
12. O'Ballance, *Indo-China War*, p. 214.
13. Roy, *Dien Bien Phu*, p. 138.
14. Fall, *Hell in a Very Small Place*, p. 90; O'Neill, *General Giap*, pp. 151–52.
15. Fall, *Hell in a Very Small Place*, pp. 104, 126.
16. Roy, *Dien Bien Phu*, p. 60.
17. Ibid., p. 76.
18. Bernard Fall, *Vietnam Witness, 1953–1966* (New York: Praeger, 1966), p. 35.
19. Fall, *Hell in a Very Small Place*, p. 451.
20. Ibid., p. 85; O'Neill, *General Giap*, p. 145.

21. Fall, *Street Without Joy*, p. 325.
22. *U.S. News & World Report*, 19 February 1954; Fall, *Hell in a Very Small Place*, pp. 107–9.
23. *Time*, 28 September 1953.
24. O'Ballance, *Indo-China War*, p. 216; Fall, *Hell in a Very Small Place*, pp. 171, 403; Georges Boudarel and François Caviglioli, "Comment Giap a falli perdre la bataille de Dien Bien Phu," *Nouvel Observateur*, 8 April 1983.
25. Roy, *Dien Bien Phu*, pp. 27, 143–45.
26. Giap, *People's War, People's Army*, p. 174.
27. Ibid., pp. 166–69.
28. Ibid., pp. 168, 170.
29. Giap PBS interview outtakes transcript; Karnow, "Giap Remembers," p. 57.
30. Giap, *People's War, People's Army*, p. 170. See also Chen Jian, "China and the First Indo-China War, 1950–54," *China Quarterly*, August 1993, pp. 85–110.
31. Giap PBS interview outtakes transcript.
32. William L. Ryan, AP press release, 21 April 1972, copy in Giap File.
33. Pisor, *End of the Line*, p. 157.
34. Giap, *People's War, People's Army*, p. 178.
35. Buttinger, *Dragon Embattled*, vol. 2, p. 802.
36. Giap, *People's War, People's Army*, pp. 178, 182–83.
37. Fall, *Hell in a Very Small Place*, p. 230.
38. Giap, *People's War, People's Army*, p. 184.
39. Ibid., pp. 174, 209.
40. Ibid., p. 199.
41. Ibid., p. 201.
42. Ibid., p. 203.
43. Ibid., p. 179.
44. Ibid., p. 204.
45. Ibid., p. 198.
46. Davidson, *Vietnam at War*, p. 224.
47. Ibid., p. 234.
48. Vo Nguyen Giap, "Dien Bien Phu," Viet Nam News Agency press release, in English, 5 May 1984, FBIS, Giap File.
49. Giap, *People's War, People's Army*, pp. 174–76.
50. Fall, *Hell in a Very Small Place*, p. 372.
51. Olson and Roberts, *Where the Domino Fell*, pp. 38–39.
52. This "gun-target, line-of-sight field artillery adjust fire technique" used by the Viet Minh required their howitzer crews to expose themselves dangerously to French counterbattery fire. Had the French been able to mount such fire in any effective way, Giap's gunners would have suffered serious casualties. Another advantage held by Viet Minh artillery crews was that they also had the advantage of firing down on the defenders at Dien Bien Phu.
53. Fall, *Hell in a Very Small Place*, p. 451.
54. Ibid., pp. 126, 264; O'Neill, *General Giap*, p. 151.
55. Giap, "Dien Bien Phu" press release.
56. Giap, *People's War, People's Army*, pp. 174–76.
57. Ibid., p. 176.

58. Fall, *Street Without Joy*, p. 321.
59. Davidson, *Vietnam at War*, p. 239.

CHAPTER FIFTEEN
"In the Heart of the Battlefield"

1. Fall, *Two Vietnams*, p. 225; Olson and Roberts, *Where the Domino Fell*, pp. 41–43.
2. Olson and Roberts, *Where the Domino Fell*, pp. 43–44.
3. Giap, *People's War, People's Army*, p. 212.
4. Ibid., p. 214.
5. Fall, *Street Without Joy*, pp. 327–28.
6. Fall, *Hell in a Very Small Place*, p. 171.
7. Giap, *People's War, People's Army*, p. 213.
8. Robert Bonnafous, "Les prisonniers du Corps Expeditionnaire Français dans les Camp Viet-Minh (1945–1954)," *Guerres Mondiales et Conflits Contemporains* 37 (1987), pp. 81–103. Bonnafous writes that of the total of 39,979 French POWs taken by the Viet Minh during the nine years of the First Indochina War, only 10,754 survived.
9. Giap, *People's War, People's Army*, p. 215; Fall, *Street Without Joy*, p. 325.
10. Giap interview in *Armee Rundschau*, pp. 24–29, 64.
11. Giap, *People's War, People's Army*, p. 184.
12. Fall, *Hell in a Very Small Place*, p. 237.
13. Ibid., p. 278.
14. Giap, *People's War, People's Army*, pp. 180–81. At least this is how Giap describes his frantic efforts to reinvigorate the morale of his men. It all sounds a little pat, however, for studies show that political cadre systems tend to break down in the heat of heavy combat, and it is doubtful that corrective measures went as smoothly as Giap would have us believe. No matter how he accomplished it, he managed to keep his men in line and willing to continue, however reluctantly, their assault on Dien Bien Phu.
15. Olson and Roberts, *Where the Domino Fell*, p. 46.
16. Giap, *People's War, People's Army*, p. 216.
17. Ibid., pp. 196, 217; Patrick Turnbull, "The Battle of Dien Bien Phu, 1954" *History Today* 29, 4 (April 1979), pp. 230–39; Boudarel and Caviglioli, "Comment Giap a failli," pp. 35–36, 90–92, 97–99; Vo Nguyen Giap, *Dien Bien Phu* (Ha Noi: Foreign Languages Publishing House, 1962), *passim;* Vo Nguyen Giap, "Thirty Years Ago: Paramount Significance of the Great Dien Bien Phu Victory and of the Winter-Spring Victories," *Vietnam Courier* 20, 4 (April 1984), pp. 7–15. Ho's joke was told to the author by Giap; interview, Ha Noi, 12 December 1988.
18. Nayan Chanda, *Brother Enemy: The War After the War* (San Diego: Harcourt Brace Jovanovich, 1986), pp. 125–26.
19. Interview, unnamed interviewer, with Vo Nguyen Giap for the weekly newspaper *African Revolution* on the occasion of the victory of Dien Bien Phu, in Ha Noi, printed in *Nhan Dan*, 9 May 1963, English translation by FBIS, Giap File.
20. Fall, *Street Without Joy*, p. 385; Pike, "Man on the Spot," p. 16; "Red Napoleon," *Time*, 17 June 1966, p. 30.

21. Giap, "Paramount Significance of the Great Dien Bien Phu Victory," pp. 7–10, *passim*.

22. Janos Radvanyi, "Dien Bien Phu: Thirty Years After," *Parameters* 15, 2 (June 1985), pp. 63–68, *passim*.

23. Currey, *Edward Lansdale, passim*.

24. John S. Bowman, ed., *The Vietnam War: An Almanac* (New York: World Almanac Publications, 1985), pp. 37–38; Olson and Roberts, *Where the Domino Fell*, pp. 46–48; interview, Mario Dolci with Vo Nguyen Giap, "The Rise of Gen. Giap," published in *Milan Giorni*, 18 May and 31 May 1972, English transcript in Giap File.

25. Fall, *Hell in a Very Small Place*, p. 51.

26. Davidson, *Vietnam at War*, pp. 278–80.

27. O'Neill, *Strategy of General Giap*, p. 4.

28. Pisor, *End of the Line*, p. 158.

CHAPTER SIXTEEN
"The Party Committed Serious Errors"

1. DIA Document.

2. Thayer, *War by Other Means*, pp. 195–96. A glance at FBIS reports for the years 1954–73 reveals the constant flow of encomiums received by Giap and other Vietnamese high-level party members from visitors to Ha Noi from third-world countries and the continuing references to his achievements during the First Indochina War which Giap received at welcoming ceremonies and official banquets during his state visits to underdeveloped nations.

3. Currey, *Lansdale*, p. 152.

4. Edward G. Lansdale, *In the Midst of Wars: An American's Mission to Southeast Asia* (New York: Harper & Row, 1972), p. 168.

5. Currey, *Lansdale*, pp. 157–58. Also see "Lansdale Team's Report on Covert Saigon Mission in 1954 and 1955," in Gravel, ed., *Pentagon Papers*, vol. 1, p. 577. Although not identified internally as such, the author of this report was Edward Lansdale. Cited hereafter as Team Report.

6. Interview, Cecil B. Currey with Edward G. Lansdale, McLean, Va., 16 May 1984; Team Report, pp. 578–79.

7. Team Report, pp. 582, 578.

8. Memorandum, "Resources for Unconventional Warfare, S.E. Asia," Edward Lansdale to Maxwell D. Taylor, undated but apparently July 1961, in Gravel, *Pentagon Papers*, vol. 2, pp. 643–49; interview, Cecil B. Currey with Lucien Conein, McLean, Va., 25 May 1987; interview, Cecil B. Currey with Joseph Baker, McLean, Va., 27 May 1987.

9. Team Report, p. 577.

10. Ibid., p. 583.

11. Interview, Cecil B. Currey with Lucien Conein, McLean, Va., 24 June 1985; Team Report, p. 579; interview, Cecil B. Currey with William Colby, 24 June 1985.

12. Interviews, Cecil B. Currey with Brigadier General Cao Pha, Vice Director, Institute for Military History, Ha Noi, 12 March 1988 and 15 December 1988.

13. Interview, Cecil B. Currey with Edward G. Lansdale, McLean, Va., 19 December 1984.

14. *Vietnam: A Historical Outline* (Ha Noi: Xunhasaba Publishers, 1966), pp. 57, 151.
15. Team Report, p. 576; Currey interview with Lansdale, 16 May 1984; Robert Scheer, *How the United States Got Involved in Vietnam* (Santa Barbara, Calif.: Center for the Study of Democratic Institutions, 1965), pp. 26ff; Robert Shaplen, *The Lost Revolution: The Story of Twenty Years of Neglected Opportunities in Vietnam and of America's Failure to Foster Democracy There* (New York: Harper & Row, 1965), pp. 114–15.
16. Team Report, p. 576; Shaplen, *Lost Revolution*, pp. 114–15.
17. Interview, Cecil B. Currey with Bui Tin, Editor, *Nhan Dan*, Ha Noi, 11 March 1988. Western sources often state that 900,000 people moved south. Vietnamese estimates, as seen here, are higher. General Tran Cong Man, commander of the 151st Engineer Regiment during the struggle at Dien Bien Phu and later editor in chief of *Quan Doi Nhan Dan* ("People's Army") newspaper, indicated that one and a half million departed the North. They were, he said, "mostly Hoa [Chinese], Catholics, merchants, and French-trained Vietnamese bureaucrats." Interview, Cecil B. Currey with General Tran Cong Man, Ha Noi, 12 March 1988.
18. Currey interview with Bui Tin; Team Report, p. 579; lecture, Edward G. Lansdale, "Military Psychological Operations," Part 2, Armed Forces Staff College, Norfolk, Va., 29 March 1960. (He gave Part 1 on 7 January.)
19. O'Neill, *General Giap*, p. 163.
20. Henry Charles Lea, *A History of the Inquisition of the Middle Ages*, 3 vols. (New York: Russell & Russell, 1958), *passim*.
21. O'Neill, *General Giap*, pp. 164, 165n.
22. *Nhan Dan*, 31 October 1956, quoted in Hoang Van Chi, *From Colonialism to Communism*, pp. 215–16.
23. Ibid.
24. Radio broadcast, Voice of Ha Noi, in Vietnamese to Southeast Asia, 4 March 1957, FBIS, Group File.
25. Interview, Cecil B. Currey with Vu Hac Bong, Director, Foreign Affairs Bureau, Ho Chi Minh City, 24 March 1988.
26. Davidson, *Vietnam at War*, p. 284; DIA Document.
27. Radio broadcast, Voice of Ha Noi, in Vietnamese to Southeast Asia, 20 December 1957, FBIS, Giap File.
28. Davidson, *Vietnam at War*, 283–86.
29. Currey, *Lansdale*, pp. 168–69.
30. Ibid., p. 180.
31. Olson and Roberts, *Where the Domino Fell*, p. 62.
32. Ibid., pp. 63–64.
33. Currey interview with Bui Tin.
34. Radio broadcast, Voice of Ha Noi, in Vietnamese to Southeast Asia, 4 March 1957, FBIS, Group File.
35. O'Neill, *General Giap*, p. 180.
36. Giap, *People's War, People's Army*, pp. 34, 49, 146.
37. Speech by Vo Nguyen Giap, published in *Addresses, Third National Congress of the Viet-Nam Worker's Party*, 3 vols. (Ha Noi: Foreign Languages Publishing House, 1960), vol. 3, pp. 43–65.

CHAPTER SEVENTEEN
"Absolute Secrecy and Security Were Our Watchwords"

1. Interview, Cecil B. Currey with Pham Binh, Director, Institute for International Relations, Ha Noi, 10 March 1988.
2. Ibid.
3. Robert F. Rogers, "Policy Differences Within the Hanoi Leadership," *Studies in Comparative Communism* 9, 1–2 (Spring/Summer 1976), pp. 108–28, *passim*.
4. Douglas Pike, "Van Tien Dung," four-page typescript biographical sketch (1985), Giap File.
5. Duiker, *Historical Dictionary of Vietnam*, pp. 143–44.
6. Truong Chinh, *Primer for Revolt* (New York: Praeger, 1963), p. 109.
7. As early as 1962, a CIA national intelligence estimate claimed, "The present conflict in South Vietnam is . . . *a purely Vietnamese civil war* with dynastic overtones. . . ." See "Prospects in South Vietnam (Draft for Board/Panel Consideration)," NIE 53-62, Office of National Estimates, Central Intelligence Agency, 19 November 1962. CIA Documents. Emphasis added.
8. Giap, *People's War, People's Army*, pp. 49, 34.
9. Ibid., p. 146.
10. "Final Declaration of the Geneva Conference on the Problem of Restoring Peace in Indochina, July 1954," in Gareth Porter, ed., *Vietnam: A History in Documents* (New York: New American Library, 1981), p. 160.
11. Olson and Roberts, *Where the Domino Fell*, pp. 66–67.
12. Ibid., p. 66.
13. Ibid., p. 67.
14. Ibid., pp. 65–66.
15. Ibid., pp. 67–68.
16. Stanley Karnow, *Vietnam: A History*, (New York: Penguin, 1984), p. 238.
17. Olson and Roberts, *Where the Domino Fell*, p. 69; "Vietnam: We Lied to You," from Paris correspondent, *Economist*, 26 February 1983, pp. 56, 58; Pike, *PAVN*, p. 32.
18. Interview, Cecil B. Currey with Dong Nghiem Bai, Director, North American Department, Foreign Ministry, Ha Noi, 10 March 1988.
19. Olson and Roberts, *Where the Domino Fell*, p. 71.
20. Currey, *Lansdale*, pp. 183–84.
21. Ibid., p. 183; Tran Van Don, *Our Endless War*, pp. 60–61.
22. Olson and Roberts, *Where the Domino Fell*, p. 99.
23. Ibid.
24. Ibid.
25. Ibid., pp. 64–65, 99–100.
26. Bowman, ed., *Vietnam War Almanac*, p. 47.
27. Davidson, *Vietnam at War*, pp. 289–90; Karnow, *Vietnam: A History*, pp. 238–39; Bowman, ed., *Vietnam War Almanac*, pp. 48–50; Duiker, *Historical Dictionary of Vietnam*, pp. 111–12.
28. Olson and Roberts, *Where the Domino Fell*, p. 70.
29. Currey, *Lansdale*, pp. 212–13.
30. Ibid., pp. 213–25, *passim*.

31. John Stirling, "Red Vietnam General Writes Guerrilla Guide," *Herald Tribune* (Paris), 16 November 1961.

32. "Vietnam: We Lied to You," *Economist*, 26 February 1983, pp. 56, 58. Colonel Hoang Xuan Dien, one of the engineers who helped build the Ho Chi Minh Trail, said that later American B-52 raids were not as much of a problem as they could have been because they came each day at the same time, "so we knew when to [take] shelter." When the route first opened, it took six months to travel from north to south. By 1975 the trip took about a week.

33. Vietnamese News Agency broadcast, Ha Noi, in English to Europe and Asia, 20 September 1962, FBIS, Giap File.

34. Vietnamese News Agency broadcast, Ha Noi, in English to Europe and Asia, 22 December 1962, FBIS, Giap File.

35. Vietnamese News Agency broadcast, Ha Noi, in English to Europe and Asia, 23 December 1962, FBIS, Giap File. The biblical paraphrase is to Hosea 8:7.

36. Vietnamese News Agency broadcast, Ha Noi, in English to Europe and Asia, 26 December 1962, FBIS, Giap File.

37. Vo Nguyen Giap, "New Year, New Successes," *Quan Doi Nhan Dan*, 29 January 1963, translation by FBIS, Giap File.

38. Bowman, ed., *Vietnam War Almanac*, p. 58.

39. Currey, *Lansdale*, p. 218–23, 283–86; interview, Cecil B. Currey with Lucien Conein, Tyson's Corner, Va., 16 March 1991.

40. Davidson, *Vietnam at War*, pp. 305–6.

CHAPTER EIGHTEEN
"Only Philosophers Talk of Laws"

1. Vietnam News Agency, Ha Noi, domestic service in Vietnamese, 23 December 1963, FBIS, Giap File.

2. Vietnam News Agency, Ha Noi, international service in English, 9 May 1964. General Earle Wheeler stated later that by the summer of 1965, "it became amply clear that it wasn't a matter of whether the North Vietnamese were going to win the war; it was a question of when." See Olson and Roberts, *Where the Domino Fell*, pp. 137–38.

3. New China News Agency, Beijing, international service in English, 1 June 1964, FBIS, Giap File.

4. Article, in French, dispatched to *L'Aurore* in Paris by Vietnam Press Agency, Saigon, 3 June 1964, FBIS, Giap File.

5. *Nhan Dan*, 19 July 1964; Vietnam News Agency, Ha Noi, international service in English, 27 July 1964, FBIS, Giap File; Bowman, *Vietnam War Almanac*, p. 64.

6. Bowman, *Vietnam War Almanac*, p. 83.

7. Speech, Vo Nguyen Giap to Anti Air Craft and Viet Nam People's Army Naval Forces, Vietnam News Agency, Ha Noi, international service in English, 8 August 1964, FBIS, Giap File; Eugene G. Windchy, *Tonkin Gulf* (Garden City, N.J.: Doubleday, 1971), *passim*. Giap gave his own version of the "Pac Bo" Gulf incident in *Once Again We Will Win* (Ha Noi: Foreign Languages Publishing House, 1966), *passim*. He claimed "the U.S. imperialists have shifted their aggressive war to a new stage" (p. 16).

8. Giap speech, 8 August 1964.

9. *Nhan Dan,* Ha Noi, 23 December 1964, FBIS.

10. O'Neill, *General Giap,* p. 192. VC main and regional forces numbered perhaps 82,000, guerrillas and self-defense forces perhaps 112,000. Other factors were more important than numbers and included leadership, equipment, logistics, morale, and training. No good DRV documentation has been found to substantiate beyond any doubt that it was Ha Noi's plan to cut the Republic of Viet Nam in half along the Pleiku–Qui Nhon axis, although Westmoreland and many American commanders believed that was the case. So also does O'Neill, *General Giap,* p. 190, and this writer concurs. The increased activities of enemy troops in the area fit well into Giap's inevitable willingness to make use of advantageous circumstances and thus this is the most plausible explanation for the increase in operations along this line.

11. Sherman Kent, Chairman, Board of National Estimates, Central Intelligence Agency, Memorandum, "The View from Hanoi," for the Director, Central Intelligence, 30 November 1966. Originally stamped "secret" but declassified 13 September 1989. CIA Documents.

12. Olson and Roberts, *Where the Domino Fell,* p. 129.

13. Interview, Japanese Suzuki Television with Vo Nguyen Giap, no date, broadcast by Vietnam News Agency, Ha Noi, international service in English, 10 March 1965, FBIS, Giap File.

14. Article by Vo Nguyen Giap in *Hoc Tap,* broadcast by Vietnam News Agency, Ha Noi, international service in English, 21 July 1965, FBIS, Giap File.

15. Seymour Topping, "Hanoi Prepares People for War," *New York Times,* 29 July 1965, pp. 1, 9.

16. Robert Taber, *The War of the Flea: A Study of Guerrilla Warfare, Theory and Practice* (New York: Citadel, 1965), p. 11.

17. Currey interview with Giap.

18. Ibid.

19. Ibid.

20. Vietnam News Agency, Ha Noi, international service in English, 10 August 1965, FBIS, Giap File.

21. "Dangerous Air War Becomes Deadly," *U.S. News & World Report,* 18 September 1967, p. 41; Ted Sell, "Air Loss Costs 3 Times More than Damage," *Philadelphia Inquirer,* 11 October 1967. Giap's statistics were as optimistic as those regularly released by the Pentagon. As early as 20 November 1965, he spoke of having downed eight hundred planes. "These victories prove that with intense patriotism, with deep hatred for the aggressors and invaders, and with their tradition of indomitable struggle . . . our Vietnamese people are fully and surely able to defeat the U.S. aggressors." Vietnam News Agency, Ha Noi, domestic service in Vietnamese, 23 November 1965, FBIS, Giap File.

22. Currey interview with Giap; Davidson, *Vietnam at War,* p. 363.

23. Intelligence memorandum, "An Appraisal of the Bombing of North Vietnam (Through 14 May [1966])," Directorate of Intelligence, Central Intelligence Agency, 21 May 1966. Originally classified "Secret. No Foreign Dissem[ination]." Declassified 30 December 1977. CIA Documents.

24. Harold G. Moore and Joseph L. Galloway, *We Were Soldiers Once . . . and Young* (New

York: Random House, 1992), *passim;* J. D. Coleman, *Pleiku: The Dawn of Helicopter Warfare in Vietnam* (New York: St. Martin's, 1988), *passim;* James Olson, ed., *Dictionary of the Vietnam War* (New York: Peter Bedrick Books, 1987), 215–16; Harry G. Summers, Jr., ed., *Vietnam War Almanac* (New York: Facts on File, 1985), 202–3; *Time,* 17 June 1966, p. 29; Davidson, *Vietnam at War,* p. 362. Davidson's figures are from the official U.S. Army report on the battle. Also see Kent, "View from Hanoi."

25. Vietnam News Agency, Ha Noi, international service in English, 31 January 1966, FBIS, Giap File.

26. Interview, William Broyles, Jr., with Hoang Anh Tuan, Vice Minister for Foreign Affairs, Ha Noi, published in the *Tampa Tribune,* 21 April 1985.

27. Interview, William Broyles, Jr., with General Nguyen Xuan Hoang, Ha Noi, published in the *Tampa Tribune,* 21 April 1985.

28. Ibid.

29. Broyles interview with Hoang Anh Tuan.

30. "Fatal Victory," *U.S. News & World Report,* 29 October 1990, p. 32.

31. Interview, Harold G. Moore and Joseph L. Galloway with Vo Nguyen Giap, in "Fatal Victory," sidebar, p. 48.

32. Broyles interview with Nguyen Xuan Hoang.

33. "Fatal Victory," sidebar, p. 48.

34. Interview, William Broyles, Jr., with General Tran Cong Man, Ha Noi, published in *Tampa Tribune,* 21 April 1985.

35. Comment by Vo Nguyen Giap in "Fatal Victory," sidebar.

36. Broyles interview with Nguyen Xuan Hoang.

37. Vo Nguyen Giap, "We Shall Win," *Vietnam Courier* (Ha Noi) 2, 12 (December 1966), pp. 4, 6.

38. *Nhan Dan,* 16, 17, 18 January 1966, published 4 February 1966 by FBIS, Giap File; *New York Times,* 6 February 1966, pp. 1, 16; Hoc Tap, 31 January 1966.

39. Interview, Jacques Decornoy with Vo Nguyen Giap, *Le Monde* (Paris), 8 December 1966, pp. 1, 2, printed in daily report, 22 December 1966, FBIS, Giap File; *New York Times,* 31 July 1966; Vietnam News Agency, Ha Noi, international service in English, 22 December 1966, FBIS, Giap File. Excerpts from Giap's speech were published under the title "North Viet Nam Army and Population's Glorious Success Is That of the Undauntedness of our People," in *Vietnam Courier,* 2 January 1967, pp. 4–5.

40. Decornoy interview with Giap.

CHAPTER NINETEEN
"Washington Cannot See the End of the Tunnel"

1. Interview, Wilfred Burchett with Vo Nguyen Giap, Ha Noi, Vietnam News Agency, domestic service in Vietnamese, 20 February 1967, FBIS, Giap File.

2. PAP, Warsaw, international service in English, 13 April 1967, FBIS, Giap File.

3. Kent, "View from Hanoi."

4. Nguyen Chi Thanh, "Ideological Tasks of the Army and People in the South," *Hoc Tap* (Ha Noi), July 1966, as quoted in Davidson, *Vietnam at War,* p. 419.

5. O'Neill, *Strategy of Giap,* pp. 9–12.

6. Jonathan Schell, *The Village of Ben Suc* (New York: Knopf, 1967), *passim.*

7. Bernard W. Rogers, *Cedar Falls—Junction City: A Turning Point* (Washington, D.C.: Government Printing Office, 1974); Davidson, *Vietnam at War*, p. 428; Andrew F. Krepinevich, Jr., *The Army and Vietnam*, (Baltimore: Johns Hopkins University Press, 1986), pp. 190–92.

8. *Newsweek*, 11 March 1968, p. 30; Intelligence Memorandum #1659/67, "North Vietnam Defense Minister Giap's Analysis of the War," 21 September 1967, prepared by the Office of Current Intelligence for the Director, CIA Documents.

9. Davidson, *Vietnam at War*, pp. 449–50. For a contemporary account, see *Newsweek*, 11 March 1968, pp. 30–31.

10. DIA Document.

11. John Albert, Voice of America news analyst, "Analysis of General Giap's 'Victory' Strategy," October 1967, typescript in Giap Files.

12. *Red Star* (Moscow), 21 October 1967, also published in *Nhan Dan* and *Quan Doi Nhan Dan*, reported 3 November 1967 by FBIS.

13. See Davidson, *Vietnam at War*, p. 443. Davidson not only writes from his own experiences but cites Pham Van Son, ed., *The Viet Cong "Tet" Offensive 1968* (Saigon: Printing and Publications Center A.G./Joint General Staff, RVNAF, 1969). Some have quibbled that the role of the border battles is "still controversial" and that everyone does not agree that the purpose of these battles was to pull American troops away from populated areas. Until we have definitive evidence from archives of the then DRV, it seems the better part of valor to accept the view of Westmoreland's G-2 on this subject.

14. Vietnam News Agency, Ha Noi, international service in English, 7 June 1977, FBIS, Giap File.

15. Allan R. Scholin, "An Airpower Lesson for Giap," *Air Force and Space Digest* 51, 6 (June 1968), pp. 90–98; Padget, "The Strategy of Vo Nguyen Giap."

16. Giap's book *Big Victory, Great Task* (New York: Praeger, 1968) appeared in its American edition in the midst of the Tet fighting; it was a set of essays previously published in *Nhan Dan* and *Quan Doi Nhan Dan*. Despite its repetitive, clichéd harangues, its slogans, occasional fictions, and sweeping generalizations, Giap's beliefs and intent still came through clearly. He claimed that in terms of America's stated goals, the war was already irremediably lost. The North was "the great rear area" to sustain the fight for unification going on within the boundaries of the Republic of Viet Nam. He exhorted his fellows to work even harder, to sustain the struggle, and to achieve eventual victory.

17. See Don Oberdorfer, *Tet: The Story of a Battle and Its Historic Aftermath* (Garden City, N.Y.: Doubleday, 1971), *passim*. Joseph Hovey of the CIA accurately predicted the offensive months before it began.

18. Davidson, *Vietnam at War*, p. 443.

19. James J. Wirtz, *The Tet Offensive: Intelligence Failure in War* (Ithaca, N.Y.: Cornell University Press, 1991), *passim*; comments by Andrew F. Krepinevich, Jr., in *Journal of American History*, March 1993, pp. 1687–88; O'Neill, *Strategy of Giap*, p. 16.

20. Davidson, *Vietnam at War*, pp. 474ff. See also review essay of Wirtz, *Tet Offensive*, by Thomas L. Cubbage II in *Conflict Quarterly* 12, 4 (Fall 1993).

21. Davidson writes, "History will applaud Giap . . . for his resolute opposition to [the Tet offensive]. History will record that it was Vo Nguyen Giap who . . . possessed that ability to sort fact from fantasy and who, like his hero, Napoleon, exhibited

that 'ineradicable feeling for reality' which is the foundation of generalship. To paraphrase Churchill's words, it was his finest hour." Davidson, *Vietnam at War*, p. 450.

22. O'Neill, *Strategy of Giap*, p. 19.
23. "The General's Gamble," *Time*, 9 February 1968, p. 26.
24. *Time*, 22 March 1954, p. 34.
25. *Newsweek*, 11 March 1968, p. 30.
26. O'Neill, *Strategy of Giap*, p. 19.
27. Interview, Madeleine Riffaud, published in *Voix Ouvrière* (Geneva) and L'Humanité (Paris), reported on 8 June 1968, FBIS, Giap File.
28. Moscow in French to Africa; Algiers domestic service in French; AFP, Paris, in French, 14 June 1968, FBIS, Giap File.
29. Interview, unnamed correspondent for NEPSZABADSAG, with Vo Nguyen Giap, Budapest, MTI, international service in English, 6 December 1969, FBIS, Giap File.
30. Hoang Ngoc Lung, *General Offensives of 1968–1969*, Indochina Monographs (Washington, D.C.: U.S. Army Center of Military History, 1981), p. 118.
31. Speech, Vo Nguyen Giap to the Second Determined-to-Win Emulation Congress, Vietnam News Agency, Ha Noi, domestic service in Vietnamese, 22 June 1969, FBIS, Giap File; "Two Speeches by General Vo Nguyen Giap," Viet-Nam Documents and Research Notes, United States Mission in Vietnam, Saigon, copy in Giap File; twenty-third anniversary of founding the Vietnamese artillery forces, Vietnam News Agency, Ha Noi, domestic service in Vietnamese, 3 July 1969, FBIS, Giap File. See also Giap's interview with Marta Rojas published in *Prensa Latina* (Havana), in Spanish, 7 August 1969, FBIS, Giap File; and his speech on the seventh anniversary of the unification of the South Vietnamese People's Liberation Armed Forces, Vietnam News Agency, international service in English, 14 February 1968, FBIS, Giap File; on the fiftieth anniversary of the founding of the Soviet army, AFP, in English, 23 February 1968, and Vietnam News Agency, Ha Noi, international service in English, 24 February 1968; on the twenty-third anniversary of the August Revolution, Vietnam News Agency, domestic service in Vietnamese, 26 August 1968; All-Army Rear Service Conference, Ha Noi, *Nhan Dan*, 27 March 1969; address to an air force congress, Vietnam News Agency, Ha Noi, domestic service in Vietnamese, 20 June 1969; and interview with *Militiarwesen* on the twenty-fifth anniversary of the founding of the People's Liberation Army, Vietnam News Agency, Ha Noi, international service in English, 26 December 1969, FBIS, Giap File.
32. Richard Helms, Director, Central Intelligence, "The Outlook from Hanoi: Factors Affecting North Vietnam's Policy on the War in Vietnam," Special National Intelligence Estimate (SNIE) 14.3-70, 5 February 1970, concurred in by the U.S. Intelligence Board. Originally "secret," this was finally declassified and a copy was supplied to me by the CIA.
33. Ibid.
34. Interview, Ferenc Hegedus, director-general of *Nephadsereg*, organ of the Hungarian People's Army, with Vo Nguyen Giap, Ha Noi, no date, Vietnam News Agency, international service in English, 9 December 1969, FBIS, Giap File; Tad Szulc, "Giap Indicates a Change in Hanoi's Battle Tactics," *New York Times*, 28 December 1969.

CHAPTER TWENTY
"Rivers May Dry Up and Mountains May Erode"

1. "Foreign Report," *Economist*, London, 21 January 1970.
2. Tad Szulc, "Hanoi Sees All Indochina as an Arena," *New York Times*, 17 June 1970.
3. Chanda, *Brother Enemy*, p. 67.
4. Currey interview with Giap.
5. Nabil Zaki visited Ha Noi in January, and Giap told him that successes in Viet Nam could not be separated from "the success scored by other people or from the valuable experiences of these people." Interview, Nabil Zaki, Foreign Affairs Editor, with Vo Nguyen Giap, Ha Noi, January 1970, printed in *Al-Akhbar* (Cairo), 4 February 1970, FBIS, Giap File.
6. Remarks by Giap published in *Ad-Dustur* (Amman, Jordan), 14 April 1970, FBIS, Giap File.
7. That same day, Miroslav Tuleja and Jiri Prazak, correspondents for Prague's *Obrana Lidu*, met with Giap, who told them, "The American imperialists are facing defeat." Perhaps he had not yet received radio reports from the Cambodian front announcing the sudden excursion by U.S. and ARVN forces into his sanctuaries.
8. Jean Lacouture, "From the Vietnam War to an Indochina War," *Foreign Affairs* 48, 4 (1970), pp. 617–28.
9. Tad Szulc, "Hanoi Sees All Indochina."
10. Vo Nguyen Giap, speech to military conference, Vietnam News Agency, Ha Noi, domestic service in Vietnamese, 5 October 1970, FBIS, Giap File.
11. Giap's talk was published in *Quan Doi Nhan Dan*, 30 October 1970; released by Vietnam News Agency, Ha Noi, domestic service to the Republic of Viet Nam in Vietnamese, 28 and 30 October 1970, FBIS, Giap File.
12. Vietnam News Agency, Ha Noi, domestic service in Vietnamese, 22 December 1970, FBIS, Giap File.
13. Ibid., 29 January 1971, FBIS, Giap File.
14. Interview, Masana Wada with Vo Nguyen Giap, Ha Noi, 21 January 1971, published in *Akahata* (Tokyo), 25 and 26 January 1971, FBIS, Giap File.
15. Olson and Roberts, *Where the Domino Fell*, pp. 239–40.
16. After-Action Report, "LAMSON 719," Headquarters, Department of the Army, Washington, D.C., 1971. Copy supplied by U.S. Army.
17. Vietnam News Agency, Ha Noi, domestic service in Vietnamese, 20 March 1971, FBIS, Giap File.
18. Note, Frank Margiotta to Cecil B. Currey, 29 June 1995.
19. Davidson, *Vietnam at War*, pp. 673–74.
20. Ibid., p. 675. See also Ngo Quang Truong, *The Easter Offensive of 1972* (Washington, D.C.: U.S. Army Center of Military History, 1980), *passim*. Lieutenant General Truong, an ARVN officer, closely observed the fighting on the northern front.
21. Davidson, *Vietnam at War*, p. 676.
22. Brian Jenkins, "Giap and the Seventh Son," September 1972, P-4851, typed analysis of the 1972 campaign, Giap File.
23. Davidson, *Vietnam at War*, pp. 676, 683–88.

24. Interview, Kamil Tangri with Vo Nguyen Giap, Ha Noi, 27 April 1972, published in *Vorwaerts* (Bonn), 18 May 1972, FBIS, Giap File.
25. *Time*, 8 May 1972, p. 8.
26. Davidson, *Vietnam at War*, pp. 688–93.
27. *Time*, 8 May 1972, p. 8.
28. Davidson, *Vietnam at War*, pp. 693–99.
29. Ibid., p. 703.
30. Vietnam News Agency, Ha Noi, domestic service in Vietnamese, 23 December 1972, FBIS, Giap File.
31. AFP, Paris, in Spanish, 23 December 1972, FBIS, Giap File.

CHAPTER TWENTY-ONE
"They've Had Me in My Grave a Dozen Times"

1. Vietnam News Agency, domestic service in Vietnamese, 27 January 1973, FBIS, Giap File.
2. AFP, Paris, in French, 22 January 1973, FBIS, Giap File.
3. Vietnam News Agency, domestic service in Vietnamese, 27 January 1973, FBIS, Giap File.
4. Ibid., 4 February 1973, FBIS, Giap File.
5. Interview, unnamed correspondents for *Obrana Lidu, Pravda,* and *Cteka* with Vo Nguyen Giap, CTK, Prague, in English, 24 May 1973, published in *Pravda* (Bratislava) on 25 May 1973, pp. 1, 7, FBIS, Giap File.
6. Philip A. McCombs, "Gen. Giap's Role Cut; Cancer Thought Reason," *Washington Post*, 23 July 1974, p. A-15; David K. Shipler, "Top Hanoi Officer Described as Ill," *New York Times*, 4 September 1974, p. 7.
7. Yoshihisa Komori, "Gen. Vo Nguyen Giap, NVN's Defense Minister, Stepped Down from the First Line," *Mainichi Shimbun* (Tokyo), 4 May 1974, p. 2, Giap File; Shipler, "Top Hanoi Officer," *New York Times*, 4 September 1974.
8. Vietnam News Agency, Ha Noi, domestic service in Vietnamese, 7 May 1974, FBIS, Giap File.
9. *Kyodo* (Tokyo), in English, 25 May 1974, FBIS, Giap File.
10. *Frankfurter Allgemeine*, 12 July 1974, FBIS, Giap File.
11. Shipler, "Top Hanoi Officer."
12. Interview, Berengère d'Aragon with Vo Nguyen Giap, Ha Noi, no date, published in *Paris Match*, 14 October 1977, p. 92, copy in Giap File.
13. Davidson, *Vietnam at War*, pp. 738, 742, 747, 749–50.
14. Tran Van Tra, *History of the Bulwark B-2 Theatre: Concluding the 30-Years War* (Ho Chi Minh City: Van Nghe Publishing Plant, 1982), p. 33.
15. Davidson, *Vietnam at War*, pp. 738, 752–53.
16. Tra, *Bulwark*, p. 125.
17. Davidson, *Vietnam at War*, p. 770.
18. Boudarel, *Giap!*, p. 127. See also Van Tien Dung, *Our Great Spring Victory: An Account of the Liberation of South Vietnam*, trans. John Spragens, Jr. (New York: Monthly Review Press, 1977).
19. Tra, *Bulwark*, p. 125 and *passim*.
20. Lomperis, "Giap's Dream," p. 19.

21. Gates, "People's War in Vietnam," pp. 338–39.

22. Vo Nguyen Giap and Van Tien Dung, *How We Won the War* (Ypsilanti, Mich.: RECON Publications, 1976), p. 41. Emphasis in original.

23. Ibid., and Van Tien Dung, *Great Spring Victory, passim.*

24. Giap and Dung, *How We Won,* p. 42.

25. Van Tien Dung, *Great Spring Victory;* Duiker, *Communist Road to Power;* Cao Van Vien, *The Final Collapse* (Washington, D.C.: U.S. Army Center of Military History, 1982), *passim;* Davidson, *Vietnam at War,* pp. 789–90.

26. Currey interview with Giap; Karnow, "Giap Remembers," p. 58.

27. Currey interview with Giap.

28. Ibid.

29. Fish interview with Conein.

30. Interview, unnamed interviewer, with Vo Nguyen Giap, 1982, transcript of *Vietnam: A Television History.*

31. Vietnam News Agency, Ha Noi, in English and Vietnamese, daily reports of 16–31 December 1975 and 1–4 January 1976, FBIS, Giap File. The speech was printed in *Quan Doi Nhan Dan,* 8 January 1976, pp. 1–2, FBIS, Giap File.

32. Currey interview with Giap.

33. Vietnam News Agency, Ha Noi, in English and Vietnamese, daily reports of 5–20 January 1976, FBIS, Giap File.

34. Vo Nguyen Giap, speech to all-army cadre conference, Vietnam News Agency, Ha Noi, domestic service in Vietnamese, 19 April 1976, 28 January 1976, 29 January 1976, 26 February 1976, 22 March 1976, 26 March 1976, 29 March 1976, 20 September 1976, 22–25 November 1976; *Tien Phong* (Ha Noi), 29 April 1976, p. 2, FBIS, Giap File.

35. Gareth Porter, *Vietnam: The Politics of Bureaucratic Socialism* (Ithaca, N.Y.: Cornell University Press, 1993), p. 83.

36. Two-page (CIA?) intelligence analysis, typed, dated 11 May 1977, in Giap File; *Far Eastern Economic Review,* 10 June 1977, p. 35.

37. Vietnam News Agency, Ha Noi, international service in English, 4 January 1977, and domestic service in Vietnamese, 5 January 1977, FBIS, domestic service in Vietnamese, 3 February 1977, 7 March 1977; international service in English, 12 February 1977 and 4 March 1977, FBIS, Giap File.

38. AFP, Hong Kong, 8 March 1977; Vietnam News Agency, international service in English, 11 and 18 March 1977; USSR domestic service in Russian, 11, 13, 14, 16, and 19 March 1977; *Krasnaya Zvezda* (Moscow), 11 and 17 March 1977; Vietnam News Agency, international service in English, 12, 18, 22, 25, and 29 March 1977; domestic service in Vietnamese, 7 March 1977; Tass (Moscow), 21 and 28 March 1977; ADN, East Berlin, international service in English, 1 and 2 April 1977, FBIS, Giap File.

39. Vietnam News Agency, Ha Noi, international service in English, 3 April 1977, FBIS, Giap File.

40. Ibid., 3, 5, 6, 8, and 12 April 1977, FBIS, Giap File.

41. Ibid., international service in English, 19, 23, and 30 April 1977, 1 May 1977; Warsaw, domestic service in Polish, 21 April 1977, FBIS, Giap File.

42. Vietnam News Agency, Ha Noi, international service in English, 5–7 May 1977, FBIS, Giap File.

43. Ibid., domestic service in Vietnamese, 29 July 1977; international service in English, 2, 3, 7, and 15 June 1977; New China News Agency (NCNA), Beijing, international service in English, 6 May 1977, 2–5, 19, and 20 June 1977; *Kiangsu* (Nanking), domestic service in Mandarin, 15 June 1977; AFP, Hong Kong, 3 June 1977, FBIS, Giap File.

44. Memorandum, Professor Harvey Nelsen, International Studies Department, University of South Florida, Tampa, to Cecil B. Currey, September 1991.

45. Vietnam News Agency, Ha Noi, international service in English, 7 June 1977, FBIS, Giap File.

46. Chanda, *Brother Enemy*, pp. 120–21.

47. Vietnam News Agency, Ha Noi, international service in English, 13 July 1977, 18 August 1977, 26 October 1977, 18 November 1977, 21 December 1977; Vietnam News Agency, Ho Chi Minh City, domestic service in Vietnamese, 2 August 1977; Vietnam News Agency, Ha Noi, domestic service in Vietnamese, 7 August 1977, FBIS, Giap File.

48. D'Aragon interview with Giap.

49. Chanda, *Brother Enemy*, p. 196.

CHAPTER TWENTY-TWO
"The Memories Have Not Faded"

1. Vo Nguyen Giap, speech at National Assembly meeting, 28 May 1979, by Vietnam News Agency, Ha Noi, domestic service in Vietnamese, 29 May 1979, FBIS, Giap File; Chanda, *Brother Enemy*, p. 216; Bowman, *Vietnam War Almanac*, pp. 346–49; Ronald J. Cima, ed., *Vietnam: A Country Study* (Washington, D.C.: Headquarters, Department of the Army, 1989).

2. Vietnam News Agency, Ha Noi, domestic service in Vietnamese, 7 February 1978, 25 February 1978, daily reports, FBIS, Giap File.

3. Ibid., 23 January 1978, daily report, FBIS, Giap File. For his other conference activities in 1978 in the field of science and technology, see ibid., 27 March, 24 April, 31 May, 8 August, 22 September, daily reports, FBIS, Giap File.

4. Vo Nguyen Giap, *Problems of the Scientific and Technical Revolution in Viet Nam* (Ha Noi: Su That [Truth] Publishing House, 1978); *On the General Strength of the Vietnamese Revolution* (Ha Noi: Su That Publishing House, 1978); *War for National Liberation and National Defence* (Ha Noi: Su That Publishing House, 1979); *The Whole People Determined to Defend Socialist Viet Nam* (Ha Noi: Su That Publishing House, 1979).

5. Giap, speech to the national assembly, 28 May 1979.

6. Vietnam News Agency, Ha Noi, domestic service in Vietnamese, 19 March 1979, FBIS, Giap File.

7. Interview, Daniela Kuneva special correspondent in Southeast Asia for BTA, Bulgarian television, with Vo Nguyen Giap, no date, published in *Pogled* (Sofia), 2 July 1979, FBIS, Giap File.

8. Vietnam News Agency, Ha Noi, domestic service in Vietnamese, 5 June 1979, FBIS, Giap File. The manager of the cooperative briefed Giap on its accomplishments the previous year and lovingly recited his statistics. Yen So's gross output in 1978 totaled 1.8 million dong, of which crops accounted for 48.5 percent, animal husbandry 14 percent, and secondary occupations 38.5 percent. It produced half a

million items the previous year, of which export goods composed more than 50 percent. Ten years later I visited that same farm and the (same?) manager briefed me in similar fashion.

9. Vietnam News Agency, Ha Noi, domestic service in Vietnamese, 22 November 1979, and international service in English, 23 November 1979, FBIS, Giap File.

10. Vietnam News Agency, Ha Noi, domestic service in Vietnamese, 7 December 1979, FBIS, Giap File.

11. Ibid., 7 February 1980; XINHUA, Beijing, international service in English, 20 February 1980, FBIS, Giap File; "Giap Reportedly Replaced," *Washington Post*, 30 January 1980, p. 8; "Giap Loses Hanoi Defense Post," *New York Times*, 8 February 1980, p. 3.

12. Vietnam News Agency, Ha Noi, domestic service in Vietnamese, 8 February 1980, FBIS, Giap File.

13. Ibid., 8 February, 9 February, 14 March, 10 April 1980; international service in English, 7 March, 18 and 29 April, 6 June, 3 November 1980, FBIS, Giap File; *Nhan Dan*, 28 September 1980, FBIS, Giap File.

14. *Nhan Dan*, 7–8 October 1980, FBIS.

15. Vietnam News Agency, Ha Noi, international service in English, 21, 26, and 27 February 1980; *Pravda* (Moscow), 26 February 1980, FBIS, Giap File.

16. Vietnam News Agency, Ha Noi, international service in English, 14 June, 23 July, 30 July 1980, FBIS, Giap File.

17. Ibid., 4 November 1980, 13 January 1981, FBIS.

18. Interview, Wilfred Burchett with Vo Nguyen Giap, no date, published in the *Guardian*, (Manchester) 7 July 1980, p. 13. Emphasis added.

19. Vietnam News Agency, Ha Noi, international service in English, 30 April 1981, FBIS.

20. See FBIS daily reports for that period, Giap File.

21. John Sharkey, "Vietnam Party Removes Giap from Key Post," *Washington Post*, 1 April 1982; David Watts, "General Giap Is Demoted by Hanoi Congress," *Times* (London), 1 April 1982.

22. Sheehan, "Reporter at Large," p. 58.

23. Interview, Cecil B. Currey with Dr. Do Trong Hieu, M.D., Ha Noi, 3 January 1990.

24. See FBIS daily reports for 1982–90, Giap File.

25. Letter, Tran Kim Dung to Cecil B. Currey, Paris, 30 August 1991.

26. Ibid.

27. *Indochina Chronology*, Fall 1992, p. 34.

28. Giap, "Pac Bo Spring," pp. 5–6.

DOCUMENT COLLECTIONS

Allison Kent Thomas Collection. Letters sent to author, dated 21 March, 2 April, 24 April, 1 May, 4 May, and 15 September 1991, accompanied by photostatted enclosures of portions of Thomas's 1945 diary, a twelve-page summary of his impressions on an early-1990 return visit to Ha Noi to see Giap, a Vietnamese-language article published in *Tap Chi* with an accompanying English-language translation, and copies of a note and two letters Thomas received from Giap, the first written in August or early September 1945, the second dated 20 November 1946, and the third 2 April 1946.

CIA Documents. On 3 April 1991 I filed a freedom of information request for material on Giap with the Central Intelligence Agency. It responded on 8 August 1994, supplying me with four documents and denying me the right to see any portion of seven others it had identified. Those supplied to me consisted of "Biographies of Key Personalities, Indochina," Section 59, National Intelligence Survey, dated 1953; "Key Personalities, North Vietnam," National Intelligence Survey 43, dated 1959; "General Giap's View of the Vietnam Situation," Intelligence Memorandum #0776/66, dated 1966; and "General Giap and Hanoi's Intentions," Intelligence Memorandum #149, dated 1970.

DIA Document. On 3 April 1991 I filed a freedom of information request for material on Giap with the Defense Intelligence Agency. It responded almost precisely two years later, 16 April 1993, with several helpful documents. One report, still partially classified, and hence with portions blacked out, has no title, no date or place of acquisition, and no preparation attribution. It is a biographical sketch of Giap, five single-space legal-size pages in length. A date stamp on the upper right of the first page shows that it was used by DIA as late as 12 January 1970. Although the agency carefully blacked out the report number on the first page, it omitted doing so on later pages. This was report #6 832 0761 69—the last two digits indicated the year it was produced. Internal evidence in this report suggests that it was derived, in large part, from material provided by French intelligence, the evidence including, among other elements, the use of "the (the abbreviation of "Monsieur") before the names of many individuals. Unlike reports on Giap produced by other American intelligence agencies (which regularly contained masses of incorrect information), this report includes many details on Giap's early years, including direct quotes from his family members, names of family friends, tutors, schoolteachers, and Giap's early associates. This is no homegrown product.

Giap File. Indochina Archive, Indochina Studies Project, Institute of East Asian Studies, University of California, Berkeley. In addition to much material of other kinds, this file contains numerous accounts of Giap's interviews, appearances, travels, and speeches drawn from the pages of the publication known as *Foreign Broadcast Information Service, Daily Report Supplement,* compiled by the National Technical Information Service (NTIS) of the United States Department of Commerce. NTIS monitors foreign radio broadcasts, news agency transmissions, newspapers, and periodicals, and regularly reproduces translations in full or in extract of those deemed to be of importance to subscribers. These documents in the Giap holdings of the Indochina Archive are cited herein as FBIS, Giap File.

Giap Questionnaire. Two single-spaced typescript pages of questions to which Vo Nguyen Giap responded orally to his daughter, Hong Anh, who wrote his responses in French on twenty-three single-spaced typescript legal-size sheets of paper.

Vinh Loc Manuscripts. A series of letters written by Lieutenant General Vinh Loc, ARVN (Ret.), to Cecil B. Currey with accompanying pages of information, dated 12 February, 3 March, 14 April, 2 May, 18 June, 21 August, 6 September, 15 September and 1 November 1991.

WRITINGS BY VO NGUYEN GIAP
(arranged chronologically)

One Year of Revolutionary Achievement: Report to the Viet Nam People at Ha Noi. Ha Noi: Viet Nam News Agency, 1946.

Ten Years of Fighting and Building of the Vietnamese People's Army. Ha Noi: Foreign Languages Publishing House, 1955.

The Party's Great Experiences in Leadership over Armed Struggle and the Building of Revolutionary Armed Forces. Ha Noi: Su That Publishing House, 1961.

People's War, People's Army. New York: Praeger, 1962.

Dien Bien Phu. Ha Noi: Foreign Languages Publishing House, 1962.

"The Lessons Taught by Dien Bien Phu." *Nhan Dan* (Ha Noi), 7 May 1964.

"The Founding of the Vietnamese People's Army." *Nhan Dan* (Ha Noi), 14 December 1964.

"Promote the People's War." *Tuyen Huan* (Ha Noi), October 1965.

"Stemming from the People," in [no ed. listed] *A Heroic People: Memoirs from the Revolution.* Ha Noi: Foreign Languages Publishing House, 1965. Pp. 91–149. Published as "Naissance d'une Armée" in *Récits de la Résistance Vietnamienne.* Paris: Maspero Publishers, 1966.

The South Vietnamese People Will Win. Ha Noi: Foreign Languages Publishing House, 1965.

"Let the Entire People Resolutely and Unanimously Step Up Their Great Patriotic War." *Hoc Tap* (Ha Noi), Vietnamese Studies #1, January 1966.

Once Again We Will Win. Ha Noi: Foreign Languages Publishing House, 1966.

"We Shall Win." *Vietnam Courier* (Ha Noi), 2, 12 (December 1966).

Big Victory, Great Task. New York: Praeger, 1968.

"The Brilliant Victories and Great Power of the People's War in the Local Areas." *Hoc Tap* (Ha Noi), Vietnamese Studies #8, August 1969.

Viet Nam People's War Has Defeated the U.S. War of Destruction. Ha Noi: Foreign Languages Publishing House, 1969.

"President Ho: A Strategic Genius." *Nhan Dan* (Ha Noi), 31 May 1970.

Banner of People's War: The Party's Military Line. Preface by Jean Lacouture; introduction by Georges Boudarel. New York: Praeger, 1970.

The Military Art of People's War Selected Writings of Vo Nguyen Giap. Ed. and introduction by Russell Stetler. New York: Monthly Review Press, 1970.

The Strategic Position of the Local People's War and the Local Armed Forces. Ha Noi: Quan Doi Nhan Dan Publishing House, 1970.

"Study the Development of Vietnamese Military Science." *Hoc Tap* (Ha Noi), Vietnamese Studies #11, November 1970.

"Arm the Revolutionary Masses and Build the People's Army." 4-part article. Part 1, *Hoc Tap* (Ha Noi), January 1972; Part 2, *Quan Doi Nhan Dan* (Ha Noi), January 1972; Part 3, *Quan Doi Nhan Dan* (Ha Noi), February 1972; Part 4, *Hoc Tap* (Ha Noi), April 1972. Published in translation by FBIS on 27 April, 2 June, and 18 October 1972.

People's War on the River and Sea Battlefield. Ha Noi: People's Army Publishing House, 1972.

Those Unforgettable Months and Years. Ed. by Huu Mai. Ha Noi: Van Nghe Quan Doi, 1972.

Unforgettable Months and Years. Trans. and introduction by Mai Van Elliott; foreword by George McT. Kahin. Ithaca, NY: Cornell University Southeast Asia Program Data Paper #99, May 1975.

Victory of the People's War Against the War of Destruction in the Towns and Industrial Centers of Socialist Viet Nam. Ha Noi: People's Army Publishing House, 1972.

National Liberation War in Viet Nam. Ha Noi: Foreign Languages Publishing House, 1973.

"The Invincible Strength of the Vietnamese People's War in the New Era." *Hoc Tap* (Ha Noi), Vietnamese Studies #12, December 1974.

People's War Against the U.S. Aero-Naval War. Ha Noi: People's Languages Publishing House, 1975.

To Arm the Revolutionary Masses to Build the People's Army. Ha Noi: People's Languages Publishing House, 1975.

Unforgettable Days. Ha Noi: Foreign Languages Publishing House, 1975.

Selected Writings, 1969–1972. Ha Noi: Foreign Languages Publishing House, 1977.

Problems of the Scientific and Technical Revolution in Viet Nam. Ha Noi: Su That Publishing House, 1978.

On the General Strength of the Vietnamese Revolution. Ha Noi: Su That Publishing House, 1978.

Essential Tasks of the Scientific and Technical Revolution in Our Agriculture. Ha Noi: Su That Publishing House, 1979.

War for National Liberation and National Defence. Ha Noi: Su That Publishing House, 1979.

The Whole People Determined to Defend Socialist Viet Nam. Ha Noi, Su That Publishing House, 1979.

The People's War for the Defence of the Homeland in the New Era. Ha Noi: Foreign Languages Publishing House, 1981.

"Thirty Years Ago: Paramount Significance of the Great Dien Bien Phu Victory and of the Winter-Spring Victories." *Vietnam Courier* (Ha Noi), 20, 4 (April 1984).

"Pac Bo Spring." *Nhan Dan* (Ha Noi), 24 December 1989.

————and Truong Chinh. *The Peasant Question, 1937–1938.* Trans. and introduction by Christine Pelzer White. Ithaca, N.Y.: Cornell University Southeast Asia Program, Data Paper #94, 1974.

————and Van Tien Dung. *How We Won the War.* Ypsilanti, Mich.: RECON Publications, 1976.

LETTERS

Will Brownell, Director, Vietnam Bibliographical Project, Columbia University, to author, 1 February 1991, 13 February 1991 and 1 July 1991.

INTERVIEWS BY CECIL B. CURREY
(arranged chronologically)

Edward G. Lansdale, McLean, Va., 16 May 1984 and 19 December 1984.

William Colby, Georgetown, Va., 24 June 1985.

Joseph Baker, McLean, Va., 27 May 1987.

Lucien Conein, McLean, Va., 24 June 1985, 25 May 1987, Tysons Corner, Va., 26 April 1990, 16 and 17 March 1991.

Pham Binh, Director, Institute for International Relations, Ha Noi, 8 and 10 March 1988.

Bui Tin, Editor, *Nhan Dan*, Ha Noi, 9 and 11 March 1988.

Tran Cong Man, Editor-in-Chief, *Quan Doi Nhan Dan*, Ha Noi, 9, 12, and 17 March 1988.

Dong Nghiem Bai, Director, North American Department, Foreign Ministry, Ha Noi, 10 March 1988.

Cao Pha, Vice Director, Institute for Military History, Ha Noi, 12 and 17 March 1988, 15 December 1988.

Chau Phong, Deputy Director, Institute for International Relations, Ha Noi, 14 March 1988, and, as Acting Director, 8 December 1988.

Vu Hac Bong, Director, Foreign Affairs Bureau, Ho Chi Minh City, 24 March 1988.

Vo Nguyen Giap, Government House, Ha Noi, 12 December 1988.

Do Trong Hieu, M.D., Ha Noi, 3 January 1990.

Nguyen Dinh Tu, Vienna, Va., 26 April 1990.

Le Si Ngac, McLean, Va., 16 March 1991.

Christine Pelzer White, Honolulu, 10 May 1991.

Allison Kent Thomas, Tampa, Fla., 21 February 1992.

Sigmund Klaussner, Tampa, Fla., 26 March 1993.

Phan Quang Dan, Tampa, Fla., 8 April 1993.

INTERVIEWS BY OTHERS
(arranged chronologically)

Unnamed correspondent for the weekly *African Revolution* with Vo Nguyen Giap, Ha Noi, undated, published in *Nhan Dan*, 9 May 1963, FBIS, Giap File.

Wilfred S. Burchett with Vo Nguyen Giap, Ha Noi, 13 April 1964. Released by Viet Nam News Agency, International Service in English, 9 May 1964, FBIS, Giap File.

Unnamed correspondent for *Verde Olivo* (Havana) with Vo Nguyen Giap, Ha Noi, 15 May 1964. Released in English by Viet Nam News Agency, 15 May 1964, FBIS, Giap File.

Huu Mai with Vo Nguyen Giap, Ha Noi, 14 December 1964, published in *Nhan Dan* (Ha Noi), FBIS, Giap File.

Unnamed Japanese television delegation with Vo Nguyen Giap, Ha Noi, 7 March 1965, FBIS, Giap File.

Jacques Decornoy with Vo Nguyen Giap, printed in *Le Monde* (Paris), 8 December 1966, FBIS, 22 December 1966, Giap File.

Wilfred Burchett with Vo Nguyen Giap, Ha Noi. Released by Viet Nam News Agency, domestic service in Vietnamese, 20 February 1967, FBIS, Giap File.

Ladislaw Mnacko, Czechoslovakian journalist, with Vo Nguyen Giap, Ha Noi, December 1967, published in *Jerusalem Post*. Copy in Giap File was clipped in such a way that no publication date remained.

Madeleine Riffaud, correspondent for *L'Humanité* (Paris) with Vo Nguyen Giap, Ha Noi, undated, published 4 June 1968, FBIS, Giap File.

Unnamed correspondent for *El Moudjahid* (Algiers), with Vo Nguyen Giap, Ha Noi, 2 June 1968, published 14 June 1968, p. 6, FBIS, Giap File.

Oriana Fallaci, correspondent, in Ha Noi, undated, with Vo Nguyen Giap, published 6 April 1969 as "Americans Will Lose, Says Gen. Giap" in *Washington Post* Outlook Section, Op-Ed page, Sunday, 6 April 1969.

Marta Rojas, with Vo Nguyen Giap, published in *Prensa Latina* (Havana), 7 August 1969, FBIS, Giap File.

Unnamed correspondent for NEPSZABADSAC, with Vo Nguyen Giap, Budapest, MTI, international service in English, 6 December 1969, FBIS, Giap File.

Ferenc Hegedus, director-general of *Nephadsereg*, organ of the Hungarian People's Army, with Vo Nguyen Giap, Ha Noi, no date, Viet Nam News Agency international service in English, 9 December 1969, FBIS, Giap File.

Unnamed correspondent for *Militiarwesen*, (German Democratic Republic), with Vo Nguyen Giap, Ha Noi, December 1969, FBIS, Giap File.

Nabil Zaki, with Vo Nguyen Giap, Ha Noi, January 1970, printed in *Al-Akhbar* (Cairo), 4 February 1970, FBIS, Giap File.

Unnamed correspondent for *Armee Rundschau (Army Review)*, East Berlin, Deutsche Demokratische Republic, with Vo Nguyen Giap, Ha Noi, undated, published in November 1970, pp. 24–29, 64, in FBIS, Giap File.

Joaquin Crespo Daga, correspondent for *Prensa Latina* (Havana) with Vo Nguyen Giap, Ha Noi, published 20 December 1970, FBIS, Giap File.

Masana Wada, correspondent for *Akahata* (Tokyo), organ of the Japanese Communist Party, with Vo Nguyen Giap, Ha Noi, 22 January 1971, published 25 January 1971, FBIS, Giap File.

Volker Ott, correspondent for DDR television, (German Democratic Republic) with Vo

Nguyen Giap, Ha Noi, undated, broadcast on East Berlin domestic television service, 6 July 1971, FBIS, Giap File.

Kamil Tangri with Vo Nguyen Giap, Ha Noi, 27 April 1972, published in *Vorwaerts* (Bonn), 18 May 1972, FBIS, Giap File.

Mario Dolci, correspondent for *Giorni* (Milan), with Vo Nguyen Giap, Ha Noi, undated, published 18 and 31 May 1972 as "The Rise of Gen. Giap," FBIS, Giap File.

Miroslav Tuley, editor, *Obrana Lidu,* Julius Loerincz, editor, *Pravda,* and Jozef Belicek, resident CTK correspondent, with Vo Nguyen Giap, Ha Noi, undated, published in *Pravda* (Bratislava), 25 May 1973, pp. 1, 7, FBIS, Giap File.

Marta Rojas, correspondent for *Granma Weekly Review,* (Havana) with Vo Nguyen Giap, undated, published 18 January 1976, FBIS, Giap File.

Tihomir Ilievski, correspondent for *Nova Makedonija* (Skopje), with Vo Nguyen Giap, Ha Noi, 23 May 1976, FBIS, Giap File.

Unnamed correspondent for *Krasnaya Zvezda* (Moscow), with Vo Nguyen Giap, Ha Noi, undated, published 30 March 1977, p. 3, FBIS, Giap File.

Berengère d'Aragon, correspondent for *Paris Match* with Vo Nguyen Giap, Ha Noi, 14 October 1977, FBIS, Giap File.

Daniela Kuneva, special correspondent in Southeast Asia for BTA, Bulgarian television, with Vo Nguyen Giap, Ha Noi, undated, published in *Pogled* (Sofia), 2 July 1979, broadcast 3 July 1979, FBIS, Giap File.

Miguel Rivero, correspondent for *Verde Olivo* (Havana) with Vo Nguyen Giap, Ha Noi, undated, published 10 February 1980, pp. 4–7, FBIS, Giap File.

Wilfred Burchett with Vo Nguyen Giap, undated, published in *Guardian* (Manchester), 7 July 1980, p. 13.

William Broyles, Jr., with Hoang Anh Tuan, vice minister for foreign affairs; General Tran Cong Man, editor-in-chief of *Quan Doi Nhan Dan;* and General Nguyen Xuan Hoang, Ha Noi, undated, published in *Tampa Tribune,* 21 April 1985.

Lydia Fish in McLean, Virginia, 30 July 1989, with Lucien Conein, Dan Johnson, and Joe Baker.

Stanley Karnow with Vo Nguyen Giap, Ha Noi, undated, published as "Giap Remembers," in *New York Times Magazine,* 24 June 1990.

Harold G. Moore and Joseph L. Galloway with Vo Nguyen Giap, Ha Noi, undated, published in *US News & World Report,* 29 October 1990 in sidebar, p. 48, of article entitled "Fatal Victory."

Virginia Gift with Kim Dung Tran-Ngoc, in Rueil-Malmaison, Paris, February/March 1991.

Unnamed Public Broadcasting System interview with Vo Nguyen Giap, Ha Noi, undated, for "Vietnam: A Television History," in William Joiner Center for the Arts, University of Massachusetts.

PAMPHLETS

Edward G. Lansdale, "Military Psychological Operations." Two speeches. Part 1 given on 7 January 1960, Part 2 given on 29 March 1960, Armed Forces Staff College, Norfolk, VA. Printed by the college. Copy in Papers of Edward G. Lansdale, The Hoover Institution for War, Revolution, and Peace, Stanford University, Palo Alto, CA.

"The United States and Vietnam: 1944–1947." Staff study based on the *Pentagon Papers,* prepared for use of the Committee on Foreign Relations, United States Senate, Study #2, 3 April 1972. Washington, D.C.: Government Printing Office, 1972.

UNPUBLISHED STUDIES

Arroyo, Javier M. "Vo Nguyen Giap: Military Operations: 1946–1954." History seminar paper, University of South Florida, Tampa, November 1989.

Barton, Terry L. "Generals Westmoreland and Giap—Two Great Commanders?" Student thesis #86-0210, Air Command and Staff College, Maxwell Air Force Base, Montgomery, Ala., 1986.

Bell, John C. "Was Dien Bien Phu Giap's Last Win?" Student essay, U.S. Army War College, Carlisle Barracks, Pa., 1967.

Clemons, James G. "The Snow-Covered Volcano." Student essay, U.S. Army War College, Carlisle Barracks, Pa., 1967.

Chu Van Tan. "Reminiscences on the Army for National Salvation: A Memoir." Trans. by Mai Elliott. Data Paper #97, Southeast Asia Program, Department of Asian Studies, Cornell University, Ithaca, N.Y., September 1974.

Eye, Douglas M., "The Generalship of Giap—the Myths and the Realities," Student thesis, Army War College, Carlisle Barracks, Pa., 1973.

Headquarters, Department of Army. LAMSON 719 After-Action Report, 1971.

J-2, U.S. Military Assistance Command, Vietnam (USMACV). "General Giap Outlines VPA Use of Party Line." 16 December 1969, Library. U.S. Army Command and General Staff College, Ft. Leavenworth, Kan.

Keaveney, Michael W. "Giap—Innovator or Imitator?" Student research report, U.S. Army Command and General Staff College, Ft. Leavenworth, KS, 1974.

———, "Unravelling the Giap Myth." Student essay, U.S. Army War College, Carlisle Barracks, Pa., 1984. Although titled differently, these works by Keaveney are identical.

Laidlaw, James R. "Modern Guerrilla Warfare: Emphasizing Mao Tse-tung and Vo Nguyen Giap." History seminar paper, University of South Florida, Tampa, November 1989.

Latimer, Thomas K. "Hanoi's Leaders and Their South Vietnam Policies, 1954–1968." Ph.D. dissertation, Georgetown University, Washington, D.C., 1972.

Levanger, John C. "General Vo Nguyen Giap: The Vietnamese Napoleon?" Student thesis #AD-761-581, U.S. Army War College, Carlisle Barracks, Pa., 1973.

Padgett, Allen T. "The Strategy of Vo Nguyen Giap." History seminar paper, University of South Florida, Tampa, November 1989.

Pike, Douglas. "General Vo Nguyen Giap—Man on the Spot." Typescript, May 1968. Giap File.

———. "Van Tien Dung." Typescript, Undated. Giap File.

Shuffer, George M. "Objective: The Population." Student essay, U.S. Army War College, Carlisle Barracks, Pa, 1967.

Staudenmaier, William O. "Vietnam, Mao, and Clausewitz." Military Issues Research Memorandum, U.S. Army War College, Carlisle Barracks, Pa. 1977.

Stotser, George R. "Concepts of Guerrilla Warfare and Insurgent War." Student monograph, U.S. Army War College, Carlisle Barracks, Pa., 1972.

"The OSS in Indochina, 1945–1946." Typescript, Giap File.

ARTICLES

Bonnafous, Robert. "Les prisonniers du Corps Expeditionnaire Français dans les Camp Viet-Minh." (1945–1954). *Guerres Mondiales et Conflits Contemprains,* 37, 147 (1987), pp. 81–103.

Boudarel, Georges. "Essai sur la pensée militaire Vietnamienne." *L'Homme et la Société,* 7 (Jan.-Feb.-Mar. 1968), pp. 183–200.

———and François Caviglioli. "Comment Giap a failli perdre la bataille de Dien Bien Phu." *Nouvel Observateur,* 8 April 1983, pp. 35–36, 90–92, 97–100.

Brittain, Victoria. "General Vo Nguyen Giap—Communist Napoleon who Conquered South Vietnam," *Times* (London), 2 June 1975.

Caratini, Marcel. "Mission Aupres de Giap." *Revue des Deux Mondes,* June 1985, pp. 611–617.

Chen Jian. "China and the First Indo-China War, 1950–54." *China Quarterly* August 1993, pp. 85–110.

Clos, Max. "The Strategist Behind the Vietcong." *New York Times Magazine* 16 August 1964, pp. 7, 9, 52–55.

Currey, Cecil B. "Edward G. Lansdale: LIC and the 'Ugly American.' " *Military Review,* 67, 5 (May 1988), pp. 44–56.

———. "Preparing for the Past." *Military Review,* 69, 1 (January 1989), pp. 2–13.

Dolci, Mario. "The Rise of General Vo Nguyen Giap, 'Red Napoleon' of Asia." *Giorni* (Milan), 18 May 1972, pp. 18–20, 31 May 1972, pp. 47–49.

Elliott, David P. "North Vietnam Since Ho." *Problems of Communism,* July/August 1975, pp. 35–52.

Fonde, Jean J. "Giap et Le maquis de Cho Ra (Mars 1945–Mars 1946)." *Revue Histoire de l'Armée,* 30, 2 (February 1976), pp. 112–127.

———. "Il y a 25 ans à Hanoi." *Revue Militaire Générale,* (June 1972), pp. 753–758.

Fox, James. "Giap—The Victor at Dien Bien Phu." *Sunday Times Magazine* (London), 5 November 1972, p. 56.

———. "The War Against America." *Sunday Times Magazine* (London), 12 November 1972.

Gates, John M. "People's War in Vietnam." *Journal of Military History,* July 1990.

Hamilton-Smith, M. L. J. "The Development of Revolutionary Warfare Strategy, Vietnam—1946–1964." *Army Quarterly and Defence Journal,* 113, 3 (September 1983), pp. 328–339; 113, 4 (December 1983), pp. 439–450.

Karnow, Stanley. "Giap Remembers." *New York Times Magazine,* 24 June 1990.

Khanduri, Chandra B. "General Vo Nguyen Giap." *Journal of the Service Institution of India,* 111, 465 (1982), pp. 267–284.

Khanh, Huynh Kin. "A Legend Demoted." *Far Eastern Economic Review,* 116, 15 (9 April 1982), pp. 32–33.

Lacouture, Jean. "From the Vietnam War to an Indochina War." *Foreign Affairs,* 48, 4 (April 1970), pp. 617–28.

Liu, T. C. "Great Retreat of South Vietnamese Forces." *Asian Outlook* 31 March 1975, pp. 33–34.

Lomperis, Timothy J. "Giap's Dream, Westmoreland's Nightmare." *Parameters: U.S. Army War College Quarterly,* 18, 2 (June 1988), pp. 18–32.

Moraes, Dom. "The Frozen Volcano." *Asia Magazine,* 17 September 1972, pp. 3–7.

Ngoc An. "Bo Doi Viet-My." *Tap Chi Lich Su Quan Su* (November 1986).

Nong Van Lac. "Diary." *Tac Pham Moi*, 34 (February 1974).

Paschall, Rod. "Low-Intensity Conflict Doctrine: Who Needs it?" *Parameters: U.S. Army War College Quarterly*, 15, 3 (September 1985), pp. 33–45.

Radvanyi, Janos. "Dien Bien Phu: Thirty Years After." *Parameters: U.S. Army War College Quarterly*, 15, 2 (June 1985), pp. 63–68.

"The Red Napoleon," *Time*, 17 June 1966, p. 30.

Rogers, Robert F. "Policy Differences Within the Hanoi Leadership." *Studies in Comparative Communism*, 9, 1–2 (Spring/Summer 1976), pp. 108–128.

Scholin, Allan R. "An Airpower Lesson for Giap." *Air Force and Space Digest* (now *Air Force Magazine*), 51, 6 (June 1968), pp. 90–98.

Sheehan, Neil and Susan. "A Reporter at Large in Vietnam." *New Yorker*, 18 November 1991.

Turnbull, Patrick. "The Battle of Dien Bien Phu, 1954." *History Today*, 29, 4 (April 1979), pp. 230–239.

"V.N. Giap appraises Americans In The V.N. War [sic]." *Free Observer: The First and Only Monthly Magazine in English in Vietnam*, May 1966, pp. 8, 24.

BOOKS

Addresses, Third National Congress of the Viet-Nam Worker's Party. 3 vols., Ha Noi: Foreign Languages Publishing House, 1960.

Armbruster, Frank E, Raymond D. Gastel, and Herman Kahn. *Can We Win in Vietnam?* New York: Praeger, 1968.

Bao Dai. *Le Dragon d'Annam: Memoirs de S.[erene] M.[ajesty] Bao Dai.* Paris: Editions Plon, 1979. Also published in Vietnamese as *Con Rong Viet Nam.* Los Alamitos, Calif.: Edition Xuan Thu, 1990.

Bodard, Lucien. *The Quicksand War: Prelude to Vietnam.* Trans. Patrick O'Brien. Boston: Little, Brown, 1967.

Boettcher, Thomas D. *Vietnam: The Valor and the Sorrow.* Boston: Little, Brown, 1985.

Boudarel, Georges. *Giap!* Paris: Editions Atlas, 1977.

Bouscaren, Anthony T., ed. *All Quiet on the Western Front: The Death of South Vietnam.* Old Greenwich, Conn. Devin-Adair, 1977.

Bowman, John S., ed. *The Vietnam War: An Almanac.* New York: World Almanac Publications, 1985.

Bui Diem. *In the Jaws of History.* Boston: Houghton Mifflin, 1987.

Butler, David. *The Fall of Saigon: Scenes from the Sudden End of a Long War.* New York: Simon & Schuster, 1985.

Buttinger, Joseph. *The Smaller Dragon: A Political History of Vietnam.* New York: Praeger, 1968.

———. *Vietnam: A Dragon Embattled.* 2 vols. New York: Praeger, 1967.

———. *Vietnam: A Political History.* New York: Praeger, 1968.

Cairns, J. F. *The Eagle and the Lotus: Western Intervention in Vietnam, 1847–1968.* Mystic, Conn.: Lawrence Verry, 1969.

Cable, James. *The Geneva Conference of 1954 on Indochina.* New York: St. Martin's, 1986.

Cao Van Vien. *The Final Collapse.* Washington, D.C.: U.S. Army Center of Military History, 1982.

Carver, Michael. *War Since 1945*. New York: G. P. Putnam's, 1981.

Chanda, Nayan. *Brother Enemy: The War After the War*. San Diego: Harcourt Brace Jovanovich, 1986.

Chanoff, David and Doan Van Toai. *Portrait of the Enemy*. New York: Random House, 1986.

Chen, King C. *Vietnam and China, 1938–1954*. Princeton, N.J.: Princeton University Press, 1969.

Cima, Ronald J. *Vietnam: A Country Study*. Washington, D.C.: Headquarters, Department of the Army, 1989.

Cincinnatus [Cecil B. Currey]. *Self-Destruction: The Disintegration and Decay of the United States Army During the Vietnam Era*. New York: W. W. Norton, 1981.

Coleman, J. D. *Pleiku: The Dawn of Helicopter Warfare in Vietnam*. New York: St. Martin's, 1988.

Currey, Cecil B. *Edward Lansdale: The Unquiet American*. Boston: Houghton Mifflin, 1988.

———. *Follow Me and Die: The Destruction of an American Division During World War II*. Briarcliff Manor, N.Y.: Stein & Day, 1984.

Davidson, Phillip B. *Vietnam at War: The History, 1946–1975*. Novato, Calif.: Presidio Press, 1988.

———. *Secrets of the Vietnam War*. Novato, Ca: Presidio Press, 1990.

Dawson, Alan. *55 Days: The Fall of South Vietnam*. Englewood Cliffs, N.J.: Prentice Hall, 1977.

Dederer, John Morgan. *War in America to 1775: Before Yankee Doodle*. New York: New York University Press, 1990.

Devillers, Philippe. *L'histoire du Vietnam de 1940 à 1952*. Paris: Editions du Seuil, 1952.

———. *End of a War, Indochina, 1954*. New York: Praeger, 1969.

Do Mau. *Viet Nam: Mau Lau Que Huong Toi [My Native Country in War]*. Calif.: 1986.

Do Quang Tien. *Vom Troi Bien Gioi*. Ha Noi: Nha Xuat Ban Viet Bac, 1972.

du Berrier, Hilaire. *Background to Betrayal: The Tragedy of Vietnam*. Boston: Western Islands Press, 1965.

Duiker, William J. *Historical Dictionary of Vietnam*. Metuchen, N.J.: Scarecrow Press, 1989.

———. *The Communist Road to Power in Vietnam*. Boulder, Colo.: Westview Press, 1981.

———. *Vietnam Since the Fall of Saigon*. Athens, Ohio: Ohio University Press, 1989.

Dunn, Peter M. *The First Vietnam War*. New York: St. Martin's, 1985.

Fall, Bernard B. *The Viet-Minh Regime: Government and Administration in the Democratic Republic of Viet-Nam*. New York: Institute of Pacific Relations, 1956.

———. *Street Without Joy*. Harrisburg, Pa.: Stackpole Press, 1961.

———. *The Two Vietnams: A Political and Military Analysis*. New York: Praeger, 1963.

———. *Vietnam Witness, 1953–1966*. New York: Praeger, 1966.

———. *Hell in a Very Small Place*. New York: Lippincott, 1967.

———. *Ho Chi Minh on Revolution: Selected Writings, 1920–1966*. New York: New American Library, 1968.

Fenn, Charles. *Ho Chi Minh: A Biographical Introduction*. New York: Charles Scribner's, 1973.

Fischel, Wesley., ed. *Vietnam Witness*. Itasca, Ill.: F. E. Peacock, 1968.

Galula, David. *Counterinsurgency Warfare: Theory and Practice*. New York: Praeger, 1964.

Gibson, James William. *The Perfect War: Technowar in Vietnam.* Boston: Atlantic Monthly Press, 1986.

Gilbert, Marc J. *The Vietnam War: Teaching Approaches and Resources.* Westport, Conn.: Greenwood Press, 1991.

Gosselin, Charles. *L'empire d'Annam.* Paris: Perrin, 1904.

Gravel, Mike, ed. *The Pentagon Papers: The Defense Department History of United States Decisionmaking on Vietnam.* 5 vols. Boston: Beacon Press, 1971.

Halberstam, David. *Ho.* New York: Random House, 1971.

Hammer, Ellen J. *The Struggle for Indochina, 1940–1955.* Palo Alto: Stanford University Press, 1955.

———. *Vietnam Yesterday and Today.* New York: Holt, Rinehart & Winston, 1966.

Henderson, William D. *Why the Vietcong Fought: A Study of Motivation and Control in a Modern Army in Combat.* Westport, Conn.: Greenwood Press, 1979.

Hoang Lac. *Nam Viet Nam, 1954–1975.* Alief, Texas: 1990.

Hoang Ngoc Lung. *General Offensives of 1968–1969.* Indochina Monographs. Washington, D.C.: U.S. Army Center of Military History, 1981.

Hoang Van Chi. *From Colonialism to Communism: A Case History of North Viet Nam.* New York: Praeger, 1963.

Honey, P. J. *Communism in North Vietnam: Its Role in the Sino-Soviet Dispute.* Cambridge, Mass.: MIT Press, 1963.

Hong Nam [Vo Nguyen Giap]. *Ca Nuoc Mot Long Bao Ve Vung Chac To Quoc Viet Nam Xa Hoi Cu Nghia.* Ha Noi: Su That Publishing House, 1979.

Hosmer, Stephen T., Konrad Kellen, and Brian M. Jenkins. *The Fall of South Vietnam: Statements of Vietnamese Military and Civilian Leaders.* New York: Crane, Russak, 1980.

Huy Phong and Yen Anh. *Nhan Dien Huyen Thoai Vo Nguyen Giap: Hoa quang vay muon cho cuoc chien tuong tan.* San Jose, Calif.: Mekong-Tynan, 1989.

Hy Van Luong. *Revolution in the Village: Tradition and Transformation in North Vietnam, 1925–1988.* Honolulu: University of Hawaii Press, 1992.

Jamieson, Neil L. *Understanding Vietnam.* Berkeley: University of California Press, 1993.

Jenkins, Brian. *Giap and the Seventh Son.* Santa Monica, Calif.: Rand Corporation, 1972.

Joes, Anthony James. *From the Barrel of a Gun: Armies and Revolutions.* Washington: Pergamon-Brassey's, 1986.

Kahin, George McTuran and John W. Lewis. *The United States in Vietnam.* Rev. ed. New York: Dell, 1969.

Kolko, Gabriel. *The Politics of War: The World and United States Foreign Policy, 1943–1945.* New York: Random House, 1968.

Lacouture, Jean. *Vietnam: Between Two Truces.* New York: Random House, 1966.

———. *Ho Chi Minh.* Paris: Editions du Seuil, 1967. Published in English, New York: Random House, 1968.

——— and Philippe Devillers. *End of a War: Geneva, 1954.* New York: Praeger, 1969.

Lansdale, Edward G. *In the Midst of Wars: An American's Mission to Southeast Asia.* New York: Harper & Row, 1972. 2d ed. Intro. by Cecil B. Currey. Bronx, N.Y.: Fordham University Press, 1990.

Lawrence, T. E. *Seven Pillars of Wisdom: A Triumph.* Garden City, N.Y.: Doubleday, Doran, 1927.

———. *Evolution of a Revolt.* Ed. and with an introduction by Stanley and Redelle Weintraub. University Park, Pa.: Pennsylvania State University Press, 1968.

Le Gro, William E. *Vietnam from Cease-Fire to Capitulation.* Washington, D.C.: U.S. Army Center for Military History, 1985.

Le Quang, Gérard. *Giap: ou, la guerre du people [Giap, or people's war].* Paris: Denoel, 1973.

Lockhart, Greg. *Nation in Arms: The Origins of the People's Army of Vietnam.* Wellington, Australia: Allen & Unwin, 1989.

Luong, Hy V. *Revolution in the Village: Tradition and Transformation in North Vietnam, 1925–1988.* Honolulu: University of Hawaii Press, 1992.

Mao Zedong. *Guerrilla Warfare.* New York: Praeger, 1961.

———. *On People's War.* Beijing: Foreign Languages Press, 1967.

———. *The Strategic Problems of the Anti-Japanese War.* 2d ed., Beijing: Foreign Languages Press, 1960.

———. *Struggle of the Chin-Kan-Shan Mountains.* Beijing: Foreign Languages Press, 1954.

McAlister, John T., and Paul Mus. *The Vietnamese and Their Revolution.* New York: Harper & Row, 1970.

McGarvey, Patrick J. *Visions of Victory: Selected Vietnamese Communist Military Writings, 1964–1968.* Stanford, Calif.: Hoover Institution on War, Revolution and Peace, 1969.

Mallin, Jay. *Strategy for Conquest: Communist Documents on Guerrilla Warfare.* Coral Gables, Fla.: University of Miami Press, 1970.

Marr, David G. *Vietnamese Anticolonialism, 1885–1925.* Berkeley: University of California Press, 1971.

———. *Vietnamese Tradition on Trial, 1920–1945.* Berkeley: University of California Press, 1981.

Matthews, Lloyd J., and Dale E. Brown, eds. *Assessing the Vietnam War.* McLean, Va.: Brassey's, 1987.

Maurer, Harry. *Strange Ground:* Americans in Vietnam, 1945–1975. New York: Henry Holt, 1989.

Melling, Phil, and John Roper, eds. *America, France and Vietnam: Cultural History and Ideas of Conflict.* London: Academic Publishing Group, 1991.

Moore, Harold G., and Joseph L. Galloway. *We Were Soldiers Once . . . and Young.* New York: Random House, 1992.

Morris, James M. *America's Armed Forces: A History.* Englewood Cliffs, N.J.: Prentice-Hall, 1991.

Ngo Quang Truong. *The Easter Offensive of 1972.* Washington, D.C.: U.S. Army Center of Military History, 1980.

Nguyen Duy Thanh. *My Four Years with the Viet Minh.* n.p., Democratic Research Service, n.d.

Nguyen Khac Huyen. *Vision Accomplished: The Enigma of Ho Chi Minh.* New York: Macmillan, 1971.

Nguyen Kien Giang. *Viet Nam Nam Dau Tien Sau Cach Mang Thang Tam [Viet Nam: The First Year Following the August Revolution].* Ha Noi: Su That Publishers, 1961.

Nhuong Tong. *Nguyen Thai Hoc.* Ha Noi: Viet Nam Quoc Dan Mang, 1980.

O'Ballance, Edgar. *The Indochina War, 1945–1954: A Study in Guerrilla Warfare.* London: Faber & Faber, 1964.

Oberdorfer, Don. *Tet: The Story of a Battle and Its Historic Aftermath.* Garden City, N.Y.: Doubleday, 1971.

Olson, James, ed. *Dictionary of the Vietnam War.* New York: Peter Bedrick Books, 1987.

Olson, James, and Randy Roberts. *Where the Domino Fell: America and Vietnam, 1945–1990.* New York: St. Martin's, 1991.

O'Neill, Robert J. *General Giap: Politician and Strategist.* New York: Praeger, 1969.

———. *The Strategy of General Giap Since 1964.* Canberra: Australian National University Press, 1969.

Patti, Archimedes L. A. *Why Vietnam? Prelude to America's Albatross.* Berkeley: University of California Press, 1980.

Pike, Douglas. *PAVN: People's Army of Vietnam.* Novato, Calif.: Presidio Press, 1986.

———. *Viet Cong.* Cambridge, Mass.: MIT Press, 1966.

———. *War, Peace and the Viet Cong.* Cambridge, Mass.: MIT Press, 1969.

Pisor, Robert. *The End of the Line: The Siege of Khe Sanh.* New York: Norton, 1982.

Porter, Gareth, ed. *Vietnam: A History in Documents.* New York: New American Library, 1981.

———. *Vietnam: The Politics of Bureaucratic Socialism.* Ithaca, N.Y.: Cornell University Press, 1993.

Race, Jeffrey. *War Comes to Long An: Revolutionary Conflict in a Vietnamese Province.* Berkeley: University of California Press, 1972.

Rice, Edward E. *Wars of the Third Kind: Conflicts in Underdeveloped Countries.* Berkeley: University of California Press, 1988.

Radvanyi, Janos. *Delusion and Reality.* South Bend, Ind.: Gateway Editions, 1978.

Rogers, Bernard W. *Cedar Falls—Junction City: A Turning Point.* Washington, D.C.: Government Printing Office, 1974.

Rosie, George. *The British in Vietnam: How the Twenty-five-Year War Began.* London: Panther, 1970.

Roy, Jules. *The Battle of Dien Bien Phu.* Trans., Robert Baldick. New York: Harper & Row, 1965.

Safer, Morley. *Flashbacks: On Returning to Vietnam.* New York: Random House, 1990.

Salmon, Malcolm. *Focus on Indochina.* Ha Noi: Foreign Languages Publishing House, 1961.

Scheer, Robert. *How the United States Got Involved in Vietnam.* Santa Barbara, Calif.: Center for the Study of Democratic Institutions, 1965.

Schell, Jonathan. *The Village of Ben Suc.* New York: Knopf, 1967.

Scott, Andrew M., *et al. Insurgency.* Chapel Hill: University of North Carolina Press, 1970.

Shaplen, Robert. *The Lost Revolution: The Story of Twenty Years of Neglected Opportunities in Vietnam and of America's Failure to Foster Democracy There.* New York: Harper & Row, 1965.

Shore, Moyers S. *The Battle for Khe Sanh.* Washington, D.C.: Government Printing Office, 1969.

Simpson, Howard R. *Dien Bien Phu: The Epic Battle America Forgot.* Washington, D.C.: Brassey's, 1994.

Smith, Ralph B. *An International History of the Vietnam War.* 3 vols. New York: St. Martin's, 1983.

Stahel, Albert A. *Marxistisch-Leninistische Konzeptionen des Terrorismus und der Revolution* [*Marxist-Leninist concepts of terrorism and revolution*]. Geneva, Switzerland: Allgemeine Schweizerische Militaerzeitschrift, 1987.

Stanton, Shelby. *The Rise and Fall of an American Army: U.S. Ground Forces in Vietnam, 1965–1973.* New York: Dell, 1985.

Starobin, Joseph R. *Eyewitness in Indo-China.* New York: Cameron & Kahn, 1954.

Sully, François. *We the Vietnamese: Voices from Vietnam.* New York: Praeger, 1971.

Summers, Harry G., Jr. *On Strategy: A Critical Analysis of the Vietnam War.* New York: Dell, 1984.

————, ed. *Vietnam War Almanac.* New York: Facts on File, 1985.

Taber, Robert. *The War of the Flea: A Study of Guerrilla Warfare, Theory and Practice.* New York: Citadel, 1965.

Tanham, George K. *Communist Revolutionary Warfare: The Vietminh in Indochina.* New York: Praeger, 1961.

Thayer, Carlyle. *War by Other Means: National Liberation and Revolution in Viet-Nam, 1954–1960.* Sydney, Australia: Allen & Unwin, 1989.

Thompson, W. Scott, and Donaldson D. Frizzell, eds. *The Lessons of Vietnam.* New York: Crane, Russak, 1977.

Todd, Oliver. *Cruel April: The Fall of Saigon.* New York: Norton, 1987.

Tonnesson, Stein. *The Outbreak of War in Indochina, 1946.* Oslo: International Peace Research Institute, 1982.

Tournoux, J. R. *Secrets d'état: Dien Bien Phu les Paras Lalger.* Paris: Editions Plon, 1960.

Tran Huy Lieu. *Cach Mang Thang Tam [The August Revolution].* Ha Noi: Su Hoc Publishers, 1960.

Tran Van Don. *Our Endless War: Inside Vietnam.* San Rafael, Calif.: Presidio Press, 1978.

Tran Van Tra. *Vietnam: History of the Bulwark B-2 Theatre: Concluding the 30-Years War.* Ho Chi Minh City: Van Nghe Publishing Plant, 1982.

Trinh Van Thao. *Vietnam du Confucianisme au communisme: un essai itinéraire intellectual.* Paris: L'Harmetton, 1990.

Truong Chinh. *Primer for Revolt.* New York: Praeger, 1963.

————. *The August Revolution.* Ha Noi: Foreign Languages Publishing House, 1947.

Truong Nhu Tang. *A Vietcong Memoir: An Inside Account of the Viet Nam War and Its Aftermath.* New York: Harcourt Brace Jovanovich, 1985.

Turley, William S. *The Second Indochina War.* Boulder, Colo.: Westview Press, 1986.

Turner, Robert F. *Vietnamese Communism: Its Origins and Development.* Stanford, Calif.: Hoover Institution Press, 1975.

Trinquier, Roger. *Modern Warfare: A French View of Counterinsurgency.* Trans. by Daniel Lee. New York: Praeger, 1964.

Van Tien Dung. *Our Great Spring Victory: An Account of the Liberation of South Vietnam.* Trans. by John Spragens, Jr. New York: Monthly Review Press, 1977.

Vietnam: A Historical Outline. Ha Noi: Xunhasaba Publishers, 1966.

Vu Anh. *Days with Ho Chi Minh.* Ha Noi: Foreign Languages Publishing House, 1962.

Warner, Denis. *The Last Confucian.* Baltimore: Penguin, 1964.

Werner, Jayne S., and Luu Doan Huynh. *The Vietnam War: Vietnamese and American Perspectives.* Armonk, N.Y.: M. E. Sharpe, 1993.

Westmoreland, William C. *A Soldier Reports.* Garden City, N.Y.: Doubleday, 1976.

Windchy, Eugene G. *Tonkin Gulf.* Garden City, N.Y.: Doubleday, 1971.

Wirtz, James J. *The Tet Offensive: Intelligence Failure in War.* Ithaca, N.Y.: Cornell University Press, 1991.

ABOUT THE AUTHOR

CECIL B. CURREY recently retired as a professor of military history at the University of South Florida in Tampa after thirty-four years of teaching. He has written about Viet Nam since 1981. An ordained clergyman and former military chaplain, he retired from the Army Reserve in 1992 with the rank of colonel. Married for forty-four years, he and his wife Laura Gene will divide their time between their home in Lutz, Florida, and their ranch in Currey Valley, Montana. They have three children and three grandchildren.